A GUIDE TO
BAROQUE ROME:

THE CHURCHES

Anthony Blunt

A Guide to Baroque Rome: The Churches

Revised by Michael Erwee
with Sebastian Wormell, Dany McNutt,
Jennifer Montagu, Jenny Wilson,
Alexander Fyjis-Walker and Lisa Adams

PALLAS ATHENE

Published by Pallas Athene (Publishers) Ltd,
2 Birch Close,
London N19 5XD

www.pallasathene.co.uk

 @pallasathenebooks

 @Pallasathene.co.uk

 @pallasathenebooks

Originally published in the English language by
HarperCollins Publishers Ltd
under the title: *A Guide to Baroque Rome*
© Anthony Blunt 1982

This edition © 2013 published under licence from
HarperCollins Publishers Ltd

Revisions and additional material
© Pallas Athene (Publishers) Ltd 2013, 2017, 2020,
2023, 2025, 2026

The author asserts the moral right to be identified
as the author of this work.

ISBN 978-1-87342-918-1

Printed in England by Blissetts

Contents

Foreword 7
Preface to the original edition 9

THE CHURCHES 15

Bibliographies and references 259
    Abbreviations 260
    References 261
    Bibliography 308

Indexes 313
    Index of artists 315
    Index of patrons and benefactors 353
    Popes 1527-1870 358
    Topographical index by street 359
    Topographical index by rione 362

Foreword

It is the task of the reference book to lead its reader efficiently and where possible enjoyably to the information required; it is certainly not to draw attention to the personality of its compilers or the many other individuals involved in its production. Yet a reference book will also fail in its task if it lacks character of its own, and however broad the subject, it must to some indefinable extent be marked with a living personality if the book is to be useful both in supplying knowledge and - its more nebulous, but equally important mission - in stimulating further interest and enquiry.

The balance is even more difficult to maintain when the book in question is a long outdated favourite that needs to be fully overhauled, and of necessity overhauled by a stranger. Anthony Blunt's A Guide to Baroque Rome was deservedly a classic, and was fully imprinted with the unsurpassable acumen, taste and judgment of one of the greatest art historians and teachers of his time. It also bore necessarily silent witness to Blunt's vast achievement in weeding out foolishness and impossibility. In this field, as in others, Blunt's work is easily overlooked and forgotten. More obvious to the purely critical eye are the carelessnesses and omissions inevitable in a book co piled hurriedly – in a race against death – from notes covering most of a lifetime. When the required corrections are added to the updatings and expansions that flow from thirty years' of scholarly research, much of it directly or indirectly stimulated by Blunt and by this very book, the impression is easily given of a work that flourishes more in the breach than in the observance. Yet in fact, as I trust this volume demonstrates, Blunt's overall conception and in many cases the acuity of his research and of his writing, remain of permanent value.

For the original edition, Blunt was persuaded to add summary entries on palaces, villas and fountains. As these were not part of his original enterprise and as research in these areas has gone so very much further than Blunt could perhaps have envisaged, it was felt that nothing useful would be achieved by reprinting them. It is hoped that we will be able to bring out companion volumes to cover these topics in the near future.

Though I did not realize it at the innocent time when, at the suggestion of Tom Jenkins, then of the Courtauld Institute, I undertook the republication of Blunt's Guide, the problems were to prove too much for any single reviser to tackle with success. Nevertheless the gigantic labour of revising Blunt's main work, that on churches, published here, was in great part completed by Dr. Michael Erwee, and we must salute the patience, tenacity and passion he deployed in revising in such minute detail this

FOREWORD

already large work. His achievement is all the more striking when on knows that the task came to him as a vocation, after he visited Rome on holiday, taking with him Blunt's book, which, though inspirational, he soon found to be in sore need of updating, expanding and correcting. Without Dr. Erwee's dedication to this self-imposed task, and without his generosity in allowing us to use the extremely extensive material he has accumulated, this book would not be possible and all readers will remain in his debt.

Many others have helped on the way, with research, editorial checking and with the arts of copy editing, picture research and layout, whose importance to a work of this nature, and this work in particular, cannot be overestimated. The principal contributors are recognised on the title page. Other crucial assistance was afforded by Joshua Drapkin and the late Ralph Davis.

Most of all, however, this volume pays tribute to the multifarious work of the immense band of scholars who have combed the archives and gazed anew at the buildings, and whose research, summarized in these pages, has reinvigorated the understanding and appreciation of this turbulent, passionate and moving architecture, some of the greatest yet produced. I very much hope that they will consider the present volume a work in progress, and help us keep future editions fully up to date and as error free as possible. All contributions would be most gratefully received.

Alexander Fyjis-Walker
London, Spring 2013

Preface to the original edition

The purpose of this book is double. It aims first at providing a guide book which the visitor to Rome who is interested in the Baroque can carry round with him on his walks through the city; but it is also intended to be useful in the study for those who want to pursue the Baroque in a more leisurely way. The individual entries contain, therefore, what I hope is accurate information about the buildings and their contents, but also a lead or leads towards the sources from which this information is derived. Where possible I have given a reference to a good modern source, such as the volumes in the series Le Chiese di Roma illustrate, from which the interested student will be able to follow up his enquiries through the bibliographies supplied, but I have supplemented these by references to books and articles which were published since the volume in question appeared or which deal with individual problems not discussed in it. Where no reliable modern monograph exists I have referred to the old guide books to Rome, to the early biographies of artists, or to any other sources that seemed to me useful. I have also given references to the early guide books of Mola and Martinelli, which have only been published within the last twenty years, and I have added references to the most important illustrated sources for the benefit of those who may want to use the book in the study rather than in the field.

One great problem was to decide what to include and what to leave out. As regards dates I have taken the Baroque to mean roughly the art of the period beginning with the election of Gregory XV as pope in 1621 and ending about the middle of the eighteenth century, but obviously precise limits of date cannot be laid down. The question of how late to carry the study was relatively easy to solve, because about the middle of the eighteenth century Roman Baroque architecture begins to wither away – mainly owing to the advent of Neo-classicism, but partly perhaps because of the removal of Vanvitelli and Fuga to Naples in 1750 – and though clearly certain latecomers like Marchionni, the builder of the sacristy of St Peter's and the Casino of the Villa Albani, had to be included, it was not difficult on the whole to decide what buildings should be excluded on the grounds that they belonged to the incipient Neo-classical movement.

The question of where to begin was much more difficult. Obviously the immediate forefathers of Baroque architecture, who worked for Paul V and his nephew Scipione Borghese – Carlo Maderno, Flaminio Ponzio and Van Santen (Vasanzio) – had to be included, and it seemed to be sensible to put in as much as possible of the work of their immediate predecessors – Giacomo della Porta, Domenico Fontana and Giacomo del

Duca – on the grounds that the first two created the Rome in which the inventors of the Baroque grew up, while the third was an important factor in the formation of Borromini's style. I have only mentioned the work of earlier artists when it is to be found in buildings which play an important part in the development of the Baroque, or which were enlarged or altered in the Baroque period and had therefore in any case to be discussed. So, for instance, Vignola's S. Andrea in via Flaminia is included as belonging to the first category, Perino del Vaga's frescoes in S. Marcello are mentioned because the church has to be discussed for its Baroque features, and even S. Sabina gets a mention because of its altarpiece by Sassoferrato and the chapel of St Dominic within the convent attributed to Borromini. I have even included the church and Oratory of S. Giovanni Decollato because they contain spectacular examples of Mannerist illusionist decoration which form a prelude to the work of the Alberti brothers and so lead on to Baroque decoration. I am aware of the fact that I have not been consistent in giving data about late sixteenth-century painting, but much of it is not really relevant to the Baroque, and I have tried to include as far as possible paintings of the last generation of Mannerists as well as the contemporaries and followers of Caravaggio and the Carracci.

The main emphasis in the book is on architecture. This is partly because of my own special interest in this aspect of Roman Baroque, but it has also a more objective basis, in that architecture was the master art in the Baroque age, and one of the most obvious characteristics of this period is the fusion of the three arts of architecture, sculpture and painting under the dominant control of the first. The entries on individual churches therefore contain a fuller discussion of architecture than of the other arts. I have, however, as far as possible included information about the paintings and sculpture in the buildings discussed. In the case of the paintings I have taken a permissibe short-cut by referring to Sir Ellis Waterhouse's lists in his Roman Baroque Painting (2nd edition, London, 1976) but they unfortunately do not cover some important painters of the eighteenth century, and do not refer to works in Roman churches by non-Roman artists. He has, however, kindly supplied me with many details from his notes and I have added others from old guide books and recent literature, but I am aware of the fact that my treatment of this aspect of the subject is a little summary. The problem of sculpture was more difficult because the modern literature on the subject is so incomplete, but here I have had the inestimable advantage of having been able to consult Dr Jennifer Montagu, the greatest expert on the subject, who generously offered to read through the whole manuscript and has not only saved me from making a number of howlers but has added much information of the greatest interest. Any facts based on unpublished documents discovered by Dr Montagu are marked with the initials J. M.

It was difficult to know how much practical information to add. The location of every monument has been given. These indications should make it possible for users of the book to find any building which interests them; but will they be able to get into it?

PREFACE TO THE ORIGINAL EDITION

Most Roman churches are open from early in the morning (6 or 7 a.m.) till midday and many reopen from about 3 p.m. onwards, but there are, as every student of Roman art knows, only too many which are only open on rare occasions, perhaps early on Sunday morning, possibly for a late mass at midday, or perhaps only on the feast of the patron saint. It was tempting to include what information I had been able to collect on this subject, but careful examination showed that it goes out of date so rapidly that it can be more misleading than helpful. The new Guide Rionali, for instance, often gives indications of when churches are open, but having made a check of about a dozen I found that two out of three were wrong – and the result was merely to add to one's sense of frustration. The only advice is 'try, try again', and ask the advice of neighbours who may know where the parocco or the sacristan lives. Some Roman churches now have notices on their doors giving their times of opening, but the information is often misleading; for instance, they often forget to mention that the timetable does not apply in, say, August and September when the parish priest and the sacristan may be on holiday, or the monks in their country retreat.

I have also added notes on some churches which no longer exist, but about which there is some visual evidence in the form of old photographs, engravings or, in one case, a foundation medal.

In the description of the interiors of churches I have followed a path starting from the entrance, going up the right wall or aisle, through the transepts (if they exist) and the choir and then down the left-hand side. The abbreviations 1 to R, 1 to L mean first chapel or altar to the right or left.

I have visited – by which I mean been inside – almost all the churches covered in this handbook. In cases where I have failed to get into them during the preparation of the book I have qualified any comment I make about the interiors with the word 'apparently', which means that I have based my statement on what appears to be the best available evidence from written or verbal sources.

I have also been round all the major churches and a very large percentage of the smaller ones with the final typescript in my hand in order to make sure that I have supplied the answers to as many as possible of the questions which the student will ask and to check that objects which I mention are in the places where I describe them. As regards the first point I have not listed altarpieces or tombs about which no information seems to be available. About the second I have no doubt made mistakes, and I should be very grateful for any corrections which users of the guidebook may care to send me. The same applies to bibliographical references which I have done my best to check, but in which mistakes are certain to have arisen in the process of copying – mainly owing to my handwriting.

I have as far as possible noted whether the marbling in a church is composed of real marble or scagliola, or is painted. The distinction is important because it affects the whole appearance of a church and is not visible in a reproduction. The result is that certain churches – for instance S. Carlo al Corso or SS. Trinità degli Spagnuoli – appear in a reproduction to be magnificently decorated but in reality the 'marbling' is painted, with the result that instead of reflecting the light, it is completely dead and produces an effect of heaviness. The finest example of the effect of luminosity produced by real marbling is Bernini's S. Andrea al Quirinale, but it is also effective in less ambitious churches, such as S. Giovanni Calabita, S. Maria dell'Umiltà or S. Caterina da Siena a Magnanapoli.

I have incurred many debts of gratitude in the preparation of this book. Some of these have been acknowledged above, but I have also gained much by discussion with my colleagues in London University, particularly Howard Burns and Bruce Boucher.

Above all I must thank Elizabeth Haslock who has patiently and uncomplainingly typed and retyped the text, deciphering my additions and corrections and detecting many mistakes and inconsistencies, and has prepared the index of artists – a formidable task. Without her help the book would have remained an untidy bundle of notes and would certainly never have reached the publisher.

When it did reach the publisher I was lucky in that it fell into the hands of Moira Johnston who not only carried out the boring process of checking spelling, typography etc. but pointed out a shameful number of inconsistencies and ambiguities. I – and my readers – owe her a deep debt of gratitude for her acute and scholarly checking of the text and index.

It would not have been possible to write this book without the existence of the Bibliotheca Hertziana, with its unrivalled collection of modern books, periodicals and old guide books dealing with Rome, many of which are difficult to find in this country and even in other libraries in Italy. In fact it might be said that it is simply a distillation of their marvellous indexes arranged according to artists and individual monuments as well as by authors. It is for this reason, and also in gratitude for the kindness and hospitality that I have invariably received there over many years, that I dedicate this book to the Library, its foundress, those who built it up, and those who administer it today.

I should also like to express my particular gratitude to the late Wolfgang Lotz, who died suddenly while this book was in the press. During the many years when he was director of the Library he found time to discuss with me problems connected with Baroque architecture with which I was faced, always providing imaginative suggestions which cleared away many clouds and led me to a fuller understanding of the whole subject.

Anthony Blunt,
London 1982

In the present edition a number of changes have been made to Anthony Blunt's layout that we hope will be of use to the reader. The bibliographical notices, and the footnotes, have been collected in a section of their own in order to free the text up and make it more legible. The start date remains unchanged, though a few more of the early buildings and decorative schemes are described; and the end date too remains

PREFACE TO THE ORIGINAL EDITION

unchanged as far as buildings are concerned, although Dr. Erwee has included statuary and some other decorative elements up to the mid-nineteenth century where this will help the visitor. Greater attention has been paid to clarifying the subject matter of paintings and sculpture. Finally, for some of the more obdurately closed churches, an attempt has been made to identify opening times, though no guarantee can of course be proferred on this score.

Like Anthony Blunt, we must also emphasize how grateful we will be to any readers who can point out errors and omissions.

THE CHURCHES

S. Adriano
Foro Romano

In Republican times this building housed the Roman Senate. Under Honorius I (625-38) it was converted into a church. It was remodelled by Martino Longhi the Younger in 1653-56, but in the 1930's all the Baroque additions were removed. They are, however, recorded in photographs which are reproduced by Pugliese and Rigano.

The holy-water stoups with angels by Orfeo Boselli formerly in the church are now in that of S. Maria della Mercede, viale Regina Margherita[1].

S. Agata dei Goti
Via Mazzarino, 14-16

A church existed on the site from very early times, and at one moment in the 5th century it was occupied by the Arians. The medieval church was restored and decorated for Cardinal Antonio Barberini under the direction of Andrea Sacchi between 1633 and 1641 and again in 1726 under the direction of Salvatore Casali, but most of the additions then made were removed in a further restoration in 1933.

The façade dates from 1726 and is attributed by Roisecco and Titi to Francesco Ferrari. The usual entrance to the church is in the via Panisperna, 29.

INTERIOR
The wooden ceiling, commissioned by Cardinal Francesco Barberini, was designed by Domenico Castelli and carved by Bartolommeo de' Rossi, 1632-33.

The organ above the entrance was commissioned by Cardinal Carlo Giacomo Bichi, 1703[1].

The painting in the half-dome of the apse and the paintings between the windows representing scenes from the *Life of St Agatha* are by Paolo Gismondi, begun c.1637 but only completed c.1672. R aisle: *St Agatha Refuses the Advances of the Consul Quintan*; *St Agatha Refuses to Worship Pagan Gods*; *St Agatha Has her Breasts Cut off*; L aisle: *St Peter Appears to St Agatha*; *Martyrdom of St Agatha*; *Death of St Agatha*; apse: *St Agatha Received into Heaven*. The gilded stucco frames date from 1709.

R aisle: Cappella di S. Agata: marble sarcophagus designed by A. Sacchi, 1636-38. Altar and wooden statue of *St Agatha*, 1681
L aisle: monument in stucco to Cardinal Carlo Bichi (d. 1718) by C. de' Dominicis[2].

S. Agata in Trastevere
Piazza di S. Giovanni de' Matha, 7

According to an inscription in the sacristy the church was founded by Gregory II in 727 but it is first mentioned in 1121. It was given by Gregory XIII in 1575 to the Congregation of Christian Doctrine who began to rebuild it in 1671, but work was delayed until 1710 when it was begun again to the designs of Giacomo Onorato Recalcati.

INTERIOR
The interior is painted marble.
Vault of nave: Girolamo Troppa, *St Agatha in Glory*, 1711[1]
3 to R: Biagio Puccini, *Madonna of the Rosary with Sts Dominic and Catherine and Souls in Purgatory*[2]
High altar: B. Puccini, *Martyrdom of St Agatha*, 1713[3]
3 to L: B. Puccini, *Crucifixion with the Virgin, Sts Mary Magdalen and John the Evangelist*[4].

S. Agnese in Agone
Piazza Navona

As an important part of his scheme to make the Piazza Navona into a monument to his family, Innocent X planned to rebuild and greatly enlarge the church of S. Agnese, which at that time faced on to the via dell'Anima with its choir abutting the Piazza Navona. In 1652 Girolamo Rainaldi, assisted by his son Carlo, provided the first plan. This consisted of a Greek cross with rounded ends to the arms and large niches in the piers, a long rectangular vestibule and a straight façade articulated with large and small columns. In February 1653 Innocent X entrusted his nephew, Camillo, to undertake the building of the church. In April 1653, as a result of the severe criticism which had been levelled at the design of the church, Rainaldi resigned and the work was left in the hands of his son. In June, however, Carlo was replaced by Borromini. A drawing by Cortona in the Staatliche Sammlung, Munich, which was originally thought to be connected with SS. Luca e Martina, is in fact for S. Agnese and shows that Cortona must have submitted a design for the church in 1652 or early in 1653.

By the time Borromini took over, the interior had nearly reached the top of the pier niches and the façade had risen to a height of ten feet. Borromini had the façade pulled down and his final plan involved important changes: a concave façade enclosing a flight of oval steps and whole columns at the corners of the main piers in the interior. Work went so fast that by the beginning of 1655 the dome was complete except for the lantern and the façade had reached the cornice; in the interior the columns and pilasters were finished up to the capitals.

It has always been thought that the curved façade and the steps were the invention of Borromini, and Karl Noehles discovered a drawing[1] which he believed to be a copy of one showing Borromini's new plan in one half and Rainaldi's plan in the other. Eimer, however, argues that the drawing shows Girolamo Rainaldi's original design together with a new design by his son. If this hypothesis is correct, the oval steps and concave façade would have to be credited to Carlo Rainaldi, but Eimer's arguments are not conclusive and the design with a concave façade has no parallel in the work of Carlo Rainaldi but is completely in accordance with Borromini's style.

In January 1655 Innocent X died and his nephew Camillo Pamphili was left to finish the church. Alexander VII appointed a commission under Cardinal Imperiali to supervise the building but relations with the architect became strained. Borromini was accused of neglecting his duties and in February 1657, in order to avoid being dismissed, he resigned. Carlo Rainaldi was recalled to complete the church. In so doing he made considerable modifications to Borromini's design, reducing the height of the lantern, giving it eight columns instead of sixteen and taking away all the fantasy of Borromini's towers, which are recorded in a drawing[2].

Preimesberger has shown that the completion of the church was not entirely due to Rainaldi. Camillo Pamphili died in May 1666 and control of the project was taken over by his widow Donna Olimpia. She appointed G. M. Baratta to supervise the building and in November added Cardinal Decio Azzolini to the commission, who called in Bernini (his name appears in December). Bernini at once ordered work on the façade to be stopped and produced a new design for it. This involved abandoning

Borromini's compound pediment, which rose from the attic, and replacing it with a straight pediment set against the attic. Above it was to be the coat of arms of Innocent X, supported by angels, and there were to be statues on the attic. Of all these features only two were carried out: the coat of arms and the statue of *St Eugenia* by Andrea Baratta, 1669[3]. In the interior Bernini made one important alteration: he removed those parts of the attic which ran over the niches of the main piers, thus enlarging the space for the pendentives. He then caused the commission to fresco them to be given to his protégé Baciccio and quite possibly supplied the iconographic programme, and perhaps even sketches, for them.

In the summer of 1668, however, the young Giambattista Pamphili, son of Camillo and Donna Olimpia, came back to Rome after a tour abroad, took control and changed all his mother's plans. According to Preimesberger (who does not unfortunately quote the documents), he replaced Bernini with Cortona and his pupil, Ciro Ferri. Ferri began frescoing the dome in 1674-75.

Innocent X intended to erect his own tomb in S. Agnese. In one of Borromini's plans, made in 1653, he shows it at the end of the right transept in a semi-circular bay cut off from the church by four columns of green marble, with behind it a door leading to the adjacent college. In 1656 or 1657 – about the time that Rainaldi took over – it was decided to place the tomb in the left transept and to convert the right transept into a chapel in honour of St Agnes. While Borromini was in charge, Bernini's rival Algardi was engaged to design the tomb and on the latter's death in 1654 the commission was passed on to his pupils, Domenico Guidi and Ercole Ferrata. In 1667 Bernini, who had just taken over control of the building, began to make his own plans for the tomb, with which two drawings at Windsor can be connected. The work was not even begun, however, and in 1698 it was decided to put the tomb over the entrance door, set against a small oratory.

The interior of the church was decorated under Rainaldi's (and for a short time Bernini's) direction by a series of sculptors and painters whose work almost completely destroyed the character of Borromini's interior with the richness of the gilding, the carved and coloured marble and the luxuriance of the frescoes. It is still possible, however, to grasp the significance of the changes which Borromini made to the design of the piers by widening them through the addition of columns, thus giving them a monumentality which they would have lacked in Rainaldi's version.

INTERIOR

The dome, showing *The Heavenly Hosts Introducing St Agnes to the Virgin,* was frescoed by Ciro Ferri, begun in 1674-75 and finished after his death in 1689 by his pupil Sebastiano Corbellini[4]. The pendentives - representing *Justice, Peace and Truth, Faith, Charity and Temperance* - were painted by the young Baciccio, 1662-72[5].

On the piers of the half-domes over the altars are reliefs of angels carrying the symbols of the saints to whom the altars are dedicated, executed by Ercole Ferrata to designs by Ferri.

Over main entrance door: monument to Innocent X (d. 1655) by Valvassori with figures of the pope and *Spiritual* and *Temporal Power* by G. B. Maini, 1723-29[6].

1 to R: Altare di S. Alessio: *St Alexius with Pope Innocent and his Father Euphemianus* by Giovanni Francesco de' Rossi, 1660-63[7]; above: angels and putti with emblems of the saint by E. Ferrata[8].

Between 1 and 2 to R: lower church: marble

relief of *St Agnes Led to Martyrdom* by Giovanni Buratti, 1662-63[9]
2 to R: Cappella di S. Agnese: designed by C. Rainaldi in 1654, altered 1657-58, dedicated 1664; statue of *St Agnes*, c.1664; above: marble angels by E. Ferrata, 1664-66, and stucco angels by Paolo Landini, 1664[10]. Sides: E. Ferrata, reliefs of the *Four Church Fathers*[11]
3 to R: *Martyrdom of St Emerentiana* by Ercole Ferrata and completed on his death by L. Retti, 1660-1709[12]; above: putti and angels with emblems of the saint by E. Ferrata[13]
Summer sacristy: built in 1658 to Borromini's design: a rectangular room with the corners cut off by convex curves. Vault fresco: Paolo Gismondi, *St Agnes in Glory*, 1664[14]. Stuccoes by Rocco Boli, 1659-62. Vault over the altar: Francesco Allegrini, *Assumption*, 1660; marble angels by Andrea Falconi, 1659[15]. Holy-water stoups by A. Baratta, 1666
High altar: ancient columns of *verde antico* bought by the pope in 1658; relief of the *Holy Family with Sts Elizabeth, Zachariah and John the Baptist* by D. Guidi, c.1683-88[16]; *Angels and Glory* by G. B. Maini and F. Moderati, 1721[17]
3 to L: Altare di S. Cecilia: relief of *The Dying St Cecilia Visited by Pope Paschalis and St Maximus* begun by Giuseppe Peroni and completed by A. Raggi, 1662-65[18]; above: putti with emblems of the saint by E. Ferrata, 1670
2 to L: Cappella di S. Sebastiano: statue of *St Sebastian* by P. P. Campi, 1719[19]
Between 2 and 1 to L: Cappella di S. Francesca Romana: fresco, *Ascension of St Frances of Rome* by F. Cozza, 1660[20]
1 to L: Altare di S. Eustachio: *St Eustace and his Family Exposed to Wild Beasts*. Commissioned in 1660, the relief was begun by Melchiorre Caffà (d. 1667) but finished by E. Ferrata and G. F. de' Rossi[21]. Above: angels and putti by P. Legros, 1717-19[22].

S. Agostino
Piazza di S. Agostino

The site was given to the Augustinian Hermits in 1286 and a church was begun in the following year. It was rebuilt in 1479-83 by the French Cardinal d'Estouteville, chamberlain to Sixtus IV. The masons were Jacopo da Pietrasanta and Sebastiano Fiorentino. Vasari attributes the design to Baccio Pontelli, probably wrongly. The church was restored between 1756 and 1763 by Vanvitelli, who added the sacristy. Restored again in 1856-68[1].

INTERIOR
The nave and piers were frescoed by Pietro Gagliardi, 1855-61.
Nave: scenes from the *Life of the Virgin*[2]; piers: *Prophets*; on crossing piers: *Four Latin Fathers*; pendentives: *Four Evangelists* and dome: *Apostles* with *Christ* in the lantern
Entrance wall: Altare Martelli: Jacopo Sansovino, *Madonna del Parto*, 1518-21[3]. L of altar: monument to Francesca Faggioli (d. 1661) with a portrait by her husband Francesco Cozza[4]; to L: monument to Alessandro Saracinelli (d. 1669)[5]
3rd pier to L: above: Raphael, *Isaiah*, 1512; below: Andrea Sansovino, *Virgin and Child with St Anne*, 1510-12, both commissioned by the humanist Johann Goritz[6]. This group was moved by Vanvitelli to the third chapel left but in 1981 the niche was reopened and restored and the group replaced in its original position below the Raphael

The two angels holding the holy-water stoups are by Cosimo Fanzago (*Raphael*, 1650; *Gabriel*, 1660). A third smaller angel in the left aisle is also attributed to him[7]. The pulpit is by Carlo Spagna to a design by Vincenzo della Greca, 1664.

1 to R: Cappella di S. Caterina d'Alessandria/Mutini: decorated by Marcello Venusti; altarpiece: *Coronation of St Catherine of Alexandria*; to L: *St Stephen* and to R: *St Lawrence*, c.1550-60[8]. Monuments to L: Stefano Mutino (d. 1485) and Lorenzo Mutino (d. 1509) and to R: Stefano Mutino (d. 1585), Clemenza Cafarelli and Giovanni Battista Mutino (d. 1609)

Between 1 and 2 to R: monument to Cardinal Fabrizio Veralli (d. 1624)[9].

2 to R: Cappella di S. Giuseppe/Castanga: built by Giacomo della Porta. Apse medallions: L: *Visitation*; C: *Annunciation*; R: *Presentation* by Avanzino Nucci. Altarpiece: Domenico Spagnolo, *Madonna of the Roses*. Stucco by Giovanni Giacomo, 1588[10]. Side walls: P. Gagliardi, L: *Death of St Joseph* and R: *Marriage of the Virgin*

Between 2 and 3 to R: monument to Cardinal Girolamo Veralli (d. 1555)

3 to R: Cappella di S. Rita: architecture and decorations by G. B. Contini, 1674[11]. Altarpiece: G. Brandi, *St Rita of Cascia in Ecstasy*[12]; frescoes by P. Lucatelli, vault: *Vision of St Rita*; side walls: L: *Death of St Rita* and R: *The Young St Rita Covered with Bees*[13]

4 to R: Cappella di S. Pietro/Casali: apse fresco: G. Vasconio, *Angels in Glory*; L wall: *Assumption*; R wall: *Immaculate Virgin*. Over altar: G. B. Cassignola, marble group of *Christ Giving the Keys to St Peter*, 1596, which originally stood in a niche in one of the nave piers

Between 4 and 5 to R: monument to Baldassare Ginanni (d. 1595)

Between 6 to R and sacristy: monument to Alberto Splawski (d. 1596) with bust by A. Casa (1866)

R of sacristy door: bust of Onofrio Panvinio, distinguished ecclesiastical historian and Augustinian monk (d. 1568), by G. Sibilla, 1758

Above door: memorial to Cardinal Guillaume d'Estouteville with bust by Pietro Galli

Sacristy passage: monument to Ambrogio Landucci (d. 1669)[14]

Sacristy: by Carlo Murena to Vanvitelli's design, 1756-60[15]. Altarpiece: copy after Romanelli's *St Thomas of Villanova Distributing Alms*, c.1660[16]

L of sacristy door: bust of Cardinal Henry Noris (d. 1704) by Francesco Maratta, erected 1759[17]. Further: monument to Leopoldo Ratti and Angelo Righi by T. Rabacchi

6th pillar to R: monuments to Cardinal Antonio Ghirlandaio (d. 1669) attributed to Bernardo Fioriti[18], Cardinal Giovanni Giacomo Baldini (d. 1675)[19] and Cardinal Tommaso Maria Martinello

R transept: Cappella di S. Agostino: built by V. della Greca, 1636. Altarpiece by Guercino, *Sts Augustine, John the Baptist and Paul the Hermit*, 1637-38[20]; on walls: paintings by Lanfranco, R: *St Augustine Destroys the Manicheans* and L: *St Augustine Washes the Feet of a Pilgrim (Christ)*, 1637-38[21]

L wall: monument to Cardinal Giuseppe Renato Imperiali (d. 1737) by Paolo Posi; statues by Pietro Bracci, L: *Charity* and R: *Fortitude*; portrait by Pietro Paolo Cristofari to a design by L. Stern, 1741-45[22]

Chapel to R of high altar: Cappella di S. Nicola da Tolentino/d'Estouteville: vault: scenes from the *Life of St Nicholas* by G. B. Ricci, V. Conti and G. B. Cavagna; pendentives by A. Lilli, *Four Latin Fathers*[23]. Altarpiece: Tommaso Salini, *St Nicholas of Tolentino with the World and the Devil*[24]. Wall frescoes by P. Gagliardi, L: *Vision of St Nicholas during the Celebration of Mass* and R: *End of the Plague in Córdoba*

High altar: by Orazio Torriani, 1628. The

two angels by Giuliano Finelli to Bernini's designs are the first work by Bernini to have been executed entirely by studio assistants, 1626-28[26]
Over doors in choir: pairs of putti, those on the left by P. Bracci[27], those on the right by Pincellotti
1 to L of high altar: Cappella di S. Monica: Giovanni Gottardi, *Madonna of Consolation with Sts Augustine and Monica*[28]. Vault frescoes of scenes from the *Life of St Monica* by G. B. Ricci[29]; side walls by G. Gagliardi, L: *St Monica Consoled by a Bishop* and *St Monica's Vision*; R: *St Monica Receives the News of her Son's Conversion* and *Death of St Monica*[30]
2 to L of high altar: Cappella di SS. Agostino e Guglielmo/Buongiovanni: on walls, R: *Vision of St William* and L: *St Augustine Meditates on the Trinity*; altarpiece: *Coronation of the Virgin with Sts Augustine and William*; vault: *Assumption*; lunette: *Apostles by Mary's Tomb*; pendentives: *Prophets* by Lanfranco, 1616[31]
Over entrance to chapel: tomb of Cardinal Lorenzo Imperiali (d. 1673), Governor of Rome under Alexander VIII by Domenico Guidi, 1676[32]
L transept: Cappella di S. Tommaso da Villanova/Pamphili: built for Principe Camillo Pamphili and decorated by G. M. Baratta 1660-69[33]. The figure of *St Thomas Distributing Alms* was begun by Melchiorre Caffà but the whole group was finished after his death in 1667 by Ercole Ferrata, who also executed the angels and *God the Father* over the pediment. The reliefs on the side walls are by Andrea Bergondi: R: *Apparition of St Thomas* and L: *St Thomas Exorcising a Demon*[34]
L wall: monuments to R: Bishop Giuseppe Eusanio (d. 1692) by C. Rusconi[35] and L: Adeodato Nuzzi (d. 1720)
R of door: bust of Cardinal Girolamo Seripando (d. 1759) by Gaspare Sibilla, 1758-59[36]
L of door: bust of Gregorio da Rimini (d. 1759) by G. Sibilla, 1758[37] and monument to Alessandro Saracinello by G. Trabacchi, 1871
6th pillar to L: monuments to Giuseppe Francesco Mazio by R. Francisi, 1870, Cardinal Filippo Maria Visconti (d. 1664)[38] and Cardinal Fulgenzio Petrelli (d. 1648)
5 to L: Cappella di S. Giovanni da San Facondo: G. Brandi, *St John of San Facondo Rescues a Drowning Child*, before 1674[39]
Between 4 and 5 to L: monument to Fulgenzio Bellelli (d. 1742)
4 to L: Cappella di S. Apollonia/Marliani: altarpiece: Girolamo Muziano, *St Apollonia Prays whilst in Prison*[40]; vault frescoes of *St Apollonia in Glory*; side walls: allegorical figures of L: *Innocence* and R: *Martyrdom* by Francesco Rosa c.1660-63[41]
3 to L: Cappella di S. Chiara da Montefalco/Mauro: altarpiece: Sebastiano Conca, *Christ Appears to St Clare of Montefalco*, c.1751-52[42]
2 to L: Cappella di S. Anna/Pio: designed by Bernini, 1643-49[43]. Vault fresco and stuccoes by Abbatini, *Angels in Glory*[44]. The altar originally had an *Assumption* by Giacinto Gimignani which was removed by Vanvitelli and replaced by Andrea Sansovino's *Virgin and Child*. The present altarpiece is by Ventura Salimbeni, *Crucifixion*, 1589-90[45]. R wall: monument to Angelo Pio (d. 1649); L wall: monument to Baldassare Pio (d. 1643) in the manner of Bolgi[46]
1 to L: Cappella della Madonna di Loreto/Cavaletti: altarpiece: Caravaggio, *Madonna of the Pilgrims*, 1604-05[47]; frescoes and stuccoes by C. Casolani, L wall: *Mary Magdalen* and R wall: *St William*; in the half-dome are scenes from the *Life of the Virgin*

The cloister and vestibule, which originally opened onto the via della Scrofa (now accessible from the via dei Portoghesi, 12), are by Vanvitelli, 1746-56[48]. On the staircase is a statue of *Benedict XIV* by G. B. Maini, 1747[49]. In the ex-refectory, leading out of the vestibule onto the via della Scrofa, is a fresco of the *Feeding of the Five Thousand* by Gregorio Guglielmi.

SS. Alessio e Bonifazio all'Aventino
Piazza di S. Alessio

The foundation of the church probably goes back to the 4th century. It was originally dedicated to St Boniface but the name of St Alexius was added by Honorius III in 1217. In 1426 it was given by Martin V to the Hieronymite Hermits. At the end of the 16th century it was in a dangerous condition and was restored in 1582. Between 1743 and 1753 it was completely remodelled for Cardinal Angelo Maria Quirini of Brescia, initially on a plan by Nolli and later by Tommaso de' Marchis, who preserved the original plan of the church, including the atrium, but left nothing of the medieval building visible except the campanile.

In the vestibule is a stucco statue of *Benedict XIII*, 1752[1].

INTERIOR

The interior was restored in 1852-60, when Carlo Gavardini decorated the pendentives, *Four Evangelists*, and the apse, *Resurrected Christ*. The vault was painted by Michele Ottaviani.

R aisle: monument to Cardinal Metello Bichi (d. 1619)[2]
4th bay: monument to Eleonora Buoncompagni, wife of Giovanni Battista Borghese, Principe di Sulmona (d. 1695). This was moved here in 1936 from the church of S. Luca dei Ginnasi, which was demolished when the via delle Botteghe Oscure was widened in 1935. The tomb was originally set up in 1702-03 to the designs of G. B. Contini, the figure sculpture being by Andrea Fucigna[3]
R transept: ciborium by D. Ferrerio
High altar: built 1582-1603; on floor to R: monument to Cardinal Giovanni Vincenzo Gonzaga (d. 1591) by N. Pippe, 1592[4]
Passage to sacristy: R wall: monument to Cardinal Giovanni Francesco de' Bagni (d. 1641) by Domenico Guidi, c.1650[5]
Chapel to L of choir: Cappella di S. Girolamo Emiliani/Guidi di Bagno: built by Carlo Murena, 1736. Altarpiece: C. Gavardini, *Virgin and Child with St Jerome Emiliani and Orphans*
L aisle, 2nd bay: J. F. de Troy, *The Blessed Jerome Emiliani Presenting Orphans to the Virgin*, 1749[6]
L of entrance wall: stucco group by Andrea Bergondi, 1755, showing *St Alexius* lying dead under the staircase where he lived for seventeen years. The putti support the relic of the stairs[7].

S. Ambrogio della Massima
Via di S. Ambrogio, 3

Now attached to a Benedictine congregation, the church was rebuilt in 1606, probably to designs by Maderno. The dome was built by Orazio Torriani in 1633. It suffered much from heavy restoration in the 19th century. It still contains, however, some good 17th century altars, though most of the original paintings have been removed. The church is open on Monday afternoon at 5 pm for Mass.

INTERIOR

In the pendentives of the dome are the four Cardinal Virtues - *Justice, Prudence, Fortitude* and *Temperance* - by Francesco Cozza, 1634-35[1]

2 to R: Cappella di S. Benedetto: designed by G. B. Mola, 1635. Marble statue of *St Benedict* by Orfeo Boselli after a stucco model by François Duquesnoy [2]
R transept: Cappella della Croce: altarpiece: *Crucifixion* after Trevisani
High altar: by G. P. Morandi (with modern painting)
L transept: Cappella di S. Mauro: altarpiece: Pierre Subleyras, *St Maurus Heals a Sick Man* [3]
The two transept altars are from Genoa and were installed in 1863.
2 to L: Cappella della Madonna: built in 1631
1 to L: Cappella di S. Giuseppe: fine inlaid altar frontal
In monastery: Baccio Ciarpi, *Death of St Benedict* [4]; Fedele di San Biagio, *Pius V in Glory*.

S. Anastasia al Palatino
Piazza di S. Teodoro

A church has probably stood on this site since the 4th century but it was rebuilt from 1606 onwards at the expense of Cardinal Sandoval y Royas, during which time the façade and portico were rebuilt by Giovanni Maria Bonazzini, probably following a design by F. Ponzio. The portico was destroyed by a cyclone in 1634 and on the order of Urban VIII, whose arms it bears, the present severe brick façade was built, completed in 1636. Martinelli ascribes the façade to Luigi Ariguicci; Titi, Cappello and Crescimbeni to Domenico Castello (payments are recorded to both). Mola attributes it in one passage to Ariguicci and in another to Castello. The church has been closed for many years.

INTERIOR
Between 1644 and 1645 the apse and choir were remodelled for Cardinal Ulderigo Carpegna by Borromini. A restoration programme of the choir and transepts, initiated in 1677 by Monsignor Francesco Maria Febei, resulted in the dismantling of Borromini's choir, parts of which were reused in the transept and high altar. At the same time the *confessio* was built after the relics of St Anastasia were found. Finally the church was restored by Cardinal Nuñez da Cuña de Attayde in 1722[1] to the designs of Carlo Gimac, an amateur architect from Malta[2]
Ceiling: Michelangelo Cerruti, *Martyrdom of St Anastasia*, 1722[3]

Between the nave windows are paintings of a number of saints, of which *St Damasus* in the right aisle and *The Blessed Sancha of Portugal* and *The Blessed Teresa of Portugal* in the left aisle are by M. Cerruti, 1721-22[4].
1 to R: P. F. Mola, *St John the Baptist*, c.1650[5]
Chapel to R of choir: Cappella di SS. Carlo Borromeo e Filippo Neri: L. Baldi, L wall: *St Charles Borromeo Distributing Alms* and *Anointing the Sick with Chrism*; R wall: *Death of St Philip Neri* and *St Philip in Ecstasy*, 1679-80[6]
R transept: Cappella di S. Torbio/Valladolid: designed by M. de' Rossi and executed by G. B. Casella; restored in 1870[7]; altarpiece: F. Trevisani, *St Turibius of Lima*[8]
Choir: high altar designed by G. R. Ripoli; altarpiece: L. Baldi, *Adoration of the Shepherds*, 1680-85; vault: L. Baldi, *Anastasia in Glory with Music-making Angels*, c.1679-81 and stuccoes by Giacomo Pozzi, 1682

The *confessio* below the altar table was designed by M. de' Rossi and built by G. B. Casella, 1682-86; the marble figure of *St Anastasia* was begun by Francesco Aprile (d. 1686) and finished after his death by Ercole Ferrata, 1685-86[9]. Tombs of members of the Febei family designed by M. de' Rossi and executed by G. B. Casella with busts by

G. Lucenti, set up in 1684 by Tommaso Ripoli; R: Monsignor Francesco Maria Febei (d. 1680) and L: Archbishop Pietro Paolo Francesco Febei (d. 1649)

L transept: Cappella del Rosario/ de' Sanctis: altar attributed to G. T. and P. A. Ripoli. Altarpiece: L. Baldi, *Madonna of the Rosary with Sts Catherine of Siena and Peter Martyr*, after 1683[10]; R wall: monument to Cardinal Angelo Mai (d. 1857) by G. M. Benzoni

Chapel to L of choir: Cappella di S. Girolamo: rebuilt to a design by G. T. Ripoli and executed by P. A. Ripoli, 1678-79. Altarpiece: F. Chiari, *St Apollonia Directs the Burial of St Anastasia*; lunette: D. Ponti, *Martyrdom of St Anastasia*, 1677[11]

L nave: Cappella di S. Giorgio: designed by C. Gimac, 1722. Altarpiece: Etienne Parrocel, *Sts George and Publius*.

SS. Andrea e Claudio de' Borgognoni *see* SS. Claudio e Andrea de' Borgognoni

S. Andrea delle Fratte
Piazza di S. Andrea delle Fratte

A church dedicated to St Andrew, with an Augustinian convent attached, existed on this site by 1370. It then passed to the Scottish community but after the Reformation was given to the Confraternita del SS. Sacramento, who still reside in it. The church became a *parocchia* in 1584 and in 1585 was given to the Minims of St Francis of Paola. Rebuilding began in 1604[1] to the designs of Gaspare Guerra but was interrupted in 1609 owing to lack of funds. In 1612 the Marchese Ottavio del Bufalo, whose palace stood nearby, promised a large donation but by the time he died the next year just a small part had been paid. In 1622 Guerra died when only the nave was finished. The Minims themselves completed the nave vault. In 1653 the Marchese Paolo del Bufalo supplied further funds and Borromini was commissioned to complete the church. The campanile and the dome were built between 1653 and 1659 (when they appear in an engraving by Falda) but the projected lantern was never carried out. It seems probable that Borromini followed Guerra's designs in the plan of the transept and the choir but the exterior of the dome and the campanile are entirely from his designs[2].

Borromini had several ancient models in mind when he designed these features. The false drum, which actually encloses the dome – according to a system common in Lombardy since Bramante's dome of S. Maria delle Grazie in Milan but rare in Rome – is close in its general configuration to the ancient tomb near Capua called *La Conocchia*[3], though Borromini introduced an extra curve into the central section. The circular columnar section of the campanile is close to ancient works such as the choragic monument to Lysicrates in Athens. Though Borromini is unlikely to have known this, similar monuments are to be seen in Roman reliefs[4]. By contrast the top section is built of piers faced with the type of cherubim of which Borromini was so fond (cf. the Lateran and the niche on the façade of S. Carlino). There was to have been a lantern over the dome, which would have made the dome dominate the campanile in height as well as in bulk. In view of the roughness of the brickwork (particularly in the capitals) it is likely that Borromini intended to cover the dome with stucco.

The lower part of the façade dates from the period when Guerra was in charge but the upper storey was built in 1826 by

S. Andrea delle Fratte

Pasquale Belli, probably to Guerra's designs, owing to a bequest to the church from Cardinal Ercole Consalvi[5].

INTERIOR

Entirely decorated with painted marble.

Entrance wall: R: tombs of Livia del Grillo (d. 1746) and her daughter the Duchessa d'Avello (d. 1750) by Francesco Queirolo, 1749[6]. L: tomb of Cardinal Carlo Leopoldo Calcagnini (d. 1746) by P. Bracci, 1748[7]

1 to R: baptistery: altarpiece: *Baptism of Christ* by L. Gimignani, 1683[8]. The font cover was painted by Guglielmo Cortese: *Baptism of Christ, St Andrew* and *St Francis of Paola*, 1642[9]. L wall: Marcantonio Bellevia, *St Lucy*; R wall: Domenico Jacovacci, *St Agatha*; altar lunette: *God the Father* by Jacovacci[10]

2 to R: Cappella di S. Michele Arcangelo: altarpiece: *St Michael* by L. Gimignani; frescoes by Cozza, R: *Vision of St Frances of Rome* and L: *St Charles Borromeo Distributing Alms during the Plague*, 1657[11]

3 to R: Cappella di SS. Francesco di Sales e Giovanna di Valois: the chapel was refurbished in 1759[12]. Altarpiece: *St Francis of Sales Receives the Cord from St Francis of Paola in the Presence of the Blessed Jane of Valois* by Marcantonio Romoli. L wall: monument to Cardinal Pier Luigi Carafa by Paolo Posi; R wall: monument to Judith Falconet by Harriet Hosmer[13]; monument to Gioacchino Pessuti (d. 1814) by Teresa Benincampi, 1815[14]

4 to R: Cappella dei Beati dell' Ordine dei Minimi: altarpiece: Giuseppe Cades, *The Virgin Appears to the Blessed Caspar de Bono and Nicholas Saggio*, 1793[15]; R wall: Apollonio Nasini, *Vocation of St Rosalia*; L wall: O. Noleti, *St Rosalia before the Virgin*; L pillar: monument to Michaela Fauvet (d. 1845) by G. M. Benzoni, 1847[16]; R pillar: monument to Oreste Kiprenskij (d. 1836) by Nicolai Iefimoff, 1836[17]

Over entrance door: F. Cozza, *St Charles Borromeo's Vision of St Frances of Rome and Christ*, 1657[18]

L of door: monument to Rudolph Schadow (d. 1822) by Emil Wolff, 1822-24[19]

R transept: Cappella di S. Francesco di Paola: altar by F. Barigioni, 1726-36; altarpiece of *St Francis of Paola* by P. Nogari; stucco angels supporting the painting by G. B. Maini, as well as the stucco putti above the altar, which incorporates two marble putti left unfinished by Bernini and completed by Maini[20]

Ante-sacristy: monument to Monsignor Giuseppe Baviera (d. 1756) and Monsignor Domenico Tomati (d. 1711)

Chapel beyond sacristy: Cappella di S. Francesco di Paola: G. Odazzi, *St Francis of Paola*, c.1723[21]

Sacristy: on ceiling: Giacomo Fuga, *St Francis of Paola*[22]

To L and R of high altar: two *Angels* carved by Bernini himself for the Ponte S. Angelo, 1667-69[23]

Over R door: *Flagellation of St Andrew* by Giovanni Antonio Crecolini, c.1704-08[24]

Apse: R wall: G. B. Leonardi, *Burial of St Andrew*, c.1700[25]; over altar: L. Baldi, *Martyrdom of St Andrew*, 1686-88[26]; L wall: F. Trevisani, *St Andrew Tied to the Cross*, 1695-97[27]. Frescoes by P. A. Marini: in the apse: *Multiplication of the Loaves and Fishes*; over the crossing: *Redemption*; dome: *Celestial Glory*; pendentives: *Sts Jerome and Cyril of Alexandria*; *Sts Ambrose and John Chrysostom*; *Sts Augustine and Basil*; *Sts Gregory the Great and Gregory of Nazianzen*, 1700-08[28]. High altar by F. Ferruzzi, 1728

Over L door: *Condemnation of St Andrew*, attributed to Giovanni Antonio Crecolini[29]

L transept: Cappella di S. Anna: commissioned in 1749, the design of the chapel is by Luigi Vanvitelli, though the building was not finished until 1857 by G. Valadier and his son Luigi[30]. Altarpiece: G. Bottani, *Education of the Virgin*, 1758[31]. Below the *mensa* is a recumbent statue of *St Anne* variously attributed to C. Pacetti and G. B. Maini. Neither attribution is certain but it is an interesting variation on Bernini's *The Blessed Ludovica Albertoni* in S. Francesco a Ripa. The stucco of the *Assumption of St Anne* is by L. Fontana and the stuccoes on either side of the window and soffit are by G. B. Maini: L: *Angel Appearing to Joachim and Anne* and R: *Presentation of the Virgin*[32]

L of left transept: monument to Duchessa Marianna del Bufalo Caffarelli (d. 1816) by Gaetano Giorgieri, 1819[33]

R of side entrance: R: monument to Albert Bertin (d. 1830) by A. Etex, 1831[34]

4 to L: Cappella di S. Giuseppe: F. Cozza, *St Joseph and the Christ Child*, 1632[35]; side walls: G. Capparoni, R: *Sacred Family* and L: *Marriage of the Virgin*[36]

3 to L: Cappella della Beata Vergine: restored by A. Sarti in 1849. Altarpiece: Natale Carta, *The Virgin Appears to Alphonse Ratisbonne*[37]

2 to L: Cappella del Crocifisso/Accoromboni: on the walls of the chapel are marble portrait medallions of four members of the Accoromboni family: R: Cristoforo (d. 1621) and Roberto (d. 1663) and L: Ottavio, Archbishop of Urbino (d. 1645), and Ottavio (d. 1637). The medallions hang on white marble ribbons against a surface of Sicilian jasper and are in many ways reminiscent of the Spada chapel in S. Girolamo della Carità and even more so of some of the unexecuted drawings for this and other Spada chapels, published by Portoghesi[38]. The connection with the Spada designs is confirmed by the fact that the altar of the chapel was made by Giovanni Somazzi, called 'Il Moretto', a *maestro scalpellino* whose name appears frequently as working for the Spada[39], particularly in connection with the decoration of the chapel in S. Girolamo[40]. Portoghesi tentatively ascribes the Accoromboni chapel to Borromini but now that it is generally recognised that the Spada chapel was not designed by him, the basis for the attribution collapses. Whether Virgilio Spada or his brother Orazio, who seems to be responsible for the design, had a hand in the Accoromboni chapel is not clear but it seems fairly certain that the decoration was carried out by Somazzi. The vault fresco of *God the Father and Angels Holding the Instruments of the Passion* is sometimes attributed to Guglielmo Cortese but is not listed by Waterhouse

1 to L: side walls by A. Nucci, L: *Annunciation* and R: *Nativity*[41]

CONVENT

The Doric cloister has an attractive garden and provides a good view of Borromini's dome. The frescoed lunettes illustrate scenes from the *Life of St Francis of Paola* by Raffaello Vanni, Giovanni da San Giovanni, P. A. Marini and others[42]. On the second floor is a gallery with frescoes by Francesco Cortese and Christian Meder, between 1685 and 1729.

S. Andrea al Quirinale
Via del Quirinale, 28-30

In his biography of his father, Domenico Bernini tells us that the architect regarded this as one of his most successful works and that in his old age he sometimes came to sit here and enjoy it; and we may well endorse his judgement. Its plan is simple but original in having the short axis of the oval leading to the high altar; its architecture is pure and conceived in almost unbroken surfaces of delicately coloured marble. Moreover, it contains one of the most brilliant examples of Bernini's device of carrying the action through the whole building: the martyrdom of the saint is depicted in the painting over the high altar, he appears again in the round, rising to Heaven, over the opening to the chancel, while the Heavenly Host awaits him around the base of the lantern, at the top of which is the dove of the Holy Spirit.

The Jesuit Novitiate was founded in 1566 on the south side of what was then the via Pia (via Quirinale), opposite the gardens of the Quirinal, and in 1658 Alexander VII approved an offer by Principe Camillo Pamphili, nephew of Innocent X, to build a new church here. The commission was given to Bernini and the foundation stone laid in November 1658. The dome and vault were completed the following year. The lantern was completed in 1661 and the decoration of the dome was carried out between 1660 and 1666. The convex colonnaded porch was added in 1670.

The old church was at the north-west corner of the site but for the new one a site at the north-east was chosen. Eimer[1] published a plan for the church based on a pentagon, which may be the first design presented, but its attribution to Bernini is open to doubt[2].

The site, enclosed by the existing buildings, was long and shallow, which led Bernini to use an unusual plan. From the *Diary of Alexander VII*[3] we learn that Bernini discussed his plans with the pope on 9 August and 2 September 1658 and on 8 August 1659, and that on 9 September 1658 the architect submitted a model. The entry for 2 September[4] refers to the fact that the church had been moved back in the new plan, which seems to imply that it may originally have been planned to stand right on the street.

In Bernini's first plan the church was enclosed in a court separated from the road by a wall with two gates, one near either end. The basic features of the design were already established: there were to be four chapels on each side of the church, leaving a solid instead of a void at each end of the long axis, but all the chapels, as well as the chancel and the entrance bays, were to be of uniform trapezoidal shape (with the outer wall curved) and there was to be no lantern. No elevation drawing of the façade survives but it is clear from the plan that it was to be flat and articulated with pilasters.

INTERIOR

On the floor is the inlaid marble tomb of Cardinal Sforza Pallavicini (d. 1667) by M. de' Rossi to a design by Bernini. The stucco putti on the vault and the figure of *St Andrew* over the opening to the chancel are by Antonio Raggi[5], and the architectural stuccoes are by Pietro Sassi. The Pamphili arms with two figures of *Fame* over the entrance door and the gilt stucco angels, putti and cherubs around the high altar are by Giovanni Rinaldi, 1668-70[6]. G. M Baratta was responsible for the architectural decorations and oversaw the placing of the *cottonella* marble columns adjacent to the high altar and the attachment and polishing of the other stone surfaces.

1 to R: Cappella di S. Francesco Saverio: altarpiece: Baciccio, *Death of St Francis Xavier*, 1676; on walls, R: *St Francis Preaching* and L: *St Francis Baptising a Heathen King and Queen*, 1705-09[7]; vault: Filippo Bracci, *St Francis Xavier in Glory*

2 to R: Cappella della Passione: decorated by G. Brandi; altarpiece: *Pietà*, 1676; L wall: *Christ and St Veronica*; R wall: *Flagellation*; vault: F. Bracci, *God the Father*

High altar[8]: in 1668 Bernini was recalled to design the high altar, which was executed by M. de' Rossi and G. M. Baratta, with stuccoes by G. Rinaldi. Altarpiece:

Guglielmo Cortese, *Crucifixion of St Andrew*, 1668-71[9]; fresco of *God the Father* in the dome. The tabernacle was made in 1697 and paid for out of a bequest from the General of the Order, Padre Oliva[10]

Room to L of high altar: L wall: monument to Carlo Emmanuele IV di Savoia (d. 1819) by A. Testa, 1821-22[11]

2 to L: Cappella di S. Stanislao: altar by Etienne François, 1716. Altarpiece: C. Maratta, *The Virgin and Child Appear to St Stanislaus Kostka*, before 1687[12]; wall frescoes: Ludovico Mazzanti, R: *St Stanislaus Receives the Host from an Angel while Ill in Vienna*; L: *St Stanislaus Tries to Cool the Heat of Ecstasy*; vault: *St Stanislaus in Glory* by Giovanni Odazzi[13]

1 to L: Cappella dei Santi Fondatori: altarpiece: L. Mazzanti, *Virgin and Child with Sts Ignatius, Francis Borgia and Aloysius Gonzaga*, 1721-25[14]; wall frescoes by Ludovico Antonio David, L: *Adoration of the Magi* and R: *Adoration of the Shepherds*[15]; frescoes on vault: Giuseppe Chiari, *Music-making Angels*, after 1713[16]

Sacristy: vault frescoed by Jean Delaborde, *St Andrew in Glory*, 1669-70[17]; stuccoes by Pietro Sassi

In the novitiate itself (access through the sacristy) are the rooms lived in by St Stanislaus. On the walls are watercolours by Giacomo Zoboli of scenes from the *Life of St Stanislaus*[18]. In the cell is the statue by Pierre Legros, 1702-03, of the saint lying on his death bed, one of the most remarkable examples of Baroque illusionism in the use of coloured marble[19]. Behind: *The Virgin, Sts Agnes, Cecilia and Barbara Appear to St Stanislaus* by Tommaso Minardi, 1825[20].

S. Andrea della Valle
Piazza di S. Andrea della Valle, Corso Vittorio Emanuele

The design of this church, despite being the result of a series of compromises between the projects of different architects, each supported by his own particular patron, is remarkably harmonious. The decoration, on the other hand, records the profound differences which existed within the arts in the first half of the 17th century. Lanfranco's fresco in the dome – the first fully illusionist treatment of a dome to be painted in the 17th century – was a direct challenge to the classical principles illustrated by Domenichino's decoration of the vault of the choir, and was seen as such by contemporary critics (see below). Unfortunately the vault of the nave never received its intended decoration and the frescoes added in the early 20th century do not harmonise with either the purity of Domenichino or the Baroque exuberance of Lanfranco. It is not known how the architects involved in the original design of the church intended to treat the apse but it is almost certain that there would have been a monumental marble altar enclosing a painted altarpiece. The existing arrangement, with frescoes by Mattia Preti and his pupils between the pilasters, bears some resemblance to a formula often adopted in the late 17th and early 18th centuries (cf. SS. Apostoli), though rarely quite so completely denuded of architecture; in this case, however, it was almost certainly dictated by lack of funds.

The Theatine Order, founded in 1524 by S. Gaetano Thiene (St Cajetan) and Gian Pietro Carafa, later Paul IV, and confirmed by Paul III in 1540, was established at S. Silvestro al Quirinale in 1557. In 1586 the Order took possession of the palace given to it by Donna Constanza Piccolomini on the site of the present church and began planning a larger church to the designs of the Neapolitan architect Fabrizio Grimaldi. In 1588-89 Cardinal Alfonso Gesualdo offered to supply funds for the church but commissioned his architect, Giacomo della Porta, to make the plans. In the end Grimaldi was appointed architect but his plan was subjected to revision by Della Porta. The old parish church of S. Sebastiano, which stood on this site, was pulled down (the parish was transferred to S. Susanna) and the foundation stone of the new church was laid in 1591. The nave and first four chapels were built between 1591 and 1599, initially under the supervision of Francesco da Volterra (d. 1594). In 1599-1600 a competition was held for the design of the façade but work had to be stopped for lack of funds. Gesualdo died in 1603 and his estate was not settled until 1605. In 1608 Cardinal Alessandro Peretti-Montalto, nephew of Sixtus V, agreed to complete the church and appointed Maderno as architect in charge. The dome, which was designed by Maderno, was raised between 1620 and 1623 and the nave was finished in 1621.

The problem of the façade is as complicated as that of the design of the church. The façade was begun in Maderno's lifetime and the plan of the lower storey must therefore be his. A drawing for the façade (Florence, Uffizi) carries annotations by Maderno comparing the dimensions of his new design with those of the recently completed Gesù. Borromini demonstrated his ideas in a drawing now in the Ashmolean, datable to 1623 and thought to be his first presentation drawing. The final design was, however, altered while the façade was being built but critics are not in agreement about what share of the final form should be attributed to Carlo Rainaldi and what to Carlo Fontana. Fasolo[1] emphasizes Rainaldi's share but Noehles in his review of Fasolo[2] calls attention to the differences between Rainaldi's design of 1662 and the façade as built and attributes these changes to Fontana, who was in charge in 1663. Rainaldi was much the senior, however, and the character of the façade as it stands today is more in conformity with his style than with Fontana's.

The sculptures on the façade are by Ercole Ferrata (the angel standing on the lower storey where one would expect a volute, *St Andrew*, *The Blessed Andrew Avellino* and the two pairs of putti carved in full), Domenico Guidi (*St Sebastian* and *St Cajetan of Thiene*, studio works) and G. A. Fancelli (*Hope* and *Prudence*); they were all made according to the directions of Rainaldi, 1664-66[3].

INTERIOR

The interior was heavily restored in 1905 when the pilasters were fluted and gilded, the angels in the spandrels added, the frieze and vault of the nave decorated, and a new pavement laid.

In 1614 the tombs of the two Piccolomini popes, Pius II (1458-64) and Pius III (1503), were moved here from old St Peter's, to commemorate the fact that the church was built on the site of the palace given by Donna Constanza Piccolomini.

1 to R: Cappella Ginetti[4]: granted to Cardinal Marzio Ginetti in 1651, built to the designs of Carlo Fontana from 1670 and consecrated in 1684. The chapel decorations, however, were not completed until 1703. The chapel is magnificently lined with marble, which even covers the dome and the pendentives, the earliest example of this kind of decoration introduced by Fontana (see also S. Maria del Popolo, Cappella Cybò).
Altarpiece: A. Raggi, *Virgin and Child with the Infant St John the Baptist and St Joseph*

in Glory, 1671-73; allegorical figures of L: *Humility* and R: *Vigilance*, and over the altarpiece: *Angel* by A. Rondone, 1690
L wall: monument to Cardinal Marzio Ginetti (d. 1671) by A. Raggi, 1683-84; the allegorical figures of *Fame* in the lunette and L: *Immortality* and R: *Religion* are by A. Rondone, 1677-78
R wall: monument to Cardinal Giovanni Francesco Ginetti (d. 1691) and allegorical figures of L: *Justice* and R: *Fortitude* by A. Rondone, 1683-84; the allegorical figure in the lunette of *Fame* is by A. Raggi, 1677-78.
Either side of altar: R: bust of Marchese Marzio Ginetti and L: Monsignor Giovanni Paolo Ginetti by A. Rondone, 1703
2 to R: Cappella Strozzi[5]: this chapel is also richly marbled and contains bronze figures by Gregorio de' Rossi after statues by Michelangelo. The figures were cast in 1616, which is probably the date when the whole chapel was decorated[6]. Restored for Ferdinando Strozzi in 1819[7]
3 to R: Cappella della Vergine: rebuilt in 1887-89 by Aristide Leonori and decorated by Silverio Capparoni. L wall: monument to the Contessa Prassede Tomati di Robilant (d. 1824) by Giuseppe de' Fabris, 1824-25[8]

To the left of the chapel is the monument to Pius III (d. 1503) from old St Peter's.
R transept: Cappella di S. Andrea Avellino: altarpiece: Lanfranco, *St Andrew Avellino Suffers a Stroke of Apoplexy while Saying Mass*[9]. R of altar: monument to P. Gioacchino Ventura di Raulico (d. 1861) by Stefano Galletti, *c.*1870[10]
Chapel to R of choir: Cappella del Crocifisso/Confraternita del Divino Amore: decorated in 1647 with fine black marble columns. According to Mola[11] the altar, and therefore probably the whole chapel, is by Orazio Torriani
Choir: Maderno planned a screen and high altar to cut off the choir from the crossing[12] but these were never built. The apse was frescoed in 1650-51 by Mattia Preti, L: *St Andrew Tied to the Cross*; C: *St Andrew Crucified*; R: *Deposition and Burial of the Saint*[13]. The vault of the choir was decorated by Domenichino, 1622-27, who executed the frescoes and designed the stuccoes, which were carried out by Jacques Sarrazin[14]. The frescoes represent scenes from the *Life of St Andrew*. In the centre of the under-arch: *The Baptist Revealing Christ to Sts Peter and Andrew*; in the canopy of the apse: L: *Flagellation of St Andrew*; C: *Calling of Sts Andrew and Peter*; R: *St Andrew Adoring the Cross*. Below are allegorical figures of (left to right) *Prayer*, *Fortitude*, *Hope*, *Religion*, *Charity*, and *Faith*[15]. The decoration was completed with two frescoes on the side walls by Carlo Cignani with the assistance of Emilio Taruffi: R: *Cardinal Bessarion Arriving in Ancona with the Head of St Andrew* and L: *St Andrew before his Judge*, 1662-65[16]. The *Four Evangelists* in the pendentives of the dome are also by Domenichino, 1622-27, but the dome itself was frescoed by Lanfranco in 1625-27[17]

Lanfranco's fresco in the dome, which is strongly influenced by Correggio's dome of the Cathedral and S. Giovanni in Parma, is one of the earliest manifestations of the full Roman Baroque in ceiling painting and was seen as a novelty which shocked the conservative party but was vigorously defended by others[18].

High altar and tabernacle by Francesco Fontana[19].
L of high altar: Cappella della Purità: restored and marbled for Cardinal Giovan Francesco Stoppani in 1774, whose funeral monument (d. 1774) is in the left chapel niche. Altarpiece: *Virgin and Child* by Alessandro Francesi, 1647[20]
Sacristy: Giovanni de' Vecchi, *Crucifixion*

with St John and the Virgin[21]
L transept: Cappella di S. Gaetano: decorated by Mattia de' Mare and Alessio d'Elia with scenes from the *Life of St Cajetan*, 1764-70: L wall: *Charity of St Cajetan*; *Approval of the Order by Paul III*; R wall: *St Cajetan Preaching in Naples*; *St Cajetan Intercedes for the Plague Victims*[22]. The altar was designed by Cesare Bazzani and erected in 1912. Altarpiece: *The Virgin and Child Appear to St Cajetan* by M. de Mare, 1770. The statues of L: *Abundance* and R: *Wisdom* are by Giulio Tadolini
4 to L (side entrance): L wall: monument to Gaspare Thiene (d. 1676) with statues of R: *Rectitude* and L: *Prudence* by Domenico Guidi, 1676[23]; above, outside the chapel: monument to Pius II
3 to L: Cappella di S. Sebastiano: redecorated in 1869 by Filippo Martinucci with wall frescoes by Guido Guidi: R wall: *St Roch* and L wall: *Christ with Martha*[24]. Altarpiece: Giovanni de' Vecchi, *St Sebastian*, 1614[25]. R wall: monument to Luisa and Pellegrina Cini (d. 1841, 1854), 1841-44[26], and Vincenzo and Raffaello Cini by Scipione Tadolini, 1844-46
2 to L: Cappella Rucellai/Ruspoli: built by Matteo Castello[27], 1603-05, for Orazio Rucellai. Dome fresco: Roncalli, *Angels with Musical Instruments* but poorly preserved. The putti on the pendentives are by Giovanni Battista Crescenzi[28]. R wall: *Martyrdom of St Lawrence*; L wall: *St Sebastian Tended by St Irene*, attributed to D. Seiter but rejected by Kunze[29]
1 to L: Cappella Barberini: begun in 1604 by Cardinal Maffeo Barberini, later Pope Urban VIII, in accordance with the will of his father, Francesco (d. 1600), and consecrated in 1616. Attributed by Baglione[30] and Martinelli[31] to Matteo Castello but according to Hibbard Maderno, and possibly even Ponzio, may have had a hand in the design.

In 1618-19 Pietro Bernini made models for some of the putti which were carved by himself and his son, Gian Lorenzo. The left putti on the left wall pediment is attributed to G. L. Bernini, while that on the right is given to Mochi[32]

The altarpiece of the *Assumption*, 1616; dome frescoes, *Four Virtues with God the Father*; pendentives, *Prophets and Kings*; L wall: *Visitation*; lunette: *Birth of the Virgin* and R wall: *Presentation in the Temple* and lunette: *Annunciation* are all by Domenico Cresti[33]. The angels holding the cross on the pediment of the tabernacle are by Cristoforo Stati.

The statues of R: *St Martha* is by Francesco Mochi, *St John* by Ambrogio Buonvicino and L: *Mary Magdalen* by C. Stati. Nicholas Cordier began a statue of *St John the Baptist* but did not complete it and the existing statue was carved by Pietro Bernini, 1614-15, from a new block[34]. Marble decorations by B. Basso[35].

In the small chapel of S. Sebastiano on the left, attached to the Cappella Barberini, are statues of Carlo Barberini (d. 1630) by Giuseppe Giorgetti, 1665-75[36], and Monsignor Francesco Barberini (d. 1600) by C. Stati, 1616[37]. Altarpiece: *St Sebastian Removed from the Cloaca Maxima* by Cresti[38].

In the passage between the Barberini and the Rucellai chapels are medallions of Antonio Barberini and Camilla Barbadora, parents of Urban VIII, by T. Fedeli, 1626-27[39].

The monastic buildings to the left of the church were probably begun by Giuseppe Calcagni in 1602 and continued by Paolo Maruscelli after 1629[40].

S. Andrea in via Flaminia
Via Flaminia, 208

Built in 1550-53 by Vignola for Julius III to commemorate his release from capture by imperial troops during the Sack of Rome on St Andrew's Day and as part of the scheme to develop the Valle Giulia and the area between it and the Tiber. The church is mentioned by Palladio[1] but he does not name the author. The attribution goes back to Baglione.

This is the earliest surviving church built with an oval dome, though Peruzzi, a generation earlier, had left many designs for oval churches. Vignola carried the idea a stage further in S. Anna dei Palafrenieri where the church itself is an oval.

The main altar panel of the *Assumption* was painted by Sicciolante but is no longer extant. All that remains is the *God the Father* in the vault[2]. The church is open for early morning Mass.

S. Andrea in Vincis
(destroyed)

The church stood in the old via di Tor de' Specchi, below the Capitol. A church had stood on the site from the 15th century but it was rebuilt in the 16th century and again between 1735 and 1773. It was destroyed when the via del Mare was built in 1929 but its façade is recorded in a photograph.

SS. Andrea e Bartolomeo
Via di S. Giovanni in Laterano, 280a

A small church attached to the Ospedale Lateranese (S. Salvatore) was built in 1642 with a very simple front articulated by Ionic pilasters. The interior, which is in the shape of a trapezium, is of little interest, except for the fine 15th century marble altar and floor.

Only open when funerals are taking place.

S. Angelo Custode
(destroyed)

Built on the via del Tritone for the Confraternita dei Santi Angeli Custodi about 1675 to the designs of Felice della Greca. The façade was by Mattia de' Rossi (1668-1676) and the high altar by Carlo Rainaldi (1681). Measured drawings and photographs are reproduced by Matthiae.

S. Angelo in Pescheria
Via Tribuna di Campitelli, 6

Founded in 770 and built into the ruins of the Portico of Octavia; restored in 1610, according to Mola by Giovanni Fontana, again in 1700 under the direction of Carlo Maratta and finally in 1864 for Pius IX by Alessandro Betocchi and decorated by L. Fontana. Usually open on Wednesday and Saturday late afternoons.

INTERIOR

Entrance wall: Francesco Manno, R: *St Francis Caracciolo Adores the Eucharist*; L: *St Francis Caracciolo Converts a Courtesan*, 1808[1].

1 to R: G. B. Brughi, *Sts Lawrence and Cyrus of Alexandria with the Trinity*[2]

End of R aisle: Cappella di S. Andrea/dei Pescivendoli: the right aisle was rebuilt by Martino Longhi, 1583, and the chapel was decorated by I. Tacconi; vault: scenes from the *Life of St Andrew*, 1618-19[3]. Altarpiece: *St Andrew*, attributed to Marco Tullio Montagna[4]. To R of altar: B. Cesari, *Miracle of the Fishes*, 1619[5]

High altar: copy of Reni's *St Michael Defeats Lucifer* by Angelo Augero
Sacristy: copy of Marco Benefial's *Baptism of Christ*[6]

To the right of the church is the small Oratorio dei Pescivendoli, or fish-sellers, built by Filippo Tittoni, 1688-90, with a façade decorated with good stucco work by L. Ottoni and M. Maglia, *c.* 1689[7]. It is now secularised.

S. Anna dei Bresciani *see* SS. Faustino e Giovita (destroyed)

S. Anna dei Palafrenieri
Via di S. Anna

The church was built at the expense of the grooms (*palafrenieri*) of the papal court. According to the life of Vignola with which Vincenzo Danti prefaced his edition of the architect's *Due Regole della Prospettiva Pratica* (Rome, 1583), the plans of the church were made by Vignola and put into execution by his son Giacinto. Probably begun about 1568, the church had reached the main cornice by 1576 when building ceased. The interior was altered in the 17th century when the door in the right wall was blocked up and replaced by an altar. The upper part of the façade was added by A. Specchi between 1700 and 1725. The dome was built by Navone between 1744 and 1755.

The church marks a stage beyond S. Andrea in via Flaminia in the use of the oval. Here for the first time the plan of the church is oval, though it is enclosed in an outer rectangular shell. The interior is articulated with full columns set in niches and these are unequally spaced so that they form an alternation of wide and narrow bays. The exterior has Vignola's usual flat pilasters.

INTERIOR

Restored for Gregory XVI by S. Ferretti, 1842[1]; the interior was redecorated with painted marble during a further restoration in 1897. The frescoes are by Ignatius Stern, R: *Education of the Virgin, St Anne in Glory*; L: *Charity of St Anne, Prophecy of the Virgin's Birth*[2]. Stucco work by G. B. de' Rossi, 1746-47.

The Palafrenieri sold the only painting of importance that they ever owned, Caravaggio's *Virgin with St Anne*, which was paid for in April 1606 and sold to Cardinal Scipione Borghese in June of the same year.

SS. Annunziata
Vicolo dell'Annunziatella, 99

The church, which is attached to a hospital, was founded in 1220 and given to the Arciconfraternita del Gonfalone in 1448. It was used by St Philip Neri to house pilgrims during visits to the seven basilicas of Rome. It was restored for Cardinal Francesco Barberini by F. Peparelli in 1638, and was restored again in 1722.

INTERIOR

1 to R: *St Aloysius Gonzaga in Ecstasy*, attributed to Ottavio Vannini[1]
R of high altar: copy of Maratta's *Adoration of the Magi*
1 to L: *Madonna del Gonfalone*, R. Vanni, *c.* 1640[2]

Oratory of the SS. Annunziata (S. Spirito in Sassia)
Lungotevere Vaticano, 1

The 1763 edition of Titi states that the oratory was 'di nuovo rifabbricato', and a manuscript note in a copy in my possession adds 'col disegno di Pietro Paassalacqua Siciliano'. These facts are confirmed by R. Venuti and Vasi. Passalacqua died in 1748, so Titi's use of the phrase '*di nuovo*' suggests that the oratory must be a late work. It was pulled down when the via della Conciliazione was laid out and rebuilt, apparently exactly as it was, on a nearby site. In its general design the façade is close to that of S. Croce in Gerusalemme, which is, I believe, also due to Passalacqua.

The church has the form of a rectangle with rounded corners used by Borromini for the Re Magi and the Oratory of St. Philip Neri.

INTERIOR
Paintings by Angelo Masserotti.
High altar: *Annunciation*
R: *Christ Taken from the Cross* and *Dormition of the Virgin*
L: *Birth of the Virgin* and *Adoration of the Shepherds*.

SS. Annunziata a Tor de' Specchi
Via del Teatro di Marcello, 32

The church of the convent of Tor de' Specchi, founded in 1433 by Francesca Bussa di Leoni (d. 1440), later canonised (1608) as S. Francesca Romana (see the church of that name), was built at an uncertain date in the 17th century; it was richly decorated as the result of a bequest received from Anna Maria Ludovisi in 1668. The marbling shows some traces of the Neapolitan style introduced by Cosimo Fanzago in about 1650[1].

The church is only open to the public on 9 March, the Feast of St Frances of Rome. Over the door to the convent is a relief of *St Frances and the Angel* by A. Bergondi, 1756.

INTERIOR
Choir: altarpiece: *Annunciation*, Alessandro Allori. Apse decoration by Lorenzo Gramiccia, *Archangel Michael Flanked by Angels Playing Musical Instruments*; on side walls: Sebastiano Ceccarini, *Angels with Instruments of the Passion*, 1749[2]. The tabernacle dates from 1610.

Within the convent are the altarpieces from the church of S. Maria Liberatrice by E. Parrocel: *The Virgin Presents the Rule to St Frances of Rome, with Sts Mary Magdalen, Paul and Roch and a Cistercian Monk*, 1749, and *The Annunciation*; S. Ceccarini, *St Anthony Abbot, St Michael, Tobias and the Angel*[3].

The convent chapel is decorated with a magnificent fresco cycle depicting scenes from the *Life of St Frances of Rome* by the workshop of Antoniazzo Romana, 1468[4].

S. Antonio Abate
Via Carlo Alberto, 2

A church stood on this site from the 6th century but was rebuilt in 1481 and the side chapels were added in 1583. The church was restored and redecorated in 1724 on the orders of Prior Jean von Chores. It is usually open for Sunday morning Mass.

INTERIOR
The fine stucco decorations date from the 1724 restoration. Nave and side chapels frescoed by G. B. Lombardelli and N. Circignani

with scenes from the *Life of St Anthony Abbot*, 1585-86.
1 to R: Cappella di S. Antonio: built by D. Fontana
High altar: altarpiece: G. Odazzi, *Crucifixion*[1].

S. Antonio dei Portoghesi
Via dei Portoghesi, 2

The church was built originally under Eugenius IV in 1429-47 for the Portuguese colony in Rome but was completely rebuilt in the 17th century. According to Mola the church was designed by Gaspare Guerra and the nave seems to have been finished before 1636, but the choir and transepts were only built much later. They were probably begun by Carlo Rainaldi, who was in charge during the years 1674-76, though the work appears to have been completed by Christoph Schor, who was in charge in 1686 when the choir and the dome were still unfinished. The decoration of the interior had begun by 1692.

The most interesting feature of the church is the façade. The foundations were being laid in 1631 and it was described with admiration in 1636 and 1638 by writers of two guide books, who ascribe it to Martino Longhi the Younger, an attribution which is confirmed by Martinelli and Mola. Work on it was, however, still being done in 1692, though this may refer to sculpture only, since in that year the cherubim over the main door by Cristoforo Muti were paid for. De' Rossi says it was finished 'circa l'anno 1695'. There is reason to think that Longhi's design was followed in all its essentials, and the façade of S. Antonio can be regarded as, in many ways, a preparation for that of SS. Vincenzo e Anastasio, with which it has in common the unusual feature of anthropomorphic elements instead of scrolls linking the two storeys, atlantes in the former and caryatids in the latter.

INTERIOR
Restored by Francesco Vespignani, 1868-69, during which time the vault decorations and stucco were added by Giuliano Corsini and Andrea Bevilacqua.
Vestibule: L wall: monument to António de Almeida Borges (d. 1657) and Martín de Azpilcueta Navarro (d. 1586)[1]; R wall: monument to Orazio Maria Battaglia (d. 1679)[2]
Vault: Salvatore Nobili, *Apparition of the Cross to King Alfonso of Portugal*; pendentives: Francesco Grandi, *Sts Mancius, Gerald, Damasus and Victor*
1 to R: Cappella di S. Caterina: R wall: monument to Alessandro de Souza Holstein (d. 1803) by A. Canova, 1805-07[3]
2 to R: Cappella di San Giovanni Battista/Cimini: designed by Cesare Corvara, 1682-88. Altarpiece: *Baptism of Christ*; R lunette: *Sacred Family with St John the Baptist*; L lunette: *Beheading of the Baptist* and vault: *God the Father* by Giacinto Calandrucci c.1682[4]. L wall: Nicholas Lorrain, *Birth of the Baptist*; R wall: Francesco Graziani, *Preaching of the Baptist*[5]; monument to Catherine Raimondi (d. 1703) with bust attributed to Andrea Fucigna. L wall: monument to G. B. Cimini (d. 1683) by A. Fucigna[6]
R transept: Cappella di S. Elisabetta: redecorated to a design by F. Navone and executed by D. Magnani and D. Romagnoli, 1777-89. The commission for the altarpiece was given to Giuseppe Cades but when he died in 1799 he had only completed the *modello*. The actual altarpiece, *St Elizabeth Queen of Portugal Reconciles the Warring Parties of Castile and Aragón*, is by Luigi Agricola, 1803[7]
High altar: designed by C. Schor, 1686.

The presbytery was remodelled to a design by F. Navone and executed by F. Ferrari, including the marble wall decorations and *coretti*, 1774. Altarpiece: Calandrucci, *Virgin and Child with St Anthony*, 1687[8]. R: M. Cerruti, *The Blessed Jane of Portugal Refuses the Crown* and L: G. Odazzi, *The Blessed Teresa and Sancha of Portugal, c.* 1725[9]

L transept: Cappella dell'Immacolata Concezione/Sampajo[10]: completed in 1756; architecture by L. Vanvitelli, who had already left for Naples and was therefore assisted by Carlo Murena[11]. Altarpiece: Giacomo Zoboli, *Immaculate Virgin*, 1756[12]. Tomb of Emanuel Pereira de Sampajo (d. 1750) by Filippo della Valle and dated from 1756 when the chapel was consecrated[13]. Above: allegorical figures of R: *Purity* and L: *Charity* attributed to G. Sibilla.

2 to L: Cappella del Presepe/della Beata Vergine di Betlemme: built in 1783 to the designs of F. Navone; altarpiece: *Adoration of the Shepherds*; R wall: *Holy Family*; L wall: *Adoration of the Magi* by Antonio Concioli, 1782[14].

1 to L: Cappella di S. Antonio Abate: A. Antoniazzo: *Virgin and Child with Sts Anthony of Padua and Francis c.*1490-1500[15]; L wall: M. Venusti, *Sts Anthony Abbot, Sebastian and Vincent*[16]

Within the Istituto Portoghese: Venusti's *St Anthony of Padua and the Christ Child*, which was once on the former high altar[17].

S. Apollinare
Piazza di S. Apollinare

The church was probably founded in the 7th century by Basilian monks. By 1284 a college of canons was attached to it. In 1574 the church and college were given by Gregory XIII to the German Jesuit College (later the German-Hungarian College), which held it until the Order was suppressed in 1773. In 1742 the foundation stone of the new church was laid by Benedict XIV who had promised to pay for the high altar and the chancel. The architect for the church and high altar was Ferdinando Fuga, some of whose drawings survive. The church was consecrated in 1748. The plan is unusual in having a large narthex for the use of the general public while the church itself could be cut off for the use of the college. The façade shows Fuga's rejection of the High Baroque style and his return to a flatter, more classical design. The outer bays end in curved blocks which were perhaps intended to support statues. Though the atrium is open every morning, the church is only open on Sunday mornings.

INTERIOR

Atrium: L wall altar: built to house a miraculous image of the Virgin (*Madonna di S. Apollinare*); altar frontal designed by P. Camporese and executed by A. Cappelletti and S. Borgognoni, 1815[1]. Above: stucco angels by Filippo de' Castro with putti by Peter Anton Verschaffelt, 1748[2]. To left of entrance to church: monument to Giuseppe Calendrelli (d. 1827) by A. d'Este, 1828[3].

Nave painting: *St Apollinaris in Glory* by Stefano Pozzo, 1746[4]

Above entrance: organ case by Girolamo Carpi, 1749[5]

1 to R: Cappella di S. Luigi Gonzaga: altarpiece: Lodovico Mazzanti, *St Aloysius Gonzaga Adores the Crucifix*, 1748[6]

2 to R: Cappella di S. Giuseppe: altarpiece: Giacomo Zoboli, *Holy Family*, 1747[7]; altar frontal by A. Cappelletti, 1815[8]

3 to R: Cappella di S. Francesco Saverio: statue of *St Francis Xavier* by Pierre Legros, 1702[9], stuccoes by Francesco Guidotti

Choir: high altar commissioned by Benedict XIV. It is a lavish structure of marble

columns with gilt bronze capitals, between which are marble panels cut to make a symmetrical pattern; made by Bernardino Ludovisi to Fuga's design, with marble decorations by P. Blasi[10]. The putti on the *mensa* are by Filippo della Valle, 1746[11]. Altarpiece: Ercole Graziani, *St Apollinaris Consecrated Bishop of Ravenna by St Peter*, 1746[12]; candlesticks and cross by L. Valadier[13]. Apse stuccoes by Giacomo Galli, 1747 and stucco angels over the altar by B. Ludovisi
3 to L: Cappella di S. Ignazio di Loyola: C. Marchionni, statue of *St Ignatius*[14].
1 to L: Cappella di S. Giovanni Nepomuceno: altarpiece: Placido Costanzi, *St John Nepomuk with the Virgin and Child*, 1748 [15]

Over the triumphal arch: stucco angels holding the arms of Benedict XIV by P. A. Verschaffelt, 1748[16].

In the college attached to the church is a ceiling fresco by an imitator of A. Pozzo of the *Coronation of the Virgin*.

S. Apollonia
(destroyed)

The church, which stood in Trastevere opposite S. Margherita, was built in 1582 and consecrated in 1585 for the Tertiary Franciscan nuns. Its rather simple façade is recorded in an engraving by Vasi (opposite, church to the right).

SS. Apostoli
Piazza di SS. Apostoli

The church was probably founded in the 6th century by Pope Pelagius to commemorate Narses' defeat of Totila and the Ostrogoths and was completed by John III. It was given to the Conventual Franciscans by Pius II in 1463. The church was restored by many popes, including Sixtus IV, who added the portico, probably to the designs of Baccio Pontelli. Carlo Rainaldi added the windows to the upper level in 1682[1]. In 1701 it was decided that the church was in such a dangerous condition that it could not be saved and Francesco Fontana, son of Carlo, was commissioned to rebuild it, but on the death of Francesco in 1708 his father took over. He was assisted by Niccolò Michetti, who replaced him in 1712, and to a lesser extent by Francesco Ferrari. The church was consecrated in 1724. The façade above the portico was added by G. Valadier, 1827.

Vestibule: L wall: Canova's memorial to Giovanni Volpato (d. 1803), 1804-07[2]; entrance wall: Luigi Roversi, *tondi* of *Sts Joseph of Copertino, Bonaventure, Francis, Clare, Louis of Toulouse* and *The Blessed Duns Scotus*[3]. Tondi of L: *St Philip* and R: *St James* by D. Guidi[4].

INTERIOR
Some of the marbling is painted. The fresco on the vault of the nave, *Christ Receiving the Saints of the Franciscan Order,* is by Baciccio, 1707[5]. Between 1869 and 1875 Luigi Fontana frescoed panels at the sides of Baciccio's fresco with figures of the *Evangelists* and in the area beside the windows with the *Apostles*. The apse fresco by Odazzi shows the *Fall of the Rebel Angels*, not before 1713.

On the inner side of the façade are four allegorical statues: *Religion* by P. Legros; *Charity* by G. Napolino; *Faith* by P. Papaleo and *Prayer* by P. E. Monnot, *c.*1709[6].

1 to R: Cappella di S. Bonaventura/Mendosi: designed by Michelangelo Simonetti, 1771. Altarpiece: N. Lapiccola: *Virgin and Child Adored by Sts Bonaventure and Andrew Conti*, 1771-75[7]; below: Antoniazzo Romano, *Virgin and Child*[8]. Over life-size

statues either side of the altar by Paolo Cavaceppi, L niche: *Faith* and R niche: *Wisdom*, c.1721[9]
2 to R: Cappella dell'Immacolata: built by S. Cipriani for G. B. Rambotti between 1718 and 1744 and modified in 1858 by Louis Gabet. Altarpiece: C. Giaquinto, *Immaculate Virgin*, 1749-50[10]; angel to L of altar by Luigi Roversi, 1860; angel to R by Domenico Morani, 1859[11]
2nd pier L: monument to Maria Clementa Sobieska (d. 1735), wife of the Old Pretender, James Stuart (d. 1766), by Filippo della Valle, 1738-39[12]
3 to R: Cappella di S. Antonio da Padova/Odescalchi: built by Ludovico Rusconi Sassi for Livio Odescalchi and his heir Baldassare, c.1719, completed in 1722[13]; altarpiece: B. Luti, *St Anthony of Padua with the Christ Child*, 1721; the two stucco angels above the altar are by Bernardino Cametti; dome: *St Paul Shipwrecked in Malta* and *St Anthony Received into Heaven*; spandrels: *Personifications of the Cardinal Virtues* by Giuseppe Nasini, 1722[14]
Chapel to R of high altar: Cappella del Crocifisso: built by Sebastiano Cipriani, 1721-23, but transformed in 1858 by Luca Carmini; the fresco to the side of the altar of *Sts Anthony and Francis* and the scenes on the walls depicting the *History of the Franciscan Order* are by Domenico Bruschi[15]
Apse: this is one of the earliest examples of an apse being built without a full altar, the altar being merely indicated by the flanking pilasters of the main order
High altar: Muratori, *Martyrdom of Sts Philip and James*, 1715-16[16]. The *confessio* was excavated and decorated between 1873 and 1886. It contains statues of R: *St Claudius* by Domenico Guidi, c.1650[17], and L: *St Eugenia* by Giuseppe Peroni, which were once part of Rainaldi's altar in the Cappella di S. Antonio da Padova[18]

Choir: R wall: monument to Count Giraud d'Ansedun (d. 1505); above: monument to Raffaele Riario (d. 1521); above: organ case by S. Cipriani, 1726[19]. L wall: monument to Cardinal Pietro Riario (d. 1474) by Mino da Fiesole and Andrea Bregno, 1474-75[20]
End of L aisle: monument to Clement XIV (d. 1774) with allegorical figures of L: *Temperance* and R: *Humility* by Canova, 1783-87, commissioned by Carlo Giorgi[21]
Sacristy: designed by Francesco Fontana, together with the cupboards, which were carved by Modesto Scaramella and his son Lazzaro. Vault: *Ascension* by Sebastiano Ricci, 1701[22]
3 to L: Cappella di S. Francesco/Colonna: altarpiece: G. Chiari, *St Francis in Ecstasy*, 1726[23]. Monuments to L: Cardinal Carlo Colonna (d. 1739) by G. B. Grossi, 1753[24], and R: Maria Lucrezia Rospigliosi Salviati (d. 1740) by Bernardino Ludovisi, 1749[25]
Between 3 and 2 to L: monument to Principe Filippo Colonna (d. 1821) and his wife, Caterina Colonna Savoia Carignano, by Francesco Pozzi, 1822[26]
2nd pier to L: monument to Bessarion of Trebisond (d. 1473); pulpit by Sebastiano Cipriani, 1736
2 to L: Cappella di S. Giuseppe da Copertino: designed by M. Simonetti, 1779. Altarpiece: G. Cades, *St Joseph of Copertino Levitating at Mass thereby Converting the Duke Johann Friedrich of Braunschweig-Hannover*[27]. Vault fresco: L. Fontana, 1865[28]
Between 2 and 1 to L: monument to Giuseppe Vannutelli and Clara Girometti by Vincenzo Luccardi, 1861[29]
1 to L: Cappella della Pietà: F. Manno redesigned the chapel in 1807-15 and painted the altarpiece, *Deposition*, 1815.

S. Atanasio dei Greci
Via del Babuino, 150b-c

Built in 1580-83 by Gregory XIII under the supervision of Cardinal Santori for members of the Eastern Church who had joined the Roman Church, partly with the intention that they should foster their union. Though Martino Longhi the Elder is recorded as working on it by Titti, all other early authorities agree that the architect of the church, including the façade, was Giacomo della Porta. This church ranks with S. Maria dei Monti among the most harmonious works of Roman architecture of the last decades of the 16th century. The interior is disturbed by the iconostasis inserted in 1876.

The façade is unusual in having two flanking towers, a form not often found in Roman churches at this date (but cf. S. Trinità dei Monti).

INTERIOR
1 to R: Francesco Traballesi, *Annunciation*
R transept: Giuseppe Cesari, *Coronation of the Virgin with the Apostles around her Empty Tomb*
L transept: G. Cesari, *Crucifixion*, 1588-91
1 to L: F. Traballesi, *Christ amongst the Doctors*, 1584[1].

S. Balbina
Piazza di S. Balbina, 8

This ancient church, founded in the 4th century, was restored for Cardinal Pompeo Arrigoni in 1600. It was radically restored in 1929.

INTERIOR
Apse vault: *Christ in Glory with St Balbina* by Anastasio Fontebuoni, who frescoed the figures of *St Peter* and *St Paul* flanking the arch, 1569[1].

Bambino Gesù
Via Urbana

Founded in 1671 for the Congregazione delle Zitelle del Bambino Gesù, mainly owing to the devotion of a pious servant of the Serlupi family, Anna Moroni, with the help of Cosimo Berlinzani, parish priest of S. Maria in Portico.

In the early years of the 18th century it was planned to build a convent and a new church, and about 1708 the architect Alessandro Specchi was asked to produce designs, which survive in drawings but were never executed owing to a lack of funds. In 1731 Clement XII made a generous donation and work was begun on a more modest project by Carlo Buratti, who, however, died the next year and was replaced by Ferdinando Fuga, who completed the church in 1736. It is not clear how far Fuga modified Buratti's designs but the façade is characteristic of the former's style. It originally had a double flight of stairs leading up to it.

The most interesting feature of the interior are the six doors – two in the vestibule and four in the main body of the church – which incorporate interesting variations on Borrominesque forms, suggesting the authorship of Fuga.

INTERIOR
The interior is decorated with painted marble.
Altar to R: D. M. Muratori, *St Augustine Triumphant over Heresy*, 1736[1]
High altar: Filippo Evangelisti, *Adoration of the Shepherds*, c.1730
Altar to L: Altare di S. Andrea Corsini: built by E. Rodriguez, c.1736[2]; altarpiece: Giacomo Zoboli, *The Virgin Appears to St Andrew Corsini*, 1736[3]
L of entrance: Cappella della Passione: built by Virginio Vespignani, 1856; paintings by

F. Grandi, side walls: R: *Betrayal of Judas* and L: *Flagellation*; pendentives: *Old Testament Prophets*[4]; niches: *Four Evangelists* by S. Galletti, 1856[5]

S. Barbara dei Librai
Largo dei Librai, off via dei Giubbonari

The church was given to the Confraternita dei Librai in 1601 and restored between 1674 and 1686 by Giuseppe Passeri at the expense of Zenobio Masotti. Externally it has good stucco figures of angels that support a niche containing a travertine statue of the saint by A. Parisi[1]. The church is usually open for Sunday evening Mass.

INTERIOR
The vestibule vault fresco of *St Barbara in Glory* is by Luigi Garzi, c.1680[2].
R transept: L. Garzi, altar: *Sts John and Mary Magdalen at the Crucifixion*; L wall: *St Anthony of Padua*; R wall: *St Teresa with the Virgin and Child*
Choir: altarpiece: L. Garzi, *St Barbara's Vision of Christ*. R lunette: D. Monacelli, *St Barbara Flees her Father*; below: attributed to C. Mellan, *St Barbara with St Thomas Aquinas and Members of the Confraternita dei Librai*; L lunette: D. Monacelli, *Sts Stanislaus Kostka Receives the Host from St Barbara*. L wall: monument to Zenobio Masotti (d. 1688). Vault: D. Monacelli, *God the Father*
Lunette above high altar: D. Monacelli, *Martyrdom of St Barbara*
L transept: F. Ragusa, altar: *Virgin and Child with Sts Paul, Jerome, Peter* and below: *Thomas Aquinas and John of God with an Angel*; L wall: *St Philip Neri*; R wall: *Ecstasy of St Francis*, L. Garzi[3]
L side chapel: Cappella Specchi: altarpiece: G. B. Brughi, *St Sabas Adoring the Crucifix.*

S. Bartolomeo all' Isola
Piazza di S. Bartolomeo all' Isola

The church goes back at least to the late 10th century but was badly damaged by a flood in 1557. It was rebuilt from 1583 onwards to the designs of Martino Longhi the Elder at the expense of Cardinal Giulio Antonio Santorio. Titi says that the façade is by Longhi the Elder but it cannot be of such an early date and Mola is almost certainly right in stating that it was erected by Orazio Torriani (in 1624-25 according to Buchowiecki).

INTERIOR
Drastically restored in 1865-68. The wooden ceiling dates from 1624 but was altered in the 19th century restoration, when the painted panels by B. Loffredo were added: *St Francis Receives the Stigmata*; *St Bartholomew Refuses to Worship Idols*; *Virgin in Glory*. The stucco decorations in the nave date from 1721-39 under Cardinal Alvaro de Cienfuegos.
2 to R: Cappella di S. Carlo Borromeo: decorated by Antonio Carracci, probably in 1608-11. Altarpiece: *St Charles Borromeo in Prayer*; L wall: *St Charles Administers the Sacraments to the Plague Victims*; R wall: *St Charles Exorcises a Demon*; vault: L: *Almsgiving of St Charles*; *Christ in Glory*; R: *St Charles in Prayer*. Entrance arch: *Bernardino Tarugi and Giuseppe Cavaliero Miraculously Spared from Drowning by St Charles* and landscapes[1]
3 to R: Domenico Antonio Fiorentini, *St Francis Appears to St Bonaventure*, 1796[2]; side walls by A. C. Carlini, R wall: *St Francis Receives the Stigmata* and L wall: *Death of St Francis*
R of high altar: Cappella della Madonna/Orsini: built 1601 and frescoed by G. B.

41

Mercati with scenes from the *Life of the Virgin*; R wall: *Visitation*; *Nativity*; *Marriage*; L wall: *Annunciation; Birth of the Virgin; Presentation in the Temple*, c.1628-31[3]

Presbytery: vault decorated by B. Loffredo, R: *St Francis Venerating the Cross*; C: *St Francis Sending Friars on a Mission*; L: *St Francis Adores the Host*. Altarpiece: F. Manno, *Martyrdom of St Bartholomew*, 1806[4]. Paintings over end chapels by B. Loffredo, L: *Christ Commands the Apostles to Evangelise* and R: *St Bartholomew Preaching*

L of high altar: Cappella di S. Paolino da Nola/Molinari: decorated by an unknown artist in 1704. The altarpiece of the *Virgin with Sts Paulinus, Alabert, Marcellus and Esuperantius* dates from 1655

L transept: monument to Cardinal Lorenzo Cozza (d. 1729)

3 to L: Cappella della Passione: much restored frescoes by Antonio Carracci; L wall: *Flagellation*; R wall: *Crowning with Thorns*; altar: *Crucifixion*; vault: L: *Daniel*; C: *God the Father*; R: *Moses*[5]

2 to L: Cappella della Madonna della Pace: decorated A. Carracci: R wall: *Birth of the Virgin*; L wall: *Annunciation*; vault: L: *Immaculate Virgin*; C: *Dove of the Holy Spirit*; R: *Assumption*, 1609-10

1 to L: Cappella di S. Antonio: altarpiece: Francesco Manno, *St Anthony of Padua*, 1801.

SS. Bartolomeo e Alessandro dei Bergamaschi (S. Maria della Pietà)
Piazza Colonna, 361

Initially founded in 1548 by Ferrante Ruiz, Diego Bruno and his son, Angelo, as the Compagnia dei Povereri Forestieri and officially approved in 1561 as the Confraternita di S. Maria della Pietà, whose task it was to look after the insane. The Jesuit leader Diego Lainez secured them a hospital near the Piazza Colonna, where their church was built by Francesco de' Gnocchis. The interior was redesigned by G. B. Conti, the confraternity's architect, and continued after his death by Carlo de' Dominicis, who was also responsible for the façade. In 1726 the Confraternity of the Bergamasques, which was founded in 1539, took over the church and hospital after their church, S. Macuto, had been given to the Jesuits. In 1729 the interior was radically transformed, probably by Valvassori, the confraternity's architect. Raguzzini also submitted a design for a new church but it was not accepted. The church is usually open in the late afternoons.

The college attached to the church was built by Valvassori from 1730 onwards.

INTERIOR

As built, the church consists of a simple rectangular nave with side chapels. The church was restored by G. Valadier, 1836-39[1], and again in 1884 by Francesco Ceribelli and finally in 1902 by Giuseppe Sacconi from which time the vault decorations by Emilio Restrosi date.

2 to R: Giovanni Antonio Valtellina, *Sts Firmus and Rusticus Refuse to Worship Idols*, 1732[2]

R of high altar: monument to Cardinal Giuseppe Alessandro Furietti (d. 1764), noted archaeologist, by Carlo Sala, 1771-72

Between 2 and 3 to L: painted wooden sculpture by Filippo dal Borgo, *Christ at the Column*, 1574

2 to L: Aureliano Milani, *Beheading of the Baptist*, 1732[3]

Sacristy: G. Muziano, *Beheading of St John the Baptist*, 1578-82
Oratory: above door: D. Alberti, *Virgin and Child with Sts Bartholomew, Francis and Alexander*, 1574-75; end wall: P. Bianchi, *Pope Alexander VIII*, 1690.

S. Basilio
Via di S. Basilio, 51

Built by Innocent XI for the Greek Catholic (Basilian) monks of Grottaferrata. A simple façade (dated 1683) of two almost equal storeys. The interior, restored in 1962, is dominated by the iconostasis and little of the 17th century decorations remains visible.

S. Bernardino ai Monti
Via Panisperna, 257

A small church erected on the foundation of an ancient Roman circular building and consecrated in 1625. The church, which was almost derelict, was restored in 1965.

In 1658 Domenico Caroli, brother of one of the nuns, Maria Chiara, left money to build a high altar. Two years later Maria Chiara decided to have one made to the designs of Bernini, incorporating some columns and coloured marbles already prepared by Pietro Vitale, but nothing came of this scheme.

INTERIOR

The interior is decorated with painted marble.
Dome fresco: B. Gagliardi, *St Bernardine Received into Heaven*, c.1639[1]
1 to R: Cappella di S. Francesco: Giovanni de' Vecchi, altarpiece: *St Francis Receives the Stigmata*; R wall: *St Francis Gives his Rule to Christ*; L wall: *St Francis' Rule Approved*

Between 1 and 2 to R: Giovanni de' Vecchi, *Sts Helena and James*
Apse: altarpiece: A. Amorosi, *St Bernardine in Glory*. Clemente Maioli: R wall: *Preaching of St Bernardine* and L wall: *Funeral of St Bernardine*, 1663[2]
Over L door: G. Baglione, *God the Father with Sts Agatha, Anthony and Clare*, 1617[3]
2 to L: altarpiece: Biagio Puccini, *Virgin and Child*, 1717
1 to L: architecture attributed to Palombi.

S. Bernardo alle Terme
Piazza di S. Bernardo

The church was built in 1598-1600 after Caterina de' Nobili Sforza purchased one of the circular chambers (*torrioni*) of the Baths of Diocletian from the monks of S. Maria degli Angeli, for the Reformed Cistercians (Feuillants or Foglianti) whose prior was the Frenchman, Jean de la Barrière. This particular *torrione* and the area around it had formed part of the famous *vigna* laid out from 1535 onwards by Cardinal Jean du Bellay, the friend of Rabelais and Philibert de l'Orme.

The façade, formed by the door and flanking niches, is decorated with light plaster work in the style current about 1600, but the blind oval panels round the false drum, which encloses the actual dome, seem to date from the restoration of 1670. The ancient coffered dome survives almost intact but is now covered with stucco, probably dating from the restoration carried out in 1857 for Pius IX after the church was occupied by the French in 1803.

INTERIOR

The eight stucco statues of saints in the niches are by Camillo Mariani; from entrance R to L: *Sts Augustine, Monica, Mary Magdalen,*

Francis of Assisi, Bernard of Clairvaux, Catherine of Alexandria, Catherine of Siena and *Jerome*, 1599-1602. The *St Francis* was most probably executed by Mariani's pupil, Francesco Mochi. The stucco angels and the cartouche above the inner portal are ascribed to Mariani[1].
R of entrance: monument to Claudio Benci (d. 1626)
1 to R: Altare di S. Bernardo: G. Odazzi, *St Bernard's Vision of the Crucified Christ*, c.1718[2]
R of choir: portrait of Jean de la Barrière (over his funeral monument), traditionally ascribed to Sacchi but the attribution is rejected by Harris[3]
Chapel to R of high altar: Cappella di S. Francesco/Nobili: built in 1647 for Vincenzo Nobili, with monuments to members of the Nobili family by G. A. Finelli, 1647-c. 49. Entrance wall: Cardinal Vincenzo (d. 1626); R wall: Pierfrancesco (d. 1593) and Sforza (d. 1624); L wall: Cardinal Roberto (d. 1559); Vincenzo the Elder (d. 1560)[4]. Altarpiece: attributed to G. A. Finelli, *St Francis Receives the Stigmata*[5]. Fine *scagliola* altar frontal. Other monuments: L wall: Friedrich Overbeck (d. 1869) by Karl Hoffman, 1870; R wall: Tommaso Mossi by F. Mercandetti[6]
High altar: paid for by Cardinal Giovanni Bona, c.1670
Choir: Saraceni, *Madonna di Loreto*, 1600-05[7]; *Death of St Alexius*, P. Larcan, 1766
To L of sacristy door: monument to Carlo Finelli (d. 1853) by Rinaldo Rinaldi, 1857[8]
1 to L: Altare di S. Roberto: G. Odazzi; *St Robert of Molesmes with the Holy Family and St Benedict*, c.1705[9]
L of entrance: monuments to Alfonso Vidasco (d. 1659)[10] and Antonio Benci (d. 1703).

S. Biagio in Campitelli *see* S. Rita da Cascia

S. Biagio della Pagnotta
Via Giulia, 63-66

A church stood on this site from very early times and was to have been rebuilt as part of the Palazzo dei Tribunali planned by Bramante for Julius II. The project, however, was not carried out and the church was rebuilt in 1730 by G. A. Perfetti. The presbytery was remodelled by Filippo Navone in 1833-34 to meet the ritual needs of the Armenians, to whom the church was given[1].

SS. Biagio e Carlo ai Catinari *see* S. Carlo ai Catinari

SS. Biagio e Cecilia dei Materassai *see* Madonna del Divino Amore

S. Bibiana
Via Giolitti, 150

The church was founded in the 5th century and restored in 1224. In March 1624 the remains of St Bibiana (St Vivian), her mother and sister were discovered under the high altar and Urban VIII immediately decided on the restoration of the church, which was carried out in the years 1624-26.
  Bernini was commissioned to add a portico and a façade and to carve the statue of the saint for the high altar in collaboration with G. Finelli[1]. The church is important as being one of the earliest

ventures of both Bernini and Pietro da Cortona into work of this nature, and one of the rare examples of their collaboration (another is the *Salone* of the Palazzo Barberini). In his frescoes Cortona came close to evolving a fully Baroque formula but in the façade Bernini used a curiously dry idiom which is featured on a medal by Gaspare Mola (University of Glasgow, Hunterian Museum), issued as part of a series in the mid 1630's to commemorate Oraban's interest in restoring buildings connected with the Early Church. The general design with a three-bay portico below is based on the façade of S. Sebastiano by Ponzio and Vasanzio, and can be traced further to a kind of loggia frequently found in the 16th century in the Veneto, for instance in Sansovino's S. Spirito in Isola (now destroyed) and Trissino's Villa at Cricoli; but the actual arches, cut out of the wall as if with a razor, without any mouldings, recall Vignola's colonnade in the Villa Giulia. What is original is the treatment of the central bay of the upper storey, used for displaying relics on particular holy days, which breaks through the upper entablature and forms a prominent central feature; but this feature does not seem to have been completely integrated into the design and almost gives the impression of having been slipped down over the façade as an afterthought. Bernini used a somewhat similar arrangement, but with much greater success, at S. Andrea al Quirinale.

The architecture of the high altar is so different from that of the façade that it is hard to believe both were designed by the same artist at the same time. The façade is thin and papery, conceived in flat surfaces broken only by pilasters, whereas the altar has full columns, an entablature with a convex frieze and a rich and rather heavy pediment. The evidence as regards date is, however, final, since it appears in an engraving of the altar in Fedini's *Vita di S. Bibiana*, published in 1627, and it is hard to believe that Bernini would have allowed anyone else to design it (unless it was Borromini, who was working as his assistant at St Peter's, but it bears no resemblance to his work). It is closer in style to altars of the previous generation, such as Maderno's in the Cappella Salvia in S. Gregorio Magno, that in the Cappella Silvia in the grounds of the same church and that round Annibale Carracci's *St Margaret* in S. Caterina dei Funari.

INTERIOR

Over the colonnade of the nave are frescoes of scenes from the *Life of St Bibiana*, between which are single figures of her relations who were martyred with her. Those on the right wall are by Ciampelli: *St Bibiana's Body Exposed in the Forum*; *St Olympiana*; *St Bibiana is Buried Next to her Mother by the Priest John*; *St Dafrosia*; *St Olympiana Builds a Chapel to Honour Sts Bibiana, Demetria and Dafrosia*, 1624-26.

Those on the left wall are by Cortona: *Martyrdom of St Bibiana*; *St Demetria*; *Rufina Tries to Persuade St Bibiana to Abjure Christianity and Worship the Idols*; *St Flavianus*; *Sts Bibiana and Demetria Confess their Faith before the State Prefect Apronianus*.

Over entrance wall: Ciampelli, *Angels*
Chapel at end of R nave: Cappella di S. Dafrosa: Cortona, *St Dafrosia*[2]
High altar: *St Bibiana* by Bernini, 1626. Vault fresco: G. D. Marziani, *God the Father and Angels with Musical Instruments*
Chapel at end of L nave: Cappella di S. Demetria: A. Ciampelli, *St Demetria*, 1626-27[3]
1 to L: Cappella di S. Gertrude Magna/Pacetti: altarpiece: Jacopo Verona, *Ecstasy of St Gertrude the Great*[4]; R wall: monument to Vincenzo Pacetti (d. 1674).

SS. Bonaventura e Croce dei Lucchesi *see* SS. Croce e Bonaventura dei Lucchesi

S. Bonaventura al Palatino
Via di S. Bonaventura, 7

Approaching the church: *Stations of the Cross* by Antonio Bicchierai.

The church was built by Cardinal Francesco Barberini in 1676-77 for a body of Spanish Discalced Friars and consecrated in 1689. It was transformed by a restoration for Gregory XVI of 1839[1].

INTERIOR
R of entrance: monument to Giuseppe Agostino Chiaveri (d. 1783)
1 to R: G. B. Beinaschi, *Crucifixion with the Virgin, St John the Evangelist and Mary Magdalen*, soon after 1675[2]
2 to R: G. Calandrucci, *Virgin and Child with Sts Anne, Didacus and the Blessed Salvatore of Orta with St Pascal Baylon below*, before 1686[3]
After 2 to R: copy of S. Conca's *Virgin and Child*
Chapel at end of R aisle: A. Kuchler, *St Anthony of Padua*, 1867
High altar: Filippo Micheli, *Immaculate Conception with Sts Bonaventure, Louis of Toulouse, Bernardine of Siena, Peter of Alcantara, John of Capistrano, James of the Marches, Clare, Louis IX of France and Ferdinand III of Spain*[4]
Chapel at end of L aisle: A. Kuchler, *St Francis*, 1869
2 to L: G. B. Beinaschi, *Annunciation with God the Father and the Dove of the Holy Spirit*, soon after 1675[5]
1 to L: G. B. Beinaschi, *St Michael*, soon after 1675[6]

L of entrance: monument to Francesco Mancini (d. 1758)

MUSEUM
L. Garzi, *St Anthony of Padua*[7]

S. Brigida
Piazza Farnese

Built in the 15th century for the Swedish colony in Rome on the site of a house in which St Bridget lived until her death in 1375. Rebuilt in 1614 (according to Mola by Francesco Peparelli) and restored by Cardinal Francesco Albani (begun before he became Pope Clement XI in 1700), who added the façade in 1705 and commissioned B. Puccini to fresco the interior. The architect was Pietro Giacomo Patriarca, *capo maestro* of St Peter's[1].

On the façade are figures of R: *St Catherine* and L: *St Bridget* by A. Fucigna, 1705[2].

INTERIOR
Frescoes by B. Puccini; vault: *Apotheosis of St Bridget*, begun 1707, and *Four Evangelists*.
Nave: L wall: *Mystic Communion of St Bridget*; *Christ and St Bridget*; R wall: *The Virgin Crowns St Bridget*; *Virgin and St Bridget*, 1705
Choir: L wall: *Christ Appears to St Bridget*, 1705; R wall: *Ecstasy of St Bridget*, 1702[3]
Before 1 to R: monument to Count Nils Bielke (d. 1765) erected in 1768 to a design by Pietro Camporese the Elder and executed by Tommaso Righi[4].

S. Caio
(destroyed)
Built in 1631 on the site of the via Milano on the orders of Urban VIII by Vincenzo della

Greca and Peparelli. Demolished in 1878, the façade is recorded in a medal reproduced in the *Guide Rionali*, and in an engraving reproduced by Armellini.

S. Callisto
Piazza di S. Callisto

In 1608 Paul V granted the church and the adjacent palace to a body of Benedictine monks and both were rebuilt by Orazio Torriani, 1608-09. The church has been closed to the public for many years.

INTERIOR
Completely restored in 1854 and again in 1938.
1 to R: the altar is ascribed to Bernini. Fagiolo dell'Arco[1] accepts the attribution but it is rejected by Mano and implicitly by Wittkower, who does not mention the work. Altarpiece: P. L. Ghezzi, *Miracle of St Maurus*[2]
High altar: A. Nucci, *Madonna of Mercy and Sts Callistus, Palmatius, Calepodius and Privatus*[3]
1 to L: Giovanni Biliverti, *Martyrdom of St Callistus*, 1610[4].

Cappuccini *see* S. Maria della Concezione

Oratorio del Caravita (S. Francesco Saverio)
Via del Caravita, 7

Founded by the Spanish Jesuit Father Pietro Gravita (Caravita) and built in 1631-33. The latter date is on the frieze of the lower storey of the façade, which is an example of the severe style still current in Rome at that time. The upper storey appears to date from the 18th century.

INTERIOR
The vault fresco in the vestibule and the scenes from the *Life of St Francis Xavier* are by L. Baldi. R lunette: *St Francis Xavier Baptising a Heathen Queen*; L lunette: *St Francis Resurrecting a Man*; vault: *St Francis' Vision of Christ*; C: *Angels with the Chalice and Host*; L: *St Francis' Vision of the Virgin and Child*; back wall: *St Francis Succouring the Plague Victims*; *The Saint Preaching*; L: *The Saint Assisting the Dying*; entrance wall: *Temptation of St Francis*; L: *A Crab Retrieves St Francis' Lost Crucifixion*, 1671-73[1]. The oratory itself was completely repainted between 1858 and 1875 and little remains of its 17th century character except some stucco decorations in the apse and the high altar by Clemente Orlandi[2].

In the second oratory (Ristretto degli Angeli): frescoes by G. Sortini, L wall: *St Bernard of Clairvaux*; R wall: *St Jerome*; entrance wall: R: *St Francis of Assisi* and L: *St Francis di Paola*, 1745-46[3]. Stucco altar and wall decorations by G. B. Maini[4].

SS. Carlo e Ambrogio al Corso
Via del Corso, 128

Built by the Confraternity of the Lombards on the site of an earlier church dedicated to St Nicholas, granted to them in 1471 by Sixtus IV and replaced in 1513 by one dedicated to St Ambrose, patron saint of Milan. On the canonisation of S. Charles Borromeo in 1610 the confraternity decided to build a new and larger church, of which the foundation stone was laid in 1612. A large donation towards construction was made

SS. Carlo e Ambrogio al Corso

by Cardinal Paolo Emilio Sfondrati, nephew of Gregory XIII and the restorer of S. Cecilia. The architect was Onorio Longhi and the church was continued after his death in 1619 by other architects, including his son Martino Longhi the Younger and Francesco Contini, who modified his design[1]. His plan was of a medieval type rare in Rome, a three-aisled church with side chapels, an ambulatory around the choir and transepts which did not project beyond the line of the chapels. In 1665 a panel of architects, including Borromini and Pietro da Cortona, were asked to examine the crossing piers and in 1668, after some strengthening had been carried out, the latter was commissioned to build the dome which, externally, is one of the most harmonious in Rome. In 1682-84 the façade was built, unhappily to the designs of the new benefactor of the church, Cardinal Luigi Omodei, who fancied himself as an amateur architect. The result is the present clumsy structure. Carlo Bizzacheri made a design for it, preserved in a drawing, but it was presumably rejected[2]. Longhi's original design for the church is preserved in a medal struck by Paul V in 1612 and engraved by Claude du Molinet in his *Historia summorum pontificum*, Paris, 1679[3]. In his text[4], Du Molinet explicitly connects the medal with the church: 'In via quae vulgo Cursus dicitur'. It seems clear that Omodei knew this design and imitated it to the extent of using Longhi's general pattern with a colossal order enclosing two storeys of equal width, though he replaced Longhi's attic with the existing heavy pediment covering the whole width of the façade, introduced three doors instead of one and abolished the high pedestals shown in Longhi's design, which would have taken away the heaviness of the columns.

INTERIOR

The nave is vast and curiously inhuman. The effect of the whole is seriously diminished by the very coarse painted marble, which probably dates from the 19th century. The vaults of the nave, choir and transepts are decorated with fine gold and white stuccoes by G. A. and C. Fancelli to designs by Cortona, probably modified by Ciro Ferri in the form of coffering[5]. They enclose a fresco of the *Fall of the Rebel Angels* by G. Brandi[6]. Baldi also decorated the apse to imitate a tapestry, *St Charles amongst the Plague-Stricken*, with four stucco figures by Girolamo Gramignoli supporting the fictive tapestry; on the vault of the choir, *St Charles in Glory*, surrounded by stucco angels by Francesco Poli; in the pendentives of the dome, *Jonah*, *Jeremiah*, *Daniel* and *Hosea*. This work was unveiled in 1677. The reliefs of *Angels Playing Musical Instruments* at the crossing are by C. Fancelli.

The inscription over the arches of the nave and choir refer explicitly to the Old and New Dispensations and suggest that the church was conceived to represent the advance from the one to the other. This idea is rare in Roman iconography but it can be paralleled in a group of 18th century Neapolitan churches[7].

The vaults of the aisles and the ambulatory were decorated from 1677 onwards with a series of frescoes representing various virtues. Below them are statues of *Sts Matrona, Barnabas, Stephen, Peter, Joseph, John the Baptist, Thelca, Sebastian, Philip Neri* and *Marcellina* by F. Cavallini, 1679-82[8]

1 to R: Cappella del Crocifisso: aisle vault: Paolo Albertoni, *Temperance Bridles Desire*; R wall: Francesco Rosa, *St Benedict Appears to St Henry*, 1666[9]; L wall: G. Troppa, *Christ with Sts Ambrose and Charles*, c.1678; wooden crucifix in the manner of Algardi

(late 17th or early 18th century)
2 to R: Cappella della Madonna Auxilium Christianorum: L wall: monument to Francesco Antonio Gugliemi (d. 1854) by G. de' Fabris, 1854[10]. Aisle vault: Girolamo Troppa, *Justice, Peace, Law and Virtue*, 1678
2nd pier to R: monument to Caterina Giovanetti (d. 1857) by F. Gnaccarini
Between 2 and 3 to R: monument to Giovanni Rotti (d. 1839) by C. Benaglia, 1845[11]
3 to R: Cappella della Sacra Famiglia: aisle vault: G. B. Beinaschi, *Religion, Fortitude, Purity and Chastity*; L wall: Morazzone, *Virgin and Child with St Francis*, c.1620[12]
R transept: Cappella della Beata Vergine: altar designed by Paolo Posi and executed by Innocenzo Spinazzi with stucco angels by Tommaso Righi, 1768-77. Altar cross designed by Posi and executed by Leonardo Gagliardi. The angels above the right door are by Agostino Penna and those above the left door by Pietro Rudez; above: *Angels with Marian Medallion* by I. Spinazzi. The altarpiece is a mosaic copy of Maratta's altarpiece in the Cappella Cybò in S. Maria del Popolo, *Immaculate Virgin with Sts Gregory, John Chrysostom, John the Evangelist and Augustine*. Statues of R: *Judith* by Pietro Pacilli and L: *David* by A. J. Lebrun[13]
R ambulatory vault: Carlo Ascenzi, *Penitence*; Giovan Battista Buoncuore, *Prayer, Humility, Perfection and Fortitude*, 1679[14]
L ambulatory vault: L. Garzi, *Angels*; Ludovico Gimignani, *Vigilance*, 1680; Fabrizio Chiari, *Patience, Tolerance and Discretion*
High altar: the original structure was by C. Fancelli and F. Cavallini, 1677 but was later replaced. The painting of *Sts Ambrose and Charles Borromeo with St Sebastian* is by Maratta, 1685-c.86[15]. Crucifix after Algardi[16]
2nd pillar in choir: monument to Francesco Righetti (d. 1819) by Francesco the Younger and Luigi Righetti, 1826-31[17]
L transept: altar built in 1929 as an exact copy of the one in the right transept. The altarpiece by Tommaso Luini representing *God the Father Adored by Angels*, 1627-32, was originally designed for the high altar and then stood over the altar of the right transept[18]
3 to L: Cappella di S. Olaf: aisle vault: Luigi Garzi, *Faith*; R wall: C. Roncalli, *Holy Family with St Anne and Joachim*[19]; below: monument to Lorenzo and Serafina Mencacci (d. 1838 and 1832) by Filippo Gnaccarini, 1834-38[20]; L wall: Pasquale de' Rossi, *Agony in the Garden*, c.1675[21]
Between 3 and 2 to L: monument to Conte Carlo Curt Lepri (d. 1841) by P. Lemoyne, 1841-42[22]
2 to L: Cappella di S. Filippo Neri: aisle vault: Francesco Rosa, *Charity*, 1677; altarpiece: F. Rosa, *St Philip Neri in Ecstasy*, 1668[23]. Side walls: G. Zoboli, L: *St Stanislaus Kostka Receives the Blessed Sacrament from an Angel*; R: *St Aloysius Gonzaga Succours the Plague Victims*, 1726[24]
1 to L: Cappella di S. Barnaba: aisle vault: Pio Paolini, *Faith, Time and Truth*; altarpiece: P. F. Mola, *St Barnabas Preaching*, after 1652[25]; behind Mola's altarpiece is F. Rosa's *The Virgin and Child Appear to St Henry*, c.1666[26]
Sacristy: busts of R: Cardinal Ferdinando d'Adda and L: Luigi Omodei (d. 1707) by A. Cornacchini[27]; fine *lavamano* with dolphins (18th century); Tommaso Luini, *St Ambrose and Deacons*[28]
Oratory: sculpture of the *Descent from the Cross* and *Two Sibyls* by Tommaso della Porta, 1583[29]; above: A. Tofanelli, *Virgin with Sts Ambrose and Charles Borromeo*, 1821[30]. Walls and ceiling, *Coronation of the Virgin with Sts Ambrose and Charles Borromeo* by Eraldo Moscatelli, 1928-40[31]

Casa di S. Carlo: François Pourbus, *Margaret of Savoy*, 1606[32]

To the left of the church is a building containing the premises of the Confraternity of St Ambrose, which is attached to the church. It has frescoes attributed to L Gimignani, *c.*1677. Its cloister has windows and memorial tablets which are purely Cortonesque in style but since they are dated 1679, that is to say ten years after Cortona's death, it is to be supposed that they were designed by Ferri. The door to the buildings of the confraternity on the street to the left may well also be by him.

S. Carlo ai Catinari (SS. Biagio e Carlo ai Catinari)
Piazza Benedetto Cairoli

In 1574 the Barnabites, an Order founded in 1532 in Milan by St Antony Zaccaria, established a house in Rome, when Gregory XIII granted the monks the little church of S. Biagio dell'Anello. In 1611 the foundation stone of the new church, dedicated to the recently canonised St Charles Borromeo, was laid[1]. The architect was Rosato Rosati of Macerata, who soon afterwards left Rome to return to his native city. The nave and dome were finished by 1620 but the transepts and choir were not begun until after 1627, when a bequest from Cardinal G. B. Leni, which came through his executor, Cardinal Scipione Borghese, made the completion of the church possible. The façade was begun in 1636 and the choir was finished in 1646. According to Mola, Rosati intended it to have a longer choir.

The façade, built between 1636 and 1638, was designed by G. B. Soria, who was undoubtedly chosen by Cardinal Borghese, his best patron. It is a variant of the type used by him for two other churches commissioned by the cardinal (S. Gregorio Magno and S. Caterina da Siena a Magnanapoli).

INTERIOR

Restored by V. Vespignani for Pius IX from 1860-61[2]. The pilasters of the main order are of yellow *scagliola*. The angles of the crossing piers are of panelled marble and the walls of the transepts painted.

Over entrance doors: L: Gregorio Preti, *St Charles Borromeo Authorising Dominic Boria to Combat Heresy in Grison*; R: Mattia Preti, *St Charles Distributing Alms to the Plague Victims in Milan*, 1652[3]; lunettes: F. Coghetti, L: *Beheading of St Paul* and R: *Giving of the Keys*, *c.*1860.

The dome was to have been painted by G. Semenza, a pupil of Guido Reni, but Cardinal Scipione Borghese insisted that Domenichino should replace him, and he executed the four pendentive frescoes of the Cardinal Virtues (*Fortitude, Justice, Prudence* and *Temperance*), 1628-30. The figure of *Temperance* was completed by Domenichino's pupil Francesco Cozza[4]. In the event, the dome was decorated with stuccoes, and Martinelli states that these were designed by Domenichino. The stucco decoration of the vaults of the nave, choir and transepts is probably also to his designs. Like his wooden ceiling in S. Cecilia these stuccoes are based on a design at the end of Serlio's fourth book.

1 to R: Cappella Costaguti: decorated by Simone Costanzi, 1698-1702; altarpiece: Lanfranco, *Annunciation c.*1624[5]

R transept: Cappella di S. Biagio: altar by Carlo Rainaldi; altarpiece: Giacinto Brandi, *Martyrdom of Sts Blaise and Sebastian*, 1674[6], replacing one by Cerrini; lunettes: F. Coghetti, R: *Martyrdom of St Blaise* and L:

St Blaise Raising a Dead Boy[7]
Chapel to R of high altar: Cappella di S. Cecilia[8]: designed by Antonio Gherardi for the Congregazione dei Musicisti and executed between 1691 and 1700. The stucco decorations were executed by Michele Maglia, Jean-Baptiste Théodon and Lorenzo Ottoni, Simone Giorgini, and Giuseppe Bilancioni. Gherardi is also responsible for the *St Cecilia* over the altar, 1689-90. One of the most original late Baroque chapels in Rome, it has a cut-off dome, on which sit splendid *Music-making Angels*, and which leads to a rectangular chamber, lit by partially concealed windows.
Chapel further R of high altar: built in 1841 by L. Boldrini; altarpiece: Pietro Valentini, *Madonna of Providence*[9]
Choir: fresco in the half-dome of the apse: Lanfranco, *St Charles Borromeo in Glory*, his last work, 1646-47[10]
High altar[11]: in 1637 Cardinal Giovanni Battista Colonna bequeathed four ancient porphyry columns to be used for the altar, and in 1639 Filippo Colonna bequeathed further money for its construction, with the request that it should be designed by Girolamo Rainaldi. As we know on the authority of Boselli, however, who carved the statues of the *Virtues of Charity towards God and towards One's Neighbour* over the altar to the designs of Martino Longhi the Younger, the actual altar was also designed by Longhi[12]. Figures of L: *St Peter* by G. de' Fabris and R: *St Paul* by A. Tadolini, *c.*1835[13]. Above: two *tondi* by E. Ruspi of *St Francis of Sales* and *The Blessed Alexander Sauli*, 1861. Two altarpieces representing St Charles were painted in succession – by Gaspare Celio and Andrea Commodi – but neither was satisfactory, and the present altarpiece of *St Charles Borromeo Carrying the Holy Nail in Procession during the Plague* was painted by Cortona in 1651-67[14]. The ciborium is by Simone Costanzi, 1702. The two *cantorie* are by Carlo Fontana, 1685. Bronze work by Pasquale Pasqualini[15]
Sacristy: begun in 1640[16]; fine marble *lavamano*, 1675; cupboards and holy-water stoups, 1690; bronze crucifix by Algardi, given by Cardinal Lambertini, later Benedict XIV, in 1730[17]; *Mocking of Christ* by Giuseppe Cesari[18]; Andrea Commodi, *St Charles Borromeo Prays for the Cessation of the Plague*[19]; copy of Sicciolante's *Crucifixion* in S. Giovanni in Laterano[20]
Passage behind high altar leading from sacristy to monastic buildings: Reni's *St Charles in Prayer*, 1613, originally on the inside of the façade[21]
2 to L: Cappella Filonardi: built 1636 by Maruscelli and dedicated to the four Persian martyrs, Sts Marius, Martha, Habakkuk and Andofax. The altarpiece representing them, which now hangs on the R wall, is by Romanelli. The frescoes are by Giacinto Gimignani, L lunette: *Martyrdom of the Saints* and R lunette: *The Saints Relieving Prisoners*, 1641[22]
Passage between 2 to L and L transept: R wall: monument to Monsignor Carlo Zeni (d. 1825) by R. Rinaldi[23]
L transept: Cappella di S. Anna: A. Sacchi, *Death of St Anne*, 1648-49[24]; L wall: monument to Cardinal Francesco Fontana (d. 1822) by G. de' Fabris, 1822[25]; lunettes: F. Coghetti, R: *Presentation of the Virgin* and L: *Marriage of Anne and Joachim*. R wall: monument to Cardinal Giacinto Gerdili with bust by C. Prosperi[26]
1 to L: Cappella Cavallerini: architecture by Mauro Fontana, 1739-40; dome and wall frescoes by F. Mondelli, 1746: L wall: *St Paul Visits Ananias to Heal his Blindness*; R wall: *St Paul Preaching in Athens*; dome: *Angels in Glory*. Altarpiece: Gaetano Sortini, *Sts Alexander Sauli and Paul*, 1760[27]. Stucco decorations by A. Corsini and G. Lironi, 1739

Convent choir: G. Calandrucci, vault: *St Paul Rapt into the Third Heaven*; lunettes: *Charity; Hope; Faith*[28]
Former refectory: Giacinto Gimignani, *Supper at Emmaus*, 1678[29].

S. Carlo al Corso *see* SS. Carlo e Ambrogio al Corso

S. Carlo alle Quattro Fontane
Via del Quirinale, 23-25

In 1611-12 the Discalced Spanish Trinitarians, whose function was to collect money to buy the freedom of Christians captured by the Moors, bought a small plot of ground on the south-west corner of the crossroads of the Quattro Fontane where the Strada Pia met the Strada Felice. The monks at first received some financial help from Cardinal Francesco Barberini, whose palace lay opposite, but he then lost interest. Later they received help from the will of Pietro Soderini and the Spanish Ambassador, the Marquis of Castelrodrigo, but he was recalled in 1660 and the building was not finished until after 1682 (when the accounts finish).

The commission to design the church and the monastery was given to Borromini in 1634. He first built the dormitory quarters, the refectory (now the sacristy), the library in 1634-35 and then the cloister in 1635-36. He must also have made a plan for the church at the same time, though he did not actually begin building it until 1637. The church was consecrated in 1646. The drawings show that the cloister was conceived from the beginning almost exactly as it was executed, and they record only very small variations; but those for the façade of the monastic building facing the garden prove that Borromini tried out a number of projects. This façade was much altered in the 18th and 19th centuries when further blocks of monastic buildings were put up round the garden. For the latter Borromini made several projects which were never carried out.

The history of the church has been bedevilled by the fact that the generally reliable Hempel suppressed the most important drawings for it and published as studies for it four drawings (his figs 6-9) which, as has been shown by Steinberg, are certainly not for S. Carlo (they would not fit on the site) and are probably by Borromini's nephew, Bernardo Castello.

The four preparatory drawings[1], though difficult to read owing to the degree to which they were reworked by the architect, show that originally he planned a church, abutting the Strada Felice edge of the site, with two rectangular bays for the altar and the entrance and two semi-circular bays on the cross-axis. At a later stage he moved the whole church some twenty feet to the west and flattened the bays on the cross-axis to parts of ovals and so was able to insert a sacristy between the church and the Strada Felice. The drawings also show that he was experimenting with designs for the façade as he developed the plans for the church, and it can be shown that he had reached the double S-curve on which it is actually based before he made the final plan for the church itself. It is therefore certain that, though the façade was not begun until 1665, it was planned in the 1630's and was not, as has often been said, a creation of Borromini's last years. At the time of his death only the lower storey was built; the upper part was completed by his nephew Bernardo Castello in 1675-77, almost certainly not according to Borromini's designs, since it includes one motif – the oval painting supported by angels – which is taken directly from Bernini's altars at Castelgandolfo and in the Fonseca chapel in S. Lorenzo in Lucina. The statue of *St Charles Borromeo* over the door is by Raggi (1676)[2]; those of *St John of Matha* and *St Felix of Valois*, the founders of the Order, are by Sillano Sillani (1682) and the angels supporting the fresco are by G. C. Dona and F. A. Fontana (1676). The painting itself of *The Trinity* is by P. Giarguzzi (1677), but is now ruined. The capitals of the lower order were carved by Lorenzo Dini. The stags' heads are by Simone Giorgini. The façade with the entrance to the cloister was executed in the very last years of Borromini's life. The original triangular campanile was pulled down and replaced by the existing four-sided one between 1667 and 1670 by Bernardo Castello. The original campanile can be seen in a drawing by Lieven Cruyl.

S. Carlo, together with its monastic buildings, was Borromini's first independent commission but it contains many of the essential features of his later and more mature works. The general plan makes brilliant use of a limited site of irregular shape: the cloister, at first sight simple and straightforward, is in fact extremely subtle in its variation on traditional forms; internally the church shows Borromini's inventiveness in the designing of a ground plan and in the treatment of space with combinations of curves, convex and concave, with straight lines, and of a complete oval with parts of the oval covered by coffered part-domes of unusual flattened forms, the whole giving the effect of movement for which his architecture is famous. Externally this movement is even more apparent in the double S-curve of the plan of the façade, the stepped dome and the re-entrant bays which enclose the lantern. It is characteristic of Borromini's style that the interior should be entirely in white stucco with only a few touches of gilding. The monk who wrote the history of the church soon after Borromini's death comments on the architect's ability to reduce the cost of the building without diminishing its beauty or its practical efficiency, and also on the care with which he guided all the individual craftsmen involved in the building. The beauty and consistency of the detail confirm his testimony.

INTERIOR

The statues of the founding saints of the Order in the niches are by Isidoro Uribesalgo. The stucco medallions on the pendentives show: *The Meeting of Sts John of Matha and Felix of Valois*; *Pope Innocent III Approves the Order*; *The Founding Saints Receive the Habit* and *Ransoming of Captives*, D. Rossi.

R transept: altarpiece: Amalia de' Angelis, *The Blessed Michael de' Santi in Ecstasy*, 1847[3]

High altar: Pierre Mignard, *St Charles Borromeo Contemplates the Trinity with Sts John of Matha and Felix of Valois*, 1645-46

L transept: the small Barberini chapel was decorated by Borromini with motifs taken from Late Antique architectural ornamentation. Altarpiece: *Rest on the Flight into Egypt* by Romanelli, 1642[4]

1 to L: altarpiece: Prospero Mallerini, *Ecstasy of the Blessed John Baptist of the Conception*, 1829[5]

Passage leading to monastery: Cerrini, *St Ursula* and *Holy Family with Sts Agnes and Catherine of Alexandria*, 1643, which were the original paintings over the side altars[6]

The old sacristy is of little interest but the present sacristy (originally the refectory) has an unusual form with rounded corners. It is probable that the stucco decoration of the central field was added when the room was converted to its present use.

It contains the painting of *St Charles Borromeo Adoring the Trinity* by Orazio Borgianni, 1611-12, originally over the high altar of the church[7].

The lower church follows the upper one in plan but is much lower. The walls are flat and only articulated with pilaster bands, and the ridges of the vault are entirely without moulding, with the result that the space is even more sharply defined than in the upper church. To the left of the altar is a chapel Borromini probably intended as his own funerary chapel. It is small but contains some of Borromini's most beautiful play with curved surfaces and undulating architraves.

S. Caterina dei Funari
Via dei Funari

The Compagnia delle Vergini Miserabili, founded by St Ignatius Loyola in 1542-43 and formally approved by Pius IV in 1560, was a lay confraternity which provided shelter and education in a conservatory setting to girls in danger of prostitution. They were given the medieval church of S. Maria Dominae Rosae. The expense of the new church was undertaken by Cardinal Federico Cesi, the confraternity's first cardinal protector. Work began in 1559 and was completed in 1564. The traditional attribution is to Giacomo della Porta but Giovannoni discovered the real architect, Guidetto Guidetti, and the date 1564 on the frieze of the lower order of the façade. The belfry was built some time after the completion of the church. The monastery was sold in 1937. The church is open to the public on Monday mornings and Wednesday afternoons and for Sunday morning Mass.

INTERIOR
This is one of the few Roman churches of its date to have survived without the addition of Baroque decoration and with its simple architecture and white walls gives a clear impression of what many of the late 16th century churches (including the Gesù) and oratories looked like.

Over entrance door: F. Zuccaro, *St Catherine in Prison Converting the Empress Faustina*, 1571-72

1 to R: Cappella Bombasi: the chapel was sponsored by Gabriele Bombasi. Altarpiece: Annibale Carracci, *St Margaret*, c.1598; above: *Coronation of the Virgin* by Innocenzo Tacconi to a design by Carracci[1]

2 to R: Cappella della Pietà/Ruiz: built by Giacomo Barozzi da Vignola for Abbot Filippo Ruiz, c.1565-66. Decorated by Girolamo Muziano; altarpiece: *Burial of Christ*; L wall: *Christ Healing the Blind*; above: *St John*; R wall: *Christ Healing at the Pool of Bethesda*; above: *St Matthew*; L: *The Woman Taken in Adultery*; C: *Raising of Lazarus*; R: *Christ Healing the Centurion's Servant*; above: *Old Testament Prophet*; arch: L: *St Jerome*; C: *God the Father*; R: *St Francis*; entrance arch: L: *Christ Carrying the Cross* and R: *Christ before Herod*[2]. The figures of *St Luke* on the right pier pilaster and of *St Mark* on the left are by F. Zuccaro, 1571. Stucco decorations designed by Vignola

3 to R: Cappella dell'Assunta/Solano: the chapel was sponsored by Giovanni Solano. Altarpiece: Scipione Pulzone, *Assumption*, unfinished at his death in 1598; R wall: *St Lucy*; L wall: *St Catherine of Alexandria*; apse: Giovanni Zanna, L: *Mary Queen of Heaven*; C: *Coronation of the Virgin*; R: *Assumption*

Choir: Cappella Maggiore/Cesi[3]: altarpiece: Giovanni Sorbi, *Martyrdom of St Catherine*, 1760; to R of altarpiece: *St Monica*; to L: *St Augustine* by Alessio d'Elia. Altar wall lunette: A. d'Elia, *The Body of St Catherine*

Transported to Mount Sinai, 1771. Side walls: F. Zuccaro, R: *Martyrdom of St Catherine of Alexandria*; L: *St Catherine of Alexandria Disputing with the Philosophers*, 1571-72; below: saints by Raffaellino Motta da Reggio, R: *Sts Sisinius and Saturninus*; L: *Sts Augustine and Romanus*, 1571-72
3 to L: Cappella di S. Giovanni Battista/Torres: commissioned by Ludovico de' Torres, Archbishop of Monreale, and decorated by Marcello Venusti with scenes from the *Life of St John the Baptist*; R wall: *Beheading of the Baptist*; L wall: *Baptism of Christ*; altarpiece: *St John the Baptist*; 2nd register of apse: *Zachariah in the Temple*; below, L: *Visitation*; C: *Birth of the Baptist*; R: *St John Preaching*, between 1564-65 and 1570[4]
1 to L: Cappella dell'Annunziata/Canuto: commissioned by Andrea Canuto, Bishop of Oppida, and decorated by Girolamo Nanni with scenes from the *Life of the Virgin*; arch: *David*; *Assumption*; *God the Father*; *Marriage of the Virgin*; *Moses*. 2nd register of apse: *Coronation of the Virgin*; below R: *Birth of the Virgin* and *Washing of the Child*; R oval: *Visitation*; R wall: *St Andrew*; L wall: *St Augustine*, c.1590-1600. Altarpiece: copy of Marcello Venusti's *Annunciation*.

S. Caterina della Rota
Piazza di S. Caterina della Rota

A church has stood on the site since the 12th century but it was replaced in the late 16th century by the present one, almost certainly designed by Ottaviano Mascarino. The façade, which is in the lively style of the early 18th century, is first recorded in an engraving of 1756 by Vasi. The church, which belongs to the Arciconfraternita di S. Anna dei Palafrenieri, is seldom open to the public.

INTERIOR
Nave: fine carved and gilt wooden ceiling with the arms of Sixtus V, moved here from the demolished church of S. Francesco a Ponte Sisto.
1 to R: G. Muziano, *An Angel Warns Joseph to Flee to Egypt*; lunette: *Two Prophets*, first half of the 1550's[1]
R niche at end: apse: F. Nappi, *God the Father*
L niche at end: apse: F. Nappi, *Angels*
3 to L: designed by Guglielmo della Porta; altarpiece: Michele Grechi, *Virgin and Child with Sts Catherine and Apollonia*[2]; above: *Annunciation*, possibly by Michele Grechi
1 to L: copy of G. A. Galli's *St Valeria of Limoges Carries her Head to the Altar where St Martial is Celebrating Mass*[3]
1st pillar to L: monument to Giuseppe Vasi (d. 1782), the celebrated engraver during the pontificate of Clement XII.

S. Caterina da Siena
Via Giulia, 161

Originally built under Leo X for the Sienese colony, but rebuilt in 1766-75 by Paolo Posi. The façade is one of the latest Roman examples of a firmly curved concave design, which was at the time being superseded by flatter, more classical forms. Stucco reliefs by Joseph Wander Elsken.

INTERIOR
Nave fresco: *Music-making Angels*, 1771, by Ermenegildo Costantini; stucco decorations by Elsken
The holy-water stoups were made by Francesco Antonio Franzoni.
1 to R: Salvatore Monosilio, *St Bernardine Preaching*, 1768-71
2 to R: N. Lapiccola, *Christ Appears to the Blessed Bernard Tolomei*, 1774-76[1]

Apse: L. Pécheux, *Return of Gregory XI from Avignon*, 1773[2]
High altar: G. Lapis, *Mystic Marriage of St Catherine*, 1768-70[3]
2 to L: Tommaso Conca, *Assumption*, 1768-70[4]
1 to L: Domenico Corvi, *Gregory VII Extinguishes the Fire Lit by the Troops of Henry IV in the Vatican (Fire in the Borgo)*, 1769-70[5]; L wall: tomb of Paolo Posi (d. 1778) with bust by his pupil Giuseppe Palazzi. Oval scenes from the *Life of St Catherine*: R wall: Giovanni Sorbi and Ignazio Marta, *St Catherine Receiving the Stigmata*; Etienne Parrocel, *St Catherine Receiving the Cross*, 1768-69; Pietro Angeletti, *The Young St Catherine in Prayer*, 1769; G. Lapis, *Christ Appearing to the Penitent St Catherine*. L wall: G. Lapis, *Christ Showing St Catherine His Wounds*; P. Angeletti, *St Catherine Receives the Crown of Thorns*, 1769[6]; E. Parrocel, *St Catherine Receiving the Host from Christ*; T. Conca, *St Catherine and the Sacred Heart*
Sacristy: remodelled by Paolo Posi and completed in 1776. Attributed to A. Grammatica, *Virgin and Child with Sts Bernardine, Catherine of Siena and other Saints of the Order*[7], from the earlier church; R. Vanni, *Mystic Marriage of St Catherine*[8]
Oratory: Girolamo Genga, *Resurrection*[9]. Vault fresco: Taddeo Kuntz, *Angels with the Instruments of the Passion*. Walls: decorated by Giovanni Battista Marchetti.

S. Caterina da Siena a Magnanapoli
Piazza Magnanapoli

In 1563 Porzia Massimo (née Colonna) gave money to build a convent for the nuns of the Tertiary Dominican Order founded by St Catherine of Siena, who had previously been housed in the convent of S. Caterina da Siena in the via Chiara. In 1574 they were moved to their present site and in 1628 Urban VIII authorised the construction of a new church. Their protector Cardinal Scipione Borghese was probably responsible for obtaining the services of G. B. Soria. According to Mola, Soria built the façade and 'parte della chiesa'. The choir was finished in 1631 and the church was consecrated in 1640. The façade probably dates from after 1638[1]. The cutting of the via XXIV Maggio and the via IV Novembre in the late 19th century involved lowering the level of the Piazza Magnanapoli and necessitated the construction of the steps leading up to the church. In the portico are stucco statues of R: *St Catherine* and L: *St Dominic* by Giovanni Francesco de' Rossi, c.1640[2].

INTERIOR
Over the entrance is a fine nun's choir and beside it two *coretti*.

Titi[3] records a series of early 17th century altarpieces which were replaced in the late 17th and early 18th centuries by more up-to-date paintings. The choir was decorated before 1667 and the whole church was marbled with Sicilian jasper, probably in the late 17th century.

Nave vault: frescoed by Luigi Garzi, *St Catherine Received into Heaven*, before 1713[4]
1 to R: Cappella della Maddalena: Benedetto Luti, *Last Communion of Mary Magdalen*, c.1706-08; vault: *Putti in Adoration*[5]
2 to R: Cappella d'Ognissanti: decorated by Luigi Garzi, altarpiece: *Triumph of St Catherine and All Saints*; ceiling fresco: Giuseppe Passeri, L: *Mystic Marriage of St Catherine*; C: *Christ in Glory*; R: *Martyrdom of St Lawrence*[6]
3 to R: Cappella di S. Domenico/Caetani/Pallavicini: decorated by Filippo Vasconi; altarpiece: Biagio Puccini, *St Dominic Raises*

a Boy from the Dead, 1706; vault, R: *Madonna of the Rosary*; C: *St Dominic in Glory*; L: *St Dominic and St Francis Adore the Cross*

Over doors to sacristy and convent: G. Passeri, R: *St Catherine in Prayer before her Surprised Father*; L: *St Catherine Receives Two Crowns from Christ, c.*1703[7]

Choir: the high altar has black marble columns; relief by Melchiorre Caffà of the *Ecstasy of St Catherine*, 1660-67[8]. Reliefs on either side, L: *St Agnes of Montepulciano with the Christ Child* and R: *St Rosa of Lima*, added by Pietro Bracci in 1755[9]. Gilt bronze tabernacle with lapis lazuli columns by Carlo Marchionni, cast by Giuseppe and Nicola Giardoni, 1786-87[10]. Lantern frescoes of *God the Father* by F. Rosa[11]

3 to L: Cappella del Rosario/Bonanni: ceded to Giuseppe Bonanni and decorated between 1640 and 1650. Altarpiece: G. Passeri, *Madonna of the Rosary with Sts Dominic and Catherine of Siena*, 1700-03[12]; vault: G. P. Speranza, R: *Adoration of the Shepherds*; C: *Assumption*; L: *Annunciation*; over entrance: *Prophets;* arch: Giovanni Battista Ruggieri, L: *St John the Baptist and St Dominic*; C: *St Catherine of Siena and St Mary Magdalen*; R: *St John the Evangelist and St Philip Neri*. Monument to L: Giuseppe Bonanni (d. 1648) and R: his wife Virginia Primi (d. 1650) by G. Finelli, *c.* 1651-53[13]

2 to L: Cappella Patrizi: decorated by Johann Paul Schor, *c.*1654-56; arch, outer band: L: *Dream of Joseph*; C: *Virgin and Child*; R: *Liberation of Peter*; inner band: L: *St John on the Isle of Patmos*; C: *God the Father* and R: *St Catherine with an Angel* (the *St John* and *God the Father* were probably painted by Egid Schor); entrance to chapel: *Music-making Angels*[14]. Altarpiece: G. Passeri, *Three Archangels, c.* 1700-03[15]

1 to L: Cappella di S. Nicola di Bari: altarpiece: Pietro Nelli, *Virgin and Christ with St Nicholas of Bari*; vault: G. Passeri, *Angels, c.* 1700-03[16].

S. Cecilia
Piazza di S. Cecilia, Via dei Vascellari

Founded before the 5th century on the site of St Cecilia's house and restored by Paschal I (817-24); the portico and campanile were added in the 12th century. The church and monastery were given in 1530 to the Benedictine nuns by Clement VII. In 1599 the body of the saint was discovered intact by Cardinal Paolo Emilio Sfondrati, nephew of Gregory XIV. This event led to a restoration of the church and to the commissioning of the statue of the saint from Stefano Maderno. In the early 18th century a further restoration of the interior was undertaken for Cardinal Francesco Acquaviva, whose name appears on the frieze of the portico, by Domenico Paradisi and Luigi Berettoni, who also remodelled the upper part of the façade. In 1741-42 another member of the Acquaviva family, Cardinal Troiano, commissioned Ferdinando Fuga to build the façade on the street. Over the central arch are the arms of Cardinal Francesco Acquaviva, carved by Agostino Corsini.

In 1822 a survey of the church, ordered by Cardinal Giorgio Doria, showed that the columns of the nave were seriously out of the vertical and that the building was in danger of collapsing. As a result the architect F. Salvi was instructed to carry out a drastic restoration, which involved enclosing the ancient columns in a series of piers between round and flat headed openings[1]. This restoration involved concealing the last features of the medieval building, except for the tabernacle by Arnolfo di Cambio and the 8th century mosaic in the apse

(Cavallini's frescoes had been covered up in the restoration of 1725 and were not uncovered until 1901).
Portico: R wall: tomb of Cardinal Paolo Emilio Sfondrati (d. 1618) by Girolamo Rainaldi[2] with figure of R: *St Cecilia* and L: *St Agnes* by Angelo di Pellegrino, 1623-27[3].

INTERIOR
The frescoed illusionistic architecture on the vestibule ceiling is by Marzio Ganassini and the side lunettes by Fabrizio Parmigiano[4]. L of entrance: monument to Cardinal Forteguerri (d. 1473) by Mino da Fiesole[5].
Vault: frescoed by S. Conca, *Coronation of Sts Cecilia and Valerian with her Brother Tiburtius and Pope Urban I*, 1723-24[6].
1 to R: Cappella del Bagno: Guido Reni, *Coronation of Sts Cecilia and Valerian*, 1601[7]. The frescoes of scenes from the *Lives of Sts Cecilia and Valerian* are attributed to Antonio Circignani[8]. Landscapes by Paul Bril, 1600[9]
2 to R: Cappella dei Ponziani: vault: Antonio del Massaro, *Four Evangelists, Saints and God the Father*, c.1480[10]
3 to R: Giuseppe Ghezzi, *St Benedict*, 1676[11]
4 to R: Cappella delle Reliquie: designed and decorated by L. Vanvitelli, R wall: *An Angel Appears to Sts Cecilia and Valerian*, c.1725; vault: *St Cecilia in Glory*[12]
Before last chapel to R: monument to Cardinal Giuseppe Maria Feroni (d. 1767) designed by G. B. Ceccarelli and bust by A. Lebrun, 1768[13]
Last chapel to R: monument to Cardinal Mariano Rampolla (d.1913) by E. Quattrini, 1929[14]
High altar: the statue of the dead *St Cecilia* and the setting with gilt bronze angels are by Stefano Maderno, completed 1600[15]. On the wall behind are busts of L: Innocent XII and R: Clement XI by G. Mazzuoli, commissioned, probably in 1700, by Cardinal Francesco Acquaviva, whose career they had furthered[16]. The busts stand on oval pedestals like those in Borromini's Re Magi.
Chapel at end of L nave: Baglione, *Sts Peter and Paul*, before 1600[17]
3 to L: Antonio Circignani, *St Agatha*, 1600-1[18]
Between 2 and 3 to L: monument to Cardinal Luigi Brignole (d. 1853) by S. Revelli, 1855
2 to L: Baglione, *St Andrew*, 1601[19]
Between 1st and 2nd altars: monument to Cardinal Gregorio Magalotti (d. 1538)
1 to L: Giuseppe Ghezzi, *Sts Stephen and Lawrence*, 1676[20].
Within the convent: G. Baglione, *Virgin and Child with St Agnes* and *Virgin and Child with St Catherine of Alexandria*, 1600[21].

SS. Celso e Giuliano
Via del Banco Santo Spirito, 6

Founded probably in the 6th century when the relics of the two saints were brought from Antioch to Rome and deposited in S. Paolo fuori le Mura. The old church was pulled down during the widening of the via Banchi by Julius II, who in 1513 promised to build a new one. The designs supplied by Bramante are known from the drawings but very little was actually built and that little was pulled down in 1733 when the present church was begun on the orders of Clement XII to the designs of Carlo de' Dominicis. Payments to him continued until 1743 though the structure seems to have been finished by 1735, the date on the façade[1].

The church is built on an oval plan with the shorter axis leading to the altar, as in S. Andrea al Quirinale, but with large chapels on the ends of the cross-axis. The façade, particularly in its upper part, shows interesting adoptions of Borrominesque ideas.

A note by P. L. Ghezzi, dated 1733, on a drawing of Cardinal Neri Corsini's villa at Anzio designed by Alessandro Galilei, states that the latter was working on the church in 1733 but his share is not defined[2].

INTERIOR

The church has a nearly complete set of altarpieces dating from 1736-38. Restored in 1868[3].

1 to R: Gaetano Lapis, *Pope Cornelius with Sts Artemia and Januaria*, 1737[4]
2 to R: Emanuele Alfani, *Vision of the Magdalen*, 1736[5]
Choir: high altar: Pompeo Batoni, *Christ in Glory with Sts Celsus, Julian, Marcionilla and Basilissa*, 1736-38[6]. To R: Francesco Caccianiga, *St Celsus Victorious over the Pagan Priests*, 1736-38[7]; to L: Giacomo Triga, *St Julian Raises a Man from the Dead*, 1736[8]
2 to L: Giuseppe Valeriani, *Virgin and Child with St Liborius*, 1736[9]
1 to L: Giuseppe Ranucci, *Baptism of Christ*, 1736-37[10]
Sacristy: monument to Giovanni Bissaga (d. 1691)[11].

S. Cesareo
Via di Porta S. Sebastiano, 6

A church has stood here from very early times, though it was first recorded in 1192. It was restored under Clement VIII between 1597 and 1603 for Cardinal Cesare Baronio. This restoration is an important example of the interest in the Early Christian church in which Baronio, as a great ecclesiastical historian, played an important part (cf. SS. Nero e Achilleo). The cosmatesque screens and *amboni* were preserved, though they were rebuilt to fit their new setting, and other fragments were used for the altar frontal.

The architect in charge of the restoration was probably Giacomo della Porta, though Buchowiecki quotes payments to Stefano Longhi and Battista Prata, who may only have been the executants.

INTERIOR

The fresco decoration of scenes from the *Lives of Sts Cesarius and Hippolytus* were executed by Giuseppe Cesari (Cavaliere d'Arpino) and Cesare Rosetti. Francesco Zucchi was responsible for the apse mosaic, *God the Father with Angels*, based on G. Cesari's cartoon[1]. The fresco of the *Virgin and Child* above the cathedra is by the workshop of Antoniazzo Romano[2].

The painted and gilded wooden ceiling dates from the same time and bears the arms of Clement VIII.

1 to R: altarpiece: P. Gabrini, *Holy Family*.

Chiesa Nuova *see* S. Maria in Vallicella

S. Chiara
Piazza di S. Chiara

According to Baglione, the church was rebuilt to the designs of Francesco da Volterra from 1582 onwards; the façade, which was added in 1627-28, is recorded in an engraving by Vasi. The convent buildings, designed by Carlo Maderno, are also shown in the engraving. The church and convent were completely rebuilt and reconsecrated in 1881. The façade was added in 1888 by Luca Carimini. The church is not open to the public.

INTERIOR

2 to L: V. Pasqualoni, *Holy Family*, 1863.

SS. Claudio e Andrea de' Borgognoni
Piazza di S. Claudio

The church of the Burgundian colony in Rome, mentioned by Titi in 1686, was rebuilt by the French architect, Antoine Dérizet, in 1728-29.

An unexecuted plan for the church made by G. B. Contini in 1708 shows a curved convex central bay to the façade[1].

On the façade are statues of L: *St Andrew* by Luc-François Breton and R: *St Claudius* by G. A. Grandjacquet, 1771.

INTERIOR

The interior is decorated with painted marble.
R transept: altarpiece: Placido Costanzi, *St Claudius Appears to Charles Borromeo*, 1731[2]
High altar: lunette: A. Bicchierai, *God the Father*, c.1728[3]
L transept: altarpiece: J. F. de Troy, *Resurrection*[4]
Sacristy: Pietro Barbieri, *Immaculate Virgin with Sts Andrew and Claudius*, c.1730[5].

S. Clemente
Piazza di S. Clemente, Via di S. Giovanni in Laterano

One of the most famous Early Christian churches of Rome, built over the remains of a Mithraeum and other Roman buildings. It was rebuilt in the 12th century and though much work of this period is still visible – as well as Masolino's frescoes in the chapel of St Catherine – a good deal must have disappeared by the time of the restoration carried out in 1716-19 by Carlo Stefano Fontana for Clement XI, whose *monti* and star appear on the side door dated 1719[1]. Fontana built a new façade, rebuilt the adjacent cloister and remodelled the atrium.

INTERIOR

The wooden ceiling dates from the restoration of Clement XI. It encloses a painting of *St Clement in Glory*, after 1715, by G. Chiari. The paintings over the nave arcade illustrating the *Lives of St Clement of Antioch and Servulus* are as follows: R from entrance: 1: Tommaso Chiari, *Death of St Servulus*; 2: G. D. Piastrini, *Sentencing of St Ignatius by the Emperor Trajan*; 3: Giacomo Triga, *St Ignatius Bidding St Polycarp Farewell in Smyrna*; 4: P. L. Ghezzi, *Martyrdom of St Ignatius of Antioch*; L: 1: P. de' Pietri, *St Clement Giving the Veil to St Flavia*; 2: S. Conca, *Miracle of St Clement*; 3: G. A. Crecolini, *Martyrdom of St Clement*; 4: G. Odazzi, *Reception of the Relics of St Clement*[2]. Stucco frames designed by C. S. Fontana.
Above entrance wall: P. Rasina, R: *St Methodius* and L: *St Cyril*[3]
Chapel at entrance end of R aisle: Cappella di S. Domenico: restored 1715 by Carlo Fontana for Cardinal Tommaso Ferrari, 1716; altarpiece: *St Dominic in Ecstasy*; L wall: *St Dominic Raises Napoleone Orsini from the Dead* both by Carlo Roncalli[4]; R wall: *St Dominic Raises a Builder from the Dead*, S. Conca[5]
R aisle vault: Pietro Rasina, *St Servulus in Glory*, c.1714[6]
R aisle: monument to Federick Ambrose Ramsden (d. 1859) and his wife Catherine by T. Forlivesi, 1874. Further: monument to Cardinal Francesco Brusati (d. 1485) by Luigi Capponi; monument to Cardinal Bartolomeo Roveralla (d. 1476) by Andrea Bregno and Giovanni Dalmata, 1476-c.78[7]
L aisle vault: Pietro Rasina, *Coronation of the Virgin*, c.1714[8]
1 to R: altarpiece: Sassoferrato, *The Virgin*

Chapel to L of entrance: Cappella di S. Caterina: frescoes by Masolino; R wall: scenes from the *Life of St Ambrose*; altar wall: *Crucifixion*; L wall: scenes from the *Life of St Catherine*[9]
Chapel to L of high altar: altarpiece: S. Conca, *The Virgin Gives the Rosary to Sts Dominic and Catherine*, 1714[10]
L wall: monument to Cardinal Jacopo Venerio (d. 1479); on pillar opposite: J. Zucchi *Virgin and Child with St John the Baptist*[11]
L aisle: monument to Bartolomé Conte de Basterot (d. 1888) and his wife Pauline de la Tour by T. Forlivesi, 1874.

S. Cosimato (SS. Cosma e Damiano in Mica Aurea)
Via Roma Libera, 76

A church has stood here since the 9th century and in 1234 it was given to the Order of Poor Clares, who remained in the monastery until it was suppressed in 1873. The church was restored a number of times – the last under Pius IV. The carved wooden door, donated by Sister Diodora Terzi, dates from 1661.

INTERIOR
The interior decorations date from the 1871 restoration by Bonaventura Loffredo, assisted by Andrea Fiorani.
Ceiling: *Virgin and Child with Sts Severa, Christine, Francis and Clare*. Side walls, R: scenes from the *Life of St Clare* and L: scenes from the *Lives of Sts Cosmas and Damian*
L altar: B. Loffredo, *Sts Cosmas and Damian*
High altar: donated by Sister Costanza Androsilla in 1639. L of altar: attributed to Antonio del Massaro, *Virgin and Child with Sts Francis and Clare*; R of altar: attributed to B. Loffredo, *Holy Family*; above: B. Loffredo, L: *St Peter* and R: *St Paul*
ToL of choir: Cappella di S. Severa: R wall: monument to Cardinal Lorenzo Cybò (d. 1503), originally found in the Cappella Cybò in S. Maria del Popolo
Sacristy: canvases from the Oratory of the Pescivendoli, which include: L. Baldi, *Christ's Charge to St Peter*; *Flagellation of St Peter*; *St Andrew Adores the Cross*; *Martyrdom of St Andrew*, 1687-92[1]; G. Cortese, *Transport of St Andrew to his Grave*; *Burial of St Andrew*, 1667; G. Ghezzi, *Calling of Sts Peter and Andrew*[2].

SS. Cosma e Damiano
Via dei Fori Imperiali

This church is built in two Roman temples which were adapted to Christian worship by Pope Felix IV (526-30), who commissioned the celebrated mosaic in the half-dome of the apse. A project for restoring the church was produced for Urban VIII by Orazio Torriani in 1626, but between 1629 and 1633 this was replaced by one designed by Luigi Ariguccio for Cardinal Francesco Barberini. (Mola, however, ascribes the remodelling to Domenico Castello.) The new work, apart from a fine wooden ceiling and the high altar by D. Castello himself (1638), was of mediocre quality but was a manifestation of the interest shown by the popes of the early 17th century in restoring Early Christian churches. The church is served by Franciscans of the Third Order Regular.

INTERIOR
R of entrance: monument to Cardinal Fabio Carandini (d. 1600)[1]
Vault: Marco Tullio Montagna, *Sts Cosmas and Damian in Glory*, 1632[2]
1 to R: Cappella della Passione: vault: scenes

from the *Passion* by G. B. Speranza, L: *Agony in the Garden* and *Arrest of Christ*; C: *Resurrected Christ*; R: *On the Road to Calvary* and *Crowning with Thorns*, 1636[3]
2 to R: Cappella Baglione: paintings by G. Baglione: altarpiece: *Sts Peter and John Healing the Lame*; on walls: R: *Adoration of the Magi*; L: *Presentation*; vault: *Assumption*, 1630[4]
3 to R: G. A. Galli, *St Anthony of Padua*[5]; frescoes on walls by Francesco Allegrini; R wall: *St Clare of Assisi*; R lunette: *Doctors of the Church*; L wall: *St Louis IX*; L lunette: *Evangelists*; vault: *Trinity*[6]
4 to R: altarpiece: attributed to G. Muziano, *St Francis in Prayer before the Crucifix*[7]
2 to L: frescoes by Francesco Allegrini, R wall: *Martyrdom of St Alexander*; L wall: *Judgment of St Alexander*; vault: L: *Torture of the Saint*; C: *God the Father*; R: *Miracle of the Saint*[8]
1 to L: copy of Giuseppe Cesari's *St Barbara* in S. Maria Traspontina

In the cloister are frescoes depicting scenes from the *Life of St Francis* by F. Allegrini
Sacristy: half-length portrait of an unknown man by G. Finelli, 1651-53[9]

In the circular chapel (now a shop) attached to the west end of the church (originally the Temple of Romulus, son of Maxentius) is a huge and magnificent Neapolitan *presepe*, or creche, dating from the 18th century, with hundreds of little wooden figures enacting the *Adoration of the Magi*, which was given to the church in 1939.

SS. Cosma e Damiano de' Barbieri (Gesù Nazareno)

Via dei Barbieri, 22
A small church built by the Guild of Barbers in 1724, as recorded in an inscription in the church, to the designs of an architect called Carnevale and dedicated to Sts Cosmas and Damian, the two brother apothecaries. For a time the parish of S. Elena was transferred here from the nearby church of that name which was demolished in the 19th century.

The church is not open to the public.

INTERIOR
Decorated with good stuccoes, enclosing on the right wall a painting of the *Virgin and Child* carried by two angels.
Vault: Giovanni Antonio Crecolini, *Sts Cosmas and Damian in Glory*
Choir: A. Bicchierai, R: *Sts Cosmas and Damian Thrown into the Sea*; to L: *Sts Cosmas and Damian within the Fire*, 1724[1].

S. Crisogono
Viale Trastevere, 47

The church is first recorded in 499, and was rebuilt in 1123-29 by Cardinal Giovanni de' Crema (the campanile survives). In 1618 Cardinal Scipione Borghese, whose titular church it was, undertook its complete renovation. This was carried out by G. Vasanzio, who added the carved wooden roof, replaced all the capitals of the re-used Roman columns, modified the entablature (into which he introduced the Borghese arms), inserted large windows in the clerestory, and redecorated the transepts, the arches at the crossing and the aisles. On his death in 1621 the project was taken over by G. B. Soria until the completion of the restoration in 1629.

The portico and façade were also added by Scipione Borghese, whose name appears on the frieze of the portico with the date 1626, while his arms fill the centre of the pediment of the façade. Most early authorities ascribe the portico to Soria but Mandl maintains that he was only the executant working to the designs of Sergio Venturi. The grille has the arms of Clement XI. The church has been served by the Trinitarians since 1847.

INTERIOR

The interior underwent extensive restoration between 1860 and 1863.

In the ceiling is a copy of Guercino's *St Chrysogonus in Glory*[1] and in the central transept panel of the *Virgin with Child* by G. Cesari.

1st bay to R: Domenico Valeriani, *Sts John the Baptist, Catherine of Alexandria, Nicholas of Bari, Barbara and other Saints*, 1624

2nd bay to R: Giovanni da San Giovanni, *The Three Archangels*[2]

3rd bay to R: Ippolito Provenzale, *St Frances of Rome*, 1624

4th bay to R: Paolo Guidotti, *Crucifixion*, 1624[3]

Chapel to R of high altar: Cappella del Sacramento/Poli: attributed by Titi[4] and De' Rossi[5] to Bernini and possibly based on a sketch by him, but executed entirely by assistants, 1677-81[6]. R: monument to Monsignor Gaudenzio Poli (d. 1679) and L: Cardinal Fausto Poli (d. 1653)[7]; vault fresco: G. Gimignani, *Trinity with the Virgin*, after 1641 and much repainted[8]

High altar: inscribed with the name of Cardinal Borghese and probably by Soria with putti by Domenico Prestinaro. The apse stucco depicting scenes from the *Life of St Chrysogonus* were executed by Marcantonio Fontana, as were the clerestory stucco decorations. The choir stalls were designed by F. Fontana with sculptured figures by P. Galli, 1863[9]

4th bay to L: G. B. Mercatti, *St Charles Borromeo*, 1624

3rd bay to L: P. Guidotti, *Meeting of Sts Francis, Dominic and Angelo*, 1624

1st bay to L: *St Angelo of Sicily* to a design by Guidotti

L of entrance: tomb of Cardinal Giacomo Millo (d. 1757) by Pietro Pacilli, 1760[10]

S. Croce in Gerusalemme
Piazza di S. Croce in Gerusalemme

The church is said traditionally to have been founded by Constantine and it is certain that it existed in the 4th century. It was rebuilt by Lucius II in 1144, and of this building the campanile survives. In 1482 during further restorations workmen discovered a box containing the label INRI from the cross and this relic rapidly increased the popularity of the church. In 1495 Cardinal Bernardino Lopez de Carvajal became titular cardinal of the church and carried out an extensive restoration, including the fresco in the apse. His successor, Cardinal Francesco Quiñones, gave the splendid tabernacle by Jacopo Sansovino (1536). In 1561 Pius IV transferred the Carthusians, who had previously held the monastery of S. Maria degli Angeli, and gave S. Croce to the Cistercians, who still serve it.

In 1602, on the orders of Archduke Albrecht, Rubens painted three compositions of the *Crucifixion*, *Descent from the Cross* and *St Helena*. These were removed when the church was restored in the mid 18th century, and are now at Grasse.

In 1741-44 a complete restoration of the church was carried out for Benedict XIV, including the stuccoing of the interior and the addition of a portico and façade, dated 1744.

All the guide books ascribe the church to Gregorini, except Vasi, who in 1753 attributes it to Gregorini and Pietro Passalacqua and in 1777 mentions Passalacqua alone. Documentary evidence, however, shows Gregorini was responsible for the restoration and that Passalacqua acted only in a minor capacity[1].

Above the façade is a series of statues: *Angels* by B. Ludovisi; *St Matthew* by Marchionni; *St John the Evangelist* by P. Verschaffelt; *St Luke* by A. Corsini; *St Mark* by G. B. Grossi (who also made the group of cherubim); *St Helena* by T. Brandini; *Constantine* by P. Lestache, c.1743. Façade and portico stuccoes by B. Mattei[2].

INTERIOR
Vault: Corrado Giaquinto, *The Virgin Presenting St Helena and the Emperor Constantine to the Trinity*; over high altar: *Adoration of the True Cross*; 1741-43[3]. Four stucco reliefs in the nave with putti carrying the *Instruments of the Passion* by P. Verschaffelt
1 to R: Giovanni Bonatti, *St Bernard Retrieves the Head of St Cesarius*
2 to R: Carlo Maratta, *St Bernard Induces the Antipope Victor to Submit to Innocent II*, 1656-59[4]
3 to R: Raffaelle Vanni, *A Vision of the Mother of St Robert of Molesme*[5]
Choir: in the half-dome of the apse is a fresco of the *Legend of the True Cross* by Antoniazzo and his workshop, c.1492-1495, commissioned by Cardinal Carvajal[6]. On the walls frescoes are by Corrado Giaquinto: R: *Moses Drawing Water from a Rock* and L: *The Brazen Serpent*, 1752[7]. Apse: monument to Cardinal Francesco Quiñones (d. 1540) with tabernacle by Jacopo Sansovino, 1536[8]. The *baldacchino* dates from the restoration by Gregorini but incorporates the four columns of the medieval ciborium.
End of R aisle: lower church: Cappella di S. Elena: frescoes by Niccolò Circignani: altar wall: *St Helena Adoring the Cross*; L wall: *Proof of the True Cross*; R wall: *Division of the Holy Wood*; portal wall: *Discovery of the True Cross*, completed in 1593; vault: mosaics of *God the Father* and *Four Evangelists* and allegorical figures attributed to F. Zucchi[9]
Cappella di S. Gregorio: frescoes by Francesco Nappi and Girolamo Nanni, vault: *Trinity with the Virgin and Sts Peter, Paul, John the Baptist, Benedict, Robert of Molesme, Bernard and Gregory the Great*; pendentives: scenes from the *Life of St Bernard*[10]. Marble relief of the *Pietà* by Archangelo Gonelli, 1628-29[11]. R wall: monument to Cardinal Gioacchino Besozzi (d. 1755) by Innocenzo Spinazzi; L wall: monument to Cardinal Girolamo Souchiers (d. 1571)
3 to L: Luigi Garzi, *St Sylvester Showing the Portraits of Sts Peter and Paul to Constantine*, between 1675 and 1686[12]
1 to L: G. Passeri, *Incredulity of St Thomas*, between 1675 and 1686[13]

In the monastery library built by S. Cipriani is a seated statue of *Benedict XIV* by Carlo Marchionni[14]; vault fresco: G. P. Pannini, *Exaltation of the Cross*.

SS. Croce e Bonaventura dei Lucchesi
Via dei Lucchesi, 1

The medieval church of S. Nicola de Portis which stood on this site was given in 1536 to the Capuchins and in 1631 Urban VIII ceded it to the Lucchesi, who restored it between 1691 and 1695. The façade was designed by Giovanni Coli and Filippo Gherardi and built in 1695-96[1].

INTERIOR
The interior, which consists of a single nave with three side chapels on either side, was redecorated in 1692 to a design by Cardinal

Francesco Buonvisi, their cardinal protector. This involved the construction of little galleries (*coretti*) in the broad piers which separate the side chapels. The interior was radically restored for Pius IX between 1858 and 1863 by Virginio Vespignani, when the pilasters were decorated and the *coretti* embellished[2]. The presbytery walls were frescoed with stories of the *Holy Face* by Francesco Grandi, with the help of Ercole Ruspi, who painted the tribune vault. The walls are decorated with painted marble.

The ceiling paintings are by Giovanni Coli and Filippo Gherardi, both of Lucca, 1674-75; *Heraclius Brings the Cross Back from Persia*; *The Holy Face of Lucca Supported by Angels*; *The Sudarium Supported by Angels*

Entrance wall: R: monument to Fabio Guinigi (d. 1691) designed by Domenico Guidi, 1692; L: monument to Fantinello de' Fantinelli (d. 1719); above: stucco statues of L: St *Paulinus* and R: St *Fredianus*, patron saints of Lucca, by Francesco Baratta the Younger, 1692-93[3]

1 to R: Cappella Fantinelli: built for Monsignor Fantinello de' Fantinelli and decorated in 1695-99. Altarpiece: Lazzaro Baldi, *St Zita Giving Water to a Beggar, which Changes into Wine*, c.1695; putti above the altar by L. Ottoni[4]

2 to R: Cappella della Concezione/Castagnori: designed by Simone Costanzi, 1701-05; altarpiece: *Immaculate Virgin* by B. Puccini, 1701[5]. L wall: D. M. Muratori, *St Lawrence Justinian Healing a Possessed Woman*; R wall: Francesco del Tintore, *Miracle of St Fredianus Diverting the River Sechio*, c.1700-10[6]; putti above altar by L. Ottoni and stuccoes by Andrea Bertoni

3 to R: Cappella Tofanelli: altarpiece: Agostino Tofanelli, *Tobit with the Archangel Raphael Heals his Father's Blindness*, 1822

High altar: built in 1745[7] and attributed to G. A. Perfetti. Side walls frescoed by Francesco Grandi, R wall: *Seleucius, the Guardian of the Holy Statue in the Holy Land Reveals Where it is to be Found*: L wall: *The Ship with the Holy Face Lands at Luni*, c.1862

3 to L: altarpiece: Antonio Barbalonga and Giovanni Battista Quagliata, *Virgin with Sts Jerome and Bonaventure*[8]

2 to L: L wall: monuments to Cardinal Lorenzo Prospero Bottini (d. 1818) by R. Rinaldi, 1818, and Filippo Buonamici (d. 1780); R wall: monuments to Monsignor Alessandro Buttaoni (d. 1826) by Adam Tadolini, 1826[9], and Stefano Tofanelli (d. 1812) by Agostino Tofanelli, 1812[10]

1 to L: decorated in 1723.

S. Croce alla Lungara (S. Croce delle Scalette)
Via della Lungara, 19

Founded in 1615 by the Marchese Baldassare Paluzzi Albertoni as a convent for penitent women. The façade was modified in 1854 by Virginio Vespignani.

INTERIOR

The chapel was drastically restored in the 19th century when presumably the *Crucifixion* by Troppa, recorded by Titi and mentioned by Waterhouse, was removed.

Oratorio del SS. Crocifisso
Piazza dell'Oratorio

Built for the Confraternita del SS. Crocifisso, which was founded in 1519 and attached to S. Marcello. The architect was Giacomo della Porta who was apparently making designs in 1559[1]. Work on the actual building was begun in the next year and finished in 1568. The most distinguished feature of the building is the façade, which was traditionally ascribed to Vignola but is in fact one of Della Porta's most successful early works.

INTERIOR
The oratory is of a simple rectangular form, with a carved wooden ceiling by Flamen Boulanger, 1573-84, given by Cardinal Alessandro Farnese. The walls are frescoed with scenes from the *Legend of the True Cross*. The main narrative proceeds from the right of the altar in a clockwise direction around the nave of the oratory.
R nave wall from altar: *St Helena Orders the True Cross to be Found*; *Prophet*; *Discovery of the True Cross*; *Sibyl with a Prophet*, all by Giovanni de' Vecchi; *Miracle of the True Cross*, Niccolò Circignani
Entrance wall: R: *The Miraculous Cross Taken in Procession during the Plague of 1522*, P. Nogari; L: *The Miraculous Cross Survives the Fire in S. Marcello*, Roncalli; L nave wall: *Founding of S. Chiara al Quirinale and Founding of the Confraternity*, Roncalli
L nave wall: *Battle of Heraclius against the Persian King Chosroes*; *Prophet*; *Heraclius Attempts to Bring the Holy Cross into Jerusalem on Horseback*, Niccolò Circignani; *Prophet*; *Heraclius Enters Jerusalem as a Penitent with the Holy Relic*; *Sibyl with Prophet*, Cesare Nebbia
Altar-room: R: *St Mary Magdalen*; L: *St John the Evangelist* by Roncalli.

S. Dionigi alle Quattro Fontane (destroyed)

Built between 1619 and 1637 on the via Felice (now the via delle Quattro Fontane) near the Quattro Fontane. Pulled down in 1939 and replaced by a block of offices. Photographs of it are reproduced by Matthiae. The façade was designed by Giovanni Antonio Masi shortly before 1686 when the church was redecorated.

SS. Domenico e Sisto
Largo Angelicum

The church of S. Maria ad Nives stood on this site from the late 10th century. In 1569 it was given by Pius V to the Dominican nuns of S. Sisto Vecchio, which lay in a dangerously malarial part of the city. Rebuilding of the church and the construction of the convent began soon after under the direction of Domenico Dario de' Mezzana, who was succeeded by Giacomo della Porta. The campanile, which was attached to the church, was built before 1574 probably by Della Porta, who is also responsible for the choir and much of the convent. After Della Porta's death in 1602 he was replaced in 1609 by Niccolò Torriani, who completed the nave and added the façade in 1628; work was finished in 1652-53. The steps and main entrance were added in 1654-57 by Vincenzo della Greca. The effect of the steps was greatly damaged when the ground in front of the church was lowered in 1876 for the cutting of the via XXIV Maggio. The church was finally completed under Felice della Greca in 1664.

On the façade are statues of, above: *Sts Thomas Aquinas* and *Peter Martyr* by Stefano Maderno, 1636, and below: *Sts Dominic* and *Sixtus* by Marc Antonio Canini, *c*.1654; above entrance door: *Madonna of the Rosary*, attributed to M. A. Canini[1].

INTERIOR
The final decoration of stucco and marble was added to the nave and side chapels between 1636 and 1652. The *scagliola* pilasters were added in 1851.
Vault: fresco: Domenico Maria Canuti and Enrico Haffner, *St Dominic in Glory* (*The Dream of the Prior Guala of Brescia*) and scenes from the *Life of St Dominic*; window arches: *Cardinal Virtues*; entrance wall: *St Dominic Overcomes Heresy*; L: *Institution of the Rosary*; R: *Introduction of Sts Francis and Dominic*[2]
1 to R: Cappella della Maddalena/Alaleoni[3]: marble group, *Noli me tangere*, commissioned by Sister Maria Alaleoni from Bernini, who supplied the design and supervised the execution of the group by Antonio Raggi, 1649-52. The coloured background is a modern addition[4]. In arch above: stucco figures of R: *Chastity* and L: *Temperance* by A. Raggi[5]
2 to R: Cappella di S. Pietro Martire: decorations completed in 1648
3 to R: Cappella di S. Domenico/Costaguti: decorations completed by 1648; altarpiece: P. F. Mola, *The Picture of St Dominic Carried to Soriano by the Virgin and Sts Catherine of Alexandria and Mary Magdalen*, 1648[6]. Stuccoes by Battista Petraglia
Cappella Maggiore: the marble revetment and side doors were designed by Giovan Battista Soria. The high altar was commissioned by Sisters Lucrezia and Antonia Leni. In 1652 it was attributed to Bernini by Sister Maria Domenica Salamonica (d. 1672), a nun of the convent and historian of the community. It was said by Fagiolo[7] to have been executed between 1636 and 1640. Not mentioned by Wittkower, it is stylistically quite unlike Bernini. The altar once housed a much venerated image of the *Madonna Avvocata*. The marble angels were only installed in 1819, replacing the original gilt ones, which were removed by the French in 1796
Altar wall: L. Gentile, scenes from the *Life of the Virgin*; to R from top: *Presentation in the Temple*; *Annunciation* and *Adoration of the Shepherds*; to L from top: *Birth of the Virgin*; *Marriage* and *Visitation*. Above: D. M. Canuti, apse: *St Dominic's Vision of the Madonna of Mercy*, 1673-75; R wall: *Mystic Lactation of the Virgin to St Dominic*; L wall: *Pope Honorius III Presenting Letters Confirming the Order to St Dominic*[8]. Stuccoes by Francesco and Battista Petraglia, 1624-39
L wall: L. Gentile, *Miracle of the Fire of St Dominic*, 1638-40
R wall: P. P. Baldini, *St Dominic at the Battle of Muret*, 1639[9]
3 to L: Cappella del Crocifisso/della Madonna/Altemps: decorated by P. P. Baldini, 1646, with scenes from the *Passion*; L wall: *Flagellation*; R wall: *Garden of Gethsemane*; vault: R: *Crowning with Thorns*; C: *God the Father*; L: *Christ Carrying the Cross*[10]. Altarpiece: Giovanni Lanfranco, *Crucifixion*, now in the Sala Capitolare[11]
2 to L: Cappella di S. Caterina da Siena/Giustini: altarpiece: Francesco Allegrini, *Mystic Marriage of St Catherine*, 1632. Side walls: scenes from the *Life of St Catherine of Siena*. Stuccoes by G. B. Petraglia
1 to L: Cappella del Rosario/Celsi: decorated in 1652; altarpiece: Romanelli, *Madonna of the Rosary*, 1652
Nuns' choir: restored by Domenico Costa in 1749, from which time the altar dates. The choir is decorated with scenes from the New Testament, some dating from the early 17th century, by an anonymous artist.

Domine Quo Vadis (S. Maria in Palmis)
Via Appia Antica, 51

Founded at a very early date (at the latest about 9th century) on the spot where St Peter escaping from prison is said to have met Christ and addressed him with the words which give the church its name. It collapsed during a violent storm in January 1637 and was restored by Cardinal Francesco Barberini, whose arms appear on the façade. This is composed of two pairs of giant pilasters supporting a straight broken pediment, a pattern very close to that of S. Egidio, which may have been designed by the same architect. The interior is simple and contains no works of art of importance.

S. Dorotea
Via di S. Dorotea, 22

Built 1751-56 on the site of a much earlier church, which had been given to the Padri Minori Conventuali di S. Francesco by Benedict XIII in 1727. The architect was G. B. Nolli, famous for his plan of Rome published in 1748. This is his only architectural achievement. The façade is plain but impressive with four giant composite pilasters on a simple concave plan. The interior, almost a Greek cross with an added apse, is dominated by the central space, covered not by a dome but by a vault with four heavy ribs, a feature which in some ways recalls Piedmontese churches of the same period, such as Vittone's S. Chiara at Brà.

INTERIOR
The painting on the nave vault dates from 1931.

1 to R: G. Martorana, *Sts Cajetan and Joseph Calasanctius*, c.1751-56[1]
R transept: L. Gramiccia, *Vision of St Anthony of Padua*, c.1751-56[2]
3 to R: Georg von Prenner, *Immaculate Virgin*, c.1747[3]
High altar: Michele Bucci, *Sts Dorothy and Sylvester*, enclosing an earlier painting of *The Virgin*[4]
3 to L: M. Bucci, *Crucifixion with Sts Cajetan, Dorothy and an unknown Bishop*[5]
L transept: Liborio Marmorelli, *Ecstasy of St Francis*, 1760[6]
1 to L: Vincenzo Meucci, *Levitation of St Joseph of Copertino*, 1746-47[7].

S. Egidio (S. Maria del Carmelo)
Piazza di S. Egidio

A small church originally dedicated to St Lawrence. In 1610 it was given to Agostino Lancellotti, who established a convent of Carmelite nuns and restored the church. It was restored again in 1630 at the expense of Filippo Colonna, whose daughters were members of the convent, and dedicated to S. Maria del Carmine. The façade is similar to that of Domine Quo Vadis and the two churches may have been designed by the same architect.

INTERIOR
Entrance wall: to R of door: monument to Petronella Paolina Massimo (d. 1663). To L of door: monument to Marchesa Veronica Rondanini Origo (d. 1705) designed by C. Fontana[1]
High altar: A. Camassei, *The Virgin Giving the Scapular to St Simon Stock*, 1630[2]
Choir: attributed to Luc de la Haye, R: *Investiture of St Teresa* and L: *Coronation of the Virgin*

1 to L: C. Roncalli, *St Giles*[3].
Nuns' choir: R wall: Andrea Pozzi, *St Teresa*, 1826.

S. Eligio dei Ferrari
Via di S. Giovanni Decollato, 9

Built 1561-62 for the Guild of Iron Workers (*ferrari*) and restored in 1723 by F. Ferrari and L. Barattone and again by Carlo Busiri Vici in 1905. The façade was rebuilt in 1905, apparently on the lines of the original. The church is only open for weddings.

INTERIOR
Fine gilt wooden ceiling by Francesco Nicolini, 1602-04, and restored in 1723-24 when the ceiling was painted and gilded[1]. The organ-gallery over the entrance dates from 1690 and the two *coretti* were added by Gaetano Fabrizi in 1738. The marbling and stucco decorations in the apse date from the 1905 restoration. The oratory ceiling was made by Giuseppe Bianchi in 1589.
1 to R: Altare di S. Antonio Abate/dell' Università dei Marescalchi: dates from 1730-36; wooden statue of *St Anthony Abbot*, 1622-26
2 to R: Altare della Sacra Famiglia/dell' Università dei Chiodaroli e Rivela: dates from 1726; altarpiece: attributed to M. Venusti, *Holy Family*
3 to R: Altare di S. Francesco/dell' Università dei Giovani Ferracocchi: dates from 1748; altarpiece: Terenzio Terenzi, *St Francis in Ecstasy*, now in the oratory; underneath is an earlier fresco of *Christ Carrying the Cross* by an unknown artist[2]
Apse and high altar: built by G. B. Mola, 1640-41; the alabaster altar frontal dates from 1794; altarpiece: *Virgin and Child Enthroned with Sts Eligius, Martin and James* by Sicciolante da Sermoneta, c.1563[3]

3 to L: Altare del Crocifisso/dell' Università degli Spadari: altar by Giuseppe Valadier, 1827; altarpiece: attributed to S. Pulzone, *Crucifixion with the Virgin and St John the Evangelist*
2 to L: Altare di S. Orsola/dell' Università dei Calderari: dates from 1745; altarpiece: A. Mattei, *St Ursula*, 1764
1 to L: Altare di S. Ampelio/dell' Università dei Giovani Lavoranti dei Chiavari: built by Antonio Blasij in 1725; altarpiece: *St Ampelius and Angels* by an unknown artist, 1748

In the oratory (accessible from the choir) is a banner painted on both sides by Pompeo Batoni. On one side is *The Virgin Appearing to St Eligius* and on the other *Christ Appearing to St Ampelius*, 1748-50[4].

S. Eligio degli Orefici
Via di S. Eligio, 9

Begun to the designs of Raphael in 1514-15 for the Guild of Goldsmiths. Construction progressed very slowly, the dome being completed in 1536 and the cornice in 1542. The vault and dome were rebuilt in 1602-04 by Flaminio Ponzio, but much of the church remains one of the purest expressions of the ideals of the Roman High Renaissance. The façade was rebuilt by Giovanni Maria Bonazzini, 1621. The church is open 10.00 am to noon on weekdays and for Sunday morning Mass.

INTERIOR
To R of sacristy: Filippo Zucchetti, *Sts Andronicus and Athanasia*[1]
R transept: altarpiece: Romanelli, *Adoration of the Magi*; frescoes of *Sibyls* in the spandrels, 1639[2]; L wall: monument to Giovanni Giardini (d. 1722)
Apse: frescoes by Marco Pino, *Virgin and*

Child with Sts Stephen, John the Baptist, Catherine, Mary Magdalen, Eligius and Lawrence; above: *Holy Trinity*[3]
Triumphal arch: spandrels: M. da Lecce, R: *The Virgin*; L: *Angel of the Annunciation*; vault: R: *Pentecost*; C: *Dove of the Holy Spirit*; L: *Pentecost*
L transept: Romanelli, frescoes of *Sibyls* in the spandrels[4]; fresco over the altar: Giovanni de' Vecchi, *Adoration of the Shepherds*, 1574-74[5].

S. Eligio dei Sellari
(destroyed)
The church stood in the Piazza delle Gensole in Trastevere, near the Ponte S. Bartolomeo. It was built in 1740 to the designs of Carlo de' Dominicis. From the old photograph reproduced by Armellini it seems to have been oval in plan with a convex façade of unusual design.

S. Eufemia
(destroyed)
This church stood on the Forum of Trajan. It was rebuilt by Cardinal Baronio and Fulvio Sforza under Clement VIII. The façade was by Mario Arconio. The church was pulled down in the early 19th century in the course of the excavations carried out in the Forum of Trajan.

S. Eusebio
Piazza Vittorio Emanuele II, 12b

A church has stood on this site since the 4th century; in 1471 it was given to the Celestines by Sixtus IV. It was restored in 1588 and again in 1600 when Onorio Longhi built the choir, high altar and transepts. The façade was built by Carlo Stefano Fontana in 1711, though without the steps, which had to be added when the Piazza Vittorio Emanuele was laid out and the ground lowered in 1873.

The church itself was almost totally rebuilt on the orders of Cardinal Enrico Henriquez to the designs of Niccolò Picconi in 1753-60.

INTERIOR
Nave vault: fresco by A. R. Mengs with the assistance of Anton von Maron, *St Eusebius in Glory*, 1757-58[1]
Over triumphal arch: two angels holding a cartouche by T. Righi, 1759-60
R transept altar: C. Rossetti, *St Benedict Receives Placidus and Maurus into the Order*
Choir: fine 16th century choir-stalls (1556); Cesare Rossetti, *Crucifixion*[2]
High altar: by Onorio Longhi[3]; above altar: B. Croce, *St Eusebius*
L transept altar: Karl Andreas Ruthart (a German-born painter who became a monk here), *St Peter Celestine*[4].

S. Eustachio
Piazza di S. Eustachio

A church has stood on this site at least since the 8th century but by the middle of the 17th century it was in a dangerous condition. Various architects, including Borromini, were asked to produce designs for a restoration but nothing was done until 1700 when Cesare Corvara was entrusted with the job. He began work in 1701 and was succeeded in 1703 by G. B. Contini, who completed the portico and nave[1]. By 1706 only the portico and crossing were completed and worked stopped due to lack of funds. Between 1714 and 1719 the chapel of S. Michele was completed to a design by Alessandro Sperone. In 1723 Innocent XII provided funds for the completion of the church under the direction of Antonio Canevari, briefly in 1727 under N. Salvi and finally under Domenico Navone[2]. The church was consecrated in 1730. The architecture of the church is undistinguished but it contains a few altars of interest.

ATRIUM
L of entrance: monument to Giovanni Giraud (d. 1834) by G. Barba, 1839-43[3]

INTERIOR
L of entrance: monument to Constantino Theodorus (d. 1718)
Above entrance: organ case by Francesco Michetti, 1747-49[4]
R of entrance: monument to Angelo Maria Lucatelli (d. 1730); monument to Angelo Magnonus, set up in 1705 (d. 1716)[5]

1 to R: Cappella della Sacra Famiglia: P. Gagliardi, *Sacred Family*, 1855[6]. R wall: monument to Luigi Greppi (d. 1673), workshop of G. Finelli, 1651-53[7]
2 to R: Cappella dell'Annunziazione/Ciogni: altarpiece: O. Leoni, *Annunciation*
Passage between 2 and 3 to R: monument to Pietra Ruga by A. Laboureur[8]
R transept: altarpiece: Giacomo Zoboli, *St Jerome*, 1729[9]
High altar: the altar is in the form of a sarcophagus, and was commissioned by Cardinal Neri Corsini, nephew of Clement XII, in 1739 and designed by Nicola Salvi. The candlesticks are by the same artist (1749). Altarpiece: *Martyrdom of St Eustace and his Family* by Francesco Fernandi, called 'Imperiali' (1725-26)[10]
L transept: altarpiece: G. Zoboli, *Visitation*, 1729[11]
3 to L: Cappella della Madonna: designed in 1771 by Melchiorre Passalacqua with sculpture by Agostino Penna. L wall: Michele Paolini del Possenet, *Flight into Egypt*; R wall: T. Conca, *Rest on the Flight*, 1774[12]
2 to L: Cappella di S. Michele Arcangelo: built 1716-19 under the direction of Alessandro Sperone. Altarpiece: Giovanni Bigatti, *St Michael*, 1818[13]; L of altar: *St Raymund Nonnatus*; R of altar: *St Frances of Rome* by Giovanni Bigatti. R wall: monument to Silvio de' Cavalieri by Lorenzo Ottoni to a design by Alessandro Sperone[14]
1 to L: Cappella di S. Giuliano: altarpiece: B. Puccini, *St Julian Attends the Sick*, c.1707[15]
L of entrance: monument to Constantinus Theodorus.

SS. Faustino e Giovita (S. Anna dei Bresciani) (destroyed)

Built in the 16th century as part of the Palazzo dei Tribunali, planned by Bramante for Julius II but never completed. In 1664 it was given a new façade by Carlo Fontana, known from drawings and engravings. The church was pulled down in 1890 when the Lungotevere was built.

S. Filippo Neri
Via Giulia, 134

In 1623 the Congregazione delle Piaghe di Gesù Cristo built the church dedicated to St Philip Neri. It was later restored by F. Raguzzini in 1728. The façade was added by G. F. Fiori in 1767-68 and has a fine oval stucco bas-relief of *The Virgin and Child Appearing to St Philip Neri* by Tommaso Righi, 1769. Secularised in 1942 and abandoned for many years, it has recently been restored.

S. Filippo Neri, Oratory of
see S. Maria in Vallicella

S. Francesca Romana (S. Maria Nova)
Piazza di S. Francesca Romana, 4

Founded on the site of a Roman temple by Paul I (757-67) and dedicated to Sts Peter and Paul. The church changed hands several times but in 1352 it was given to the Olivetans who held it until the suppression of 1873. In 1421 Francesca Buzzi de' Ponziani founded a congregation of Oblates in the church and when she was canonised as S. Francesca Romana in 1608 her name was added to that of the original dedication. The 12th century campanile still stands but the church itself was remodelled for Cardinal Sfondrato between 1608 and 1615 by Carlo Lambardi (or Lombardo), who designed the façade, which is unusual for Rome in being an adaptation of Palladian motifs (S. Giorgio Maggiore and the Redentore). The church was restored between 1816 and 1829 after being damaged by French troops in 1798. The date 1615 appears on the façade.

INTERIOR
The wooden ceiling dates from the 17th century restoration. Some of the walls are decorated with painted marble.

3 to R: Cappella di S. Francesca Romana: built by Francesco Ferrari, 1727-28[1]; vault: stucco reliefs of allegorical figures of *Prudence, Penitence* and *Humility*; altarpiece: *Virgin and Child with St Frances of Rome*, attributed to M. Rocca[2]

Before entrance to choir: R wall: copy of Reni's *St Andrew Being Led to his Martyrdom*; L wall: copy of Domenichino's *Flagellation of St Andrew*, both after the oratory of St Andrew[3]

Confessio[4]: St Frances of Rome (d. 1440) was first buried under the high altar but when in 1634 her body was found there it was decided to build a *confessio* in her honour[5]. Bernini's original gilt bronze statues (1644-49) were destroyed by the French but replaced by copies by Giosuè Meli, 1866[6]. Within the crypt, which was built by A. Busiri Vici in 1869[7], is a relief of the saint by Ercole Ferrata[8]. The work was paid for by Donna Agata Pamphili, sister of Innocent X, who was a nun at Tor de' Specchi, a convent founded by St Frances[9]

Apse: D. M. Canini, *Martyrdom of Sts Nemesius, Olympius, Sempronius, Lucilla, Esuperia and Theodolus*, before 1663[10]

Choir: R side: monument to Gregory XI (d. 1378), last of the Avignon Popes and brought back to Rome by the pleading of St Catherine of Siena, by Paolo Olivieri; relief of *Gregory XI Entering Rome*; on side walls: figures of L: *Faith* and R: *Prudence*, 1584[11]

L side of choir: R wall: S. Pozzo, *The Blessed Bernard Tolomei Succours the Plague Victims*, c.1744[12]

Sacristy: Pierre Subleyras, *St Benedict of Norcia Resurrecting a Child*[13]; Brandi, *Holy Trinity with the Dead Christ Mourned by the Blessed Bernard Tolomei*[14]; Cerrini, *Tobias and the Angel*(?)[15]; Jacopino del Conte, *Pope Paul III*[16]

4 to L: vault of chapel copied exactly from a plate in Pozzo's *Perspectiva pictorum*[17]; altarpiece: Giuseppe Pirovani, *The Blessed Bernardo Tolomei Assisting the Sick in Sienna*[18]

3 to L: altarpiece: Pietro Tedeschi, *St Emidius*, 1797[19]

2 to L: altarpiece: Angelo Caroselli and Filippo Lauri, *Mass of St Gregory*, 1620-23[20]

1 to L: altarpiece: copy of Maratta's *Adoration of the Shepherds*; L wall: Domenico

Maria Canuti, *The Blessed Bernard Tolomei Exorcising a Demon*[21].

S. Francesco d'Assisi a Monte Mario
Piazza diMonte Gaudo, 8

Built in 1669-76 as the result of a bequest from a priest named Bartolomeo Neri, for the benefit of those living on the Monte Mario, who had no church nearby, and made into a parish church in 1708. The façade was added in 1728-29 to the designs of Pietro Passalacqua. It is an unusually simple work for that architect but the funds available were limited.

INTERIOR
High altar: *Virgin and Child with St Francis and the Blessed Jordan of Pisa*, Giuseppe Cacci, 1675-76. Choir stuccoes by Marcantonio Baragiolio.

S. Francesco di Paola
Piazza di S. Francesco Paola, 10

The church was given to the Order of Minims, founded by St Francis of Paola, by Gregory XV in 1622. It was rebuilt between 1645 and 1650 to the designs of G. P. Monaldi at the expense of Donna Olimpia Aldobrandini-Pamphili, wife of Camillo, nephew of Innocent X. At this stage the lower half of the façade was built. It was completed by Nicola Lorenza Piccioni in 1764[1], though it is described as complete by Roisecco in 1750. The convent was being built by Domenico Castello when Baglione wrote in 1642.

If shut, ring at the door of the monastery to the left of the church.

INTERIOR
The interior was redecorated between 1723 and 1728 to designs by Luigi Barattone, a pupil of Ludovico Rusconi Sassi, for the General of the Order, Francesco Zavarroni. It was restored in 1952 when the vault was given its present decoration. The side chapel stucco decorations are by the brothers Carlo and Pietro Porciani.

1 to R: Cappella di S. Anna: altarpiece: Filippo Luzi, *Holy Family with St Anne*; vault: Onofrio Avellino, *St Anne in Glory*, 1730-35[2]

2 to R: Cappella di S. Francesco di Paola: frescoes by Giuseppe Chiari, L wall: *St Francis of Paola Raises a Dead Labourer*; R wall: *St Francis Restores the Features to a Deformed Child*; vault: *St Francis in Glory*, c.1726[3]

3 to R: Cappella di S. Francesco di Sales: Antonio Crecolini, altarpiece: *St Francis of Sales Receives the Cord of the Third Order from St Francis of Paola*; L wall: *St Francis of Sales Writing*; R wall: *Charity of St Francis of Sales*[4]

R wall: monument to Monsignor Lazzaro Pallavicini, erected in 1744 by Benedict XIV, designed by F. Fuga with bust by Agostino Corsini[5]

Choir: the bottom of the wall was covered with *cippolino* in 1952
High altar: by G. A. de' Rossi, c.1655. The wooden tabernacle was added in 1663 to a design by Mattia de' Rossi, and the screen gilded and painted by Antonio Ronca, 1668[6]
L wall: monument to Giovanni Pizzullo (d. 1646) attributed to Agostino Corsini
Sacristy: vault: Sassoferrato, *St Francis of Paola before the Virgin and Child*, 1641[7], one of his finest works, set in a rich but severe stucco frame by F. Braccioli, a rare example of pure *quadro riportato* from the mid 17th century. Lunettes by Agostino

Masucci and Filippo Luzi of scenes from the *Life of St Francis of Paola*, 1729[8]
Sala del Capitolare: altarpiece: Cozza, *Crucifixion with St Francis of Paola*, 1640-42[9]; walls: S. Pozzo, L: *Agony in the Garden*; R: *Carrying the Cross*, back: *Pietà*; vault: *Instruments of the Passion*[10]
Corridor off sacristy: S. Pozzo, *Immaculate Virgin*[11]
3 to L: Cappella di S. Michele Arcangelo: altarpiece: Stefano Perrugini, *St Michael*; R wall oval: G. B. Brughi, *St Michael Gives St Francis the Insignia of the Order*; L wall oval: G. A. Crecolini, *St Michael Gives St Francis the Cowl*, 1721-22
2 to L: Cappella del Beato Nicola dei Longobardi: decorated in 1733. The altar dates from 1787. Altarpiece: Francesco Manno, *The Blessed Nicholas Saggio Longobardi Receives the Cross from Christ in a Vision*, 1792[12]; S. Pozzo, L wall: *Adoration of the Magi*; R wall: *Adoration of the Shepherds*
1 to L: Cappella di S. Gaspare de Bono: altarpiece: O. Avellino, *St Caspar de Bono*; S. Pozzo, L. wall: *Flight into Egypt*; R wall: *Joseph's Dream*; vault: *God the Father*.

S. Francesco a Ripa
Piazza di S. Francesco d'Assisi

The church and monastery are built on the site of an earlier Benedictine church and hospital, S. Biagio, in which St Francis stayed when in Rome. In 1229 it was given by Gregory IX to the Franciscan Friars Minor, who rebuilt the church on a larger scale and still serve it today. In 1579 a theological college was attached to the church, adding greatly to its importance. The choir was rebuilt in 1603 by Onorio Longhi and the whole church was remodelled after 1682 by Mattia de' Rossi, who added the meagre façade.

INTERIOR
Entrance wall: monument to R: Tommaso Raggi (d. 1679) and L: his wife Ortensia Spinola (d. 1672)[1]
1 to R: Cappella del Crocifisso/Ricci: Pesci attributes this chapel to Carlo Fontana but this seems incorrect. Vault frescoes by Fra' Emanuele da Como. L wall: monument to Cardinal Michelangelo Ricci, member of the Congregation of the Inquisition under Innocent XI (d. 1682), by Domenico Guidi[2]. R wall: monument to Stefano Brandi (d. 1794)[3]. Over altar: crucifix by Fra' Angelo da Pietrafitta[4]
Between 1 and 2 to R: monument to Michelangelo Mattei (d. 1702), one of a number of Baroque monuments in this church of which nothing is known
1st pillar: monuments to Maria Costa (d. 1852) by Camillo Pistrucci with bust by Domenico Morani
2 to R: Cappella di S. Giovanni da Capistrano: the chapel was begun in 1681 to a plan attributed to Carlo Fontana but work was interrupted and only began again in 1693, when the chapel was marbled; it was finally completed under Filippo Leti in 1698. The paintings in the chapel are by Domenico Maria Muratori. Altarpiece: *St John Capistrano Directing the Battle of Belgrade*; L wall: *Consequences of the Saint's Preaching in Perugia*; lunette: *Miracle of the Saint at his Death*; R wall: *Miracle of the Saint during the Siege of Vienna*; lunette: *Last Communion of St John Capistrano*; vault: *St John Capistrano in Glory*, before 1698[6]
Between 2 and 3 to R: monument to Cesare Gherardi (d. 1623)
3 to R: Cappella di S. Giuseppe/Papi/Ludovisi: by Giovanni Corbelli, including stucco decorations, 1686; altarpiece: *Holy Family with God the Father*, 1685, by Stefano Legnani; frescoes by Giuseppe Passeri, L wall: *Joseph's Dream*; R wall:

Flight into Egypt; vault: *Angels in Glory*, c.1705[7]
L of 3 to R: monument to Nicola Grappelli (d. 1690)
3rd pillar: monuments to Gioacchino Costa (d. 1841) by C. Pistrucci, 1841[8], and Ulisse Calvo (d. 1694)
R transept: Cappella di S. Pietro d'Alcantara/Pallavicini Rospigliosi[9]: begun by N. Michetti in 1710 from a model which survives and is on loan to the Museo di Roma, Palazzo Braschi[10]. The monument was completed in 1725 by Girolamo Caccia and L. Rusconi Sassi after Michetti departed for Russia in 1718. R wall: monument to Maria Camilla Pallavicini (d. 1710) and G. B. Rospigliosi (d. 1722) with allegorical figures of R: *Charity* and L: *Prudence* and busts of the deceased by G. Mazzuoli, 1714-19; bronze figures of *Death* on both monuments by Francesco Maglia, 1716. L wall: monument to Stefano (d. 1687) and Cardinal Lazzaro Pallavicini (d. 1680) with allegorical figures of R: *Justice* and L: *Fortitude* by G. Mazzuoli and the *Lion* by F. Pincelotti, 1715-19[11]. Altarpiece: G. Chiari, *Vision of the Trinity Vouchsafed to Sts Peter of Alcantara and Pascal Baylon*, 1725[12]; pendentives: Tommaso Chiari: *Faith, Hope, Charity* and *Patience*[13]
High altar: designed by F. Ferruzzi and erected in stucco in 1737 and then in marble in 1744 by Fra' Secondo da Roma; modified by Carlo de' Dominicis in 1746[14]. The wooden statue of *St Francis in Ecstasy* dates from before 1588 and is ascribed to Fra' Diego da Careri. The present arrangement was designed by Agostino Masucci and the *Angel* carved by G. Frascari[15]
L of high altar: Fra' Diego da Careri, statue of *St Anthony of Padua*, c.1578-88
Sacristy: remodelled by Mattia de' Rossi in 1696, with fine woodwork; bronze crucifix by Algardi[16]
4 to L: Cappella Albertoni[17]: the structure dates from the 16th century (two frescoes survive from it) but the chapel was remodelled in 1622 by Giacomo Mola on the orders of the Marchese Baldassare Paluzzi Albertoni, who wished to honour his relative the Blessed Ludovica Albertoni. The frescoes are by Gaspare Celio, 1625[18], though the frescoes which flank the altar, R: *St Clare* and L: *The Blessed Ludovica Albertoni*, are from an earlier campaign and by an unknown hand. The cult of the Blessed Ludovica was confirmed by Clement X in 1671, who was related to the Albertoni family, and on this occasion Cardinal Angelo Paluzzi Albertoni commissioned Bernini to make a statue of *The Blessed Ludovica Albertoni*, 1671-74. This is one of the most moving renderings of a mystical ecstasy in Baroque art. It shows the Blessed Ludovica in the extreme state of mystical union with the Divine, beyond even the tangible vision of St Teresa which Bernini evoked so vividly in the Cornaro Chapel at S. Maria della Vittoria. The effect is marred by the fact that one of the side windows which light it has been walled up. Bernini's original terracotta model for the statue was acquired in 1980 by the Victoria & Albert Museum, London[19]. Baciccio's altarpiece of the *Virgin and Child with St Anne* was painted to complete the decoration of the chapel, 1675[20].
On pier outside chapel: monument to Giulia Ricci, wife of the Marchese Francesco Paravicini (d. 1662), by E. Ferrata[21]
3 to L: Cappella della Pietà/Mattei: by Francesco Peparelli[22] but restored in 1882 by Paolo Belloni. Altarpiece: copy of Reni's *St Michael*. L wall: monument to Laura Frangipani Mattei (d. 1635) to a design by F. Peparelli and bust by Andrea Bolgi, 1637[23]; R wall: monument to Cardinal Orazio Mattei, Majordomo to Innocent XI (d. 1688), by Lorenzo Ottoni[24]; lunettes painted

by Marcello Sozzi with scenes from the *Life of St Charles of Sezze*, whose relics lie below the altar
Between 2 and 3 to L: monument to Pietro Carcarsi (d. 1716)
2 to L: Cappella dell'Annunciazione/Castellani: probably built *c*.1530-40; altarpiece: F. Salviati, *Annunciation*, *c*.1532-35[25]; frescoes by G. B. Ricci: R lunette: *Visitation*, flanked by *Sibyls*; below, R: *Solomon* and L: *Jeremiah*; L lunette: *Birth of the Virgin*, flanked by *Sibyls*; below, L: *Isaiah* and R: *David*; vault: *God the Father with Music-making Angels*; pendentives: *Four Evangelists*, 1555
2nd pillar: monument to Innocenzo da Chiusi (d. 1630) to a design by G. B. Mola
Pier between 2 and 1 to L: monument to Monsignor Giuseppe Paravicini (d. 1695) by C. Rusconi[26]
1 to L: Cappella dell'Immacolata: decorated under the direction of Simon Vouet. Altarpiece: Antoon Sallaert, *Immaculate Conception*,[27]; L wall: S. Vouet, *Birth of the Virgin*, 1627-30[28]; R wall: *Assumption* ascribed to Sandart[29]; vault: *Coronation of the Virgin*, Vouet and workshop; pendentives: *Sibyls* to a design by S. Vouet[30]

From the sacristy a staircase leads to the chapel of Cardinal Alessandro Montalto and Cardinal Ranuccio Pallavicini.

S. Francesco di Sales *see*
S. Maria della Visitazione
Via S. Francesco di Sales, 61

S. Francesco Saverio *see*
Oratorio del Caravita
Via del Caravita, 7

S. Gallicano
Via di S. Gallicano, 26

The hospital of S. Gallicano was founded by Benedict XIII in 1724 and built by F. Raguzzini. One of his simplest buildings, consisting of a long, straight front, broken only by the projecting façade of the church, the side bays of which are on concave curves but which is topped by a somewhat fanciful attic composed of scrolls supporting a cross. Internally the church is a simple Greek cross with very shallow arms. The church was built in 1725-26.

INTERIOR
Decorated by Marco Benefial on the orders of Cardinal Piermarcellino Corradini.
Altarpiece: *St Gallicanus Recommends the Sick to the Virgin*
R lunette: *Vision of St Philip Neri*
L lunette: *The Virgin of the Snows Appears to St Gallicanus*, 1725-26.

Il Gesù (SS. Nome di Gesù)
Piazza di Gesù

The Jesuit Order, founded by St Ignatius of Loyola, was approved by Paul III in 1540 and was given the little church of S. Maria della Strada near the palaces of the Altieri and Astalli families. In 1551 Nanni di Baccio Bigio was commissioned to design a larger church but owing to difficulties in collecting funds and in acquiring the necessary land nothing was built. In 1554 Michelangelo was asked to provide an alternative plan but this is lost[1].

In 1565 Francesco Borgia, later beatified, became the General of the Order. In 1561 a new patron appeared in the person of Cardinal Alessandro Farnese, who supplied funds generously, partly on the recommendation of his secretary, Giulio Folchi (buried in the first chapel on the right of the church), and with this help the complete site needed for the church was acquired.

At this time the architect of the Company was Giovanni Tristano but in 1563 Farnese imposed his own architect, Vignola, who prepared the design, though Tristano remained in charge of the actual building operations. The foundation stone was laid in 1568; by the time of Vignola's death in 1573 the nave was structurally complete and the façade begun. Vignola's original design for the façade, shown on the medal of 1568, had a high attic running the whole width of the building with a Serliana window in the middle under a broad pediment. This was immediately abandoned, and Vignola provided another design; this too was rejected, and other architects, including Galeazzo Alessi and Giacomo della Porta, were asked to submit designs. In 1571 Della Porta's was chosen and Vignola was only able to preserve his design for posterity by having it engraved by Mario Cartari (1573). The drawing made for the engraving, probably by Giacinto Vignola to his father's design, is in the Kunstbibliothek, Berlin[1]. The existing façade was finished in 1577; Ammanati's over-door panel with the name of Jesus and the choir and transepts were finished by 1582, when work on the high altar was started. In 1583 the pendentives of the dome were frescoed by an artist named in the documents as 'Andrea', whose identity is uncertain, and the dome was begun by Giovanni de' Vecchi. The dome was left unfinished and all these frescoes disappeared when the church was redecorated by Baciccio.

In its plan and structure the Gesù was more influential than any other Roman church of the 16th century. It satisfied all the requirements of liturgy and ecclesiastical practice as laid down by the Council of Trent and the exponents of Tridentine doctrine, such as Carlo and Francesco Borromeo. Its broad nave was suitable for preaching to large congregations; the choir was clearly cut off from the nave – as was not the case with centrally planned churches – and so emphasised the distinction between priest and laity; the long axis of the church led the eye firmly towards the altar; the chapels flanking the aisles provided for altars devoted to the worship of individual saints (and could be sold to individual families); and the sacristy was set far enough away from the apse to enable the priest carrying the Host for the celebration of the Mass to make an impressive procession to the high altar. Vignola's design for the façade was also imitated all over Europe for several centuries – more in fact than the façade as executed by Giacomo della Porta. It provided an ideal solution to the problem of binding into a single whole the higher central section covering the nave and the lower side sections corresponding to the aisles – a problem that had exercised architects since the 15th century, when Alberti invented the earliest formula in the façade of S. Maria Novella in Florence.

As it was first conceived the interior of the church was to have been almost bare, the pilasters were of stucco, with capitals and bases of travertine, and the only marbling would have been on the altars and the inside of the entrance doors, with frescoes in the dome and pendentives. It is clearly shown in this state in Sacchi's painting of the centenary celebrations of 1639, now in the Museo di Roma[2]. This simplicity was universal in early Jesuit churches and was laid down by Giuseppe Valeriano (who became the official architect of the Order after Tristano's death in 1565) in connection with the Jesuit churches in Genoa and Naples[3].

In this context it is worth emphasising that the Jesuits, who are often regarded as the early protagonists of the Baroque, to the extent that in French the style was for long known as 'le style jésuite', were in fact slow in taking it up. They never employed Borromini, and Bernini only built one church for them – the Novitiate of S. Andrea al Quirinale – and that not until the late 1650's. In fact it was not until the election of Giovanni Paolo Oliva as General of the Order in 1664 that a new policy in church building and decoration was inaugurated[4]. He at once determined on a much grander scheme of decoration for the Gesù. For this purpose he enlisted the services of the most distinguished artists working in Rome at the time: Cortona for the chapel of St Francis Xavier; Maratta to paint its altarpiece; the Jesuit Guglielmo Cortese to fresco the apse; Baciccio to fresco the dome, pendentives and nave vault; and another Jesuit, Andrea Pozzo, to design the altar of St Ignatius. Cortese died in 1679 before he began his work, and in the event Baciccio replaced the earlier frescoes in the dome and pendentives and frescoed the vault of the nave with one of the most spectacular illusionist schemes in the whole of Baroque art.

The chapel decorations were begun in 1584[5]. The iconography was conceived by the Jesuits themselves under the direction of Giuseppe Valeriano and Giovanni de' Rossi, and the design and planning were by the Jesuit painter G. B. Fiammeri. The first chapel to be decorated was the Cappella della Madonna in the left transept, which stood more or less on the site of the old church of S. Maria della Strada and perpetuated its dedication; the last to be finished (1639) was the chapel of St Ignatius in the left transept, decorated by Cortona. All this work was, however, swept away by the later redecoration.

In 1767 the Jesuits were expelled from Spain and the Kingdom of the Two Sicilies, and money had to be raised to help the Fathers, for which purpose many of the precious objects in the treasury of the Gesù were sold. In 1773 the Company was finally suppressed by Clement XIV. The Fathers were, however, allowed to continue serving the church but with the French occupation in 1798 almost everything of value in the church was either sold or carried off.

In 1814 Pius VII re-established the Company and an attempt was made to restore to the church some of its splendour and to complete the decoration of the apse (the high altar was unfinished and the walls bare). This job was entrusted in 1841 to the architect Antonio Sarti by the General Jan Roothaan. Sarti made a new high altar (criticised at the time as being merely 'a door') and marbled the walls of the apse. In 1858 Prince Torlonia gave money to carry the restoration into the nave where the travertine and stucco pilasters were replaced with marble. The last trace of the original simplicity had vanished.

INTERIOR

Frescoes by Baciccio, nave vault: *Triumph of the Name of Jesus*, 1676-79; dome: *Glory of Heaven*, 1672-75; pendentives: *Evangelists; Fathers of the Latin Church; Prophets and Law Givers*, 1675-76; choir: *Choir of Angels*, c.1683; apse: *Adoration of the Lamb*, 1680-83[6]. The stucco decorations on the window embrasures and the frieze of putti are by A. Raggi[7]. The statues in the dome are by P. Naldini: *Temperance* and *Justice*, and Retti: *Prudence* and *Fortitude*; those in the right transept are by Michele Maglia and those in the left by L. Retti[8].

A drawing at Düsseldorf[9] shows that originally Baciccio intended to decorate the cove of the vault with circular panels supported by painted figures, which would have left a much narrower field for the main fresco, and it was almost certainly Bernini who suggested the scheme as executed, with a vast central fresco extended outside the frame by clouds which appear to throw shadows on the gilt stuccoes of the cove. This device heightens the dramatic effect of the whole scheme in which the light streaming from the IHS, signifying the name of Jesus, drives heretics and unbelievers out of heaven so that they seem to be hurtling down into the world of the spectator. Many of the frescoes and altarpieces in the side chapels are illustrated in Hibbard.

1 to R: Cappella di S. Andrea/Folchi/Cerrini: decoration of the chapel began in 1588, but was not completed by Giulio Folchi's death in 1591. Salustio Cerrini took over the chapel in the same year and saw the decoration finished in 1601. Frescoes by Agostino Ciampelli, vault: *Mary Queen of Martyrs*; pendentives: *Sts Clement, Ignatius of Antioch, Cyprian* and *Polycarp*; R wall: *Martyrdom of St Stephen*; lunette: *St Catherine*; L wall: *Martyrdom of St Lawrence*; lunette: *St Agnes*. Altarpiece: *St Andrew Adoring the Cross*

2 to R: Cappella della Passione/Mellini: decoration of the chapel began in 1590 to G. B. Fiammeri's design, and was executed by Gaspare Celio; L wall: *Christ Carrying the Cross*; lunette: *Christ in the Garden*; R wall: *Christ Nailed to the Cross*; lunette: *Kiss of Judas*; vault: *Glory of the Cross*; pendentives: *Four Evangelists*. Final payment 1597. Altarpiece: Pietro Gagliardi, *Virgin and Christ with Jesuit Saints*; to L: *Christ at the Column* and to R: *Christ Crowned with Thorns*, G. Celio.

3 to R: Cappella degli Angeli/Garzonia/Vittorio: the frescoes in the chapel were completed in the mid 1590's by Federico Zuccaro. Altarpiece: *The Seven Archangels Adoring the Trinity*, c.1600[10]; vault: *Triumph of the Virgin*; L wall: *Souls Purified in Purgatory Presented to Heaven*; lunette: *The Prodigal Son Comforted by an Angel* (also attributed to V. Salimbeni); R wall: *Fall of the Rebel Angels*, F. Zuccaro; lunette: *Angels Gathering the Praises of the Faithful for Presentation to the Lord*. Pendentives: *Habakkuk and the Angel*; *Shadrak, Meshak and Abednego amongst the Flames*; *Jacob's Ladder* and *Tobias and the Angel*, all attributed to Salimbeni. The four palm-bearing angels are by Silla Longhi and Flaminio Vacca, the vault stuccoes are by Mariani[11]; marble revetment by Giovanni de' Rossi

R transept: Cappella di S. Francesco Saverio/Negroni[12]: altar designed by Cortona in the last years of his life (1669), but executed after his death by his nephew Luca Berrettini (finished 1679). The arms on the base of the columns are those of Clement IX and Innocent XI. Altarpiece: C. Maratta, *Death of St Francis Xavier*, 1674-79[13]; vault frescoes: G. A. Carlone, L: *St Francis Finds his Lost Crucifix*; C: *St Francis in Glory*; R: *St Francis Baptising*, 1695[14]

Chapel to R of high altar: Cappella di S. Francesco d'Assisi/del Sacro Cuore/Orsini: attributed to Giacomo della Porta[15]; altarpiece: *Sacred Heart of Jesus* by Pompeo Batoni, 1765-67[16]. The paintings in the vault are by B. Croce, *Evangelists* and *Doctors of the Church*, 1599. The scenes from the *Life of St Francis* are ascribed to Paul Bril and Joseph Heintz the Elder. To R of entrance and moving anticlockwise: *St Francis Renounces his Worldly Goods*; *Preaching to the Birds*; *St Francis Preaching to the Sultan of Egypt*; *Apparition of St Francis in the Fire*; *St Francis Appears to Brother John*; *St Francis and the Wolf of Gubbio*; *Death of St Francis*, 1588-89[17]. Marble decorations by G. Valeriano

Choir: high altar: A. Sarti, 1841. The original

tabernacle ascribed to Giacomo della Porta is now in the Cathedral of Thurles[18]. Altarpiece: A. Capalti, *Circumcision*, 1843. The original altarpiece by G. Muziano is held in the Galleria dei Marmi. Pozzo designed two magnificent high altars for the church, one of which he actually executed in false perspective for the ceremony of the *Quarant'ore*, but he was unable to carry out either in permanent form[19]. In 1755 a new tabernacle was added by Giuseppe Silvestro, an artist who is only known from the drawings for this church and other buildings in Rome preserved in the Kunstbibliothek, Berlin[20]

To R: monument to the Blessed Giuseppe Maria Pignatelli (d. 1811) by L. Simonetti, 1811[21]

To L: monument to Cardinal Robert Bellarmine (d. 1621) with bust by Bernini, c.1624. It originally formed part of a larger monument with allegorical figures by Pietro Bernini, which was destroyed in the restoration of 1841[22]. The monument is usually ascribed to Girolamo Rainaldi but Mola[23] attributes it to Francesco Peparelli. It was completed by A. Tadolini[24]

Chapel to L of choir: Cappella di S. Maria della Strada/Caetani Orsini: originally the left transept was dedicated to S. Maria della Strada but later it was given to St Ignatius and the dedication transferred to this chapel. The chapel is attributed to Giacomo della Porta[25] and according to Pecchiai the dome was built by Valeriano. Work began on the chapel in 1584 and by 1587 was completed to the vault. In 1587-88 the dome was decorated with stuccoes and frescoes by Giovanni Battista Pozzo of *Music-making Angels*. The altarpiece, a detached fresco of the *Virgin and Child*, is from the old church of S. Maria della Strada. The canvases decorating the walls are by Giuseppe Valeriano, with the collaboration of S. Pulzone; from the R passage wall: *Birth of the Virgin*; R wall: *Presentation*; R of altar: *Dormition of the Virgin*; L of altar: *Death of St Joseph*; L wall: *Marriage of the Virgin*; *Annunciation*; *Visitation*; L passage wall: *Assumption*[26]. The rich wall marbling is by B. Basso, 1584-87[27]

L transept: Cappella di S. Ignazio[28]: this chapel was originally dedicated to the Crucifixion and given to Cardinal Giacomo Savelli, who commissioned Giacomo della Porta to design a rich decoration for it. Work was interrupted, however, by Savelli's death in 1587. In 1629 a gilt urn to contain the remains of St Ignatius was executed to the designs of the Jesuit architect Orazio Grassi, with decorative details by Alessandro Algardi, including the relief of Jesuit Saints[29], but it was not actually installed until 1637, when Pietro da Cortona was commissioned in March 1636 by Francesco Giattino to design the altar frontal which was executed by Santi Ghetti, Giovanni Pilotti and Francuccio Francucci. In 1696 the whole altar was replaced by a new one designed by Andrea Pozzo, one of the most sumptuous Baroque works in any Roman church. L. A. Acquisti's *St Ignatius*, 1804, is a reproduction of Pierre Legros' original silver statue, which was melted down by the French in 1798; only the chasuble and maniple are original[30]. The altar frontal was remade in 1737.

R: *Triumph of Religion over Heresy*, 1695-97/98 by P. Legros[31]; L: *Triumph of Faith over Paganism* by Jean-Baptiste Théodon; above: *Trinity* by Bernardino Ludovisi and Lorenzo Ottoni[32]. Reliefs over altar: L to R: René Frémin, *St Ignatius Miraculously Extinguishing a Fire*; Angelo de' Rossi, *St Ignatius Exorcises a Possessed Man*; Pietro Reyff, *St Ignatius Healing a Nun*; Lorenzo Merlini, *St Peter Appears to St Ignatius*; Francesco Nuvolone, *St Ignatius Meets St*

Philip Neri; R. Frémin, *St Ignatius Cures the Sick with Oil from the Altar Lamp*; P. E. Monnot, *Liberation of Captives*. To the side of the altar are two reliefs, 1695-99, L: Angelo de' Rossi, *Paul III Approving the Jesuit Order* and R: Bernardino Cametti, *Canonisation of St Ignatius by Gregory XV*, 1695-98[33]. The two angels on the R wall above the door are by Rusconi, 1691-99[34]. Within the lunettes are stucco reliefs of scenes from the *Life of St Ignatius* attributed to A. Raggi and L. Retti[35].

The bronze altar-rail, 1695-99, is of exceptional splendour. It was probably designed by Carlo Fontana, modified by Francesco Maglia and modelled by G. B. Antonini, P. Legros, A. de' Rossi, C. Lobelli, P. Reyff, P. Papaleo, D. Melussi and F. de' Vecchi, 1695-99[36]. The *Crucifixion* and *Pietà* on the altar are by P. Reyff[37].

3 to L: Cappella della Trinità/Taro/Arrigoni: decoration of the chapel began in 1584 and was completed in 1589. Altarpiece: Francesco Bassano, *Holy Trinity*, 1589; frescoes painted from Giovanni Battista Fiammeri's cartoons by B. Baldi, F. Fenzoni, V. Salimbeni and D. Alberti. L wall: Durante Alberti, *Transfiguration*; R wall: B. Baldi, *Baptism of Christ*; L lunette: *God the Father* and R lunette: *Abraham before the Angels*, both by Salimbeni; vault: G. B. Fiammeri with the assistance of Pietro Fiammingo, *The Creation*; pendentives and other vault decorations by Salimbeni[38].

2 to L: Cappella della Natività di Maria/Cerri: the chapel originally belonged to the Braghesi family but passed to the Cerri family in *c.*1639 and was restored to the designs of Pietro da Cortona from 1640 onwards. Decoration of the chapel began in 1584, including the vault fresco by Niccolò Circignani. The frescoes include, R wall: *Adoration of the Magi*; lunette: *Annunciation to the Shepherds*; L wall: *Presentation in the Temple*; lunette: *Massacre of the Innocents*; vault: *Heavenly Celebration of the Birth of Christ*; pendentives: *David*, *Isaiah*, *Zachariah* and *Baruch* – all heavily restored in the 19th century. Altarpiece: Giovanni Gagliardi, *Holy Family*[39].

The chapel contains four allegorical figures, inserted by the Cerri: *Justice* by Cosimo Fancelli, *Fortitude* by Giacomo Antonio Fancelli, *Prudence* by Giovanni Lazzoni and *Temperance* by Domenico Guidi[40]. It also contains four monuments by Pietro da Cortona, each designed to contain a bust: R back: Monsignor Antonio Cerri (d. 1642) with a bust executed in the studio of Algardi, possibly by Domenico Guidi, after one by the master which is now in the Manchester Art Gallery[41]; R front: Monsignor Carlo Cerri (d. 1726) by Filippo della Valle, *c.*1729[42]; L back: Cardinal Carlo Cerri (d. 1690) attributed to Guidi[43]. The fourth niche was filled in the 19th century with a bust of a member of a different family.

1 to L: Cappella degli Apostoli/Borgia/Morelli/Ravenna: vault frescoes begun in 1585 by Niccolò Circignani, called 'Il Pomarancio', and completed in 1587: *Pentecost*; R lunette: *Martyrdom of St Paul with Religion and Love*; L lunette: *Martyrdom of St Paul with Faith and Hope*; pendentives: *Prudence*, *Justice*, *Fortitude* and *Temperance*. Wall frescoes by P. F. Mola, R: *Conversion of St Paul* and L: *St Peter Causes Water to Spring in the Prison in Order to Baptise Sts Processus and Martinian*, *c.*1656-57[44]. Altarpiece by A. Pozzo, *St Francis Borgia Adores the Eucharist*, altered in the 19th century by the addition of a group of Japanese martyrs after their canonisation in 1862[45].

The church also contains an important series of inlaid tomb slabs, of which the most interesting, in front of the altar rail to the right, is that of *Carlo Pio*, probably Cardinal Pio (d. 1641). This was designed by Bernini c.1649-50, probably as a wall monument (a drawing for it exists at Holkham) but eventually carried out as a floor slab, with the life-size figures in brass inlaid in the marble, a technique very rare in Italy and much more frequent in Northern Europe, particularly England, though it had gone out even there by this date. The result cannot be regarded as one of Bernini's triumphs, though as a smaller wall monument it might have been successful[46].

Sacristy: ceiling: A. Ciampelli, *Adoration of the Blessed Sacrament*; Giovanni Baglione, *Cardinal Sfondrato with Sts Cecilia, Valerian, Maximus and Tiburtius*[47]; Giovanni Antonio Galli ('Lo Spadarino') *Sacrifice of Isaac*[48]. Statues of *St Francis Xavier* and *St Francis Borgia*, C. Ferri, c.1687-89[49]

Casa Professa (to R of church): this contains the rooms of St Ignatius decorated with *trompe-l'oeil* frescoes begun by Giacomo Cortese in 1675 and finished by A. Pozzo between 1681 and 1686. Pozzo also frescoed the Cappella della Vigna[50]

Cappella di Odoardo Farnese: by Girolamo Rainaldi[51]. Altarpiece: copy of Domenichino's *Vision of St Ignatius at La Storta*. The room is decorated with canvases relating to scenes from the *Life of St Ignatius*: upper L wall: *St Peter Appears to St Ignatius*, B. Ciarpi; lower: *Senator Marcantonio Trevison Finds St Ignatius under the Portico*; back wall; *Mass at Manresa*; upper R wall: *The Virgin Appears to St Ignatius*, all by Commodi; lower: *Death of St Ignatius*, Ciarpi; above door: *The Trinity Appear to St Ignatius*, Commodi[52].

Gesù e Maria
Via del Corso, 45

The church, which belongs to a house of Discalced Augustinian Friars, was built by 'Carlo Butio Milanese' at the expense of Cardinal Scipione Borghese. Plans for the church were made in 1619 but only approved in 1629, and the foundation stone was laid in 1632 by Monsignor Giambattista Altieri. The church was officially opened in 1637 but was incomplete owing to a building dispute with the Fathers of S. Giacomo degli Incurabili across the road. In 1671 Carlo Rainaldi was commissioned to complete the two western chapels and the façade, based on Butio's original plan. The façade is unusual, being a variant of Palladio's church façades with a smaller order playing against a larger one.

INTERIOR

The interior decorative programme, including the high altar, was begun in 1678 under the direction of Rainaldi and completed in 1686. It was made possible by the patronage of Giorgio Bolognetti, the retired Bishop of Rieti.

In 1681-83 the interior was decorated under the direction of Francesco Perini with unusually rich marbling, partly of Sicilian jasper. The pilasters are outlined in black and range from yellow through orange to red, except those flanking the chancel arch, which are entirely black.

The most interesting feature of the church is the series of monuments commissioned by Giorgio Bolognetti for members of his family and set in the four piers separating the side chapels[1]. The monuments transform the whole church into a family chapel, a sort of oratory in which all the deceased play their part, an extension of the method employed by Bernini in his Cornaro and

Fonseca chapels.
Nave: vault: G. Brandi, *Assumption of the Immaculate Virgin*, 1684-86; between the windows: *Evangelists*. The vault stuccoes are by G. Gramignoli and M. Maglia, 1683. Stucco figures in niches: entrance wall, R: F. Cavallini, *St Anne*; above: M. Maglia, *Moses*, 1684; L: M. Maglia, *St James*; above: M. Maglia, *David*, 1684; R wall, 1st niche: L. Ottoni, *The Virgin*; 2nd niche: F. Cavallini, *St Elizabeth*; L wall, 1st niche: *St Joseph*; 2nd niche: M. Maglia, *St Zacharias*, 1682-86

Beside the nave windows are stucco figures of *Old Testament Prophets*, those on the right by G. Gramignoli and those on the left by M. Maglia, 1684-86.
Above entrance: organ by G. B. Testa. 1750[2]
R entrance wall: monument to Canon Camillo del Corno (d. 1680) by Domenico Guidi with putti by Francesco Aprile, c.1680-86
1 to R: Cappella del Crocifisso: R wall: monument to Conte Giuseppe Cini (d. 1830) by R. Rinaldi[3]
1st pier to R: monument to Pietro (d. 1680) and Francesco Bolognetti (d. 1671) by F. Aprile, 1682-86[4]
2 to R: Cappella di S. Nicola da Tolentino: restored by Francesco Ferraris, completed in 1795. altarpiece: Raffaele Minossi: *The Virgin Appears to St Nicholas of Tolentino*; L wall: *St Nicholas of Tolentino Distributes Alms*; R wall: *St Nicholas of Tolentino Frees Prisoners*; vault: *St Nicholas in Glory*, 1795[5]
2nd pier to R: monument to Francesco Mario Bolognetti (d. 1677) by Francesco Cavallini, 1682-86
3 to R: Cappella di S. Anna: altarpiece: Ermenegildo Costantini, *St Anne and the Immaculate Virgin with St Anthony Abbot*, 1765[6]
High altar: by Carlo Rainaldi, with angels holding the globe by P. Naldini and the two putti above the pediment by F. Cavallini,

1678-80. Altarpiece: G. Brandi, *Coronation of the Virgin*, 1678-79, and vault: *God the Father and the Holy Spirit*; on either side: marble statues, L: *St John the Baptist* and R: *St John the Evangelist* by Giuseppe Mazzuoli, 1680-81[7]. Tabernacle by Giuseppe Silvestro to a design by Rinaldi, 1754. In the monks' choir: Lazzaro Baldi, *The Virgin Dividing her Girdle between Sts Augustine and Monica*, 1690-c.92[8]
Sacristy: L. Baldi, *Virgin of the Girdle*[9]
3 to L: Cappella della Madonna del Divin Aiuto: redecorated by Giacomo Paticchio, 1793; Pietro Labruzzi, R lunette: *Adoration of the Shepherds* and L lunette: Angelo Campanelli, *Flight into Egypt*. Memorials to L: Francesco Romolini (d. 1795) and R: Flavia Bonelli (d. 1691), the latter by Bizzacheri with putti by G. P. Mauri and bust by G. Cartari, 1691[10]
2nd pier L: monument to Monsignor Giorgio Bolognetti (d. 1686), Bishop of Rieti, by Cavallini, 1682-87 (mentioned as not yet finished by Titi in 1686)
2 to L: Cappella di S. Giuseppe: designed by G. Valadier, 1823[11]. Altarpiece: G. Brandi, *Holy Family*, before 1663[12]
1st pier to L: monument to Ercole (d. 1678) and Luigi Bolognetti (d. 1678) by M. Maglia, 1682-86
1 to L: Cappella di S. Tommaso da Villanova/Ferrini: Felice Ottini, R wall: *Mary Magdalen* and L wall: *Ecstasy of St Francis*[13]
Entrance wall to L: monument to Monsignor Giulio del Corno (d. 1662) by E. Ferrata with putti by F. Aprile, c.1680-86.

S. Gesù Nazareno *see* SS. Cosma e Damiano de' Barbieri
Via dei Barbieri, 22

S. Giacomo Augusta see S. Giacomo degli Incurabili
Via del Corso, 499

S. Giacomo degli Incurabili (S. Giacomo in Augusta)
Via del Corso, 499

The hospital, also known as S. Giacomo in Augusta, owing to its proximity to the Mausoleum of Augustus, was founded in the 14th century by the terms of the will of Cardinal Pietro Colonna (d. 1326). In 1515 Leo X raised it to an *arciospedale* with the particular charge of looking after those suffering from syphilis, which had been rampant in Italy since the 1400's. During the succeeding decades a number of distinguished architects, including Antonio da Sangallo the Younger and Baldassare Peruzzi, made designs for the new building but nothing was done until the Florentine Cardinal Anton Maria Salviati was put in charge.

Salviati first rebuilt the hospital, which runs in two wings between the via del Corso and the via di Ripetta, during the 1580's and just before 1590 commissioned Francesco da Volterra to design the church. Volterra first planned a conventional Latin cross church but soon abandoned it in favour of an oval scheme. The building was unfinished at the time of Volterra's death in 1594 and Maderno was appointed to replace him. Some parts of the building, including the upper part of the façade, have been attributed to him but, though he unquestionably supervised the building of the façade and dome, Hibbard argues convincingly that he followed Volterra's design. The structure of the church was finished by 1601 and the steps in front of the church were built in 1608[1].

INTERIOR
The church marks an important step in the development of churches based on an oval plan in that the tall chancel arch, which breaks through the main entablature, gives a greater emphasis to the longitudinal axis than in Vignola's two oval churches (S. Andrea in via Flaminia and S. Anna dei Palafrenieri). Wittkower argues that the fact that the middle chapels – on the ends of the short axis of the oval – have higher arches than those which flank them (they do not break through the entablature) establishes an emphasis on the cross-axis, but it is possible to see the succession of low-high-low arches as a variation on the normal regular repetition of equal arches which actually accentuates the movement of the eye towards the high altar. The interior was restored in 1861, when the dome fresco of *St James in Glory* was painted by Silverio Capparoni, and again in 1910 when the painted marble was added.

Room to R of entrance: C. Roncalli, *Resurrection of Christ*, completed 1602[2]; Francesco Zucchi, *Virgin with St James and the Donor Vittoria Tolfa*

2 to R: Cappella di S. Francesco di Paola/dei Miracoli: chapel designed by P. Legros who also carved the marble relief of *St Francis of Paola Adoring the Madonna dei Miracoli* and above: *Dove of the Holy Spirit*, 1711-14[3]. Side wall paintings by G. Passeri, L wall: *St Francis of Paola Restores a Stonemason to Life* and R wall: *The Saint Miraculously Raises Water*[4]

3 to R: D. Cresti, *Baptism of Christ*, c.1610[5]

Tribune: altarpiece: F. Grandi, *God the Father*, 1860. Tabernacle by B. Basso[6]. R wall: Vespasiano Strada, *Melchizedek Gives the Blessed Bread to Abraham*; L wall: Francesco Nappi, *Fall of Manna*; apse: *Angels in Glory*[7]. Above: organ originally by Girolamo Borghese with carved organ case

by Johann Jacob Reth, 1660[8]
3 to L: Cappella del Rosario: R wall: A. Grammatica, *Adoration of the Shepherds*, c.1621-26[9]. L wall: copy of Murillo's *Immaculate Virgin*
2 to L: Cappella di S. Giacomo: Ippolito Buzio, *St James*, 1601[10].

S. Giacomo alla Lungara (S. Giacomo in Settimiano)
Via della Lungara, 140

A church has stood on this site at least since the 12th century and the present church was given by Urban VIII in 1628 to the Augustinian nuns of S. Maria Maddalena delle Convertite al Corso. They rebuilt the church between 1635 and 1643 at the expense of Cardinal Francesco Barberini, probably to the designs of Luigi Arigucci working in collaboration with Domenico Castello.

INTERIOR
Choir: high altar: G. F. Romanelli, *St James*[1]. R wall: monument to Ippolito Merenda, who died in 1636 and left 20,000 scudi for the convent[2]. The monument, which is entirely of white marble, consists of a skeleton holding a piece of windswept drapery on which is incised an inscription celebrating the deceased. It was designed by Bernini on a commission from Cardinal Francesco Barberini but executed by Lorenzo Florij, 1641[3]. For the skeleton cf. Bernini's tomb of Alessandro Valtrini in S. Lorenzo in Damaso; for the windswept drapery cf. the same monument and also that of the Blessed Maria Raggi in S. Maria sopra Minerva. The iconography probably signifies the idea of death sweeping all away, as the wind blows away the dead leaves[4].

S. Giacomo in Settimiano *see* S. Giacomo alla Lungara
Via della Lungara, 140

S. Giacomo degli Spagnuoli (Nostra Signora del Sacro Cuore)
Piazza Navona, 105

Virgilio Spada records that when Innocent X was building his palace on the Piazza Navona and rebuilding S. Agnese the Spanish colony added a new, very simple façade to their church.

In 1878 the orientation of the church was changed and the building was restored by Luca Carimini, who added the façade facing Piazza Navona[1]. The main entrance is now from the Corso del Rinascimento.

INTERIOR
2 to L: Cappella di S. Giacomo/Alborense: commissioned in 1518, architecture and stucco designed by Antonio da Sangallo the Younger. Altar niche: copy of Jacopo Sansovino's *St James*, now in S. Maria di Monserrato. Frescoes by Pellegrino Tibaldi: L and R of altar: *St Peter* and *St Paul*; L wall: *Freeing of Philetus and the Repentant Magician*; *Repentance of Hermogenes and the Destruction of Heretical Books Thrown into the Sea*; *St James Led to his Execution*, ruined; R wall: *St James Appears at the Battle of Clacijo and Leads the Spanish Troops against the Moors*[2]
3rd bay to L: choir loft by Pietro Torrigiani, 1506.

SS. Gioacchino e Anna
Via del Quirinale, 24-26

Built for the Reformed Spanish Carmelites in 1611, the date over the door, but rebuilt by Paolo Maruscelli; completed in 1638 after his death. The church has a central dome over a square structure. Titi, writing in 1686, says the church had recently been decorated but this work was swept away in a drastic restoration in 1846 when the church became the property of the Belgian College. It is now deconsecrated and used as offices.

INTERIOR
Pendentives: E. Dobbelaer, *Sts Willibrord, Landoald, Eleutherius and Rumwold*, 1853
R altar lunette: Pietro Nelli, *Death of St Rita* [1]
Choir: monuments to R: Auguste Victor Misson (d. 1861) and L: Alfred de Limminghe (d. 1861) by Pietro Galli, 1861[2]
L altar lunette: P. Nelli, *Sts Rita and Teresa*.

S. Gioacchino in Selci
Via Selci, 96

Built in 1770-c.78 on a simple Greek cross plan by Francesco Fiori for a community of Tertiary Franciscans founded in 1730. The church is open for Sunday morning Mass.

INTERIOR
High altar: designed by Giovanni Vinelli, with stuccoes by Domenico Coraducci. The altarpiece, representing *The Virgin with her Parents*, a good example of mid 18th century Roman painting, was inserted only shortly before the first edition of this work, and the author's name has not since been vouchsafed
L chapel: Cappella del Crocifisso: built by G. Vinelli, 1780[1]

S. Giorgio in Velabro
Via del Velabro, 3

An ancient church, situated near the Arch of Janus, which was Cardinal Newman's titular church. It contains no works of the Baroque or later periods. The iron lattice portico was donated by Cardinal Renato Paolucci, 1703.

S. Giovanni Battista dei Genovesi
Via Anicia, 12

The church, which is attached to a hospital belonging to the Genoese community, was built in 1481 but completely remodelled by Francesco Cellini and Luca Carimini, 1843-76.

INTERIOR
The painted marble dates from the 19th century restoration.
1 to R: Filippo Zucchetti, *St George and the Dragon*, 1696[1]
High altar: rebuilt in 1876 to a design by Luca Carimini. Altarpiece: Nicholas Règnier, *Baptism of Christ*[2]
1 to L: Giovanni Odazzi, *Apparition of the Madonna of Mercy of Savona*, 1698[3]
Chapel to L of entrance: Cappella di S. Caterina Fieschi: built in 1738/39-45; altarpiece: Odoardo Vicinelli, *Death of St Catherine Fieschi*, 1737[4]; vault: Vicinelli, *St Catherine in Glory*[5].

S. Giovanni Calabita
Via di Ponte Quattro Capi, 39

A church dedicated to St John the Baptist stood on this site from Early Christian times but the dedication was later changed to one of the presumed Roman martyrs, St John Calabytes. In 1582 Gregory XIII gave the church and the attached hospital to the Fatebenefratelli (an Order founded in the 16th century by the Portuguese St John of God), who rebuilt the church in 1640. Borromini was asked to produce plans for the façade[1], as was Martino Longhi the Younger in 1644, but these were not carried out and the existing façade was built in 1711, probably by the architect Romano Carapecchia, who worked mainly in Malta[2]. Between 1736 and 1742 the interior was given its present magnificent marble decoration by Carapecchia, which was completed by a series of frescoes and paintings by Corrado Giaquinto. The result is one of the richest interiors of any 18th century church in Rome[3]. It was visited by Clement XII in 1742 and is now open for Sunday morning Mass.

INTERIOR

Nave and choir vaults: Corrado Giaquinto, *St John of God in Glory*, 1741-42, and *God the Father with the Dead Christ*[4]
1 to R: miraculous icon of the *Madonna della Lampada*, set up in 1741
Sacristy: vault fresco: *The Fatebenefratelli Ministering to the Sick*, attributed to Baldi
2 to R: Altare di S. Giovanni Calabita: G. B. Lenardi, *Death of St John Calabytes*, after 1690[5]
Choir R: C. Giaquinto, *Martyrdom of Sts Marius, Martha, Audifax and Habakkuk*, 1741-42[6]. Stucco frames on either side of choir attributed to Gabriele Borghini
High altar: A. Genaroli, *Virgin and Child with St John of God*, 1640, enlarged at the top by C. Giaquinto, 1741[7]
Choir L: C. Giaquinto, *Martyrs of Porto, Sts Hippolytus, Taurinus and Herculanus*, 1741[8]
2 to L: Altare di Antonio Abate: C. Giaquinto, *Death of St Anthony Abbot*, 1741[9].

HOSPITAL
For entry apply in the sacristy or at the door of the hospital to the left of the church:
Sala Verde: Gregorio Preti, *Flagellation*, c.1650[10]; Marcello Sozzi, *The Blessed John Grande*, 1853
Sala dell'Assunta: magnificent stucco altar with painted curtain held by angels by B. Cametti, with the arms of Clement XI, 1700-02[11]. Ceiling fresco: scenes from the *Life of St John of God* by J. P. Schor, 1654-56[12]. Fine and unusual *scagliola* altar frontal.

S. Giovanni Decollato
Via di S. Giovanni Decollato, 22

The Confraternita di S. Giovanni Decollato detta della Misericordia was formally founded in 1488 by a body of Florentines to attend those condemned to death. Michelangelo, Antonio da Sangallo, Bandinelli and Pietro da Cortona were amongst its members. The church was begun almost immediately but not finished until the mid 1550's. The oratory was begun in 1535 and completed in 1536-37. Weisz has put forward Battista da Sangallo, brother of Antonio and an active member of the confraternity, as a possible architect for the church.

The bronze group of the *Beheading of the Baptist* attributed to F. Duquesnoy and mentioned by Toesca appears to be missing[1].

The church is only open on the morning of 24 June, the feast of the Birth of St John the Baptist, but may be visited after seeking permission in writing from the *governatore* of the confraternity.

INTERIOR

1 to R: Jacopo Zucchi, *Birth of the Baptist*, c.1585; above: L: *St Thomas* and R: *St Philip*[2]
2 to R: altarpiece: J. Zucchi after a copy by F. Salviati, *Doubting Thomas;* above: L:

St *Thaddeus* and R: *St Bartholomew*
3 to R: Cappella Rucellai: C. Roncalli, *Visitation*, 1589; above: L: *St Matthew* and R: *St Simon*
Choir: high altar rebuilt by Ignazio Brocchi in 1775, with sculpture by Pietro della Valle[3]; altarpiece: Vasari, *Beheading of the Baptist*, 1552-53[4]. L wall: *Raising of Lazarus*, G. Balducci, 1584[5]; R wall: copy of G. Muziano's *Beheading of the Baptist*
Lunette over vestibule door to L: Balducci, *Raising of Lazarus*, 1584[6]
3 to L: Cappella del Crocifisso: decorated in 1582-83; above: L: *St Andrew* and R: *St Peter;* modern crucifix
2 to L: G. B. Naldini, *St John the Evangelist in Boiling Oil*, 1579-81; above: L: *St Matthew* and R: *St James the Greater*
1 to L: Cappella della Madonna della Misericordia: J. Zucchi, surrounding the altar and filling the arched bay is a canvas of the *Assumption*; above: *Sts John the Evangelist and James the Lesser*

The six saints on the wall strips at the end of the nave (3 on each side) are by Giovanni Balducci, called Giovanni Cosci, L: *Sts Gregory, Athanasius* and *Bernard* and R: *Sts Jerome, Augustine* and *Thomas*
1st bay to L: G. Balducci, *St John the Baptist Preaching*, 1592.

Oratorio di S. Giovanni Decollato
Via di S. Giovanni Decollato

The oratory is remarkable for its frescoes, which form one of the most complete examples of Mannerist illusionism. They were begun about 1536 by Jacopino del Conte, continued by Francesco Salviati and completed in the 1550's by Pirro Ligorio. They show one of the most ingenious schemes of Mannerist illusionism, with fictive architecture and figures apparently walking into the pictures from the real space of the chapel, devices which were to be widely employed by Baroque artists. The narrative cycle begins on the right wall at the altar end of the oratory and continues in a clockwise direction.

R wall: Jacopino del Conte, *Annunciation to Zachariah of the Birth of St John*, 1536-37; F. Salviati, *Visitation*, 1538; F. Salviati, *Nativity of the Baptist*, 1551; false window with a *tondo* of *Truth Revealed by Time* by Salviati[1]
End wall: Jacopino del Conte, *Preaching of the Baptist*, to Perino del Vaga's design, 1538; statue of *St John the Baptist* by an unknown artist; R; Jacopino del Conte, *Baptism of Christ*, 1541
L long wall: Battista Franco, *Arrest of the Baptist*, c.1541-44; attributed to Pirro Ligorio, *Dance of Salome*, c.1550; *Beheading of the Baptist*, to a design by Salviati and executed by a member of his workshop, possibly Jan van der Straet, 1553[2]
Altar wall: L: *St Andrew* and R: *St Bartholomew* by Salviati, 1550
Altarpiece: Jacopino del Conte, *Descent from the Cross*, 1551
Office: C. Nebbia, *Crucifixion*[3].

S. Giovanni dei Fiorentini
Piazza dell'Oro, Via Giulia

The church of the Florentine community. A competition for the church was held in 1519 and the winner was Jacopo Sansovino, but his plans were never used. The foundation stone was laid by Cardinal Giulio de' Medici in 1519 and the actual church was built to a design by Antonio da Sangallo the Younger. Under Sangallo's direction the nave was completed to the level of the clerestory and the decoration of the lower part of the façade was started, while the crossing, transepts and choir had yet to be built. After the Sack of Rome building stopped. In 1559 Michelangelo submitted plans for a centralised building but these were not executed and in 1583 work resumed under Giacomo della Porta to Antonio da Sangallo's original Latin cross plan. By 1593 the nave was finished but work had apparently stopped for lack of funds. In 1599 Maderno is mentioned as the architect but little was done until 1610-14, when the church was finished. The transepts were being stuccoed in 1618.[1]

Maderno's main alteration to the earlier plans seems to have been to make the transepts and the choir square-ended instead of apsed.

The façade was added by Alessandro Galilei in 1734 for Clement XII. Reliefs: *St John Preaching* by F. della Valle; *Baptism* by Bracci; *Beheading of the Baptist* by Scaramucci; *Visitation* by P. Benaglia. Statues over entablature (left to right): *St Mary Magdalen dei Pazzi* by S. Sanni; *St Philip Benizi* by F. Queirolo; *St Peter Igneus* by Simone Martines; *St Bernard degli Uberti* by G. Altobelli; *The Blessed Eugene the Deacon* by C. Pacilli; *St Catherine de' Ricci* by G. Cornaro, all 1734-35[2]; over door: *Charity* and *Fortitude* by Filippo della Valle, 1749-51[3].

INTERIOR

The organ is said to have been made in 1673[4]

1 to R: Cappella di S. Vincenzo Ferrer/Fantonir: D. Cresti (rejected by Nissman), *St Vincent Ferrer Preaching*

2 to R: Cappella di SS. Simone e Giuda/later S. Filippo Benizi/Firenzuola: frescoes by Orazio Gentileschi; R wall: *A New Born Child Proclaims the Deacon Euphorines Innocent of its Bastard Birth when Asked by Sts Simon and Jude*; L wall: *Sts Simon and Jude Baptising the King of Persia and his General Barbadach c*.1606-09[5]

In passage to sacristy: L: bust of Antonio Coppola (d. 1612) by Pietro Bernini, 1612, and R: Antonio Cepparelli (d. 1622) by G. L. Bernini, 1622-23[6]. L wall: bust of Clement XII by Filippo della Valle, 1742, but only erected in 1750[7]

Sacristy: built by Giuseppe Palazzi, 1795[8]. Attributed to R. Vanni, *St John the Baptist Preaching*[9]

3 to R: Cappella di S. Girolamo/Mancini: altarpiece: Santi di Tito, *The Penitent St Jerome*, 1599[10]; R wall: Cigoli, *St Jerome Writing the Vulgate*, 1599[11]; L wall: D. Cresti, *St Jerome with Sts Paula and Eustochium Supervising the Construction of a Monastery*, 1599[12]

4th pillar to R: monument to Monsignor Ugolino Mannelli Galilei (d. 1784) by Giuseppe de' Fabris, 1821[13]

4 to R: Cappella di S. Filippo Neri/Torrigiani: redecorated in 1774 after the chapel was ceded to Luca Torrigiani in 1740. Altarpiece: copy of C. Maratta's *The Virgin Appearing to St Philip Neri*

5th pillar to R: monument to Gaetano Forti (d. 1771)

Before R transept: monument to the Marchesa Francesca Calderini Pecori-Riccardi (d. 1655) with bust by L. Merlini, c.1700[14]

R transept: Cappella di SS. Cosma e Damiano/Nerli: ceded to Piero Nerli in 1667. Altarpiece: Salvator Rosa, *Martyrdom of Sts Cosmas and Damian*, 1669. Monuments to R: Ottaviano Acciaioli (d. 1695) by Ercole Ferrata[15] and L: Ottaviano Corsini (d. 1641) by Algardi[16]

Chapel to R of choir: Cappella del Sacramento: decorated by Matteo Castello, 1612-14, with elaborately inlaid marble altar and tabernacle attributed to Marco Gamberucci[17]. R wall: Anastasia Fontebuoni, *Death of the Virgin*, 1617-18[18];

L wall: Ciampelli, *Birth of the Virgin*; dome fresco: Ciampelli, *Coronation of the Virgin*
Choir: in the 17th century this was in effect turned into a family chapel by the Falconieri, whose palace stood at the end of the via Giulia and who were of Florentine origin[19]

In 1634 Orazio Falconieri commissioned Pietro da Cortona to make the high altar, the design of which is held at Windsor[20]. Cortona is known to have made a full-scale model of it in wood, which was erected in 1634, but no work seems to have been done on the marble altar itself. In 1655 Falconieri took up the scheme again but this time he entrusted the execution of it to Borromini, in spite of the fact that Cortona was still alive.

For the high altar Borromini used Cortona's design but modified it in several ways. He abolished the attic over the main order and continued the order itself to the full height available, thus producing a design commensurate with the unusual height of the nave and choir of the church. He replaced Cortona's simple curved pediment with one of his favourite compound forms (cf. Oratory façade) and moved the outer columns forward, giving them his most elaborate fluting (as in the fireplace in the Oratory). Francesco Mochi was originally commissioned to make a relief of the *Baptism* for the altar (now in the Museo di Roma) but this was never used and the existing group of the *Baptism of Christ* in coloured marble is by Antonio Raggi, completed in 1676 or 1677[21]. The seated statues of R: *Fortitude* and L: *Justice* were added after Borromini's death, when Cortona's pupil Ciro Ferri completed the scheme (unveiled 1683, Cartari-Febei). *Fortitude* is by Leonardo Retti and *Justice* by an artist referred to by Titi in 1686[22] as 'Monsù Michele' and identified in the 1763 edition as Michel Anguier. This cannot be correct, since Anguier left Rome in 1651. The artist may possibly be Michel Maille, known in Italian as Michele Maglia.

On the two walls of the choir are monuments to the Falconieri family. These were begun by Borromini but the crowning sections, which do not carry the Borrominesque movement of the main order, were completed by Ferri[23]. The right-hand monument is that of Orazio Falconieri (d. 1664) and his wife Ottavia Sacchetti, with a statue of *Charity* holding a portrait medallion by Domenico Guidi[24] and, below, of Paolo Francesco Falconieri and his wife Vittoria del Bufalo by an unknown artist, 1733. The two stucco youths holding medallions are attributed to F. Carcani[25].

The left-hand monument to Orazio's brother Cardinal Lelio (d. 1648) has a statue of *Faith* by Ercole Ferrata, 1665-69[26]; below is a monument to Cardinal Alessandro Falconieri (d. 1734) and, to the left, a monument to another Alessandro Falconieri and his wife Marianna Lante by Pietro Benaglia, 1845[27]. The stucco figures of youths holding medallions on either side of the monuments are attributed to P. Balestra, before 1686[28].

Orazio Falconieri also planned a mortuary chapel under the choir[29]. From a drawing in Berlin[30] it is clear that Borromini was involved in the designing of the chapel, but as it stands it is far more Cortonesque than Borrominesque in character (compare the lower church of SS. Luca e Martina) and it must have been finished by Ferri after Borromini's death. It is worth noting that the Doric columns have no bases and therefore correspond to the Doric used by Borromini on the façade of the Palazzo di Propaganda Fide, but the floor of the chapel is not the original one and may have been raised, perhaps owing to flooding from the Tiber.

In the pavement under the crossing, near the arch leading to the left transept, is the tomb of Carlo Maderno (d. 1629).

Chapel to L of high altar: Cappella del Crocifisso/Sacchetti: bronze crucifix modelled by Prospero Antichi and cast after his death in 1592 by Paolo Sanquirico, 1624[31]. Paintings by Lanfranco, vault: *Ascension* and *Four Evangelists*; R wall: *Garden of Gethsemane*; R lunette: *Mocking of Christ*; L wall: *Christ Carrying the Cross*; L lunette: *Arrest of Christ*, 1621-24[32]. Fine stuccoes of scenes from the *Passion*[33]

L transept: Cappella di S. Maria Maddalena/Caponi: altarpiece: Astolfo Petrazzi, *Assumption of Mary Magdalen*, 1662-65; monuments to R: Antonio Barberini the Elder (d. 1629) by F. della Greca and bust attributed to F. Dieussart, after 1630[34], and L: Pietro Francesco de' Rossi (d. 1673) by an unknown sculptor

L aisle, last pier to R: monument to Girolamo Samminiati (d. 1733) by Filippo della Valle, 1733[35]

5th pillar to L: monument to Alessandro Capponi (d. 1746) designed by Fuga, sculpture by M. Slotz, 1746[36]

5 to L: Cappella di S. Francesco/Scarlatti: altarpiece: J. Ligozzi, *St Francis Adoring the Crucifix*. Frescoes and stucco by Niccolò Circignani, R wall: *St Francis before the Sultan of Egypt*; L wall: *Approval of the Franciscan Rule by Honorius III*; vault: L: *St Francis Preaching*; C: *Angels*; R: *St Francis before Pope Honorius*, 1586-87[37].

4th pillar to L: monument to Marco Panvini (d. 1826) by G. Ceccarini, 1827[38]

4 to L: Cappella di S. Antonio Abate/Benozzi: altarpiece: Ciampelli, *Death of St Anthony Abbot*, 1612[39]; R wall: *Conversion of St Paul* and L wall: *Christ's Charge to St Peter* by Giovanni Angelo Canini. Vault: Antonio Tempesta, R: *St Lawrence before the Emperor Valerian*; C: *St Lawrence in Glory*; L: *St Lawrence with Pope Sixtus II*[40]

3 to L: altarpiece: G. B. Naldini, *St John the Baptist Preaching*[41]

2nd pillar to L: monument to Pietro Vallentini by M. Mori[42]

2 to L: Cappella di S. Maria Maddalena dei Pazzi/Cavalcanti: altarpiece: Francesco Curradi, *The Virgin Gives the Veil to St Mary Magdalen dei Pazzi*, before 1661; flanking the altarpiece: Ciampelli, *St Anne* and *St Joseph*; walls by Giovanni Balducci, R: *The Virgin Dictates the Early Life of Christ to St Luke* and L: *Charlemagne at Monte Cassino*; vault: scenes from the *Life of Charlemagne* by A. Tempesta after 1592[43]

1 to L: Cappella di S. Sebastiano/Montauti: altarpiece: G. B. Vanni, *St Sebastian Tended by St Irene*, 1626[44].

S. Giovanni in Laterano
Piazza di S. Giovanni in Laterano

The Cathedral of Rome and first church of Christendom, founded by Constantine the Great on the property of the Plauti Laterani, a wealthy Roman family, and the barracks of the Equites Singulares. After being sacked and burnt a number of times it was rebuilt by Urban V (1362-70) and Gregory XI (1370-78), and restored by Martin V (1417-31). Finally it was remodelled by Borromini for Innocent X for the Holy Year of 1650. The Benediction Loggia on the north transept was built in 1586-89 by Domenico Fontana for Sixtus V.

The façade was built in 1733-35 by Alessandro Galilei, who won a competition instituted by Clement XII in which all the leading architects of Rome took part[1]. The statues on the top of the façade represent: on the central section (L to R) G. B. de' Rossi, *St Gregory the Great*; B. Pincellotti, *St John*

S. Giovanni in Laterano

the Baptist; P. Benaglia, *Risen Christ*; D. Scaramucci, *St John the Evangelist*; A. Corsini, *St Jerome*. On the right side: B. Ludovisi, *St Augustine*; G. Frascari, *St Basil*; P. Lestache, *St Athanasius*; B. Casoni, *St Bonaventure*; T. Brandini, *St Bernard*. On the left side: P. Bengal, *St Ambrose*; C. Tantardini, *St John Chrysostom*; G. Riccardi, *St Gregory Nazianzen*; G. F. Lazzoni, *St Eusebius of Vercelli* and P. Latour, *St Thomas Aquinas*, 1734-35[2].

VESTIBULE

The vestibule contains an ancient statue of Constantine set up here in 1737 to replace one of Clement XII. The reliefs over the door with scenes from the *Life of St John the Baptist* are: L side: Filippo della Valle, *Beheading of St John the Baptist*; over L door: B. Ludovisi, *Zachariah Writes the Name he Intends for his Son*; over R door: G. B. Maini, *St John Preaching in the Desert*; R side: P. Bracci, *St John Reproaches Herod for his Adultery*[3]. The bronze doors dating from the reign of Diocletian were taken by Alexander VII from the Curia (later converted into the church of S. Adriano) and given to the Lateran in 1637 but they had to be enlarged to fit the door frames by the addition of outer bands with stars. This operation was carried out by Girolamo Ferreri and other craftsmen between 1657 and 1661 to the designs of Borromini. References to the installation of the doors occur in the *Diary* of the pope[4].

INTERIOR

The carved wooden roof was begun under Pius IV in 1562 and finished under Pius V in 1567, restored for Pius VI by G. B. Ceccarelli, 1788[5].

The floor was originally laid by Martin V, the crowned column of whose arms appears three times in it. The sections under the arches of the nave have the arms of Innocent X and near the main door are those of Alexander VII. Payments to Borromini for the floor are recorded in 1654[6].

In 1646[7] Innocent X decided to restore the church, which was in danger of collapsing, and he gave the commission to Borromini with the condition that the work be finished by the Holy Year of 1650. The architect was also instructed to preserve as much of the old structure as possible, for reasons of piety, not on aesthetic grounds. In general the pope had no objection to the old parts being concealed within the new but he insisted that some parts should be left visible. Borromini satisfied this demand by leaving the ovals, which now contain reliefs of prophets added in the 18th century, open to show the old walls 'come gioia nell'anello, accio resti e perpetua memoria la fabrica fatta da Costantino', as is recorded by Virgilio Spada[8]. Borromini pulled down the aisles, strengthened the walls of the nave (which were dangerously out of the vertical), removed one column out of three of the old arcade and embedded the remainder in his new piers. He produced three designs which are often said to have been made in succession but were actually alternatives presented simultaneously to the pope. He planned to vault the nave with a series of ribs, of which the first were to spring from the canted bays next to the main doors to the church and would have come down on the second pair of pilasters along the nave. How he would have dealt with those which would have come down at the crossing is not clear, because his designs seem to show that he was going to preserve the colossal ancient granite columns which existed at that point in the old church and he would therefore not have been able to have canted bays. The pope decided, however, that he did not want to touch the coffered ceiling put up under Pius IV and finished under Pius V, executed by

F. Boulangier, Vico di Raffaelle and A. Bonazzino, 1564-66[9]. It was restored for Pius VI by G. B. Ceccarelli, 1788[10].

The work was carried out at incredible speed in spite of difficulties which arose owing to Borromini's temperament; because though very practical and easy with his own workmen he was incredibly touchy about outside interference and on several occasions stopped work altogether until his grievances were settled[11]. The structure was finished by the end of 1647 and most of the stucco decoration by October 1649, two months before the opening of the Holy Year. Borromini hoped to continue his restorations round the transepts and choir but lack of funds – and after the death of Innocent X possibly lack of enthusiasm for the architect – frustrated the project. The result is that, though the articulation of the nave is one of Borromini's most mature achievements, the effect is incomplete because the huge pilasters clearly need to run into a vault, and there is a complete break between the nave and the transepts and choir.

The detail of the interior is of superb quality. The bases of the nave pilasters have an almost Michelangelesque richness, whereas those of the aisles are much more delicate. The sides of the piers are decorated with bands of laurel and palm-leaves in Borromini's crispest manner and the grey marble bases of the niches containing the statues of the *Apostles* are decorated with garlands of palm-leaves in the same style. The vaults of the aisles are peopled with a host of Borromini's winged cherub heads.

After 1650 work was more or less suspended, though Borromini began to plan the project for bringing back into the church fragments of the medieval and Renaissance tombs which had been removed during the restoration of the building – some of which are recorded in the summary drawings in the MSS of Virgilio Spada[12] – and incorporating them in settings of his own design. A few of the drawings connected with this project bear the arms of Innocent X but nothing was actually carried out until after his death and the actual monuments all bear the arms of Alexander VII (the project is mentioned a number of times in entries in Alexander's diary for 1658-59[13]). Borromini showed the utmost ingenuity in incorporating the old fragments and producing designs which would fit the awkward spaces below the oval windows in the outer wall of the aisles. The tombs are engraved in De' Rossi, *Architettura Civile*, II, pls. 37-44, and reproduced in Portoghesi, *Borromini*, pls. 105-19.

The niches of the main piers of the nave are of grey marble and are flanked by columns of *verde antico* taken from the aisles of the old church. They contain statues of *Apostles* commissioned by Clement XI in 1703 and executed to designs by Carlo Maratta between 1703 and 1708 by a team of sculptors under the general direction of Carlo Fontana[14]. To right: 1: L. Ottoni, *Judas Thaddeus*; 2: C. Rusconi, *St Matthew*; 3: G. Mazzuoli, *St Philip*; 4: P. Legros, *St Thomas*[15]; 5: C. Rusconi, *St James the Greater*. To left: 6: P. E. Monnot, *St Peter*; 5: C. Rusconi, *St Andrew*; 4: C. Rusconi, *St John*; 3: A. de' Rossi, *St James the Lesser*; 2: P. Legros, *St Bartholomew*[16]; 1: F. Maratta, *St Simon*.

The oval pictures of *Old Testament Prophets* in the nave are to R: 1: D. M. Muratori, *Nahum*; 2: M. Benefial, *Jonah*; 3: G. Nasini, *Amos*; 4: G. Odazzi, *Hosea*; 5: G. P. Melchiorri, *Ezekiel*; 6: S. Conca, *Jeremiah*; to L: 1: P. L. Ghezzi, *Micah*; 2: G. Chiari, *Obadiah*; 3: L. Garzi, *Joel*; 4: A. Procaccini, *Daniel*; 5: F. Trevisani, *Baruch*; 6: B. Luti, *Isaiah*, all 1718[17].

The reliefs above the arches were not

intended to remain in stucco but were planned to be executed in mosaic. The programme was devised by Annibale Albani: right from entrance: *Resurrection* by G. Lazzoni; *Christ in Limbo* by G. F. de' Rossi; *Christ Betrayed* by Alexander Jacquet; *Christ Falling under the Cross* attributed to A. Raggi; *Baptism of Christ* attributed to Algardi; *Crucifixion* by M. Anguier. Left from entrance: *Jonah and the Whale* by an unknown artist; *Passage of the Red Sea* attributed to M. Anguier; *Joseph Sold into Slavery* attributed to A. Raggi; *Sacrifice of Isaac* by D. de' Rossi; *The Flood* attributed to M. Anguier; *Expulsion from the Garden* attributed to Giovanni Battista Morelli[18].

The confessionals were designed by Andrea Busiri Vici, 1859[19].

RIGHT AISLE

Over the doors leading from the vestibule to the inner aisles are stucco panels with very elaborate curved and broken pediments erected by Cardinal Benedetto Pamphili in 1729. Beside them are doors by Borromini leading to a small spiral staircase[20]. Over the doors leading from the vestibule to the outer aisles are stucco panels with the arms of Alexander VII designed by Borromini.

1 to R: Cappella Orsini: one of the three chapels completely rebuilt by Borromini. The altar-rail shows a variant of the form of balustrade with alternating balusters which he used in the cloister of S. Carlo and the gallery of the oratory. Here, in addition to making the balusters alternate in their vertical disposition, Borromini set them alternately with the flat face or a sharp edge facing into the aisle, thus introducing the maximum liveliness. Indeed, the balusters seem almost to be rotating as one walks past them. Similar balustrades occur in the other two chapels which Borromini rebuilt. Altarpiece: Placido Costanzi, *Immaculate Virgin* with *Sts Barbatus and Fidelis of Sigmaringen* 1742[21]

1st pier to R of nave: Borromini, monument to Boniface VIII (d. 1303) incorporating four grey marble columns and a fragment of the Trecento fresco showing the *Pope Proclaiming the Holy Year of 1300*

Between 1 and 2 to R: Borromini, monument to Cardinal Giulio Acquaviva (d. 1574), incorporating statues of *Temperance* and *Prudence* by Isaia da Pisa from the monument to Cardinal de Chiaves (see below)

2 to R: Cappella Torlonia[22]: built by Q. Raimondi between 1838 and 1850 in the form of a Greek cross. Altar-relief: *Deposition* by P. Tenerani, 1846. R wall: monument to Principe Giovanni Torlonia (d. 1829) by Luigi Maioni with allegorical figures of R: *Charity* and L: *Industry*, completed after his departure from Rome by G. Chialli and G. Barba, 1830-33. L wall: monument to Anna Torlonia (d. 1840) by G. Barba with allegorical figures of R: *Guardian Spirit of History* and L: *Clemency* and a relief of the *Charity of Anna Maria Torlonia*, 1845[23]. In the niches: *Justice* by V. Gaiassi, *Temperance* by A. Stocchi, *Fortitude* by F. Gnaccarini and *Prudence* by A. Bezzi, 1845[24]. Pendentives: stucco reliefs of the *Evangelists*, P. Galli

3 to R: Cappella Massimo: by Giacomo della Porta, 1565-71[25]. Its entrance had to be displaced when Borromini restored the church and he balanced the new door with a grille composed of the *monti* and the stars of Alexander VII's arms. Altarpiece: Sicciolante da Sermoneta, *Crucifixion*, 1573[26]; L wall: monument to Domenico Massimo by G. della Porta; R wall: G. Cesari, *St John the Baptist Led to his Tomb*

3rd pier: Borromini, monument to Alexander III (d. 1181) in black and yellow marble with a medallion of the pope by Guidi, 1657-59[27]

Between 3 to R and entrance to Palace: monument to Cardinal Cesare Rasponi (d. 1675) and Clarice Vaini (d. 1670) by Filippo Carcani[28]

Between 3 and 4 to R: bay containing the entrance to the Lateran Palace, bearing the date of the Holy Year 1650 and the arms of Innocent X (much criticised by Visentini[29]). The swags with the Pamphilli dove on the side walls and the leaves spread over the ceilings above the windows are to be found almost exactly repeated in Borromini's decoration of the Villa Giustiniani. The other side of the door, which also bears the arms of Innocent X, can be seen from the cloister of the Lateran Palace

4th pier: Borromini, monument to Pope Sergius IV (d. 1012) incorporating an earlier relief

Between entrance to Palace and 4 to R: Borromini, monument to Cardinal Casate, Conte di Giussano (d. 1287), in pale grey marble. It incorporates fragments of the medieval altar from the chapel of the Magdalen, which is surprising since it was Cardinal Bianco who was buried under the altar, not Cardinal Casate

4 to R: Cappella di S. Giovanni Evangelista: altarpiece: L. Baldi, *St John on Patmos*, c.1660-65[30]; R wall: monument to Cosmo Inghirano

5th pier: monument to Cardinal Ranuccio Farnese (d. 1565), ascribed by Martinelli[31] unconvincingly to Vignola and by Baglione to G. della Porta[32]. The statues of L: *Faith* and R: *Prudence* are signed by Antonio Petrarca[33]

Between 4 to R and transept: Borromini, monument to Cardinal Antonio Martinez de Chiaves, called the Cardinal of Portugal (d. 1447), incorporating the sarcophagus and recumbent figure from his original monument and three other 15th century figures.

TRANSEPTS

The transepts were decorated for Clement VIII under the direction of Giacomo della Porta and Giuseppe Cesari between 1597 and 1600. The lower parts of the walls have inlaid marbling and the frescoes above are painted as feigned tapestries with the Aldobrandini arms in the border. These represent scenes from the *Life of Constantine*; they begin on the left wall next to the high altar and continue in chronological order into the right transept and end opposite the first scene. L wall: C. Nebbia, *Sts Gregory the Great and Ambrose*; B. Cesari, *Triumphal Entry of Constantine*; B. Cesari, *St Peter*; C. Nebbia, *Constantine's Dream*; G. B. Ricci, *St Andrew*; C. Roncalli, *St Simon*; P. Nogari, *Constantine Seeks St Sylvester on Mount Soratte*; P. Nogari, *St Bartholomew*; C. Roncalli, *Pope Sylvester Baptises Constantine*; Orazio Gentileschi, *St Jude Thaddeus*. R wall: G. B. Ricci, *St Matthias*; P. Nogari, *Foundation of the Lateran*; C. Nebbia, *St Thomas*; G. B. Ricci, *Consecration of the High Altar*; Baglione, *St Philip*; P. Nogari, *St James the Greater*; P. Nogari, *Apparition of Christ*; C. Nebbia, *St Paul*; Baglione, *Constantine's Donation to the Lateran*; C. Nebbia, *Sts Augustine and Jerome*. Paul Bril was responsible for the landscape and Francesco Zucchi for the painted garlands that frame the frescoes.

L transept wall: Giuseppe Cesari, *Ascension*. The frescoes in the triumphal arch by A. Ciampelli; before transept: R: *Zachariah*; L: *St John the Baptist*; between nave and transept: R: *St Luke* and L: *St Mark*; between transept and tribune: R: *St Matthew* and L: *St John*

The sculptures of the *Angels* in the transepts are by Cordier, Paracca, Buonvicino, Mariani, T. della Porta, G. van den Vliete, F. Landini, S. Longhi and I. Buzio. The transept ceiling was designed by Taddeo

Landini, 1595-96.

In the vestibule to the transept, outside the basilica (below the Benediction Loggia) is a statue of Henry IV of France by Nicholas Cordier, 1606-09, set up by Clement VIII to record his absolution and reception into the Roman Church[34].
Corridor to R of choir: L wall: monument to Gabriele Filipucci (d. 1706) by B. Cametti, after 1706[35].

CROSSING

Under the crossing stands the papal altar at which only the pope can celebrate Mass. Alexander VII planned to replace it in 1657. Borromini submitted designs[36] but, as an entry in Alexander's *Diary* shows[37], he did not get the commission. The pope adds: 'si vuol morire di dolore'. In fact nothing was done at that time but the *baldacchino* was rebuilt by Pius IX in 1851, incorporating parts of the original tabernacle[38].
R transept: the organ was built by Luca Blasi and the case carved by G. B. Montano[39]. Below are two statues, R: *Solomon* by Francesco Landini and L: *David* by Ambrogio Buonvicino, 1597-99
Chapel in R transept: R wall: monument to Cardinal Carlo Rezzonico (d. 1799) by Antonio d'Este, 1804[40]
Over the Porticus Leonina to R of chapel: monument to Innocent III (d. 1216) with figures by Giuseppe Luchetti, 1891[41].

CHOIR

In 1763 Pope Clement XIII commissioned Piranesi to make designs for the remodelling of the choir to complete the work undertaken by Borromini for Innocent X, but though the architect produced brilliant drawings (in the Pierpont Morgan Library, New York), nothing was actually built and the project was abandoned in 1767[42]. In 1876 Pius IX commissioned A. Busiri Vici to extend the choir, but he was later dismissed and it was Virgilio Vespignani who – disastrously – rebuilt and lengthened it, a task completed in 1886[43].
Passage leading to sacristy: monuments include those to Giuseppe Cesari (d. 1640) by N. Menghini and Andrea Sacchi (d. 1661) by Pietro Paolo Naldini[44]
Over door to L of choir: monument to Leo XIII (d. 1903) with figures of L: *St Joseph* and R: *Religion* by Giulio Tadolini, 1906-07[45]
Sagrestia dei Canonici/Sala Clementina[46]: rebuilt in 1592-94. The end walls were frescoed by Agostino Ciampelli, *Miracle and Martyrdom of St Clement*, and the vault by Giovanni and Cherubino Alberti with brilliant *quadratura* compositions, c.1600[47]. Over door: bust of Clement VIII by Taddeo Landini, 1595
Cappella di S. Anna: in the chapel off the sacristy and over the door is a monument to Louis XV by A. Corsini, 1730[48]
Sagrestia Vecchia: altarpiece: S. Pulzone, *St Mary Magdalen*[49]; L wall: M. Venusti, *Annunciation*[50]; G. Cesari, *St John the Evangelist Led to his Grave*[51]; Andrea Lilli, *Miracle of the Fishes*[52]; B. Spranger, *Miracle of the Fishes* and *St John the Evangelist in Boiling Oil*, before 1575[53]. Over door: monument to Clement XII with bust by P. Bracci and cast by Pietro Ceci; stucco work by G. B. de' Rossi, 1733-34[54]
Cappella Colonna/Coro: according to Martinelli[55] the architect is Girolamo Rainaldi. Altarpiece: Giuseppe Cesari, *Christ with St John the Evangelist*[56]. To L: monument to Lucrezia Tomacelli Colonna (d. 1625) designed by Teodoro della Porta and executed by Giacomo Laurenziano, 1625[57]
L transept: Altare del SS. Sacramento: Altar of the Blessed Sacrament of 1600 set up by Clement VIII for the Holy Year of 1600 to the designs of Padre Paolo Olivieri, who

incorporated four ancient columns of colossal size, thought to have come from the Temple of Jupiter Capitolinus. The Altar of the Blessed Sacrament was built to honour the relic of the Table of the Last Supper. The tabernacle, made from semi-precious stones, is by Pompeo Targone and executed by Curzio Vanni. The silver relief of the *Last Supper* over the altarpiece, also by Curzio Vanni, was melted down by the French in the 1790's and replaced in 1860 by a copy[58]. The two angels flanking the silver relief are by A. Buonvicino[59]. In the tympanum of the pediment: C. Roncalli, *God the Father*. This was one of the first major altars to be devoted to the worship of the Blessed Sacrament, a rite that became increasingly important during the 17th century

To R of altar: *Moses*; above: relief of the *Harvest of Manna* by G. van den Vliete; *Elijah*; above: relief of *Elijah Fed by an Angel in the Desert* both by P. P. Olivieri and completed on his death by Mariani

To L of altar: *Melchizedek*; above: *Meeting of Abraham and Melchizedek* by Nicholas Pippe; *Aaron*, above: *Jewish Passover* by Silla Longhi.

LEFT AISLE

5th pier: monument to Elena Savelli by Giacomo del Duca, 1570[60]. The bronze medallions were cast by his brother Ludovico[61], one of the few works in sculpture by this highly talented pupil of Michelangelo

R of 5 to L: monument to Clement Argenvilliers

5 to L: Cappella di S. Ilario/Mauri: Guglielmo Cortese, *St Hilary Meditates on the Trinity*, c.1660[62]

Between 5 and 4 to L: monument to Cardinal Girolamo Casanate (d. 1700), founder of the Casanate Library; figure by P. Legros, 1700-03[63]

4th pier: monument to Cardinal Lucio Sasso (d. 1604)

4 to L: Cappella Lancellotti[64]: the original chapel, probably built by Maderno, was pulled down as part of Borromini's restoration and the present one was built by G. A. de' Rossi, probably between 1674 and 1686[65]; stuccoes of angels and medallions with scenes from the *Life of St Francis* by Filippo Carcani[66]; altarpiece: G. B. Puccetti, *St Francis Receives the Stigmata*[67]. L wall: monument to Giuseppe Massimo Lancellotti by G. Meli, 1862; Filippo Agricola, *Christ with Sts John the Evangelist and Baptist*. R wall: Giovanni Piancastelli, *Martyrdom of John Nepomuk*

3rd pier: monument to Cardinal Alessandro Burghi (d. 1615)

3 to L: Cappella del Crocifisso/Santori: designed by Onorio Longhi, 1600-c.02[68]; L wall: monument to Cardinal Giulio Antonio Santori (d. 1602) with bust by Finelli, 1634[69]; altar vault: B. Ciarpi, L: *Betrayal of Christ*; C: *Resurrection*; R: *Agony in the Garden*[70]

Between 3 and 2 to L: Borromini, monument to Cardinal Bernardo Caracciolo (d. 1255) incorporating the recumbent figure from the original monument

2nd pier: monument to Girolamo Garimberti (d. 1575)

2 to L: altarpiece: begun by G. Odazzi and completed by I. Stern, *Assumption with Sts Philip Neri and Dominic*. L wall: monument to Cardinal Nicola Antonelli, Secretary of the Propaganda under Clement XIII, by Gaspare Sibilla, 1777[71]

Between 2 and 1 to L: Borromini, monument to Cardinal Gerardo Bianco (d. 1062), incorporating the incised slab from his original monument

1st pier: monument to Giuseppe Lanciuti (d. 1625)

1 to L: Cappella Corsini[72]: the chapel was ceded to Clement XII in 1731 as a

mausoleum for himself and other members of his family, and built to the designs of Galilei from 1732 onwards. It marks the transition from the late Baroque to early Neo-classicism. **Pendentives:** *Gifts of the Holy Spirit* by Agostino Corsini and Bernardino Ludovisi. The stucco reliefs in the lunettes depicting the *Beatitudes* are by G. B. de' Rossi, A. Corsini, B. Ludovisi, S. Martini, G. M. Frascari and C. Tantardini **R wall:** 1st niche: G. Rusconi, *Fortitude*; above: P. Lestache, *St Andrew Corsini Heals a Blind Man*; 2nd niche: G. Lironi, *Justice*; above: Lambert Sigisbert Adam, *The Virgin Calls St Andrew to the Priesthood*; monument to Cardinal Neri Corsini, uncle of the pope (d. 1678); statues of the cardinal and *Religion* by G. B. Maini
Altar: mosaic after Reni's *St Andrew Corsini in Prayer* by P. P. Cristofari[73]; above: statues of R: *Penitence* and L: *Modesty* by B. Pincellotti; lunette: A. Cornacchini, *St Andrew Appearing at the Battle of Anghiari*, 1734-36
L wall: 1st niche: F. della Valle, *Temperance*[74]; above: P. Benaglia, *St Andrew Distributing Bread During the Famine of Florence*; 2nd niche: Cornacchini, *Prudence*, 1734-36; above: P. Bracci, *St Andrew Healing a Plague Victim with a Kiss*. Monument to Clement XII (d. 1740); the ancient porphyry sarcophagus came from the portico of the Pantheon; bronze statue of Clement XII cast by Francesco Giardoni on a model by Maini, 1735, and installed in 1736, replacing an earlier statue by Monaldi; R: *Abundance* and L: *Magnificence* by C. Monaldi, 1736[75]
Pendentives: *Gifts of the Holy Spirit* by Agostino Corsini and Bernardino Ludovisi. The stucco reliefs in the lunettes depicting *Beatitudes* are by G. B. de' Rossi, A. Corsini, B. Ludovisi, S. Martini, G. M. Frascari and C. Tantardini.[76] The bronze angels bearing lamps are by Angelo Spinazzi and A.

Cornacchini, 1734-35[77]. The magnificent grills were designed by Galilei, modelled by Paolo Campana and Simone Martini, and cast by Giacomo and Pietro Ceci, 1734[78]
In crypt: *Pietà* by A. Montauti, 1733-40, a plaster cast of which has also been placed in the chapel[79]
To L of entrance to church: Borromini, monument to Cardinal Riccardo Annibaldi della Molara, incorporating fragments probably by Arnolfo di Cambio.

The Baptistery (S. Giovanni in Fonte)
Piazza di S. Giovanni in Laterano

Founded by Constantine and rebuilt by Urban III (432-40). It was restored under the direction of Francesco da Volterra on the orders of Gregory XIII for the Holy Year of 1575. Further restorations were undertaken by Urban VIII and Alexander VII, who commissioned Borromini to replace the roof, which was collapsing, and make the stucco frieze round the exterior of the building, which incorporates the keys, tiara, *monti* and oak-trees of the Chigi arms[1].

The frieze was restored in the late 1970's when one incomprehensible change was made: on one of the eight faces Borromini introduced, instead of the tiara and keys, a *Chi-rho* in a laurel wreath (visible in old photographs – there is one in the Biblioteca Hertziana), but in the restoration this was replaced by the tiara and keys which appear on all the other faces.

INTERIOR
This was restored by Urban VIII, who commissioned Andrea Sacchi to paint scenes from the *Life of St John the Baptist* round the drum of the dome: *Annunciation to Zachariah*; *Visitation*; *Birth of the Baptist*;

Naming of the Baptist; *Blessing of the Baptist before his Departure*, 1641-49[2]; the originals have been replaced by copies and are now in the Lateran Palace.

Round the walls of the ambulatory are frescoes illustrating scenes from the *Life of Constantine*; from right to left of entrance: adjacent to door: C. Maratta, *Constantine and Pope Sylvester*; G. Gimignani, *Constantine's Vision of the True Cross at the Milvian Bridge*; A. Camassei, *Constantine Defeats Maxentius*; Camassei, *Constantine's Triumphal Entry into Rome*; adjacent doors: C. Maratta, *Sts John the Baptist and Evangelist*; Maratta, after a cartoon by Sacchi, *Constantine Establishing the Christian Religion*; C. Magnoni, after a cartoon by Sacchi, *Destruction of the Pagan Writings at the Council of Nicæa*[3].

The balustrade has the arms of Gregory XIII. The font, commissioned by Cardinal Francesco Barberini, was designed by Ciro Ferri with reliefs of the *Baptism of Christ* and the *Baptism of Constantine* and was cast by Carlo Spagna in 1677-78[4].

The original narthex of the baptistery was converted into two chapels:
R bay: Cappella dei SS. Seconda e Rufina/Lercari: the chapels date from when the portico of the baptistery was converted into a chapel by Pope Anastasius (1153-54). Decorated by N. L. Piccioni, 1764[5]; L of altar: fresco of the *Virgin with Christ and St John* by Sassoferrato; R: *St Philip Neri* by Guido Reni (but not listed by Pepper), supported by stucco putti; monument to L: Cardinal Nicola Maria Lercari (d. 1757), Secretary of State under Benedict XIII, 1761, and R: Nicola Lercari (d. 1757), Archbishop of Rhodes, 1760, by T. Righi[6].
L bay: Cappella di SS. Cipriano e Giustina/Borgia: restored 1754. L wall: monument to Cardinal Alessandro Borgia (d. 1767) by T. Righi, 1767[7]; altarpiece: *Martyrdom of St Justina*
2 to L: Cappella di S. Venanzio: restored after 1672 for the Ceva family by C. Rainaldi, who designed the altar and the monuments flanking it; to R: Marchese Francesco Adriano Ceva (d. 1672) and to L: Cardinal Francesco Adriano Ceva (d. 1655). The monuments were executed by Cosimo Fancelli and the putti above them by P. P. Naldini, 1673-99[8]. On the left wall is a tablet to Cardinal Francesco Adriano Ceva (d. 1655) by Borromini, 1650. The designer has used a particularly delicate selection of marbles, including the rare *pavonalezza* for parts of the frame and *rosso antico* for the red elements in the crowning feature, but the effect of the monument was greatly damaged during the 20th century restoration which, in order to reveal the Early Christian brickwork, removed the white stucco which provided an appropriate background for Borromini's carefully chosen materials and colours. The carved wooden ceiling dates from Gregory XIII's restoration of the baptistery
1 to L: Cappella di S. Giovanni Evangelista: this chapel, built by Pope Hilary (461-68) and notable for the 5th century mosaics on its vault, was redecorated with fine stuccoes and marbling under Clement VIII, 1596-97. Restored by G. B. Ceccarelli in 1780[9]. Anteroom of chapel: A. Ciampelli, five scenes from *Revelation*. Altar: bronze statue of *St John the Evangelist* by Taddeo Landini and A. Buonvicino; frescoes by A. Tempesta of scenes from the *Life of the Saint*[10].

The Scala Santa
Piazza di S. Giovanni in Laterano

This building incorporates the Sancta Sanctorum of the Early Christian Lateran Palace and the staircase approaching it, which is supposed to have been brought from the Praetorium of Pontius Pilate in Jerusalem by St Helena. The original structure, dating from the time of Constantine, was remodelled by Nicholas III (1277-81) and again by Sixtus V when he pulled down the old Lateran Palace and built the new one to the designs of Domenico Fontana. Fontana is also responsible for the new setting of the Scala Santa and for the two chapels (L: S. Silvestro and R: S. Lorenzo) which flank the Sancta Sanctorum, finished 1589. Restored by Giovanni Azzurri for Pius IX, 1852-56, when the arches of the loggia were bricked up and the Passionist Convent built adjoining the Scala Santa.

INTERIOR
ATRIUM
R of entrance: *Kiss of Judas*, I. Jacometti, 1855
L of entrance: *Ecce Homo*, I. Jacometti, 1855
L wall: *Christ at the Column*, G. Meli, 1874
R wall: *Pope Pius VI in Prayer*, Oscar Sosnowski, 1877

The walls and vault of the central Holy Stairs, which led up to the chapels, were frescoed with thirty-three scenes from *Christ's Passion* based on an iconographical programme by Angelo Rocca, whilst the staircase flanking the Holy Stairs were frescoed with Old Testament scenes by a team of artists, which included F. Fenzoni, G. Baglione, Paul Bril, Angelo da Orvieto, A. Lilli, A. Nucci, A. Righi, V. Conti, P. Nogari, P. Orsi, G. B. Ricci, B. Croce, G. Stella and P. Guidotti.
Cappella di S. Silvestro: decorative vault fresco attributed to Giovanni and Cherubino Alberti. Tommaso Conca, *Mary Magdalen before Christ*.
Cappella di S. Lorenzo: vault fresco of *Doctors of the Church* and lunettes by P. Bril.

The Triclinium of Leo III

The apse represents the only surviving fragment of the hall in the papal palace attached to the Lateran and built by Leo III (795-816). It was saved when Sixtus V built the new palace. The mosaic was restored in 1625 by Cardinal Francesco Barberini, who had an aedicule built over it. Clement XII pulled down the monument, while enlarging the square in front of the Lateran, but Benedict XIV had a copy made, based on fragments still preserved at the time, and set it up at a point near the Scala Santa between 1741 and 1744. The architect was Fuga.

S. Giovanni in Mercatello (destroyed) *see* SS. Venanzio e Ansovino

S. Giovanni in Oleo
Via di Porta Latina

In 1509 the Burgundian Benoît Adam built a small octagonal chapel on the site on which St John was said to have been plunged into boiling oil. Adam's arms and the date 1509 appear above the door. The architect was probably a member of the circle of Antonio da Sangallo the Younger. In 1658, according to an inscription inside the chapel, it was restored by Borromini on the orders of Cardinal Francesco Paolucci. A drawing in the Albertina[1] shows that originally Borromini planned to make the roof curved and would have decorated the ribs with palm-branches. A second variant on the same drawing shows the roof stepped, but finally

Borromini built a simple conical roof without either ribs or steps. The attic is decorated with palmettes and roses, the latter being an allusion to the arms of the patron. The frieze is typical of Borromini's late, almost classical, decoration and is very similar to the one which he added to the Lateran baptistery for Alexander VII.

INTERIOR
L. Baldi, frescoes of the *Life of St John the Baptist*, c.1658[2].

S. Giovanni della Pigna
Piazza della Pigna

A medieval church on the site was given by Gregory XIII in 1585 to the Arciconfraternita della Pietà dei Carcerati, who ministered to those in gaol. The church was rebuilt, probably c.1690, by Angelo Torrone.

INTERIOR
The interior was wholly restored and redecorated by V. Vespignani in 1836 and again in 1860.
1 to R: G. Zoboli, *Martyrdom of St Eleutherius of Tournai*, 1738[1]
High altar: N. Lapiccola, *St John the Baptist*, c.1776[2]; fresco above: L. Garzi, *Pietà*, before 1686[3]
2 to L: manner of Antonio Gherardi, *Christ Appears to St Teresa*[4]
1st bay to L: monument to Gaspare Elia (d. 1624).

SS. Giovanni e Paolo
Via di SS. Giovanni e Paolo

This church, which contains remarkable remains of ancient Roman and Early Christian frescoes, was disastrously restored first for Cardinal Philip Howard in 1677 and later by Antonio Canevari, assisted by Francesco Ferrari in 1715-18, for Cardinal Fabrizio Paolucci. Nothing of the medieval church is to be seen in the interior – except the Cosmatesque floor – and the Baroque remodelling is heavy and pedestrian. In 1773 Clement XIV gave the church to the Passionists, who still serve it.

INTERIOR
The wooden ceiling dates from 1598 and contains the arms of Cardinal Agostino Cusani.
Over door to sacristy: *Sts Francis of Sales, Vincent de Paul, Jane de Chantal* by Jean Barbault, 1748[1], but appears to be missing
Vestibule to sacristy: busts of Cardinal Fabrizio Paolucci and Innocent XII by P. Bracci, 1725[2], and Clement XIV, 1775[3]; busts of Pius IX and Pius VI by unknown artists
Sacristy: side walls painted by A. Milani, R: *St Charles Borromeo* and L: *Conversion of St Paul*[4]
1st pillar to R: monument to Cardinal Roberto de' Roberti (d. 1867) by Giuseppe Luchetti[5]
1 to R: M. Benefial, *St Saturninus Smashes the Idols and Refuses to Worship*, 1716[6]
2nd pillar to R: monument to Count Gustav von Stackelberg (d. 1847) by A. Veyrassat, 1848[7]
2 to R: A. Milani, *St Pammachius Builds the Church of SS. Giovanni e Paolo*, c.1722[8]
3 to R: Cappella di S. Paolo della Croce: by Filippo Martinucci, 1857-80; altarpiece: F. Coghetti, *The Crucifix Appears in a Vision to St Paul of the Cross*. Coghetti was also responsible for the decoration of the dome, *St Paul of the Cross Received into Heaven*, 1869-70[9]. Side walls by Francesco Grandi, R: *Pietà* and L: *Christ in the Garden*. The saint's body lies beneath the altar
4th pillar to R: monument to Monsignor Lorenzo Litta (d. 1820) by G. de' Fabris, 1827[10]

Apse: rebuilt by F. Ferrari. Apse frescoes: scenes from the *Martyrdom of Sts Peter and Paul*, frescoed in 1725-26. R: P. A. Barbieri, *Conversion of Terentian*; C: G. Triga, *Martyrdom of Sts John and Paul*; L: D. Piastrini, *Charity of Sts John and Paul*; apse: *Celestial Glory* by Niccolò Circignani, 1587[11]. The stucco angels in the apse are probably by P. Bracci. The high altar was consecrated by Benedict XIII in 1726[12]
Chapel at end of L aisle: altarpiece: Felice Torelli, *Assumption*, 1716[13]
4 to L: T. Conca, *Crucifixion*[14]
4th pillar to L: monument to Cardinal Giuseppe Lorenzo Garampi (d. 1782) by C. Prosperi and G. Ravaglini, 1793[15]
3 to L: A. Milani, *St Joseph with the Christ Child*[16]
2 to L: A. Milani, *Scillitan Martyrs*, 1722[17].

SS. Giovanni e Petronio dei Bolognesi
Via del Mascherone, 61a

A medieval church on this site was given by Gregory XIII in 1581 to the Arciconfraternita delle Stimmate della Nazione Bolognese, who rebuilt it in the last years of the 16th century, almost certainly to the designs of the Bolognese architect Ottaviano Mascarino. It was restored in 1696-1700, the latter date being inscribed on the frieze.

INTERIOR
R transept: F. Gessi, *Death of St Joseph*, 1696
High altar: the original altarpiece was Domenichino's *Virgin with Sts John and Petronius*, removed by the French in 1797 and now in the Galleria Nazionale d' Arte Antica. It has been replaced by a copy
L transept: G. del Sole's *St Catherine* is now covered by an anonymous painting of *The Virgin* brought from the sacristy. Giovanni Sirani, *Virgin and Child with Sts Ludwig, Alexius, John the Baptist, Clare and Anthony of Padua*[1]
If shut, ring at No. 61 (to the left of the church).

S. Girolamo della Carità
Via Monserrato, 62

The church originally belonged to the Franciscan Observants but in 1524 it was handed over to the Arciconfraternita della Carità, a company of non-Roman nobles founded in 1519 by Cardinal Giulio de' Medici, later Clement VII, and approved by Leo X in 1520[1]. After a fire destroyed the oratory and several adjoining buildings it was decided completely to rebuild the church. The task was undertaken by Domenico Castello – who is mentioned in the accounts in 1654 – and it is said to have been finished in 1660. The façade has frequently been attributed to Carlo Rainaldi. Fasolo gives it to Martino Longhi the Younger, but Noehles[2] has shown that it was built, like the church, by Castello[3]. Though Castello died before the completion of the façade, his plan was carried out with modifications, except that most of the planned sculptural decoration was omitted. The church is open on Wednesday morning and for Sunday morning Mass.

INTERIOR
Coffered ceiling by Andrea Tozzi with the arms of Cardinal Giulio Antonio Severina, 1587.
1 to R: Cappella della Madonna/Spada[4]: the chapel was granted to Orazio Spada in 1595 and some restoration was carried out soon afterwards. In 1654-57 the whole chapel was redecorated under the direction of Borro-

mini's friend, Virgilio Spada, and his brother Bernardo, to contain the monuments to two members of the family, Bernardino Lorenzo and Giovanni Spada, and medallions of other members of earlier generations. The chapel, which is frequently ascribed to Borromini, is in fact the invention of Virgilio Spada, who habitually submitted his designs to a number of professional architects, including Borromini, who supplied a drawing for the altar frontal which was not exactly followed.

The chapel has always stood out from Borromini's work – and indeed from Roman architecture of the period – on account of the very elaborate marble inlay with which its walls and floors are covered and which suggests a Neapolitan rather than Roman origin (though the colours, yellow and brown, are more subdued than those in most Neapolitan *commessi*). The inlay has now been explained by the fact that the documents and Virgilio Spada's letters about the chapel refer to a 'Cavalieri Cosimo' – the Neapolitan architect Fanzago – who was at that time working in Rome on the decoration of S. Lorenzo in Lucina, and to the craftsman actually executing the marble inlay, called Giovanni Battista Scala.

The most remarkable feature of the chapel is the 'altar-rail' formed by two angels carrying a heavy piece of drapery composed of sheets of jasper so ingeniously fitted together that at first sight the 'shroud' seems to be a single solid piece. This is the work of Antonio Giorgetti, a pupil of Bernini. The wings of the right-hand angel are of wood and hinged to allow access to the chapel.

Altar wall: P. Naldini, reliefs of R: *St Bonaventure* and L: *St Francis*. L wall: monument to Bernardino Lorenzo Spada, Bishop of Calvi (d. 1247), by E. Ferrata and reliefs of Amadore I and Alerano Spada (d. 1087) by P. Naldini; Amadore II Spada (d. 1226) by F. Baratta; Amadore III (d. 1275) and Mengo Spada (d. 1313) by A. Raggi. R wall: monument to Giovanni Spada (d. 1543) by Cosimo Fancelli and reliefs of Pietro di Cecco (d. 1413) and Serronedi Pietro Spada by P. Naldini; Ghino di Mengo Spada (d. 1340) by G. Peroni and Mutio (d. 1360) and Antonello Spada (d 1477) by E. Ferratta. Crucifix by F. Duquesnoy and candle-holders by F. Traviani

2 to R: Cappella del Crocifisso/Speziali

R transept: monument to Conte Asdrubale di Montauto (d. 1629) to a design by Pietro da Cortona[5]

Chapel to R of high altar: Cappella di S. Giovanni Battista/Marescotti: decorated by D. Alberti. Altarpiece: *Holy Family with Sts John the Baptist and Evangelist*; L lunette: *Baptism of Christ*; vault: *Ascension* and *Four Evangelists* [6]

High altar: Cappella Renzi: by Carlo Rainaldi[7]. It contains a copy (1797) by Antonio Corsi of Domenichino's *Last Communion of St Jerome*, of which the original was removed by the French in 1797 and is now in the Vatican Gallery[8]. Monuments to L: Fantino Renzi (d. 1647) and R: Scipione Gisleni Renzi[9]

Chapel to L of high altar: Cappella di S. Filippo Neri/Antamoro[10]: dedicated to St Philip Neri, who belonged to the Community before founding the Oratory. Designed by Filippo Juvarra and executed 1708-10; Juvarra's only work in Rome. The statue of the saint, the putti and vault decorations are by Pierre Legros; vault: L: *St Philip Neri in the Catacombs of S. Sebastiano*; R: *St Philip Neri's Vision of Souls in Heaven*

L transept: monument to Cardinal Paolo Odescalchi (d. 1585) attributed to L. Sormani[11]

2 to L: Cappella di S. Carlo Borromeo/Magalotti: altarpiece: Pietro Barbieri, *Virgin with Sts Charles Borromeo and Philip Neri*[12]; painted architecture and allegorical figures by G. Mengozzi, before 1750

1 to L: Cappella di S. Pietro/Sanpieri: altarpiece: G. B. Ricci, *Christ's Charge to St Peter*[13]
Sacristy: designed by Matteo Sassi in 1717: altarpiece: P. A. Barbieri, *Virgin and Child with Sts Philip Neri and Jerome*, c.1716; vault: *Angels in Glory with Dove of the Holy Spirit*[14].

The oratory behind the church facing the Piazza di S. Caterina della Rota was built between 1632 and 1637 by Peparelli[15]. Over the entrance is an oval bas-relief of the *Dead Christ* by Pietro Bracci, 1734[16]. Within the convent is a series of frescoes depicting scenes from the *Life of St Philip Neri* by G. B. Speranza[17].

S. Girolamo degli Schiavoni (S. Girolamo dei Croati)
Via di Ripetta, 75

The church of S. Marina and the hospital attached to it were given by Nicholas V in 1453 to the colony of Slavs – or Illyrians – who had fled from their countries in the face of the Turkish advance in the late 14th century, and today it is the church of the Croatian community. The church was begun in 1588 on the orders of Sixtus V, whose titular church it had been, probably to designs by Martino Longhi the Elder, though Mola says it was designed by Giovanni Fontana. The structure was apparently finished by 1589.

The façade, which is certainly by Martino Longhi the Elder, is characteristic of his style in its avoidance of all monumentality and its skilful treatment of the design in an almost unbroken plane. There are no columns or half-columns and only the flattest of pilasters, and the central section only breaks forward very slightly from the side bays. The pediment is unbroken and light in its moulding. Longhi seems to have been defiantly reacting against Giacomo della Porta's façade of the Gesù, and even Vignola's unexecuted design for that church looks massive in comparison with his façade. In its delicacy and restraint it shows the particular talent of the architect, which is also shown in his decorations, for instance, in the Cappella Altemps in S. Maria in Trastevere.

INTERIOR

A single nave with shallow transepts and three chapels on each side, a spacious example of this familiar late 16th century design. The nave vault was frescoed by P. Gagliardi, *Exaltation of the Cross*; nave pillars: *Apostles*, 1848-52[1]. The fresco in the dome with fictive architecture is probably by Paolo Guidotti, and those in the choir – treated as imitation tapestries – are ascribed to A. Viviani and A. Lilli, L: *St Jerome in the Desert Disputing the Scriptures*; C: *Ordination of St Jerome*; R: *Sts Jerome, Gregory of Nazianzen and Basil Debate the Scriptures*[2]. The six side altars were designed by N. Michetti and executed by P. Blasi, 1749.
R of entrance wall: monument to Paolo Gozzi (d. 1683), almost as moving in its restraint as Bernini's monument to Fonseca in S. Lorenzo in Lucina[3]
1 to R: Cappella dell'Annunziata: altarpiece: M. Cerruti, *Annunciation with Sts Philip Neri, Francis of Paola and Anthony of Padua*[4]. Monuments on R wall: Fortunatus Rudel and Maria Jacoangeli and L wall: Bartolomeo Rudel and Teresa Gatti by D. Carnevale, 1869
2 to R: Cappella della Madonna della Stella: altarpiece: Filippo Bracci, *Madonna della Stella*, c. 1745. Wall frescoes by P. Gagliardi, R: *Birth of the Virgin* and L: *Assumption*
3 to R: Cappella di S. Anna: altarpiece: G. Puglia, *Virgin and Child with St Anne*, 1631[5]; L wall: monument to Luigi Lezzani (d. 1861)

by Ignazio Jacometti[6]
R transept: P. Gagliardi, *Adoration of the Magi*
High altar: erected in 1749 by P. Blasi to a design by N. Michetti, 1749[7]
L transept: P. Gagliardi, *Crucifixion*; figure to left of sacristy door: *St Jerome* by Francesco Grassia[8]
Sacristy: bust of Sixtus V by G. Plancic[9]
3 to L: altarpiece: G. Puglia, *St Jerome*; below: C. Giaquinto, *St Francis of Assisi*. Wall frescoes: P. Gagliardi, R: *St Paul at the Gate of the Areopagus* and L: *St John the Baptist in the Desert*
2 to L: altarpiece: G. Puglia, *Pietà*, 1633[10]; below: G. Corrado, *St Joseph*; vault fresco: landscapes and oval with the *Trinity* by A. Lilli[11]; wall frescoes by P. Gagliardi, R: *Crowning with Thorns* and L: *Agony in the Garden*.

S. Giuliano dei Fiamminghi
Via del Sudario, 40-42

The church was restored in 1675-80 and again in 1713-20. The façade was added by Camillo Arcucci, 1661-63, and has rather elegant carved stone decorations round a niche which encloses a bronze cast of the original wooden statue of *St Julian* by F. Diessart, 1631-34, preserved from an earlier church. The original is housed within the church, which is open for Sunday morning Mass.

INTERIOR
The interior probably dates from the 1715 campaign and appears to be by a Flemish architect. The *St Julian in Glory* on the vault was painted c.1717-18 by William Kent who offered to do the job without payment in order to establish his reputation in Rome[1].
Entrance wall: R: monument to Jacob Strum (d. 1844) by J. Tuerlinck, 1844[2]
R altar: altar by M. Asprucci, 1739-40; altarpiece: M. de Haese, *Sts Peter and Paul*, 1743, stucco decoration by S. Porciani
High altar: rebuilt in 1648-52 to a design attributed to Arcucci; altarpiece: Dirk Helmbreker, *Conversion of St Julian*, 1695; vault: G. Giabazzi, *Glory of Angels*, 1842; altar lunette: J. B. Capronnier, *St Joseph and the Christ Child*
L of entrance to tribune: monument to Ludovica Timbrune Valence, Countess of Celles (d. 1828) by L. M. Kessels, 1828-36[3]
L altar: altar by M. Asprucci, 1739-40; altarpiece: copy of Sassoferrato's *Virgin and Child*
L wall past 1 to L: the monument, attributed to D. Guidi, to Vinoco de Valle (d. 1663) is of some interest in showing the influence of the Neapolitan style introduced to Rome in about 1650 by Cosimo Fanzago[4].

S. Giuseppe a Capo le Case
Via Francesco Crispi, 22-24

Founded in 1598 by Francesco de Soto, the Italian translator of many of St Teresa of Avila's writings, as the first Discalced Carmelites convent in Italy, responsible for the care of poor girls. In 1619 it was placed under S. Giacomo degli Spagnuoli, and in 1628 rebuilt at the expense of Cardinal Marcello Lante. The façade is a severe design executed in fine brick, with the unusual arrangement of a Tuscan order over an Ionic. This may, however, be due to the fact that the two storeys appear to be of different dates, and there may originally have been a project for building the upper storey conventionally with a Corinthian order, which was abandoned for reasons of economy, since a Tuscan order would be lower and would have involved less elaborate details than a Corinthian. The same arrangement occurs on the façade of S. Maria di Grottapinta and on S. Maria in Publicolis. In the case of the latter the façade is by a single hand, G. A. de' Rossi, and the architect must therefore have deliberately intended the arrangement.

INTERIOR
High altar: designed by Bartolomeo Breccioli[1]. It contains a ruined fresco of *Joseph's Dream*, painted by Andrea Sacchi and restored by Maratta[2]. It was for a long period covered by a modern painting but is now once again exposed to view.
Comunichino: Maria Eufrasia della Croce, *God the Father* and the *Annunciation*; R wall: *Repentant Magdalen*; L wall: *Christ with the Woman from Samaria*, c. 1630-40
Winter choir: Maria Eufrasia della Croce, *Virgin with St John and Mary Magdalen*, c. 1640

Behind the altar (door to left of choir) is the nuns' choir off which leads a small Scala Santa with fine mid 18th century stuccoes. The Scala Santa was commissioned in 1717 and is attributed by Donati[3] to Carlo Stefano Fontana.

S. Giuseppe dei Falegnami
Clivo Argentario, 1

The church of the Guild of Carpenters (*falegnami*), built over the Mamertine prison in which St Peter is supposed to have been incarcerated. Begun in 1597 to a design by G. B. Montano, a member of the guild, whose reconstructions of ancient Roman buildings, published by his pupil, G. B. Soria, were to be of great influence on Baroque architects. The building was completed by Soria and Antonio del Grande, and the church was consecrated in 1633.

The interior was restored and largely redecorated in 1880.

The façade, which was finished by 1602, has many features in common with Montano's designs for tabernacles, some of which are included in books of his work as published by Soria, particularly the unusual relation of the small upper storey to the tall lower one and the two smaller pediments subsumed under the main pediment. The double staircase in front of the church was removed in 1932. The church is open for weddings.

INTERIOR
The coffered ceiling was erected by Francesco Fangerilli, probably to a design by G. G. Montano, 1611-13. Carved relief of the *Nativity* by G. B. Montano, 1612, with figures of *Sts Peter and Paul* and *St Joseph with the Christ Child* by Melchior van Bon, 1613[1]. Over the door is an organ gallery by G. B. Vannelli, 1713, and an organ by F. Testa[2].
1 to R: wooden altar carved by B. de' Rossi, 1627-29; altarpiece: Bartolomeo Colombo, *Death of St Joseph*, 1648[3]
Coretto to R: G. B. Speranza, *Joseph's Dream*, 1634
2 to R: G. Ghezzi, *Holy Family with St Anne*, 1692[4]
Choir: decorated by C. Mariani, R wall: *Sixtus V Blesses Slaves Liberated by the Confraternity*; L wall: *Giovanni Cerrone Elected Governor of Rome*; apse: *The Virgin Appears to St Bonaventure*[5]. High altar by Giuseppe Rinaldi
2 to L: C. Maratta, *Adoration of the Shepherds*, 1651[6]
Coretto to L: G. Puglia, *Rest on the Flight*[7]
1 to L: O. Bianchi, *Marriage of the Virgin*.

ORATORY
The oratory (accessible from the right aisle),

added in 1627, was frescoed with scenes from the *Life of St Joseph* by M. T. Montagna, 1631-37[8]. The altar was designed by Tiberio Calcagni and the painting of the *Immaculate Virgin with Sts Joseph and Joachim* is by P. L. Ghezzi[9]. The ceiling, erected by Giovan Antonio Giani and Giovanni Salvatori, dates from 1628-29, with reliefs of the *Rest on the Flight into Egypt, Marriage of the Virgin* and *Jesus with the Doctors*[10].

Within the Mamertine prison is the chapel of SS. Pietro e Paolo in Carcere; over the altar: relief of the *Baptism of Sts Processus and Martinian by St Peter*, J. Bonnassieux, 1842[11].

S. Giuseppe alla Lungara
Via della Lungara, 43-46

Built for the Pii Operai della Dottrina Cristiana, a body founded by the Neapolitan Carlo Carafa in 1600, which was established in Rome in 1689. The present church was begun in 1729 to the designs of Ludovico Rusconi Sassi, and was consecrated in 1734, but the pavement was not finished until 1736. At first sight the church appears to be an oval but it is in fact a rectangle with its corners cut off.

INTERIOR

The church was restored by Antonio Cipolla in 1860 when the vault was rebuilt and painted by Vincenzo Palliotti with the *Doctors of the Church* in the pendentives, 1859. The painted marble dates from this time.

The choir on the entrance wall was built by Giovanni Francesco Fiori, 1764-65, and decorated by M. Rossi, *Christ and the Twelve Apostles*; in the four corners are ovals of R: *St Joseph with Jesus; Death of St Joseph*; L: *Marriage of the Virgin and Joseph; Holy Family*[1].

1 to R: altarpiece: stucco decoration by Pietro Galli under Ricciolini's direction, 1753-54, when the architectural surrounding of the altarpiece was added; altarpiece: N. Ricciolini, *Deposition*, 1754[2]
High altar: by F. Navone, 1767. Altarpiece: Mariano Rossi, *St Joseph's Dream*, between 1764 and 1774. To R: *Massacre of the Innocents* and to L: *Adoration of the Magi* by M. Rossi, 1767
1 to L: Girolamo Pesci, *Education of the Virgin*, 1735[3]
Sacristy: vault: M. Rossi, *Triumph of the Church*, 1768.

Oratorio del Gonfalone (*See also* S. Lucia del Gonfalone)
Via del Gonfalone, 32

Now used as a concert hall. The church was rebuilt by an unknown architect, beginning in 1544, and was consecrated in 1551. The building was destroyed by fire in 1555 but immediately rebuilt in the same style, reopening in 1557. The façade was built by Domenico Castello. Between 1569 and 1576 the oratory was decorated with one of the most complete cycles of late 16th century frescoes to have survived in Rome. It depicts the entire Holy Week from Palm Sunday to Easter Sunday. Restored in 1957.

INTERIOR

Carved and gilded ceiling by Ambrogio Bonazzino, 1568.
Altarpiece: Pedro de Rubiales, *Crucifixion*, 1568
R wall from altar to entrance: Jacopo Bertoia, *Entry into Jerusalem*; above: *Prophets and Sibyls*, 1568-69; Livio Agresti, *Last Supper*; above: *Prophets and Sibyls*,

1570-71; Domenico da Modena (attributed), *Agony in the Garden*; Marcantonio del Forno, *Arrest of Christ*, 1574-75; above: *Prophets and Sibyls* by J. Bertoia, 1571-72; Raffaellino da Reggio, *Christ before Pilate*; above: *Prophets and Sibyls*, 1574-75
Entrance wall: R: F. Zuccaro, *Flagellation*[1]; above: *Prophets and Sibyls*, 1573; centre: Cesare Renzi, *The Trinity and the Virgin with the Company of the Gonfalone*, 1575; above: Matteo da Lecce, *Solomon*, 1575-76; L: Cesare Nebbia, *Crowning with Thorns*, 1576; above: M. da Lecce, *Prophets and Sibyls*, 1576
L wall: C. Nebbia, *Ecce Homo*, 1576; above: M. da Lecce, *Prophets and Sibyls*, 1575; L. Agresti, *Road to Calvary*; above: *Prophets and Sibyls*, 1571; unknown artist, *Crucifixion*, 1575; Giacomo Rocca (attributed), *Deposition*, 1572; above: *Prophets and Sibyls*, 1569-71; Marco Pino, *Resurrection*; above: *Prophets and Sibyls*, 1572-75.

S. Gregorio al Celio
Piazza di S. Gregorio

Founded by Gregory the Great, who converted his own house into an oratory dedicated to St Andrew. A large church was built, probably by Paschal II in 1108, on the site of the existing building. In 1573 the church and monastery were given to the Camaldolese, having previously belonged to the Benedictines. In 1595 Cardinal Antonio Maria Salviati began the restoration of the church – work that was continued by Cardinal Baronio[1] and finished by Cardinal Scipione Borghese, who was responsible for the restoration of the atrium and the building of the façade, which was begun in 1629. The façade has the date 1633 inscribed on it but it was not finished until 1642, nine years after the cardinal's death. The architect was Giovanni Battista Soria – a protégé of Cardinal Borghese – who followed, with variations, the pattern which he had used at S. Carlo ai Catinari[2]. Between 1725 and 1734 a further restoration of the interior was begun by Fra Giuseppe Sorratini and completed by Francesco Ferrari, who is mainly responsible for its present appearance. The side chapels were not finished until 1757.

PORTICO
Entrance: monuments to R: Pietro Beltramo (d. 1543) and L: Robert Peckham (d. 1564)
R wall: monument to Porzia del Drago Santacroce (d. 1614)[3]
L wall: monuments to Sir Edward Carne (d. 1561), English ambassador to the Holy See; Giacomo Bespino (d. 1645) attributed to A. Bolgi[4]; Emilia Lomelli (d. 1592); Giovanni di Ottone Niccolini by G. A. Dosio[5]; Virgilio Crescenzi (d. 1592) by Onorio Longhi, 1592-1602[6]; Lelio Guidiccioni (d. 1643)

INTERIOR
Nave vault: *Triumph of Sts Gregory and Romuald* and the *Triumph of Religion over Heresy* by Placido Costanzi, 1727[7]
1 to R: Cappella di S. Silvia: altarpiece: John Parker, an English pupil of M. Benefial, *Sts Benedict, Sylvia and Gregory*, c.1749[8]
2 to R: Cappella di S. Pietro Damiani: altarpiece: Francesco Mancini, *Pope Alexander II Gives the Discipline to St Peter Damian*, c.1751[9]
3 to R: Cappella di S. Romualdo: altarpiece: Francesco Fernandi, *Death of St Romuald*, 1733[10]
Chapel to R of high altar: Cappella di S. Gregorio: altar frontal with scenes from the *Life of St Gregory* by Luigi Capponi, 1485-1490; altarpiece: *St Gregory*, A. Fontebuoni[11]

High altar: by Cav. Dalmazzoni, 1735; apse stucco decoration by C. Porciani and F. Ferrari, 1725[12]; altarpiece: Antonio Balestra, *Sts Andrew and Gregory with the Virgin and Child*, 1735[13]; above triumphal arch: relief by G. B. de' Rossi, *St Gregory and the Monks of St Augustine*, 1725

Chapel at end of L aisle: Cappella del SS. Sacramento: L wall: monument to Cardinal Placido Zurla (d. 1834) by G. de' Fabris, 1835[14]

Off L aisle: Cappella Salviati:[15] built by Carlo Maderno for Cardinal Antonio Maria Salviati, possibly using a design by Francesco da Volterra, though Hibbard[16] believes that it is entirely Maderno's invention. According to the inscription it was finished in 1600. The marble inlay is by B. Basso[17]. Over the altar is a copy of Annibale Carracci's *St Gregory in Prayer*[18]. Frescoes by G. B. Ricci; pendentives: *Angels Carrying the Instruments of the Passion*; vault: *Christ in Glory*; lunettes and spandrels: *Church Fathers and Evangelists*; L wall: *An Archangel Appearing to St Gregory at the Top of Castel S. Angelo during the Plague*; L wall: *Virgin*[19]; original marble tabernacle from the high altar by Andrea Bregno, 1469. R wall: Christen Kobke, *God the Father and Angels*, 1839

3 to L: Cappella Fioravanti: altarpiece: F. Mancini, *Immaculate Virgin with the Trinity*, 1739[20]

2 to L: Cappella Gabrielli: altarpiece: Pompeo Batoni, *Virgin with the Blessed Peter, Castora, Fortis and St Ludolph*, 1732-33, Batoni's first public work[21]

1 to L: altarpiece: G. B. Bonfreni, *The Blessed Michael of Monte Corona in Adoration of Christ*, c.1755[22]

In the grounds to the southwest of the church are the oratories of S. Andrea and S. Barbara dating to the 6th century, restored by Cardinal Cesare Baronio, who commissioned the third oratory, S. Sylvia[23].

S. Barbara: restoration completed in 1607. The oratory, dedicated to Gregory's mother, incorporates part of a 6th century house and contains the table at which St Gregory is said to have served food to the poor and to an angel (Christ). Frescoes of scenes from the *Life of St Gregory* by Antonio Viviani, 1602. R entrance wall: *St Gregory Giving Alms*; L wall: *Election of Probus as Abbot of S. Andrea and S. Lucia*; *Apparition of an Angel at the Supper of St Gregory*; *St Gregory Writing*; R entrance wall: *Vision of St Gregory*; R wall: *Procession of St Augustine and his Companions before King Ethelbert*; *St Gregory Giving a Hortatory Epistle to St Augustine and his Companions*. Statue of *St Gregory* by Nicholas Cordier, completed 1602[24] (sometimes but wrongly said to have been begun by Michelangelo)

S. Andrea: probably on the site of Gregory the Great's original oratory of S. Andrea. Restoration begun in 1602 for Cardinal Baronio by Stefano Longhi and later (1608) under Flaminio Ponzio for Cardinal Scipione Borghese. Frescoes: R wall: Domenichino, *Flagellation of St Andrew*, 1609[25]; L wall: Guido Reni, *St Andrew Led to his Execution*, 1609[26]. The two frescoes were for a long time regarded as rivals, Reni's being more widely acclaimed, Domenichino's being admired by a group of more austere artists, including Poussin. On entrance wall: chiaroscuro frescoes of *St Gregory* and *St Sylvia* by Lanfranco[27]. Altarpiece: *Virgin and Child with Sts Andrew and Gregory* by C. Roncalli, 1602[28]. On either side: frescoes of *St Peter* and *St Paul* by Reni[29]. Ceiling by Vittorio Ronconi, 1607

S. Sylvia: built for Cardinal Baronio in 1604 and continued after his death in 1607 for Cardinal Borghese by Flaminio Ponzio. Fine fresco with *Angels Playing Musical*

Instruments by Guido Reni, 1609[30], an unusually illusionistic composition for this artist. Statue of *St Sylvia* by Cordier, 1603-04[31]; to L: *David* and to R: *Isaiah* by S. Badalocchio, 1608-09. Ceiling by V. Ronconi, 1607.

S. Gregorio a Ponte Quattro Capi
Via di Monte Savello

The church stands on the edge of the Ghetto and has over the door inscriptions in Latin and Hebrew directed against the Jews, and sermons designed for their conversion to Christianity were frequently preached here. Benedict XIII gave the church to the Congregazione degli Operai della Divina Pietà in 1727 and the medieval church was replaced by the present building in 1727-29 to a design by Filippo Barigioni. Restored in 1858.

INTERIOR
Vault: Giuseppe Serene, *Virgin in Glory*, 1858
1 to R: Andrea Casali, *Ecstasy of St Philip Neri in S. Maria sopra Minerva*, 1729
High altar: stucco *Glory of Angels* by Pietro Bracci enclosing a picture of the *Virgin and Child* by G. Hallet; lunette: P. Marini, *God the Father*, 1858
1 to L: E. Parrocel, *Supper of St Gregory*, 1727-29[1].

S. Ignazio
Piazza di S. Ignazio

In 1626 Cardinal Ludovico Ludovisi decided to build a church for the Collegio Romano at which his uncle, Gregory XV, had been a student. It was to replace the old church of the Annunziata and was to rival Cardinal Farnese's Gesù and Cardinal Montalto's S. Andrea della Valle. It was dedicated to St Ignatius, who had been canonised by Gregory XV in 1622. Various architects were asked to submit designs, including Domenichino. The design chosen was almost certainly that of Orazio Grassi, who was responsible for the wooden model made in 1628. His authorship is confirmed by Giovanni Simone Ruggieri in his account of the consecration of the church in his *Diario dell'anno del Santissimo Giubileo MDCL*[1], where he writes; 'Intona il vespro il medesimo Padre Architetto di detta Chiesa, il Padre Horatio Grassi'. Maderno, however, was certainly consulted by Ludovisi and his project is recorded in a drawing by Borromini[2]. Grassi was absent from Rome for most of the decade following 1633 and the church was built by Antonio Sassi, who introduced many changes, including an increase in the height of the façade, reputedly on the instructions of the new patron, Principe Niccolò Ludovisi. The planned dome was never built. The church was opened for worship in 1650, though it was complete only as far as the transepts, and was not consecrated until 1722.

INTERIOR
The nave arcade is unusual in that it consists of columns of Sicilian jasper standing free from the main piers and forming a series of Serlianas.

The stucco frieze of putti on the entrance wall and over the first three chapels on either side, together with the inscription tablet on the entrance wall supported by figures of *Religion* and *Magnificence*, were designed by Algardi[3].

The vaults were painted by Andrea Pozzo[4]. The first part to be undertaken was the false perspective of the dome over the crossing,

1684-85. This was painted on canvas and replaced in 1823 by Francesco Manno's copy, after the original was damaged when a powder magazine near S. Paolo fuori le Mura exploded. It was restored in 1961-63. On the pendentives are four Old Testament figures: *Judith*, *David*, *Samson* and *Jael*, all of whom prefigure Christ. The half-dome of the apse shows *St Ignatius Helping the Sick*, 1685-88. Below are three paintings also by Pozzo; over altar: *St Ignatius Adoring the Trinity*; to R: *St Francis Borgia Received into the Order*; to L: *St Ignatius Sending St Francis Xavier to India*; on vault over choir: *St Ignatius Receives the Call at the Siege of Pamplona*. Funding for the interior decoration of the church was raised through sales of Pozzo's *Perspectiva* .

Nave vault: by Pozzo: *St Ignatius in Glory* with the effects of the Jesuits' mission in the four parts of the world shown on the cove, 1694. This is one of the most elaborate programmes of religious paintings of the period, expounding the whole early history of the Society of Jesus. It is also one of the most dazzling pieces of illusionism in the whole of Baroque art, but it must be looked at from a point in the middle of the nave (indicated by a yellow metal disk in the floor), seen from which all the perspective falls into place.

1 to R: Cappella di S. Stanisla Kostka: altarpiece: *The Virgin with Sts Stanislaus Kostka and Francis Regis* by Alessandro Salini, 1763; above altar: stucco angels by Filippo della Valle, 1763[5]

2 to R: Cappella di S. Giuseppe/Sacripanto: originally built by Carlo Rainaldi for the Lancellotti family and decorated in 1712 by Niccolò Michetti for Cardinal Giuseppe Sacripanto[6]; altarpiece: Trevisani, *Death of St Joseph*, 1712[7]; L lunette: Giuseppe Chiari, *The Blessed Lucy of Narni Receiving the Stigmata*; R lunette: Trevisani, *Last Communion of St Aloysius Gonzaga*[8]; dome: L. Garzi, *St Joseph Received into Heaven*; pendentives: *Christ amongst the Doctors*; *Adoration of the Shepherds*; *Joseph's Dream*; *Marriage of the Virgin*, begun soon after 1712[9]

3 to R: Cappella di S. Gioacchino: altarpiece: S. Pozzo, *St Joachim Presenting Mary to God the Father*, 1765[10]. Beneath the altar lies the body of St Robert Bellarmine (d. 1621).

R transept: Cappella di S. Luigi: the altar was built to receive the remains of St Aloysius Gonzaga (d. 1591) and was financed by Principe Scipione Lancellotti, whose arms are on the altar. Designed and directed by A. Pozzo and executed by Carlo Mauro Bonacina[11]. Pierre Legros was responsible for the relief of the *Apotheosis of St Aloysius Gonzaga*, 1697-99, the figures of *Innocence* and *Penitence*, the two putti seated on the pediment, the putto with the scourge and the putto with a globe seated below the altar[12]. The marble angels on the balustrade are by Bernardino Ludovisi. The altar is second only to the altar of St Ignatius in the Gesù as an example of Roman Baroque sumptuousness. Vault: A. Pozzo, *St Mary Magdalen dei Pazzi's Vision of St Aloysius Gonzaga*; L lunette: *The Virgin Appears to St Aloysius*; R lunette: *St Aloysius Receives his First Communion from St Charles Borromeo*

Chapel to R of high altar: Cappella Ludovisi: monument to Gregory XV (d. 1623) and Cardinal Ludovico Ludovisi by Pierre Legros, who executed the greater part of the monument, including the figure of the pope, the allegorical figures of L: *Religion* and R: *Peace*, and below: the *Cardinal* in profile. The figures of *Fame* are by Monnot, c.1709-14[13]. In the four corners of the chapel are allegorical figures by Camillo Rusconi: *Prudence*, *Temperance*, *Fortitude* and *Justice*, 1685-86[14]

SS. Ildefonso e Tommaso di Villanova
Via Sistina, 11

Founded in 1619 by the Spanish Augustinians. Titi in 1674 says that the church had just been rebuilt to the design of a Sicilian Dominican named Giuseppe Paglia (recorded 1662-82). The façade was added by Francesco Ferrari in 1725. Buchowiecki gives 1667 as the date for the laying of the foundation stone.

INTERIOR
The nave elevation consists of rather correct coupled Ionic pilasters, but the vault is an imitation of Borromini's in the Re Magi chapel (Collegio di Propaganda Fide).

Stucco figures and decoration in the nave by Antonio Cometti, R: *St Rita of Cascia*; *St Fulgentius*; *St Ferdinand, King of Castile*; L: *St Louis IX*; *St Alipius*; *St Clare of Montefalco*

1 to R: marble bas-relief of the *Nativity* by Francesco Grassia[1]

2 to R: altarpiece: Juan Correa, *Immaculate Virgin with Sts Augustine and Monica*

The altars have fine *scagliola* frontals.

Sacristy (off L transept): frescoes of scenes from the *Life of St Ignatius* by Pierre de Lattre. Ceiling fresco: *The Virgin Appearing to St Ignatius during Mass*. Walls: A. Pozzo, *Deposition of Christ* and *St Francis and Brother Leo Adore the Cross*[15]. Fine wooden cupboards

Chapel to L of choir: four allegorical statues: S. Giorgini, *Faith*; G. A. Lavaggi, *Hope*; F. Nuvolone, *Charity*; F. Rainaldi, *Religion*, before 1688[16]. Stucco model by Giuseppe Rusconi for the statue of *St Ignatius* in the series of Founders in St Peter's executed by Giuseppe from the design of his master, Camillo Rusconi[17]

L transept: Cappella dell' Assunta: carved decoration by F. Cerruti, c.1747[18]; altarpiece: architecture and marble relief of the *Annunciation* by Filippo della Valle, 1750[19]; above are allegorical figures of *Chastity* and *Humility* which, together with the marble angels on the altar rails, are by Pietro Bracci[20]. Vault decoration by Ludovico Mazzanti; R window lunette: *Presentation in the Temple* and L window lunette: *Adoration of the Shepherds*; in blind windows; R: *Moses* and L: *David*; vault: *Assumption*, 1720[21]

2 to L: Cappella dell' Immacolata: altarpiece: P. de Lattre, *Sts Francis Xavier and Francis Borgia*; below: P. Gagliardi, *Virgin of the Immaculate Conception*

1 to L: Cappella di S. Gregorio Magno: altarpiece: P. de Lattre, *Sts Gregory the Great and Gregory Nazianzen*, 1649-50

Attached to the church is the Cappella della Prima Primaria with frescoes by Giacomo Cortese[22].

S. Isidoro
Via degli Artisti, 41

Founded in 1622 on the edge of the Villa Ludovisi by the Spanish Discalced Franciscans. In 1625 it was taken over by the Irish Franciscans to whom it still belongs. The church and monastic buildings are generally said to have been designed by Antonio Casone and finished by Mario Arconio, 1630, but Mola attributes the church to Domenico Castello. It was completed in 1630. The steps and portico are certainly by Castello but the upper half of the façade was built by Carlo Bizzacheri in 1714-15. The statues in the niches of L: *St Patrick* and R: *St Isidore* are by S. Giorgini, 1704[1], and the stucco work is by Andrea Bertoni. The pediment is a sort of inversion of Borromini's at the Oratory, straight at the sides and curved in the middle.

INTERIOR

Nave vault: Charles van Loo, *St Isidore in Glory*, 1729[2]. Dome fresco of the *Virgin and Saints* by Domenico Bartolini, 1856
1 to R: Cappella di S. Giuseppe/Alaleoni: decorated by C. Maratta in 1652, but the paintings on the walls have been replaced by copies. R: *Death of St Joseph*; lunette: *Adoration of the Shepherds*; L: *Flight into Egypt*; lunette: *Joseph's Dream*; altarpiece: *Marriage of Joseph*; L wall: monument to Isabella Ball-Sherlock by Giovanni Maria Benzoni, 1847[3]
2 to R: Cappella di S. Anna/Barberini: by Castello; decorated with scenes from the *Life of St Anne* by P. P. Baldini, before 1633; altarpiece: *St Anne with the Virgin and Child*; L wall: *Birth of the Virgin*; lunette: *Meeting of Joachim and Anne*; R wall: *Presentation of the Virgin*; lunette: *An Angel Appearing to Joachim and Anne*; dome: *Four Evangelists*[4]
R transept: monument to Alfonso Mansanedo de Quiñones (d. 1627) with bust attributed to Giuliano Finelli[5] and more recently to Algardi[6]
Chapel to R of high altar: Cappella dell' Immacolata Concezione/de Sylva: the dedication of the chapel may be connected with the fact that Wadding first came to Rome with a mission sent by Philip III of Spain to promote the doctrine of the Immaculate Conception.

In 1661 the chapel was acquired by the De Sylva family and redecorated. It was dedicated in 1663. The painting over the altar is by C. Maratta of the *Immaculate Virgin and Child*, c.1663[7], and the decoration was commissioned from Bernini. It consists of portraits of the De Sylva family, allegorical figures of *Mercy* and *Truth* and a bas-relief of Rodrigo de Sylva and his wife Beatriz on the L, *Justice* and *Peace* and a bas-relief of Francisco de Sylva and his wife Juana on the R. Draperies were later added to these figures. Drawings for the walls of the chapel by Bernini are known[8] but the work was executed largely by G. Cartari[9]. The oval medallions with bas-reliefs were inserted in the 18th century to replace coats of arms flanked by flying angels[10]. Fagiolo dell'Arco[11] points out that the bas-reliefs with pairs of portraits do not appear in the engraving of 1699 and concludes that they too must be later. The frescoes on the right entrance pillar of *St Anthony of Padua* and left pillar of *St Francis*, as well as the left lunette of *Music-making Angels*, are attributed to G. Gimignani[12].
High altar: by Marco Arconio, 1630; altarpiece: Andrea Sacchi, *The Virgin Appears to St Isidoro*, 1622-23[13]; lunette: D. Bartolini, *Agony in the Garden*, 1856
Over door: Fra' Ippolito di Poggio Bustone, *St Patrick Expels the Snakes from Ireland*, 1861
L of entrance door: monument to Monsignor Pietro Pavonio (d. 1626)[14]
R of entrance door: monument to Antonio Borani (d. 1677) by G. F. de' Rossi[15]
2 to L: Cappella di S. Antonio da Padova: partly decorated c.1655 by Cosimo Fanzago, who designed the marble inlay of the floor, the altar and the lower part of the walls. The decoration was completed in the 1680's by Carlo Bizzacheri[16]. Altarpiece: G. D. Cerrini, *Vision of St Anthony*, c.1663[17]; side wall decorated by Pietro Paoletti, L: *St Anthony Raises a Dead Boy* and R: *St Anthony Confronts the Tyrant Ezzelino III*

da Romana, 1830[18]; lunettes by G. Hallet, L: *St Anthony Raises a Dead Child* and R: *St Anthony Preaching to the Fishes*[19]. Monuments to R: Benedetto Cappelletti, Archbishop of Siponto (d. 1681), and L: Pietro Carlo Cappelletti[20]

1 to L: Cappella della SS. Croce/Ludovisi: frescoes in lunettes by Maratta, L: *Agony in the Garden*; R: *Christ Crowned with Thorns*; ceiling: *Angels Bearing the Cross and Crown of Thorns*; above entrance: *Two Putti Holding the Veronica Veil*, c.1655-57[21]; bronze crucifix by Algardi[22].

S. Ivo alla Sapienza
Corso del Rinascimento, 40

The Arciginnasio of Rome – later raised to the status of University – was founded by Boniface VIII in 1303 and moved to the site of the Sapienza under Eugenius IV (1431-47). In 1935 it was moved to the new university near S. Lorenzo fuori le Mura, though the university continues to serve the church. After 1935 the Archivio di Stato was installed in the main rooms but they are now being expropriated so that the palace can be used as an extension of the Senate.

The present building was begun by Pirro Ligorio for Pius IV and continued by Giacomo della Porta for his successors, whose arms appear on the arcades of the court. Borromini, who was appointed to the Arciginnasio in 1632, intended to make radical alterations to Della Porta's façade, replacing his central door by two aligned on the cloisters, and he would have added an extra storey to Della Porta's tower, but none of this was carried out. Della Porta planned a circular church at the end of the court, but the building of the church did not start until 1643 under Borromini. The basic structure took a year to build and reach the level of the drum; the vaulting was completed in the same year. Building ceased with the death of Urban VIII and was resumed by Innocent X in 1652, who undertook the completion of the church, including the lantern and spiral. The church was consecrated in 1660.

The decoration of the interior was not begun until 1659, and the altarpiece of *St Ivo with Sts Luke, Pantaleon, Leo the Great and Fortunatus* was begun by Cortona in about 1661 and finished after his death by Giovanni Ventura Borghesi, after 1764[1]. A highly worked drawing for this survives in Edinburgh, National Gallery of Scotland, and also in the Uffizi; an oil *bozzetto* is in the collection of the Confederazione Nazionale di Coltivatori Diretti. The history of the altarpiece is complex. The upper part and group of supplicants on the right was the only part completed before Cortona's death in 1664. At this point Cortona's assistant, Ciro Ferri, was employed to complete it but demanded an excessive 900 *scudi*. It was then passed on to G. V. Borghesi.

The frame of the altar was erected by G. B. Contini in 1685, when the bay which contains it was altered and a window removed. The present altar was erected by Nicola Forti, the Sapienza's architect, 1783-84.

This is Borromini's boldest and most inventive building. All the features present in his earlier church of S. Carlo alle Quattro Fontane are here developed and given more mature expression. The church is brilliantly designed to fit a cramped site between the two existing blocks. The plan is formed by the intersection of two equilateral triangles. These form a six-pointed star (of Wisdom) and a central hexagon, to each side of which a bay is added. Three of these are semi-circular, and the other three are triangles with their points cut off by convex arcs of circles drawn with the points of the basic triangles as centres. The structure of the building follows this plan up to the top of the dome, producing an effect of uniformity instead of the variety shown in the three stages of S. Carlino. In this scheme there is one small variation, carefully concealed. In the triangular bays the convex parts are continued up to and including the entablature, but above the window the vault emerges concave, the change being concealed by the neutral character of the window, neither convex nor concave. The restoration of the 1960's gave back to the interior its whiteness, characteristic of Borromini, which had been destroyed by the painted marbling added in the 1850's, and the quality of the carefully thought out detail can now be fully seen. The decoration of the dome includes the *monti*, stars and oak trees of Alexander VII's arms, but there are also allusions to the Temple of Solomon (or Temple of Wisdom) in the palms, cherubim and pomegranates[2]. The symbolism of the interior has given rise to much discussion.[3]

The exterior, designed to make a striking climax to the court in which the church stands, consists of a cylindrical element of six convex bays, which looks like the drum of the dome but in fact encloses the cupola and contains the solid masonry which takes the lateral thrust of the dome (the site did not allow space for buttressing). Above this is a convex stepped zone (cf. the Pantheon) up which run concave buttresses, ending in Ionic volutes supporting balls, a motif borrowed from Michelangelo's Porta Pia. The lantern consists of a series of concave bays between coupled columns, like some late antique 'temples' in reconstructions by Montano (whether Borromini knew drawings of the circular temple of Baalbek is a matter of speculation, see Blunt[3]). Above this comes a spiral ramp reminiscent of a ziggurat, the symbolical meaning of which has led to even more speculation than the interior of the church.

The Biblioteca Alessandrina (on the left side of the *cortile* and not open to the public) was added under Alexander VII. At the end of the library is a tablet with an inscription and a bust of Alexander by Domenico Guidi, 1660-61. Ceiling fresco: Clemente Maioli, *Religion with the Evangelists, Theological Virtues and Doctors of the Church*, 1661-65.

S. Lorenzo in Damaso
Piazza della Cancelleria, 1

Built in 1486-95 for Cardinal Raffaele Riario, nephew of Sixtus IV, who also built the Palazzo della Cancelleria in which it is enclosed. The door was designed by Vignola and engraved, together with an unexecuted design for the door of the palace, at the end of his *Regola delle Cinque Ordini*.

INTERIOR

The church was restored and altered in the 17th and 18th centuries. The choir was remodelled by Bernini on the orders of Cardinal Francesco Barberini in 1640[1] and the *confessio* was built in 1730 by Gregorini[2] but both were completely transformed in the restoration by Giuseppe Valadier, 1807-18[3] and again in 1868 by V. Vespignani. The church was damaged by fire in 1939.

The nave was decorated by Luigi Fontana with scenes from the *Life of St Lawrence*.
R entrance wall: monument to Alessandro Valtrini (d. 1634) designed by Bernini following a commission from Cardinal Francesco Barberini and executed by Lorenzo Florij, Giacomo Razzinello and Niccolò Sale[4]. For the symbolism see the similar tomb of Ippolito Merenda in S. Giacomo alla Lungara

L of entrance: copy of Bartolomeo Pincellotti's *St Hippolytus*
Piers in vestibule: 1 to R: monument to Giovanni Pacini (d. 1567) by G. A. Dosio, 1566-68[5]. 2 to R: statue of *St Charles Borromeo* by Stefano Maderno[6]
1 to R: Cappella Ruffo[7]: decorated by Nicola Salvi for Cardinal Tommaso Ruffo and consecrated in 1743. Vault: frescoes by Corrado Giaquinto, *Moses Receives the Tablets of the Law* and pendentives: *Ruth, Esther, Rebecca* and *Rachel*, 1641-43[8]; altarpiece: *Virgin with Sts Philip Neri and Nicholas of Bari* by Sebastiano Conca, 1741-43[9]. On the floor is the inlaid marble tombstone of Cardinal Ruffo (d. 1753). On the pillar: monument to Tullio Sicciolante (d. 1582)
Between 1 and 2 to R: above side entrance: G. Cesari, *Angels*, 1587-89

RIGHT AISLE
1st pier: monument to George Conn, Scottish secretary to Cardinal Francesco Barberini (d. 1640) by Giuseppe Giorgetti and Lorenzo Ottoni, 1678[10]. Opposite: monument to Principe Camillo Massimiliano Massimo (d. 1839), 1839[11] and Principessa Cristina Massimo Sassonia (d. 1837) by G. Gnaccarini, 1840[12]
2nd pier: monument to Principessa Maria Gabriella di Savoia Massimo (d. 1837) by P. Tenerani, 1837-38[13]
2 to R: Cappella del Crocifisso: altar by G. D. Navone, 1758
3 to R: Cappella del Sacro Cuore: transformed in 1820; decorated by Pietro Gagliardi, altarpiece: *Sacred Heart*; R wall: *Rinaldo de' Giovanni Preaching in S. Lorenzo*; L wall: *Pope Leo XIII Approves the Society of the Sacred Heart*
After 3 to R: monument to Cardinal Francesco Saverio Massimo by Antonio Moretti and executed by his brother Scipione;

mosaic portrait of the cardinal by Michelangelo Barberi, 1851[14]. Further: monument to Cardinal Antonio de' Lucca by Giuseppe Prinizi. To L: monument to Pellegrino Rossi by P. Tenerani, 1851[15]
High altar: commissioned by Cardinal Alessandro Farnese; Federico Zuccaro, *Coronation of the Virgin with Sts Lawrence, Paul, Peter and Damasus*, c.1568-70[16]
End of L aisle: Cappella della SS. Concezione: restored in 1634-35 by Cortona for Cardinal Francesco Barberini[17]. The vault frescoes of *God the Father* were destroyed in the 1859 restorations but the fine stucco decorations remain. Passeri clearly states that Cortona was also responsible for the marbling of the walls

LEFT AISLE
Between 1st bay and corner: monument to Annibale Caro (d. 1566), chief secretary to Cardinal Alessandro Farnese, by Giovanni Dosio[18]
3rd bay to L: monument to Antonio Cepparello (d. 1607)
1 to L: Cappella del SS. Sacramento/Ottoboni[19]: decorated for Cardinal Pietro Ottoboni by Ludovico Rusconi Sassi and consecrated in 1736. The tabernacle and balustrade date from the 1816-20 restoration. Altarpiece: Vincenzo Berrettini, *Last Supper*, 1818; vault fresco: Andrea Casali, *Adoration of the Lamb*, 1735[20]

In 1633 Cardinal Francesco Barberini commissioned Cortona to design an *apparato* for the *Quarant'ore* in the church, which is known from a drawing at Windsor[21].

S. Lorenzo in Fonte
Via Urbana, 50

The church was restored and partly rebuilt for Cardinal Juan Alvarez in 1543 by Domenico de' Ario. The choir and sacristy were built in 1628 by Domenico Castello for Urban VIII.

INTERIOR
The interior was many times restored, last in 1959-60, and now has little architectural character.
Choir: Marco Caprinozzi, L wall: *Charity of St Lawrence*; R wall: *Martyrdom of St Lawrence*, 1773[1]
High altar: Andrea Camassei, *St Lawrence Baptises the Centurion Hippolytus*[2]
In a small room adjoining the church is a bust of Urban VIII by Bernini, *c*.1620[3].

S. Lorenzo in Lucina
Piazza di S. Lorenzo in Lucina, 6

Originally built in the 4th or 5th century. According to one legend this was the site of a temple of Diana Lucina, according to another the church was founded by a Roman lady called Lucina who gave hospitality to Pope Marcellus I. Rebuilt under Paschal II (1099-1118), to whose time the portico belongs. As a parish church, it was handed over in 1606 by Paul V to the Chierici Regolari Minori (Clerks Regular Minor), an Order founded by St Francis Caracciolo. Cosimo Fanzago was invited by the Prior Raffaele Aversa to restore the church on the occasion of the Holy Year of 1650, at a time when he had taken refuge in Rome after the Masaniello revolt in Naples. The work, which was completed in 1652, involved an almost complete redecoration of the church, but most of this was swept away in a further decoration in 1857-58[1] under the direction of Andrea Busiri Vici, leaving only the magnificent pulpit, the holy-water stoups and pavement of the presbytery. The black and white marble pavement of the nave is dated 1734. Carlo Rainaldi submitted a plan for a new façade but it was never built[2].

VESTIBULE
R wall: monument to Clelia Severini (d. 1822) by Pietro Tenerani, 1823-25[3].

INTERIOR
The ten monochrome ovals on the nave walls depicting scenes from the *Life of St Francis Caracciolo* are by Francesco Manno, 1808-9[4].
Vault: *Ascension with Sts Lawrence, Francis Caracciolo, Lucina and Pope Pascal II*, Roberto Bompiani, 1857
Entrance wall: L: monuments to Bernardo Pasquini (d. 1710), Domenic Cunego (d. 1803) – the relief is dated 1784[5] – and Cardinal Luigi Capponi (d. 1667)[6]; R: monument to Cardinal Silvio Passerini (d. 1529), 1587
1 to R: Cappella di S. Lorenzo: restored for Cardinal Boschi in 1788-89; side walls decorated by Taddeo Matteini, R: *Martyrdom of St Lawrence*; L: *St Lawrence Displays the Poor to the Emperor*, 1789[7]. Altarpiece: Sigismondo Rosa, *St Lawrence in Glory with St Lucy*, 1716[8]
2 to R: Cappella di S. Antonio da Padova: architecture by C. Rainaldi, *c*.1655[9]. Above altar: Domenico Rainaldi, *Holy Family*. Wall frescoes: J. Miel, R: *St Anthony of Padua Makes a Donkey Kneel before the Host*; L: *St Anthony Heals the Foot of a Boy*[10]
Between 2 and 3 chapel to R: monument to Nicolas Poussin (d. 1665) with a relief of *Et in Arcadia Ego* by Louis Desprez; the bust is by Paul Lemoyne and the architectural elements by Louis Vaudoyer, erected by Chateaubriand, 1829-32[11]
3 to R: Cappella di S. Francesco Caracciolo: the altar dates from 1784. Altarpiece: L. Stern, *St Francis Caracciolo Adores the Host*, 1752; pendentives: scenes from the *Life of St Francis Caracciolo* by Teodoro Matteini, 1784[12]
4 to R: Cappella dell'Annunziata/Fonseca[13]: the chapel was designed by Bernini and executed in 1660-64. The bust of Gabriele Fonseca, doctor to Innocent X, was executed

by Bernini, but the exact date of its execution is a matter of dispute. It was certainly begun by 1668, the date of Fonseca's death, but it was probably not finished till later. (Wittkower argues that it may only have been put in place after 1674, because Titi does not mention it in that year, but it is also – unaccountably – omitted in all later editions.) The three other busts were added in the 18th and 19th centuries and Bernini's original design altered. The altarpiece of the *Annunciation*, 1664, by Ludovico Gimignani is a variant of Reni's painting in the Quirinal chapel. R wall: Giacinto Gimignani, *Elisha Pouring Salt into the Waters of Jericho in Order to Purify them*, 1664[14], no doubt in allusion to the fact that Fonseca was much concerned with purifying the malarial waters of Rome and the Campagna. Bernini's bust of Fonseca, which is one of his most deeply felt late works, shows the doctor in impassioned prayer, gazing towards the altar. Curiously enough Specchi's engraving in De' Rossi's *Altari*[15] shows Fonseca's arms surmounted by an ecclesiastical hat, in spite of the fact that he was – *pace* Ms Dobia – a layman, and the arms in the chapel are surmounted by a knight's helm. The bust of an unknown woman opposite the Fonseca monument is attributed to G. Cartari[16]

Room leading to sacristy: R wall: monument to Cardinal Giovanni Davia (d. 1740), erected by Benedict XIV with bust by Agostino Corsini, 1742[17]; facing wall: monument to Giuseppe Zignoni by V. Pacetti, 1805[18]

High altar: by C. Rainaldi, 1669, as a setting for the *Crucifixion* by Reni, 1637-38, bequeathed to the church by the Marchese Angelelli[19]

Chapel to L of high altar: monument to Cardinal Gabriele Filippo della Genga (d. 1861) by Astro Peruzzi, 1869[20]; L wall: monument to Carlo Fea (d. 1836) by I. Rivi

5 to L: Cappella di S. Francesco d'Assisi e della Beata Giacinta Marescotti/Alaleoni: altarpiece: M. Benefial, *Death of the Blessed Hyacinth Marescotti*, 1738[21]; paintings on vault and side walls by Simon Vouet: vault: *Assumption, Annunciation, Presentation, Birth of the Virgin;* centre *tondo: God the Father;* pendentives: *Evangelists;* R wall: *St Francis Taking the Vow of Poverty;* lunette: *Visitation;* L wall: *Temptation of St Francis;* lunette: *Marriage of the Virgin,* 1623-24[22]. The paintings around the chapel walls of *Sts Mary Magdalen, Lucy, Peter, Paul, Catherine of Alexandria* and *Clare* are attributed to F. Manno[23]

4 to L: Cappella di S. Giuseppe: altarpiece: Alessandro Turchi, *Holy Family with God the Father and the Holy Spirit*

3 to L: Cappella di S. Giovanni Nepomuceno: statue of *St John Nepomuk* by Gaetano Altobelli, 1737[24]

2 to L: Cappella di S. Carlo Borromeo: altarpiece: Carlo Saraceni, *St Charles Borromeo Prepares for the Procession of the Holy Nail,* c. 1619[25]; L wall: *Charity of St Charles;* R wall: *St Charles Giving the Sacrament to the Plague Stricken.* The chapel contains four fine busts of the Pasqualoni family dating from the first half of the 17th century but about which nothing is known[26]

1 to L: baptistery by Giuseppe Sardi, between 1713 and 1721[27]. Altarpiece: G. N. Nasini, *Baptism of Christ,* 1722; walls: Antonio Crecolini, L: *Baptism of St Lucy* and R: *Baptism of St Sabina by St Peter,* 1721[28]

Sala Capitolare: Onofrio Avellino: *Virgin and Child Enthroned with Sts Michael and John Nepomuk,* c.1732[29]

The convent attached to the church was rebuilt by C. F. Bizzacheri, 1690-1700. It has a fine door on the via Lucina[30].

S. Lorenzo in Miranda
Via Sacra al Foro Romano

The temple dedicated by Antoninus Pius to the memory of his wife Faustina was converted into a Christian church at an early date. The *cella* was rebuilt at the expense of the Nobile Collegio degli Aromatori Speziali, the association of Roman pharmacists, in 1610-14, by Orazio Torriani, who built the lower half of the façade and renovated the interior, 1613-16. The upper half of the façade was finished by Matteo Sassi, 1722. Torriani was also involved in the restoration of the neighbouring church of SS. Cosma e Damiano; thirty-three drawings by him are in the Kunstbibliothek, Berlin[1]. The church is usually open to the public on Thursday mornings between 10 and 12 am.

INTERIOR
1 to R: L wall: monument to Valentino Sbardella (d. 1670)[2]
3 to R: altarpiece: Alessandro Fortuna, *Annunciation*, c.1617-23[3]; L wall: G. de' Vecchi, *St Catherine Contemplates the Wounds of Christ*[4]; R wall: Ida Botta, *Virgin and Child*
Choir: high altar by O. Torriani, 1637[5]. Altarpiece: Cortona, *Martyrdom of St Lawrence*, 1646[6]. L wall: Raffaele Vanni, *Virgin and Child with Sts Philip and James the Lesser*[7]
2 to L: R wall: monument to Nicola Marra (d. 1677)
1 to L: the two stucco figures flanking the altar are by Jacques Sarrazin to designs by Domenichino[8]; altarpiece: Domenichino, *Virgin and Child with Sts Philip and James the Lesser*, 1626-27[9].

S. Lorenzo fuori le Mura
Piazzale di S. Lorenzo

One of the most important of the Early Christian churches and one of Rome's five patriarchal basilicas. It was severely damaged by aerial bombing in 1943. It contains a certain number of Baroque tombs and paintings.

INTERIOR
Restored for Pius IX by Virginio Vespignani, 1862-70.
R aisle: inlaid tomb of Giuseppe Rondinini (d. 1640) with mosaic portrait in the same style as that on the tomb of Ottaviano Ubaldini della Gherardesca in S. Maria sopra Minerva by G. B. Calandra and probably by the same hand
Chapel to R: Cappella di S. Tarciso: altarpiece: Emilio Savonanzi, *St Cyriaca Burying a Martyr*, 1580-1660[1]; L wall: Giovanni Serodine, *Beheading of the Baptist*, damaged in the bombing of 1943[2]
L aisle: monuments to G. Aleandro and B. Guglielmi designed by Cortona. The monuments were commissioned by Cardinal Francesco Barberini in 1627 and were originally intended to commemorate Bernardo Guglielmi (d. 1623) and John Barclay (d. 1621), who had been the cardinal's teachers in jurisprudence and letters. Both contained busts by Duquesnoy but that of Barclay was stolen by his widow and is now in the Museo Tassiano at S. Onofrio. It was replaced by one of the cardinal's secretary Girolamo Aleandro (d. 1629) by A. Giorgetti, 1660-61[3]

Between the monuments is a door leading to a staircase which goes down to the chapel of S. Ciriaca and the entrance to the catacombs. The chapel has an inscription with the date 1677, which is no doubt also that of the door and stairs.
Monument to Michele Bonelli (d. 1604)[4].

S. Lorenzo in Panisperna
Via Panisperna, 90

Built by Pope Silvester I on the site of St Lawrence's martyrdom. The church was rebuilt in 1574 for Cardinal Sirleto, perhaps by Francesco da Volterra, though the façade is dated 1684. It stands at the end of a small forecourt now approached by a flight of steps and a gate built – very skilfully – in 1892 when the level of the via Panisperna was lowered.

INTERIOR
Much of the marbling is painted. The six side chapels were redecorated under the direction of M. Fontana in 1757[1]. The altarpieces are all listed in the 1763 Titi but are not mentioned in 1745 by Roisecco, who records a few 16th century paintings, which no doubt they replaced.

Nave vault: A. Bicchierai, *Apotheosis of St Lawrence*, 1757[2]
1 to R: Antonio Nessi, *St Clare Drives Back the Troops of the Emperor Frederick II with a Monstrance*, 1756[3]; R wall: monument to Cardinal Guglielmo Sirleto (d. 1585) attributed to G. Paracca[4]
2 to R: Giovanni Francesco Romano, *Sts Crispin and Crispinian*, 1757[5]
3 to R: altarpiece: Giuseppe Ranucci, *Immaculate Virgin*, 1757[6]
Altar wall: Pasquale Cati, *Martyrdom of St Lawrence*, 1577[7]
Choir: L wall: Antonio Bicchierai, *Tobias and the Angel*, 1757[8]
3 to L: Giovanni Bigatti, *Crucifixion with God the Father, the Dove of the Holy Spirit, the Virgin and St John*[9]
2 to L: Giuseppe Montesanti, *St Bridget Adores the Crucifix*, 1757[10]
1 to L: Nicola Lapiccola, *St Francis Receives the Stigmata*, c.1757[11].

S. Lorenzo in Piscibus
Via Pancrazio Pfeiffer, 10

In 1659 this church was given to the Scuole Pie (Scolopi). In 1672 it was altered by Francesco Massari, described as 'compagno del Borromini'. The façade was erected in 1733 to the designs of Giovanni Domenico Navone. It is shown in a drawing published by Armellini and was an imitation of a single bay of Michelangelo's Palazzo dei Conservatori. Navone added the portico, ingeniously designed to join the church to the Borgo Vecchio, from which it was set back at a considerable distance. Battaglia gives the plan and good photographs of the interior. The façade was pulled down in 1938 when the via della Conciliazione was laid out. The interior has been stripped of all its Baroque decorations and many of the Baroque altarpieces are kept in the Istituto dei Padri Scolopi. The church now belongs to the Centro Internazionale Giovanile.

SS. Luca e Martina
Clivo Argentario, 3

In 1588 the Accademia di S. Luca, which had been founded in 1577 as the academy of painters, sculptors and architects, was given possession of the small but ancient church of S. Martina in the Forum, built on the site of the Secretarium Senatus between the Forum Romanum and the Forum Caesaris. Part of the earlier church is preserved in the foundations of the choir. In 1589 the church was renamed S. Luca after the patron saint of painters; land adjacent to it was bought and a wooden model for the new church was made by Giovanni Battista Montano, who was lecturing at the Academy on architecture at the time, but the money necessary to carry out these schemes was not forthcoming and nothing was done.

Noehles[1] published various drawings which he identified as designs by Mascarino for the rebuilding of the church at this stage, but the attribution is, in my opinion, very doubtful. He also published[2] as being for this church a drawing by Cortona in Munich which can be identified as dating from the pontificate of Innocent X and as being, in my view, for S. Agnese in Piazza Navona. A design for a circular church which he also publishes[3] as being for SS. Luca e Martina is more problematic, but the identification is far from certain.[4]

In 1627 Cardinal Francesco Barberini, nephew of Urban VIII, was made protector of the Academy and in 1634 Pietro da Cortona was elected *principe* (director). These two events led to the last and most important chapter in the history of SS. Luca e Martina. Cortona immediately decided to restore the crypt, partly to strengthen the foundations of the church, which was in danger of collapsing, and partly in order to build there a tomb for himself, but also in all probability in the hope of finding the remains of S. Martina, which would be a sure way of attracting the interest and support of the pope (as at S. Bibiana). His hopes were fulfilled on 25 October 1634. In November 1634 the pope visited the church to inspect the relics and Cardinal Francesco Barberini undertook to pay for the high altar.

A survey plan dating from before July 1635 shows that the foundations of the façade were already laid and the plans of the whole building must already have been completed. They must therefore have been made in the last months of 1634 or early in 1635. At first the work proceeded quickly: the relics were buried again in the lower church in January 1635; the high altar of the upper church was begun during the same year, and a drawing made by Cortona before he left for Florence in June 1637[5] shows that the apse was completed, but only part of the lower storey of the façade was completed before June 1637.[6]

There are no documents to show exactly when construction of the lower church was begun, but it is likely to have been started about 1635 and was in the main finished by 1647, though the sculptural decoration was not completed till much later.

Work on the church was held up for two reasons: Cortona was in Florence from 1639 till 1647, and after the death of the pope in July 1644 Cardinal Francesco Barberini had to flee Rome and take refuge in Paris from the threats of Innocent X in January 1646. During Cortona's absence work continued on the lower church under the direction of his nephew Luca Berrettini and largely at his own expense, but the construction of the upper church seems to have been halted. Only after the cardinal returned from France in February 1648 did he undertake to finance the completion of the upper church and work begin.

It was probably at this stage that Cortona produced his plan to enlarge the façade of the church to the width of the transept by adding two side bays either in the same plane as the central section[7] or sloping back at 45°.[8] This scheme was not carried out, presumably because the site could not be acquired, and in the event the façade was built as it appears in the survey drawing of 1635.

By the time of Cortona's death in 1669 the construction of the church was complete, except for the top of the façade. This was finished under the direction of Ciro Ferri. The coat of arms was set up in 1671 and the angels supporting it (by Giuseppe Giorgetti) were put in place in 1673[9], as were the flaming urns. It is not certain whether the façade was completed according to Cortona's final design or whether he intended to add a broad straight pediment over the existing curved one (as at S. Maria della Pace) and over the coat of arms, as Noehles[10] convincingly suggests.

The external appearance of the church has suffered severely from the clearing of the area. In the early 19th century the excavation of the Forum lowered the level of the ground so that it is now completely dissociated from the church, which originally grew out of it but now stands on a macadamised street. In 1932 the buildings immediately surrounding it were pulled down to lay bare the ancient ruins below them and at the same time the adjacent church of S. Adriano, built in the Republican Senate House, was stripped of its Baroque decoration. The result of removing the houses which flanked the church was to emphasise the fact that Cortona had not been able to complete the façade and to make its unusual proportions even more conspicuous. The removal of the buildings around the apse made the dome more visible but necessitated the addition of much modern brickwork. As it now stands the church is in many ways awkward and naked.

The façade of the church is the earliest surviving example of Cortona's 'close-packed' design, which he had employed earlier in secular architecture in the destroyed Villa del Pigneto, built for the Sacchetti. The columns of the lower storey and the pilasters of the upper are set under straight unbroken entablatures and the spaces between them are filled with panels which squeeze up against them and even overlap them. Cortona conceives of the wall as something to be carved out, almost like sculpture, an effect which is intensified by the choice he has made of a particularly rough type of travertine.

INTERIOR

The church – the only complete building by Cortona to survive – is in the form of a cross of which the arms are almost equal – the nave and choir being in fact slightly longer than the transepts – and is dominated by the heavy Ionic columns, typical of Cortona, which the architect has disposed in such a way that the walls are carved into a series of layers, ranging from the outer shell, behind the columns set into the walls of the choir, to the front layer formed by the entablature over the pilasters flanking the columns of the crossing piers. The windows in the vault and dome are composed of heavy Michelangelesque forms, typical of Cortona's work in the 1630's.

The decoration of the vault and dome was not finished at the time of Cortona's death but was continued for many years under Luca Berrettini and Ciro Ferri, the latter being responsible for the stuccoes in the dome, which were still being worked on in 1679. It is not certain therefore that all the work was carried out according to Cortona's design. The question is of some importance, because it is generally said that Bernini borrowed from SS. Luca e Martina the idea of combining ribs and coffering for the decoration of a dome, which he applied at Castelgandolfo (1658-61) and his other later churches; but if in fact the decoration of the dome at SS. Luca e Martina was an invention of Ferri – and it has a certain softness which is more typical of him than of his master – then Bernini's churches may have been completed before SS. Luca e Martina. Cortona's priority, however, remains certain because he employed a simplified version of the same scheme in the dome of S. Maria della Pace on which he was probably working c.1656-57.

The reliefs of the *Four Evangelists* in the pendentives were added in 1730 under the artistic direction of Sebastiano Conca: *St Matthew*, Giuseppe Rusconi; *St Mark*,

Filippo della Valle; *St Luke* and *St John*, G. B. Maini[11].

Immediately inside the main door, which has over it an inscription dated 1650, is a simple memorial slab to Cortona. To the right is a monument to Carlo Pio Balestra (d. 1763) by Tommaso Righi, 1776-77[12].

R transept: Cappella di S. Lazzaro: Lazzaro Baldi, *Martyrdom of St Lazarus*, 1681-82[13], and monument to Baldi and his sister, designed by the artist. The chapel also contains the tomb of Girolamo Rainaldi (d. 1655) and his father Adriano[14]

High altar: begun in 1635 to a design by Cortona, the execution being in the hands of Luca Berretini and Domenico Tavolaccio. The work was, however, interrupted and the altar was only completed after Cortona's death to a design slightly modified by Cirro Ferri. The altarpiece, *St Luke Painting the Virgin*, is traditionally ascribed to Raphael and was presented to the Academy by Federico Zuccaro; it has now been replaced by a copy by Grammatica, 1622-23[15]. Below the *mensa* is the statue of *The Dead St Martina* by N. Menghini, 1643-51[16]

L transept: Cappella dell'Assunta e S. Sebastiano: altar designed by Carlo Buratti, 1722, perhaps incorporating elements from a design presented by Carlo Fontana in 1696; altarpiece: S. Conca, *Assumption with St Sebastian*, 1733[17]

In the sacristy is a terracotta relief by Algardi of *Mary Magdalen in Ecstasy*, a *bozzetto* for a relief now in Saint-Maximin, Provence[18].

Access to the lower church is through a small room to the left of the choir, which contains the tomb of the architect G. B. Soria (d. 1651), a friend of Cortona, who was *principe* of the Accademia di S. Luca in 1648 and also died in 1651. The bust is attributed to G. Finelli, 1652-53[19].

LOWER CHURCH
The lower church, which is accessible on the feast of St Martina (30 January), consists of two main chapels linked by a corridor. Over the altar of the first chapel is a relief by Algardi of the *Holy Trinity*; it has now lost the arched top which contained the Dove of the Holy Spirit[20]. In the niches are the statues of *Sts Sabina*, *Theodora* and *Euphemia* by Cosimo Fancelli, and *St Martina* attributed to Pompeo Ferrucci[21].

In the inner chapel the altar contains the relics of St Martina. It was designed by Cortona in 1641-42, but was not completed until 1656 and involved at least ten founders and sculptors, though their individual contributions are not known. The pairs of angels on the front and back of the altar and the putti on the sides are attributed to G. Finelli[22]. The altar supports two alabaster reliefs of *The Virgin Appearing to St Martina* by Fancelli[23]. In a shallow apse behind the altar is an Early Christian throne preserved from the old church. In a side chapel is a terracotta group by Algardi of *Sts Concordius, Epiphanius and a third unidentified Saint*[24]. The lower church also contains a wall monument with a bust of Cortona begun by Bernardo Fioriti[25] and an inscription recording his bequest to the church.

In contrast to the upper church the inner chamber of the lower church is of rich marble and the altar is of elaborately worked gilt bronze, alabaster and precious stones. Cortona has set the four Ionic columns at the corners of the chapel on the diagonals, as Michelangelo had done in the Cappella Sforza, but he softened the effect by setting them in shallow niches and flanking them with pairs of pilasters, whereas in the Cappella Sforza they project alone into the central space of the chapel. The pediments over the central panels are also Michelangelesque but Cortona has added mouldings in the field of the pediment which in the middle break forward into what seems to be the vestigial peak of another pediment.

The outer chamber is made of simpler material and is much less ornate in detail. Eight Tuscan columns support the low vault, in the centre of which is a broad stucco wreath of flowers and fruit surrounding an opening which allows a view straight up into the dome of the upper church.

S. Lucia del Gonfalone
(See also **Oratorio del Gonfalone**)
Via dei Banchi Vecchi, 12

Built by Marco David in 1761-65, under the patronage of Cardinal Flavio Chigi, to replace an earlier church belonging to the Roman confraternity of the Raccomandati di S. Maria, which was absorbed in 1470 into the Raccomandati della Vergine, later known as the Gonfalone.

INTERIOR
The interior was restored in 1863-65 by Francesco Azzurri so that all that remains of the 18th century church is the sober façade. The *Prophets* on the pilasters and the *Old Testament Women* on the entrance wall are by Cesare Mariani.
1 to R: altarpiece: Salvatore Monosilio, *Virgin and Child with Sts Thomas of Villanova and Francis of Sales*, 1765; R wall: monument to Monsignor Nicola Maria Nicolai (d. 1833) by Giuseppe de' Fabris, 1833[1]
2 to R: statue of *St Lucy* by Scipione Tadolini[2]
3 to R: altarpiece: Mariano Rossi, *Sts Peter and Paul on their Way to Martyrdom*, 1765[3]
Choir: L wall: *Jesus in Joseph's Workshop*; R wall: *The Holy Family Arrive in Bethlehem*, C. Mariani[4]; apse: *The Virgin Appears to St Bonaventure*[5]. High altar by Giuseppe Rinaldi
3 to L: altarpiece: E. Costantini, *St Bonaventure Prays at the Feet of St Francis*, 1766[6]
1 to L: altarpiece: Eugenio Porretti, *St Charles Borromeo with the Blessed Cardinal Gregory Barbarigo*
Sacristy: F. Costantini, *Crucifixion*, 1766.

S. Lucia in Selci
Via Selci, 82

According to Hibbard, begun by Maderno in 1603 for the convent of Augustinian nuns and consecrated in 1619, though Baglione says that the convent was modernised by Felice Antonio Casone. The church is only open to the public for Mass on Sunday morning at 9.30 am.

INTERIOR
A single nave with shallow side chapels, the usual form in the late 16th and early 17th centuries.
1 to R: Lanfranco, *Martyrdom of St Lucy*, c.1632[1]
2 to R: A. Camassei, *St Augustine's Vision of the Virgin and Christ*[2]
High altar: G. B. Fontebuoni, *Annunciation*, 1606; the grille over the *mensa* is by Borromini
2 to L: A. Camassei, *St John the Evangelist Gives the Host to Mary Magdalen*[3]
1 to L: Cappella Landi: decorated by Borromini in 1637-39; altarpiece by Giuseppe Cesari, *Sts Nicholas of Tolentino and Monica with the Trinity*, 1639. In this chapel Borromini uses for the first time a device which he repeats later in the cornice on the exterior of S. Ivo: he converts the egg-and-dart moulding into a series of cherubs' heads (the eggs) and wings (the darts)
Nuns' choir: B. Ciarpi, *St Monica*; Conver-

sion of St Augustine; Adoration of the Shepherds; St Charles Borromeo; St Lucy Receives the Host from St Ambrose; St Clare of Montefalco, 1614-15[4].

S. Lucia della Tinta
Via di Monte Brianzo, 62

This ancient church was rebuilt in 1278 and restored in 1580 for the Compagnia dei Cocchieri and again in 1628, when it was granted to the Borghese family by Paul V. Redecorated by Thaddäus Kuntz on the orders of Principe Marcantonio Borghese in 1781.

INTERIOR
Vault: T. Kuntz, *St Lucy's Vision of the Assumption*
3 to L: Giacomo Triga, *Virgin and Child with Sts Ivo, Genesius and Giles with Souls in Purgatory.*

S. Luigi dei Francesi
Piazza di S. Luigi dei Francesi

In 1478 the French colony acquired a small 14th century church dedicated to S. Salvatore near this site. In the first years of the 16th century it was decided to build a new church which was to be dedicated to St Louis. This church, designed by Jean de Chènevière, was to be circular. It was never finished but a number of decorative panels from it were incorporated in the façade of the existing church, including two salamanders, the emblem of Francis I, and the element which crowns the pediment. The foundation stone was laid by Leo X in 1518. Work on the church was suspended and it never rose more than six feet above the ground. The form of this church was no doubt suggested by Bramante's Tempietto, but it is interesting to note that eight years earlier another northern patron, the Burgundian Benoît Adam, used a similar form, though octagonal instead of circular, for the little church of S. Giovanni in Oleo. The form was mainly used for *martyria* to which class S. Giovanni, but not S. Luigi, belonged. The reasons for the choice of this form for the church are unknown. Work on the church was abandoned in 1524.

At an unknown date – presumably after 1524 – Antonio da Sangallo the Younger produced a basilical plan, which was not executed, and the church was actually begun on the plans of a little known architect, Giovanni Mangone, who died in 1543, and it is not known who took over. The evidence about who completed the church is somewhat confusing. Cametti published documents which showed that in the 1570's Giacomo della Porta was in charge with Domenico Fontana working under him. Mola says that the façade was begun by 'M.re Gio: francese', no doubt meaning Jean de Chènevière, and adds that it was finished by Della Porta, and both Baglione and Martinelli ascribe the façade to this architect. On the other hand Bousquet has shown that Fontana was paid 300 scudi in 1585 and 220 scudi in 1588 for his work on the façade, whereas Della Porta was only paid 6 scudi per month, which suggests that Fontana was the actual designer and directing architect of the façade. A decision on stylistic grounds is difficult to arrive at, but the evidence seems to point to him rather than to Della Porta as the designer. Della Porta never built a church with a façade composed, like S. Luigi, of two equal storeys and though there is nothing precisely similar to be found in Fontana's work – he never built a complete church – the broad-shouldered squareness of S. Luigi recalls his style in general and has something in common with the external elevation of his Sistine Chapel in S. Maria Maggiore[1]. Furthermore, the very heavy pediment over the doors, niches and windows are closer to his manner than to that of Della Porta as, for instance, at the Gesù, S. Maria ai Monti or S. Atanasio dei Greci. The two *ignudi* in the pediment were designed for the top of the Porta Pia but were never set up there. They were tentatively ascribed by Schwager[2] to Daniele da Volterra, but documents published by Bousquet seem to show that they, and the coat-of-arms which they support, are by the French sculptor Nicholas Pippe of Arras. The figures by Pierre Lestache are set into niches on the façade; lower L: *Charlemagne*; upper L: *St Clotilde*; lower R: *St Louis*; upper R: *St Joan of Arc*, 1746-48[3].

The church was consecrated in 1589 and when Fontana left Rome for Naples in 1594 his place was taken by Maderno, who is recorded as receiving a payment of 10 scudi in 1606 and was still in charge in 1626, but since the building was by then complete his function was probably supervision of its upkeep.

INTERIOR

The present appearance of the interior is due to a redecoration by Antoine Dérizet between 1751 and 1756[4]. Designs for the decoration held at Windsor, however, show that Andrea Sacchi was commissioned by Cardinal Antonio Barbarini to decorate the interior. Based on Annibale Carracci's ceiling decorations in the Farnese Palace, the series of monumental nudes, unusual as church decoration, and an iconographic programme more secular than religious may partly have prevented the scheme from being carried out. Bellori notes in his biography of Sacchi that the artist lamented never carrying out a major fresco cycle. The painting on the vault of the nave of the *Death and Transfiguration of St Louis* is by A. Bicchierai to a design by Natoire, 1755-56[5]. This redecoration of the vault altered the original barrel shape. The reliefs on the pendentives of the dome are by: G. B. Maini, *St Gregory the Great*; Filippo della Valle, *St Jerome*; N. Gillet, *St Augustine* and Simone Challe, *St Ambrose*, 1750-52.

1 to R: Cappella di S. Dionigi: altarpiece: Reynaud Levieux, *St Denis Heals a Blind Man*, 1676[6]; L wall: monument to Colin d'Ernest (d. 1851) by C. Soulacroix, 1853

Between 1 and 2 to R: monument to Charles Errard (d. 1689), Director of the French Academy in Rome from 1666 to 1683

2 to R: Cappella di S. Cecilia/Polet: Domenichino, scenes from the *Life of St Cecilia*: L wall: *Death of St Cecilia*; R wall: *St Cecilia Distributing Alms*; vault: R: *Sts Cecilia and Valerian Crowned by an Angel*; C: *St Cecilia in Glory*; L: *Condemnation of St Cecilia*, 1612-15. One of the purest expressions of the classical tendency in early 17th century Roman painting. Poussin drew on these frescoes in several of his compositions[7]. Altarpiece: copy of Raphael's *Vision of St Cecilia* by Reni, 1600[8]

Between 2 and 3 to R: monument to Nicholas Vleughels (d. 1737), Director of the French Academy from 1724 to 1737, by M. A. Slodtz, 1738-40

2nd pillar to R: monument to Xavier Sigalon (d. 1837) by V. Baltard and A. Ottin, 1837-38 [9]

3 to R: Cappella di S. Giovanna di Francia: altarpiece: Etienne Parrocel, *The Blessed Jane of Valois*, c.1743

3rd pillar to R: monument to Nicholas Didier Boguet (d. 1839) by Antoine-Laurent Dantan with relief by P. Lemoyne, 1839-41[10]

4th pillar to R: monument to the Marquis Just de la Tour-Maubourg (d. 1837) and Nicholas Dider Boguet (d. 1839) by P. Lemoyne[11]

4 to R: Cappella di S. Remigo/Dupre: altarpiece: Jacopino del Conte, *St Remigius*

Baptising the Franks. R wall: Pellegrino Tibaldi, *King Clovis Prepares for War*; L wall: Girolamo Sicciolante, *Baptism of King Clovis by St Remigius*, c.1547-48. Vault: R: *Battle of Tolbiac* by an unknown artist; C: *The Sacred Vase of Rheims*, P. Tibaldi; L: *Capture of Soisson (Rheims)* ascribed to Perino del Vaga[12]

Between 4 and 5 to R: monument to Charles François Poerson (d. 1725), Director of the French Academy from 1704 to 1725

5 to R: L wall: monument to Pierre Guérin (d. 1833) by P. Lemoyne with bust by A. Dumont (copy)[13]; R wall: monument to Giuseppe Sisco (d. 1820) by R. Rinaldi, 1830[14]; monument to Jean Baptiste Wicar (d. 1834) by F. Gnaccarini, 1834-35[15]; monument to Jean Baptiste Deschamps (d. 1867) by E. Delaplache

End of R aisle: over door to sacristy: P. Lestache, bust of Cardinal de la Grange d'Arguien, c.1725[16]

Sacristy: P. Batoni, *Holy Family with the Infant St John the Baptist*, 1758[17]; C. Maratta, *Holy Family with St John*, 1695[18]; B. Lamberti, *Annunciation*, 1696[19]

Choir: high altar: Francesco Bassano, *Assumption*, 1585-90[20]. Side walls: *Putti with Instruments of the Mass* by P. Lestache. Over altar: *Holy Trinity* by Gian Giacomo Caffieri, 1752[21]

End of L aisle: bust of Cardinal Joseph François de la Trémouille (d. 1770) by an unknown sculptor

5 to L: Cappella di S. Matteo/Contarelli[22]: commissioned by Cardinal Matteo Contarelli. The vault was decorated by Giuseppe Cesari, *St Matthew Raises the Ethiopian King's Daughter from the Dead*, 1591-93; on the wall and over the altar are canvases by Caravaggio: L wall: *Calling of St Matthew*, 1599-1600; R wall: *Martyrdom of St Matthew*, 1600; altarpiece: *An Angel Dictates the Gospel to St Matthew*, 1602. The first version of the altarpiece (destroyed during the Second World War) was too brutal for the clergy of S. Luigi, who sold it to the Marchese Vincenzo Giustiniani and commissioned Caravaggio to paint the version which is in the chapel today. These paintings were Caravaggio's first commission for a Roman church[23]

Between 5 and 4 to L: monument to Eléonore Blount by Jean-Baptiste Carpeaux, 1862-63[24]

4 to L: Cappella della Vergine: frescoes by Charles Mellin, who obtained the commission in 1630 in a competition in which Poussin took part unsuccessfully. Altarpiece: *Birth of Christ*; R wall: *Annunciation*; vault, R: *Visitation*, 1630-31; L: Baglione, *Presentation*; C: G. Manno, *Coronation*, 1826[25]; L wall: Baglione, *Adoration of the Magi*, 1630-31[26]

3 to L: Cappella di S. Louis IX/Benedetti: designed by Plautilla Bricci, 1675-880[27]. Altarpiece: P. Bricci, *St Louis IX*, 1680[28]. Gilt-bronze tabernacle attributed to Jacob Cobaert, originally in the Contarelli chapel[29]; R wall: Lodovico Gimignani, *St Louis Hands the Crown of Thorns to the Archbishop of Paris*, 1680[30]; L wall: Nicholas Pinson, *Catherine de' Medici Presenting St Louis the Plans for the New Church*, 1680[31]

2 to L: Cappella di S. Nicola di Bari: altarpiece: Girolamo Muziano, *St Nicholas of Bari*; altar wall: Girolamo Massei, L: *St Barbara*; R: *St Catherine of Alexandria*[32]. Side walls: Baldassare Croce, R: *Death of St Nicholas*; L: *Birth of St Nicholas*. Vault: R: *St Nicholas Saves a Condemned Innocent Man from Death*; L: *The Saint Helps the Poor*; C: *St Nicholas in Glory*[33]

Between 1 and 2 to L: monument to Pierre de Rochechouart by Nicholas Pippe, 1593

1st pier: monument to Claude Lorrain (d. 1682) by P. Lemoyne, 1836-40[34]

1 to L: Cappella di S. Sebastiano: altarpiece: *Martyrdom of St Sebastian*, Girolamo Massei (or N. Boucoiran, 1838); R wall: monument to Cardinal François de Pierre de Bernis (d. 1794) by F. M. Laboureur, c.1805[35]; L wall: monument to the Countess Pauline de Monmorin de Beaumont (d. 1803) by J. Marin, 1805[36]; upper wall frescoes by Giuseppe Manno, L: *Justice* and *Peace*, R: *Truth* and *Mercy*, 1833[37]

To the right of the church in the via Giovanna d'Arco is the Palazzo di S. Luigi built by Carlo Bizzacheri in 1709-12 to house a college attached to the church[38].

S. Macuto
Piazza di S. Macuto

The church was rebuilt for the Arciconfraternita dei Bergamaschi in 1561-62, possibly by Martino Longhi the Elder or Francesco da Volterra. Alberto Galvani's name appears in the confraternity's records but his role in the building of the church is unclear. It was restored in 1730 and again in the 19th century. It has a very simple façade with one unusual feature, a Serliana in the upper storey. This might be taken for a 19th century insertion but it appears in Vasi's engraving.

The church contains two unusual altars, probably dating from the late 16th century restoration and in character Venetian rather than Roman. The church now serves as the chapel to the seminary (via del Seminario, 120) through which it can be visited.

INTERIOR
The barrel vault dates from the 1818 restoration under Benedetto Piernicoli. Both side chapels are by Francesco da Volterra, c. 1574.
R altar: M. Cerruti, *St Joseph in Glory*[1]
High altar: M. Cerruti, *Virgin with St Macutus*[2]
L altar: M. Cerruti, *Sts John Nepomuk and Aloysius Gonzaga Adore the Sacred Heart*[3].

Madonna dell'Archetto see S. Maria dell'Archetto
Via di S. Marcello, 41b

Madonnella di S. Marco see Madonna delle Grazie
Piazza Venezia

Madonna del Divino Amore (SS. Biagio e Cecilia dei Materassai)
Vicolo del Divino Amore, 12

The church belonged to the Confraternita dei Materassai (mattress makers) from 1575. It was rebuilt by Raguzzini in 1729-31. The façade is of great simplicity and the interior was restored in 1865-74.

INTERIOR
Vault: F. Prosperi, *Virgin and Child with Sts Blaise and Cecilia* , 1866
R altar: Sigismondo Rosa, *St Blaise Healing a Child*
High altar: G. Bombelli, *Virgin and Child*
L altar: P. Costanzi, *Sts Cecilia and Valerian*, 1729[1].

Madonna delle Grazie (Madonnella di S. Marco)
Piazza Venezia

The chapel originally formed part of the Palazzetto Venezia and when this was pulled down and rebuilt on the other side of the Palazzo Venezia in 1911 the chapel was moved to the right-hand end of the main front of the Palazzo.

INTERIOR
Altar: erected in 1682 by G. B. Contini; the

angels on either side are by Filippo Carcani, completed 1683[1]; altarpiece: Bernardino Gagliardi, *Virgin and Child*, c.1655-57
Side walls: Alessandro Grimaldi, R: *Birth of the Virgin* and *Flight to Egypt* (the latter painting is also given to F. Cozza); L: *Assumption*[2].

Madonna dei Monti *see* S. Maria dei Monti
Via della Madonna dei Monti, 39-41

Madonna del Pascolo *see* SS. Sergio e Bacco
Piazza della Madonna dei Monti, 3

SS. Marcellino e Pietro
Via Merulana, 161

A church with the dedication to these two martyrs has probably stood on this site since the last years of the 4th century. The restoration was undertaken in 1703 by Carlo Fontana for Clement XI, but under Benedict XIV a completely new church was built in 1750-53 to the designs of Girolamo Theodoli. The plan of the church – a Greek cross – and the façade are strictly classical but the architect has allowed himself a flight of fancy in the stepped dome, which owes its origins ultimately to the Pantheon, but more immediately to Borromini's dome of S. Ivo.

INTERIOR
R transept: F. Evangelisti, *St Gregory Frees a Soul from Purgatory by his Mass*, 1754[1]
High altar: Gaetano Lapis, *Martyrdom of Sts Marcellinus and Peter*, 1751[2]
L transept: Copy after Reni, *Virgin with Sts Joseph and Teresa*[3].

S. Marcello
Piazza di S. Marcello, Via del Corso

A church on the site is first mentioned in 418. Later it became the titular church of a cardinal and from 1369 it belonged to the Servites (Servants of Mary). The old church was destroyed by fire in 1519. Rebuilding was begun immediately to plans by Jacopo Sansovino and continued by Antonio da Sangallo the Younger after Sansovino's departure for Venice in 1526. The apse was added by Annibale Lippi in 1569 and the church was completed in 1592.

The façade was added in 1682-83 by Carlo Fontana[1]. Fontana accepted the principle of the curved façade introduced by Borromini and Cortona in the 1630's but applied it in a simpler way. Instead of the double-S curve of S. Carlino or the play of convex against straight or concave of SS. Luca e Martina or S. Maria della Pace, he planned his front on a single steady curve. The result proved enormously successful and the façade was probably more frequently imitated – often with variations – during the late 17th and 18th centuries than any other in Rome, except the Gesù (Juvarra's S. Christina in Turin, the Neumünster in Würzburg to quote two widely separated examples). S. Marcello seems to have been the first church façade actually built on this design but two architects had experimented with it on paper at an earlier date: Borromini for S. Carlino[2] and Martino Longhi the Younger for S. Giovanni Calabita in 1644[3].

The relief over the door showing *St Philip Benizi Renouncing the Tiara* is by Antonio Raggi, 1684[4]. The statues represent R: *St Marcellus* and L: *St Philip Benizi* by F. Cavallini (c.1683). Above: *The Blessed Joachim Piccolomini* and *The Blessed Francis Patrizi* and the allegorical figures of *Faith* and *Hope* on the pediment are by Andrea Fucigna[5].

S. Marcello

INTERIOR
Restored in 1861-67 by V. Vespignani. The ceiling was put up in 1592 by Carlo Lambardi at the expense of Monsignor Giulio Vitelli (d. 1600), who paid for the frescoes on the vault of the choir, apse and clerestory: R clerestory: *Entombment*; *Christ in Limbo*; *Resurrection*; *Noli me tangere*; *Ascension*; *Trinity in Glory*; L clerestory: *Ecce Homo*; *Crowning with Thorns*; *Flagellation*; *Christ before Herod*; *Arrest of Christ*; *Agony in the Garden*; entrance wall: *Crucifixion* by G. B. Ricci
R entrance wall: monument to Cardinal Francesco Cennini, Papal Nuncio to Spain under Paul V (d. 1645) by Giovanni Francesco de' Rossi[6]
L entrance wall: monument to Cardinal Angelo Giovanni Michiel (d. 1503) and Bishop Antonio Orso (d. 1511), traditionally ascribed to Jacopo Sansovino but rejected by Boucher[7]
Room to R of entrance: above door: monument to Virginia Rasponi Mangelli (d. 1836) by Gaetano Sarrocchi, 1836[8]
1 to R: Cappella dell' Annunciazione/Alli Maccarani: built in 1593 and decorated in 1666. Altarpiece: L. Baldi, *Annunciation*, 1684-86[9]; vault: frescoed in the early 17th century by Tarquinio Ligustri da Viterbo, 1607[10]
2 to R: Cappella di SS. Degna e Merita/ Muti Bussi: designed by Francesco Ferrari and opened 1727[11]; vault fresco: *Sts Digna and Emerita in Glory* by Ignatius Stern[12]; altarpiece: P. A. Barbieri, *Martyrdom of Sts Digna and Emerita*, 1727. Monuments to L: Giovanni Muti and R: his wife Maria Colombia Vincentini by Bernardino Cametti, 1725[13]. Brilliant variants in an 18th century spirit of the ideas invented by Bernini in the Cornaro Chapel (S. Maria della Vittoria) and Fonseca Chapel (S. Lorenzo in Lucina) and developed in the Bolognetti tombs in the Gesù e Maria.

Between 2 and 3 to R: pulpit designed by G. M. de' Rossi, executed by Carlo Torriani with a stucco angel seated on a globe supporting the pulpit by Paolo Naldini, 1673[14]
3 to R: Cappella della Madonna delle Grazie/ Grifoni: Marian cycle on the altar wall by Francesco Salviati, c.1554-63, completed by G. B. Ricci on Salviati's death in 1563; altar wall: L: *Annunciation*; *Birth of the Virgin*; C: *Coronation*; R: *Purification*; *Presentation in the Temple*; vault: L: *Marriage of the Virgin*; C: *Assumption*; R: *Pentecost*. Side walls: R: *Adoration of the Magi*; L: *Adoration of the Shepherds*[15]. R wall: monument to Bishop Matteo Grifoni (d. 1567) by Stoldo Lorenzi; L wall: monument to Cardinal Thomas Weld (d. 1837) by Thomas Hill[16]
4 to R: Cappella del Crocifisso[17]: the crucifix survived the fire of 1519; the screen which covers the crucifix is by Luigi Garzi, before 1686. The tabernacle is by Bizzacheri, 1691[18]. Vault: *Creation of Adam and Eve*, 1525-27, and *St Mark* and *St John* by Perino del Vaga[19]. The rest of the vault was completed after Del Vaga's death by Daniele da Volterra using Del Vaga's designs: *St Matthew* and *St Luke*, 1540-43[20]. L wall: monuments to Cardinal Ercole Consalvi (d. 1824)[21] and the Marchese Andrea Consalvi (d. 1827) by Rinaldo Rinaldi, 1824-31[22]
5 to R: Cappella di S. Pellegrino/Paolucci: restored in 1723-24 by Rusconi Sassi for Cardinal Fabrizio Paolucci (d. 1726), Secretary of State to Clement XI; P. Bracci's monument to Paolucci, 1729, stands against the right wall[23]. The paintings are by Aureliano Milani; altarpiece: *St Peregrinus Cured by Christ*, 1725; R wall: *The Dead Saint Rises from his Funeral Bier to Heal a Blind Boy*; L wall: *Miracle of the Madonna del Fuoco*[24]
Over sacristy door: monument to Cardinal Camillo Merlin Paolucci (d. 1763), Papal Nuncio to Vienna under Clement XIII, by Tommaso Righi, 1776[25]

Sacristy: vault: G. B. Ciocchi, *St Marcellus in Glory* and *Four Cardinal Virtues*
Apse: apse frescoes by G. B. Ricci, L: *Death of the Virgin*; C: *Coronation of the Virgin*; R: *Assumption*; arch: *Visitation*; *Annunciation*; *Marriage of the Virgin*; *Presentation in the Temple*; *Birth of the Virgin*. High altarpiece: Silverio Capparoni, *St Marcellus in Glory*, 1867; between windows: L: *Sts Francis Patrizi and Philip Benizi*; R: *Sts Juliana Falconieri and Joan Sonderini*, Giovan Battista Polenzani, 1867

6 to L: Cappella di S. Filippo Benizi/Dandini/ de' Sylva: restored in 1725 for Cardinal Alessandro Falconieri. Altarpiece: P. L. Ghezzi, *St Philip Benizi Assisted by St Alexius Falconieri Gives the Rule to St Juliana Falconieri in the Presence of the Virgin*, 1725[26]. Side walls frescoed by Bernardino Gagliardi, R: *Death of St Philip Benizi* and L: *Multiplication of the Loaves by the Saint*, 1652[27]

5 to L: Cappella di S. Paolo/Frangipane: decorated by Taddeo Zuccaro with scenes from the *Life of St Paul*; altarpiece: *Conversion of St Paul*, 1564-66; L wall: *Blinding of Elymas*; R wall: *St Paul Healing the Cripple*; vault: R: *St Paul Raises Eutychus*; C: *Beheading of St Paul*; L: *Sea Storm near Malta*, c.1557-66[28]. Monuments to members of the Frangipane family: L wall: Mario (d. 1568), Curzio (d. 1555) and Antonio (d. 1546)[29]; R wall: busts of Lelio (d. 1605) and Roberto (d. 1622) and their father Muzio (d. 1588) by Algardi, probably between 1630 and 1640[30]

4 to L: Cappella della Madonna dei Sette Dolori: designed by Filippo Zenobio del Rosso and marbled in 1762 by Alberto Fortini; altarpiece: P. P. Baldini, *Seven Sorrows of the Virgin*; sculpture by Tommaso Righi; gilded stucco ornamentation by Cinzio Ferrari. Vault fresco: Antonio Bicchierai, *Presentation of Christ in the Temple*; side walls by D. Corvi, L: *Abandonment of Moses*, 1762[31] and R: *Sacrifice of Isaac*, 1762[32]

3 to L: Cappella di S. Maria Maddalena/ Parisani: altarpiece: G. Triga, *Death of Mary Magdalen*; Tommaso da Pesaro, R wall: *The Blessed Joachim Piccolomini*; L wall: *The Virgin Appears to the Blessed Francis Patrizi*; vault: Giovanni Paolo del Colle, L: *Annunciation* and R: *Adoration of the Shepherds*, 1550

2 to L: Cappella dei Sette Santi Fondatori/ Cesi/Orsa: begun in 1593 and completed in 1634 by F. A. Casone; altarpiece: A. Masucci, *Virgin with the Founding Saints of the Servite Order*, 1727[33]; frescoes by P. P. Baldini: L wall: *Entombment* and R wall: *Christ Falling under the Cross*[34]

1 to L: Cappella Nuova del Buon Pastore: over entrance: monument to Domenico Morichini (d. 1836) by Adam Tadolini[35]

Within the monastery of S. Marcello is a series of paintings commissioned for the canonisation of St Philip Benizi. N. Berrettoni, *Miracle of St Philip Benizi as a Child*, 1671; L. Baldi and workshop, *St Philip Benizi Strikes Water from Mount Senario*, 1670; F. Rioli with C. Maratta, *St Philip Benizi Strikes a Blasphemer with Lightning*, 1671; F. Rioli, *St Philip Benizi Refuses the Papacy*; L.Garzi, *St Philip Benizi Mediates the Peace between Rudolph I and the King of Bohemia* and *St Philip Benizi Heals a Leper*, 1671[36].

S. Marco
Piazza di S. Marco

Built on the site of the house belonging to Pope Mark I (337-40), the church was transformed completely in the second half of the 15th century by the Venetian Cardinal Pietro Barbo, later Pope Paul II, who also built the adjacent Palazzo Venezia, later the seat of the Venetian ambassador to the Holy See. The interior was redecorated in 1653-57 by

S. Marco

Orazio Torriani on the orders of Niccolò Sagredo, the Venetian ambassador to Rome, and again by Filippo Barigioni in 1735-36 and 1743-49 at the expense of Cardinal Angelo Maria Querini, when the columns veneered with Sicilian jasper were added[1].

The portico dates from the 15th century restoration, as does the coffered wooden ceiling of the nave. The only visible remains of the medieval church are the mosaics in the apse and on the arch over it, which date from the 9th century.

INTERIOR

The ceiling was erected for Paul II, 1467-69.

The paintings on the wall of the nave, which illustrate on the right wall the *Lives of Sts Abdon and Sennen* and on the left wall *The Early History of St Mark*, belong to the 1653-59 restoration. Those on the right are totally ruined by damp[2].

RIGHT NAVE
1 to R: G. Cortese, *Sts Abdon and Sennen Bury the Bodies of Martyrs*[3]
2 to R: G. A. Canini, *Sts Abdon and Sennen Refusing to Worship Idols*[4]
3 to R: F. Allegrini, *Sts Abdon and Sennen Chained to the Emperor's Chariot*
4 to R: P. F. Mola, *Martyrdom of Sts Abdon and Sennen*[5]

LEFT NAVE
1 to L: Cortese, *St Mark Crowned as Pope*[6]
2 to L: G. A. Canini, *St Mark Approving the Plan of the Church*[7]
3 to L: F. Allegrini, *Consecration of an Altar in S. Marco*
4 to L: F. Chiari, *Translation of the Body of St Mark*[8]

The stucco reliefs between the paintings represent scenes from the *Lives of the Twelve Apostles* and were added by C. Monaldi, P. Pacilli, J. Le Doux, A. Bercari, A. Bergondi and M. A. Slodtz, c.1743-44[9]

Entrance wall: R: monument to Agostino Tofanelli (d. 1834) with bust by A. Stocchi and L: monument to Virginio Bracci (d. 1815) with bust by R. Tuccimei, 1834[10].

RIGHT AISLE
Between 1 and 2 to R: monument to Cardinal Francesco Pisani (d. 1570) and Girolamo Quirino (d. 1571) with an unusual superstructure in the form of a temple façade
2 to R: altarpiece: Louis Cousin, called Luigi Gentile, *Virgin and Child with Sts John the Baptist and Anthony of Padua*
3 to R: altarpiece: C. Maratta: *Adoration of the Magi*, c.1656[11]; wall frescoes: Baldi, L: *St Francis* and R: *St Nicholas of Bari*, c.1653-56, almost totally ruined by damp[12]
Between 3 and 4 to R: monument to Cardinal Christoph Vidman (d. 1660) by C. Fancelli[13]
4 to R: altarpiece: Bernardino Gagliardi, *Pietà*; wall frescoes, R: *St John the Baptist* and L: *Mary Magdalen*
Beyond 4 to R: monument to Francesco Erizzo (d. 1700) by F. Maratta[14]
5th niche: monument to Leonardo Pesaro (d. 1796) by A. d'Este, 1796-97[15]
Before Cappella del SS. Sacramento: monument to Cardinal G. B. Rubino (d. 1707); further: monument to Maria Teresa Gennotte-Merkenfeld (1828) by G. de' Fabris[16]
Chapel to R of choir: Cappella del SS. Sacramento[17]: Casale states that the chapel was restored to the designs of Pietro da Cortona. He affirms that the artist's name occurs in the documents, but it does not do so in those that he quotes; and he attributes to him the two drawings for the chapel which he publishes but which are too weak to be from Cortona's own hand. He gives the date 1661 for the chapel but Del Piazzo[18] gives 1655 as the date of a drawing for the chapel, presum-

ably one of those reproduced by Casale. The attribution of the decoration to Cortona is confirmed by the style and also by the fact that Cortona's nephew, Luca Berrettini, is recorded as being in charge of the work. Moreover, the chapel is attributed to him by Titi[19] and Venuti[20]. The frescoes on the walls are by Guglielmo Cortese, L wall: *Aaron Collecting the Manna in a Vase* and R wall: *Sacrifice of Aaron*, 1653-57[21]. The altar is much earlier in style and is attributed by Venuti[22] convincingly to Orazio Torriani; altarpiece: Melozzo da Forli, *St Mark*, 1469-70[23]

Choir: remodelled and decorated in 1735 by Barigioni, who altered the shape of the last arches in the arcade. The high altar (round a magnificent ancient porphyry bath which contains the relics of St Mark) and the fine marble structure which supports it are ascribed to Barigioni[24]

Apse: Romanelli, *St Mark* (badly damaged)[25]; wall frescoes by Cortese, L: *St Mark's Body Dragged along the Ground* and R: *Martyrdom of St Mark*[26]

Sacristy: tabernacle by Mino da Fiesole with the assistance of Giovanni Dalmata, 1474, which was given by Cardinal Marco Barbo and once stood over the high altar, was moved here in the 17th century[27]. G. Cortese, portrait of Niccolò Sagredo, 1656[28]; Bartolomeo Cavarozzi, *St Ursula and her Companions*, 1608[29]; Ciro Ferri, *Virgin and Child with St Martina*[30]; T. Bigot, *Adoration of the Magi*, c.1634[31]

L of sacristy: monument to the Contessa Gabriella Scaglia di Saluzzo (d. 1796) by G. Gardelli and F. Festa, 1798[32]

LEFT AISLE

Before 4 to L: monument to Cardinal Pietro Basadonna (d. 1684); the statues by Filippo Caracani were being executed in 1686[33]
4 to L: altarpiece: Mola, *St Michael*, 1655-59[34]; walls: G. Cortese, L: *St Vincent Levita* and R:

St Anastasius
Between 3 and 4 to L: monument to Cardinal Luigi Prioli (d. 1720)[35]
3 to L: altarpiece: attributed to Cristofano Allori, *St Dominic Resurrects the Son of Gertrude dei Bubaleschi*[36]
2 to L: Cappella di S. Gregorio Barbarigo/Rezzonico: altar erected in 1765 to the designs of Francesco Sintes[37]. Marble relief by Antonio d'Este, after a design by Canova, *Almsgiving of St Gregory Barbarigo*, 1802[38]
Between 2 and 1 to L: monument to Cardinal Marco Antonio Bragadin (d. 1658) by Alessandro Vitale, with busts and putti by Lazzaro Morelli[39]. Westin[40], however, upholds Titi's attribution to Raggi[41]
1 to L: side walls: C. Maratta, L: *Prudence* and R: *Innocence*.

S. Margherita in Trastevere
Piazza di S. Apollonia, Via della Lungaretta

Rebuilt in 1564 on the site of a 13th century church, and again in 1678-80, to the designs of Carlo Fontana for Cardinal Girolamo Gastaldi, who also contributed to the completion of S. Maria dei Miracoli and S. Maria di Montesanto. The façade and interior are typical of Fontana's severe style, here manifesting itself at a very early date.

INTERIOR

The marbling is painted.
Apse: Fra Umile da Foligno, *St Margaret in Glory*[1]
Choir: the high altar dates from 1728. Altarpiece: copy after G. Brandi, *St Margaret's Vision of the Cross while in Prison*, after 1686
L of high altar: G. Ghezzi, *Martyrdom of St Margaret*[2]
R of high altar: copy after Ghezzi, *Torture of St Margaret*
1 to L: Baciccio, *Immaculate Conception*

133

with Sts Francis and Clare (or *The Blessed Angelina da Marsciano*), c.1685[3].

S. Maria degli Angeli
Piazza delle Repubblica

In 1561, partly at the instigation of a Sicilian priest called Antonio del Duca (uncle of the architect Giacomo del Duca), who was passionately devoted to the worship of angels, Pius IV decided to convert the vast tepidarium that formed the central chamber of the baths of Diocletian into a church to be dedicated to S. Maria degli Angeli and to be served by the Carthusians of S. Croce in Gerusalemme. Such a conversion of a pagan building into a Christian church had been a regular practice in Early Christian times, but had lapsed for many centuries.

The remodelling of the church was placed in the hands of Michelangelo, who converted the building with a minimum of construction. He chose to place the entrance and the high altar on the shorter axis of the complex, leaving the main hall as a vast transept, at each end of which he enclosed a square space to form an entrance vestibule. In what had been the passage to the frigidarium he built a choir for the monks. He placed the high altar, flanked by two columns, between the choir and the body of the church. This arrangement satisfied the demands of the Carthusians for complete seclusion from the laity, a demand which would not have been met by the alternative project of treating the great hall as a nave, since the choir would not have connected directly with the cloister, built over the frigidarium. Later – probably in 1565 when Pius declared the church a titular church – the altar was moved to the end of the choir, which then became open to the church.

The interior was completely transformed in the 18th century. In 1700 and 1746 the two vestibules at the end of the great hall were closed and turned into chapels. In 1727 the bays opening off the hall were closed to provide wall space for the altarpieces from St Peter's, which had been replaced by mosaics, and in 1749 Vanvitelli was commissioned by Benedict XIV to carry out a complete remodelling of the building. It is said that Vanvitelli suggested opening up these chapels again, but the Carthusians refused. To the existing eight ancient granite columns Vanvitelli added eight more (in *scagliola*) in the two bays on the short axis, and over the long axis he erected depressed arches imitating those used by Maderno in the aisles of St Peter's. He also redecorated the circular vestibule and added a very simple façade. This was removed in the restorations of 1909-13 when the present arrangement and a niche – totally unjustified archaeologically – was invented. Vanvitelli's impressive door to the cloister is now within the Museo delle Terme.

INTERIOR
VESTIBULE
R: monument to Carlo Maratta (d. 1713) designed by the artist himself, 1704; bust by Francesco Maratta, before 1708[1]
Chapel to R: Cappella del Crocifisso/Cevoli: altarpiece: Giacomo Rocca, *Crucifixion with St Jerome and Girolamo Cevoli*, 1572-74; vault and lunettes by G. Rocca: *Sibyls, Prophets* and *Angels with the Instruments of the Passion*; *Last Supper* and *Washing of the Feet*; stucco work, including the angels, by Michele Alberti, 1572-74[2]. L wall: monument to Pietro Tenerani (d. 1869). Further: monument to Cardinal Francesco Alciati (d. 1580) by G. B. della Porta
L: Cappella di S. Maria Maddalena: altarpiece: Hendrik van den Broecke, *Noli me tangere*[3]; baptistery font by Vanvitelli[4]. Further: monument to Salvator Rosa (d.

S. Maria degli Angeli

1673), erected by his son, Augusto; bust and putti representing *Painting* and *Poetry* by B. Fioriti[5]. Further: monument to Cardinal Pietro Parisi (d. 1580)

Bay between vestibule and great hall: holy-water stoups by G. B. de' Rossi

R: Houdon, *St Bruno*, 1766[6]

Chapel to L: Cappella di S. Pietro: altarpiece: G. Muziano, *Christ Giving the Keys to St Peter*, c.1585[7]. This and a number of the altarpieces in the church were originally painted for St Peter's and were moved here when they were replaced by copies in mosaic. Side walls: M. Carloni, R: *Sts Peter and Paul* and L: *Liberation of St Peter from Prison*

Above entrance to great hall: F. Trevisani, *Expulsion of Adam and Eve*[8]

GREAT HALL

Pavement designed by Giuseppe Barberi, 1778[9]. Across the right half of this lies the meridian laid out by Francesco Bianchini for Clement XI in 1702.

Right half

1 to R: N. Ricciolini, *Crucifixion of St Peter*, 1728-29[10]

2 to R: P. C. Trémolières after Francesco Vanni, *Fall of Simon Magus*

Clerestory: Niccolò Ricciolini, L of window: *Philosophical Wisdom* and R: *Fear of God*, 1730-34[11]

Chapel at end: Cappella del Beato Niccolò Albergati: built 1746-50. Vault: A. Bicchierai, *Four Church Fathers* and the *Holy Spirit*[12]. Side walls: L: Trevisani, *Baptism by Water*, 1738-39 and R: *Baptism by Desire*, 1740; altarpiece: Ercole Graziani, *The Blessed Nicholas Albergati Refuses the Bishopric*, 1749[13]. Figures of L: *Justice* and R: *Peace* on either side of altar by Ferdinand Pettrich[14]

Clerestory: N. Ricciolini, L of window: *Intellect* and R: *Strength*[15]

1 to L: F. Mancini, *Miracle of St Peter*, copy after G. Baglione

2 to L: Girolamo Muziano, completed after his death by C. Nebbia, *St Jerome Preaching in the Wilderness*, c. 1584-92

R choir chapel: Cappella di S. Giacinto/Litta: decorated by Giovanni Baglione; altarpiece: *Virgin and Child with Sts Raymund and Hyacinth*; L: *St Cecilia and Valerian Crowned by an Angel*; R: *St Francis Receives the Stigmata*; vault: *God the Father*, 1608[16]

Choir: R wall: Romanelli, *Presentation of the Virgin in the Temple*, 1638-42, and Domenichino, *Martyrdom of St Sebastian*, 1625-30[17]. L wall: C. Maratta, *Baptism of Christ*, 1696-98[18], and Cristofano Roncalli, *Death of Ananias and Sapphira*, 1599-1603[19]; apse: D. Seiter, *Virgin in Glory* and medallions of L: *St Anthelmus*; C: *St Bruno*; R: *St Hugh*, 1680-81[20]. Monument to Pius IV (d. 1565) by Alessandro Cioli[21]. Angels and putti surrounding the altarpiece by Bernardino Ludovisi[22]

L choir chapel: Cappella del Salvatore/Catalani: built by Giacomo del Duca, 1572-74; altarpiece: Domenico da Modena, *The Christ Child Adored by Angels*, 1573-74; side walls: R: Giulio Mazzoni, *Scene of Hell*, 1574-75; L: *Pius IV and a Group of Devotees*. Around altarpiece: attributed to Van der Broecke, *Story of Christ*; vault: Van der Broecke, R: *Defeat of the Rebel Angel* and L: *Allegory of Salvation*, 1574-75[23]

Left half

1 to R: P. Bianchi, completed by Gaetano Sardi, *Immaculate Virgin with Sts Gregory Nazianzen, Francis and Anthony of Padua*, 1730-c.35[24]

2 to R: P. Costanzi, *Resurrection of Tabitha*, 1740[25]

Clerestory: N. Ricciolini, L of window: *Piety* and R: *Virgin in Glory*, 1730-34[26]

Chapel at end: Cappella di S. Bruno: *quadratura* and allegorical figures by Domenico Belletti[27]; altarpiece: G. Odazzi to a design by Maratta, *The Virgin Appearing to St Bruno*,

soon after 1700[28]. Side walls: Trevisani, *Baptism by Blood*, 1738-45[29]; vault: A. Procaccini, *Evangelists*, soon after 1700[30], but Negro[31] ascribes them to A. Bicchierai, c.1750
2 to L: P. Subleyras, *Mass of St Basil*, 1743[32]
1 to L: Pompeo Batoni, *Fall of Simon Magus*, 1746-55[33]
Clerestory: N. Ricciolini, L of window: *Practical Wisdom* and: R: *Counsel*[34]
Sacristy/Cappella dell' Epifania: Odazzi, *Rest on the Flight into Egypt*[35]. Off this is the *Sala dei Certosini* with 18th century frescoes and fine stalls. The vault fresco of *St Bruno in Glory* has been ascribed to Odazzi and by Matthiae to Garzi

To the left of the church is a door with the arms of Gregory XIII, who transformed part of the baths into a granary in 1575, the architect being Martino Longhi the Elder[36]. Round the corner in the via Parigi are the arms of Paul V connected with the same project and those of Clement XIII (dated 1764) on the entrance to the oil-store which he made there, apparently designed by Vanvitelli[37].

Also to the left of the church is another door by Pietro Bracci, his only surviving architectural work[38], which originally led to the orphanage founded there by Clement XIII, whose arms it bears.

S. Maria dell'Anima
Via di S. Maria dell'Anima, 66

Built as the German national church in 1431-46 but rebuilt between 1500 and 1523 and consecrated in 1542. It contains important 17th century monuments and frescoes.

INTERIOR
R of main entrance: monument to Archduke Andreas von Austria (d. 1600) by G. van den Vliete
L of main entrance: monument to Cardinal Willem von Enkevoirt (d. 1534), Datary to Hadrian VI, by Giovanni Mangone, 1536-38
1 to R: Cappella di S. Benno: altarpiece: Saraceni, *St Benno Restores the Cathedral Keys to the City of Meissen*, 1617-18[1]
1st pier to R: monument to Jan Nolen (d. 1726), erected 1726
2 to R: Cappella di S. Anna: altarpiece: Giacinto Gimignani, *Virgin and Child with St Anne*, 1640[2]; frescoes of the *Story of Joachim* by Giovanni Francesco Grimaldi, R wall: *An Angel Appears to Joachim in the Desert*; L wall: *Meeting at the Golden Gate*; vault: *Virgin and St Anne in Glory*[3]; R wall: monument to Giovanni Savenier (d. 1638) by Algardi, c.1640[4], and bust of Cardinal Gualtiero Gualtieri (d. 1659) by Ercole Ferrata; L wall: monument to Cardinal Johann Walter Sluse, Secretary of Briefs under Innocent XI (d. 1687), attributed to Domenico Guidi[5]
2nd pier to R: monument to Jean Théodore Jacquet (d. 1715), erected 1737
3 to R: Cappella di S. Marco/Fugger: Giulio Romano's *Holy Family*, now over the high altar, originally stood in this chapel; walls: frescoes by Sicciolante of scenes from the *Life of the Virgin*, R wall: lower: *Presentation in the Temple*; upper: *Dedication*; L wall: lower: *Birth of the Virgin*; upper; *Visitation*; vault: *Assumption*, c.1560-63[6]. Wooden crucifix by Giovanni Montana, 1584
3rd pier to R: monuments to Adraen Vryburgh (d. 1628) by François Duquesnoy[7] and Johann Benedikt Gentilott von Engelsbrunn (d. 1725)
Between 3 and 4 to R: monument to Carolus Micault (d. 1577)
4 to R: Cappella della Pietà: altar built by Ottavio Perini and Antonio Baldi, 1791. Lorenzetti, *Pietà*, 1530-32
End of R aisle: monuments to Nikolaus L'Hoste (d. 1533), Johannes Emerix (d. 1669), Jacob Emerix von Matthys (d. 1696) and

Franz Oranus (d. 1599), erected 1622
Choir: redecorated in 1750-51 by Paolo Posi. Side walls: frescoes by Ludwig Stern, L: *Death of the Virgin*; R: *Birth of the Virgin*[8]; in the niches are allegorical figures of L: *Religion* and R: *Faith* from the monument to Prince Karl Friedrich of Julich-Cleve-Berg. R wall: monument to Hadrian VI (d. 1523) commissioned by Cardinal Enkevoirt, designed by Peruzzi and executed by Angelo di Mariano with a relief of *Adrian VI Entering Rome* by Niccolò Tribolo, c.1524-27[9]; L wall: monument to Prince Karl Friedrich of Julich-Cleve-Berg (d. 1575) by G. van den Vliete, Nicholas Pippe and Pietro della Motta, 1577-79[10]

High altar: by F. G. Mangone, 1542, but altered in the 18th century by the addition of allegorical figures. A new *mensa* was added by Filippo Baldi in 1781. Altarpiece: Giulio Romano, *Holy Family with Sts James, Mark and John the Baptist*, the lower part repainted by C. Saraceni after being damaged in a flood in 1598[11]

Sacristy: built by Paolo Maruscelli, 1636-44[12]; ceiling frescoed by Romanelli, *Assumption*, 1634-38; on walls: G. M. Morandi, *Annunciation and Marriage of the Virgin*, 1682[13]; Gilles Hallet, *Birth of the Virgin*; G. Bonatti, *Annunciation* and *Visitation*; Anton von Maron, *St John Nepomuk Adores the Virgin*, 1782[14]; Theodor van Loon, *Education of the Virgin*, 1628[15]. Vault: stucco decorations by G. A. Fancelli, Matteo Bonarelli and collaborators, 1640-47[16]

End of L aisle: L of side door: monument to the archaeologist Luca Holste (or Holstenius), librarian to Cardinal Francesco Barberini (d. 1661), by Antonio Giorgetti, erected 1663[17]

R of L side door memorial to Pope Clement II (d. 1046) erected in 1613; monument to Count Egone Fürstenberg (d. 1586) by N. Pippe[18]

4 to L: Cappella della Pietà: decorated by F. Salviati; altarpiece: *Deposition with Cardinal Johann Albrecht von Brandenburg*; above: *Resurrection*; semi-dome: *Pentecost*; L wall, upper: *St Maurice*; lower: *St Albert Siculus with Prudence and a She-Devil*; R wall, upper: *St Stephen*; lower: *St John the Almoner with Charity and a Beggar*, 1549-50[19], but have also been dated 1561-63[20]

Between 3 and 4 to L: monument to Johann Baptist Wentzl von Stock and Sternbach (d. 1725)

3 to L: Cappella di S. Barbara: commissioned by Cardinal Willem von Enkevoirt. Decorated by Michiel Coxie; altarpiece: *Trinity with St Barbara and Cardinal Enkevoirt*; scenes from the *Life of St Barbara*; lower L wall: *St Martin of Tours and the Beggar*; above: *St Barbara before the Heathen Judge*; *St Barbara Captured by her Father*; lower R wall: *St Lambertus*; above: *Torture of the Saint*; *Burial of St Barbara*; walls: upper central wall: *Martyrdom of St Barbara*; semi-dome: *Transfiguration*, c.1532-34[21]

3rd pier to L: monuments to Ferdinand van den Eynden (d. 1630) by Duquesnoy, 1633-41[22], Georg Meisel[23] and Olaus Magnus (d. 1557)[24]

Between 2 and 3 to L: monument to Georg Piscator (d. 1625)[25]

2 to L: Cappella di S. Giovanni Nepomuceno: built in 1779 by D. Romagnoli. Frescoes by Ludwig Seitz of scenes from the *Life of St John Nepomuk*, c.1880; altarpiece: *St John Nepomuk and the Blessed John Sarkander* by L. Seitz, 1906

2nd pier to L: monuments to Jodokus Pfingsthorn (d. 1606) and Franz Sacrati (d. 1623)

Between 2 and 1 to L: monument to Anton von Ohms (d. 1843) by M. Nussbaumer, 1844[26]

1 to L: Cappella di S. Lamberto: altarpiece: Carlo Saraceni, *Martyrdom of St Lambert*, 1618[27]; walls frescoed by Jan Miel replacing

137

those commissioned from Pietro Testa; L: *St Lambert Consecrated Bishop*; C: *Death of St Lambert*; R: *St Lambert Baptises New Converts*; apse: *St Lambert in Glory*[28]. R: monument to Gilles van de Vivere (d. 1647) by G. Finelli[29] and L: monument to Lambertus van de Vivere (d. 1619)[30]
1st pier to L: monument to Alexander Paul Maximilian von Bode (d. 1725).

S. Maria Annunziata delle Turchine (destroyed)

The church, which stood in the via Sforza, was founded in 1675 by Camillo Orsini. The façade is shown in Vasi's engraving. The church was secularised in the 19th century and has now disappeared.

S. Maria Antiqua (S. Maria Liberatrice)
Foro Romano

This Early Christian church was remodelled in 1617 by Onorio Longhi for Cardinal Marcello Lante. All his work was removed in a restoration of 1900 in order to reveal the Early Christian frescoes. The façade is recorded in engravings by Falda and Vasi, and the high altar is reproduced from an old photograph in Pugliese and Rigano[1]. See also SS. Annunziata a Tor de' Specchi.

S. Maria in Aquiro
Piazza Capranica

Built by Cardinal Antonio Maria Salviati for the Confraternita degli Orfanelli on the site of an earlier church, from about 1584 onwards, to the designs of Francesco da Volterra, but completed in 1620 after his death by Filippo Breccioli, working under Maderno[1].

The façade, begun in 1620, was designed by Breccioli to be of two almost equally broad storeys with campaniles (his design is known from a drawing) but only the lower storey was built to his design and the upper one was added by P. Camporese the Elder in 1774 with sculptural decoration by F. Lisandroni[2]. The interior was restored for Pius IX by Gaetano Morichini between 1861 and 1866.

INTERIOR
Central nave: frescoed by Cesare Mariani; entrance wall: *Visitation*; piers: *Doctors of the Church* and nave: scenes from the *Life of the Virgin*; R: *Adoration of the Shepherds*; *Pietà*; *Dormition of the Virgin*; L: *Birth of the Virgin*, *Marriage of Mary and Joseph*; *Annunciation*; triumphal arch: *Assumption*; vault: *Four Evangelists*; pendentives: *Sts Joseph*; *Joachim*; *John the Evangelist* and *Zachariah*[3]; stucco angels in the nave by Luigi Fontana
Vestibule: to R: monument to Bishop Blosio Palladio (d. 1550), Secretary of Latin Briefs under Paul III; to L: monument to Giovanni Stefano Roccatagliata (d. 1652)[4]
1 to R: decorated in 1866 by Raffaele Francisco, but now in ruins. L wall: monument to Francesco Rota (d. 1866) by M. Carpi
2 to R: vault: Carlo Gavardini, *St Jerome Emiliani in Glory*
3 to R: Cappella dell'Annunziata/Ferrari: entrance piers: M. Bassetti, *Sts Martha and Mary Magdalen*, *Sts Lucy and Agatha* and *Sts Lawrence and Stephen*[5]. Altarpiece: Cosimo Piazza da Castelfranco, *Annunciation*[6]. Side walls and vault: frescoes by Saraceni, R wall: *Nativity of the Virgin*; lunette: *Assumption*; L wall: *Presentation in the Temple*; lunette: *Death of the Virgin*; vault: *Coronation of the Virgin with Angels Playing Musical Instruments*, 1616-17[7]
R transept: Cappella di S. Benedetto Giuseppe Labre: altarpiece: Vincenzo Pasqualoni, *St Benedict Joseph Labre with the*

Virgin and the Trinity, 1877; side walls: P. Gagliardi, scenes from the *Life of St Benedict Joseph Labre*: R wall: *St Benedict Joseph Labre in Ecstasy during Mass*; L wall: *Death of the Saint*
L of sacristy door: monument to Nicola Modetti by S. Galletti, 1872[8]
High altar: M. de' Rossi's high altar and tribune decorations were replaced by those of Luca Carimini[9]. L of choir: monument to the Marchesa Nicolilla Puccetti by Carlo Chelli, 1868[10]. Further: monument to Maria Belli Modetti by S. Galletti, 1874[11]
L transept: Cappella di S. Girolamo Emiliani: altarpiece: C. Mariani, *St Jerome Emiliani Presents Orphans to the Virgin*; side walls: P. Gagliardi, scenes from the *Life of the Saint*; L wall: *Miracle of the Saint*; R wall: *St Jerome's Miraculous Liberation by the Virgin*
3rd pier to L: monument to Odoardo Paolo, 1619
2 to L: Cappella della Pietà: altarpiece: *Deposition* by an unidentified follower of Caravaggio, 'Maestro Jacopo'; L wall: Trophime Bigot, *Crowning with Thorns*, c.1634-35[12]; R wall: *Mocking of Christ*, Antonio Circignani[13]. L wall: monument to Joseph Sennius by E. Wolff[14]; vault: G. B. Speranza: *Christ Nailed to the Cross*[15]
2nd pier to L: monument to Monsignor Carlo di Montecatini (d. 1699) attributed to L. Ottoni[16]
1 to L: Cappella dell'Angelo Custode: by G. Morichini with marble work by L. Carimini. Altarpiece: I. Zapponi, *Guardian Angel*. Stucco decorations and figures of L: *St Peter* and R: *St Paul* by D. d'Amico[17]
In the institute: Placido Costanzi, *Holy Family* and *Crucifixion*; G. B. Fiammeri, *Immaculate Conception*[18]; F. Cozza, *Finding of Moses*[19]

S. Maria in Aracoeli
Piazza d'Aracoeli

The church, which is traditionally said to stand on the site of the altar at which the sibyl appeared to Augustus and foretold the birth of Christ, was originally built by the Benedictines in the 9th and 10th centuries but was given by Innocent IV in 1250 to the Franciscans, who completely rebuilt it. It was frequently modified later and the steps leading up to it were added in 1348.

INTERIOR

The church was redecorated in honour of the Victory of Lepanto, which was attributed partly to the skills of Marcantonio Colonna and partly to the intervention of the Virgin. A new roof was built by the Flemish woodcarver referred to as 'Flaminio Bolangier' – no doubt Flamen Boulanger – who also worked on the ceiling of S. Giovanni in Laterano, and was decorated by Sicciolante, 1572-75[1]. The ceiling incorporates allegorical allusions to the victory. The upper part of the nave walls was altered in 1686. Rectangular windows were inserted to replace gothic openings and frescoes were added between them. This restoration was unveiled in 1690.

Entrance wall: the wall contains four commemorative inscriptions. The one at the top spreading across the whole nave, with the Barberini bees in a window of blue glass, was erected in 1634-36 by the Senate in honour of Urban VIII and designed by Bernini with allegorical figures of L: *The Church Militant* by S. Speranza and R: *The Church Peaceful* by A. Bolgi[2]. Below to the left is one to Urban's brother, Carlo Barberini, put up on his death in 1630 and also designed by Bernini[3]. Over the door and to the right are tablets recording the Victory of Lepanto, set up in 1586. L of entrance: monument to Bartolomeo Baccinio

(d. 1597); R of entrance: monument to Cardinal Louis d'Albert (d. 1465) by Andrea Bregno, 1466-68[4], and monuments to Giulio Pietropaoli (d. 1588)[5] and Ludovico Grati Margani (d. 1531)

Clerestory: R side: *Adoration of the Shepherds, Visitation, Annunciation, Presentation, Birth of the Virgin, Immaculate Virgin* by Fra Umile da Foligno, 1689; L side: *Adoration of the Magi* and *Flight into Egypt*, Giovanni Odazzi; *Death of the Virgin* and *Assumption*, G. Passeri, 1686[6]; *Coronation of the Virgin* and *Protector of Rome*, Atanasio da Coriano. Below these frescoes is a series of Franciscan Saints by Fra Umile da Foligno. On tribune arch: G. Passeri, *Sibyl* and *Augustus*, c.1686. Against a pier to the left is a fine wooden pulpit bearing the arms of Urban VIII.

1 to R: Cappella di S. Bernardino/Bufalini: frescoes of scenes from the *Life of St Bernardine of Siena* by Pinturicchio, c.1485-86[7]

2 to R: Cappella della Pietà: altarpiece, Marco Pino, *Pietà*, c.1571 (or 1585[8]). The chapel was decorated by Roncalli in 1588-90; L wall: *Descent from the Cross*; lunette: *Veronica Veil*; R wall: *Entombment*; lunette: *Crowning with Thorns*; vault: back: *Christ in the Garden*; R: *Arrest of Christ*; L: *Christ Scourged*; front: *Christ before Pilate*; pendentives: *Four Evangelists*[9]. R wall: busts of L: Paolo Mattei (d. 1592) and R: Tuzia Colonna Mattei attributed to T. della Porta[10]

Between 2 and 3 to R: statue of Gregory XIII by P. P. Olivieri

3 to R: Cappella di S. Girolamo/Delfini: the chapel dates from 1570-71 and was completed in 1573. Altarpiece: G. de' Vecchi, *The Penitent St Jerome in the Desert*. L wall: monument to Gentile Delfini (d. 1559); R wall: monument to Mario Delfini. Pinelli[11] attributes the vault fresco of *Saints in Landscapes* to De' Vecchi, but this is rejected by Heideman[12]. Side walls and lunettes: Ludwig Seitz, L wall: *Sts Anthony of Padua and Alexander of Hales*; lunette: *St Jerome*; R wall: *The Blessed John of Parma and the Blessed John Duns Scotus*; lunette: *St Bernard*, 1875

Between 3 and 4 to R: monument to Michele Corniat (d. 1594[13])

4 to R: Cappella del Crocifisso: R wall: Girolamo Sicciolante da Sermoneta, *Transfiguration*, c.1573-75, formerly in the Armentieri chapel, 2 to L[14]

5 to R: Cappella di S. Matteo/Mattei: built in 1564-65 by Giacomo del Duca, decorated in 1586-89 by Girolamo Muziano and restored in 1680–86 by Tommaso Mattei. Stucco decoration by S. de' Rossi following Muziano's design. Altarpiece: Giovanni Angelo Canini, *Translation of the Holy House of Loreto with St Matthew*[15]; L wall: *St Matthew Raises the Son of the Ethiopian King from the Dead*; lunette: *St Matthew Preaching*; R wall: *Martyrdom of St Matthew*; lunette: *Calling of St Matthew*[16]; L wall: monument to the Marchese Carlo Teodoro Antici (d. 1849) by A. M. Laboureur, 1852[17]

6 to R: Cappella di S. Pietro d'Alcantara/de' Angelis: restored by G. B. Contini[18] and consecrated in 1684; stucco altarpiece by Michele Maglia, *St Peter of Alcantara in Ecstasy before the Crucifixion*[19]; R wall: *Angel Holding a Medallion of St Ranier*; L wall: medallion of *St Stephen*, 1682. Vault: stucco work by Francesco Cavallini, frescoes by Marcantonio Napoletano: *St Peter of Alcantara in Glory* and pendentives: *Allegorical Figures*[20]

7 to R: Cappella di SS. Lorenzo e Diego/Cenci: altarpiece: G. de' Vecchi, *St Didacus Heals a Blind Man*, c.1597-98[21]. Side walls: Vespasiano Strada, R: *St Didacus Exorcises a Demon*; L: *St Didacus Turns Bread into Flowers*, 1600-01; lunettes: Avanzino Nucci, L: *St Didacus Saves a Child Fallen into a Fire*; R: *St Didacus Teaching*, 1597-1610[22]

Between 7 to R and side entrance: monument to Michele Antonio, Marchese di Saluzzo (d. 1528), with bust by Giovanni Antonio Dosio[23]

Bay leading to side door: R wall: monuments to Giuliano Valentini (d. 1615), Luca Antonio Fabi (d. 1613)[24] and Cecchino Bracci (d. 1545) based on a design by Michelangelo; L wall: monument to Cesare Valentini (d. 1607)

8 to R: Cappella di S. Pasquale Baylon: remodelled by Antonio Stanghellini, 1679-86. Altarpiece: Vincenzo Vittoria, *St Pascal Baylon*; side walls: Daniele Seiter, *Two Posthumous Miracles of St Pascal Baylon: St Pascal Heals the Archduke Leopold of Austria*; *St Pascal Heals a Young Girl*, before 1686[25]; stucco putti and garlands by Antonio Stanghellini; putti around window by Francesco Cavallini, 1679-86[26]. Busts of R: Girolamo Buti (d. 1717) and Pietro Buti (d. 1665); L: Pietro Sante Buti (d. 1655)[27] and Lorenzo Buti (d. 1722)

Last pier to R: monument to Alessandro Camerini (d. 1621)

R transept: Cappella di S. Francesco/ Savelli: restored in 1728 by F. Raguzzini for Benedict XIII[28]; altarpiece: F. Trevisani, *St Francis in Ecstasy*, 1729[29]; to R: *St Francis Receives the Stigmata*; to L: M. Caldarani, *The Virgin and Christ Appear to St Francis*; side walls, R: *St Francis Enters the Lateran* and L: *Confirmation of the Franciscan Rule* by Mariano Rossi[30]

10 to R: Cappella di S. Rosa da Viterbo: remodelled by Antonio Stanghellini[31]. Decorated by Pasqualino de' Rossi: R wall: *Preaching of St Rose*; L wall: *St Rose Heals a Blind Boy*; oval in R lunette: *Death of the Saint*; L lunette: *Miracle of Flowers*; vault: *St Rose in Glory*[32]

Chapel to R of high altar: Cappella del Sacramento/Astalli: remodelled by Antonio Gherardi[33], c.1674-75, but the chapel was damaged in the 1882 restoration during which time his frescoes were removed, except for the left lunette: *Death of St Francis Salano*, c.1675[34]. Vault: Giuseppe Ghezzi, *Immaculate Virgin*; pendentives: *St Joseph, St Francis Salano, St Anne* and *St Joachim*[35]. Above the chapel: memorial to Francesco Aldobrandini by G. Rainaldi with sculpture by I. Buzio, 1603[36]

Last pier before R transept: Giovanni de' Vecchi, *Procession with the Miraculous Icon during the Plague of 1590*, 1603-04[37]

High altar: commissioned by the Senate in 1563, modified in 1732 and restored in 1801[38]. On either side of the high altar are statues by Vincenzo da Bassiano of R: *St John of Capestrano* and L: *St Bernardine of Siena*

Choir: vault frescoes by Niccolò Martinelli, *Virgin and Child in Glory*; R wall: *Augustus Sacrifices on an Altar*; L wall: *Augustus and the Sibyl*; over altar: *Birth of the Virgin*; over organ: *Presentation of the Virgin*

Chapel to L of high altar: Cappella di S. Gregorio/Maffei: altarpiece: Vincenzo Milione, *Virgin in Glory with Sts Francis and Gregory*, c. 1771[39]. L wall: monuments to Emilio de' Cavalieri (d. 1602) and Clelia Sannesi (d. 1673); R wall: monuments to Cardinal Jacopo de' Cavalieri (d. 1629) and Federico de' Cavalieri (d. 1637). Above the chapel are memorials to Cardinal Francesco Aldobrandini by G. Rainaldi, 1602, and Cardinal Pietro Aldobrandini attributed to G. Rainaldi

L transept: shrine of St Helena, 1605-24. Damaged by the French in 1797 and restored in 1832-33 by Pietro Holl

Against transept wall: monument to Alessandro Farnese by Roger Bascapé and Vincenzo da Montepulciano, 1596[40]. Below: monument to Alessandro Crivelli (d. 1574) with relief of the *Trinity* attributed to Giacomo del Duca[41] and portrait of the cardinal by M. Venusti[42]. L wall: statue of *Leo X*

by Domenico Aimo, c.1520[43]
Last pier of nave: altare di S. Giovanni da Capestrano: by F. Guidotti, 1682
9 to L: Cappella della Madonna di Loreto: remodelled by Onorio Longhi[44]; altarpiece: Marzio Ganassini, *Madonna di Loreto*; wall frescoes: M. Ganassini, R: *Dormition of the Virgin*; R lunette: *Flight into Egypt*; L: *Birth of the Virgin*; L lunette: *Joseph's Dream*; vault: *Coronation of the Virgin*; *Presentation in the Temple*; *Marriage of the Virgin* and *Annunciation*; pendentives: *Four Sibyls*, c.1620[45]
8 to L: Cappella di S. Margherita da Cortona/Boccapaduli: redecorated in 1729 in honour of St Margaret of Cortona, who had been canonised the previous year. Walls decorated by Marco Benefial, R: *Conversion of St Margaret on Finding her Lover Dead*; L: *Death of St Margaret*, 1729-32[46]. Altarpiece: Giuseppe Sales, *St Margaret in Prayer*, 1827.
7 to L: Cappella di S. Michele Arcangelo/Mancini/Clarelli: redecorated c.1670-71 by Carlo Rainaldi for Cardinal Francesco Maria Mancini (d. 1672). Rainaldi remodelled the left wall monument to Faustina Mancini (d. 1544) from which he reused the obelisk and added the surrounding architectural setting. The putti were carved by Francesco Brunetti. The right wall monument, originally by Rainaldi for Cardinal Mancini, was totally removed when the Cavalier Luigi Marini acquired the chapel in 1822, after which time the chapel was rededicated to St Michael and a new altarpiece inserted. A new monument by Francesco and Alessandro Laboureur was installed for Marini's wife Settimia Maffei (d. 1823) and their son Pietro, c.1823. The chapel was again refurbished by Marini's son from his second marriage to Barbara Clarelli – another Pietro. On her death in 1870 Pietro replaced the portrait of Faustina Manchini with that of his mother and added a new inscription[47]. Altarpiece: *St Michael Vanquishing Lucifer*, Giovanni Silvagni, 1851[48]. Vault: stucco work executed by G. B. Buoncuore[49]
6 to L: Cappella dell'Ascensione/Orsini: altar by Martino Longhi the Elder, 1582-83; altarpiece: G. Muziano, *Ascension*; L wall: monument to Camillo Pardi Orsini (d. 1553); R wall: monument to Vittoria della Tolfa (d. 1586) attributed to Martino Longhi the Elder. Frescoes by Niccolò Martinelli; side walls: *Allegorical Figures*; R lunette: *Ascension*; L lunette: *St Paul Preaching*, 1582-84[50]
5 to L: Cappella di S. Paolo/della Valle: altarpiece: G. Muziano, *St Paul*, 1582-83; frescoes by Roncalli, L wall: *St Paul Preaching in Athens*; lunette: *Conversion of St Paul*; R wall: *Martyrdom of St Paul*; lunette: *Baptism of St Paul*; L of altar: *St John the Baptist*; R of altar: *St Nicholas*, c.1584-86; L wall: monument to Filippo della Valle (d. 1494)[51]
4 to L: Cappella di S. Anna/Cesarini: remodelled by Domenico Gregorini in 1743[52]. Altarpiece: F. Trevisani, *Holy Family and St Anne with the Blessed Seraphina Sforza*, c.1730[53]; L wall: F. Bertosi, *The Blessed Andrew Conti Exorcises a Demon*
3 to L: Cappella di S. Antonio da Padova: built by Giacomo della Porta, 1572; altarpiece: Benozzo Gozzoli, *St Anthony of Padua with Two Donors*; vault: N. Martinelli, *Christ Seated in Heaven*; pendentives: *The Blessed Ludovica Albertoni, St Frances of Rome, St Agnes and St Cecilia*, c.1573; walls attributed to Charles Mellin: R: *The Ass of Rimini Kneeling before the Host*; L: *St Anthony Healing the Leg of the Irascible Son*[54]
Between 2 and 3 to L: statue of *Paul III* by Guglielmo della Porta
1 to L: Cappella dell'Immacolata Concezione/Serlupi: decorated by Francesco Pichi; L wall: *Antithesis between Eve and the Virgin*; lunette: *The Virgin as the Woman of the Apocalypse*; R wall: *Antithesis between Adam and Eve and Christ and the Virgin*;

lunette: *Adoration of the Virgin*; vault: *Solomon Receiving the Queen of Sheba*; *Solomon with his Bride*; *Esther before Ahasuerus*; *Bathsheba Pleading with David to Proclaim her son Solomon as his Successor*, 1551-54[55]
Entrance wall: above left door: Paolo Mattei, *Martyrdom of the Blessed John of Prado*.

S. Maria in Aventino *see* S. Maria del Priorato
Piazza dei Cavalieri di Malta

S. Maria in Campitelli
Piazza di Campitelli, 8-10

A small church was built on this site by Paul V in 1619 but in 1657 Alexander VII approved the transfer of a holy image of the Virgin housed in the nearby church of S. Maria in Portico (now destroyed) and said to have been responsible for the cessation of the plague the previous year. At the same time it was agreed that the church should be extended or rebuilt. Carlo Rainaldi was chosen as the architect and at first produced a series of designs on an oval ground plan, but these were abandoned in favour of the one actually built, which consists of a cross with nearly equal arms to which is added a square choir with an apse. The building was not begun till 1663. By this time Giovanni Antonio de' Rossi had been appointed joint architect with Rainaldi, but it does not seem likely that he exercised much influence on the design of the church as a whole. The façade and sanctuary were largely completed by the time of Alexander VII's death in 1667 and the icon was installed in October. The nave was completed in 1674.

Wittkower has pointed out that the plan is derived from northern Italian models, such as Magenta's S. Salvatore at Bologna, but that Rainaldi translated it into Roman terms by the use of giant free-standing columns which break forward over the entablature to an almost uncomfortable extent. The most successful feature of the interior is the dramatic effect of the brilliantly lit dome over the choir – not, as was normal, over the crossing – as the climax to the church. The façade has a Baroque liveliness in its free treatment of the wall with inset columns and broken entablatures and pediments, but the movement is disjointed compared to the work of Borromini or Cortona. A feature peculiar to Rainaldi is the emphasis on the aedicules which dominate the centre of the design on both storeys.

INTERIOR
Restored in 1824 by Andrea Pozzi, who added the stucco decoration in the dome[1].
Passage to R of entrance: L wall: monument to Luisa de Brinder Kriegelstein (d. 1851) by Pietro Tenerani[2]
1 to R: Sebastiano Conca, *St Michael*, 1735[3]
2 to R: Cappella di S. Anna/Barsotti/Conti: altarpiece: Luca Giordano, *Sts Anne and Joachim with the Virgin*, 1685[4]; vault: attributed to M. Ricciolini, *St Anne in Glory*; angels by Lorenzo Ottoni (R) and Michele Maglia (L)[5]
Before choir: monument to Cardinal Bartolomeo Pacca (d. 1844) by Ferdinand Pettrich, 1862[6]
High altar[7]: Spagnesi[8] has shown that De' Rossi was responsible for the general design of the altar in collaboration with G. P. Schor, though Rainaldi may have given some indication of what was wanted. Melchiorre Caffà made the wax model on De' Rossi's instructions and Ercole Ferrata was responsible for modelling the angels[9]
Choir: L wall: Baciccio, *Birth of the Baptist*, c.1698[10]
3 to L: Cappella di S. Paolo/Capizucchi:

S. Maria in Campo Marzio

Piazza di Campo Marzio, 45

Attached to a Benedictine convent of which the origin goes back at least to the 10th century. The existing church was begun in 1681 and finished in 1685[1], though the charming and unusual courtyard in front of it, one side of which contains a loggia balancing the portico of the church, may have been begun earlier in the century. The architect of the church was Giovanni Antonio de' Rossi, whose name appears in the documents at the relevant period. The church is open for Sunday morning Mass.

architecture by Mattia de' Rossi, 1685, who also designed the monument to Cardinal Raimondo Capizucchi, Master of the Apostolic Palace under Innocent XI (D. 1691)[11]; altarpiece: Lodovico Gimignani, *Conversion of St Paul*, before 1686[12]; vault: Michelangelo Ricciolini, *St Paul in Glory*; putti over the chapel, Filippo Carcani[13]

2 to L: Cappella di S. Giovanni Battista/Altieri: decorated by G. B. Contini, commissioned in 1692 and completed in 1697[14]; altarpiece: Marcello Sozzi, *Virgin and Child with Sts John Leonardi and John the Baptist*, 1860; the two angels on either side of the altar are by Giuseppe Mazzuoli; vault: L. Gimignani, *St John the Baptist in Glory*

1 to L: Cappella Albertoni/Altieri[15]: decorated by Sebastiano Cipriani, completed 1710; altarpiece: L. Ottoni, *The Blessed Ludovica Albertoni's Vision of the Holy Family while Distributing Bread to the Poor*, 1702-08; vault fresco: Giuseppe Passeri, *Assumption*, c.1702[16]; apse: *Angels on Clouds*, c.1710[17]. L wall: monument to Prince Angelo Altieri (d. 1706), with bust and left putto by G. Mazzuoli, right putto by Andrea Fucigna; above: putto by Giuseppe Napolini. R wall: monument to Vittoria Altieri (d. 1687) with bust and putti by G. A. Lavaggi; above: putti by G. Raffaelli

Passage to L of entrance: R wall: monument to Cardinal Giuseppe Bofondi (d. 1867) by Francesco Fabi Altini

Sacristy: R. Vanni, *Immaculate Conception*[18].

S. Maria in Campo Carleo
(destroyed)

The church, which stood since early times near the Forum of Trajan, was restored by Clement XIII in 1727. He presumably added the simple façade shown by Vasi. The church was pulled down in 1862.

INTERIOR

Dome: of unusual form, a type with flattened sides and ends, also used by De' Rossi in the Cappella delle Grazie at S. Rocco, but not found in the work of any other major Roman architect of the period

1 to R: altarpiece attributed to L. Baldi, *Birth of the Virgin*

R transept: P. Marini, altarpiece: *Baptism of Christ*; L wall: *Birth of the Baptist*; R wall: *Beheading of the Baptist*, c.1700[2]

3 to R: altarpiece: L. Garzi, *St Gregory Nazianzen*, 1686[3]. An oratory dedicated to this saint stood on this site from very early times

Apse: an early example of the type of design which consists of two columns attached to the walls of the apse, without any central architectural element (cf. Fontana at SS. Apostoli); in the half-dome: frescoes by Placido Costanzi, R: *St John the Baptist*; C: *Immaculate Virgin*; L: *Isaiah*, 1730[4]. High altar by Tommaso Mattei, 1703-08; altar-front by Clemente Orlandi, 1752-53

3 to L: crucifix overaltar by Algardi[5]. Side walls: Angelo Soccorsi, L: *Noli me tangere* and R: *The Penitent Magdalen*[6]

L transept: decorated by L. Baldi, altarpiece:

Death of St Benedict; L wall: *St Benedict Writing his Rule*; R wall: *Virgin and Child with St Gertrude (Scholastica?) and other Benedictine Nuns*, 1686-88
1 to L: altarpiece: Baccio Ciarpi, *Pietà*[7].

S. Maria in Camposanto
Piazza dei Protomartiri Cristiani, Vaticano

The church, which was later associated with a German confraternity, was rebuilt from 1476. Work progressed slowly; the high altar was consecrated in 1500 and the Swiss altar in 1517. Restored in 1972-74.

INTERIOR
Former Swiss Chapel: detached frescoes by Polidoro da Caravaggio: L of window: *Arrival of the Magi*; R of Window: *Adoration of the Magi*; below: *Scenes from Christ's Passion*. R wall: paintings by Liborio Marmorelli of scenes from the *Life of Old Testament Joseph*, 1780
Pier to L of high altar: monument to Laurentius Rues (d. 1690). Rues produced the design of his tomb and commissioned Giovanni Battista Giorgi to execute it, 1689
Pier to R of high altar: monument to Georg Meisel (d. 1710). Monument to Jacobus de' Hase (d. 1634) with putto on top of the inscription by F. Duquesnoy[2].

S. Maria dei Cappuccini *see* S. Maria della Concezione
Via Vittoria Veneto

S. Maria del Carmelo *see* S. Egidio
Via della Scala

S. Maria del Carmine
Piazza Costaguti

The chapel is now secularised but the porch, composed of Tuscan columns, stands against the back of the Palazzo Costaguti and is dated 1759. It is a variant of Cortona's porch of S. Maria della Pace.

S. Maria del Carmine alle Tre Cannelle
Via del Carmine, 3

Built by Cardinal Odoardo Farnese for the Congregazione di S. Maria del Carmine between 1605 and 1623. Its interior was transformed by Giacomo Ciolli, 1724-33, and damaged by fire in 1772. The church was restored in 1862 by V. Martinucci. The façade was added in 1750 to the designs of Michelangelo Specchi and is an example of the increasing severity of style which became prominent in the 18th century.

INTERIOR
High altar: built by G. Ciolli
L of high altar: Giovanni Pirri, *St Simon Stock Receives the Scapular from the Virgin*, 1776[1]

Within the church is a banner painted by C. Giaquinto, depicting on one side *Elijah on Mount Carmel* and on the other *St Simon Stock Receives the Scapular from the Virgin*, 1729-30[2].
In the oratory: G. Celio, *Virgin and Child*[3].

S. Maria della Concezione (Cappuccini)
Via Vittorio Veneto, 25

Founded for the Capuchins by Cardinal Antonio Barberini, brother of Urban VIII, in 1626 and built to an austere design by

Antonio Casone; consecrated in 1636. In 1890 the cutting of the new street, now the via Vittorio Veneto, involved the removal of the double flight of curved steps in front of the church and the destruction of the square in front of it. The façade was modified in 1925.

INTERIOR
Vault of nave: L. Coccetti, *Assumption and Coronation of the Virgin*, 1796[1]
1 to R: Cappella di S. Michele: altarpiece: Guido Reni, *St Michael*, c.1635[2]; L wall: Honthorst, *Mocking of Christ*, c.1614[3]
2 to R: Cappella della Trasfigurazione: altarpiece: Mario Balassi, *Transfiguration*; L wall: Lanfranco, *Adoration of the Shepherds*, 1631[4]
3 to R: Cappella di S. Francesco: altarpiece: donated by Domenichino after his recovery from an illness, *St Francis Receiving the Stigmata*, 1628-30[5]; R wall: Luigi da Crema, *St Crispin of Viterbo Discusses Theology with Raimondo Berolati and Sebastiano Maria Correa*, 1806[6]
4 to R: Cappella di Gesù: altarpiece: Baccio Ciarpi, *Agony in the Garden*, 1632[7]; R wall: P. Herzog, *Christ Crowns St Veronica Giuliani*, 1853. L wall: monument to Giovanni and Costanza Serafini by Antonio Bisetti, 1855
5 to R: Cappella di S. Antonio da Padova: wooden altar designed by Andrea Sacchi and carved by Alessandro Nave, 1632; altarpiece: Sacchi, *St Anthony of Padua Revives a Dead Man*, 1631-33[8]. On the floor is the tomb of the sculptor Camillo Rusconi (d. 1728)
To R of choir: monument to Cardinal Jan Freiherr von Goessen (d. 1696) by F. M. Laboureur, 1824[9]
High altar: designed by Michele da Bergamo, altarpiece: copy of Lanfranco's destroyed *Immaculate Virgin*
To L of choir: monument to Alexander Sobieski (d. 1714) by C. Rusconi, 1727-28[10]
5 to L: Cappella di S. Bonaventura: wooden altar designed by A. Sacchi and carved by A. Nave, 1632; altarpiece: A. Sacchi with the assistance of F. Gagliardi, *The Virgin and Child Appear to St Bonaventure*, 1634-36[11]
3 to L: Cappella della Pietà: altarpiece: Andrea Camassei, *Pietà* 1635[12]; L wall; G. Muziano, *St Francis Receives the Stigmata*[13]
2 to L: Cappella di S. Felice da Cantalice: altarpiece: Alessandro Turchi, *St Felix of Cantalice Worshipping the Christ Child*; R wall: Fra Semplice da Verona, *St Felix Heals a Sick Man*, 1625-c.26[14]; L wall: Luigi da Crema, *St Felix Restores the Sight of a Blind Boy*, c.1810
1 to L: Cappella di S. Paolo: wooden altar carved by Pietro Paolo Giorgetti[15]; altarpiece: Cortona, *St Paul's Sight Restored by Ananias*, 1631-32[16]
Choir: altarpiece: Terenzio Terenzi, *Virgin in Glory with Sts Francis, Bonaventure, Michael and Margaret and Members of the Peretti Family*[17]. Antonio Alberti, *Cardinal Antonio Barberini*, 1633[18]; Sicciolante, *Annunciation*[19]; Lionello Spada, *St John the Evangelist*[20]; studio of Reni, *St Matthew*[21]; M. Pino, *Noli me tangere*[22]
Sacristy: Caravaggio, *St Francis in Prayer*[23]
To R of choir: Oratorio di Urbino VIII: G. B. Maini, *Immaculate Virgin*[24]; in the corridor are the rooms of the Blessed Crispin, decorated by Luigi da Crema[25], and of St. Felix of Cantalice

Below the church (entrance from the steps on the right) is the cemetery composed of the bones of the Capuchins.

S. Maria della Consolazione
Piazza della Consolazione, 84

The church was begun, probably about 1470, to commemorate a miracle worked by the image of the Virgin below the Tarpeian Rock, and was attached to a hospital. Various chapels were added in the mid 16th century and the choir was built in 1581-85 to the designs of Giacomo della Porta. The architect in charge of the actual building was Martino Longhi the Elder. He was probably responsible for the design of the nave, which was rebuilt in the following years, incorporating some of the earlier chapels. He also built the lower storey of the façade. The upper storey was not built till 1828 by Pasquale Belli, who may have been working after a drawing by Giuseppe Valadier[1]. The addition has been made with such tact that it suggests that Valadier or Belli may have known of a drawing by Longhi. The door on the façade may be by Francesco da Volterra, who is recorded as working at the Consolazione just after Longhi's death in 1591.

INTERIOR

Three aisles separated by broad and open arches with light decoration typical of Longhi.

1 to R: Cappella Mattei: decorated by Taddeo Zuccaro, altarpiece: *The Virgin and Holy Women at the Foot of the Cross*; altar wall: *Sibyls and Prophets*; L wall: *Flagellation*; lunette: *Christ before Pilate*; R wall: *Ecce Homo*; vault: *Last Supper*, *Washing of the Feet*, *Agony in the Garden*, *Betrayal of Christ*; pendentives: *Evangelists*, 1553-56[2]

2 to R: Cappella Pelucchi: altarpiece: L. Agresti, *Virgin Enthroned with Christ, Sts Joseph and Anne, and Andrea Pelucchi*, 1575; L wall: Agresti, *Martyrdom of St Andrew*, 1570-77; R wall: Cesare Nebbia, *Calling of St Peter*, 1578-c.80[3]. L wall: monument to Andrea Pelucchi (d. 1575) and R wall: Lucrezia dei Conti Pierleoni (d. 1582)

3 to R: Cappella degli Affidati/dei Pastori: built c.1632 by A. Ferreri and decorated by Giovanni Baglione; altarpiece: *Adoration of the Magi*; side walls: R: *Adoration of the Shepherds*; L: *Presentation in the Temple*[4]

Choir: the diamond-shaped coffering of the half-dome over the apse, based on that of the Temple of Venus in the Forum, is ascribed to Martino Longhi the Elder. The high altar, by Longhi and built by G. B. Montano, holds Antoniazzo's *Virgin and Child*, 1465-70[5]

Side walls: C. Roncalli, R: *Birth of the Virgin* and L: *Assumption*[6]

Chapel at end of L aisle: second half of the 19th century, but still in a semi-Baroque, semi-classical style by Augusto Carnevali

5 to L: Cappella dei Vignaroli: decorated by Antonio Circignani; entrance pillars: *Sts Peter and Paul*; altarpiece: *Virgin and St John the Baptist*; R wall: *Marriage at Cana*; lunette: *Presentation of Christ in the Temple*; L wall: *Raising of Lazarus*; lunette: *Massacre of the Innocents*[7]

4 to L: Cappella dei Pescatori: altar attributed to Martino Longhi the Elder and decorated by Marzio Ganassini; altarpiece: *St Andrew*; L wall: *Martyrdom of St Peter*; lunette: *St Peter before the Emperor*; R wall: *Martyrdom of St Andrew*; lunette: *Judgement of St Andrew*, c.1597[8]

3 to L: Cappella dei Garzoni degli Osti: decorated by Francesco Nappi, c.1600-10; altarpiece: *Assumption*; L wall: *Adoration of the Magi*; lunette: *Dormition of the Virgin*; R wall: *Adoration of the Shepherds*; lunette: *Birth of the Virgin*; vault: *Presentation*; *Visitation*; *Marriage of the Virgin*; *Annunciation*[9]

2 to L: Cappella Sacchi: altarpiece: Durante Alberti, *St Francis Receives the Stigmata*[10]

1 to L: Cappella Dondoli: chapel attributed by Marcucci to Francesco da Volterra. Altarpiece: relief of *Mystic Marriage of St Catherine of Alexandria* by Raffaello da Montelupo[11].

S. Maria in Cosmedin
Piazza della Bocca della Verità

Built on the site of a temple of Ceres, the present church dates mainly from the 8th-13th centuries.

In 1715 the church was restored for Clement XI and on his death was taken over by his nephew Cardinal Annibale Albani. The restoration included decorating the upper nave walls with stucco, the addition of a winter choir and the restoration of the crypt. The façade was remodelled by G. Sardi in 1718[1], but this work, together with most of the interior decoration, was removed in 1899 when the church was restored to its medieval state. The façade is recorded in engravings and old photographs[2].

INTERIOR
Off R aisle: winter choir built by Tommaso Maffei and decorated with frescoes by Giuseppe Chiari to designs by C. Maratta, now in ruins
1 to L: the baptistery stucco decoration dates from the restoration of Cardinal Albani

S. Maria di Costantinopli *see* S. Maria d'Itria
Via del Tritone, 79

S. Maria in Domnica
Via della Navicella

An ancient church, first mentioned in the 8th century. Partly rebuilt under Innocent VIII (1484-93) and restored in 1513-14 on the orders of Cardinal Giovanni de' Medici, later Pope Leo X, whose titular church it was. During this restoration the façade was erected to designs by Andrea Sansovino and the coffered vault built. Later restored by F. Raguzzini for Benedict XIII, 1725.

S. Maria delle Grazie alle Fornaci
Piazza di S. Maria alle Fornaci, Via delle Fornaci

Founded in 1552 by the Università dei Fornaciari (Guild of Brickmakers) who had their kilns in this district. The existing church was begun in 1694 but was not completed till much later, by which time it had been handed over by Clement XI to the Trinitarians in 1721. According to a not very clear reference in De' Rossi the architect appears to have been Francesco Bufalini. As shown in the foundation medal of 1694 the façade of the church would have presented an interesting continuation of Seicento ideas (the dome and flanking towers of S. Agnese in Agone and the porch of S. Maria della Pace) but, as built in 1727 by Francesco Multo, it is an unfortunate adaptation of Borrominesque motifs. This is particularly obvious in the pediment, a version both mean and lumpish[1] of the one used in the Oratory.

INTERIOR
The interior, which was still being finished in 1750[2], is a typical but pedestrian example of the vernacular architecture of the period. The marbling is painted.
1 to R: Cappella di S. Giovanni Nepomuceno: Domenico Scaramuccia, scenes from the *Life of St John Nepomuk* based on a sketch by G. B. Maini. Altarpiece: *St John Nepomuk Adores the Cross*; R wall: *St John Nepomuk Confronts King Wenceslaus IV*; L wall: *The Saint Refuses to Break the Silence of Confession*[3]. Above altar: stucco angels and cherubs by Maini[4]
2 to R: Cappella della SS. Trinità: altarpiece: O. Avellino, *Sts Felix of Valois and John of Matha Adore the Trinity*, 1737[5]
3 to R: Cappella di S. Giovanni de' Matha: built by Andrea Molto, 1726. Altarpiece: Francesco Fusio, *Virgin and Child with St*

John of Matha and Liberated Slaves[6]
High altar: 1724-26, modified in 1958. Altarpiece: G. Hallet, *Virgin and Child*
3 to L: Cappella Asnaghi (1713): altarpiece: Giuseppe Chiari, *Holy Family with St John the Baptist*, c.1726-27[7]; dome fresco: Pietro de' Pietri, *Assumption*, 1712-c.1716[8]; lunettes: Marco Benefial, R: *Beheading of the Baptist*; L: *Preaching of the Baptist*[9]; below, R: N. Ricciolini, *Adoration of the Shepherds*[10] and L: P. Bianchi, *Rest on the Flight into Egypt*[11]
1 to L: Cappella del Crocifisso: completed in 1747; altarpiece: O. Vicinelli, *Crucifixion with the Virgin, Mary Magdalen and St John*.

S. Maria delle Grazie a Porta Angelica (destroyed)

The church, which stood near the Porta Angelica, was pulled down early in the 20th century. It was built in 1588 but rebuilt in 1618 at the expense of Cardinal Lante. The façade, shown in an engraving by Vasi, was like that of S. Sebastiano, with an open three-bay loggia below and a closed upper storey of equal width.

S. Maria di Grottapinta
Via di Grottapinta, 21

A small church, which was in the gift of the Orsini, now secularised and used as a store. The façade, of extreme severity, has a lower storey with rather fine Ionic pilasters and above it an attic with Tuscan pilaster bands – perhaps an economy on a projected Corinthian order (cf. S. Giuseppe a Capo le Case).

S. Maria d'Itria
Via del Tritone, 80

The original church, which belonged to a Sicilian and Aragonese confraternity, was built in 1596. It was desecrated by the French, but then rebuilt to a plan by Francesco Manno and consecrated in 1817. It was redecorated in 1840 under the direction of Biagio Lipari.

INTERIOR
2 to R: altarpiece: Natale Carta, *St Rosalyn*, 1841[1]; Giovanni Valesio, *St Rosalyn with Two Angels*

S. Maria delle Lauretane *see* S. Maria di Loreto
Via di S. Giovanni in Laterano, 33

S. Maria Liberatrice *see* S. Maria Antiqua

S. Maria di Loreto
Via di S. Giovanni in Laterano, 33

The monastery was pulled down in the late 19th century, leaving only the façade of the church, attributed to Giuseppe Sardi.

S. Maria di Loreto
Piazza della Madonna di Loreto, 26

The church was begun in 1507 for the Università dei Fornari by Antonio Sangallo the Younger, who constructed the building up to the bottom of the drum of the dome. After a long interruption it was completed by Giacomo del Duca, who built the campanile, 1525, and the dome and added the two side doors between 1573 and 1577[1]. In the doors and the windows he invented a number of variations on themes by his master Michelangelo (with whom he had collaborated on the Porta Pia) which were to influence Borromini[2]. In the lantern he created a brilliant but fantastic structure which deeply shocked his successors and was never imitated.

INTERIOR
The drum of the dome was frescoed with scenes from the *Life of the Virgin* by C. Mariani: *Annunciation*; *Adoration of the Shepherds*; *Flight into Egypt* and *Pietà*; stuccoes by D. d'Amico, 1870-73[3]
Above entrance: lunette: C. Mariani, *Translation of the Holy House of Loreto*
Over side entrance: organ originally by L. Blasi and carved organ case by G. B. Montano
1 to R: Cappella di S. Caterina: mosaic decoration by Paolo Rossetti; apse: *St Catherine*; R: *St Francis* and L: *St Mary Magdalen*, 1594[4]
2 to R: Cappella dei Re Magi/Marzetti: frescoes and stucco by Niccolò Circignani; altarpiece: *Adoration of the Magi*; to L: *St Peter*; to R: *St Paul*; apse: L: *Angel of the Annunciation*; R: *Virgin*; C: *Trinity*, 1585[5]
Choir: decorated in 1628-30 by G. de' Vecchi. The frescoes, L: *Birth of the Virgin* and R: *Death of the Virgin*, are by Giuseppe Cesari, 1629[6]. In the first niches are figures of angels by Stefano Maderno, 1628-29[7], and in those nearer the altar of R: *St Cecilia* by Giuliano Finelli, 1629-33[8], and L: *St Susanna* by François Duquesnoy, 1630[9]. The latter was originally intended to be in the niche on the right, where she would have looked down onto the altar. On either side of altar, R: *St Flavia Domitilla* by Domenico de' Rossi, 1629, and L: *St Agnes* by Pompeo Ferrucci, 1630[10]. Duquesnoy's *St Susanna* was long admired as the embodiment of a classical ideal, as opposed to the Baroque of Bernini
Sacristy: built by L. Carimini, 1871-73[11]; Pietro Tedeschi, *Sacred Heart*, 1796; Faustina Concioli, *Virgin and Child with Sts Anthony of Padua, Catherine of Alexandria and Onuphrius*, 1806[12]
2 to L: Cappella del Crocifisso: decorated by C. Mariani, R: *Agony in the Garden*; C: *Risen Christ*; L: *Three Maries at the Empty Tomb*; stuccoes designed by L. Carimini
1 to L: Cappella del Sacro Cuore: decorated by Pietro (Filippo?) Tedeschi; altarpiece: *St Charles Borromeo Distributes the Blessed Sacrament*; apse: R: *St Andrew* and L: *St John the Baptist*, 1795.

S. Maria Liberatrice *see* S. Maria Antiqua
Foro Romano

S. Maria della Luce
Via della Luce, 68

The church was originally called S. Salvatore in Corte. In 1595 it was made a parish church and in the late 17th century it was served by the Minims. In 1730 a miraculous figure of the Virgin in a nearby chapel was transferred to the church and its dedication changed to S. Maria della Luce. Soon after this date the church was rebuilt and only the Romanesque apse and campanile survive from the earlier building. The façade was never completed.

The documents show that building was taking place in the years 1738-41 and various altars were executed in the years 1752-54, which suggests that building probably continued till about 1750. In 1777 Giuseppe Vasi wrote that the church was not yet finished, but he was no doubt referring to the decoration, or to the absence of the façade.

Roisecco and Melchiorri both name Valvassori as the architect and in the absence of other evidence their attribution must be accepted; but if it is correct the severe rectilinear planning of the church and the use of a flat trabeation over the openings to the side chapels (cf. Gregorini and Passalacqua at S.

Croce in Gerusalemme) prove that Valvassori was a more classical architect than one would have supposed from the works securely ascribed to him, such as the remodelling of the Palazzo Doria-Pamphili on the Corso.

The church is unusual in plan, having an extra pair of transepts – smaller than the main transepts – next to the high altar. This might possibly have been dictated by the necessity of using the foundations of the old church.

INTERIOR
The almost neoclassical character of the decoration can be explained by the fact that it was mainly carried out from 1768 onwards.
2 to R: Giovanni Conca, *Death of St Joseph*, 1754[1]
3 to R: C. Labruzzi, *Virgin with Sts Anne and Joachim*, 1753
High altar: designed by Nicola Lorenzo Piccioni, 1768[2]
Apse: Sebastiano Conca, fresco of *God the Father*, before 1763; door of tabernacle: *Christ the Saviour* [3]; fresco to L of high altar: Onofrio Avellino, *St Francis of Paola*, c.1729[4]
2 to L: Giovanni Conca, *Sts Francis of Paola, Francis of Sales and Jane of Valois*, 1752[5].

S. Maria Maddalena
Via della Maddalena

There has been a church on this site since the 15th century. In 1585 it was granted to Camillus de' Lellis (beatified 1742, canonised 1746), founder of the Ministri degli Infermi. In 1673 a new church was begun to the designs of Carlo Fontana, but only the left transept chapel was built. In 1680 the Palermitan architect, Paolo Amato, also produced a design for the church, but this does not seem to have been followed. There was an interruption till the 1690's, when work was taken up again with G. A. de' Rossi in charge. He built the apse, right transept and the dome, but died in 1695 and the remainder of the church was built by Carlo Quadri. The elongated octagonal nave, which fits awkwardly onto the chancel and crossing, is not to be found in De' Rossi's churches, but the unusual manner in which the main arches cut into the entablature has a parallel in an early work, S. Maria in Publicolis. The lower part of the façade was built during the same campaign, but the decoration was not finished till about 1735[1]. The early guides attribute this decoration to Giuseppe Sardi, but Mallory has argued convincingly that this is stylistically impossible. She further points out that the coverings of the windows and niches and the 'pediment' which covers the whole façade – some of the most fantastic variations on Borrominesque models to be found in Rome – are very close in character to the organ gallery over the entrance door, which has recently been ascribed to Emanuele Rodriguez[2]. The church was consecrated in 1727.

On the façade, upper R: *St Martha* and L: *St Mary Magdalen* by Filippo Canarte; lower R: *St Camillus* and L: *St Philip Neri* by Paolo Campana.

INTERIOR
The interior of the church was simply decorated with stucco figures in niches and the walls were devoid of marbling, but between 1753 and 1758 it was transformed by a series of frescoes, rich marbling and stucco decorations.

The magnificent gilded choir above the entrance with figures of *Charity*, *Hope*, *Faith* and *Religion* is by Domenico Barbiani, 1729-32. Organ by Johann Conrad Werle, completed 1735[3].

The nave vault was frescoed by M. A. Cerruti: *Resurrection of Lazarus with Sts Mary Magdalen, Camillus and other Saints*, and scenes from the *Life of St Mary*

S. Maria Maddalena

Magdalen, 1730-32[4].
Dome fresco: *Trinity in Glory with Sts Mary Magdalen, Camillus de Lellis, Teresa, Philip Neri, Anthony of Padua and Cajetan* and pendentives of *Four Church Fathers* by Etienne Parrocel, 1739. On the piers of the nave are niches with six allegorical figures connected with Confession. Those on the right are by Paolo Morelli: 1 R: *Shame*; 2 R: *Faith*; 3 R: *Remorse*; on the left: 3 L: Giuseppe Raffaelli, *Simplicity*; 2 L: P. Morelli, *Secrecy*; 1 L: C. Monaldi, *Humility*[5]. The confessionals are by Joseph Palma, 1762
1 to R: Cappella di S. Francesco di Paola: marble and stucco decoration designed by Antonio Cipolla, 1837-67. Altarpiece: Biagio Puccini, *St Francis of Paola Restores the Features to a Deformed Child*, 1720[6]. Side walls: monument to R: Agostino Rem-Picci (d. 1867) and L: Antonia Rem-Picci (d. 1850) by Giuseppe Palombini
2 to R: Cappella della Madonna della Salute: decorated by G. and G. B. Luraghi to designs by F. Ferruzzi, 1718; altar lunette: G. Ghezzi, *Angel and Dove of the Holy Spirit*, 1712[7]
R transept: Cappella di S. Camillo: begun in 1742 to a design by Francesco Rosa, but completed by F. Nicoletti in 1757. Altarpiece by P. Costanzi, *St Camillus' Vision of the Crucifixion*, 1749. Below the altar is an urn containing the relics of St Camillus by Luigi Valadier, 1770[8]. R wall: Giovanni Pannozza, *St Camillus with St Philip Neri Caring for the Sick*, 1742; L wall: Gaspare Serenari, *St Camillus and St Philip Neri Assist a Dying Man*, 1742[9]; vault: S. Conca, *St Camillus in Glory* and *Allegorical Figures*, c.1746[10]
To R of high altar: Cappella del Crocifisso: designed by F. Nicoletti and executed by Carlo Calderari, 1762-64
High altar: designed by F. Nicoletti, 1750-57; angels carrying the cross by P. Pacelli; altarpiece by M. Rocca, *St Mary Magdalen Contemplates the Crucifixion*, 1698; reliefs on the side walls by F. Gesuelli, R: *Noli me tangere* and L: *Three Maries at the Tomb*, 1756[11]
Choir: fresco of *Jesus in the House of Simon with Mary Magdalen at His Fee*t by Michelangelo Cerruti, 1732; apse: *Christ Preaching* by Aureliano Milani, 1732
Sacristy: built by C. Marchionni, 1738-41; vault: G. Pesci, *Immaculate Virgin with St Philip Neri in Glory Welcoming St Camillus de Lellis*, 1739[12]. Cupboards by Domenico Barbiani, 1740
To L of high altar: Cappella delle Reliquie: built by C. Marchionni, 1730-39; altarpiece: Agostino Gagliardi, *Death of St Joseph*, 1868
L transept: Cappella di S. Nicola da Bari: begun by Mattia de' Rossi in 1694, completed by Carlo Bizzacheri in 1694-96[13]; altarpiece: Baciccio, *The Virgin Presents St Nicholas of Bari to Christ*, c.1697-98; side walls: Bonaventura Lamberti, L: *St Nicholas Restores Three Murdered Boys to Life*; R: *St Nicholas Appears from Heaven to Save a Soldier*, c.1700[14]
2 to L: Cappella di S. Lorenzo Giustiniani/Farsetti: Luca Giordano, *St Lawrence Justinian Adores the Christ Child*, 1704[15]; monuments to R: Antonio Farsetti (d. 1677) and L: Matteo Farsetti (d. 1699) by G. Mazzuoli; vault: A. Orazi, *Putti and Dove of the Holy Spirit*[16]
1 to L: Cappella dell'Assunta: designed by Francesco Nicoletti; altarpiece: Girolamo Pesci, *Assumption*, before 1727[17]

The monastic buildings to the left of the church, which were probably designed by Paolo Amato, were begun in 1678 under his direction, but were finished by C. F. Bizzacheri in 1680-84[18]. In the entrance to the convent is a stucco sculpture of St Mary Magdalen by P. Morelli, 1699.

S. Maria Maggiore
Piazza di S. Maria Maggiore

The church was founded in the 4th or 5th century and the main structure is a survival from the 5th century. The portico added by Eugenius III (1145-53) was replaced in 1575 by one designed by Martino Longhi the Elder[1], recorded in a drawing by Carlo Fontana at Windsor[2]. This in turn was destroyed when Fuga built the present façade for Clement XII (later modified by Benedict XIV), which was planned in 1735 and built in 1741[3]. The statues on the upper attic of four papal saints are 1 to R: B. Ludovisi, *Sixtus III*; 2 to R: C. Marchionni, *Paschal I*; 1 to L: C. Monaldi, *Gregory the Great*; 2 to L: Corsini, *Pius V*, 1742, with the *Virgin and Child* by G. Lironi in the centre. On lower attic: L: *St Charles Borromeo* by F. Queirolo, 1741, and R: *The Blessed Cardinal Nicholas Albergati* by Filippo della Valle, 1742. Over entrance: allegorical figures of L: *Purity* by G. M. Maini, 1743, and R: *Humility* by P. Bracci, 1742[4]. The block to the right of the façade was built in the early 17th century by Flaminio Ponzio[5].

The apse, which was added by Nicholas IV (1288-92), was transformed into a second façade under Clement X by Carlo Rainaldi whose design was preferred to Bernini's much bolder and more Baroque scheme. On the apse are statues of *Sts Peter, Paul, Dominic* and *David* by F. Fancelli, 1672-73.

On the outside of the Cappella Paolina are statues set in niches: *St Luke* and *St Jerome* by Paracca the Younger; *St Matthew* by Mochi and *St Epaphra*; *St Matthias* by Stefano Maderno and Caporale[6]

Vestibule: rebuilt by Fuga with the façade. On the right is a bronze statue of Philip IV of Spain by Girolamo Lucenti after a sketch by Bernini, 1666[7], and on the walls are four reliefs: R wall: Bernardino Ludovisi, *Giovanni Patrizi Offers his Riches to the Pope*; 1743; Pietro Bracci, *Pope Flavius at the Council of 465*, 1743; G. B. Maini, *Gelasius I Burns the Books of the Heretics*, 1743; L wall: Giuseppe Lironi, *The Exarch Olympus and Pope Martin V*[8]. To the left of the vestibule is the entrance to the Canons' Palace. On the staircase landing is a bronze sculpture of *Paul V* by P. Sanquirico, 1619-20[9]. The stairs lead to the loggia where the *Angels* by Pietro Bracci and F. Giardoni, 1749, which were once part of the high altar, have been stored[10].

INTERIOR

The character of the medieval church was completely transformed by later alterations. Only the 5th century mosaics on the nave walls and over the choir arch and those of Jacopo Torriti in the apse have survived more or less intact. The magnificent gilt wooden ceiling was put up for Alexander VI, initially under the direction of Giuliano da Sangallo but later taken over by Antonio da Sangallo, 1492-1503[11]. The major changes were made between 1746 and 1751 by Fuga, who regularised the spacing of the nave colonnade and gave the columns new bases, cut the arches in the colonnade opposite the Sistine and Pauline chapels, added the *baldacchino* and relaid the floor, dated 1750 (in an inscription, but also containing a panel with the arms of Innocent X, who may have carried out an earlier restoration on it). The result did not please Benedict XIV, who had become pope while the work was in progress and said that Fuga had reduced the church to a ballroom. **Nave:** the clerestory frescoes, initiated under Cardinal Domenico Pinelli and depicting scenes from the *Life of the Virgin*, were painted by artists who included B. Croce, F. Fenzoni, V. Salimbeni, O. Gentileschi and G. B. Ricci. Lilli's fresco above the entrance to the Sistine Chapel was destroyed during Fuga's restoration and replaced by A. Milani's

Nativity of the Virgin, 1742[12]
R of entrance: monument to Clement IX (d. 1669) commissioned by Clement X and designed by C. Rainaldi. Figure of the pope by Domenico Guidi with allegorical figures of L: *Charity* by E. Ferrata and R: *Faith* by Cosimo Fancelli. The two medallions above, showing the *Dedication of the High Altar in S. Maria Maggiore* and the *Ponte S. Angelo*, are by Pierre Montenois, 1671[13]
L of entrance: monument to Nicholas IV (d. 1292) designed by Domenico Fontana and executed by Alessandro Cioli for Cardinal Felice Peretti, later Pope Sixtus V, 1574. Allegorical figures of R: *Justice* and L: *Truth* by Leonardo Sormani. The monument originally stood against the right wall of the choir[14]. Over the side entrance door: monuments to Pier Francesco Ferreri (d. 1566) and Cardinal Guido Ferreri (d. 1585)[15]

RIGHT AISLE
End wall: to R of altar: monument to Costanzo Patrizi (d. 1623) by Algardi[16]
Cappella Patrizi: altarpiece: P. Puglia, *Founding of the Basilica*, 1634-35[17]. To L of altar: monument to Patrizio Patrizi (d. 1611)[18]. Further: monument to Massimiliano Pernestani (d. 1593)
1 to R: built by Paul V and attributed to Flaminio Ponzio[19], but transformed into the baptistery by Giuseppe Valadier for Leo XII, 1825-27. Font designed by Valadier and bronze decorations by G. Spagna, 1825-27[20]. Relief of the *Assumption* over the altar by Pietro Bernini, originally on the outside wall of the Pauline Chapel, 1606-11[21]. R wall: monuments to Odoardo Santarelli (d. 1620) by Algardi, 1640-42[22]; Lodovico Sarego (d. 1625)[23]; Francesco Herrera (d. 1636); Giovanni Cristoforo Battello (d. 1725). L wall: monuments to Innocenzo Merla (d. 1704); polychrome marble bust by F. Caporale of Antonio Emanuele Ne Vunda, called il Nigrita (d. 1608), who came to Rome as ambassador of the King of the Congo to Paul V and was converted to Christianity. The bust by Caporale was set up in 1629[24]. It is an early and important example of the revival in the 17th century of the ancient Roman practice of making polychrome busts or statues (for an earlier example see the tomb of Paul IV by Ligorio in the Carafa chapel in S. Maria sopra Minerva). Over the entrance are busts of R: Benedict XIV and L: Clement XII and over the door is a relief of Clement XI. Frescoes designed by D. Cresti but executed with the help of assistants. Vault: *Immaculate Conception*, 1608-19[25]
Sacristy: fine wooden cupboards, apparently early 18th century; ceiling: D. Cresti, *Coronation of the Virgin*
2nd altar to R: Agostino Masucci, *Holy Family with St Anne*, 1743[26]
3rd altar to R: Stefano Pozzo, *St Nicholas Albergati*, 1749[27]
2 to R: Cappella delle Reliquie: attributed to Fuga[28]
4th altar to R: P. Batoni, *Annunciation*, 1743[29]
3 to R: Cappella del Presepe/Sistina[30]: the chapel was ceded to the Peretti family in 1581 and the foundation stone for the new chapel was laid in 1585 with Domenico Fontana in charge of its design and construction. The shell was completed in 1586 and work on the internal decoration continued from 1586 to 1590. It was to house the relic of the Crib of Christ from the former Cappella del Presepe, which was moved in its entirety from its original position and placed in a subterranean *confessio* in the centre of the new chapel. A new altar was built directly above this. The tabernacle was most probably designed by D. Fontana and executed by L. del Duca, 1587-89. The supporting *Angels* were cast by Bastiano Torrigiano. Many of the *Apostles* on the balustrade were

replaced during the 1870 restoration carried out by Alberto Galli, when the entire tabernacle was gilded[31]

Within the *confessio* Fontana reinstalled Arnolfo di Cambio's *Adoration of the Magi* (*c.* 1290) at the rear and added a new sculptural group of the *Nativity*, attributed to Francesco da Pietrasanta and Prospero Antichi.

L wall: monument to Pius V (d. 1572), completed 1587; figure of the pope by Leonardo Sormani; lower L: Andrea Brasca, *Pius V Presenting the Papal Standard to Marcantonio Colonna*; top L: Francesco di Pietrasanta, *Battle of Lepanto*; lower R: *Pius V Presenting the Baton of Command to Count Sforza di Santa Fiore*, attributed to Nicholas Pippe; top R: *Count Sforza Victorious over the Huguenots in France*, attributed to N. Pippe; top C: A. Brasca, *Coronation of Pius V*. Below: sarcophagus of Pius V with a relief of the pope lying on his tomb by P. Legros, 1697-98[32]. To L: G. Paracca, *St Peter Martyr*; to R: G. B. della Porta, *St Dominic*, 1587-88

Throne area: L: Leonardo Sormani, *St Paul* and R: Prospero Antichi, *St Peter*

R wall: monument to Sixtus V (d. 1590) completed 1589; figure of the pope by Paracca; above: G. van den Vliete, *Coronation of Sixtus V*; lower L: Paracca, *Charity of the Pope*; top L: G. van den Vliete, *Canonisation of St Diego of Alcalà*; lower R: N. Pippe, *Justice of Sixtus V*; top R: *Peace between King Sigismund of Poland and Emperor Rudolph II of Austria*, probably a collaboration between N. Pippe and G. van den Vliete. To L: Flaminio Vacca, *St Francis*; to R: P. P. Olivieri, *St Anthony of Padua*

The painted decoration, which was under the direction of C. Nebbia and G. Guerra, was devised by Silvio Antoniano and embodies a complicated iconographical scheme with the *Ancestors of Christ* and scenes from the *Nativity* cycle. The artists include Lattanzio Mainardi, Hendrik van der Broecke, Paris Nogari, Giacomo Stella, Angelo d'Orvieto, Ercolino Bolognese, Salvatore Fontana, Andrea Lilli and G. B. Pozzo.

Entrance to vestibule: A. Lilli and F. Sermei, *Four Evangelists*. The *Nativity* cycle begins above the entrance to the Cappella di S. Girolamo on the left with the *Annunciation* by S. Fontana and continues in a clockwise manner: E. Bolognese, *Journey of Mary and Joseph*; G. Pozzo, *Visitation*; *First Dream of Joseph*; *Mary and Joseph Paying the Census Tax*; *Nativity*; A. Lilli, *Annunciation to the Shepherds*; *The Magi Questioning Herod*; G. B. Pozzo, *Second Dream of Joseph*; E. Bolognese, *Flight into Egypt*; the series ends above the Cappella di S. Lucia with *Herod Ordering the Massacre of the Innocents* by S. Fontana. Throne wall: L: *St Paul Writing his Epistle*: R: *St Peter Entering Rome* by G. B. Pozzo

The *Ancestors of Christ* cycle begins with *Abraham and Isaac* by G. Stella in the left half of the lunette on the entrance wall and continues chronologically in a clockwise direction onto the adjoining arches, then onto the adjacent pendentive and so on. The series continues: G. Stella, *Jacob and his Brothers*; pendentive: L. Mainardi, *Thamar, Phares and Zara*; H. van der Broecke, *Erson and Aram*; H. van der Broecke, *Aminadab and Naason*; L. Mainardi, *Salmon, Rahab and Booz*; P. Nogari, *Obed with his Mother Ruth and Naomi*; pendentive: P. Nogari, *Jesse and David*; P. Nogari, *Solomon and Roboam*; A. d'Orvieto, *Abias and Asa*; G. Stella, *Josaphat and Joram*; A. d'Orvieto, *Ozias and Joatham*; pendentive: C. Nebbia, *Achaz and Ezechias*; A. d'Orvieto, *Manasses and Amon*; A. d'Orvieto, *Josias and Jechonias*; A. d'Orvieto, *Jechonias, Salathiel and Zorobabel*; A. d'Orvieto, *Abiud and Eliacim*; pendentive: C. Nebbia, *Azor, Sadoc and Achim*; S. Fontana,

Eliud, Eleazer, Mathan and Jacob. The cycle concludes in the right lunette on the entrance wall: P. Nogari, *Holy Family*. The dome of *Angelic Hierarchies and God the Father* was frescoed by P. Nogari, L. Mainardi and G. P. Pozzo. The marble decoration was carried out by Lorenzo Bassani, 1585-98.
L of chapel entrance: Cappella di S. Girolamo: frescoed and stuccoed 1586-87; altarpiece: G. Micocca, *St Jerome Hearing the Trumpet of the Last Judgement*, 1718. R wall: A. Lilli, *St Jerome Washing the Feet of a Pilgrim*; L lunette: A. Lilli, *St Jerome Studying Hebrew*
R of chapel entrance: Cappella di S. Lucia: altarpiece: *Communion of St Lucy*, P. Nogari; L wall: *Massacre of the Innocents*; R lunette: *Martyrdom of St Lucy*, G. B. Pozzo

Entrance grille by Bastiano Torrigiano, 1589.
End of R aisle and to R: monuments on L wall: Cardinal Giovanni Pierro Moretti (d. 1646)[33] and R wall: Ludovico Cerasala (d. 1511)
End of R aisle and to L: monument to Cardinal Marcello Crescenzi (d. 1552) by B. Basso, 1586[34]

On the floor to the right of the high altar is the tomb of the Bernini family.
High altar: the *baldacchino*, composed of four magnificent porphyry columns with gilt-bronze palm leaves round them, is Fuga's near-classical reply of 1749 to Bernini's *baldacchino* in St Peter's. Altarpiece: F. Mancini, *Adoration of the Shepherds*, 1750. The two bronze putti holding candelabra either side of the high altar were designed by F. della Valle, 1751[35]

The *confessio* was commissioned by Pius IX in 1862 and designed by Virginio Vespignani[36]. Within the *confessio* is the reliquary of the Holy Crib by G. Valadier[37]. The figure of *Pius IX in Prayer* before the reliquary, by Ignazio Jacometti, was erected in 1880[38].
End of L aisle and to R: monument to Cardinal Prospero Santacroce (d. 1589), attributed to Prospero Antichi[39]
End of L aisle and to L: monuments to Francesco Pasqualini (d.1582); L wall: Girolamo Manili (d. 1634); R wall: Clemente Merlini (d. 1642). The latter is attributed to Borromini by Martinelli[40], who explains that the colours of the marbles of which the monument is composed are symbolic, red for the strength of character and white for the purity of Merlini. The drawings of the tomb and that of Manili, however, are certainly not by Borromini, but are more likely to be by Gregorio Spada, brother of Borromini's patron Virgilio[41]. The bust of Merlini is ascribed to Andrea Bolgi[42], while the bust of Manili is by G. Finelli[43]. The wreath surrounding it and many of the details of the monument are in the style of Borromini, who may well have designed them for Spada

LEFT AISLE
3 to L: Cappella Paolina[44]: designed by Flaminio Ponzio, the chapel was planned by Paul V as a counterpart to the Sistine Chapel, but his intention was clearly to outdo his predecessor, and the chapel is in fact richer than its counterpart in its marbling and lavish use of sculptural decoration. The foundation stone was laid in 1605 and the structure was completed in 1610, but the decoration continued till 1615
L wall: monument to Paul V (d. 1621); statue of the pope by Silla Longhi; reliefs, top: I. Buzzi, *Coronation of Paul V*; upper L: Paracca the Younger, *Canonisation of Sts Charles Borromeo and Frances of Rome*[45]; lower L: S. Maderno, *Papal Army Fighting against the Turks*; upper R: Cristoforo Stati, *The Persian Ambassador Received by Paul V*; lower R: Buonvicino, *Fortification of Ferrara*; four caryatids between reliefs in upper regis-

ter by Buzio. Flanking the monument: R: *David* and L: *Dionysius the Areopagite* by Cordier

R wall: monument to Clement VIII (d. 1605); figure of the pope by Silla Longhi; reliefs, top: *Coronation of Clement VIII*, Pietro Bernini[46]; lower L: *Surrender of Ferrara*, A. Buonvicino; upper L: *Reconciliation of Philip II of Spain and Henry IV of France*, Buzio; upper R: *Canonisation of Sts Raymund and Hyacinth*, Paracca the Younger[47]; lower R: *Gian Francesco Aldobrandini Fighting the Turks at Graz*, C. Mariani, completed by Mochi. Caryatids by Pietro Bernini. Flanking the monument: R: *St Bernard of Clairvaux* and L: *Aaron* by Cordier

Against altar wall: R: *St Joseph* by Buonvicino and L: *St John the Evangelist* by Mariani, 1610-11[48]

The central feature of the chapel is the *Hodegetria* icon of the Virgin and Child known as the *Salus Populi Romani*, traditionally attributed to St Luke and particularly venerated by the people of Rome. Girolamo Rainaldi made the original design for the altar, which was executed with modifications by Pompeo Targone. Camillo Mariani provided the models for the *Angels* and the *Dove of the Holy Spirit* that surround and support the icon. Guillaume Berthelot was responsible for the models of the two large angels that rest on the pediment. The bronzes were cast by Domenico Ferrerio and Orazio Censore. The relief in the pediment, showing the *Miracle of the Snow* (the foundation of the church) is by Stefano Maderno. The altar tabernacle was begun in 1608 and the icon inserted on 27 January 1613. The altar was replaced in 1749 to a design by Antonio Asprucci as a gift from Principe Camillo Borghese and his wife, Agnese Colonna.

The frescoes in the chapel were carried out under the direction of Giuseppe Cesari[49]. They celebrate the virtues of the Virgin, expound the worship of holy images reaffirmed by the Counter Reformation theologians and celebrate those who fought heresies. Mâle, in one of the earliest attempts to analyse this new iconography, gives a detailed account of these frescoes, which include stories of God's vengeance on the iconoclasts and of the miracles wrought by images. The programme for the whole cycle was prepared by a member of the Oratory, Tommaso Bozzio, who based his choice of subjects on his historical apologetics *De signis Ecclesiæ Dei contra omnes haereses* (1591).

Entrance arch: frescoes by G. Baglione, R: *Death of Emperor Constantine V Copronymus*; C: *Emperor Julian the Apostate Killed by Sts Mercurius and Artemius*; L: *Death of Emperor Leo V the Armenian*. The frescoes were completed in 1612

Entrance vestibule: G. Baglione, *St Gregory Nazianzen*; *St Athanasius*; *St Gregory the Great* and *St Jerome*

To R: frescoes by G. Reni, arch: R: *Sts Pulcheria of Byzantium, Ediltrude of England and the Blessed Cunegunda of Poland*; C: *Dove of the Holy Spirit*; L: *St Cyril of Alexandria*; R lunette: *Miraculous Robing of St Ildephonsus*; L lunette: *Miraculous Restitution of St John Damascene's Hand*

Altar wall: frescoes by G. Cesari, arch: R: *St Irenaeus of Lyons and Cyprian of Carthage*; C: *St Luke*; L: *St Ignatius of Antioch and Theophilus of Antioch*; lunette: *The Virgin and St John the Evangelist Appear to St Gregory the Thaumaturge*

To L: frescoes by G. Reni, arch: R: *St Dominic*; C: *Christ Enraged*; L: *St Francis*; lunettes: R: *Heraclius's Victory over Chosroes of Persia*; L: *Narses' Victory over Totila*; dome frescoed by Cigoli, *Virgin with Apostles*, 1610-12[50]; pendentives: *Isaiah*; *Jeremiah*; *Ezekiel* and *Daniel* by G. Cesari

L of chapel entrance: Cappella di S. Francesca Romana: decorated by G. Baglione,

R wall: *Miracle of St Frances of Rome*; vault: *Glory of Angels* [51]
R of chapel entrance: Cappella di S. Carlo Borromeo: decorated by B. Croce

These two chapels are dedicated to two saints canonised under Paul V, St Frances of Rome and St Charles Borromeo.
Sacristy: decorated by D. Cresti, ceiling: *The Virgin Gathers Flowers from the Lap of Christ*; *Founders of Monastic Orders* and *Old Testament Scenes*; walls: *King Manuel of Portugal Builds a Church in India Dedicated to the Virgin*; *Foundation of the Fort of the Teutonic Knights*; altarpiece: *Christ Appears to the Virgin after His Resurrection*, c.1611-12[52]. Entrance grille by Giacomo Laurentiani and Gregorio de' Rossi
2 to L: Cappella Sforza[53]: commissioned from Michelangelo in the last years of his life by Cardinal Guido Ascanio Sforza (d. 1564). According to Vasari, Michelangelo made the designs but handed over the execution to Tiberio Calcagni. After the latter's death in 1565 the chapel was completed by another architect, generally assumed to be Giacomo della Porta. According to the inscription the chapel was finished by Cardinal Alessandro Sforza, brother of Ascanio, and the chapel was consecrated in 1573. The tombs of the two cardinals stand in the curved side-bays of the chapel, L: Cardinal Guido Ascanio Sforza and R: Cardinal Alessandro Sforza (d. 1581), attributed to Paracca the Elder[54], with portraits by Sicciolante[55]. That of Alessandro is dated 1582, and neither has any connection with Michelangelo. Altarpiece: Sicciolante, *Assumption*, c.1570-73[56]; above: C. Nebbia, *Coronation of the Virgin*, and *Prophets* on either side of the windows

Ackerman points out the poor quality of certain details (e.g. the capitals) as evidence for the fact that Michelangelo cannot have been responsible for the detail (which, it may be added, is not at all like Della Porta's work), but the design of the whole is certainly due to Michelangelo.

The chapel contains many completely new features. The main piers are set on the diagonals of the crossing instead of on one or other of the main axes and the two apsed transepts are formed of arcs less than a semicircle. With these innovations Michelangelo prefigured features which were to be fundamental in Baroque architecture, above all the use of incomplete forms leading into one another.

The first architect who really understood these revolutionary features was Borromini, who derived many ideas from them. He followed up Michelangelo's use of incomplete forms in the plans of the side chapels in S. Carlino and the canting of the columns at 45° in his monument to Cardinal Caracciolo in the Lateran[57].

The façade of the chapel facing the aisle of the church was destroyed by Fuga, but is recorded in an engraving[58]. According to Ackerman, it was designed after Michelangelo's death.
2nd altar to L: P. Costanzi, *St Francis in Ecstasy*, 1743[59]
1st altar to L: S. Ceccarini, *St Leo Kneels before the Virgin*, 1750[60]
1 to L: Cappella Cesi/Massimo: attributed to Martino Longhi the Elder[61]; altarpiece: Sicciolante, *Beheading of St Catherine*, c.1566-67. Between the paired pilasters: L: *St John the Evangelist* and R: *St Matthew* by Sicciolante[62]; below: L: *St Peter* and R: *St Paul* attributed to G. B. Ricci. R wall: Canini, *St Catherine Disputing*, c.1600[63]; Luigi Gentile, *Martyrdom of St Catherine*; L wall: C. Cesi, *Mystic Marriage of St Catherine*, c.1660[64]. Monuments to R: Cardinal Federico Cesi (d. 1565) and L: Cardinal Paolo Cesi (d. 1537) by G. della Porta[65]. R wall: Luigi Gentile, *Martyrdom of St Catherine*
To L of Cappella Cesi: monuments to Cardi-

nal Mariano Perbenedetto (d. 1611)[65]; Monsignor Antonio Maria Traversi (d. 1842) by G. de' Fabris, 1843[67]
1st bay to L: monument to Cardinal Agostino Favoriti (d. 1685) with figures of L: *Faith* and R: *Fortitude* by Filippo Carcani, c.1685. The monument is attributed to Ludovico Gimignani[68]. Opposite: monument to Cardinal Francesco Toledo (d. 1596), the first Jesuit cardinal, designed by G. della Porta and executed by G. van den Vliete, 1598[69].

S. Maria ad Martyres (The Pantheon)
Piazza della Rotonda

The temple was originally part of the Baths of Agrippa but was rebuilt by Hadrian between 118-25 and dedicated to the seven major gods worshipped by the Romans. It was converted into a Christian church and dedicated to S. Maria ad Martyres by Boniface IV in 609. Urban VIII removed the bronze supports in the portico to make the *baldacchino* in St Peter's. In 1612 he caused two towers to be added to the façade (pulled down in 1883). These are generally ascribed to Bernini but the drawings for them are by Borromini and were made while he was still working for Maderno[1]. The three left-hand columns of the portico were replaced under Urban VIII and Alexander VII, whose arms appear in their capitals.

INTERIOR
The attic was altered to its present form by Paolo Posi in 1756-58, but one section was restored to its original form in 1932.

RIGHT HALF
1st aedicule: *Virgin and Christ with St Nicholas of Bari*, anonymous, 17th century

1 to R: R of altar: Paolo Bonzi, *Incredulity of St Thomas*; L of altar: Clemente Maioli, *Sts Lawrence and Agnes*; L wall: L niche: bust of Pompilio Zuccarini (d. 1662) by F. Mochi[2]; R niche: bust of Giacomo Gamba (d. 1661). R wall, R niche: bust of James Gibbs (d. 1677) by Paolo Naldini, 1667[3]; L niche: bust of Antonio Baldani (d. 1765) by unknown artist[4]
2nd aedicule: *Coronation of the Virgin*, 15th century, Tuscan School
2 to R monument to Vittorio Emmanuele II (d. 1878) by Manfredo Manfredi, 1886-87
3rd aedicule: Lorenzo Ottoni, *Virgin and St Anne*[5]
3 to R: *Madonna of Mercy with St John the Baptist and St Francis*, 15th century, Umbro-Lazian School; R wall: *Donation of the Pantheon to Boniface IV*, anonymous, c.1750
4th aedicule: *St Anastasia*, B. Cametti, 1725-27
High altar: this includes fragments of one designed by Alessandro Specchi, built 1719-24 but dismantled and rebuilt in 1934[6].

LEFT HALF
4th aedicule: *St Rasius*, Francesco Moderati, 1727
3 to R: 15th century crucifix; L wall: Pietro Labruzzi, *Pentecost*; R wall: monument to Cardinal Ercole Consalvi (d. 1824), Secretary of State under Pius VII. The relief depicts the *Restitution to Pius VII of the Papal States Liberated from Foreign Occupation* by Bertel Thorvaldsen, 1824[7]
3rd aedicule: Lorenzetti, *Madonna del Sasso*; to L: bust of Raphael; below: tombs of Raphael (d. 1520) and Annibale Carracci (d. 1609)
2 to R: monument to Umberto I (d. 1900) and Margherita di Savoia (d. 1925)
2nd aedicule: Vincenzo Felici, *St Agnes*[8]; to L: monument to Baldassare Peruzzi (d. 1536)
1 to L: Vincenzo de' Rossi, *St Joseph with*

Jesus; L: *Adoration of the Shepherds*; F. Cozza, R: *Adoration of the Magi*, c.1662[9]; above, G. A. Carlione, R: *David*; C: *God the Father*, 1674[10]; L: *Moses*, c.1675[11]; L wall: Paolo Benaglia, *Joseph's Dream*; above: *Cumaean Sibyl* by Ludovico Gimignani[12]; R wall: Carlo Monaldi, relief of *Rest on the Flight into Egypt*[13]; above: *Erythraean Sibyl*, Giovanni Antonio Carlione[14]
1st aedicule: A. Camassei, *Assumption*, 1638[15].

S. Maria sopra Minerva
Piazza della Minerva

Founded in the 8th century by Pope Zacharias on the ruins of a temple of Minerva Calcidica and given by Gregory XI (1370-78) to the Dominicans, who rebuilt it on a much larger scale and in the gothic style. It was frequently altered and restored, but in 1848-55 a disastrous attempt was made to restore it to its original state, which included encasing the gothic piers in dark grey marble.

The façade was never completed. In 1725 a design for it was made by F. Raguzzini for Benedict XIII but it was never executed.

INTERIOR
Entrance wall: monument to Virginia Pucci-Ridolfi (d. 1568), c. 1568-71[1]. Holy-water stoups by Ottaviano Lazzari, 1638[2]
1 to R: baptistery by Filippo Raguzzini, 1724, but altered in 1850[3]; L wall: bust of Cardinal Ladislao d'Aquileo, Papal Nuncio to Switzerland under Clement VIII (d. 1621), by Francesco Mochi[4]; R wall: monument to Alberto Gallo (d. 1641)[5]
1st pier of nave: monument to Natale Mongardi (d. 1831) by Pietro Tenerani, 1831[6]
2 to R: Cappella di S. Antoninus/S. Ludovico Bertrando/Caffarelli: built in 1498 for Prospero Caffarelli and restored by Cardinal Scipione Borghese, who also paid for the monument on the left wall to his father Francesco Caffarelli (d. 1615) and rebuilt the altar, 1620[7]. The chapel was restored by Giuseppe Paglia in 1670-71 and re-dedicated to St Louis Beltran. Altarpiece: Baciccio, *St Louis Beltran*, 1671-74[8]. Vault: Gaspare Celio, R: *St Dominic Exorcises a Demon*; L: *St Dominic Resurrects a Boy*[9]; lunettes: *Two Figures Holding the Attributes of St Dominic*, attributed to G. Cesari
Between 2 and 3 to R: monument to Uberto Strozzi (d. 1553)
3 to R: Cappella di S. Rosa da Lima/Colonna: L. Baldi; altarpiece: *St Rose of Lima Venerated by the Natives of Peru*; L wall: *The Virgin Appears to St Rose*; R wall: *Christ Commands St Rose to Destroy the Idols*; vault: *Coronation of St Rose*, 1668-71[10]. R wall: monument to Isabella Alvarez-Colonna (d. 1857) by Pietro Tenerani[11]
2nd pier of nave: monument to Carlo Emanuele Vizzani (d. 1661) by Domenico Guidi, erected by his brother[12]
4 to R: Cappella di S. Pietro Martire/ Gabrielli: altar by C. F. Bizzacheri, 1688; altarpiece: B. Lamberti, *St Peter Martyr*, 1688[13]; wall frescoes by G. B. Franco, L: *Adoration of the Shepherds*; lunettes: *Prophet and Sibyl*; R: *Resurrection of Christ*; lunette: *St John the Evangelist and Mary Magdalen*. Vault by G. Muziano: *Pietà*; *Pentecost*; *Ascension*; *Adoration of the Magi* and pendentives: *Four Evangelists* and entrance arch figures, c.1551[14]
Between 4 and 5 to R: L wall: monument to Francesco del Nero, Secretary to Clement VIII (d. 1563), designed by Bartolomeo Ammanati, executed by Bastiano Bruschini with bust by Giulio Mazzoni[15]. Above entrance: monument to Bernardino Riccardi by T. Barlocci, 1857. Further: monument to Girolamo Ameto (d. 1608)
3rd pier of nave: monument to Alessandro Valtrini (d. 1633) attributed to Bolgi, set up in 1637[16]

5 to R: Cappella dell'Annunziata/Torquemada: wall and vault frescoes by C. Nebbia of scenes from the *Life of the Virgin*: R wall lunette: *Adoration of the Shepherds*; above: *Presentation*; L wall upper lunette: *Circumcision*; vault: R: *Dormition*; C: *Coronation*; L: *Pentecost*[17]; altarpiece: Antoniazzo Romano, *Annunciation with Cardinal Juan de Torquemada Presenting Poor Girls to the Virgin*, 1500[18]. To sides of altar: L: monument to Cardinal Juan de Torquemada (d. 1468) and R: monument to Cardinal Benedetto Giustiniani (d. 1621)[19]. L wall: monument to Urban VII (d. 1590) by A. Buonvicino, c.1614[20]

4th pier of nave: monument to Francesco de' Ginnasi (d. 1637)

6 to R: Cappella Aldobrandini[21]: ceded in 1587 to Cardinal Ippolito Aldobrandini, later Clement VIII. In 1600 he decided to erect monuments to his parents and brother in it. The chapel was consecrated in 1611. The original architect was Giacomo della Porta, possibly assisted by Girolamo Rainaldi. On Della Porta's death in 1602 he was succeeded by Maderno, who designed the altar in 1603, when Barocci's *Last Supper* was commissioned[22]. Della Porta must have been responsible for the decoration up to the cornice but Maderno probably designed the vault

L wall: monument to Louisa Deti (d. 1555); the reclining figure of the pope's mother is by Nicholas Cordier, 1604-08, with figures of L: *Charity* and R: *Religion* by Cordier and Camillo Mariani respectively. The angels above the monument are attributed to Mariani[23]. To the right of the monument is a figure of Clement VIII attributed to I. Buzio[24]

R wall: monument to Silvestro Aldobrandini (d. 1558); the reclining figure of the pope's father is by Cordier, 1604, with figures of L: *Justice* attributed to Paracca the Younger[25] and R: *Prudence* by Ippolito Buzzi; the angels above the monument are by Stefano Maderno. To the left of the monument is the figure of *St Sebastian* by Cordier, 1604. On either side of the altar: C. Mariani, L: *St Peter* and R: *St Paul*; the two angels above the altar are by Ambrogio Buonvicino. Below are four busts of the Aldobrandini family, of which only that of Cardinal Giovanni Aldobrandini (d. 1573) below the *St Paul* has been identified and attributed to A. Buonvicino

The decoration of the walls is a fine early example of the use of coloured marbles. Vault: *Triumph of the Cross* and lunettes, R: *Ezekiel* and L: *Sibyl* frescoed by Cherubino Alberti in 1604 and 1606-10 respectively[26].

Between 6 and 7 to R: monument to Cardinal Francesco Bertazzoli (d. 1831) by Rinaldo Rinaldi, 1831[27]

7 to R: Cappella di S. Raimondo da Peñafort/dei Planca degli Incoronati[28]: altarpiece: Nicholas Magny, *Sts Raymund of Peñafort and Paul*. R wall: monument to Bishop Juan Díaz de Coca (d. 1477) by A. Bregno[29]; to R: monument to Natalie Komar-Spada (d. 1860) by Pietro Tenerani[30]

To R of chapel: monument to Giuseppe Pighinio (d. 1708)

Aisle chapel before transept: Cappella di SS. Lucia e Agata/Marsiliana: altarpiece: Girolamo Sicciolante, *Sts Lucy and Agatha*, c.1560[31]

R transept: Cappella di S. Tommaso d'Aquino/Carafa[32]: frescoed by Filippino Lippi; altarpiece: *Annunciation with Thomas Aquinas Presenting Cardinal Carafa to the Virgin*; altar wall: *Assumption*; R wall: *Triumph of St Thomas Aquinas*; lunette: *Miracle of Chastity*; vault: *Sibyls*, 1488-93. L wall: monument to Paul IV (d. 1559) designed by Pirro Ligorio and executed by G. B. Cassignola[33]. An important example of the revival of the use of coloured marbles in sculpture.

To R of chapel: monument to Emilio Pucci (d. 1595) and to L: monument to Onofrio Camiani (d. 1574)

2 to R of high altar: Cappella d'Ognissanti/Altieri: according to T. Magnuson[34], designs for the chapel were prepared by Camillo de' Massimi for Clement X, completed in 1672. Altarpiece: C. Maratta, *St Peter Presenting Sts Louis Beltran, Rose of Lima, Philip Benizi, Francis Borgia and Cajetan Thiene to the Virgin*; lunette by Baciccio, *Holy Trinity*, 1671-72[35]; monuments to R: Lorenzo Altieri (d. 1638) and L: Cardinal Giovanni Battista Altieri (d. 1654), father and brother of Clement X, with busts by C. Fancelli.[36]

Between the 1st and 2nd chapels and in the corresponding position on the left transept are organs by Ennio Bonifazi with carved cases by Pietro Maruscelli, donated by Cardinal Scipione Borghese, 1628[37].

Chapel next to high altar: Cappella del SS. Rosario/Capranica: the chapel, which housed the relics of St Catherine, was originally used by the Compagnia di S. Caterina da Siena but from 1573 they shared the chapel with the Confraternita del Rosario. Wall frescoes by Giovanni de' Vecchi depict scenes from the *Dialogue of Divine Providence* that Catherine wrote in 1377-78 and represent the visions she recorded. R wall: *St Catherine Receiving the Eucharist from Christ*; *St Catherine Receiving the Stigmata*; *St Catherine before Pope Gregory XI*. L wall: *Mystic Marriage of St Catherine*; *Charity of St Catherine as a Child*; *St Catherine Drinks Blood from the Wound in Christ's Side*, 1578-79. Flanking the altar: L: *St Dominic* and R: *St Catherine*, 1639[38]. Vault: Marcello Venusti, *Mysteries of the Rosary*; L: *Annunciation*; *Visitation*; *Adoration of the Shepherds*; *Presentation in the Temple*; *Jesus Teaching in the Temple*; R: *Agony in the Garden*; *Flagellation*; *Crowning with Thorns*; *On the Road to Calvary*; *Crucifixion*; C: *Resurrected Christ*; *Ascension*; *Pentecost*; *Assumption*, 1573[39]; *Crowning with Thorns* by Carlo Saraceni, 1576-78[40]

Pier separating Cappella Capranica from tribune: *St John the Baptist* by Giuseppe Obici, 1858[41]

Choir: R wall: monument to Clement VII (d. 1534) designed by Antonio da Sangallo the Younger; statue of the pope by Nanni di Baccio Bigio. The reliefs of R: *St Benedict Meeting King Totila*; C: *Coronation of Charles V* and L: *Preaching of John the Baptist* and other statues of R: *John the Baptist* and L: *St Jerome* are by Baccio Bandinelli[42]. L wall: monument to Pope Leo X (d. 1521) designed by Antonio da Sangallo the Younger; figure of the pope by Raffaello da Montelupo. The reliefs of R: *Miracle of St Julius*; L: *Baptism of Christ*; C: *Meeting of Leo X with Francis I in Bologna* and statues of R: *St Paul* and L: *St Peter* are by Baccio Bandinelli.[43]

Pier to L of choir: Michelangelo, *Risen Christ*, 1521.[44]

Passage to L of choir: over the door: monument to Cardinal Carlo Bonelli, Papal Nuncio to Madrid under Alexander VIII (d. 1676), designed by Carlo Rainaldi with allegorical figures of L: *Charity* by F. Carcani and R: *Religion* by M. Maglia; seated figures of R: *Prudence* by G. F. de' Rossi and L: *Justice* by C. Fancelli. Angels holding the bronze medallion with the relief of the cardinal by E. Ferrata; putti above attributed to F. Aprile[45]. L wall: monument to Cardinal Michele Bonelli (d. 1598) by Giacomo della Porta, 1604; figure of the cardinal by Silla Longhi; R: *Prudence* by Stefano Maderno and L: *Religion* by Pompeo Ferrucci[46]. R wall: monument to Cardinal Domenico Pimentel (d. 1653) designed by Bernini; statues of the cardinal and *Faith* (R) and *Wisdom* (L) are by E. Ferrata; R: *Justice* by G. A. Mari and L: *Charity* by Raggi.[47]

Passage to sacristy: two statues of *Faith* and *Religion* by Tommaso della Porta, which come from the monument to Paul IV; Marcello Venusti, *Virgin and Child with Sts Dominic and Catherine*[48]

Sacristy: above door: G. B. Speranza, *Conclave of 1431 and 1447 in S. Maria sopra Minerva*; above: *Landscape with the Martyrdom of the Papal Legate: the Blessed Peter of Castelnau* by Herman van Swanvelt[49]. Altarpiece: Reni, *Crucifixion with Sts Dominic, Thomas Aquinas, Peter Martyr and an unidentified Dominican Saint*. The fresco of *Putti and Angels Carrying the Attributes of Dominican Saints* on the vault over the altarpiece is by Andrea Sacchi, 1637-38[50]. He may also have designed the doors. The author of the fresco on the vault of the sacristy, *St Dominic in Glory*, is not documented, but it is attributed to Jacques Stella, who worked in Rome from 1623 to 1635[51], and to P. P. Baldini[52]. In the sacristy is a painting of *St Dominic* recently attributed to S. Vouet[53]. Reliquary cupboards designed by A. Sacchi, 1640.

Behind the altar in the sacristy is the room in which St Catherine of Siena died (1380) in the convent of the Minerva; it was moved here in 1638 by Cardinal Antonio Barberini and given an enclosing shell designed by Andrea Sacchi in a style of extraordinary classical delicacy. The stucco work was executed by Arcangelo Gonelli, whilst the door leading to the sanctuary was carved by his brother Filippo Gonelli[54]. Frescoes by Antoniazzo Romano and his workshop; altar wall: *Crucifixion with the Virgin and Sts John the Baptist, John the Evangelist, Mary Magdalen and Dominic*; L wall: *Annunciation*; *Sts Jerome and Paul the Hermit*; R wall: *St Peter and other Saints*; *Sts Lucy and Apollonia*; entrance wall: L: *St John the Baptist*; R: *St Augustine*; above door: *Christ in the Tomb*.[55]

In the *Sala dei Papi* between the sacristy and the cloister is an over-life-size unfinished marble statue of the *Madonna and Child* by P. Benaglia, which was part of an unexecuted project for the Trevi fountain[56].

L transept: Cappella di S. Domenico/Alberini: begun by Martino Longhi the Younger in 1649 but mainly built by Giuseppe Paglia in the 1670's, when the black and white columns were set up[57]. The chapel owes its present rich appearance to the decoration which it received from Filippo Raguzzini in the 1720's[58]. R wall: monument to Benedict XIII (d. 1730) designed by Carlo Marchionni with statues of the pope and *Purity* or *Humility* on R by Pietro Bracci and on L: *Religion* by Bartolomeo Pincellotti, 1734-37[59]. Altarpiece: *The Virgin with an Image of St Dominic* by Paolo de' Matteis[60]. R wall: Carlo Roncalli, *Sts Francis and Dominic Embracing*. L wall: marble group of the *Virgin and Child with Sts John the Evangelist and John the Baptist* by Francesco Grassia, 1670[61]. Vault: Carlo Roncalli, *Holy Ghost and Angels in Glory*, 1725[62]

To L of chapel: altare di S. Giacinto/Cesi: Ottavio Leoni, *The Virgin and Child Appear to St Hyacinth*, 1598

Before 6 to L: monument to the Podesti family by Andrea Podesti, 1854

6 to L: Cappella di Pio V: altarpiece: A. Procaccini, *St Pius V Triumphant over the Turks*, c.1712[63]; R wall: L. Baldi, *Pius V with an Angel at the Battle of Lepanto*, 1672[64]. Vault: M. Cerruti, *Angels in Glory*[65]

5th pier of nave: monument to the Venerable Maria Raggi (d. 1600) designed by Bernini and executed with assistance by Antonio Raggi[66]. The monument is usually dated 1643, but Bernstock has pointed out that the inscription refers to Lorenzo Raggi, who erected it as cardinal, which he only became in 1647. Documents quoted by her show that the monument was finished before 1653.

It incorporates wind-swept marble drapery, which no doubt symbolises the idea of death sweeping men away as the wind carries off dead leaves, a theme which Bernini had already introduced in two earlier monuments – to Valtrini in S. Lorenzo in Damaso and Merenda in S. Giacomo alla Lungara[67]. The effect of the monument has been greatly damaged by the addition of grey marble to the presumably travertine pier against which it should stand out in contrast. Monument to Girolamo Gabrielli (d. 1587)[68]

Between 5 and 6 to L: monument to Ottaviano Ubaldini della Gherardesca (d. 1632), commander of the papal troops under Urban VIII, with mosaic portrait by G. B. Calandra and putti by G. Finelli, 1619-22[69]

5 to L: Cappella di S. Giacomo Apostolo/Lante della Rovere: altarpiece and stucco: M. Venusti, *St James*, 1570[70]; R wall: monument to Maria Colonna (d. 1840); L wall: monument to Guido Lante della Rovere and his daughters Carlotta and Livia by Pietro Tenerani[71]

Between 4 and 5 to L: monument to Bishop Girolamo Melchiorri (1583) and his brother Benedetto (d. 1585) with a portrait of Girolamo by J. del Conte[72]

4 to L: Cappella di S. Vincenzo Ferreri/Giustiniani: altarpiece: Bernardo Castello, *St Vincent Ferrer Preaching at the Council of Constance*, c.1584[73]. Wall monuments of L: Cardinal Vincenzo Giustiniani (d. 1582) and R: Giuseppe Giustiniani (d. 1600)

Between 3 and 4 to L: monument to Giovanni Vigevano (d. 1630); the bust is by Bernini but was probably made some time before the sitter's death, about 1617-18[74]

3rd pier of nave: monuments to L: Fabio and R: Ippolito de' Amicis (d. 1596 and 1651) designed by Pietro da Cortona[75]. The bust of Fabio is attributed to Camillo Mariani[76]

3 to L: Cappella del SS. Salvatore/Grazioli/Lante: over altar: sculpture of *St Philip Neri* given to the church by Benedict XIII. L of altar: *St John the Baptist* attributed to Buonvicino, 1603[77]

2 to L: Cappella di S. Giovanni Battista/Naro: restored by Flaminio Ponzio for Fabrizio Naro, who gained jurisprudence of the chapel in 1588. The chapel contains a number of monuments to members of the Naro family from the early 17th to the late 18th centuries. The most important is that of Cardinal Gregorio Naro (d. 1634) on the left wall, designed by Bernini and executed by Matteo Albertini in 1638-40, with the bust of the cardinal by G. A. Fancelli[78]. That of the cardinal's younger brother, Bernardino (d. 1671), the last bust left of the altar, is attributed to Andrea Bolgi[79]. Frescoes attributed to Francesco Nappi, vault: *David, Zachariah, Isaiah* and *Jeremiah*; pendentives: *Evangelists*; lunette: *St John the Baptist Preaching*. Altarpiece: Giuseppe Bastiani, *St John the Baptist*, 1602[80]. To L of altar: monument to Orazio Naro (d. 1575) and R: Giulia Cenci Naro[81]

Between 1 and 2 to L: monument to Cesare Magalotti (d. 1602)[82]

1st pier of nave: monument to Raffaello Fabretti (d. 1700) with bust by Rusconi[83]

1 to L: Cappella S. Maria Maddalena/Visconti

The main building of the convent, to the left of the church, now contains offices connected with the Chamber of Deputies. Some of the rooms contain frescoes by Francesco Allegrini[84]. In the cloister (late 16th century; accessible from the *sala dei papi*) is a small museum containing some chalices, vestments and lamps dating from the 17th and 18th centuries.

The wing originally containing the noviciate and running along the via S. Ignazio was built at the expense of Cardinal Antonio Barberini. It is now incorporated in the Biblioteca Casanatense, which is housed in a vaulted hall, built in 1719, in the southern part of the range[85].

S. Maria dei Miracoli *see* **S. Maria di Montesanto and S. Maria dei Miracoli**
Piazza del Popolo

S. Maria di Monserrato
Via Monserrato, 115

Built for the Spanish confraternity of S. Maria di Monserrato (founded in 1506), the church was built under the direction of Antonio da Sangallo the Younger in 1518-1520, but was not finished until 1582 under the direction of Giovanni Antonio Dosio, apparently still according to Sangallo's plans. The apse was built by G. B. Contini in 1673-75[1]. The façade was begun by Francesco da Volterra, who built the lower storey in 1585-93, but the whole design is preserved in engravings in the early guide books (reproduced in the *Guide Rionali*); the upper storey was only built in 1926-28. The freely designed group of the *Virgin and Child on the Rock of Monserrato* over the door is by C. Monaldi[2].

INTERIOR
The interior was restored by Giuseppe Camporese and Pietro Camporese the Younger in 1820-22, from which time the decorations date. It was restored again in 1926-29.
1 to R: Cappella di S. Diego: Annibale Carracci (with the help of assistants), *St Diego of Alcalà Recommending Juan de Herrera's Son to Christ*, c.1606-07[3], from the church of S. Giacomo degli Spagnuoli; R wall: monument to Popes Callistus (d. 1458) and Alexander VI (d. 1503) by Filippo Moratilla, 1881
2 to R: Cappella dell'Annunziata: designed by Giovanni Antonio Ferrer, 1625-26; stucco by Francesco Bizzacheri; frescoes by Francesco Nappi; altarpiece: *Annunciation*; R wall: *Birth of the Virgin*; lunette: *Visitation*; L wall: *Assumption*; lunette: *Virgin of the Apocalypse*[4]
3 to R: Cappella della Madonna del Pilar/ Gómez Garzía: restored by Giuseppe Marchetti with stucco and sculptural decoration by Pietro Rudiez, 1768; altarpiece: Francesco Preciado, *Madonna del Pilar with Sts Vincent Ferrer and James the Elder*[5]; L wall: Luigi Gentile, *Triumph of the Immaculate Conception*, 1633; R wall: Francesco da Castello, *Assumption*[6]
High altar: Sicciolante, *Crucifixion with the Virgin and St John*, 1564-65[7]
Room to L of choir: monument to Cardinal Pedro de Montoya (d. 1630) designed by Niccolò Torriani with bust by Bernini, one of his earliest works, executed in 1621[8]
Sacristy: built to a design by Bernardino Valperga, 1601-03. Pedro de Rubiales, *Virgin and Child*[9]
3 to L: Cappella di S. Giacomo: Jacopo Sansovino, *St James*, 1518-20[10]; R wall: monument to Antonio Vargas y Laguna (d. 1824) by José Alvarez Cubero and José Antonio Alvarez Bouquel; L wall: above: monument to Felix de Aguirre (d. 1832) by A. Sola, 1832[11]
1 to L: Cappella di S. Anna: Tommaso Boscoli, *St Anne with the Virgin and Child*, 1544[12]
Refectory: reconstructed half-length portrait of Francesco de Vides (d. 1633) from the church of S. Giacomo degli Spagnuoli by G. Finelli, 1651-53[13].

S. Maria di Monterone
Via Monterone, 75

The medieval church was restored by Innocent XI (1676-89), when the present very simple façade was built. To the right of it is an interesting tall *barocchetto* façade covering the premises attached to the church, possibly to a design by D. Gregorini[1].

INTERIOR
Entrance wall: L: monument to Cesare Eugerio Planetti (d. 1726)
1 to R: altarpiece: G. Gagliardi, *Assumption with Souls in Purgatory*
End of R aisle: R wall: monument to Anna Moroni (d. 1647)[1]
Choir: L wall: monument to Cardinal Stefano Durazzo, archbishop of Genoa (d. 1667), with a skeleton holding a medallion with a portrait of the deceased attributed to F. Parodi[2]. R wall: monument to Giovanni Rinuccini (d. 1730)
End of L aisle: Cappella di S. Alfonso Maria de' Liguori: built by Pietro Camporese the Younger, 1848. Decorated by Donato de' Vivo; altarpiece: *St Alphonus Maria de' Liguori*, 1848; R wall: *St Alphonus Levitates before the Virgin*; L wall: *St Alphonus with the Rule of the Redemptorist Congregation*
Before last chapel: monument to Vincenzo Belli (d. 1859) by Pietro Camporese the Younger[3]
1st bay to L: monument to Caterina Gondi (d. 1867) by Domenico Pierani, 1869.

S. Maria di Montesanto and S. Maria dei Miracoli
Piazza del Popolo

Till the early 16th century the area within the Porta Flaminia, later called the Porta del Popolo, was an irregular space, marked by a monument, sometimes thought to be the tomb of Nero or Marcellus, which stood near the point where the via Lata (called the Corso since the time of Paul III) runs into the open area (this monument was destroyed in the first half of the 16th century). In 1518, on the orders of Leo X, Raphael and Antonio da Sangallo the Younger laid out the via Leonina (called the via Ripetta since the time of Clement XI) running down to the Porta Fluviale beside the Mausoleum of Augustus. In the Holy Year of 1525 the third street, called the via Clemenza, was opened by Clement VII. It was completed by Paul III and renamed the via Paolina, and later the via del Babuino. In 1573 Giacomo della Porta set up a fountain in the middle of the area (replaced in the 19th century) and in 1589, on the orders of Sixtus V, Domenico Fontana erected the obelisk brought by Augustus from the Circus of Heliopolis to Rome and set up in the Circus Maximus. The area is marked as the Forum Populi in Bufalini's map of 1551 and as Piazza del Popolo in Tempesta's of 1593. A drawing published by Hager (fig. 136) shows the area c.1610.

In 1658 Alexander VII commissioned Carlo Rainaldi to build two churches flanking the opening of the Corso, both to be dedicated to the Virgin. This scheme was designed to create a fine symmetrical effect for travellers arriving from the north along the via Flaminia. The *piazza* was given its present form between 1816 and 1830 by Giuseppe Valadier, who added the two curved bays at the sides and the terraces leading up to the Pincio.

At the time of Alexander's commission there were already two churches at the entrance to the Corso: to the left S. Maria di Montesanto served by Discalced Carmelites and to the right S. Orsola, which was given by Alexander to the Tertiary Franciscan nuns, though the latter had its axis at right angles to the street and did not reach to the end of the block facing the ,. In order to make the execution of the scheme as symmetrical as possible more land had to be acquired and this caused delays.

Rainaldi, probably working in collaboration with the much younger Carlo Fontana, produced a design which included two almost identical circular domed churches with small apsed arms, whose façades were to be articulated with pilasters. Later this design was modified and coupled columns replaced the pilasters. The foundation stones of the two churches were laid in 1661 and 1662 respectively. In the latter year an important change was made in the design by Rainaldi who planned to add free-standing porticos, which are the most unusual feature of the churches. In 1644 Fontana introduced further modification by heightening the drums, thereby making the churches more impressive and improving the relationship of domes to portico. It was, however, Rainaldi who made the decision to design the Montesanto on an oval plan, with the long axis leading to the altar, to make better use of the long but narrow site. Financial problems, coupled with the death of the pope in 1677, led to great slowness in the building of the two churches, but in 1671 the newly created Genoese Cardinal Girolamo Gastaldi offered substantial help. At this stage Fontana replaced Rainaldi, but he was made subordinate to Bernini. It was probably the latter who designed the adjustments needed to make the two domes – one oval and one circular – look as far as possible identical externally, by thickening the masonry of that of the Montesanto on the cross-axis and making both domes polygonal outside, that on the left having twelve sides, that on the right having eight. As designed in 1622 the pediments over the porticos were to stand against a high attic, but in execution this was omitted. In 1674 Cardinal Gastaldi made a further donation so that work could start seriously on the Miracoli and in the following year Prince Camillo Pamphili also gave money. In 1676 work started under the direction of Rainaldi, though the inner dome of the Montesanto was finished under the direction of Bernini, who was probably largely responsible for its decoration. The church was finished by Fontana to whom Rainaldi had handed over effective control. Work on the Miracoli proceeded rapidly and in 1677 the interior of the dome was being stuccoed.

The belfry of S. Maria di Montesanto is by Gerolamo Theodoli and was erected in 1761[1].

S. Maria dei Miracoli

The statues on the attic are by Lazzaro Morelli, Cosimo Fancelli, Michele Maglia, 'il Tedesco' and Ercole Ferrata.

INTERIOR
Over choir arch: arms of Cardinal Gastaldi by Antonio Raggi
1 to R: Cappella dell'Assunta: R wall: monument to Aurelio Guglielmi by Cesare Benaglia, 1869[1]
Choir: sculpture by Raggi, begun 1679, completed before 1684. R wall: monument to Benedetto Gastaldi (d. 1681) with figures of L: *Prudence* and R: *Temperance* by Raggi and bust by Girolamo Lucenti[2]; L wall: monument to Cardinal Girolamo Gastaldi (d. 1685) with figures of R: *Hope* and L: *Faith* and bust of the cardinal originally in bronze, now replaced by a stucco copy, by G. Lucenti[3]
2 to L: Cappella del Rosario: altarpiece: copy of Sassoferrato's *Madonna of the Rosary* in S. Sabina
1 to L: Cappella di S. Antonio: altarpiece: Henry Gascard, *Virgin and Child with Sts Anthony Abbot and Anthony of Padua*[4]. R wall: monument to Antonio d'Este (d. 1837)[5].

S. Maria di Montesanto

The statues on the attic are by Alessandro

Rondone, Lazzaro Morelli, Sillano Sillani, Francesco Fontana, Giovanni Maria de' Rossi and others.

INTERIOR
Dome: figures in the niches by Filippo Carcani, *Sts Elijah, Angelus of Jerusalem, Elisha* and *Albert*, 1679[1]
1 to R: Cappella del Crocifisso/de' Rossi: by Alessandro Cassani, 1677-79; stucco figures by P. Papaleo[2]. Side walls by Ludovico Venuti, L: *Ahijah of Shiloh Receives Jeroboam's Wife*; R: *The Prophet of Bethel Recovers the Body of the Prophet of Judah*, 1822-25[3]; above L: *Judith and Holofernes*; R: *David and Goliath* by Fernando Cavalleri, 1825[4]
3 to R: Cappella di S. Anna/Vivaldi: architecture by Carlo Bizzacheri, 1679[5]; stuccoes by Pietro Paolo Naldini; decorated by Niccolò Berrettoni; altarpiece: *Holy Family with St Anne*; R lunette: *An Angel Appears to Joachim*; L lunette: *Meeting at the Golden Gate of Joachim and Anne*; vault: *God in Glory*, 1679-82[6]
High altar: by Mattia de' Rossi, 1677; angels by Filippo Carcani; side walls: terracotta busts (after lost bronzes) of L: Urban VIII and Clement IX and R: Alexander VII and Clement X, after Girolamo Lucenti[7]. The bust of Urban VIII and possibly some of the others were originally after models by Bernini[8]
Sacristy: Biagio Puccini, *Deposition*[9]
3 to L: Cappella Montioni: architecture by Tommaso Mattei from a design by Carlo Fontana, 1677-79; altarpiece: C. Maratta, *Virgin and Child with Sts James and Francis*, 1686[10]. R wall: Luigi Garzi, *The Virgin and Child Appear to St Francis*; L wall: D. Seiter, *Charity of St James*, before 1686[11]; vault: Baciccio, *Assumption*[12]
Sacristy of Cappella Montioni: frescoes by Baciccio; vault: *Symbols of the Passion*; wall: *St James*, 1691-92[13]; altarpiece: Giuseppe Chiari, *Deposition*[14]
2 to L: Cappella di S. Maria Maddalena dei Pazzi/Aquilanti: architecture by Carlo Rainaldi; paintings by Ludovico Gimignani: altarpiece: *The Virgin Covers St Mary Magdalen dei Pazzi with a Veil*; L wall: *St Augustine Appears to the Saint*; R wall: *Mystic Communion of the Saint*; vault: *Christ in Glory*, 1680-86[15]; stuccoes by Filippo Carcani[16]
1 to L: Cappella di S. Lucia: R wall: monument to Francesco Palombi (d. 1831) and Isabella Palombi Moroni (d. 1831) by A. M. Laboureur, 1832[17].

S. Maria dei Monti (Madonna dei Monti)
Via della Madonna dei Monti, 39-41

The church, which was attached to a convent that looked after non-Christian girls who intended to become converted to the Christian faith, was begun in 1580 to house a miraculous image of the Virgin. The architect was Giacomo della Porta and the church is one of the most complete examples of late 16th century Roman architecture and decoration. The façade was paid for by Cardinal Sirleto. It is of the familiar Roman type, with a narrow upper storey joined to a wider lower one by a scroll, and is articulated only with pilasters. It is an early and unusually harmonious example of the form.

INTERIOR
The church consists of a broad nave, with three chapels on either side, a dominant domed crossing, shallow transepts and an apse that contains a free-standing high altar designed by Giacomo della Porta enclosing the holy image. The vault of the nave was frescoed by Cristoforo Casolani (*c.*1620) with

the *Ascension*. It is one of the first instances of an artist breaking with the traditional method of decorating a vault bay by bay and extending his main fresco to unite all three bays[1]. Spandrels: R: *St Jerome*; *St Augustus*; L: *St Gregory*; *St Ambrose*; nave stuccoes by Giovanni Casolano

The dome has frescoes of scenes from the *Life of the Virgin* by B. Croce, M. Ganassini, V. Conti, C. Torelli, P. Guidotti and others, 1599-1600[2]; above these are *Angels with Musical Instruments* by O. Gentileschi and C. Nebbia[3]. The stucco angels are by Ambrogio Buonvicino. Pendentives: C. Casolani, *Evangelists*. The half-dome is decorated with stuccoes designed by Della Porta enclosing frescoes by Casolani, R: *Birth of the Virgin*; C: *Presentation in the Temple*; L: *Marriage of the Virgin*, completed 1603; below are frescoes by G. Gimignani; from left to right: *St Michael Fights the Demons*; *Crucifixion*; *St Peter Baptising in Prison*; *The Resurrected Christ Appearing to the Virgin*; *Baptism of Christ*, 1676[4]. The interior walls are decorated with painted marble.

1 to R: Cappella di S. Carlo Borromeo/Buccini: built for Andrea Buccini in 1621 and decorated in 1622. Altarpiece: Innocenzo Tacconi, *The Virgin and Child Appear to St Charles Borromeo*. Stuccoes and frescoes by Giovanni da San Giovanni: above chapel arch: *Calling of Sts Peter and Andrew*; R wall: *Assassination Attempt on St Charles's Life*; L wall: *St Charles Attends the Plague Victims*[5].

3 to R: Cappella della Pietà/Falconi: decorated in 1584 by Giacomo della Porta, who also designed the stuccoes; altarpiece: Antonio Viviani, *Descent from the Cross*, c.1590; L wall: Lattanzio Mainardi, *Flagellation*; R wall: Paris Nogari, *Christ Carrying the Cross*; ceiling arch: Giovanni Battista Lombardelli, L: *Christ before Caiaphas*; C: *Agony in the Garden* (ruined); R: *Kiss of Judas*

R transept: R wall: monument to Tommaso Sergi (d. 1752)

L transept: beneath the altar: reclining figure of *St Benedict Joseph Labre* by Achille Albacini, 1892[6]

3 to L: Cappella del Presepe/Sabbatini: altar by Giacomo della Porta; altarpiece: Girolamo Muziano, *Adoration of the Shepherds*, 1582; side walls by Cesare Nebbia, L wall: *Adoration of the Magi*; R wall: *Joseph's Dream*; pillars: *Prophets*; above altar: Paris Nogari, L: *Visitation*; C: *Annunciation*; R: *Circumcision*; vault stuccoes executed by Giovanni Casolano and Giovanni Solari, probably to Della Porta's design, 1581; above chapel entrance: C. Nebbia, *Coronation of the Virgin*

Passage to sacristy: L wall: monument to Luca Cappelli (d. 1682)

Sacristy: D. Alberti, *Road to Calvary*

1 to L: Cappella dell'Annunciazione/Buoncompagni/del Monte: altarpiece: decorated by Durante Alberti, *Annunciation*, 1588; side walls, R: *Sts Andrew and Bartholomew* and L: *Sts Peter and Paul*; vault, R: *Flight into Egypt*; C: *Last Supper*; L: *Immaculate Virgin*; entrance pier, R: *St Francis*; above, *St Dominic*; L: *Franciscan Saint*; above, *St Lucy*; above chapel entrance: Paolo Guidotti, *Marriage at Cana*[7]

Mariano Rossi, *Stations of the Cross*.

The noviciate attached to the church was built in 1635-39 at the expense of Cardinal Antonio Barberini, to the designs of Gaspare de'Vecchi[8].

S. Maria in Monticelli
Via di S. Maria in Monticelli

The medieval church was restored for Clement XI in 1715 by Matteo Sassi and Giuseppe Sardi[1]. In 1725 it was granted by Benedict XIII to the French Pères de la

Doctrine Chrétienne. It was restored in 1857-60 by Francesco Azzurri.

INTERIOR
Nave vault decorations by C. Mariani; spandrels: *Old Testament Women*, 1860[2].
Lunette over organ loft: C. Mariani, R: *Jacob's Dream*; L: *Moses and the Burning Bush*; organ loft: T. Minardi, *St Cecilia with Angels*
1 to R: Odoardo Vicinelli, *Agony in the Garden*[3]
2 to R: attributed to Antonio Carracci, *Flagellation*
3 to R: Cappella di S. Ninfa: G. B. Puccetti, *St Nympha Refuses to Worship Idols*, c.1717[4]; L wall over door: Baccio Ciarpi, *Virgin and Child with Sts Maximilian, Nympha, Eustasius, Proculus and Quodvultdeus*, 1613[5]
High altar: rebuilt in 1788; made of Sicilian marbles presented by Sicilian members of the Order. Altarpiece: A. Bea, *Presentation of the Virgin in the Temple*. Tabernacle, 1727.
Wall frescoes by C. Mariani, R: *Jesus with the Children* and L: *Jesus Preaching*
Room to L of high altar: *Assumption*, attributed to Sacchi (but not mentioned by Harris)
3 to L: G. B. Pacetti, *St John the Baptist Preaching*[6]; R wall: E. Parrocel, *Holy Family with Sts Philip Neri and Francis*[7]
1 to L: J. B. van Loo, *Flagellation*; L wall over door: G. Prinetti, *Martyrdom of St Erasmus*.

S. Maria della Neve
Via del Colosseo, 19

Originally called S. Andrea di Portogallo, this church, which belonged to the Confraternita dei Rigattieri (sellers of old mens' clothes), was rebuilt in 1706 to the designs of Francesco Fontana. The façade is unusual in having a parapet over the pediment (cf. S. Pasquale Baylon). The church contains three fine Baroque altarpieces, apparently without attribution. The church appears to be permanently closed.

S. Maria Nova *see* S. Francesca Romana
Piazza di S. Francesca Romana

S. Maria dell'Orazione e della Morte
Via Giulia, 262

Built for the Confraternita di S. Maria dell' Orazione e della Morte to ensure Christian burial for those unable to afford to pay for it. Founded as an informal body in 1538, it was approved by Julius III in 1552. In 1572 they bought two houses in the via Giulia on the site of the present church. The first church was built in 1575-76 with a burial place beneath it. Designs for the existing church were presented by Ferdinando Fuga and approved in 1722, but the foundation stone was not laid till 1733 and it was only consecrated in 1737.

The site was small and awkward, because it was limited on the north (right) by the party-wall of the Palazzo Falconieri which formed a slightly acute angle with the street. Remembering no doubt Borromini's solution at S. Carlo alle Quattro Fontane, Fuga chose an oval plan with the long axis running to the altar, round which he was just able to squeeze in four shallow chapels and a sacristy (for the right-hand chapels the confraternity had to acquire a narrow strip of land from the Falconieri).

The façade of the church is without curves in plan, but is richly articulated with pairs of full columns set between pilasters in a manner which recalls Cortona's SS. Luca e Martina and Martino Longhi the Younger's SS.

Vincenzo e Anastasio, and the lines of the entablature are broken consistently backward and forward at four points, corresponding to the junctions of the outer piers and central aedicules, an arrangement reminiscent of Della Porta's Gesù façade. The interior is dominated by an order of Corinthian columns which support, over the entrances to the chapels, pediments broken like that over the choir opening in Bernini's S. Andrea al Quirinale. In the latter church the short axis leads to the high altar, but the two plans have in common the fact that the cross axis of the oval ends in solids and not in the opening to a chapel. The design of the dome also owes much to S. Andrea.

This was Fuga's first church design in Rome and it shows that he was capable of making an impressive design from an intelligent choice of elements from the three 'Founding Fathers' of Roman Baroque – Bernini, Borromini and Cortona. It remains one of the most accomplished buildings of the late 'classicising' Baroque inaugurated in Rome by Carlo Fontana in the last decades of the 17th century.

The church is usually open for Mass on Sunday evenings at 6 pm.

INTERIOR

Between 1 and 2 to R: G. Lanfranco, *Meeting of St Anthony Abbot* and *St Paul the Hermit*, c. 1611. These detached frescoes come from the Camerino degli Eremiti, which was attched to the earlier church[1]
2 to R: Cappella di S. Michele: architecture by Paolo Posi, 1741[2]; altarpiece: copy of Reni's *St Michael* in S. Maria della Concezione
High altar: Ferri, *Crucifixion*, 1680
2 to L: P. L. Ghezzi, *St Juliana Falconieri Receiving the Habit from St Philip Benizi in the Presence of her Uncle St Alexius Falconieri*, c.1737[3]

Between 2 and 1 to L: Lanfranco, *St Simeon Stylites*
1 to R: Cappella della Sacra Famiglia: L. Masucci, *Rest on the Flight into Egypt*, 1750[4]
Behind organ: Lanfranco, *Count Roger Visits St Bruno*[5]

S. Maria dell'Orto
Via Anicia, 9-10

The church – with a hospital attached to it – was founded by a group of thirteen local guilds, which included fruiterers, poulterers, millers and local gardeners. It was canonically approved in 1492 and raised to an archconfraternity in 1558. The documents give the essential dates connected with the building of the church, but supply only tantalising indications of the artists involved. By 1525 the church was far enough advanced for some of the altars to be consecrated, and the whole structure was finished by 1563. The lower part of the façade was built in 1566-67, and the upper part begun in 1568 and finished in 1579. Over the door to the oratory is the date 1563, and the church was consecrated in 1585. In the earlier phases of the building no architect's name is given. Between 1556 and 1560 the name 'Guidetto' appears in the documents. This must be Guidetto Guidetti, the architect of S. Caterina dei Funari, but it is not clear whether he was the designer of the parts being built – probably the aisles and tribunes – or whether he was following the plan of the original architect. In 1560 'Raffaello' is mentioned as making a survey but he cannot be identified. In 1567 there is mention of 'Ms Jacinto' as taking measurements of the façade and this confirms the idea, originally put forward by Giovannoni on purely stylistic grounds, that the designer of the façade was Vignola, whose son and assistant was called Giacinto. The

S. Maria dell'Orto

suggestion is confirmed by the fact – unknown to Giovannoni and Fasolo – that Martinelli names Vignola as the author (contemptuously rejecting the generally accepted attribution to Martino Longhi the Elder). The documents clearly state that drawings for the upper part of the façade were made by Francesco da Volterra, but it is so unlike him in style that it seems almost certain that he was following Vignola's design, at least in its main outlines. The whole façade is shown – though with the proportions falsified – in a woodcut by Girolamo Francini reprinted in Roman guide books from at least as early as 1589. The façade appears – more accurately – in Falda's engraving of the 1660's (it is often stated wrongly that the upper part of the façade dates from the 18th century).

There seems to be no solid evidence about the original designer of the church and it is at least possible that the design was altered during the course of execution. Some 17th century writers of guide books attribute the design to Giulio Romano but this is unlikely, since he was only born in 1499. In general the indications of both date and authorship given in the guide books are confused and conflict with the facts known from the documents. It is, however, worth noting that Palladio[1] mentions the church in 1540, when it must have been still unfinished. The façade clock was added by N. Giansimoni, 1765[2].

INTERIOR

The decoration of the interior, which was begun by 1686 and finished in the first decades of the 18th century, is described in detail in the 1763 Titi. The fresco of the *Assumption* on the vault of the nave is by Giacinto Calandrucci, c.1700-05[3], and that of the *Immaculate Conception* over the crossing together with the pendentives is by Andrea and Giuseppe Orazi, 1703[4]. The stuccoes of the crossing and choir are by Simone Giorgini and Leonardo Retti, 1699-1706. Those on the vault of the nave are more classical and probably later, possibly by Valvassori, who is recorded as working in the church in the 1730's and later, and who designed the marble floor, 1747.

Entrance wall: G. and A. Orazi, L: *Adoration of the Shepherds* and R: *Joseph's Dream*[5]

1 to R: Cappella dell'Annunciazione: Federico Zuccaro, *Annunciation*, 1561[6]; aisle fresco: A. and G. Orazi, *Virgin in Glory*, 1703[7]

2 to R: Cappella di S. Caterina d'Alessandria: decorated probably by Luigi Barattone, 1708-11, but altered by G. Valvassori, 1750; altarpiece: Filippo Zucchetti, *Mystic Marriage of St Catherine with St Francis*, 1709-11; walls: F. Zucchetti, R: *St Paul* and L: *St Peter*; vault: *Putti with the Instruments of the Passion*, T. Cardani, 1711; aisle vault: A. and G. Orazi, *St Catherine in Glory*, 1703[8]

3 to R: Cappella di SS. Giacomo, Bartolomeo e Vittoria: decorated by G. Baglione. Altarpiece: *Virgin with Sts James, Bartholomew and Victoria*, c.1630; L wall: *Martyrdom of St Andrew*; L wall: *Beheading of a Deacon*[9]; aisle vault: G. and A. Orazi, *St Bartholomew in Glory*[10]

R transept: Cappella del Crocifisso: vault fresco: Calandrucci, *Resurrection*, c.1700[11]; walls: Niccolò Martinelli, scenes from the *Passion*: R wall: *Descent from the Cross*; above: *Pietà*; L wall: *Christ Carrying the Cross*; above: *Flagellation*, c.1591[12]

Over oratory door: A. Procaccini, *Pentecost*[13]; stucco angel holding a *tondo* by Legros, 1702[14]

The oratory has elaborate 18th century decoration, including a carved ceiling and frescoes of remarkable gaiety on the walls[15].

Within confraternity building: *Pietà*, Sodoma[16]

Apse: frescoes next to altar: lower L: Taddeo Zuccaro, *Adoration of the Shepherds*; upper

L: F. Zuccaro, *Marriage of the Virgin*; lower R: F. Zuccaro, *Rest on the Flight into Egypt* painted from Taddeo's design; upper R: *Visitation*, 1556-57[17]; side walls: Baglione, R: *Birth of the Virgin* and L: *Presentation*; apse: L: *Assumption*; C: *Coronation of the Virgin*; R: *Dormition*; R lunette: *Meeting at the Golden Gate*; L lunette: *Annunciation to Joseph of the Flight into Egypt*, 1598[18]

The high altar is datable to 1703 but was modified in 1755 by Valvassori.

Over door to sacristy: A. Procaccini, *The Virgin Appears to Joachim and Anne*[19]; stucco angel holding a *tondo* by Legros, 1702[20]

L transept: Cappella di S. Francesco d'Assisi: decorated by N. Martinelli with scenes from the *Life of St Francis*: lower R: *Confirmation of the Rule by Innocent III*; upper R: *Dream of Innocent III*; lunette: *Birth of the Virgin*; lower L: *Holy Family Adored by St Francis*; upper L: *St Francis Renounces his Worldly Goods*; lunette: *Dormition*; vault: Mario Garzi (son of Luigi), *St Francis in Glory*

3 to L: Cappella di SS. Carlo, Bernardino e Ambrogio: altar by Luigi Barattone; chapel decorated by G. Baglione: altarpiece: *Virgin and Child with Sts Ambrose, Charles Borromeo and Bernardine of Siena*, c.1641; R wall: *St Ambrose at the Defence of Milan against the Arians*; L wall: *Charity of St Charles Borromeo*[21]; aisle vault: G. Parodi, *St Charles Borromeo in Glory*

2 to L: Cappella di S. Giovanni Battista: restored in 1750 by Valvassori[22]; altarpiece: C. Giaquinto, *Baptism of Christ*, 1749-50[23]; side walls: G. Ranucci, L: *Beheading of the Baptist* and R: *Preaching of the Baptist*, 1749; aisle vault: G. Parodi, *St John the Baptist in Glory*

1 to L: Cappella di S. Sebastiano: decorated by Baglione; altarpiece: *St Sebastian*, 1624; R wall: *St Anthony of Padua*; L wall: *St Bonaventure*[24]; aisle vault: G. Parodi, *St Sebastian in Glory*

The hospital attached to the church, now dwelling houses, is dated 1739. It is attributed by Fasolo to Luigi Barrattone and by Barroero to Valvassori. It is probably by Valvassori, who was architect to the confraternity at that time.

S. Maria della Pace
Piazza della Pace

A church, S. Maria della Virtù, stood on this site in the 15th century and was granted to the Canons Regular of the Lateran. In 1482 Sixtus IV visited it to celebrate the peace which he had established after the troubles following the assassination of Giuliano de' Medici in the Pazzi conspiracy. On this occasion he changed the name of the church to S. Maria della Pace and ordered its reconstruction. The work was continued by his successor Innocent VIII. The author of the new church is said in the old guides to be Baccio Pontelli, but there does not seem to be any evidence for this attribution. The cloister was built in 1500 by Bramante. In the first years of the 16th century Agostino Chigi, the banker and friend of Julius II, nephew of Sixtus IV, was granted a chapel in the church, and the link with the Chigi family led to the restoration of the church and the construction of the façade by Alexander VII in 1656-57 to the designs of Pietro da Cortona.

The building of the façade was connected with the development of the area in front of the church and this in turn involved consideration of the circulation of traffic. As a result of Alexander VII's interest the church became fashionable, particularly because it was possible to attend Mass there in the afternoon. On the other hand the approach to the church was difficult. The street leading to the front of the church from S. Tommaso in Parione was narrow and those on either side of the

S. Maria della Pace

church were worse. That on the east passing below the apse of S. Maria dell'Anima would not admit a coach at all and that on the left allowed passage for one, but not two, which led to quarrels over precedence. By pulling down some houses Cortona was able to make a symmetrical *piazza* of unusual shape which made a fine approach to the church and allowed room for the turning of coaches, and he produced a design which brought the church and adjoining streets into a single architectural unit.

The upper part of the façade of the church itself he articulated with an order of Corinthian pilasters and columns which are laid out on the same kind of curved plan that he employed at SS. Luca e Martina. Below this he set a bold half-oval porch composed of massive Tuscan columns, which may have been inspired by a reconstruction of the Baths of Diocletian by Etienne Dupérac[1], though the uneven spacing of the columns is based on Peruzzi's Palazzo Massimo alle Colonne. At the lower level he extended the line of the façade by a wall which contained an opening for the right hand street, and this he balanced by a blind door. Above the wall he constructed two quarter-oval bays which mask the adjacent buildings, including the apse of S. Maria dell'Anima. The result was a brilliant solution to an extremely difficult problem. An unusual feature of the façade is that in the upper storey Cortona cut the very rough travertine that he chose as the material so that the 'graining' forms symmetrical patterns, thus giving an unusually rich texture to the surface. Cortona seems to have been alone in applying this technique to the rough Roman stone. The medallions of Alexander VII and Sixtus IV are by A. Raggi[2].

The complicated and rather amusing story of the financial manipulations involved in the construction of the *piazza* is recounted by Hans Ost.

INTERIOR

The nave remains basically as it was in the 16th century, except for the ribs on the vaulting and the window surrounds, which were added by Cortona. Over the arch leading to the octagon he added the arms of Sixtus IV and the figures of *Fortitude* and *Prudence* (a drawing for this exists at Windsor)[3], and on the entrance wall *Peace* and *Justice* by C. Fancelli[4].

The alterations which Cortona made to the octagonal sections were more considerable. Here he extended to the ground the 15th century pilasters which stood on high pedestals (recorded in drawings[5]), preserving the original capitals. In the drum he transformed the earlier *bifori* into single windows, covered with typical Cortonesque hoods, and in the dome, originally plain, he applied a mixture of ribs and coffering which seems to be the earliest example of this combination of the two systems of dome articulation, and was later followed by Bernini at Ariccia and Castelgandolfo (cf. also SS. Luca e Martina). He preserved the 15th century architect's unusual vertical division of the walls with a series of spaces for large canvases over four of the chapels (over the other two are organs, one real, the other sham to balance it).

1 to R: Cappella Chigi: decorated by Raphael for Agostino Chigi with frescoes of Sibyls, 1513-14, left unfinished at his death; the upper part finished by Sebastiano del Piombo. *Prophets* by Timoteo Viti: L to R; *Hosea, Jonah, David* and *Daniel*[6]. The chapel itself was altered under Alexander VII to the designs of Cortona, who inserted the bronze relief of the *Deposition* by Cosimo Fancelli (to Cortona's design) and the kneeling statues of R: *St Catherine of Siena* by C. Fancelli and L: *St Bernardine* by A. Raggi and the reliefs in front of the chapel of *Putti with the Instruments of the Passion* by E. Ferrata and C. Fancelli[7]

2 to R: Cappella Cesi: built by Antonio da Sangallo the Younger, c.1524. Over chapel entrance: Rosso Fiorentino, L: *Creation of Eve* and R: *Original Sin*, 1524[8]. Altarpiece: C. Cesi, *Holy Family with St Anne*[9]. Simone Mosca sculpted the pilasters, 1545-50. He was succeeded by Vincenzo de' Rossi, who completed the sculptural decorations with *Prophets* on the chapel façade, the figures of *Sts Peter* and *Paul* and the tombs of Angelo (d. 1528) and Francesco Cesi, 1550-60. Vault: Girolamo Sicciolante, R: *Nativity*; C: *Massacre of the Innocents*; L: *Flight into Egypt*; entrance: *Adoration of the Magi*, c.1549-50[10]. During the restoration under Alexander VII the chapel was slightly reduced in size in order to widen the vicolo della Pace which runs along the right hand side of the church, with the result that the decoration was truncated; two of the stucco *ignudi* vanished and one of the oval frescoes was replaced by a panel of architectural decoration clearly designed by Cortona

Octagon: lantern: F. Cozza, *God the Father*[11]; on walls: C. Maratta, *Visitation*, 1656-57; Peruzzi, *Presentation in the Temple*, c.1523[12]; Raffaele Vanni, *Birth of the Virgin* and G. M. Morandi, *Death of the Virgin*, 1657-71

4 to R: Cappella Benigni: monuments to L: Giacomo Benigni (d. 1588) and R: Giulio Benigni (d. 1611)[13]

5 to R: Cappella Olgiati: altarpiece: Orazio Gentileschi, *Baptism of Christ*, c.1600-05[14]; walls painted by Bernardino Mei, R: *The Baptist Prophesying before Herod*; L: *The Baptist on his Way to his Martyrdom*, 1659[15]

Choir: Cappella Rivaldi: enlarged and rebuilt by Maderno for Gaspare Rivaldi, 1611-14, as a setting for a miraculous image of the Virgin[16]. On the altar pediment are statues of R: *Peace* and L: *Justice* by Stefano Maderno, 1614[17]; entrance pillars: Lavinia Fontana, L: *St Catherine of Siena* and *St Cecilia*; R: *St Agatha* and *St Clare*, 1611-14[18]; on walls: D. Cresti (Il Passignano), L: *Annunciation* and R: *Nativity*, c.1612-14[19]; vault: Francesco Albani, *Assumption*; pendentives: *Angels with Musical Instruments*; apse: *God the Father Sending Gabriel to the Earth*; spandrels, L: *David* and R: *Isaiah*, 1612-14[20]. L wall: monument to Gaspare Rivaldi; R wall: monument to Ortensia Mazziotta (d. 1573) with portraits of the deceased by L. Fontana, c.1614[21]

3 to L: Cappella del Presepe: decorated by Girolamo Sicciolante; altarpiece: *Adoration of the Shepherds*; vault: L: *Creation of Adam*; C: *Temptation of Eve*; R: *Expulsion from Paradise*; walls: R: *St Sebastian* and L: *St Andrew*, c.1560[22]

Passage to sacristy: R wall: monuments to Cardinal Flaminio del Taja (d. 1682) and Cardinal Giovanni Bartoli (d. 1699)[23]

2 to L: Cappella Mignanelli: altarpiece: M. Venusti, *Virgin and Child with Sts Jerome and Ubald*[24]; above altar: F. Lauri, L: *Expulsion from Paradise* and R: *Adam and Eve with their Children*, 1668-70[25]. To L of chapel: monument to Girolamo de' Giustini da Castello (d. 1548) by Raffaello da Montelupo[26]

1 to L: Cappella Ponzetti: altarpiece: B. Peruzzi, *Virgin and Child with Sts Bridget and Catherine of Alexandria and the Donor Ferdinando Ponzetti*; half-dome: scenes from the *Old and New Testament*[27]; on chapel entrance wall: Pietro Machuca, L: *Liberation of St Peter*; R: *Conversion of St Peter* (or *Quo Vadis?*), 1516[28]. R of chapel: monuments to Beatrice and Lavinia Ponzetti (d. 1505) and L of chapel: Cardinal Ferdinando Ponzetti's monument to other members of his family who had died in Rome, erected 1509.

S. Maria in Palmis *see* Domine Quo Vadis
Via Appia Antica, 51

S. Maria del Pianto
Via di S. Maria de Calderari, 1b

The first part of the church, begun in 1608, was built to the designs of Niccolò Sebregondi, an architect from the Valtellina, and was completed in 1612 when the miraculous image of the Virgin, which gave its name to the confraternity of S. Maria del Pianto, was installed. The choir and sacristy were added by G. B. Mola in 1642; the nave was never built, but the executed parts are impressive, simple and spacious. The present dome was built by Mario Bernardi, 1734-35. Restored in 1817-18 by Pietro Holl. The church is usually open for early morning Mass.

INTERIOR
Near entrance: F. Simoncelli and B. Cibocchi, *Miracle of the Madonna del Pianto*, 1700; on reverse side: F. Simoncelli, *Virgin and Child in Glory*, 1700
1 to R: Cappella di S. Francesca Romana: altar attributed to F. Tittone, 1702; altarpiece: L. Baldi, *Virgin and Child with Sts Francis of Assisi, Anthony of Padua and Frances of Rome*, c.1695[1]. L of altar: monument to Pompeo Palmieri (d. 1647) by G. B. Mola, 1647
Choir: according to Martinelli the apse was decorated by Giacomo Mola, 1642-44. The high altar was restored in 1785; the stucco angels over the high altar are by Vincenzo Pacetti[2]. R choir wall: A. Ciampelli, *Christ Appears to St Martin*[3]
1 to L: Cappella del Crocifisso: altar designed by F. Tittone, 1692; to L: monument to Luigi Zannini (d. 1641) by Giovanni Pagni and portrait by Benigno Angiolini

Sacristy: vault: Camillo Marini, *Emblems of the Arciconfraternita della Dottrina Cristiana*, 1817.

S. Maria della Pietà *see* SS. Bartolomeo e Alessandro dei Bergamaschi
Piazza Colonna

S. Maria del Popolo
Piazza del Popolo

There is said to have been a church on this site since 1099, built over an ancient tomb, thought to be that of Nero, but the first certain documents refer to the consecration by Gregory IX in 1266 of a new church erected at the expense of the Roman people – hence its present name. It was served by a body of Augustinian Observants and was rebuilt between 1472 and 1480 by an unknown architect for Sixtus IV, but the apse is due to Bramante, working on the orders of Sixtus' nephew Julius II (or possibly his predecessor Alexander VI). In about 1513 Raphael began the construction of the Cappella Chigi, commissioned by Agostino Chigi, the celebrated banker to Julius II (who allowed him to quarter his arms with the Della Rovere arms), and in 1655-57 another Chigi, Pope Alexander VII, commissioned Bernini to restore and embellish the church. This restoration included the alterations to the nave arcade and the interior of the entrance wall, and the addition of the shield and figures over the arch between the nave and the crossing (all in stucco), the organ and marble altars in the transepts.

Before Bernini's intervention the nave arcade consisted of the existing arches separated by columns with fragments of entablatures over them. Bernini linked the

S. Maria del Popolo

columns by a continuous entablature which, however, he had to bend because the arches – surprisingly – came above the level of the top of the entablature. The result was the present somewhat weak line which the architect sought to work into the whole scheme by the addition of stucco figures of saints nearly reaching up to the windows above, which he enlarged.

The sculptors involved in the execution of the scheme were Ercole Ferrata, G. A. de' Rossi, P. Naldini, G. A. Mari, A. Raggi, L. Morelli and G. Peroni [1].

Bernini also added the curved half-pediments at the sides of the façade and the candelabra and Chigi *monti* on the central pediment[2].

INTERIOR

Over nave arches: female saints in stucco: R nave: 1st arch: F. de' Rossi, *Sts Catherine of Siena* and *Teresa*; 2nd arch: L. Morelli, *St Pudentiana* and P. Naldini, *St Praxedes*; 3rd arch: G. A. Mari, *Sts Cecilia* and *Ursula*; 4th arch: F. de' Rossi, *Sts Agatha* and *Martina*; L nave: 1st arch: E. Ferrata, *Sts Clare* and *Scholastica*; 2nd arch: A. Raggi, *Sts Barbara* and *Catherine*; 3rd arch: G. Peroni, *Sts Dorothy* and *Agatha*; 4th arch: A. Raggi, *Sts Tecla* and *Apollonia*[3]

1 to R: Cappella del Presepe/Della Rovere: frescoes by Pinturicchio assisted by Tiberio d'Assisi, 1485-89. L wall: monuments to Cardinal Cristoforo della Rovere (d. 1477) by Andrea Bregno and Mino da Fiesole[4] and his brother Cardinal Domenico (d. 1501). R wall: monument to Cardinal Giovanni de' Castro (d. 1506) attributed to Francesco da Sangallo

Between 1 and 2 to R: monument to F. Catel (d. 1856) with bust by Julius Troschel, 1857[5]

1st pier: monument to Galeotto Bernardino (d. 1591)

2 to R: Cappella di S. Lorenzo/Cybò[6]: built in 1681-86 by Carlo Fontana for Cardinal Alderano Cybò, Secretary of State under Innocent IX, whose aim it was to exceed in grandeur Raphael's Chigi chapel on the opposite side of the church. The chapel is one of the most ambitious pieces of marble decoration in Baroque Rome. As in the Cappella Ginetti in S. Andrea della Valle, Fontana has carried the marble beyond the entablature, in this case covering the barrel vault of the vestibule and the arms of the chapel. In spite of this obvious attempt at grandeur, however, the actual lines of the architecture are very simple. Altarpiece: C. Maratta, *Immaculate Virgin with Sts Gregory, John Chrysostom, John the Evangelist and Augustine*, 1686[7]. Putti supporting the altar by Francesco Cavallini, 1687[8]. Frescoes on side walls: Daniel Seiter, L: *Martyrdom of St Lawrence* and R: *Martyrdom of St Catherine*[9]; dome fresco: Luigi Garzi, *Heavenly Glory*, c.1685-86[10]. Monuments: R: Alderano Cybò (d. 1700), with bust by Antonio Francesco Andreozzi, and L: Lorenzo Cybò (d. 1503), with bust by Francesco Cavallini[11]

2nd pier: monument to Gaspar Celio (d. 1640) with portrait by Francesco Ragusa[12]

3 to R: Cappella di S. Agostino/Basso della Rovere: frescoes by the school of Pinturicchio of scenes from the *Life of the Virgin*. R wall: monument to Giovanni Basso della Rovere (d. 1483)

4 to R: Cappella di S. Caterina/Costa: marble altar with figures of *Sts Catherine, Vincent and Anthony of Padua* by Gian Cristoforo Romano[13]; L of altar: monument to Vincenzo Cascia-ni (d. 1833) by Luigi Poletti, 1833[14]; L wall: monument to Cardinal Giorgio Costa (d. 1508)

Between 4 to R and transept: monument to Caterina Balestra Marini (d. 1827) by Luigi Simonetti, 1834[15]. Monument to Cardinal Giovanni Girolamo Albani (d. 1591) by Paracca[16]

177

S. Maria del Popolo

4th pier: monument to Giovanni Battista Pallavicini (d. 1596)

R transept: organ case designed by Bernini, incorporating the Della Rovere oak, which the Chigi family were allowed to quarter. The organ itself was made in 1499-1500 by Stefano Pavoni, but was rebuilt for Alexander VII by Giuseppe Testa, who made the new organ to balance it in the left transept[17]. The two stucco angels with putti carrying the Chigi arms are by Raggi[18]. The marble altar is also to a design by Bernini. Altarpiece: G. M. Morandi, *Visitation*, 1659[19]. The angels on the altar are by L: E. Ferrata and R: Arrigo Giardé, 1658-59[20].

Passage to sacristy: monument to Bishop Bernardino Elvino (d. 1548) by Gugliemo della Porta, *c.*1548[21]

2 to R of high altar: Cappella di S. Rita da Cascia: on the floor is the tombstone of Cardinal Giovanni Battista Cicala (d. 1570) with the arms in bronze relief. R wall: monument to Archbishop Odoardo Cicala (d. 1545). Pier to R of chapel: monument to Carlo Balestra (d. 1874) by L. Simonetti, 1859[22]

1 to R of high altar: Cappella di S. Tommaso da Villanova/Feoli: altarpiece: *St Thomas of Villanova*, C. de' Rossi[23]. To L of chapel: monument to Virgilio Malvezio (d. 1691)[24]

Dome crossing: Raffaele Vanni, *The Virgin Received into Glory*, 1656-58[25]

Choir: the first bay of the choir is decorated with gold and white stucco reliefs, showing scenes from the early history of the church, which were commissioned through a bequest left by the Genoese Cardinal Antonio Sacchi (d. 1627)[26]. The high altar was paid for out of the same bequest and holds a venerated image of the Virgin, brought from the Lateran by Gregory IX. The previous high altar, commissioned by Cardinal Rodrigo Borgia from Andrea Bregno (1472-*c.*74), is now in the sacristy. The choir was extended by Bramante and converted into a family mortuary chapel for the Della Rovere family on the orders of Julius II. Vault frescoes by Pinturicchio, 1508-09; stained glass by Guillaume de Marcillat; monuments to, R wall: Cardinal Girolamo Basso della Rovere (d. 1507) by Andrea Sansovino with the allegorical figure of *Temperance* in the lower right niche by Jacopo Sansovino[27] and L wall: Cardinal Ascanio Sforza (d. 1505) by Andrea Sansovino; lunette: *Virgin and Child*; in side niches, R: *Prudence* and above: *Hope*; L: *Justice* and above: *Faith*, completed 1509[28]. Fine 17th century choir stalls

1 to L of high altar: Cappella dell'Assunta/Cerasi: founded and decorated in 1601. The frescoes on the vault of the main body of the chapel are by G. B. Ricci, lunettes: *Four Church Fathers* and vault: *Four Evangelists*. Those in the choir are by Innocenzo Tacconi after drawings by Annibale Carracci; R: *St Paul Received into Heaven*; C: *Coronation of the Virgin*; L: *'Domine quo vadis'*[29]. The gilded stuccoes depict scenes from the *Life of St Paul*[30]. Altarpiece: A. Carracci, *Assumption*, *c.*1600-01[31]. On side walls: Caravaggio, R: *Conversion of St Paul* and L: *Martyrdom of St Peter*, 1600-01[32]. Monuments to, R wall: Bartolomeo Cerasi (d. 1573) and Stefano Cerasi (d. 1575) and L wall: Tiberio Cerasi (d. 1601)[33]; beneath: monument to Theresa Pelzer (d. 1852) by Giuseppe Tenerani[34]

2 to L of high altar: Cappella di S. Caterina/Theodoli: paintings and stuccoes by G. Mazzoni: L: *St Peter* and R: *St Paul*; R oval: *St John the Baptist* and L oval: *St Jerome*; altar: *St Catherine*, 1569-70. L wall: *Angel of the Annunciation* and R wall: *The Virgin* by Giacomo Triga[35]

L transept: organ and altar to a design by Bernini; the angels holding the altarpiece are by R: Antonio Raggi and L: Giovanni. Mari, 1657-58[36]; altarpiece: Bernardino Mei, *Rest on the Flight into Egypt with Angels Holding the*

Instruments of the Passion, 1658-9[37]. L wall: monument to Cardinal Bernardino Lonate (d. 1497)
L of 4 to R: monument to Giovan Battista Robbiano (d. 1585) attributed to N. Pippe[38]
4 to L: Cappella del Crocifisso/Soderini: frescoes by Pieter van Lint, R wall: *The Emperor Heraclius Entering Jerusalem with the True Cross*; L wall: *St Helena Verifies the True Cross*; vault: *Angels with the Instruments of the Passion*; lunettes: *Prophets*, c.1637[39]
3 to L: Cappella di S. Nicola da Tolentino/Millini: frescoes of scenes from the *Life of St Nicholas of Tolentino* by Giovanni da San Giovanni; altarpiece: A. Masucci, *St Nicholas of Tolentino Introduced to the Virgin by St Nicholas of Bari*, 1745-50[40]. R wall: bust of Cardinal Savio Millini (d. 1701) erected by himself in 1699 and executed by Pierre Etienne Monnot[41]. The 15th century figures were taken from the monument – originally in old St Peter's – of Cardinal Giovanni Battista Millini (d. 1483) whose effigy now lies below the bust of Cardinal Savo. On either side of this monument are busts of L: Pietro Millini (d. 1694) and R: Paolo Antonio Millini (d. 1683) attributed to Monnot[42]. L wall: monument to Cardinal Giovanni Garzia Millini (d. 1629), commissioned in 1637 and designed by Alessandro Algardi in a markedly classical style, with a half-length figure of the cardinal by the same artist. This form of tomb sculpture, consisting of a half-length figure with one hand holding a book and the other clutching the breast, was to become very popular. It was frequently used by Finelli and was adapted by Bernini in his Fonseca monument in S. Lorenzo in Lucina, and was widely used throughout the 18th century. To the left of the altar is a bust of Urbano Millini (d. 1660) also by Algardi[43] and to the right a bust of Mario Millini (d. 1673)[44]. On floor: inlaid marble tomb of Cardinal Mario Millini (d. 1760)
2nd pier of nave: monument to Francesco Natale Rondinini (d. 1657) with bust by Domenico Guidi[45]
2 to L: Cappella della Madonna di Loreto/Chigi[46]: built and decorated by Raphael and his assistants for Agostino Chigi; begun about 1513. Altarpiece: *Birth of the Virgin*, 1533/4-55, by Sebastiano del Piombo, but completed after his death in 1547 by Salviati[47]. The mosaics in the dome (*God the Father and Planets*) are to designs by Raphael, as are the statues in the niches of *Jonah* and *Elijah*, which were executed by Lorenzetto, 1522, who was also responsible for the relief now on the altar frontal, 1519-22[48]. The lunettes were frescoed by Francesco Salviati with the *Story of Genesis* and ovals of the *Four Seasons* on the pendentives, 1522-24; those on the side wall are by Raffaele Vanni, L: *Saul and David* and R: *Samuel with Eli*, 1653.

In the same year Bernini was commissioned by Cardinal Fabio Chigi (later Alexander VII) to complete the decoration of the chapel. In that year he erected the monument to Sigismondo Chigi (d. 1526) on the left wall, added the two portrait medallions by A. Raggi (which have also been attributed to Bernini) to the obelisk-tombs and moved the bronze relief of *Christ and the Woman of Samaria* from Agostino's tomb (d. 1520) to the altar frontal. Between 1655 and 1661 he made the statues of *Daniel* and *Habbakuk*[49].

Apart from the fact that it is one of the masterpieces of Renaissance art, the Chigi chapel is important as foreshadowing many features of the Baroque, in particular the illusionism of the dome mosaics, the marble decoration of the walls and the obelisks of the tombs. If, as has been plausibly suggested by Shearman, the painting over the altar was originally intended to be an *Assumption*, then Raphael would also have forestalled Bernini

179

in the idea of continuing the action across the space of a church or chapel, since the Virgin would have been moving upwards towards the figure of God the Father in the dome, as she does in Cortona's frescoes in S. Maria in Vallicella and as St Andrew does in Bernini's S. Andrea al Quirinale.

Between 2 and 1 to L: monument to Maria Flaminia Odescalchi Chigi (d. 1771), a flamboyant example of late Baroque exuberance designed by Paolo Posi and executed partly by A. Penna; the lion and eagle are by F. A. Franzoni, the oak tree and medallion by B. Boroni, 1772[50]

1st pier of nave: monument to Francesco Mantica (d. 1614) attributed to A. Buonvicino[51]

1 to L: Cappella di S. Giovanni Battista: altarpiece: Pasqualino de' Rossi, *Baptism of Christ*[52]. R wall: monument to Cardinal Francesco Abbondio Castiglione (d. 1568)

Between 1 to L and entrance: monument to Stefano Spada (d. 1563)[53]

Entrance wall: monuments to Samuel Raphael Globicz (d. 1665); Giovanni Battista Ghisleni (d. 1672) designed by himself with a highly naturalistic skeleton in yellow marble behind a bronze grille[54]; Maria Eleonora Buoncampagni Ludovisi (d. 1745) designed by Domenico Gregorini, 1749[55].

S. Maria in Porta Paradiso
Via Ripetta, 63

A small octagonal church within the hospital of S. Giacomo degli Incurabili but accessible from the via Ripetta. Designed by Antonio da Sangallo the Younger, it was begun in 1519 and completed in 1526. It was remodelled in 1644-45 by Giovanni Antonio de' Rossi[1]. Over entrance: *Virgin and Child* by Peruzzi[2]. The church is rarely open to the public.

INTERIOR
The stuccoes of the dome are by C. Fancelli and D. de' Rossi, with frescoes by P. P. Baldini, *Assumption with Angels*, 1646[3], whilst the lunettes below depicting scenes from the *Life of Mary* are by L. Greuter, R side: *Visitation* and *Annunciation*; L side: *Dormition* and *Rest on the Flight*.

Altar to R: Domenico de' Rossi, *Holy Family with Sts Anne and John the Baptist*, 1645[4]

High altar: F. Brunetti, R: *St Dominic* and L: *St John the Baptist*[5]; decorated by L. Greuter, R wall: *Presentation in the Temple*; L wall: *Birth of the Virgin*; vault: *God the Father*

Altar to L: Cosimo Fancelli, *Risen Christ with the Virgin and Sts John the Evangelist and James*[6]. On either side of the high altar are monuments to L: Antonio de Burgos (d. 1515), designed by Peruzzi, 1534, and R: Matteo Caccia (d. 1644) by C. Fancelli[7]

Sacristy: attributed to B. Gagliardi, *St James Venerating the Madonna del Popolo*[8]

To the north of the church in the via Ripetta is another façade, dated 1589, apparently also belonging to a church but in fact closing one of the wings of the hospital. As an engraving by Falda shows, this originally stood on the Corso, to the north of the church, though its exact function there is not clear. The two bays which at present close the wings of the hospital on the Corso date from the pontificate of Gregory XVI and are by Pietro Camporese the Younger. His wooden model for them is in the museum of the Ospedale di Spirito Santo.

S. Maria in Portico (S. Galla) (destroyed)

The church stood in the via Montanara but was pulled down in the 1930's. It was remodelled in the 17th century by Mattia de' Rossi. The façade is recorded in an engraving by Vasi, reproduced by Armellini.

S. Maria del Priorato (S. Maria in Aventino)
Piazza dei Cavalieri di Malta, 4

The Priory of the Knights of Malta was established on this site in 1568. The chapel was completely remodelled by Piranesi for Cardinal Giambattista Rezzonico, Grand Master of the Order and nephew of Clement XIII, between 1764 and 1766, as is shown by the account book preserved in the Avery Library of Columbia University and drawings in the Pierpont Morgan Library. The entrance gate and the screen around the piazza in front are also by Piranesi, who incorporated in their decoration many allusions to the military and naval prowess of the Knights of Malta. The chapel and *piazza* are the only buildings that Piranesi ever actually designed and erected; they embody – particularly in their decoration – many of the most inventive features to be found in his drawings and etchings. The church is open to the public on Saturday mornings.

INTERIOR
Vault and nave stuccoes by Tommaso Righi to Piranesi's design; in the nave are *tondi* of reliefs of the *Apostles*, 1765.
2nd bay to R: statue of *Giambattista Piranesi* (d. 1778) by Giuseppe Angelini, 1779-80[1]
High altar: executed by T. Righi with figures of the *Virgin and Child* and the *Apotheosis of St Basil*, 1765; vault above altar: reliefs depicting scenes from the *Life of the Virgin*
2 to L: monument to Cardinal Gioacchino Ferdinando Portocarrero (d. 1760) by Luigi Salimei
Casa del Vescovo: A. Sacchi, *Virgin and Child with St Basil*, 1636-40[2].

S. Maria in Publicolis
Via Publicolis, 23

Built in 1640-43 almost certainly by G. A. de' Rossi for Cardinal Marcello Santacroce, whose family were patrons of the church. This is the earliest work of the architect who represents the sober, non-Baroque trend of Roman architecture of the mid 17th century. The church is simple and traditional in plan, a rectangular nave with three shallow chapels on either side, but in the façade De' Rossi has been bolder, if not always completely successful. The use of two storeys of equal width is common at this date, but the relation of the attic storey to the lower parts of the façade and the treatment of the pediments are clumsy. The fact that De' Rossi uses an Ionic order for the lower storey and a Tuscan for the upper is highly unorthodox, though the same arrangement is to be found on the façades of S. Giuseppe a Capo le Case and S. Maria di Grottapinta. The church is open for Sunday morning Mass.

INTERIOR
R of entrance: monument to Margerita Sforza (d. 1740)
1st bay to R: monument to Principe Scipione Publicola Santacroce (d. 1747) by G. B. Maini; cypress fronds by T. Righi, *c.*1748-50. The confessional which was once underneath the monument has been removed[1]
1 to R: Raffaele Vanni, *St Helena with the True Cross*, 1644[2]
Choir: high altar: R. Vanni, *Birth of the Virgin*, *c.*1644[3]. On side walls: monuments to the Publicola Santacroce family with oval painted portraits by Alessandro Grimaldi: L wall: Cardinals Marcello (d. 1674), Andrea (d. 1712), Antonio (d. 1641) and Prospero (d. 1589); R wall: Octavia Corsini (d. 1679), Scipione (d. 1568), Elena Maria Mattei di Giove (d. 1670) and Valerio (d. 1640)

1 to L: G. F. Grimaldi, *St Francis in Prayer*, 1655[4]

1st bay to L: to a design by G. F. Zannoli, 1707-08; monument to the Marchese Antonio Publicola (d. 1707) and his wife Girolama Naro (d. 1727) with busts and putti by Lorenzo Ottoni, and cloth and death's head by Andrea Fucigna. The confessional underneath is by J. Gauthier.

S. Maria della Purificazione (destroyed)

This church stood behind S. Pietro in Vincoli. It appears to have been founded in 1643 and was under the protection of Cardinal Francesco Barberini. It had a façade of five bays, the outer two not being linked to the inner ones by the usual scrolls.

S. Maria della Quercia
Piazza della Quercia, 27

The Corporazione dei Macellai (butchers) took possession of the medieval church of S. Nicola de' Curte in 1523 but were not officially confirmed as owners till 1532. Between that date and 1555 its dedication was changed to S. Maria della Quercia, in honour of the holy image of this name venerated in a church just outside Viterbo.

The foundation stone of the existing church was laid by Benedict XIII in 1727; it was opened in 1731 and consecrated in 1738. The church was restored – rather drastically – in 1864 by Andrea Busiri Vici.

All the early sources agree in ascribing the church to Filippo Raguzzini. The plan – a square with three semi-circular bays and a rectangular choir – is curiously archaic for the period, but Raguzzini used a similar, even simpler design for the chapel of the hospital of S. Gallicano, a square with shallow rectangular side bays. In plan the façade is based on an elaborate play of convex curves, as opposed to the concave curves of S. Gallicano. In elevation, however, the relation of the attic to the lower storey is somewhat clumsy. The church is usually open for Sunday morning mass.

INTERIOR

Interior decorated by Guido Molinari, vault: *Litany of the Virgin with Angels*; R lunette: *Marriage of the Virgin*; L lunette: *Presentation in the Temple*; over altar: *Coronation of the Virgin*, 1864.

1 to R: Cappella del Battesimo di Gesù: Pietro Barbieri, *Baptism of Christ*

High altar: the high altar and choir were rebuilt by Domenico Gregorini, 1731, who is also responsible for the design and construction of the organ lofts over the entrance[1]

1 to L: Cappella del Crocifisso: M. Benefial, *Crucifixion*[2].

S. Maria del Rosario su Monte Mario
Via Trionfale, 177

Built in 1628-29, but rebuilt to the designs of Camillo Arcucci from 1651 onwards and officially opened in 1700. In 1709 it was given to the Dominicans of S. Marco, Florence. The church is only open to the public for Sunday morning Mass.

INTERIOR

The interior stucco decorations date from the 18th century.

2 to L: altarpiece: M. Cerruti, *Madonna of the Rosary*, before 1726[1]; L wall: copy of Maratta's *Adoration of the Shepherds*.

S. Maria della Scala
Piazza della Scala

The church was begun in 1593 for the Casa Pia founded by Pius IV and Carlo Borromeo in 1563 to care for reformed prostitutes. The documents prove that the architect was Francesco da Volterra, but Martinelli states that he only built the church up to the entablature and that it was finished by Mascarino. Mola, however, ascribes the church to Matteo Bartolini, who may well have been the mason in charge. The dome was built in 1607-10. Martinelli adds that the convent was mainly built by Bartolomeo Breccioli.

In 1597 the establishment passed to the Discalced Carmelites, who finished the church in 1610 and began the façade in 1624, apparently still following the designs of Francesco da Volterra (the upper storey, which is in stucco, is later). The sculpture of the *Virgin and Child* over the door is by F. Cusart, 1633[1].

INTERIOR
The interior is painted marble. The magnificent choir over the entrance is by G. Pannini, 1756. On the entrance wall are monuments to L: Leonora Ferretti (d. 1697) and R: Marchese Mario Zandomarie (d. 1660).
1 to R: Cappella di S. Giovanni Battista/Sinbaldi: altarpiece: G. Honthorst, *Beheading of St John the Evangelist*, 1617-18[2]
2 to R: Cappella di S. Giacinto/Barisani: altarpiece attributed to Giovanni Sorbi, *Virgin and Child with Sts Catherine of Siena and Hyacinth*. Side walls: monuments to R: Giuseppe Sorbolonghi (d. 1758) and L: Jacopo Sorbolonghi (d. 1713).
3 to R: Cappella di S. Giuseppe/Paolelli: altarpiece: G. Ghezzi, *Holy Family*; R wall: G. Odazzi, *Joseph's Dream*; L wall: L. David, *Marriage of the Virgin*; vault: G. Odazzi, *St Joseph Received into Heaven*[3]

R transept: Cappella di S. Teresa d'Avila: rebuilt between 1734 and 1746; the architectecture is attributed to Giuseppe Pannini but archival evidence has shown that the chapel, together with the floor tombs, are by Giovanni Paolo Pannini[4]. Altarpiece: F. Mancini, *Ecstasy of St Teresa*, 1745; marble reliefs illustrating the *Life of St Teresa*; L oval: *Transverberation of St Teresa* by M. A. Slodtz; R oval: *St Teresa in Ecstasy* by F. della Valle, completed by 1738[5]; the reliefs beside the window are by G. Lironi, R: *Christ Appears to St Teresa* and L: *The Virgin Appears to St Teresa*, 1741-42[6]; stucco angels by G. Maini[7]

High altar: high altar and tabernacle commissioned by Prospero Lambertini, later Benedict XIV. They were designed by Carlo Rainaldi and the tabernacle was made by Giovanni Maniscalchi in 1747[8]. On the screen separating the sanctuary from the choir: S. Giorgini, R: *St Teresa* and L: *St John of the Cross*, 1706[9].

Choir: paintings by Luc de la Haye; R wall: *Baptism of Christ*; *Marriage at Cana*; L wall: *Ascension of Christ*; *Last Supper*, 1677[10]; between these: *Virgin and Child* by Giuseppe Cesari, 1619[11]

Chapel to L of high altar: Cappella di S. Teresa: decorated mostly by Luc de la Haye, L wall: *Transverberation of St Teresa*; R wall: *St Teresa with the Virgin and St Joseph*; *Coronation of St Teresa*; *St Teresa Receives the Stigmata*[12]

L transept: Cappella dell'Immacolata/Santacroce/Piccolomini: R wall: monument to Prospero Santacroce (d. 1643) by Algardi[13] and L wall: Livia Primi Santacroce (d. 1662) by Domenico Guidi[14]. Luc de la Haye, R wall: *Coronation of the Virgin*; L wall: *Virgin and Child in Glory*, 1678-79[15]. R of altar: monument to Tarquinio Marchioni Santacroce

3 to L: Cappella del Crocifisso/Baldi/Durani:

recorded by Titi (1763) as decorated 'di nuovo' for Cesare Baldi by Filippo Zucchetti; R wall: *Mocking of Christ*; L wall: *Christ Carrying the Cross*; vault: *Angels with Instruments of the Passion*[16]; altarpiece: marble group of *St John of the Cross in Ecstasy* by Pietro Papaleo[17]

2 to L: Cappella dell'Assunta/Cherubini: by Girolamo Rainaldi, 1603-04[18]; altarpiece: C. Saraceni, *Death of the Virgin*, c.1615, painted to replace Caravaggio's painting of the same subject which had been rejected by the authorities[19]. Side walls: G. Conca, R: *Birth of the Virgin* and L: *Marriage of the Virgin*

1 to L: Cappella del Carmine/Pandini/Ferrari: built by G. Rinaldi, 1604-05. Altarpiece: C. Roncalli, *The Virgin Gives the Scapular to St Simon Stock in the Presence of Elijah*; above: *God the Father*, 1605[20].

S. Maria Scala Coeli (*see also* S. Paolo alle Tre Fontane)
Via di Acque Salvie

The dedication of the church, Scala Coeli, records the vision seen here by St Bernard of souls walking up a ladder to Heaven. It was rebuilt in 1582 for Cardinal Alessandro Farnese and later for Pietro Aldobrandini. Baglione and Titi attribute the church to Giacomo della Porta. It was consecrated in 1584.

INTERIOR
High altar: attributed to Francesco Ragusa, *Annunciation*[1]
L apse: vault: *Virgin and Child with Sts Robert, Anastasius, Bernard and Vincent, and Clement VIII and Cardinal Pietro Aldobrandini*, executed by Francesco Zucchi after a cartoon by Giovanni de' Vecchi, 1589-1600[2]. Altarpiece: Desiderio de' Angelis, *Vision of St Bernard*, 1787.

S. Maria dei Sette Dolori
Via Garibaldi, 27

The Convent of Augustinian Oblates was founded in 1641 by Camilla Virginia Savelli, wife of Pier Francesco Farnese, duca di Laterza, and the church was begun the same year. Borromini agreed to make the design but said he was too busy – presumably with S. Ivo and the Oratory – to work out the details, which he handed over to Antonio del Grande. The whole structure was finished by 1646 and the decoration of the interior was begun in 1648-49, but was not finished till 1667 by G. B. Contini (who designed the high altar of S. Ivo).

The exterior, which is unfinished, is composed of an astonishingly rich and varied series of convex and concave forms executed in rough brick, which most likely was to have been plastered. This gives a rugged quality to the whole building, but it is so simple that we can be fairly certain that here, as at S. Andrea delle Fratte, Borromini would have plastered it. When he intended the brick to be left visible, as at the Oratory, he chose thin bricks and laid them with less mortar to make a smooth surface. The door – which is certainly not to Borromini's design – leads into a small vestibule, square, but with each side curved, convex inwards. Beyond this is a cloister probably designed by Contini.

The church belongs to a small group of those designed by Borromini in the form of a rectangle with rounded corners, the others being the Oratory of S. Filippo Neri and the Re Magi Chapel in the Collegio di Propaganda Fide, but it differs from these in that it is articulated with columns instead of pilasters and has a shallow half-oval chapel in the middle of each side.

INTERIOR
Interior disastrously repainted in 1845.

High altar: copy of Pordenone's *Deposition*[1]
L altar: C. Maratta, *St Augustine Contemplates the Trinity*, 1655[2].

S. Maria del Suffragio
Via Giulia, 59

The Compagnia di S. Maria del Suffragio was founded in 1592. The church was built by Carlo Rainaldi between 1662 and 1669, the latter date being inscribed on the frieze of the lower order of the façade. Rainaldi at first proposed an oval plan, but this was replaced by the existing design, consisting of a rectangular nave with side-chapels. The church is open for early morning Mass and on Sunday evenings.

INTERIOR
Decorated during the restoration of 1869 under the direction of Tito Armellini. Vault fresco by Cesare Mariani, *Coronation of the Virgin*.
1 to R: decorated by G. B. Natali, altarpiece: *Adoration of the Magi*, 1671; L wall: *Adoration of the Shepherds*; R wall: *Joseph's Dream*; vault: *God the Father in Glory*[1]. Monuments to, L wall: Gaspare Morone (d. 1678) and R wall: Pietro Neri (d. 1678) attributed to E. Ferrata[2]
2 to R: R wall: Calandrucci, *Jacob's Dream*; L wall: Troppa, *Sacrifice of Abraham*, both before 1686[3]
3 to R: Cappella Marcaccioni: architecture by G. B. Contini, c.1674[4]; stucco decoration and monuments to L: Gaspare (d. 1674) and R: Elena Marcacciona (d. 1703) by P. Naldini[5]; paintings on side walls by G. Chiari, L: *Birth of the Virgin* and R: *Adoration of the Magi*[6]
Oratory: altarpiece: G. Ghezzi, *Madonna of the Rosary with Sts Dominic and Joseph* (now concealed behind a cupboard)[7]; G. B. Beinaschi, *Daniel and Habakkuk*; *Raising of Lazarus*[8]
High altar: designed by Carlo Rainaldi for a painting by Giacinto Brandi, but this was replaced by one by G. Ghezzi, *Madonna del Suffragio with Souls in Purgatory*, 1672[9]; lunette: fresco of the *Assumption* and vault: *God the Father* by G. B. Beinaschi, c.1675[10]
2 to L: Cappella di S. Giuseppe da Calasanzio: restored and redecorated by Andrea Ossanni, 1783. Altarpiece: Sebastiano Ceccarini, *St Joseph Calasanctius*, 1753[11]; L wall: *Death of St Joseph Calasanctius*; R wall: *St Joseph Calasanctius Healing a Child* by Gaetano Sortini[12]
1 to L: Cappella di SS. Giacinto e Caterina/Armellini: altarpiece: D. Seiter, *Virgin with Sts Catherine and Hyacinth*, c.1685[13]; vault: Giovanni Battista Cimini, *Holy Ghost and Angels*[14].

S. Maria in Traspontina
Via della Conciliazione, 14

The present church was founded by Pius IV in 1563 but the building was not begun till 1566, using a design by Salustio Peruzzi that was preferred to one by Vignola known from a drawing[1]. In 1567 Peruzzi left for Austria and was replaced by Battista Ghioldo. In 1581 Ottaviano Mascarino took charge till 1587, when the church, still unfinished, was consecrated. The exact share of the three architects involved cannot be determined in the present state of our knowledge, particularly in connection with the façade. Baglione and, probably following him, Martinelli state that it was begun by Peruzzi and that the upper half is by Mascarino, and this statement seems convincing. The choir, transepts, dome and sacristy were finished in 1637[2]. The church has been served by the Carmelites since 1484, when it was given to them by Innocent VIII.

INTERIOR

In 1894 the interior was decorated with *scagliola*. The nave vault was frescoed by Cesare Caroselli, *St Simon Stock Receives the Scapular from the Virgin in the Presence of Saints*, and the dome by Cesare Gabrini.

1 to R: Cappella di S. Barbara: built for Cardinal Pietro Aldobrandini by Mascarino, 1581-87. Frescoed by Giuseppe Cesari and Cesare Rossetti with scenes from the *Life of St Barbara*; L wall: *Martyrdom of St Barbara*; R wall: *St Barbara before her Judges*; vault: C: *St Barbara in Glory*; R: *St Barbara Chased by her Father*; L: *Martyrdom of St Barbara*, c.1602; altarpiece: G. Cesare, *St Barbara Receives a White Robe from an Angel*, 1597[3]. R wall: monument to Oliviero Malatesta (d. 1730)

2 to R: Cappella di S. Canuto/della Nazione Danese: altarpiece: Daniele Seiter, *Martyrdom of St Canute*, 1686[4]; Alessandro Ubeleski, lunettes: putti; vault: *St Canute in Glory*[5]

This chapel and the one opposite show the influence of the Neapolitan style of marbling introduced about 1650 by Cosimo Fanzago[6].

4 to R: Cappella del Crocifisso: altar wall: Cesare Conti, *Mary Magdalen and St John*[7]; side walls: B. Gagliardi, lower R: *Christ Carrying the Cross*; upper R: *Mocking of Christ*; lower L: *Agony in the Garden*; upper L: *Scourging of Christ*[8]

5 to R: Cappella di S. Alberto: Antonio Circignani, scenes from the *Life of St Albert of Trapani*; R wall: *Death of St Albert*; L wall: *Charity of the Saint*; vault: L: *St Albert Exorcises a Demon*; C: *Birth of St Albert*; R: *Investiture of St Albert*; soffits: *Prophets*; altarpiece: *St Albert*, 1621[9].

Passage between 5 to R and transept: L wall: monument to Cardinal Francesco Albizzi (d. 1684) begun by D. Guidi, 1693, and completed by Vincenzo Felice[10]

R transept: altarpiece: Cerrini, *Christ and the Virgin Appearing to St Mary Magdalen dei Pazzi*, before 1674[11]

High altar: designed by C. Fontana in 1674[12]. Angels above altar by L. Retti[13]; figures added in 1695: *Elijah* by G. A. Lavaggi; *Elisha* by V. Felici; *St Angelo of Sicily* by A. Rondone; *St Albert* by M. Maglia[14]

Pendentives: Pietro Paolo Baldini, *Sts Elijah, Elisha, Andrew Corsini* and *The Blessed Peter Tommaso*[15]

Sacristy: built by F. Peparelli, 1635-37[16]; vault: P. P. Baldini, *St Simon Stock Receives the Scapular from the Virgin*[17]

L transept: altarpiece: G. P. Melchiorri, *Vision of St Andrew Corsini*, c.1698[18]; vault: Puccini, *Intercession of St Andrew Corsini at the Battle of Anghiari*, 1697

5 to L: Cappella di S. Angelo Martire: frescoes and altarpiece by G. B. Ricci; altarpiece: *Assassination of St Angelus whilst Preaching in Jerusalem*; R wall: *Death and Funeral of the Saint*; L wall: *Two Carmelites Embracing*; vault: L: *St Angelus Healing*; C: *Ascension of the Saint into Heaven*; R: *Vision of Christ to the Saint*[19]

4 to L: Cappella di S. Teresa: remodelled in 1697-99 by Antonio Gherardi, which involved removing the altarpiece and replacing it with one of his own, *St Teresa in Ecstasy*, as well as the addition of extensive stucco work. Luca Malmeluzzi's *tondi* on the side walls with scenes from the *Life of St Teresa* were retained, 1659. The stucco angels flanking these were executed by Giuseppe Bilancioni[20]

3 to L: Cappella di SS. Pietro e Paolo: the columns of the altar were taken from the old church; tradition holds that Sts Peter and Paul were whipped against them. Decoration by G. B. Ricci, altarpiece: *St Peter and Paul Tied to the Column*; R wall: *Beheading*

of St Paul; L wall: *Crucifixion of St Peter*; vault: L: *St Peter Receiving the Keys*; C: *Christ in Heaven*; R: *Conversion of St Paul*
2 to L: Cappella di S. Elia: altarpiece: G. Calandrucci, *Elijah between St Anthony and the Blessed Franco Lippi of Siena*; vault: *Elijah in Glory*, 1690[21]. The side walls are attributed to G. B. Calandrucci, R wall: *Angels Bring Elijah Food in the Desert*; L wall: *Elijah with the Sunamite*[22]
Oratory: attributed to Nicola Michetti, 1709-15. Vault: G. Conca, *Virgin in Glory with Carmelite Saints*. Other paintings by G. Conca, *Crucifixion*; *S. Maria Maddalena de' Pazzi Teaching*; *Death of St Joseph*; *Sacred Family*; *Souls in Purgatory*, 1715[23]. High altar: L. Garzi, *Christ Preaching*, after 1715[24].

S. Maria in Trastevere
Piazza di S. Maria in Trastevere

The Early Christian church was rebuilt by Innocent II (1130-43). It was restored probably by Martino Longhi the Elder and again by Clement XI, who added the portico, and finally by Pius IX. Certain parts of the medieval church survive: the 12th century campanile, the main colonnade of the nave, composed of reused ancient columns, the Cosmatesque pavement, the mosaics and the ciborium.

The portico was designed by Carlo Fontana and built in 1701-02[1]. The statues are by Jean Baptiste Théodon, *St Callistus*; Michele Maglia, *St Cornelius*; Lorenzo Ottoni, *St Julian* and Vincenzo Felici, *St Calapodius*, 1702-05[2].

INTERIOR
The carved wooden ceiling, a gift from Cardinal Pietro Aldobrandini, was designed by Domenichino[3], who also painted the *Assumption* at the centre, 1616-17[4]. The ceiling itself is composed of an unusually complicated series of geometrical shapes based ultimately on an engraving at the end of Serlio's fourth book.
1 to R: Cappella di S. Francesca Romana/Bussi: begun by Giacomo Recalcati and continued after his death in 1723 by F. Ferrari and F. Feruzzi, 1727[5]. Altarpiece: Giacomo Zoboli, *Last Communion of St Frances of Rome*, 1724[6]; L wall: monument to Cardinal Giovanni Bussi (d. 1726) by Francesco Ferrari with bust by Giovanni Battista de' Rossi, 1742[7]; R wall: monument to Cardinal Francesco Bussi (d. 1765)
2 to R: Cappella del Presepe: redecorated in 1739 by Filippo Raguzzini for Cardinal Antonio Fini. Altarpiece: E. Parrocel, *Adoration of the Shepherds*, after 1745[8], but also attributed to Pietro Nelli[9]
4 to R: Cappella di S. Pietro/Velli: built by Martino Longhi the Elder for Muzio Velli, 1583. Altarpiece: G. Vasconio, *Christ Gives the Keys to St Peter*, 1659
R aisle near side door: monument to Cardinal Pietro Marcellino Corradini (d. 1743) designed by Francesco Ceroti, with sculpture by Filippo della Valle, 1743-50[10]
R transept: monument to L: Cardinal Francesco Armellini Medici (d. 1528) and Bevignate Armellini, with figures of *Sts Francis and Lawrence* by Angelo and Ludovico da Siena to a design by Peruzzi, 1524[11]
Chapel to R of high altar: Cappella della Strada Cupa: built to house a miraculous image of the Virgin, which was found in 1624 at the foot of the Janiculum Hill in the Strada Cupa[12]. The chapel was ceded in 1627 to Benedetto Cecchini, who agreed to decorate the unfinished chapel, with the intention of imitating the Altemps chapel. Begun 1625, architecture and stuccoes designed by Domenichino, who was only able to execute one painting, a putto, because of his departure for Naples in 1630[13]. The stucco telamon

below the painted putto is by Algardi[14]. The altar was erected for Cardinal Henry Stuart by Zenobi Rossi with a marble *Glory of Angels* by G. Sibilla, 1762

Apse: the apse contains mosaics depicting scenes from the *Life of the Virgin* by Cavallini, mainly dating from 1140; below Cavallini's mosaics: A. Ciampelli, *Angels Carrying Symbols of the Virgin*, 1600. On either side of the apse stand two monuments to members of the Altemps family, R: Cardinal Stanislaus Osio (d. 1579) and L: Roberto, duca di Gallesi (d. 1586), the latter by M. Longhi the Elder, executed by Paracca, with bust by N. Pippe[15]

Chapel to L of high altar: Cappella del Sacramento/Altemps[16]: commissioned by Cardinal Marco Sittico Altemps (1533-95), whose family came from the Vorarlberg and who was a nephew of Pius IV and cousin of Carlo Borromeo. He played an important part in the religious reforms after the Council of Trent. The chapel was built between 1584 and 1589 by Martino Longhi the Elder to house a much venerated image of the Virgin, the *Madonna della Clemenza*. The walls and ceilings are decorated with light and delicate stuccoes, and frescoes by Pasquale Cati. Those on the ceiling show scenes from the *Life of the Virgin*; from L side: *Birth of the Virgin*; *Annunciation*; *Visitation*; *Presentation of the Virgin*; centre: *Assumption*; below, from L corner: *Meeting of Anne and Joachim*; *Marriage of the Virgin*; *Presentation of the Virgin*; *Flight into Egypt*; *Circumcision*; *Jesus Preaching in the Temple*; *Holy Family*; *Marriage at Cana*; *Crucifixion*; *Meeting of Jesus and Mary*; *The Three Maries*; pendentives: *Evangelists*. Those on the wall are much more unusual in theme; the left shows *A Sitting of the Council of Trent* and the right, *Presentation to Pius IV and Marco Sittico Altemps of the Resolutions of the Counil of Trent*. In the foreground of the former is a figure representing the papacy, surrounded by allegorical figures of *Virtues*. Over the altar is a frescoed portrait of Pius IV and the cardinal. Marbling by Stefano dello Zoppo[17]

5 to L: Cappella di S. Girolamo/Avila: remodelled for Pietro Paolo Avila by Antonio Gherardi in 1678-80; practically the entire chapel is constructed of stucco; altarpiece: Gherardi, *St Jerome in the Desert*, 1685[18]. This and the chapel of S. Cecilia in S. Carlo ai Catinari are the two boldest works by this artist, who built little but is perhaps the most original architect of his generation. In this chapel he combines architectural forms based on Borromini freely interpreted, in the false perspective over the altar, with a Berninesque use of concealed light and combination of sculpture and architecture in the dome.

3 to L: Cappella di S. Francesco/Ardizzi: restored by P. Camporese the Younger, 1834. Decorated by Ferrau Fenzoni; altarpiece: *St Francis Receives the Stigmata*, c.1595; vault: *God the Father in Glory*[19]; L lunette: *Sts Marinus and Callistus*[20]

2 to L: Cappella di SS. Mario e Callisto

1 to L: Cappella del Battistero: built by Onorio Longhi, 1592-97, and altered by Filippo Raguzzini[21]

Room behind sacristy: G. Brandi, *Martyrdom of St Frederick*, c.1660[22]

Behind the church (to the right) is the 18th century *Canonica*[23] and in the adjacent vicolo del Piede the former Oratory of the Holy Sacrament, dated 1670 on the frieze (now a *trattoria*).

S. Maria in Trivio
Piazza dei Crociferi

In 1571 the church, which was formerly known as S. Giuseppe del Bufalo or S. Giuseppe Grande, was given to the Compagnia dei Crociferi; in 1573-75 it was rebuilt to the designs of Giacomo del Duca, who was Michelangelo's assistant in some of his last works. When the Order was suppressed by Alexander VII in 1656, the church buildings were handed over to the Padri Ministeri degli Infermi (see S. Maria Maddalena), who installed their Novitiate in the monastic buildings.

Borromini, who seemed to have been an admirer of Del Duca, copied the façade in a drawing now in the Albertina (Rome 141) and was, I believe, inspired by the pediment over the door to invent his own favourite form of pediment used, for instance, over the façade of the Oratory of S. Filippo Neri[1].

In 1839 the Novitiate was moved when the fathers exchanged churches with the Chierici Regolari Minori, who held the church of SS. Vincenzo e Anastasio. In 1854 the Missionaries of the Precious Blood, an Order founded by St Caspar del Bufalo, acquired the church.

INTERIOR

The church consists of a single nave with shallow recesses for chapels separated by Ionic pilasters, which would originally have been painted white but now have coarse painted marbling. The whole interior was redecorated between 1668 and 1675 by Antonio Gherardi, who painted the ceiling, 1668-70, made a new high altar to accommodate a miraculous image of the Virgin, 1677, and designed the stucco group of the *Triumph of the Cross* over the chancel arch (*c.*1670).

The ceiling is painted with scenes from the *Life of the Virgin* arranged in an unusual scheme. Along the flat top of the ceiling are three canvases in a line, set in gilt frames, all seen *di sotto in sù* in a perspective view derived from Veronese. The cove of the ceiling is in fresco and is treated in a similar manner but with a greater effect of illusion, because the scenes are set against the sky, which suggests that the space continues from one section to another. Above the windows are pairs of angels, those at the end set against the sky, those in the middle panels against a gold ground. From the entrance: *Presentation in the Temple*; *Annunciation*; *Circumcision*; R spandrels: *Birth of the Virgin*; *Flight into Egypt*; *Adoration of the Magi*; L spandrels: *Holy Family*; *Jesus in the Temple*; *Visitation*; over door: *St John the Evangelist's Vision on Patmos of the Apocalyptic Women*[2].

Three of the altars in the nave have fine *scagliola* fronts, a fourth is in the passage to the cloister.

1 to R: canvases on sides and vault: G. F. Grimaldi, *The Seven Sorrows of the Virgin*[3]
3 to L: Paolo Piazza, *Martyrdom of St Cletus*[4]
1 to L: Luigi Scaramuccia, *Last Communion of Mary Magdalen*
Sacristy: vault fresco: Bartolomeo Merelli, *Triumph of the Cross*, *c.*1674, and wall: *Pietà*, *c.*1674

Ante-sacristy: vault: Gherardi, *A Vision of St Philip Neri*, with fictive stucco by Giacomo Amati, 1677. The small cloister is neatly designed by Del Duca to fit a confined space. The top storey is a later addition[5].

S. Maria dell'Umiltà
Via dell'Umiltà, 29

Founded in 1601 as a Dominican convent by Francesca Baglioni Orsini. The church was rebuilt in 1641-46 to the designs of Paolo Maruscelli (Baglione). The interior was originally simple, with one order of Doric pilasters and decoration in stucco only, but it was enriched with marbles – mainly Sicilian red and yellow jaspers – and gilding in the first half of the 18th century. The façade was built in 1703 by Carlo Fontana, who is recorded as architect of the convent in 1681. Early drawings and engravings show that it was a bold Baroque design with the inverted broken and curved pediment fragments used by Buontalenti in the Porta delle Suppliche in the Uffizi and by Bernini in the door of the Cappella del Crocifisso in St Peter's; this heretical feature was removed when the church was restored by Andrea Busiri Vici for Pius IX and replaced by the existing pure rectilinear pediment. Over the door is a relief of the *Assumption* by Vincenzo Felici, 1703-08[1]. The church is now part of the North American College and may be visited on request.

INTERIOR
The decoration of the interior may have been begun by Carlo Fontana, who died in 1714, but it is so much richer than his other works that much of it must be attributed to Alessandro Dori, who worked there after his death.

The fresco of the *Assumption* on the vault is dated 1726 and is probably by Cerruti[2]. The stucco statues of virgin martyrs set in niches around the nave are by A. Raggi: R aisle: *St Agnes*; *St Ursula*; *St Agatha*; L aisle: *St Barbara*; *St Catherine of Alexandria*; *St Cecilia*, 1747[3]. Above the sculptures: A. Mariani, R aisle: *Mary Magdalen* and *Education of the Virgin*; L aisle: *St Helena* and *St Catherine with Christ*.

Over entrance: magnificent gilt wooden gallery enclosing the nuns' choir, c.1735
High altar[4]: by P. Maccarano to designs by M. Longhi the Younger with marble angels by Orfeo Boselli and Arcangelo Gonelli, and metalwork surround by Pasquale Pasqualini, 1643-46[5]. Altarpiece: Antonio della Cornia, *Apostles around the Virgin's Tomb*; above: Antonio Mariani, *Assumption*. R wall: *St Catherine of Alexandria* and L wall: *St Mary Magdalen* by Francesco Cavallini, c.1686[6]
Choir: F. Cavallini, R wall: *St Catherine of Alexandria*; L wall: *St Mary Magdalen*[7]
2 to L: Cappella di S. Michele Arcangelo/Gaspardi: founded 1645 and executed in 1685-86 to Pietro Vecchiarelli's design; altarpiece: Francesco Allegrini, *St Michael*[8]
1 to L: Cappella del SS. Crocifisso/Colonna: decorated by Pietro Vecchiarelli, 1685-86; stucco figures by Francesco Cavallini; R wall: *Angel with Lance*; L wall: *Angel with Column*[9].

S. Maria in Vallicella (Chiesa Nuova)
Piazza della Chiesa Nuova, Corso Vittorio Emanuele

The Oratory was founded by St Philip Neri in 1561 as an informal gathering of men of piety and goodwill, on the model of the Oratory of Divine Love founded some forty years earlier by St Cajetan Thiene[1]. In 1575 it was established as a Congregation by Gregory XIII, who handed over to them the church of S. Maria in Vallicella and the small Franciscan convent attached to it. The foundation stone of the new church was laid in the same year, but the buildings for the fathers were not finished till the middle of the 17th century.

The church was begun in 1575 on a design with a single nave, side chapels and a low drumless dome. The author of the plan was Philip Neri's favourite architect, Matteo Bartolini, who built the nave and side chapels according to the original plan. He seems to have disappeared about 1582 and after an interval of four years Martino Longhi the Elder was put in charge of the building. At this point, probably owing to a large bequest from Cardinal Pierdonato Cesi, it was decided to give the church aisles, built on the site of existing chapels, with small semicircular chapels outside them. In 1588-90

Longhi added the choir and transepts, but he died the next year and the dome and vault of the nave were finished in 1594. In 1593 a competition was opened for designs for the façade – for which Longhi's original design was no longer suitable owing to the enlargement of the church – the winner being the little-known architect Fausto Rughesi, the candidate of the new patron, Monsignor Angelo Cesi, brother of the cardinal. The façade bears the date 1605, but it was not in fact finished till the following year. The figures of L: *St Gregory the Great* and R: *St Jerome* are attributed to Paracca.

INTERIOR

In spite of the fact that the building and decoration of the church took over a century it is one of the most complete and harmonious Baroque interiors in Rome, though it is not at all as St Philip Neri intended it to be. Like the Gesù, on which the plan is based, it was to be almost completely plain with travertine or stucco pilasters and whitewashed walls, in accordance with Philip Neri's wishes[2]. This spirit of austerity survived among the Oratorians till the 1630's when Borromini was instructed by the fathers to use brick rather than travertine on the façade of the oratory, but in the 1640's their principles changed, as those of the Jesuits were to do twenty years later, and Pietro da Cortona was commissioned to design and execute the magnificent series of frescoes enclosed in gilt and white stucco which decorate the dome, the half-dome of the apse and the vault of the nave. In the 1690's the scheme was further enriched by closing the *coretti* over the nave arcade and replacing them by stuccoes enclosing paintings[3].

St Philip Neri was responsible for the overall planning of the chapel decorations. He planned a series of coordinated altar dedications reflecting his devotions to the rosary, the side chapels being dedicated to the mysteries of the Virgin. The cycle begins on the left transept altar, dedicated to the *Presentation of the Virgin*, and proceeds left to right towards the entrance, ending on the right transept altar dedicated to the *Coronation of the Virgin*[4].

Cortona's frescoes consist of the *Intercession of Christ Surrounded by Old Testament Saints* in the dome, 1646-47; the four major prophets – *Isaiah, Jeremiah, Daniel* and *Ezekiel* – in the pendentives; the *Intercession of the Virgin in Glory Surrounded by Saints* in the half-dome of the apse, 1655-60; and *A Miracle of the Virgin during the Construction of the Church*, 1664-65, on the vault of the nave. The last is conceived as a *quadro riportato* but with a Venetian *di sotto in su* viewpoint. It is supported by stucco angels by C. Fancelli and E. Ferrata and surrounded by high relief stucco decoration of Cortona's design[5].

The stucco allegorical figures in the window lunettes of the transepts date from 1649; L: *Hope* and *Faith* and R: *Charity* by C. Fancelli and *Religion* by Ferrata. On entrance wall: allegorical figures of L: *Silence* and R: *Disdain of the World* by Ferrata.[6]

NAVE

To R: 1: *Ark of the Covenant*, D. Parodi; 2: *Judith and Holofernes*, D. Seiter; 3: *Moses Breaking the Tablets of the Law*, G. Passeri; 4: *Rebecca at the Well*, G. Ghezzi; 5: *Fall of Manna*, D. Seiter

To L: 1: *Christ Clearing the Temple*, D. Parodi; 2: *Immaculate Conception*, D. Seiter; 3: *Christ Giving the Keys to St Peter*, G. Passeri; 4: *Penitent Magdalen*, G. Ghezzi; 5: *Communion of the Apostles*, D. Seiter. The stucco angels and putti supporting the frames were designed by C. Rusconi and executed by B. Cametti, G. Raffaelli, G. Lavaggi, M. Maglia and P. Balestra

S. Maria in Vallicella (Chiesa Nuova)

Over entrance door: Daniel Seiter, *St John Preaching*[7]

1 to R: Cappella del Crocifisso/Caetani: begun in 1594 by Giovan Battista Guerra but only completed in 1621. Altarpiece: S. Pulzone, *Crucifixion*, 1583-86[8]; apse frescoes: Lanfranco, R: *Christ in the Garden*; C: *Flagellation*; L: *Crowning with Thorns*[9] and stuccoes by Stefano Longo, 1620-21: allegorical figures of L: *Justice*; C: *Faith;* R: *Fortitude*, 1620-21

2 to R: Cappella della Pietà/Cavalletti: built in 1576, chapel decoration completed in 1614; altarpiece: copy after Caravaggio's *Entombment* painted for the chapel in 1602-04, removed by the French in 1797 and now in the Vatican[10]; frescoes by Angelo Caroselli, C: *Pietà*; either side: *Prophets*, 1611-12[11]; stuccoes executed by Pietro Castelli and Pietro Intralegni

3 to R: Cappella dell'Ascensione/Ceuli: bought in 1580 by Tiberio Ceuli, and originally designed by D. Fontana and G. A. Dosio; consecrated in 1583; altarpiece: G. Muziano, *Ascension*; 1587. The apse was redecorated to a design by G. B. Guerra; the stuccoes executed by G. Guerra, 1601-07; three oval frescoes by Matteo Piccioni, R: *St Patermutius*; C: *St Alexander*; L: *St Copres*, 1624

4 to R: Cappella della Pentecoste/Campo/Giraud: designed by Gillis van den Vliete, who was also responsible for the chapel's decoration, including the stucco work and polychrome marbling, completed by 1607[12]. Altarpiece: G. M. Morandi, *Pentecost, c.*1689; vault frescoes: Cesare Torelli, R: *Moses with the Tablets of the Law*; C: *Baptism of Christ*; L: *Christ of the Apocalypse* , 1606

5 to R: Cappella dell'Assunta/Amici/Pinelli: G. della Porta was probably the architect of the chapel, the decoration of which was completed in 1587. Altarpiece: G. D. Cerrini, *Assumption, c.*1640-45; frescoes probably by Aurelio Lomi of scenes from the *Life of the Virgin*; vault ovals: R: *Burial of the Virgin*; C: *Coronation of the Virgin*; L: *Dormition of the Virgin*[13]

R transept: Cappella dell'Incoronazione/Glorieri/Carpegna: completed in 1594; altarpiece: Giuseppe Cesari, *Coronation of the Virgin*, completed 1615[14]; statues by Flaminio Vacca, L: *St John the Baptist* and R: *St John the Evangelist*; frescoes: Giuseppe Ghezzi, *Angels with Crowns*; above: *Adam and Eve with God*

Chapel to R of choir: Cappella di S. Carlo Borromeo/Spada[15]: commissioned by Orazio Spada in 1633, one of Borromini's patrons. Orazio Spada appears to have been instrumental in determining the chapel's design, basing it on Vignola's S. Anna dei Palafrenieri. The chapel was begun by Antonio Fontana as master mason but Camillo Arcucci (d. 1667) was largely responsible for its design. On his death the chapel was completed by Carlo Rainaldi, who was responsible for the fine marbling of the vestibule and chancel. Altarpiece: C. Maratta, *Sts Charles Borromeo and Ignatius Adoring the Virgin*, begun 1677-79[16]; R wall: L. Scaramuccia, *St Charles Distributing Alms*; L wall: Giovanni Bonatti, *St Charles Blessing the Sick*, both 1674[17]; vault stuccoes of scenes from the *Life of St Charles* by C. Arcucci and *Humility* by Giovanni Francesco de' Rossi

Outside the chapel and in the corresponding position on the left transept are organs, originally built by G. Alari, with cases designed by C. Rusconi and carved by Francesco Maglia, 1698-99[18].

Choir[19]: the original high altar, built in 1596-99, is by Giovanni Battista Guerra, probably to his brother's design but modified a number of times. The original is recorded in a painting of 1623[20]. The *Crucifixion* on the top is by Guillaume Berthelot, 1614-15, the two angels by Francesco Maratta were added in

1697. Ciro Ferri designed the tabernacle in 1672, assisted by Carlo Marcellini, who made the models for two adoring angels, completed in 1676. The tabernacle was cast by Stefano Benamati. The wooden upper structure was made by Francesco Nuvolone, 1684[21]. The three paintings over and on either side of the altar were executed by Rubens in 1606-08. The painting over the altar was designed to enclose the holy image of the *Virgin and Child*, the two others represent, L: *St Gregory the Great with Sts Papianus and Maurus* and R: *St Domitilla with Sts Nerus and Achilleus*[22]

Rubens originally painted a single canvas to include the holy image and the saints but it was unsatisfactory because of the way in which it reflected the light. He therefore decided to paint the existing pictures on slate, which makes their surface more matt. He took the first canvas back to Antwerp with him and it is now in the Musée des Beaux-Arts, Grenoble.

The choir, also by G. B. Guerra, contains epitaphs to Oratorian cardinals: R: Francesco Maria Tarugio and Cesare Baronio (d. 1607) and L: Pierdonato Cesi (d. 1586). On the side walls of the choir over the *coretti* are oval panels of L: *Creation of the Angels* and R: *Fall of the Rebel Angels* by L. Baldi.

Chapel to L of choir: Cappella di S. Filippo Neri[23]: designed by Onorio Longhi, 1603-04[24]. The first section of the chapel, which is octagonal and panelled with marble and semi-precious stones, is based on a design by G. Guerra. The inner circular section has a dome decorated with gilt and white stuccoes, designed by Pietro da Cortona in 1650 and completed in 1653, though the design may have been modified by Ciro Ferri[25]. The vault painting of *St Philip* and the paintings on the side walls depicting scenes from the *Life of St Philip Neri* are by Roncalli[26]. Over the altar is a mosaic copy of Reni's *St Philip Neri Kneeling before the Virgin* (the original, 1614, is now in the inner chapel, see below). In 1922 the body of the saint was transferred from its original casket to its present glass enclosure. Marble decorations by B. Basso[27]

L transept: Cappella della Presentazione/Cesi: chapel decoration attributed to Martino Longhi the Elder. Marbled and decorated in 1592 at the expense of Angelo Cesi, Bishop of Todi, a great benefactor of the Oratorians. Altarpiece: F. Barocci, *Presentation of the Virgin*, 1603[28], for whom St Philip had a particular admiration; statues by G. A. Paracca, L: *St Peter* and R: *St Paul*, 1591[29]; frescoes by G. Ghezzi, R: *Hanna before Silo in the Temple*; C: *God the Father*; L: *Samuel in the Temple*; above: *Resurrection*

Sacristy: built by Paolo Maruscelli between 1629 and 1634; marble floor, 1640; over altar: *St Philip Neri* by Algardi, 1635-38[30]. Over door: bronze bust of Gregory XV by Algardi and cast by A. Lucenti[31]. Ceiling frescoes by Cortona of *Angels Bearing the Instruments of the Passion*, 1633-34[32]

From the passage near the sacristy a door leads to the inner chapels of St Philip Neri, which incorporate the rooms in which he lived (transported from the old convent buildings to the east of the church): Girolamo da Santacroce, *Death of the Virgin*; Jan Soens, *Temptation of Christ*; Cecco del Caravaggio, *St Lawrence*; Cortona, *Virgin and Child with St Martina*; P. L. Ghezzi, *Virgin and Child with Sts Philip Neri and Ignatius*; *Miracle of St Philip Neri Involving Cardinal Orsini, later Pope Benedict XIII*[33]. In the lower chapel, *St Philip Neri in Adoration* by Guercino[34]; in the upper chapel the same subject by Reni[35]; also, L. Baldi, *Charity of St Philip Neri*, c.1680[36].

In the *sala rossa* on the ground floor is a fresco by Niccolò Tornioli of *St Philip Neri's Vision during his Illness*[37]. It also contains the urn in which the saint was enclosed till 1922[38].

5 to L: Cappella dell' Annunciazione/ Ruspoli: completed in 1591 and decorated for the brothers Alessandro and Orazio Ruspoli (cf. inscription on floor). Altarpiece: D. Cresti, *Annunciation, c.*1589-91[39]. The frescoes on the vault by A. Lilli incorporate a complex iconographical scheme alluding to the Virgin in terms of Salomonic Wisdom[40]
4 to L: Cappella della Visitazione/Pizzamiglio/Bancavalerio/Biondi: designed by G. B. Guerra and completed by 1619. Altarpiece: F. Barocci, *Visitation*, 1584-86, a painting much loved by St Philip Neri, who was frequently found in a state of ecstasy in front of it[41]; apse frescoes: Carlo Saraceni, L: *St John the Evangelist*; C: *St John the Baptist*; R: *St Matthew, c.*1617[42]; stucco by Giovanni Guerra and marble decoration by B. Basso[43]
3 to L: Cappella della Natività/Antoniani: designed by Giovanni Battista Guerra between 1597 and 1601 for Cardinal Silvio Antoniano (cf. inscription on floor); altarpiece: Durante Alberti, *Adoration of the Shepherds*; apse frescoes: C. Roncalli, R: *St Cecilia*; C: *St Catherine*; L: *St Agnes*, 1601[44]
2 to L: Cappella dei Re Magi/Ceva: the chapel was acquired by Ponzio Ceva for his tomb, begun in 1578 and completed in 1619; altarpiece: Cesare Nebbia, *Adoration of the Magi*, 1578-81; apse; *Sts Paul, Luke and Mark* attributed to Baccio Ciarpi[45]
1 to L: Cappella della Purificazione/Cusano: acquired by Cardinal Agostino Cusano, a friend of St Philip and St Charles Borromeo, who secured the relics of St Papianus and St Maurus for the church. Chapel decoration under the direction of G. Guerra. Altarpiece: Giuseppe Cesari, *Presentation of Christ*, commissioned in 1617 but only completed in 1627.

The Oratory
The history of the building of the oratory is long and complicated but has been admirably set forth by Connors. The designs had to take account of the special nature of the establishment, which was not an enclosed house, but one for priests who continued to live in the world and who, like their founder, practised preaching and disputation of an informal kind and attached great importance to the performance of religious music, often in semi-dramatic form. It was in these performances that the word 'oratorio' in its modern sense has its origins.

At first all the accommodation for the fathers was in a small area to the east of the church, but it soon became apparent that this was inadequate and, after acquiring some further houses on that side, they decided to expand to the west of the church.

The first designs for the *casa* were produced about 1621-23 by Mario Arconio but he was soon replaced by Paolo Maruscelli who, between 1620 and 1627, probably in collaboration with Virgilio Spada, who joined the Oratory in 1622, produced a series of plans which contained the essential elements for the house: oratory, library, rooms for the fathers. Work was begun in 1629 according to Maruscelli's project, the first parts to be built being the sacristy, together with the section of the corridors which separated it from the church, and the rooms around the chapel, which had been attached to the rooms occupied by St Philip in the old *casa* to the east of the church, but which had been moved, stone by stone, to the new *casa* on the west. These were finished by 1634. In 1637 Borromini was appointed to complete the execution of the design. The circumstances which led to this appointment are not clear, because the competition referred to by most writers on the subject seems to have been an invention of the architect. The change was apparently made by the *preposito* (prior), Angelo Saluzzi, possibly on the advice of Virgilio Spada, who had been invited to advise on the plan and who was to remain one of Borromini's keenest supporters (cf. S. Giovanni in Laterano).

Maruscelli had designed the *casa* round two cloisters, separated by the sacristy, the larger (north) being for the accommodation of the fathers and the smaller for the more public rooms. The oratory itself, to be used for preaching and musical performances, was to stand between the smaller cloister and the façade. Borromini was compelled to follow Maruscelli's general disposition, but he was able to introduce many modifications to individual parts of the building and so to impose his personality on them.

The first part of the complex to be built after he took over was the oratory, which was constructed in 1637-38, the vault fresco of the *Coronation of the Virgin* by Romanelli being painted in 1639-40 (removed 1788). Maruscelli had planned this as a simple rectangular space, but Borromini transformed it by putting curved pilasters in the corners which, like those on the side and end walls, lead to ribs, which are non-functional and purely decorative yet give the impression that the vault is almost like a ribbed dome. Further, he opened up the end walls with a series of arches, leading on the east to 'green rooms' for the musicians and galleries for distinguished visitors, and on the west to similar galleries (this time for musicians) and a bay for the high altar. In 1654, after Borromini had left the Oratory, the altar and singers' balconies were rebuilt to a design by Camillo Arcucci and the columns and niches, originally, like the rest of the interior, of white stucco, were faced with coloured marble.

Below the oratory is a crypt once used as an overflow hall for concerts; it is linked to the main hall by two openings in the middle of the floor, covered by gilt bronze grilles.

The galleries in the oratory are closed by balustrades of the complex form – on a triangular plan – used by Borromini in the cloister of S. Carlino. In this case he explains that he chose this type of baluster because it gave those sitting in the gallery a better view of what was happening below than if the balusters had been circular in plan. The main door to the oratory itself, from the vestibule leading off the main 'spine' of the building, is of extraordinary richness, not in its ornament but in the depth and variety of its mouldings. There are two other doors, one in the middle of the north side leading to the small cloister, the other on the south side under the gallery, which on the exterior forms the central feature of the façade. The high altarpiece is an *Assumption* by R. Vanni.

In designing the façade of the oratory, Borromini was hindered by the need to make it subsidiary to that of the church. He was instructed to use pilasters and to work mainly in brick. To conform with these instructions but at the same time make his façade effective, he designed it on a slightly concave curve – almost like a sheet of metal bent under pressure. He paid great attention to the brickwork, which is composed of very thin bricks laid with the minimum of mortar between them. In a passage in the *Opus architectonicum* Borromini explained his intention in doing this: how wonderful it would be, he exclaimed, if one could construct a whole façade out of a single piece of terracotta; but since this was not feasible he made the front as smooth and fine-grained as possible.

The oratory is probably the first curved front to be actually completed in Rome, since that of SS. Luca e Martina, though begun in 1636, was not finished till much later, and that of S. Carlino, though designed in the 1630's, was not begun till 1665. Borromini created the curvature of the façade to express the public function of the building, describing it as imitating a man, with the convex central part forming the chest and the two concave arms on either side representing his arms open to embrace the faithful. In a plan of the design[1] one can see how the entire curvature of the façade is contained only within a depth of 10 *palmi*. The difference between this drawing and the façade as built highlights the elimination in the final building of much of the ornament designed by Borromini, thought to be overly ostentatious by the Filippini.

It has been suggested by Wittkower that the unusually shaped pediment is based on the old façade of Milan Cathedral, but this is unconvincing, since the Milanese gable was composed of an ogee curve, whereas an essential feature of the oratory pediment is that it consists of a combination of straight and curved sections. The latter is more likely to be a development from Michelangelo's combination of straight and curved pediments on the Porta Pia, the intermediate stage being the design for the door of S. Maria in Trivio by Giacomo del Duca[2]. The relation of the façade to the oratory is curious, since the axis of the latter runs parallel to the façade and not, as the visitor is led to expect, at right angles to it, and the main door leads not into the oratory itself, but, as we have seen, into the vestibule below the gallery.

The next section of the *casa* to be built (1638-41) covered the area behind the apse of the church to the north. Originally this was to include the library as well as the refectory but when it was decided to move the former to a position over the oratory, Borromini had greater freedom in redesigning the buildings for this area, and in the refectory and the *sala di ricreazione* above he produced two rooms of unusually inventive design. The refectory was originally to be of simple rectangular form, but Borromini eventually changed it into a long oval, using the corners thus created for serving rooms and a small spiral staircase. Another argument in favour of the oval according to the architect, was that it was more convenient for the fathers who normally engaged in disputations while having their meals. The refectory is now used for amateur theatricals (it was once a cinema), but in the anteroom is preserved one of the beautiful *lavamani*, almost gothic in form, with a tank to hold the water in the form of a tulip. Over the refectory is the *sala di ricreazione* with a huge and superb fireplace, made out of a piece of white marble found in building the foundations of the oratory, with a Doric frieze of which the metopes contain Oratorian symbols and from which hangs a fringe of marble tassels[3].

This building campaign also included parts of the north cloister in which Borromini employed a giant order of Composite pilasters. This was to be continued round the small south cloister which, together with the main entrance between the church and the oratory, was built between 1641 and 1644. The articulation of the cloister was complicated by the fact that the windows in Maruscelli's sacristy were irregularly disposed, but Borromini got over this difficulty by an ingenious use of half-blind openings. The *foresteria* for guests was introduced over the entrance and the rooms of the porter.

During the first years of Innocent X's pontificate no building was done on the *casa*, partly no doubt because Spada, who had been appointed almoner to the pope, was engaged on other projects, including the remodelling of the Lateran, but in 1647 work was begun on the north-west part of the building, including the clock-tower.

Soon after this, difficulties began to arise between Borromini and the fathers, and in 1652 he was replaced as architect by Camillo Arcucci. Between 1656 and 1667 Spada made an energetic and ingenious attempt to have him reinstated, but he failed[4]. The *casa* was, however, finished by Arcucci according to Borromini's plans, except for certain decorative details, between 1659 and 1662, when the west wing, including the main staircase, was built.

The staircase is approached through an opening flanked by two ancient Roman columns, found during the excavation for the foundations of the building, but which Borromini had to extend to make them of the required height by adding bands of lotus leaves at the bottom – a device which he derived from a type of ancient column (cf. a set in S. Prassede). The staircase itself has both flights covered by a single vault, a form unusual in Rome at this date but already common in Venice. On the first landing is the life-size stucco made for Algardi's *Meeting of Leo I and Attila* in St Peter's[5].

The library was built between 1642 and 1644 but modified between 1665 and 1667 by extending the western wall by two bays. It contains a stucco monument to Cardinal Cesare Baronio, the first Oratorian librarian, designed by Borromini and executed by Girolamo Maggi[6].

After Borromini's departure small additions were made to the buildings to the north-east of the church by Carlo Rainaldi between 1669 and 1674, when a new thoroughfare, the via della Chiese Nuova, was opened partly on the site of the fathers' first *casa*. Various changes to the building were made, of which the most serious was closing the arches of the two cloisters. In the 19th century rooms were built on to the north side of the sacristy, thus reducing the size of the larger cloister, and many other small alterations were made. Generally speaking, however, the actual building has survived almost intact, though many parts of it have been put to unworthy uses.

The buildings of the Oratory, to which the entrance is to the left of the church, are now divided up between various authorities. The oratory itself is used for concerts and can sometimes be visited through the good offices of the *portiere* – an uncertain factor; the library, which is on the second floor and contains the Biblioteca Vallicelliana, is generally accessible; the first floor, which contains the *sala di ricreazione*, is occupied by the Archivio Capitolino. In another room on this floor is the stucco model of the *Miracle of St Agnes* in S. Agnese in Piazza Navona, executed from Algardi's model after his death by Guidi and Ferrata[7].

S. Maria delle Vergini (S. Rita da Cascia)
Via delle Vergini, 23

The Zitelle del Rifugio, a charitable foundation for young girls founded in 1593 on the Quirinal, was moved in 1613 to the present location by Cardinal Scipione Borghese because he wanted the site for the palace which he proposed to build (now the Palazzo Rospigliosi). In 1613 the foundation was changed into a convent of cloistered nuns under the rule of St Augustine. The church and convent were rebuilt in 1634 to the designs of Francesco Peparelli at the behest of Cardinal Maurizio Ginetti and the Prioress Maria Gasparini, and completed in 1636, though only officially used in 1640. The church was consecrated in 1682[1]. The façade was completed to the designs of Mattia de' Rossi in 1695-97. In 1904 the church was given to the Confraternita della SS. Spina di Nostro Gesù e di S. Rita da Cascia.

INTERIOR

Built on a Greek cross plan, unusual in Rome in the 17th century.

Vault: L. Gimignani, *Trinity in Glory*, 1682-83[2]; dome: *Saints and Angels in Glory*, 1696

1 to R: P. Lucatelli, *Sts Augustine and Monica*[3]
High altar: designed by Mattia de' Rossi, 1681-83[4]
Choir: Filippo Carcani, L wall: *St Joseph* and R wall: *St Augustine*; vault: stucco angels and festoons[5]
1 to L: decorated 1639; altarpiece: G. B. Mercati, *Noli me tangere*.

S. Maria in Via
Largo Chigi

A church has stood on this site since the 10th or 11th century. In 1513 it was given by Leo X to the Servite Fathers who still administer it. The building of the present church was apparently begun in 1579 and Tempesta's plan of Rome of 1593 shows it complete except for the upper half of the façade. It is traditionally ascribed to Giacomo della Porta but Mola says it is by Onorio Longhi. It conforms to the standard form of small Roman churches of the late 16th century, with a single nave and side chapels, in this case rather deep. Baglione ascribes the lower storey of the façade to Della Porta but the archives of the Servites mention the name Martino Longhi the Elder. The upper part is ascribed to Carlo Rainaldi[1]. It is certainly higher than would have been intended by the original architect and, with its double pediment and huge scrolls, somewhat crushes the lower storey.

INTERIOR
The choir was lengthened at the expense of Cardinal Bellarmino from 1604 onwards.
Vault: G. D. Piastrini, *First Mass of St Philip Benizi*, 1723-24[2], which may give the date for the decoration
1 to R: Cappella della Madonna del Pozzo: L wall: monument to Battista Canobi (d. 1596)

2 to R: Cappella di S. Filippo Benizi: built 1626. Altarpiece: *St Philip Benizi in Ecstasy* by an unknown artist; L wall: *Funeral of St Philip Benizi* by T. Luini; R wall: *St Philip Heals a Leper by Giving him his Tunic* by Antonio Giusani, 1632. Vault: Antonio Circignani, *Glory with Music-making Angels*, 1626, and Alessandro Vaiani, *St Philip Benizi Strikes a Spring from the Rocks at the Grotto of Montamiata* and *The Judgment of Castroleone*. Stuccoes by Marcantonio Fontana, 1627-29[3]
3 to R: Cappella dell'Annunziata/Aldobrandini: decorated by G. Cesari, altarpiece: *Annunciation*, 1597; R wall: *Adoration of the Magi*; L wall: *Adoration of the Shepherds*, 1594-96[4]; vault: Jacopo Zucchi, R: *Pentecost* and *Assumption*; C: *God the Father*; L: *Ascension* and *Noli me tangere*, 1595[5]
4 to R: Cappella della SS Trinità: built in 1608 by Carlo Lambardi (or Lombardo) as his own chapel. Altar wall: Cristofano Casolani, *Trinity with Sts John the Baptist, John the Evangelist, Francis of Assisi, and Mary Magdalen*; R wall: Francesco Lambardi, *Abraham and the Three Angels*; L wall: Cherubino Alberti, *Ark of the Covenant*, c.1610[6]
4 to L: Cappella di S. Pellegrino Laziosi: altarpiece: Giuseppe Montesanti, *Christ Appearing to St Peregrinus*[7]
3 to L: Cappella dei Sette Santi Fondatori: altarpiece: copy of A. Masucci's *Virgin with the Founders of the Servite Order in S. Marcello*
1 to L: Cappella di S. Andrea: altarpiece: Giuseppe Franco, *St Andrew*[8].

S. Maria in Via (Oratorio del SS. Sacramento)
Piazza Poli

Built in 1727-29 by Cardinal Pietro Ottoboni

for the Confraternita del SS. Sacramento, founded in 1576, the architect being Domenico Gregorini. As built the oratory was flanked by two identical blocks of secular buildings, but the one on the right was pulled down in the late 19th century for the widening of the via del Tritone. The façade is a good example of the moderate Baroque of which Gregorini was one of the most competent exponents in the early 18th century. The statues of *Faith* and *Hope* are by P. Benaglia, 1728. Internally the oratory is a rectangle with rounded corners, like Borromini's chapel in the Collegio di Propaganda Fide. It was twice restored and wholly repainted in 1865-67. It now belongs to the Corporation of Travel Agents.

INTERIOR

The high altar was made in 1843 to the designs of Luigi Valadier, son of Giuseppe. Over it hangs the *Holy Family* by F. Trevisani, 1729[1].

S. Maria in Via Lata
Via del Corso, 306

At a very early date a chapel was established in the remains of a Roman house in which St Paul was said to have stayed while awaiting trial. In 1049 the church over it was rebuilt and this was in turn replaced by another in 1491. In 1594 various alterations were made, which included raising the high altar to its present level.

Between 1636 and 1643 the choir was rebuilt and redecorated to the designs of Bernini for Francesco d'Aste and his wife, whose monuments stand in it[1]. Between 1650 and 1655 the nave was decorated by Cosimo Fanzago and though part of his work was altered or swept away in a further restoration of 1863, much of it survives, including the wooden roof, the decoration of the upper part of the wall with the windows, the encasing of the columns with Sicilian marble, the organ, the door in the aisle and probably the bronze angels standing on the altar-rails.

In 1658 Pietro da Cortona was commissioned to build the vestibule and the façade, initially financed by Canon Atanasio Ridolfi and later by Alexander VII. The lower storey was finished by 1661, when Cortona showed Alexander VII the model of the upper storey[2]. This was finished in 1663 and Cortona immediately produced plans for the campanile [3]. The grille was put in place in March 1663[4].

Cortona also restored the lower church, which was visited by Alexander VII on 31 March 1665. In so doing he preserved as much as possible of the Early Christian church, an example of the interest taken in the 17th century in the holy places of the Early Church.

The façade (dated 1662) is the latest of Cortona's work of this kind. In one way it is the simplest, because it does not incorporate any curves, a feature probably due to the fact that it had to be aligned to a long row of palaces facing onto the relatively narrow Corso. It contains, however, several novelties, in particular the breaking of the entablature over the upper order into a pediment, a device which Cortona could have known from Roman – and perhaps Hellenistic – examples (for instance, the arch at Orange). The interior of the portico with its massive columns standing against the wall of the church recalls the vestibule to the sacristy of S. Spirito in Florence by Giuliano da Sangallo and Cronaca and reminds one of Cortona's Tuscan origin. A curious feature is that the coffering of the barrel-vault seems to continue behind the arches enclosing the apsed ends of the portico.

Over the door is a relief of *The Virgin* by Cosimo Fancelli.

199

S. Maria in Via Lata

INTERIOR

The marble pavement is inlaid with heraldic elements from the arms of Aldobrandini and Pamphili and must therefore date from the time of Camillo Pamphili and his wife Olimpia Aldobrandini (married in 1647).

The organ is by Caterinazzo da Subiaco, 1652.

Vault: G. Brandi, *Coronation of the Virgin*. In the last bay the *quadratura* is attributed to V. Codazzi[5]

R entrance wall: monument to Cardinal Maurizio di Savoia set up in 1637, near Pietro da Cortona in style. A. Masucci, *Baptism*, c.1716-17[6]

Before 1st altar: A. Masucci, *Annunciation*, 1716-17

1 to R: G. Brandi, *St Andrew Adoring his Cross*, 1685[7]

Between 1 and 2 to R: Pietro de' Pietri, *Adoration of the Shepherds*

2 to R: G. Ghezzi, *St Joseph Holding the Christ Child and Adored by Sts Nicholas of Bari and Blaise*, 1686[8]

Beyond 2 to R: Pietro de' Pietri, *Presentation*; G. D. Piastrini, *Madonna of the Rosary*, 1721-c.25[9]; A. Masucci, *Adoration of the Magi*, c.1716-17[10]; below: monument to Jean Germain Drouais (d. 1788) by Claude Michallon, 1789[11]; to R: monument to Edward Dodwell (d. 1832) by L. Biglioschi, 1832[12]

High altar[13]: set up between 1639 and 1643 to a design by Bernini. On either side, monuments to the D'Aste family, the bronze bust of Giovanni Battista d'Aste (d. 1634) by Giuliano Finelli, 1651-53, and that of his wife Clarice Margana (d. 1612) probably by Andrea Bolgi, though it has recently been attributed to C. Fanzago[14]. Initially the monuments were built with the busts inserted where the present coat of arms are, but these were inverted after an Apostolic visit in 1659 criticised the former arrangement as the busts were higher than the venerated icon on the high altar. This new arrangement was the initiative of Francesco Buonaventura d'Aste. Bronze angels holding candelabra probably by C. Fanzago[15]. Apse: *Assumption*, originally painted by A. Camassei but repainted in the 19th century by Traversari.

Chapel to L of high altar: Cappella di SS. Caterina e Ciriaco: designed by D. Paradisi and built by Marcello Bigeri, 1715. Altarpiece: Giovanni Odazzi, *Virgin with Sts Catherine of Alexandria and Cyriacus*[16]. On L wall: monuments to Zenaide Bonaparte (d. 1854) by P. Tenerani and R wall: Giuseppe Napoleone by A. Tombini[17]

Between this chapel and 2 to L: Masucci, *Marriage of the Virgin*; Pietro de' Pietri, *Presentation of the Virgin*

2 to L: P. L. Ghezzi, *St Paul Baptising St Sabina*, c.1715[18]

Between 2 and 1 to L: Pietro de' Pietri, *Birth of the Virgin*

Sacristy: decorated on the order of Clement XII, from which time the wooden cupboards date. Vault: M. Cerruti, *Assumption*, 1732. L wall: attributed to Cerruti, *Deposition*[19]

1 to L: P. de' Pietri, *Virgin with Sts Lawrence, Anthony of Padua, Praxedes, Venantius and Cyrus*, c.1705[20]

L entrance wall: G. D. Piastrini, *Risen Christ Appearing to the Apostles*[21]

LOWER CHURCH

Doors and grilles by Cortona. At the top of the steps leading to the church, monument to Atanasio Ridolfi (d. 1663) to a design attributed to Cortona[22]. The bust dates from c.1640 but the sculptor is not known. Over the altar is a relief of *Sts Paul, Peter, Martial and Luke* by Cosimo Fancelli[23]. On the left wall is a fragment of a fresco painted by an assistant of Cortona, probably over the remains of a medieval fresco.

S. Maria della Visitazione (S. Francesco di Sales)
Via S. Francesco di Sales

The church was built by G. B. Contini, 1670 [1]. It is now part of the prison of Regina Coeli and is therefore not conveniently accessible.

S. Maria della Vittoria
Via XX Settembre, 15

Founded in 1607 by the Carmelites of S. Maria della Scala as a training college for missionaries. Originally dedicated to St Paul, after a small chapel on the site. The church was built between 1610 and 1612 and the design is attributed to Maderno by Baglione[1]. In 1622 its name was changed to S. Maria della Vittoria in honour of an image which is said to have caused the Count of Tilly to win the Battle of the White Mountain in 1621 and which was given to the church the next year. It perished in 1833 in a fire which destroyed the apse of the church.

In Maderno's time the interior was plain and devoid of marbling or stucco. At some date before 1663 G. D. Cerrini painted the frescoes of the dome and the vault.

The façade was built by G. B. Soria between 1625 and 1626 and paid for by Cardinal Scipione Borghese. It is Soria's earliest and least original church façade, but it was conditioned by the proximity of Maderno's S. Susanna (from which it was originally separated by a palace on the site of the Largo di S. Susanna). Soria has followed the main lines of Maderno's design but has inserted an awkwardly heavy curved pediment over the main door. He has also copied one unusual feature of S. Susanna, the introduction of a balustrade on the pediment, but he has given this a form of interlaced mouldings, apparently otherwise unknown in Rome, which was used at about the same time in France by François Mansart and which Soria could have known from engravings in Jacques Androuet du Cerceau's *Plus excellents Bastiments* (e.g. at Verneuil). The relief of the *Adoration of the Shepherds* over the door is by Domenico de' Rossi, 1627-29.

INTERIOR
The pilasters were covered with Sicilian alabaster between 1705 and 1714, and the floor marbled in 1740.
Vault: Giuseppe and Andrea Orazi, *Victory of the Virgin over Heretics*, who are also responsible for the surrounding stucco work, 1700; dome frescoes by Giovanni Domenico Cerrini, *St Paul in Glory*, shortly before 1663[2]

The organ gallery over the entrance is by Mattia de' Rossi, 1677.
1 to R: Cappella di S. Maddalena da Silvano: monuments to: R wall: Silvano Giustiniani (d. 1638) and L wall: Henri, duc de Montmorency (d. 1623)
2 to R: Cappella di S. Francesco/Merenda: commissioned by Ippolito Merenda and designed by Mario Arconio, 1629; altarpiece: Domenichino, *Virgin and Child with St Francis*, 1629-30; R wall: *St Francis in Ecstasy*; L wall: *St Francis Receives the Stigmata* by A. Barbalonga, both to Domenichino's design[3]
3 to R: Cappella Vidoni: altarpiece: A. Balzico, *St Simon Stock Receives the Scapular from the Virgin*, 1895. Monuments to L: Cardinal Girolamo Vidoni (d. 1632) and R: his nephew Giovanni Vidoni (d. 1626) by P. Ferrucci[4]
R transept: Cappella di S. Giuseppe/ Capocaccia: decorated by G. B. Contini in 1697 to balance Bernini's Cornaro Chapel opposite[5]. Over altar: *St Joseph's Dream* by Domenico Guidi[6]; on side walls: reliefs of L: *Adoration of the Shepherds* and R: *Flight into Egypt* by P. E. Monnot, 1695-99[7]. Vault frescoes:

Bonaventura Lamberti, *St Joseph in Glory*, c.1699[8]

Passage to sacristy: L wall: monument to Cardinal Sebastiano Antonio Tanara (d. 1724) set up by Fuga with bust by Agostino Corsini[9]. Room to R: relief of the *Assumption of the Virgin with Sts Jerome and John the Evangelist* by Pompeo Ferrucci, 1629[10]. *St Paul Rapt in the Third Heaven* by Gerrit van Honthorst, 1618-20[11]

Choir: rebuilt after the fire of 1833[12]. The high altar was rebuilt for Duca Alessandro Torlonia to a design by Augusto Carnevali, 1880. The tabernacle is by Luigi Castellacci, Pietro Quadroli and Francesco Conti. Apse: Luigi Serra, *Entry of the Madonna della Vittoria into Prague*, 1882-84

L transept: Cappella di S. Teresa/Cornaro: decorated by Bernini for Cardinal Federico Cornaro; begun soon after 1644, architecture finished by 1647[13]. The central group shows the *Transverberation of St Teresa*. This represents the second stage of mystical experience, beyond the act of prayer controlled by the will shown in Bernini's statue of Fonseca in S. Lorenzo in Lucina, but less complete than the total abandon of his *Blessed Ludovica Albertoni* in S. Francesco a Ripa, because though the will has withdrawn the senses are still active. On the side walls of the transept members of the Cornaro family – all deceased except for the cardinal himself, who appears second from the right in the right-hand relief – are shown disputing some theological point, no doubt connected with the saint's vision. The chapel encompasses a range of different worlds, from the heaven in the frescoed vault (by Abbatini after a sketch by Bernini), through the visionary world of St Teresa and the material world of the Cornaro family, living and dead, to Purgatory, represented by the two panels of inlaid marble in the pavement showing two skeletons, one in hopeful prayer, one in despair.

The chapel is one of Bernini's most inspired works and a brilliant expression of the fusion of the arts which was among his most personal contributions to the Baroque. The group of St Teresa and the angel express with unparalleled intensity the mystical experience which played such an important part in 17th century religious life and the combination of architecture, painting and sculpture – the last carried to the highest point of illusionism in the imitation of silk and velvet in marble – intensifies the dramatic effect of the whole and adds conviction to the dramatic unity which Bernini imposed on the different elements – divine, human and infernal – making the chapel one of the great masterpieces of Baroque art.

Frescoes and stuccoes by G. Abbatini of scenes from the *Life of St Teresa*: altar wall: L of window: *Teresa and her Brother as Children Seek Martyrdom*; R of window: *Teresa Flagellates herself with Keys before a Vision of Christ*; L side wall: *Christ Crowns Teresa for her Good Office*; R side wall: *Christ Marries Teresa with a Nail*

3 to L: Cappella della SS. Trinità/Gessi: founded by Cardinal Berlingero Gessi (d. 1639). Altar designed by Algardi and chapel decorated by Algardi and G. F. Grimaldi. Algardi was responsible for the figures of *Justice* and *Prudence* over the entrance arch to the chapel and the figurative parts of the stucco decoration of the vault[14]. The frescoes on the vault are by Giovanni Francesco Grimaldi, R: *Nativity*; L: *Baptism*; C: *Transfiguration*[15]. Altarpiece: Guercino, *Trinity*, 1638[16]. R: portrait of Cardinal Berlingero Gessi[17]

2 to L: Cappella di S. Giovanni della Croce/Bevilacqua: decorated by Nicholas Lorrain, altarpiece: *Christ Appears to St John of the Cross*; R wall: *The Virgin Saves the Young St John of the Cross after Falling into*

a Well; L wall: *Death of the Saint, c.*1675[18]
1 to L: Cappella di S. Andrea: altarpiece: copy of Reni's *St Andrew Adoring his Cross* by Pietro Camuccini, 1801[19]. Monuments to: R wall: Luca Angelo Maraldi (d. 1636) and L wall: Marco Aurelio Maraldi.

S. Marta
Piazza del Collegio Romano, 5

In 1546 St Ignatius Loyola conceived the idea of establishing a hospice for penitent women who, though wishing to reform, did not want to become nuns. The project was funded by selling some of the marbles found in the ancient ruins in front of the Gesù. In 1561 the hospice was transferred to S. Chiara and the buildings handed over to the Augustinian nuns, who built the church, which was consecrated in 1570. Between 1671 and 1674 the church was remodelled by Carlo Fontana, who had become the architect to the community and whose daughters were members of it.

The church was widened by the addition of chapels and the new vault was higher than the old. Fontana designed a new façade but this was not executed.

The church is deconsecrated and is now in the hands of the Presidente del Consiglio and closed to the public.

INTERIOR
Vault: frescoed by Baciccio, *St Martha in Glory*; the flanking *tondi* were executed by Girolamo Troppa with scenes from the *Life of St Martha*. Paolo Albertoni frescoed most of the allegorical figures. The stuccoes were executed by Leonardo Retti and Antonio Roncati, probably to Fontana's designs[1].

S. Marta in Vaticano (destroyed)
The church stood near the sacristy of St Peter's. It was built in 1538 but rebuilt by Mascarino in 1582 and restored by Clement XI, who added a new façade, presumably that shown in the engraving by Vasi reproduced by Armellini.

S. Martino ai Monti (SS. Silvestro e Martino ai Monti)
Viale del Monte Oppio, 26

A church has stood here since Early Christian times and was rebuilt by Sergius II (844-47). In 1559 it was given to a body of Carmelite monks. The interior was restored in *c.*1637 by the prior, Giovanni Antonio Filippini, the architect being Filippo Gagliardi. The façade is dated 1676.

INTERIOR
The wooden ceiling by Galeazzo Leoncino was given by St Charles Borromeo, 1640. The *confessio* is by Gagliardi.

The statues and medallions in the nave are by P. Naldini: R nave: *St Cyriacus*; *St Stephen*; *St Fabianus*; *St Nicander*. L nave: *St Theodore*; *St Martin*; *St Innocent*; *St Justa*. Entrance wall: R: *St Paul*, Naldini; above *St Anthony*, Daniele Latre; L: *St Peter*, Naldini; above: *St John the Baptist*, D. Latre, 1649[1]. The pavement was laid in 1796 to a design by Francesco Belli.

The frescoes on the aisle walls were painted between 1648 and 1651, mainly by Gaspard Dughet, brother-in-law of Nicholas Poussin, except for the two on the right wall (2nd and 3rd from entrance) which are by G. F. Grimaldi. The themes are principally taken from the *Story of Elijah and Elisha*, traditional founders of the Order, and various saints connected with it[2].

The triumphal arch and choir were painted in a later campaign under the direction of

Antonio Cavallucci. On his death in 1795 Giovanni Micocca completed the painting of saints[3].
R of entrance: baptistery chapel: G. Micocca, *Baptism of Christ*, 1797[3]
1st bay: upper: *St Simon Stock Living in a Tree Trunk*; lower: *Punishment of the Priests of Baal*, Dughet
1 to R: Matteo Piccione, *The Virgin and Child Appear to St Mary Magdalen dei Pazzi*, c.1647
2nd bay: upper: *Elijah Ascends into Heaven*; lower: *Elijah and his Servant See a Cloud Rising from the Sea*, F. Grimaldi
2 to R: G. B. Greppi, *Vision of St Teresa*, 1651
3rd bay: upper: *Elijah Fed by the Ravens*; lower: *Elijah Crossing the Jordan*, Dughet
3 to R: Fabrizio Chiari, *St Martin and the Beggar*, 1645[5]
4th bay: upper: *Elijah Fed by an Angel*; lower: *Anointing of Kings*, Dughet
4 to R: Giovanni Angelo Canini, *St Stephen Martyr*, 1646[6]
5th bay: upper: *Mass of St Cyril*; lower: *Basilicas' Prophecy to Titus*, Dughet
5 to R: Filippo Gherardi, *St Charles Borromeo*
6th bay: upper: *Vision of Elijah's Parents*; lower: *Tree of Emerentiana*, Dughet
High altar: designed by F. Belli and executed by Domenico Manzolini with metalwork and candelabra by Gioacchino Belli and tabernacle by Michele Belli, 1796. Apse: decorated by A. Cavallucci and completed on his death by G. Micocca
Crypt: monuments to the Prior Giovanni Filippini (d. 1657) by P. Naldini, 1667, and the Prior Francesco Scannapieco (d. 1676) attributed to Naldini[7]
End of L aisle: Cappella della Madonna del Carmelo: built 1790-93 by Andrea de' Dominicis to hold a venerated picture by G. Massei of the *Virgin and Child Crowned by Two Angels*, 1600[8]. The painting surrounding it of *Souls in Purgatory* is by A. Cavallucci, 1793, with a bronze frame by Giuseppe Boroni. Lunette: *Angels in Glory* by A. Penna and stucco by Filippo Godioli. L side wall: A. Cavallucci, *Elijah Sees a Cloud Rising from the Sea*; vault: *St Simon Stock Receives the Scapular from the Virgin*, A. Cavallucci.
Before 3 to L: Filippo Gagliardi, *Interior View of Old St Peter's*; above, *Elijah on Mount Horeb*, Dughet
3 to L: Giovanni Angelo Canini, *Trinity with Sts Nicholas and Bartholomew*
Over sacristy door: above: *Meeting of Elijah and Ahab*; below: *Placing the Mantle on Elisha*, Dughet
2 to L: G. Muziano, *St Albert of Trapani*[9]
Between 2 and 1 to L: Galeazzo Leoncino, *Pope Silvester Holding the Council of 324 in S. Martino ai Monti*, c.1645
After 1 to L: above: *Elisha Cursing the Mocking Boys of Bethel*; below: *Elisha Venerated after Crossing the Jordan*, Dughet
1 to L: Pietro Testa, *Vision of St Angelus of Jerusalem*, 1645-46[10]
Before 1 to L: Filippo Gagliardi, *Interior View of S. Giovanni in Laterano*; above: *Elijah's Sacrifice on Mount Carmel*, Dughet
L entrance wall: J. Miel, *St Cyril Baptising a Sultan*, 1651[11].

SS. Michele e Magno
Via del Santo Uffizio, 21

A church has stood on this site at least from the 9th century but after many restorations it was completely rebuilt and decorated by Benedict XIV and Clement XIII between 1756 and 1759, the architect being Carlo Murena. At this time it belonged to a college of canons directly dependent on St Peter's. Apart from the fine medieval campanile it has no architectural features of interest.

INTERIOR
High altar: N. Ricciolini, *Sts Gregory and Magnus with St Michael*, 1757[1]
Altar to L: Ludwig Stern, *Sts Peter and Paul*, 1757[2]
End of L aisle: monument to Anton Raphael Mengs (d. 1779) by Vincenzo Pacetti, 1784[3].

SS. Nereo e Achilleo
Via delle Terme di Caracalla, 28

A church was recorded on this site in the 4th century. It was rebuilt in 814 and restored by Sixtus IV for the Holy Year of 1475, when it was reduced to its present size. When Cesare Baronio was made cardinal in 1596 with this as his titular church he restored it, preserving as much as possible of what had survived of the earlier church (cf. S. Cesareo), including the *baldacchino*, altar frontal and screens which date from the 13th century.

INTERIOR
On the walls of the side aisles are frescoes depicting the martyrdom of the Apostles, while the lives and martyrdom of the titular saints are represented between the clerestory windows, 1596-97.
R wall: *St Thomas; St James the Lesser; St Simon; St Jude; St Matthias;* **L wall:** *St Peter; St Andrew; St James the Greater; St John; St Philip.* Entrance wall: R: *St Matthew; St Clement;* L: *St Gregory; St Bartholomew;* over the door: *Sts Flavia Domitilla, Nereus, Achilleus, Theodora and Euphrosyna*
Clerestory: R: *Sts Nereus, Achilleus and Flavia Domitilla Profess their Faith before Diocletian; St Flavia Domitilla Anointed by St Clement; St Peter Baptises Flavia Domitilla together with her Mother Plautilla and Sts Nereus and Achilleus,* attributed to G. Massei. L: *Sts Flavia Domitilla, Theodora and Euphrosyna Burnt to Death in a Burning House; Sts Theodora and Euphrosyna, Converted to Christianity by St Flavia Domitilla, Receive Baptism,* attributed to P. Nogari; *Sts Nereus and Achilleus Taken to their Martyrdom*
In the presbytery: *St Gregory Giving his 28th Homily,* attributed to G. Massei
R nave altar: D. Alberti, *Madonna della Vallicella,* 1599[1]
L nave altar: C. Roncalli, *Sts Flavia Domitilla, Nereus and Achilleus,* 1599[2].

S. Nicola in Arcione (destroyed)
The mediaeval church, which stood on the site of via del Traforo, was rebuilt several times, last in the mid 18th century by Girolamo Teodoli. It was pulled down in 1907 when the *traforo* was cut under the Quirinal, but its façade is recorded in an old photograph reproduced in the *Guida rionale*.

S. Nicola in Carcere
Via del Teatro di Marcello, 46

Built on the ruins of three Roman temples, parts of which are built into the existing structure. The ruins were converted into a Christian church, probably in the 9th century. It was restored many times, but the interior owes its present appearance largely to Cardinal Federico Borromeo, who decorated the apse and built the high altar, and Cardinal Pietro Aldobrandini, nephew of Clement VIII, who added the façade. The church was heavily restored and redecorated with frescoes under Pius IX, who replaced the old wooden ceiling with the present one. The façade by Giacomo della Porta, dated 1599, is unlike any other in Rome. Its form was partly dictated by the narrowness of the site – till the via del Mare, now the via del Teatro di Marcello, was opened up in the 1920's the church was squeezed between houses and faced onto a narrow street – which led the architect to articulate it with two tall fluted Ionic columns with Michelangelesque capitals and a rich entablature, over which rises a low attic. The stucco bas-reliefs are exceptional for the period, though they recall those by Pirro Ligorio on the Villa Pia in the Vatican gardens, and their character led one critic to make the – unfounded – suggestion that they were added in the 18th century by Piranesi.

INTERIOR
Restored several times, the last in 1851-65 by Gaspare Servi.
Nave frescoes: Guido Guidi, scenes from the *Life of St Nicholas*, 1865-66[1]
R entrance wall: copy of Guercino's *Holy Trinity with Angels* by C. Brumidi[2]
Before 1 to R: detached fresco, *Virgin and Child* by the workshop of Antoniazzo, c.1484-86[3]
Before end chapel: monument to Cardinal Giovanni Battista Rezzonico (d. 1783) by Christopher Hewetson, 1787[4]
Chapel at end of R aisle: Cappella del Sacramento/Aldobrandini: frescoes by Baglione; arch: R: *Offering of Melchizedek*; C: *Manna Descending from Heaven*; L: *Elias and the Angel with Bread*; side walls: *Prophets*, 1599[5]
High altar: the altar itself is composed of a magnificent ancient sarcophagus of green porphyry. The *baldacchino* was set up in the restoration of 1865 but incorporates the four re-used ancient columns which stood beside the medieval altar
Apse: Vincenzo Pasqualoni, *Christ in Glory with the Virgin and St Nicholas*; below: *St Nicholas at the Council of Nicaea*
L of high altar: Lorenzo Costa, *Ascension*, 1503
1 to L: L wall: copy of A. Carracci's, *Assumption*[6].

S. Nicola degli Incoronati (destroyed)

This church stood from the 12th century onwards in the piazza Padella, off the via Giulia. It was rebuilt in 1680-81 with an unusual façade of a single bay flanked by Tuscan pilasters and crowned by a broken pediment of which the curved sections end in volutes, recorded in a drawing reproduced by Incoronati.

S. Nicola dei Lorenesi
Largo Febo, 20

The confraternity of the colony of Lorrainers living in Rome was originally established in the church of S. Luigi dei Francesi, where it enjoyed the use of the second chapel to the left, but in 1623 the church of S. Nicola in Agone was allotted to it by Gregory XV. This was replaced by the existing church which was built in 1635-36, ironically exactly at the time when Lorraine was losing its independence and being absorbed into France under Louis XIII and Richelieu. The identity of the architect has been established by M. Jacques Bousquet (see note in Dumast) as the Lorrainer François du Jardin, called Francesco Giardini in Rome, where he lived from 1625 to 1661, of whom little is known. The façade indicates that he must have been trained in Rome, and he must have formed his style in studying Giacomo della Porta, whose work it closely resembles.

INTERIOR
In 1731 Corrado Giaquinto, a native of Molfetta, a town near Bari, of which St Nicholas was the patron saint, offered to fresco the vault of the nave, the choir and the dome. This, his first important commission in Rome, was unveiled in 1733. Nave: *St*

Nicholas Strikes Water from a Rock; dome: *Trinity with the Virgin; St Nicholas and other Saints*; pendentives: *Cardinal Virtues*[1]. The commission was paid for by the chaplain, Domenico Fabri, who was also responsible for the complete decoration of the church, including the marbling of Sicilian jasper, under the direction of Pietro Mariotti, 1749.

Stucco reliefs with scenes from the *Life of St Nicholas* by Giovanni Battista Grossi, 1749.
1st bay: *St Nicholas is Chosen Bishop of Myra*, Grossi
1 to R: Francesco Antonozzi, *The Blessed Peter Fourier Presents the Constitution of the Congregation of Our Lady to the Virgin*, 1730-31[2]
3rd bay to R: *The Infant St Nicholas Takes Milk from his Mother's Breast Only Once on Wednesdays and Fridays*, Grossi
R choir: copy of Giaquinto's *St Nicholas Calms a Storm*, 1827
High altar: built by C. Orlandi, 1755-61; altarpiece: Nicholas Lorrain, *St Nicholas*, 1676-86
L choir: C. Giaquinto, *St Nicholas Receives the Thanks of Constantine's Officers Nepotian, Ursus and Apilion for Saving their Lives*, 1749
3rd L bay: *The Infant St Nicholas whilst Being Bathed on his First Day Stands Upright in his Bath*, Grossi
1 to L: Nicholas Lorrain, *St Catherine of Alexandria*, 1660-74
1st L bay: *St Nicholas Distributes his Worldly Goods to the Poor*, Grossi.

S. Nicola dei Prefetti
Via dei Prefetti, 35-36

A small church of early but uncertain date, which housed St Gaetano and the first Theatines between 1524 and 1525 (before the building of S. Andrea della Valle). In 1567 it was given to the Dominicans of S. Sabina by Pius V. The façade, which has an oval with a portrait of Pius V and dates from before 1674, is unusually chaste in design. It is now held by the Congregazione dei Missionari Oblati di Maria Immacolata.

INTERIOR
Wholly restored in the 18th century and again in 1860-62 by P. Belloni.
Vault: G. Triga, *St Nicholas of Bari in Glory with the Trinity*, c.1730
High altar: the presbytery was rebuilt by P. Belloni
Between 1 and 2 chapels to L: monument to Maria Teresa Sturbinetti and Antonio Cassetta by L. Carimini, 1868[1]
1 to L: Cappella Farina: V. Pasqualoni, *Virgin and Child with Sts Joseph and Joachim*, 1869
Sacristy: Francesco Ferrari, *Miracle of St Vincent Ferrer*.

S. Nicola da Tolentino
Salita di S. Nicola da Tolentino

Founded in 1614 by the Discalced Augustinian Friars. The church was built at the expense of Don Camillo Pamphili from 1651 onwards and is traditionally attributed to Giovanni Maria Baratta, brother of Bernini's pupil Francesco Baratta. Eimer[1] argues, however, on stylistic grounds that Carlo Rainaldi was the architect of the façade[2]. The effect of the façade, which was begun in 1655, has been altered owing to the fact that extra steps had to be added to the flight approaching it when the level of the street was lowered in the late 19th century.

The church and monastic buildings attached to it now belong to the Armenian community. If shut, apply at the door of the monastery on the left. Over the door of the

S. Nicola da Tolentino

monastery is a relief of *St Nicholas of Tolentino* by G. F. de' Rossi, 1664[3].

INTERIOR
The pilasters of the nave are made of a purplish-grey substance, apparently a kind of composite of marble fragments. Holy-water stoups by G. M. Baratta, 1664.
Entrance wall: allegorical figures of R: *Charity* and L: *Religion* by Andrea Baratta, 1655[4]
Vault: P. Naldini, *St William of Aquitaine*, 1663[5]; Giovanni Francesco de' Rossi, *St Clare of Montefalco*. He is also recorded as having made ten stucco angels, probably those in the window embrasures. Figures of *St Augustine*, *St Thomas of Villanova* and *St Agnes* by Pietro Sassi, 1661, and *St Nicholas of Tolentino* by G. B. Ferrabosco, 1656
1 to R: Cappella di S. Nicola di Bari/Monanni: built and decorated by G. M. Baratta, 1666. Altarpiece: F. Laurenzi, *St Nicholas Resurrects a Child*; on side walls: G. V. Borghesi, R: *Birth of the Virgin*; L: *Christ Crowning the Virgin*, 1680[6]. An unusual altar frontal of inlaid marble, partly in relief
2 to R: Cappella di S. Gregorio Illuminatore: altarpiece: Giovanni Gagliardi, *Meeting of Pope Silvester with St Gregory the Illuminator*, 1908
3 to R: Cappella Lante della Rovere: decorated by Pietro Paolo Baldini; R wall: *Christ Appears to St Lucretia*; lunette: *Christ Embraces St Lucretia*; L wall: *Martyrdom of St Gertrude*; lunette: *St Gertrude Professing her Faith before her Judges*; vault: *Sts Lucretia and Gertrude in Glory*, before 1665[7]; altarpiece: copy of Guercino's *Sts Gertrude and Lucretia*[8]; L wall: monument to Cardinal Federico Lante della Rovere (d. 1773) designed by Virgilio Bracci with sculpture by his brother Alessandro and a portrait of the Cardinal by Filippo Bracci, 1775[9]
R transept: Cappella di S. Giovanni Battista: altar with arms of Principe Camillo Pamphili;

altarpiece: Baciccio, *St John the Baptist*, c.1670[10]; stuccoes by Ercole Ferrata; R: monument to Cardinal Nicola Oregi (d. 1672); L: monument to Giuseppe Oregi (d. 1665)[11]
Dome: Giovanni Coli and Filippo Gherardi, *St Nicholas in Glory*, 1669-70[12]; pendentives: P. P. Baldini, *Obedience*; *Poverty*; *Chastity* and *Humility*, 1643[13]
High altar: the altar and the sculpture were designed by Algardi just before his death in 1654 but were largely executed by his pupils, the relief of *God the Father* and the figure of *St Nicholas of Tolentino* being by Ercole Ferrata and the *Virgin*, *St Augustine* and *St Monica* by Domenico Guidi, the two angels by Francesco Baratta, the stucco work in the apse and the relief of *St Nicholas of Tolentino* by Giovanni Ferrabosco. Algardi makes full use of a deep curved niche, which enables him to treat his figures in full relief[14]
Chapel to L of high altar: Cappella di SS. Cecilia e Matteo/Buratti: built for Matteo Buratti by G. B. Mola and decorated by P. P. Baldini. Altarpiece: *Virgin and Child with Sts Matthew and Cecilia*; R wall: *St Cecilia before the Prefect*; lunette: *An Angel Crowns St Cecilia before Valerian*; L wall: *St Matthew Resurrects the Emperor's Son*; above door: *St Matthew*; vault: *St Cecilia in Glory*. Oil paintings on either side of altar: R: *Death of St Cecilia*; L: *Martyrdom of St Matthew* by an unknown artist, c.1640[15]
L transept: L of altar: monument to Giorgio Saphar from the demolished church of S. Maria Egiziaca, 1709
3 to L: Cappella della Madonna del Buon Consiglio: chapel designed by Pietro Camporese the Elder and completed in 1790. Altarpiece: copy of the *Madonna del Buon Consiglio* by C. Unterberger. Lunettes: *Sybils*; dome: *God the Father in Glory* by Ermenegildo Costantini. On side walls: R: G. Cades, *Holy Family*, 1790[16]; L: Raffaele

Minossi, *Annunciation*, 1789; stucco decorations by Camillo Pacetti[17]

2 to L: Cappella Gavotti[18]: founded under the will of Giovanni Battista Gavotti (d. 1661), the chapel was begun by Cortona in 1663 and completed by his pupil Ciro Ferri in 1677. Ferri was responsible for the design of the relief of the busts of two martyrs on the sarcophagus below the altar, executed by C. Fancelli. Cortona also began the vault fresco of *Angels with Musical Instruments* but it was completed by Ciro Ferri in 1669. Altar relief: *The Virgin Appears to Antonio Botta (The Madonna di Savona)* by Cosimo Fancelli; L wall: *St John the Baptist* by A. Raggi; below: monument to Giovanni Battista Gavotti (d. 1661) by C. Fancelli; above: medallion of *St Charles Borromeo* by A. Raggi[19]; R wall: *St Joseph* by Ercole Ferrata; below: monument to Carlo Gavotti (d. 1690); above: *St Philip Neri* by Ferrata. This is one of Cortona's last works of architecture, characterised, like the façade of S. Maria in Via Lata and the dome of S. Carlo al Corso, by a grand simplicity and monumentality compared with an early work such as SS. Luca e Martina

1 to L: Cappella del Santo Sepolcro.

SS. Nome di Gesù *see* Il Gesù
Piazza del Gesù

SS. Nome di Maria
Piazza del Foro Traiano, 89

On the defeat of the Turks and the raising of the Siege of Vienna in 1683 Innocent XI, who had actively supported the Emperor Leopold I and John Sobieski, declared a new feast dedicated to the Holy Name of the Virgin, to whose intervention he attributed the success over the Turks, and in 1642 the Congregazione del SS. Nome di Maria was founded by Giuseppe Bianchi. This was at first housed in the church of S. Stefano del Cacco, but was moved to that of S. Bernardo on the Forum of Trajan in 1688 and the Congregazione raised to an Arciconfraternita. In 1728 the confraternity undertook to build a new church on a site adjacent to S. Bernardo and designs were put forward but nothing was done. In 1735 the protector of the confraternity, Cardinal Lodovico Pico della Mirandola, insisted on the choice of the Frenchman Antoine Dérizet as architect. The foundation stone was laid in 1736 and the church was consecrated in 1741. Dérizet's first plans, recorded in drawings in the Kunstbibliothek, Berlin, were for a church with a low dome. Later it was decided to introduce a tall double dome with a drum, but Dérizet's foundations were discovered to be too weak to carry this and the church was finally built with a single dome.

Dérizet, though born in Lyons and trained in Paris, went to Rome when he was 26 and spent the rest of his life there, and there is nothing specifically French about the church (except the shape of the windows in the drum of the dome), which stands as a rather mediocre example of the classical strain in Roman architecture in the second quarter of the 18th century. The statues at the base of the drum are by a group of Roman artists, whose names are given by Martini and Casanova, among them being M. A. Slodtz's *St Matthew*, 1740-41.

INTERIOR
All the marbling is fictive. The interior was restored and decorated by Louis Gabet, 1858.

The eight stucco reliefs at the base of the dome depicting scenes from the *Life of the Virgin* are by Carlo Tantardini, Francesco Queirolo, Filippo della Valle, Giovanni Battista Maini, Bernardino Ludovisi and

Michelange Slodtz, 1740[1].
1 to R: Cappella di S. Luigi: Antonio Nessi, *St Aloysius Gonzaga in Adoration before the Cross*[2]
2 to R: Cappella di S. Anna: Agostino Masucci, *Education of the Virgin*, 1757[3]
3 to R: Cappella di S. Giuseppe: built by Mauro Fontana. Altarpiece: Stefano Pozzo, *Death of St Joseph*, 1755[4]
Choir: built by Mauro Fontana; 1750. high altar by Andrea Bergondi to Fontana's design, 1750[5]. Before the choir is the inlaid monument to Cardinal Lodovico Pico della Mirandola (d. 1743).
2 to L: Cappella di S. Bernardo: N. Ricciolini, *The Virgin Appearing to St Bernard*, 1751[6]
1 to L: Cappella di SS. Pietro e Paolo: L. Masucci, *Sts Peter and Paul*.

Nostra Signora del Sacro Cuore
see **S. Giacomo degli Spagnuoli**
Piazza Navona, 105

S. Omobono
Vicolo Jugario

The church was built on the site of an ancient Roman temple and incorporates part of its walls. It was originally dedicated to S. Salvatore, but the dedication was changed to St Homobonus (a Cremonese saint) at some date soon after 1573, when it was granted to the Corporation of Tailors, who remodelled it. It was frequently restored; the interior is now of little architectural interest and the church has been closed for many years.

INTERIOR
Vault: C. Mariani, *Coronation of the Virgin with Sts Anthony and Homobonus*, 1877
1 to R: Vincenzo Milone, *St Anthony of Padua*, 1767

Apse: Pietro Turini, *Christ in Glory*, 1510
1 to L: G. A. Galli, *St Homobonus Giving his Clothes to a Beggar*[1].

S. Onofrio
Piazzale di S. Onofrio, 2

The church was founded by the Poor Hermits of St Jerome in 1434 and largely decorated in the 15th century. The church is open for Sunday morning Mass.
Portico to R of entrance: Domenichino, three scenes from the *Life of St Jerome* commissioned by Cardinal Girolamo Agucchi: *Baptism of St Jerome*; *Vision of St Jerome* and *Temptation of St Jerome*, 1604-05[1]
Cappella del Rosario (at end of Portico): attributed to G. B. Soria, this was built in 1620 for Cardinal Maffeo Barberini, later Pope Urban VIII[2]. Over the door: Agostino Tassi, *Sibyls*, 1620[3]
Passage to cloister: monuments to Alessandro Guidi (1712) by Girolamo Odam[4] and Marchese Giuseppe Rondinini (d. 1801)
Cloister: frescoed lunettes of scenes from the *Life of St Onuphrius*, some by Giuseppe Cesari and V. Strada, *c.*1600[5] and others attributed to Claudio Ridolfi[6]
Museo Tassiano: devoted to the memory of the poet Torquato Tasso, who died in the monastery in 1595. It includes a bust of John Barclay (d. 1621) by F. Duquesnoy, originally in S. Lorenzo fuori le Mura[7].

INTERIOR
1 to R: Cappella di. S. Onofrio: *Annunciation*, Antoniozzi Romano and workshop[8]
2 to R: Cappella della Madonna di Loreto/Madruzzo: work on enlarging the chapel began after Carlo Madruzzo was raised to the Bishop of Trent in 1569 and the chapel decorations were completed in 1605. Frescoes by G. B. Ricci da Novara, vault: scenes from

the *Life of the Virgin*; L lunette: *Birth of the Virgin*; R lunette: *Annunciation*; pendentives: *Evangelists*; vault of chapel entrance: *Creation of Eve*. Altarpiece designed by Annibale Carracci and executed by Domenichino, *Translation of the Holy House of Loreto*, c.1604-05[9]. Monuments to R: Cardinal Cristoforo Madruzzo (d. 1578) and L: Cardinal Ludovico Madruzzo (d. 1600) attributed to the school of G. B. della Porta, probably either Tommaso or Giovanni Paolo della Porta[10]

Sacristy: F. Trevisani, *The Blessed Peter Gambacorta*, c.1720-25[11]; vault: G. Pesci, *St Onuphrius with Allegorical Figures of Hope and Charity*, 1704[12]

Apse: attributed to Peruzzi, L: *Adoration of the Magi*; C: *Virgin and Child with Sts John the Baptist, Catherine of Alexandria, Jerome and Onuphrius*; R: *Flight into Egypt*. In the arch: scenes from the *Lives of Sts Jerome and Onuphrius*, 1507-08[13]; these frescoes have also been attributed to Jacopo Ripanda and two assistants[14]. The high altar was designed by Alberto Martini, 1601

3 to L: Cappella del Crocifisso: R wall: monument to Cardinal Filippo Sega, Papal Nuncio to the Imperial Court under Sixtus V and Bishop of Piacenza (d. 1596). L wall: monument to Cardinal Giuseppe Mezzofanti (d. 1849) by Francesco Bonola, 1885

1 to L: Cappella di S. Girolamo: remodelled by Carlo Piccoli on the orders of Pius IX. Altarpiece: Filippo Balbi, *St Jerome*. R wall: monument to Torquato Tasso (d. 1595) by Giuseppe de' Fabris, 1828-57[15]

S. Pancrazio
Piazza di S. Pancrazio, 5d

A church stood on this site probably dating from the 5th century. It was extensively remodelled on the orders of the Archbishop of Monreale, Cardinal Ludovico de Torres, in 1609 and was further restored between 1662 and 1665 and in 1673 by the Discalced Carmelites to whom it had been given by Alexander VII. The church was severely damaged and plundered by the French in 1798 and only repaired and reopened in 1813-16.

INTERIOR
In one of these restorations the church received its decoration of unusually delicate stucco putti and swags and the eight stucco bas-reliefs in the aisles. R nave: *St Julius*; *Sts Processus and Martinian*; *Martyrdom of St Pancras*; *St Felix*; L: nave: *St John of the Cross*; *Prophet Elijah*; *St John the Baptist*; *Burial of St Calepodius*[1]. The frames between the swags over the main arches and the carved and gilt roof were presumably intended to contain frescoes.

End of L aisle: Palma il Giovane, *Ecstasy of St Teresa*, 1615-c.20[2].

S. Pantaleo
Piazza di S. Pantaleo

A church has stood on this site since 1216. It was dedicated to St Pantaleon, patron saint of doctors, and was at one stage attached to an English college. In 1614 it was given to the Fratelli delle Scuole Pie, an Order founded by St Joseph Calasanctius. In 1681 the church was rebuilt to the designs of G. A. de' Rossi for Cardinal Gaspare Carpegna, Protector of the Order, but was not completed until 1691. De' Rossi prepared several preliminary plans which are preserved in drawings[1]. These proceed from a circular church to a rectangle with rounded corners and finally to a simple rectangle with side chapels – a plan that minimised the number of houses that had to be demolished to clear the site. The church consists of a single nave with no transepts, a deep presbytery with a semi-circular apse and four lateral chapels. The façade was added by Giuseppe Valadier in 1806 for Principe Giovanni Torlonia[2].

INTERIOR
Nave vault: Filippo Gherardi, *Triumph of the Name of Mary*, 1687-92[3]
Entrance wall to R: monument to Aurora Berti (d. 1720) by L. Merlini[4]
2 to R: altarpiece: *Death of St Joseph*, attributed to S. Ricci, *c.*1690[5]
High altar: in 1748 Nicola Salvi was commissioned to design a new high altar but his project was abandoned. Carlo Murena was commissioned in 1763 to continue the work but he soon died and his work was carried on by Antonio Bracci between 1764 and 1767. The sarcophagus under the *mensa*, containing the relics of the saint, was designed by Vanvitelli, 1761-62[6]. Valadier finally completed the high altar in 1802, when Conca's painting of St Joseph was replaced by a bas-relief of *St Joseph Calasanctius* by Luigi Acquisti[7], but work on the altar appears to have continued until 1807[8]
2 to L: Cappella di S. Pantaleo: altarpiece: Tommaso Amedeo Caisotti, *St Pantaleon Looks after the Sick*, 1689[9]
1 to L: Cappella di S. Anna: altarpiece: Bartolomeo Bosi, *Education of the Virgin*[10]
Casa delle Scuole Pie: Cappella dell'Apparizione: altarpiece: Lorenzo Masucci, *The Virgin Appears to St Joseph Calasanctius*, 1760[11]

Pantheon *see* S. Maria ad Martyres
Piazza della Rotonda

S. Paolo fuori le Mura
Via Ostiense

The great Early Christian basilica, founded by Constantine, was destroyed by fire in 1823, only the apse and the transepts being saved. It was rebuilt under the direction of Pasquale Belli, and after his death in 1833, under Luigi Poletti.

INTERIOR
The rebuilt nave was decorated with frescoes. The cycle begins in the right transept to the right of the apse, continues in the nave and ends in the left transept. Pietro Gagliardi, *Saul Present at St Stephen's Martyrdom*; *Conversion of Saul*; F. Podesti, *Ananias Instils Saul with the Virtues of the Holy Spirit*; *Ananias Baptises Saul*[1]; G. de' Sanctis, *Paul Preaching in Damascus*; *Paul's Flight from Damascus*; N. Consoni, *Paul among the Apostles at the Council of Jerusalem*; C. Mariani, *Consecration of Paul and Barnabus*; *Paul Converts Sergius Proconsul of Papo*; *Paul and Barnabus in Lystra*; *Stoning of Paul in Lystra*; L. Cochetti, *Paul's Vision in Troas*; *Paul Exorcises a Devil from a Young Girl in Philippi*; V. Morni, *Paul and Silas Flogged in Philippi*; G. Serene, *Paul Converts the Gaoler in Philippi*; G. B. Panello, *Paul's Speech in the Aeropago of Athens*; D. Tojetti, *Paul in Corinth*; C. de' Rossi, *The Ephesians Burn their Books*; N. Carta, *Paul Brings the Young Eutiches Back to Life*; M. Sozzi, *Paul Leaving for Miletus*; R. Bompiani, *Prophecy of Agobo*; C. Dies, *Paul and James in Jerusalem*; F. Grandi, *Paul Expelled from the Temple of Jerusalem*; *Paul's Speech to the People of Jerusalem*; N. Carta, *Paul Declares himself to be a Roman and Escapes Flogging in Jerusalem*; D. Bartolini, *Paul's Vision in Jerusalem*; *Paul before Felix in Caesarea*; A. Saccioni, *Paul's Shipwreck in Candia*; *Paul and the Snakes of Malta*; N. Consoni, *Paul*

Cures the Father of Publio, the Prince of Malta; C. Garvardini, *Paul Meets the Christians of Rome on the via Appia*; *Paul in Rome*; F. Coghetti, *Elevation into the Third Heaven*; *Peter and Paul in the Mamertine Prison*; F. Baldi, *Paul and Peter Embrace each other before their Martyrdom*; *Martyrdom of Peter and Paul*.
Right transept: Altare dell'Assunta, L: F. Gnaccarini, *St Benedict*, 1837, and R: F. Baini, *St Scholastica*, 1836
1 to R of high altar: Cappella di S. Lorenzo
2 to R of high altar: Cappella di S. Benedetto: built by L. Poletti, 1843-45; over the altar: statue of *St Benedict*, P. Tenerani, 1845
Left transept: Altare della Conversione di S. Paolo: altarpiece: Vincenzo Camuccini, *Conversion of St Paul*; L: A. M. Laboureur, *St Gregory the Great*; R: A. Stocchi, *St Romuald*
1 toL of high altar: Cappella del Crocifisso: L of entrance wall: S. Maderno, *St Bridget*
2 toL of high altar: Cappella di S. Stefano: altarpiece: *St Stephen*, R. Rinaldi. R wall: *Martyrdom of St Stephen*, F. Podesti; L wall: *Judgment of St Stephen*, F. Coghetti, 1857-60
Gallery: Gaspare Giovanni Traversi, *Feast of Absalom*; *Lazarus and Dives*; *Raising of Lazarus*, 1752; *Raising of the Widow's Son at Nain*; *Departure of Tobias*; *Healing of Tobias's Father*[2]; Lanfranco, *Moses and the Bronze Serpent*; *Fall of Manna*, 1625; L. Cigoli, *Crucified Christ and St Bridget*[3]; F. Coghetti, *St Stephen*, 1853.

S. Paolo Primo Eremita
Via Agostino Depretis, 95

The house was given by Alexander VII to a body of Polish and Hungarian hermits in 1667. The church, which was begun in the following year, was replaced by the existing one designed by Clemente Orlandi in 1767-75. When the Pauline Order was abolished Pius VI gave the house and church to a conservatory for girls, but later the church was deconsecrated and given to the University of Rome. It contained a statue of St Paul by Bergondi and a painting by Guglielmo Cortese of two guardian angels, but these were removed in 1833 and sold. The façade consists of a narrow, slightly concave bay flanked by tall pilasters, between which is a flattened version of Bernini's portico of S. Andrea al Quirinale.

S. Paolo alla Regola
Piazza di S. Paolo alla Regola

The church belonged to the Tertiary Franciscans of Sicily. Titi states in 1686 that the church was being rebuilt to the designs of Padre Giovanni Battista Bergonzoni, a Bolognese Franciscan. The façade was designed by Giacomo Ciolli and executed by Giuseppe Sardi. It was finished in 1721 and consecrated in 1728.

INTERIOR
1 to R: Cappella di S. Rosalia di Palermo: altarpiece: Cristoforo Creo, *Virgin with Sts Clare of Assisi, Rose of Viterbo and Rosalia of Palermo*[1]; R wall: B. Puccini, *Martyrdom of St Erasmus*[2]
Passage between 1 and 2 to R: R: monument to Bishop Pietro Gioeni (d. 1761)
R transept: Cappella di S. Francesco: altarpiece: M. Rocca, *St Francis Receives the Stigmata*, 1695[3]
3 to R: Cappella del Crocifisso: L wall: Puccini, *St Bonaventure in Ecstasy over the Vision of St Thomas Aquinas*, 1708[4]. Bronze crucifix unconvincingly attributed to Francesco Mochi[5], but an impressive work of that period
Sacristy: built in 1712 by Alessandro de'

Grandis. Vault: Ignatius Stern, *Christ with the Virgin, St Paul and St John Chrysostom*, 1742[6]
Apse: L. Garzi; L: *St Paul Preaching*; C: *Conversion of St Paul*; R: *Martyrdom of St Paul*, soon after 1700[7]
3 to L: Cappella della Madonna delle Grazie: R wall: Puccini, *Virgin with St Clare*[8]
L transept: Cappella di S. Anna: completed in 1747. Altarpiece: G. Calandrucci, *Holy Family with Sts Anne, Joachim, Lawrence and the Infant John the Baptist*, 1700[9]; frescoes by S. Monosilio, *St Anne in Glory*, 1747[10]
1 to L: Cappella di S. Antonio da Padova: altarpiece: G. Calandrucci, *Vision of St Anthony of Padua* c.1700[11]; L wall: G. Diol, *Miracle of St Anthony of Padua*[12].

S. Paolo alle Tre Fontane
(see also **S. Maria Scala Coeli**)
Via di Acque Salvie

Three churches were erected on the site of St Paul's execution to mark the founts which sprang up when his decapitated head bounced on the ground. That of SS. Vincenzo e Anastasio has retained its medieval aspect but that of S. Paolo was rebuilt by Giacomo della Porta for Cardinal Pietro Aldobrandini in 1599-1600. The figures of *St Peter* and *St Paul* on the façade are by I. Buzio[1]. The third church is S. Maria Scala Coeli.

INTERIOR
Much of the interior is decorated with painted marble. Within the church were three reliefs of the head of St Paul by I. Buzio, marking the spots where three streams sprang up beneath the severed head of the saint, but they appear to be missing[2]. Stuccoes by Filippo Pozzo.
 Side altars by Stefano Buzio and Stefano Longo.

R Transept: Altare della Decollazione: Passarotto Passarotti, *Beheading of St Paul*[3]
L Transept: Altare di S. Pietro: copy of Reni's *Martyrdom of St Peter*.

S. Pasquale Baylon (SS. Quaranta Martiri)
Via di S. Francesco a Ripa, 20

The site was given to the Spanish Padri Minori Osservanti Scalzi in 1736, but the church was not built till 1744-47 to designs by G. Sardi, who also built the attached monastery. The façade is unusual in having a parapet running over the pediment (cf. S. Maria della Neve), a device which may ultimately go back to Maderno's S. Susanna and Soria's S. Maria della Victoria.

INTERIOR
The interior, decorated with painted marble, is one of the liveliest in Roman architecture of the mid 18th century and is unusual in the breaking of the main entablature by the insertion of oval *coretti*.
Vault fresco: Matteo Panaria (Pannaria), *St Peter of Alcantara in Glory*; crossing: *St Paschal Baylon in Adoration before the Blessed Sacrament*[1]
1 to R: G. Sorbi, *Sts Didacus and Anthony*, c.1745-47[2]
2 to R: L. Krahe, *St Teresa of Avila Receives the Host from St Peter of Alcantara*, c.1751-56[3]
3 to R: S. Monosilio, *St Paschal Baylon in Adoration before the Host*, c.1745-47[4]
End of R aisle: M. Panaria, *St John of Prado*, c.1754[5]
High altar: *The Forty Holy Martyrs*, 1747 attributed by Chracas first to Luigi Tosi[6] and then to Mariano Maella, with a new date of 1764[7]
End of L aisle: 19th century copy of Jaime Duran's *St John the Baptist*

3 to L: *Immaculate Virgin* attributed to L. Tosi
2 to L: G. Sorbi, *St Francis Receives the Stigmata*[8]
1 to L: F. Preciado de la Vega, *Holy Family*, c.1745-47[9].

SS. Petronio e Giovanni dei Bolognesi *see* SS. Giovanni e Petronio dei Bolognesi
Via del Mascherone, 61a

S. Pietro in Montorio
Piazza di San Pietro in Montorio

The medieval church was given to the Amadeiti, a reformist branch of the Franciscans, by Sixtus IV in 1472. It was rebuilt in the last decades of the 15th century with the help of Ferdinand and Isabella of Spain, possibly to the designs of Baccio Pontelli. It has always remained under the protection of the Spanish sovereign. Bramante built the circular Tempietto which stands in the cloister on the spot where St Peter was once thought to have been crucified. It was finished in 1502 and Bramante intended it to be enclosed in a circular cloister. The lower chapel was restored in 1628-29, but the stuccoes appear to be before 1600.

INTERIOR
The interior is decorated with painted marble.
R of entrance: monument to Antonio Massa da Gallese (d. 1568) by G. A. Dosio[1]
1 to R: Cappella della Flagellazione/ Borgherini: Sebastiano del Piombo, *Flagellation* based on a design by Michelangelo; L: *St Peter*; R: *St Francis*; in the half-dome, *Transfiguration*; spandrels: *Prophets*, 1516-24, oil mural[2]
2 to R: Cappella della Madonna della Lettera: altarpiece: attributed to G. B. Lombardelli, *Madonna della Lettera*
3 to R: Cappella della Presentazione: frescoes by M. Cerruti, L wall: *Annunciation*; R wall: *Immaculate Virgin*[3]
Over 2 and 3 to R: School of Pinturicchio, *Theological Virtues* and *Four Sibyls*
R transept: Cappella di S. Paolo/del Monte: designed by Vasari for Julius III, sculpture and stucco by Bartolomeo Ammanati, 1550-52; altarpiece: Vasari, *St Paul Receives his Sight from Ananias*, 1551; apse: decorated by Vasari with scenes from the *Life of St Paul*[4]; monuments to L: Cardonal Antonio del Monte, uncle of Julius III (d. 1533) and R: Vincenzo del Monte, father of Julius III (d. 1504); over the tombs are niches with allegorical figures of L: *Religion* and R: *Justice*[5]
High altar: originally contained Raphael's *Transfiguration*, now in the Vatican. The apse now contains a copy of Reni's *Crucifixion of St Peter*
L transept: Cappella di S. Giovanni Battista/Ricci: commissioned by Cardinal Giovanni Battista Ricci. Decoration of the chapel began c.1556 and was completed in 1568[6]. The architecture is an almost exact copy of the Del Monte chapel in the right transept. The whole scheme was directed by Daniele da Volterra, who provided designs for the statues of L: *St Peter* and R: *St Paul* in the niches over the monuments. These may have been executed by Leonardo Sormani, 1559-68[7]. Altarpiece: Daniele da Volterra, *Baptism of Christ*, 1555-56[8]; stuccoes and frescoes by Michele Alberti; frescoes by G. Rocca of scenes from the *Life of the Baptist*, R: *Beheading of the Baptist*; C: *St John Preaching*; C: *God the Father*, 1559-c.66[9]
4 to L: Cappella della Pietà: built for Perod de Cuside, 1615-20, with fine stuccoes in the dome; altarpiece: D. van Baburen, *Christ's Entombment*, 1617; wall paintings, L: *Christ Teaching in the Temple*; lunette: *Garden of*

Gethsemane; R: *Christ and Veronica*, D. van Baburen; lunette: *Mocking of Christ*, David de Haan[10]

3 to L: Cappella di S. Anna: workshop of Antoniazzo Romano, *Virgin and Child with St Anne*: apse: *God the Father*[11]

2 to L: Cappella di S. Francesco/Raimondi[12]: built by Bernini for Francesco Raimondi, probably between 1640 and 1648[13]. Over the altar: high relief of *St Francis in Ecstasy on Mt. Alvera*, executed by Francesco Baratta, one of the first examples of Bernini's use of concealed lighting[14]. R wall: monuments to Monsignor Girolamo Raimondi (d. 1628); L wall: Monsignor Francesco Raimondi (d. 1638), both busts by Bolgi. In both cases the deceased is shown alive and praying in the niche above but also as a corpse in the sarcophagus. The monuments and the sculptures were all designed by Bernini, but were executed by members of his studio. The reliefs on the sarcophagi by Niccolò Sale are of particularly fine quality. The one on the left represents *The Dead Rising at the Last Judgment*, the other shows three scenes of which only one, *Ash Wednesday*, is clearly identifiable, the second one being a burial and the third a Bacchic dance based on Poussin's *Bacchanal in Front of a Herm of Pan* (National Gallery, London). Vault: Romanelli, *St Francis in Glory*, surrounded by grisailles by Abbatini[15]

1 to L: Cappella delle Stimmate: Giovanni de' Vecchi, *St Francis Receives the Stigmata*, with L: *St Nicholas of Bari* and R: *St Catherine of Alexandria*; semi-dome: *Funeral of Cardinal Dolera with Franciscan Nuns and Friars*, 1594[16]

Within the cloister are a series of frescoes of scenes from the *Life of St Francis* by N. Circignani, Giovanni Battista Lombardelli and others[17].

S. Pietro in Vaticano
Piazza di S. Pietro

In 1506 Julius II laid the foundation stone for a church to replace the old Constantinian basilica, using the design of Bramante in the form of a Greek cross. From the beginning there were proposals to build the church on a Latin cross plan on the grounds that it was more suitable liturgically and that it would more completely incorporate the site of the old basilica, but they were rejected. After Bramante's death in 1514 the church was continued under the direction of various architects, including Raphael, who produced several variants of Bramante's original centralised plan. Antonio da Sangallo prepared a model on a different plan, but almost nothing of this was carried out. Michelangelo, who took over the direction of St Peter's on Sangallo's death in 1546, made radical alterations to Bramante's design, but retained the Greek cross. Three arms of the cross were completed according to his plan and the dome was begun according to his design, but there is much dispute about whether in its existing form it follows the outline which he projected or one modified after his death by Giacomo della Porta, who completed the central dome and the two small domes.

In 1602 Paul V, after long and acrimonious discussions, finally decided to add a nave, which was built to the designs of Carlo Maderno[1]. The addition of the nave sacrificed Michelangelo's conception of a great dome supported by a compact Greek cross closely related to it in its proportions and meant that from nearby the dome was almost completely obscured by the façade of the church. This was built by Maderno and the existing structure was finished in 1614. It does not, however, represent Maderno's complete intention. He planned to have two towers and in order that they should not obscure the two smaller domes he extended the front by two bays beyond the width of the church itself. In the event the towers were never built, because when in 1640 Bernini began to construct the one on the left it was realised that the foundations were too weak to support it. On the death of Urban VIII in 1644 this failure was exploited by Bernini's enemies and Bernini was removed from his post. The present aedicules with clocks were a compromise erected by Giuseppe Valadier for Pius VI, 1786-90. The angels supporting the clock are by A. Bergondi and G. Angelini[2].

The visitor is strongly urged to take the lift to the roof where s/he will get an excellent view of the main and subsidiary domes as well as a fine distant prospect of the city.

Portico[3]: begun by Maderno in 1608; vault built in 1611; stucco decoration to designs by G. B. Ricci, begun in 1618. In its general form, with five doors leading into the church, the portico provides an allusion to that of the old St Peter's. On the right is the Porta Santa with a putto in the pediment by Borromini. The bronze doors in the centre by Filarete for Eugenius IV come from the old church, 1439. The stucco decoration of the vault includes figures of canonised popes and scenes from the *Acts of the Apostles* and was executed by S. Daria, G. Caslano, R. and G. Solari and S. Fuccari to designs by G. B. Ricci da Novara, 1618-20. The relief over the central door, *Feed My Sheep*, by Bernini, was originally set up over the door on the inside of the church, 1633-46, but was moved to its present position in 1649[4]. In theme it echoes Ambrogio Buonvicino's relief on the façade representing *Christ Giving the Keys to St Peter*. When Bernini built the new entrance and the Scala Regia it was replaced by the equestrian statue of *Constantine's Vision of the Cross*, set up in 1669[5]. This can be seen from the portico through the glass doors. It is balanced at the other end by the statue of *Charlemagne* by A. Cornacchini, 1720-25[6].

A copy of Giotto's *Navicella (St Peter Walking on the Water)*, reconstructed by Orazio Manenti, 1674-75, is over the middle door on the inside of the façade.

The Benediction Loggia over the portico (only accessible from the Vatican) was vaulted in 1612. It contains Maratta's cartoons for mosaics in the interior of St Peter's.

INTERIOR

When Maderno came to build the nave, the basic decoration of the structure had been fixed. Bramante's coffering had been carried out over the first bays in the three arms of the Greek cross built by him and his successors and this set the pattern for the nave. The decoration of the arches between the nave and the aisles was designed by Bernini, who replaced the travertine columns in the nave and chapels with *cottanello* marble, decorated with emblems and 55 portraits of popes from St Peter to Benedict I, and carried out by an army of assistants from 1645 onwards for Innocent X. In the spandrels Bernini added allegorical figures of Christian virtues[7]; over the middle arches are the arms of Innocent X supported by *Fame*[8]. The piers were decorated for Clement XI to designs by Carlo Fontana[9]. In the niches between the pilasters are statues of founders of religious orders, begun in 1706 but still being executed in the 20th century[10].

RIGHT NAVE

1st pier: arch: R: *Mercy*, G. F. de' Rossi and L: *Strength*, G. F. and D. de' Rossi, 1647; lower niche: *St Teresa*, F. della Valle, 1754[11]; 2nd pier: arch: R: *Clemency* and L: *Contemplation*, C. Fancelli, 1647; lower niche: *St Vincent de Paul*, P. Bracci, 1754; 3rd pier: arch: R: *Peace*, L. Morelli and L: *Innocence*,

G. B. Morelli, 1647; lower niche: *St Philip Neri*, G. B. Maini, 1736; 4th pier: arch: R: *Faith* and L: *Charity*, Buonvicino, 1600

RIGHT TRANSEPT

R side: 1st niche: *St Cajetan Thiene*, C. Monaldi, 1738; 2nd niche: *St Jerome Emiliani*, P. Bracci, 1757[12]; 3rd niche: *St Joseph Calasanctius*, I. Spinazzi, 1755[13]; 4th niche: *St Bruno*, M. Slodtz, 1744

APSE

R side: 1st niche: *St Elijah*, A. Cornacchini, 1727; above: *St Francis of Sales*, A. Tadolini, 1845; 2nd niche: *St Dominic*, P. Legros, 1702-06[14]; above: *St Francis Caracciolo*, F. M. Laboureur, 1834[15]

L side: 2nd niche: lower: *St Francis of Assisi*, C. Monaldi, 1727; above: *St Alphonsus de Liguori*, P. Tenerani, 1839; 1st niche: *St Benedict*, A. Montauti, 1735[16]; above: *St Frances of Rome*, P. Galli, 1850

LEFT TRANSEPT

R side: 1st niche: *St Juliana Falconieri*, P. Campi, 1740; above: *St Angela Merici*, P. Galli, 1866; 2nd niche: lower: *St Norbert*, B. Cavaceppi, 1767; 3rd niche: lower: *St Peter Nolasco*, P. Campi, 1742; 4th niche: *St John of God*, F. della Valle, 1745[17]

LEFT NAVE

4th pier: arch: R: *Fortitude* and L: *Justice*, C. Mariani, 1600; lower niche: *St Francis of Paola*, G. B. Maini, 1732; 3rd pier: arch: R: *Obedience*, attributed to B. Cennini and L: *Patience*, attributed to D. Prestinaro, 1647; lower niche: *St Ignatius*, designed by C. Rusconi, executed by G. Rusconi, 1728; 2nd pier: arch: R: *Faith* and L: *Chastity*, N. Menghini, 1647-49; lower niche: *St Camillus de Lellis*, P. Pacilli, 1753[18]; 1st pier: arch: R: *Divine Justice* and L: *The Church*, A. Bolgi, 1747-49; lower niche: *St Peter of Alcantara*, F. Vergara, 1753[19]

Against the first piers of the nave are holywater stoups of colossal size by G. Lironi, F. Moderati, G. B. de' Rossi to a design by A. Cornacchini, 1725[20].

Confessio: the magnificent marbled *confessio* in front of the tomb of St Peter was built on the orders of Paul V by Maderno, 1615-18. The 89 lamps which illuminate it were added by Matthia de' Rossi in 1681. Within the *confessio* is the Niche of the Pallia, which is enclosed by bronze gates depicting the *Martyrdom of Sts Peter and Paul*, designed by N. Cordier and cast by Orazio Censore, whilst the statues on either side of the niche of L: *St Peter* and R: *St Paul* are by A. Buonvicino, 1615-18. On the landing of the staircase are two alabaster columns surmounted with statues of *St Peter* and *St Paul* by Luigi Valadier. The *confessio* and adjoining passages were frescoed by G. B. Ricci depicting scenes relating to the tomb of St Peter[21]

Crossing: the crossing itself was decorated by Bernini on the orders of Urban VIII. The scheme involved the construction of a *baldacchino* over the grave of St Peter and the decoration of the four piers[22]

Baldacchino: designed by Bernini and executed 1624-33. The angels atop the *baldacchino* are by F. Duquesnoy, A. Bolgi and G. Finnelli[23]. The papal altar under the *baldacchino* was consecrated by Clement VIII in 1594

Dome: pendentives: Giovanni de' Vecchi executed the cartoons and mosaics of *St John* and *St Luke* and C. Nebbia those of *St Matthew* and *St Mark*, 1598-99. The putti and other decorative elements were painted by C. Roncalli, 1600. The vault cartoons were executed by G. Cesari; on the lowest level are portraits commemorating popes and bishops buried in the basilica; above are *St Paul*, *St Peter*, *The Virgin*, *St John the Baptist* and the other apostles; above these are angels and seraphim and in the lantern *God the Father*, 1603-12. Restored in 1819[24]

Crossing piers: in the niches designed by Bernini stand statues connected with the four principal relics: the Veil of Veronica, statue of *St Veronica* by Francesco Mochi, 1629-32[25]; a fragment of the Holy Cross found by St Helena, statue of *St Helena* by Andrea Bolgi, 1630-39[26]; the Spear of St Longinus, statue of *St Longinus* by Bernini, 1630-39[27]; and the Head of St Andrew, statue of *St Andrew* by François Duquesnoy, 1629-40[28]. The relics themselves are now preserved in the Loggia over St Veronica

Above the niches are four galleries designed by Bernini incorporating symbols of the four relics and eight of the Salomonic columns from the screen surrounding the high altar in the old church; *The Cross of St Helena*, Stefano Speranzo, 1635; *The Spear of St Longinus*, Matteo Bonarelli, 1636-38; *The Veil of St Veronica*, M. Bonarelli, 1636 and *The Cross of St Andrew*, D. de' Rossi, 1637-38[29]. Below the piers are four chapels dedicated to St Veronica, St Andrew, St Longinus and St Helena. Sacchi was commissioned to paint the altarpieces of *Christ Carrying the Cross and St Veronica, St Andrew in Adoration before his Cross, Martyrdom of St Longinus* and *St Helena and the Miracle of the True Cross*. These were replaced in 1681 with mosaic copies; the orginals are now in the Chapter House[30].

The *baldacchino* and the decoration of the piers are the first manifestations of Bernini's genius as a decorator. In the *baldacchino* he solved the problem of constructing an altar which would have been dwarfed by Bramante's colossal order of pilasters by making his columns of dark bronze and giving them the twisted form of the columns which had stood in front of the old St Peter's and were traditionally believed to have come from the Temple of Jerusalem. In the galleries in the four piers he incorporated eight of these columns and made a crucial innovation by setting the angels bearing the relics against a background of coloured marble inlay which imitates a yellow sunset with purple clouds. The colours are echoed in the gilt of the half-dome reliefs and the purple marble of the balustrade. This is one of the first examples of the Baroque fusion of the arts, architecture blending with sculpture and using the means proper to painting, such as the use of colour and a naturalistic rendering of clouds against a sunset sky.

In the late 17th and early 18th centuries all the painted altarpieces, which had suffered badly from damp, were removed and replaced by mosaic copies. The originals are now in the Vatican Gallery and S. Maria degli Angeli. The altar frontals were renewed in 1779 on the orders of Pius VI, based on a design by G. B. Bonfreni.

RIGHT AISLE

1st bay: mosaic over the Holy Door to a design by Ciro Ferri, 1675; vault: *Mysteries of the Cross*; pendentives: *Noah; Abraham and Isaac; Moses; Jeremiah*; lunettes: *Amos, Zachariah, Phrygian Sibyl, Cumaean Sibyl, Hosea*, to designs by Pietro da Cortona, before 1669 (dome) and Ferri, 1669-71

1st chapel: originally the Cappella del Crocifisso but now called the Cappella della Pietà since Michelangelo's *Pietà*, 1499-1500, was placed there in 1749. The door to the right is by Bernini. Frescoes by Giovanni Lanfranco of the *Triumph of the Cross* and scenes from the *Passion*, 1629-31[31]. Stuccoes designed by A. Ciampelli

1st pier to L: monument to Queen Christina of Sweden (d. 1689), erected 1692-1702, designed by Carlo Fontana[32]; relief of *The Queen Abjuring Protestantism* by J. B. Théodon, putti by L. Ottone, and the bronze

parts of the tomb by G. Giardini[33]. R: monument to Leo XII (d. 1829) with allegorical figures of L: *Religion* and R: *Justice* by Giuseppe de' Fabris, 1836[34]
Passage to L of 1st chapel: Cappella di S. Nicola da Bari; L wall: *St Nicholas of Bari* by Fabio Cristofari
2nd bay: mosaics of subjects referring to the Eucharist after Cortona; vault: *Adoration of the Lamb*; pendentives: *Abel Offering a Sacrifice*; *Isaiah*; *Zachariah Stoned in the Temple*; *Jeremiah*, 1652-62[35]; lunettes: *Martyrdom of the Seven Maccabee Brothers*; *Mattathias Killing an Idolatrous Jew*, probably based on Cortona's cartoons; *Martyrdom of Two Hebrew Women*; *Eleazar Refusing to Eat Forbidden Meat*; *Daniel in the Lions' Den*; *Shadrach, Meshach and Abednego in the Fiery Furnace* by R. Vanni, 1659-63
2nd chapel: Cappella di S. Sebastiano; mosaic after Domenichino's *Martyrdom of St Sebastian*, 1628-31[36]
2nd pier to R: monument to Innocent XII (d. 1700). The pope was first buried in a simple tomb designed by Carlo Fontana which stood between the first and second chapels on the right aisle[37], but in 1746 it was decided by Cardinal Petra to give him a grander monument and the present tomb, designed by Fuga and executed by Filippo della Valle, was set up[38] with statues of L: *Charity* and R: *Justice*[39]
2nd pier to L: monument to Countess Matilda (d. 1115) commissioned by Urban VIII as a tribute to the great supporter of the temporal powers of the papacy. Designed by Bernini and executed by his studio; figure of the Countess and right putto by Luigi Bernini, 1633-37[40]. The relief on the sarcophagus shows *Emperor Henry IV Kneeling before Gregory VII at Canossa*, G. L. Bernini and S. Speranza[41]
3rd bay: vault and pendentives by Cortona, *Offering of Melchizedek*; *Elijah Restored by an Angel*; *Priest Dispensing Ceremonial Bread*; *Aaron Collecting Manna*, 1653-62; lunettes: Raffaele Vanni, *Uzzah Struck Dead*; *Isaiah*; *Offering of the High Priest*; *Return from Canaan*; *Jonathan Tasting the Honey*; *Dagon Destroyed by the Presence of the Arch*, 1659-63
3rd chapel: Cappella del SS. Sacramento[42]: grille and doors designed by Borromini, 1626[43]. Originally the sacristy but dedicated as the new Sacramental Chapel in 1638. Altarpiece: *Holy Trinity* by Cortona, 1628-31[44]. Urban VIII commissioned Bernini in 1629 to make a metal tabernacle but nothing was done. The project, still under Bernini, was revived again by Clement X in 1672 and completed in 1675. The models for the *Apostles* on the tabernacle were made by Giovanni Rinaldi and the allegorical figures of *Faith* and *Religion* by Giuseppe Mazzuoli[45]. Vault stuccoes designed by G. B. Ricci and executed by Giovanni Casolana and Simone Daria, c.1621-25. On the right wall is a mosaic copy of Domenichino's *St Francis in Ectasy*, 1628-30[46], flanked by two more of the Salomonic columns said to have come from the Temple of Jerusalem
3rd pier to R: monument to Gregory XIII (d. 1585) commissioned in 1715 by Cardinal Giacomo Buoncompagni and completed in 1723 to replace an earlier monument to Gregory XII by Prospero Antichi, of which the volutes were incorporated in the new monument. The programme was provided by the Theatine father, Alessandro Salarolo. Figures of L: *Religion* and R: *Magnificence* and relief of *The Reform of the Calendar by Gregory XIII*. The general design was given by Camillo Rusconi, though the relief was probably designed by Bernardino Cametti and executed by Carlo Francesco Mellone[47]. L: monument to Gregory XIV (d. 1591) with allegorical figures of R: *Justice* and L: *Religion* by P. Antichi

Ambulatory: Altare di S. Girolamo: mosaic after Domenichino's *Last Communion of St Jerome at the Hands of St Ephren*, 1614[48]

Cappella Gregoriana: decorated under Gregory XIII; a fine example of the early use of coloured marbles[49]. Vault: cartoon by S. Monosilio of Marian symbols: *Palm, Ark, Sun, Tower, Well, Moon* and *Cypress Tree*, 1772-75. Pendentives: *Pope Gregory the Great*; *St Jerome*; *St Gregory of Nazianzen*; *St Basil*; lunettes, *Virgin of the Annunciation*; *Angel of the Annunciation*; *Ezekiel*; *Isaiah* designed by N. Lapiccola, 1768-69. L: monument to Gregory XVI (d. 1846) with allegorical figures of R: *Prudence* and L: *Wisdom* by Luigi Amici, 1853[50]

Passage to transept: R: monument to Benedict XIV (d. 1758) by P. Bracci and assistants, 1759[51]; statues of L: *Wisdom* and R: *Disinterestedness* (a rarely represented virtue), the latter by Gaspare Sibilla[52]

Pier to L: Altare di S. Basilio: mosaic of *St Basil and the Emperor Valens* after Subleyras, 1743-47

R transept: apse stuccoes designed by L. Vanvitelli and executed by G. B. Maini, assisted by Giacomo Galli, C: *St Peter Freed from Prison*; L: *Sts Paul and Barnabas in Lystra*; R: *St Paul Preaching in the Aeropago*. R: Altare di Venceslao di Boemia: altarpieces: *St Wencelas*, after A. Caroselli, 1627-30; apse stuccoes: scenes from the *Life of St Thomas*, 1597-99. C: Altare di SS. Processo e Martiniano: Altarpiece: *Martyrdom of Sts Processus and Martinianus*, after Valentin, 1629-30; apse stuccoes: scenes from the *Life of St Paul*, 1597-99. L: Altare di S. Erasmo: altarpiece: *Martyrdom of St Erasmus*, after Poussin, 1627-29; apse stuccoes: scenes from the *Life of St James the Greater*, 1597-99

Passage to **Cappella di S. Michele:** monument to Clement XIII (d. 1769), commissioned by Abbondio Rezzonico and his brothers Cardinals Carlo and Gian Battista, by Canova, 1788-92[53]. L: Altare della Navicella: mosaic of *Christ Summoning St Peter to Walk on the Water* after Lanfranco, 1627-28

Cappella di S. Michele[54]**:** mosaics of saints on the pendentives after Sacchi, *St Leo the Great*; *St Dionysius the Areopagite*, 1631; C. Pellegrini, *St Bernard*, 1636-37 and Romanelli, *St Gregory Thaumaturgus*; lunettes: B. Lamberti, *Elijah and the Angel* and *Tobias and the Angel*, 1719-21; B. Lamberti and L. Gramiccia, *St Peter Baptising St Petronilla*, 1719-22; M. Benefial, *St Nicodemus Administering the Sacrament to St Petronilla*, 1722. Dome: *Angels with Attributes*, after N. Ricciolini, 1725-29. R: Cappella di S. Michele: altarpiece: mosaic of Reni's *St Michael*. L: Cappella di S. Petronilla: altarpiece: mosaic of Guercino's *Burial and Reception into Heaven of St Petronilla*, 1621-23

Passage to tribune: R: monument to Clement X (d. 1676) by Mattia de' Rossi, unveiled 1686. The figure of the pope is by Ercole Ferrata; L: *Clemency* by Giuseppe Mazzuoli and R: *Benevolence* by Lazzaro Morelli. The relief of the *Opening of the Porta Santa for the Holy Year of 1675* is by Leonardo Retti[55]. L: Altare di Tabita: altarpiece: mosaic of *St Peter Raising Tabitha* after Placido Costanzi, 1757

Tribune: R: monument to Urban VIII (d. 1644) by Bernini, 1627-47[56].

In 1627 Urban VIII decided to move the tomb of Paul III (d. 1549) by Guglielmo della Porta[57] which stood in the Cappella Gregoriana and to set up his own tomb to balance – and excel – it. The monument to Urban VIII is Bernini's first major tomb and shows his inventiveness in *concetti*, use of materials and dramatic treatment of gesture and draperies. The commanding figure of the pope is in dark bronze, partly gilt, as are the sarcophagus, the figure of *Death* emerging from it and the tablet on which he writes the name of the pope. The allegorical figures of *Charity* and *Justice* are in white marble. Originally the left breast of *Charity* was uncovered but stucco drapery was added, probably at the end of the 17th century. This tomb was the model which was imitated with variations for almost all papal monuments in St Peter's till it was replaced by Canova with a neoclassical type in the monument to Clement XII.

Cathedra Petri[58]: designed by Bernini and executed in 1656-66 forf Alexander VII as a setting for the wooden throne believed to have been the chair of St Peter and as the climax to the progression from the nave, through the *baldacchino* to the altar in the apse of the church.

The 'Chair' is supported by colossal figures in partly gilded bronze – *Sts Ambrose, Augustine, Athanasius* and *John Chrysostom*. Above the chair is an oval window of golden yellow glass with the dove of the Holy Spirit at its centre, surrounded by a gilded stucco setting of rays and putti. On the chair itself is a relief illustrating Christ's words to St Peter, 'Feed my Sheep'. The whole structure is therefore a dramatic testimony to the continuity of the Catholic church based on the charge to St Peter, continued by the tradition of the Fathers and guided by the Holy Spirit. The models for the four Fathers were prepared by E. Ferrata, A. Raggi, Lorenzo Morelli and Peter Verpoorten and cast by Giovanni Artusi, and the stucco *Gloria* was made by Lazzaro Morelli, A. Raggi, Pietro Sassi and P. Naldini. Apse stuccoes designed by L. Vanvitelli, L: *Crucifixion of St Peter*; C: *Christ Gives the Keys to St Peter*; R: *Beheading of St Paul*, executed by G. M. Marini, 1750

Passage to Cappella della Colonna: R: monument to Alexander VIII (d. 1691), commissioned by his nephew Cardinal Pietro Ottoboni, designed by Carlo Enrico di San Martino and executed by Angelo de' Rossi, completed after De' Rossi's death by G. Raffaelli, 1695-1725; allegorical figures of L: *Religion* and R: *Prudence*; relief of *Canonisation of Five Saints*, 1702-04. The bronze figure of the pope and cask was cast by Giuseppe Bertosi[59]; L: Altare del Paralitico: mosaic of *St Peter Healing the Cripple at the Porta Spetiosa* after Francesco Mancini, 1744-48

Cappella della Colonna/S. Leone Magno: mosaics in vault of angels and allegorical figures after G. Zoboli, 1746; pendentives: *St Bonaventure* and *St Cyril of Alexandria* by G. Lanfranco, 1629-32; *St Thomas Aquinas* and *St John Damascene* by Sacchi, 1629-34; lunettes: Romanelli, *David*; *Solomon*; *Virgin and Child*; *Joseph's Dream*, 1643-44. R: Altare di S. Leone Magno: relief of the *Encounter of Leo the Great and Attila* by Algardi, 1646-50[60]. L: Altare della Madonna della Colonna/ Mater Ecclesiae: built for Paul V to house a miracle-working image of the *Virgin and Child* taken from the old St Peter's

Passage to transept: R: monument to Alexander VII (d. 1667) by Bernini, executed 1671-78[61]; allegorical figures of *Justice* by Giulio Cartari and *Prudence* by G. Baratta, completed by Cartari, behind, and in front, R: *Charity* by G. Mazzuoli and L: *Truth* by Morelli, completed by Cartari. The figure of the pope was carved by M. Maglia. The tomb is a variant of Bernini's earlier monument to Cardinal Pimentel with the pope kneeling instead of sitting. It is exceptional among Roman tombs in being built over a door, the Porta S. Marta (actually leading to a passage out of the church), a pattern familiar in Venice, which Bernini had adopted in an unexecuted design for the tomb of Doge Giovanni Cornaro, father of Cardinal Cornaro, who commissioned the Cornaro chapel in S. Maria della Vittoria[62]

L transept: apse stuccoes designed by L.

Vanvitelli and executed by G. B. Maini, assisted by Giacomo Galli, C: *Calling of Sts Andrew and Peter*; R: *Healing of the Lame*; L: *Death of Sapphira*, 1750[63]. L: Altare di SS. Marziale e Valeria/della Crocifissione: altarpiece: *Crucifixion of St Peter*, after Reni; apse stuccoes: scenes from the *Life of St Andrew*, 1597-99. C: Altare di S. Tommaso: altarpiece: *Incredulity of St Thomas*, after Vincenzo Camuccini; apse stuccoes: scenes from the *Life of St John the Evangelist*, 1597-99

Sacristy: built by Carlo Marchionni for Pius VI, 1776-84[64]. 1st vestibule: *St Andrew*. Passage to treasury: R wall: monuments to Benedict XIII and Cardinal Francesco Barberini (d. 1679) with bust by L. Ottoni[65] and L wall: Paul IV and Mario Mattei (d. 1870). Opposite the staircase: statue of Pius VI by Agostino Penna, 1784[66]

Sagrestia: high altar: after Caravaggio, *Entombment of Christ*

Sagrestia dei Canonici: over door, J. Zucchi, *Exaltation of the Church*[67]

Sala Capitolare: D. Cresti, *Incredulity of Thomas*, 1624-26; G. A. Galli, *St Valeria of Limoges Carries her Head to the Altar where St Martial is Celebrating Mass*, 1629-32, and *St Peter* by Mino da Fiesole, 1463, modified by Niccolò Longhi, 1565[68]

Attached to the sacristy is the Treasury which contains not only important Early Christian ivories and Antonio Pollaiuolo's Tomb of Sixtus IV, 1493, but also a lifesize model for one of Bernini's angels for the Cappella del SS. Sacramento and much 17th and 18th century altar plate.

Opposite sacristy: mosaic after C. Roncalli's *Death of Sapphira*, 1599-1603. Over sacristy door: monument to Pius VIII (d. 1830) with figures of L: *St Paul* and R: *St Peter* by Pietro Tenerani[69]

Cappella Clementina[70]: decorated under Clement VIII by G. della Porta[71]. Altare di S. Gregorio Magno: altarpiece: mosaic after Sacchi's *St Gregory and the Miracle of the Corporal*, 1625-27; Altare della Trasfigurazione: altarpiee: mosaic after Raphael's *Transfiguration*. Pendentives: after Roncalli, *St Ambrose*; *St Augustine*; *St John Chrysostom* and *St Athanasius*; lunettes: *St Elizabeth*; *Joseph and Mary*; *Daniel in the Lions' Den*; *Malachi and an Angel*, 1601-02. Monument to Pius VII (d. 1823) by B. Thorvaldsen, with allegorical figures of R: *Wisdom* and L: *Strength* and sitting, R: *Time* and L: *History* 1829-30[72]

3rd pier to L: R: monument to Leo XI (d. 1605) commissioned by his nephew Cardinal Roberto Ubaldini and designed by Algardi with figures of R: *Liberality* and L: *Magnanimity*; relief below: two scenes from the *Life of Leo XI*, R: *Cardinal Alessandro de' Medici Presents Henry IV with the Articles of his Abjuration from Protestantism, which He Signs*; L: *Henry IV Swears Acceptance of the Peace of Vervins between France and Spain*, completed 1644[73]; L: monument to Innocent XI (d. 1689) commissioned by Livo Odescalchi, designed by Maratta and executed by Monnot, 1701, with figures of L: *Religion* and R: *Justice* and bas-relief of the *Liberation of Vienna from the Turks in 1683*, 1701[74]

3rd bay: pendentives: mosaic of *Prophets* to designs by Ciro Ferri, *David and Jonah*, 1681, and Maratta, *David and Habakkuk*, 1700-04; dome: M. Franceschini, *God the Father in Glory*, 1712-16; lunettes: Franceschini, *Deborah Sends for Barak*; *Judith with the Head of Holofernes*; *Jeremiah Weeps over Jerusalem*; *Deborah and Barak Give Thanks to God for Victory*, 1721; N. Ricciolini, *Moses Prays, Supported by Aaron and Hur*; *Azaria Prevents King Oziah from Burning Incense at the Altar*, 1721-23

3rd chapel: Cappella del Coro: grille by Borromini, 1626[75]; decorated in 1622; vault stuccoes designed by G. della Porta and executed by G. B. Ricci. Choir stalls by G. B. Soria and Bartolomeo de' Rossi, 1625. Altarpiece: after Pietro Bianchi, *Immaculate Conception with Sts John Chrysostom, Francis and Anthony of Padua*, 1734-40

2nd pier to L: monument to Innocent VIII (d. 1492) by Antonio and Piero Pollaiuolo, 1498; R: monument to Pius X (d. 1914), architecture by Florestano di Fausto and sculpture by Pier Enrico Astorri, 1923[76]

2nd bay: vault: G. Chiari, based on designs and sketches by C. Maratta, *God the Father with the Virgin* and *St Michael Defeats Lucifer*, 1704-13; pendentives: Maratta, *Balaam*; *Gideon*; *Aaron*; *Noah*; lunettes by Maratta, assisted by G. Chiari: *Moses Approaches the Burning Bush*; *Miriam's Thanksgiving Dance*; *Judith with the Head of Holofernes*; *Jael Killing Sisera*; *Joshua Stopping the Sun*; *Isaiah with the Cloud*, 1683-88

2nd chapel: Cappella della Presentazione: altarpiece: mosaic after Romanelli, *Presentation of the Virgin*; 1638-42; L wall: monument to Benedict XV (d. 1922) by Pietro Canonica, 1928[77]

1st pier to L: R: monument to Queen Maria Clementina Sobieska (d. 1735), wife of James III, the Old Pretender, designed by F. Barigioni, with sculpture by P. Bracci, mosaic portrait by P. P. Cristofari and bronze work by F. Giardoni, 1739-42[78]; L: monument to the last Stuarts (James III, d. 1766, Prince Charles Edward, d. 1783, and Cardinal Henry Benedict, Duke of York, d. 1807) by Canova, 1817-19[79]

1st bay: dome: *God the Father with Christ*; *Baptism by Blood*; *Water and Desire*; 1741-1745; pendentives: *America*; *Asia*; *Africa*; *Europe*, 1724-26; lunettes: *St Peter Baptising the Centurion Cornelius*; *St Philip Baptising the Eunuch of Queen Candace*; *Christ Baptising St Peter*; *St Sylvester Baptising Constantine*; *Moses Striking Water from the Rock* and *Noah Praying*, all by Trevisani, 1737-39[80]

1st chapel: Cappella del Battesimo: font designed by C. Fontana and executed by J. Théodon, M. Maglia, L. Ottoni and Giovanni Giardini, 1692-99. Originally elevated, it was lowered to its present level on the orders of Benedict XIII in 1725[81]; L walls mosaics of: *Baptism of Christ*, after Maratta, 1686-88; R wall: *St Peter Baptising Sts Processus and Martinianus*, after G. Passeri, 1709-11; *St Peter Baptising the Centurion Cornelius*, after A. Procaccini, 1710.

The crypt of the church (Grotte Vaticane) is open to visitors (entrance under the statue of *St Longinus* in one of the crossing piers) and houses a statue of Pius VI (d. 1799) by Canova and A. Tadolini, 1817-22.

The Piazza

In the Middle Ages before the Vatican became the regular residence of the popes, the area between St Peter's and the Tiber enclosed within the walls of Leo IV (847-55) was sparsely inhabited and the only ancient road was one which ran from the Mausoleum of Hadrian (Castel S. Angelo) and passed just south of the basilica. By the end of the 15th century two straight roads – the Borgo Vecchio and the Borgo Nuovo – had been laid out (the latter by Alexander VI, who also built the corridor along the top of the Leonine wall to form a direct link between the Vatican and Castel S. Angelo) and Nicholas V (1447-55) had also begun to systematise the approach to the church by building the Benediction Loggia. The area below the broad flights of steps, however, was completely irregular. The main approach to the Vatican was through a clock tower built by Martino Ferrabosca for Paul V in 1617-19.

A number of plans were submitted for the development of the *piazza*, including some by Ferrabosca, Maderno and Papirio Bartoli, but it was not until Alexander VII announced in 1656 his intention of developing the whole area in front of St Peter's and Bernini was asked to supply designs that the scheme began. The site was awkwardly restricted by the Vatican buildings to the north, the corridor running down to Ferrabosca's clock tower and various palaces and ecclesiastical buildings on the periphery of the area. In addition, the *piazza* had to be designed so that the pope could be visible to as many people as possible when he gave the blessing either from the Benediction Loggia of St Peter's or from his apartment in the block added by Sixtus V to the Vatican. Finally, the colonnade had to provide a covered way for processions, particularly that on the Feast of Corpus Christi. Additional complications were the presence of the obelisk set up by Domenico Fontana for Sixtus V in 1585-86 and a fountain built by Maderno in 1613.

Bernini's first plan is not preserved, but from descriptions it appears to have been in the form of a trapezium, which involved building a wing to correspond with the corridor to the clock tower and extending the lines of both wings to the edge of the Borgo. This plan was rapidly abandoned in favour of one in which the area before the church was made into a square; in front of the square two semi-circular arcades were planned, with a straight *terzo braccio* between their ends. This scheme was elaborated in 1657, with arcades articulated by single pilasters, but the design was soon changed in favour of one with colonnades. This change was probably made because, since the outer circumference of the covered way was larger than the inner, the outer arches would have had to be wider than the inner and would therefore have had to be either taller or depressed. In the earlier versions of the colonnade scheme the columns were coupled and depressed uniformly round the whole curve; they were then replaced by single columns, and a cross-axis was established by introducing a projecting frontispiece in the middle of each arch.

From an early stage the oval design was referred to as a 'teatro' and it was clearly meant to reflect the shape of a Roman amphitheatre. Various medals struck during this phase of the design show the oval with the *terzo braccio* straight at first but curved in the later versions. Maderno's fountain was moved to its present position and a second one added to balance it. In the final design the colonnade takes the form of an oval, as distinct from the earlier shape, which consists of two semicircles linked by a rectangular area.

This oval is drawn according to the method laid down by Serlio (Book I), using two circles, the circumference of each passing through the centre of the other. The ends of the oval were formed by arcs of these circles and the middle sections of circles drawn with their centres at the points of intersections of the two main circles. This particular form of oval used by Bernini and Borromini is especially praised by Serlio for its *dolcezza* and was described by the geometers of the time as an *ovato perfetto*[1].

In the first (arched) scheme the wings were to contain first one and then two 'aisles', but in the final scheme there are three, of which the middle is wider than the others to accommodate the processions.

In the final project of 1667 Bernini intended to set the *terzo braccio* back to the east of the line of the main colonnade, so that it would have formed a sort of propylaeum. Carlo Fontana, in an unexecuted project, planned to remove the *terzo braccio* still further east and may therefore have to take the blame for instigating the plan which led to the destruction of the buildings along the *spina* of the Borgo and the opening up under Mussolini of the via della Conciliazione.

At an early stage in the development of the scheme for the *piazza* criticisms were made of Bernini's designs and a number of counter proposals were put forward.

Construction of the *piazza* began in 1658, starting with the erection of the north corridor and colonnade; the south colonnade was begun in 1660. By the end of 1662 the north corridor was completed and the south colonnade was finished in 1664. By this time only the south corridor and the south fountain remained incomplete. Work began on these in 1666 and was largely completed by the time Alexander VII died on 22 May 1667. The statues of saints on the oval part of the colonnade were planned by Bernini, who in some cases made drawings for them, but they were executed by various members of his studio. The first statues were set up in 1662 and the last group of 96 was finished in 1673. They represent on the north arm the *Defenders of the Faith* and *Founders of the Most Ancient Religious Orders* and on the south arm *Defenders of the Primacy of Rome* and *Reformists and Founders of Religious Orders*. The artists involved include L. Morelli, Giovanni Maria de' Rossi, F. Carcani, A. Baratta, F. Mari, B. Cennini, G. A. Fancelli, F. A. Fontana and G. Angelini.

The statues on the two corridors represent *Martyred Saints*, *Saints of the Catholic Reformation* and *Miracle-working Saints* and were executed under the direction of Carlo Fontana by J. B. Théodon, L. Ottoni, G. Coscia, A. Rondini, A. Parma, F. Canusi, N. Artusi, V. Mariotti, P. Reggiani, V. Frugoni, A. Alignini, A. Gabbani, P. Cristelli, G. Riccardi, F. Pincellotti, A. Fucigna, V. Felice, G. Napolini, A. Fantasia, A. Casella, M. Tomassini, S. Giorgini, G. Raffaelli, G. Protopapa, P. P. Campi, F. Gallesini, A. Zena, G. Gramignoli, G. Ferretti, F. M. Brunetti, P. Morelli, P. Mantinovese, M. Maglia, G. M. Baratta, G. Cioli, D. Amici, B. Cametti, A. Frediani, G. B. Antonini, M. Mauri, S. P. Mauri, L. Ottoni, L. Lironi, S. Sillani, F. Marchionni, P. Monnot and F. Moderati, 1702-03.

Bernini was influenced in his design for the oval colonnade by ancient models, particularly Duperac's reconstruction of the area around the Vatican. For the covered way around the *piazza* he may also have thought of the Aviary of Marcus Varro as shown restored in the engraving in J. Lauri's *Antiquae Urbis Splendor* (1621), or the Chalcedonic portico that Alexander VII had studied thanks to Lucas Holestinius, the Vatican librarian, who produced a description for him, but he no doubt also had in mind the fact that the ancient road leading past St Peter's was a covered way.

At the beginning of the north corridor is the *portone di bronzo* built by G. B. Soria and Orazio Censore, responsible for the casting and hammering of the metal components, 1617. Above the door is a mosaic by Giuseppe Cesari, *Virgin and Child with Sts Peter and Paul*, flanked by two angels by N. Cordier and A. Buonvicino, 1607-08[2].

Cappella Sistina

The palace chapel, which stands on the site of an earlier chapel, was designed for Sixtus IV by Baccio Pontelli in 1475 and built by Giovannino de' Dolci. It consists of a single long rectangular nave surmounted by a flattened barrel vault with spandrels and a lunette above each of the twelve windows.

Side walls

The side walls are decorated with two fresco cycles from the Old and New Testaments,

1481-82, above which are a series of portraits of early popes.

Left wall
Originally, this cycle consisted of eight scenes, six on the lateral walls and two on the end walls. The first scene, on the left side of the altar, was the *Finding of Moses* by P. Perugino, which corresponded to the *Birth of Christ* on the right side. In the centre was a panel representing the *Assumption Venerated by Sixtus*. All these paintings were destroyed to make way for Michaelangelo's *Last Judgement*.

The cycle continues on the left wall:
1) 'The observance by Moses of the old rite of regeneration through circumcision' – *Circumcision of the Sons of Moses*, Pietro Perugino.
2) 'The temptation of Moses, promulgator of the written Law' – *Youth of Moses*, Sandro Botticelli.
3) 'Moses gathers the people who are to receive the Law of Scripture' – *Crossing of the Red Sea*, Cosimo Rosselli.
4) 'The promulgation of the written Law of Moses' – *Descent of Moses from Mount Sinai*, C. Rosselli.
5) 'The opposition to Moses, the bearer of the Law of Scripture' – *Punishment of Korah, Dathan and Abiram*, S. Botticelli.
6) 'The codification of the Law of Scripture by Moses' – *Testament of Moses*, Luca Signorelli.

Right wall
1) 'The institution by Christ of the new rite of regeneration in baptism ' – *Baptism of Christ*, P. Perugino and assistants.
2) 'The temptation of Jesus Christ, bearer of the Law of the Gospels' – *Temptation of Christ* and *Purification of the Leper*, S. Botticelli.
3) 'The gathering of the people to receive the Law of the Gospels' – *Calling of Sts Peter and Andrew*, Domenico Ghirlandaio.
4) 'The promulgation of the Law of the Gospel by Christ' – *Sermon on the Mount*, C. Rosselli.
5) 'Opposition to Jesus Christ, bearer of the Law of the Gospels' – *Jesus Handing the Keys to St Peter*, P. Perugino.
6) 'The codification of the Law of the Gospels by Christ' – *Last Supper*, C. Rosselli.

Back wall
The present frescoes were painted in c.1572 to replace earlier frescoes destroyed when the wall collapsed in 1522. R: *Conflict over the Body of Moses*, Matteo da Lecce and L: *Resurrection*, H. van den Broeck.

Altar wall
Last Judgment by Michelangelo, commissioned by Clement VII in 1536, who died before the project was completed in 1541. In the centre is a youthful *Christ Pronouncing Judgment*, accompanied by Mary to his left. The figures in the upper half depict various saints; to the L, below Christ, are *St Lawrence with his Gridiron*, *St Andrew with his Cross* and *St John the Baptist*. To the R of Christ are *St Bartholomew with his Knife*, *St Peter with his Keys*; *St Paul with the Red Mantle*, *St Simon with his Saw*, the *Good Thief with his Cross*, *St Blaise with his Woolcarder's Comb*, *St Catherine with the Torturer's Wheel*, *St Sebastian with his Arrows* and *St Simon of Cyrene with his Cross*. In the two lunettes are *Angels Carrying the Cross and the Column*. Below the figures of Christ and Mary are *Angels Reading from the Book of Good and Evil Deeds* and *Sounding of the Last Trumpet*; to the L of these are the *Blessed Souls Ascending into Heaven* and in the lower L corner, the *Resurrection of the Dead*. To the R of the *Angels Reading the Book* are *The Damned Dragged*

into Hell and *Charon Ferrying Souls into Hell*.

Ceiling

Julius II commissioned Michelangelo to paint the ceiling between 1504 and 1506, but work only began in May 1508 and was not completed until 1512. The central spine of the ceiling is composed of nine horizontal panels which are flanked by Old Testament prophets and Sibyls. The cycle begins from the altar wall end:

Between the pendentives; *Prophet Jonah*
L: *Prophet Jeremiah*; L medallion: *Ascension of Elijah*; C: *Separation of Light from Darkness*; R medallion: *Abraham's Sacrifice of Isaac*; R: *Libyan Sibyl*.

Creation of the Sun, Moon and Planets
L: *Persian Sibyl*; L medallion: *Elisha Cures Naaman of Leprosy*; C: *Separation of the Waters from the Firmament and Water Brings Forth Life*; R medallion: *Death of Absalom*; R: *Prophet Daniel*.

Creation of Adam
L: *Prophet Ezekiel*; L medallion: *Death of Nicanor*; C: *Creation of Eve*; R medallion: *Alexander the Great before the High Priest of Jerusalem*; R: *Cumaean Sibyl*.

Temptation and Expulsion from Eden
L: *Erythraean Sibyl*; L medallion: *Mattathias Pulls Down the Altar in Modein*; C: *Sacrifice of Noah*; R medallion: *Expulsion of Heliodorus*; R: *Prophet Isaiah*.

The Flood
L: *Prophet Joel*; L medallion: *Antiochus Epiphanes Falls from his Chariot*; C: *Drunkenness of Noah*; R medallion: *Death of Razis*; R: *Delphic Sibyl*.

Between the pendentives: *Prophet Zechariah*.

Within the lunettes and spandrels are depicted the ancestors of Christ:
Left side: *Amminadab; Salmon – Boaz – Obed; Roboam and Abias; Oziah – Joatham – Achaz; Zerubbabel – Abiud – Eliakim; Achim – Eliud; Jacob – Joseph*.
R wall: *Nahshon; Jesse – David – Solomon; Asa – Jehoshaphat – Joram; Ezechias – Manasseh – Ahaz; Josiah – Jeconiah – Shealtiel; Azor – Zadok; Eleazar – Matthan*.

Pendentives

To L of altar: *Punishment of Haman*; to R: *Brazen Serpent*.
Entrance wall: R side: R: *David and Goliath* and L side: *Judith and Holofernes*.

Michelangelo had a number of assistants who helped with the ceiling fresco and were responsible for painting the architecture, lettering and decoration, the ten bronze medallions and some of the secondary figures. These assistants included: Giuliano da Sangallo, who was responsible for estimating the cost of the work, Piero Basso and Piero Roselli, who erected the scaffolding and prepared the ceiling, Francesco Granacci and Giuliano Bugiardini, Aristotile da Sangallo, Agnolo di Donnino, Jacopo Torni and Jacopo di Sandro, Giovanni Trignoli, Bernardino Zacchetti, Giovanni Michi and Pietro Urbano.

S. Pietro in Vincoli
Piazza di S. Pietro in Vincoli

The origin of the church goes back to the 4th century. The columns of the arcade, reused from a Roman temple, are of green marble and date from the 1st century. Remodelled for Cardinal Giuliano della Rovere, later Julius II, between 1471 and 1492. In 1705 the interior was transformed – not very happily – by Francesco Fontana, who built the depressed ceiling in the centre of which is a fresco by G. B. Parodi of the *Miracle of the Chains of St Peter*, 1705. The portico in the façade dates from 1471-83 and the upper part was added in 1507-08.

INTERIOR
1 to R: Benedetto Zallone, *St Augustine*[1]
Between 1 and 2 to R: monument to Cardinal Lanfranco Margotti, Secretary of State to Paul V (d. 1611), frequently but falsely ascribed to Domenichino[2]
2 to R: copy of Domenichino's *Liberation of St Peter from Prison*[3]
After 2 to R: monument to Cardinal Girolamo Agucchi (d. 1605) erected by his brother Monsignor Giovanni Battista Agucchi, author of an important treatise on painting. The monument was designed by Domenichino, who painted the portrait of the deceased above the inscription and actually carved the two rams' heads himself, 1605-06[4]
R transept: monument to Julius II (d. 1513) by Michelangelo and others. Upper storey: L: *Sibyl*; C: *The Virgin*, 1537-42 and R: *Prophet*; these figures were initially hewn by Michelangelo. In 1542 they were given to Raffaello da Montelupo, but due to ill health they were completed by his studio; the figure of Pope Julius II is attributed to Tommaso di Pietro Boscoli. Lower storey: L: *Rachel* and R: *Leah* by Michelangelo, finished by Raffaello da Montelupo; C: *Moses* by Michelangelo[5]
R transept altar: Guercino, *St Margaret*, 1644[6]
Apse frescoes: Jacopo Coppi, scenes from the *Story of the Beirut Crucifix*; presbytery walls: R: *Eudoxia Speaks with Pope Sixtus III*; C: *Eudoxia Gives the Chains of St Peter to Sixtus*; L: *St Peter is Freed from Prison*, 1577[7]
L aisle: monuments to Cardinal Andrea Galli (d. 1767) and Mariano Vecchiarelli (d. 1639) with yellow marble skeletons, designed by Pietro Vecchiarelli and executed by P. A. Ripoli and G. Marini, 1673[8]. In front of the wall is the magnificent inlaid monument to Mariano Vecchiarelli. Further: monument to Cardinal Cinzio Aldobrandini (d. 1610) designed by C. Bizzacheri, 1707[9].

SS. Pietro e Marcellino *see* SS. Marcellino e Pietro
Via Merulana, 161

S. Prassede
Via di S. Martino ai Monti, 28

The church has stood on this site since Early Christian times and was rebuilt in the 9th century for Paschal I. In 1198 it was given to the Vallonbrosan monks who are still its custodians. Restored between 1564 and 1584 for Cardinal Charles Borromeo, whose titular church it was and who added the sacristy and the two *poggioli* on either side of the nave. It was again restored in 1594 by Cardinal Alessandro de' Medici, when the nave frescoes were executed. The church is famous for its medieval mosaics.

INTERIOR
On the clerestory and entrance walls, frescoes of scenes from the *Passion* which begin in the left nave closest to the altar. G. Balducci, *Agony in the Garden*; P. Nogari, *Arrest of Christ*; G. Massei, *Christ before Caiaphas*; A. Ciampelli, *Christ before Pilate*; R: G. Balducci, *On the Road to Calvary*; A. Ciampelli, *Ecce Homo*; B. Croce, *Crowning with Thorns*; A. Ciampelli, *Flagellation*. On either side of these frescoes are grisaille frescoes by G. Balducci depicting scenes from the *Life of Moses*[1]
Entrance: R: monument to S. Santacroce (d. 1603); beside the door: S. Pieri, *Annunciation*
1 to R: Cappella di S. Bernardo degli Uberti:

built 1716-17. Altarpiece: Filippo Luzi, *St Bernard degli Uberti Stops the River Po from Flooding*, c. 1717[2]; R wall: G. D. Piastrini, *Martyrdom of St Tesaurus Beccaria*, 1711[3]; L wall: Angelo Soccorsi, *St Peter Igneus Aldobrandini Passes through Fire Unharmed*, c.1717

2 to R: Cappella Cesi: built in 1595 for Federico Cesi; decorated by Guglielmo Cortese, R wall: *Sts Joachim and Anne See a Vision of the Immaculate Virgin*; L wall: *Adoration of the Magi*; vault: *God the Father*; pendentives *Sts Pascal, Philip Neri, Frances of Rome and Firmin*, 1661-63[4]. Lunettes by Ciro Ferri, L: *Martyrdom of Gelasius II while Saying Mass in S. Prassede*; R: *St Pulcheria Supervising the Setting up of a Statue of the Virgin*, c.1661[5]. Three of the four bronze busts set in oval niches are derived from Algardi's *St Peter* and *St Paul* and an *Angel*[6]

3 to R: Cappella di S. Zeno: L side entrance lunette: F. Gai, *Flagellation*, 1863; facing wall; monument to Federico Colonna (d. 1711)

Last pier to L in R aisle: bust of Bishop Giovanni Battista Santoni, Majordomo to Sixtus V (d. 1592), by Bernini and erected by his nephew between 1613 and 1616[7]. The heads in the decoration are also by Bernini.

To R of presbytery: monument to Cardinal Angelo Maria Quirino (d. 1755)

High altar: high altar and choir rebuilt by Francesco Ferrari for Cardinal Ludovico Pico della Mirandola, 1728-34[8]; the *baldacchino* was made by Francesco Armellini, with stuccoes by P. Porciani and four angels by Giuseppe Rusconi[9]; choir stalls by Angelo Piccardi[10]; altarpiece: *Sts Praxedes and Pudentiana Gathering the Bodies of Martyrs*, Domenico Muratori, 1735[11]; vault: Antonio Bicchierai, *Holy Spirit and Angels*, as well as *St Peter* and *St Paul* on choir pilasters[12]

Against the wall of the choir are eight ancient columns of an unusual type with bands of lotus leaves, which probably inspired Philibert de l'Orme to invent his banded columns for the 'French' order, and were imitated by Borromini in the columns leading to the staircase at the Oratory.

To L of presbytery: monument to Cardinal Ludovico Pico della Mirandola (d. 1743)

Sacristy: altar: A. Ciampelli, *St John Gualbert Receives the Assent of the Crucifixion for the Forgiveness of his Brother's Murder*, 1594 (Cantelli); Guglielmo Cortese, *St John Gualbert Treading Down the Heresies of Simony and Nicolaism*, 1661-63[13]; R wall: G. de' Vecchi, *Deposition*[14]; *Flagellation* attributed to Giulio Romano and to Peter de Kempeneer[15], showing the column preserved in the Cappella di S. Zeno

3 to L: Cappella Olgiati: commissioned by Bernardo Olgiati and built by Martino Longhi the Elder, 1590-91[16]; frescoes by Giuseppe Cesari, entrance wall: R: *Dinner at Emmaus*; C: *Last Supper*; L wall: *Noli me tangere*; above: *Assumption*; over altar: *Resurrection*; vault: *Ascension* and *Prophets* and *Sibyls*, c.1593-95. Altarpiece: Federico Zuccaro, *Christ Carrying the Cross*, 1595[17]. R of altar: G. Cesari, *St Bernard of Clairvaux* and L of altar: *St Andrew*. R wall: monuments to Settimio Olgiati, marchese di Poggio Catino (d. 1623); L wall: Marco Antonio Olgiati (d. 1627) and R: Bernardo Olgiati (d. 1627)[18]

2 to L: Cappella di S. Carlo Borromeo: built 1735. Altarpiece: E. Parrocel, *St Charles Borromeo in Prayer during the Plague of Milan*, 1739[19]; walls: L. Stern, L: *St Charles in Meditation*, 1741 and R: *St Charles in Ecstasy*, 1739[20]. In the corners are stucco figures representing the *Four Cardinal Virtues* by an unknown artist

1 to L: Cappella di S. Pietro/Falconi: built 1721-22; decorated by A. Severoni, altarpiece: *St Peter and the Senator Pudens with*

his Daughters Praxedes and Pudentiana, 1717; R wall: *Sts Emerentiana and Agnes*; L wall: *St John the Baptist*[21].

S. Prisca
Piazza di S. Prisca, 11-13

A church has stood on this site since the late 5th or early 6th century. It was restored for the Holy Year of 1600 by Cardinal Benedetto Giustiniani, who added the fine brick façade dated 1600, to the designs of Carlo Lambardi. The church was restored in the late 1930's and later.

INTERIOR
Sacristy: detached fresco: G. Odazzi, *Immaculate Virgin*
High altar: designed by Carlo Lambardi; altarpiece: Domenico Cresti, *St Peter Baptising St Priscilla*, c.1600 but heavily restored in the 18th century[1]

The frescoes in the apse depicting the events around St Priscilla's martyrdom are ascribed to Antonio Tempesta. Presbytery frescoes: L wall: *St Priscilla amongst the Lions* and R wall: *Translation of the Relics* by Anastasio Fontebuoni[2].

S. Pudenziana
Via Urbana, 158

An Early Christian church which is chiefly famous for its apse mosaic (4th-5th century). It was restored by Francesco da Volterra in 1589 for Cardinal Enrico Caetani but this façade was removed in 1870 when Antonio Manno rebuilt the present one on the orders of Cardinal Luciano Bonaparte. Most of Volterra's additions were removed in 1930. The façade frescoes are by Pietro Gagliardi[1]. It also contains, however, important works of later periods.

INTERIOR
New sacristy: L. Gimignani, *Assumption*, 1682-83[2]
2 to R: Cappella della Madonna della Misericordia: decorated by L. Baldi, entrance pier: R: *Angel of the Annunciation*; L: *The Virgin*; L wall: *Birth of the Virgin*; R wall: *Birth of Christ*; vault: *The Virgin in Glory*; lunettes: *Prophets and Sibyls*, 1690[3]
3 to R: Cappella di S. Bernardo: Michele Cippitelli, L wall: *St Catherine of Siena in Ecstasy* and R wall: *St Benedict c. 1700*[4]
Choir: dome: *Christ Surrounded by the Heavenly Host with Sts Peter, Paul and Pudens*; *Sts Timotheus and Novatus*; *Sts Pudentiana and Praxedes*; *Pius I and St Bernard of Clairvaux* by Niccolò Circignani, 1588[5]
High altar: *St Pudentiana in Glory* by Bernardino Nocchi, 1803-06, a remarkable example of how late the full Baroque still survived in Rome[6]
To L of high altar: Cappella di S. Pietro: altarpiece: G. B. della Porta, *Giving of the Keys*, 1596; stuccoes by Leonardo Retti; vault and lunette frescoes of scenes from the *Life of St Peter* by Baglione, not earlier than 1595 but now in totally ruined state[7]
2 to L: Cappella Caetani[8]: begun in 1590 by Francesco da Volterra for Cardinal Enrico Caetani, Papal Legate to France under Sixtus V, whose titular church this was, and finished after his death by Maderno in 1601[9]. The splendid marbling – mainly in green and yellow – is by G. B. della Porta and G. A. Paracca the Younger; the dome has fine stuccoes enclosing the mosaics of the *Four Evangelists* and the entrance wall lunette of *Sts Pudentiana and Praxedes Collect the Blood of the Martyrs* by P. Rossetti to designs by Federico Zuccaro[10]. Altar: relief of the *Adoration of the Magi* by P. P. Olivieri, 1599[11]. R wall: monument to Filippo, Duca di Caetani (d. 1614), bust attributed to P. P.

Naldini; figures of R: *Fortitude* attributed to A. Parisi and L: *Temperance* attributed to A. C. Brefort; *Geniuses* attributed to Mariani[12]; L wall: monument to Cardinal Enrico Caetani (d. 1599); figure of R: *Prudence* by F. Mari and L: *Justice* by C. Malavista[13]
To L of Cappella Caetani: Antonio Tanari, *Sts Pudentiana and Praxedes Collect the Blood of the Martyrs*[14]
To L of entrance: copy of Guercino's *St Augustine Contemplates the Trinity.*

SS. Quaranta Martiri *see* S. Pasquale Baylon
Via di S. Francesco a Ripa, 20

SS. Quattro Coronati
Via dei SS. Quattro Coronati, 20

Founded in the 4th century and frequently enlarged and rebuilt, the last time by Paschal II in 1111. In 1560 Pius IV gave the church and adjoining convent to Augustinian nuns, who still serve it. It was restored in 1914.

INTERIOR
R aisle: monument to Luigi d'Aquino (d. 1679)[1]
Apse: Giovanni da San Giovanni, *Saints in Glory*; apse walls: upper panels depict scenes from the *Life of Sts Severus, Severinus, Carpophorus and Victorinus*; lower panels depict scenes from the *Lives of Claudius, Nicostratus, Castor Sempronianus and Simplicius*[2]
1 to L: altarpiece: Baglione, *St Sebastian Tended by Sts Irene and Lucina*[3]

ORATORIO DI S. SILVESTRO
Celebrated early frescoes of scenes from the *Life of St Sylvester*.
Chancel: Raffaellino da Reggio, pilaster: L: *St Sylvester*; R: *Constantine*; side walls: L: *The Holy Four Crowned Martyrs Beaten before a Statue of Aesculapius*; R: *Martyrdom of the Five Pannonian Sculptors before the Statue of Apollo*, c.1570[1].

SS. Quirico e Giulitta
Via di Tor de' Conti, 31a

A small but ancient church restored on the orders of Benedict XIII, probably by Filippo Raguzzini between 1730 and 1733. The façade incorporates a 15th century door. The convent was built by Valvassori in 1750-53, to whom Rotili also ascribes the building of the church.

The door in the via S. Maria ai Monti (no. 31) appears to be by Valvassori and was apparently the main entrance to the convent.

INTERIOR
Vault: Pietro Gagliardi, *Sts Quiricus and Julitta in Glory*, 1856[1]
2 to R: Cappella di S. Domenico: altarpiece: Ercole Ruspi, *St Dominic Preaching*, 1855
High altar: *Martyrdom of Sts Quiricus and Julitta* attributed to Gregorio Preti, 1632[2].

SS. Re Magi
Via di Propaganda Fide, 1c

In 1622 Gregory XV created a Congregazione di Propaganda Fide to organise the missionary activities of the various orders and in 1627 Urban VIII attached to it a college for the training of young missionaries. The congregation and college were established in a palace (Palazzo Ferratini) at the south end of the Piazza di Spagna presented by a Spanish prelate, Juan Baustista Vives, the representative in Rome of the Lieutenant of the Netherlands, the Infanta Clara Eugenia, in 1626. In 1634 Bernini built a small chapel called the Re Magi, which was later replaced by Borromini's chapel. In 1642 it was decided to rebuild the façade on Piazza di Spagna to the designs of the Theatine priest, Padre Valerio, modified by Bernini. Between 1639 and 1645 a wing for the seminarists was begun by Gaspare de' Vecchi along the via Due Macelli. By 1646 the college had acquired the whole island and in that year Borromini was appointed architect. He proposed various plans for the completion of the building[1] which involved the destruction of Bernini's church. This was an oval with the short axis leading to the altar (cf. S. Andrea al Quirinale) the plan of which is recorded in Borromini's first drawing[2] and the façade in an elevation. Borromini first designed a longer oval with the main entrance on the street, but then chose a rectangle with rounded corners running parallel with the street, with the altar at the north-west end and the entrance from the vestibule of the college at the south-east. To the right (south-east) of the chapel he designed a court which was to have been made symmetrical by the insertion of a curved arcade that was never fully built. The façade, first designed with five and finally with seven bays, covers part of the chapel, the entrance to the college and the main staircase. Its relation to the interior is as arbitrary as in the oratory. Many drawings are known for the windows, fireplaces and other details[3]. The door and windows on the façade show a great variety of forms, and Martinelli[4] calls attention to the fact that on the *piano nobile* Borromini has used the Doric without a base (though in fact this is invisible from the street). The construction of the college went on long after Borromini's death in 1667 and the top floor of the right-hand side was added in 1705 (inscription at the top of the staircase) and has the arms of Clement XI on the outside.

INTERIOR
1 to R: Carlo Pellegrini, *Conversion of St Paul*, 1635[5]
2 to R: Carlo Cesi, *Sts Charles Borromeo and Philip Neri Adore the Virgin and Child*[6]
High altar: Giacinto Gimignani, *Adoration of the Magi*, 1634[7]; above: L. Baldi, *Christ's Charge to St Peter*, before 1674[8]; stuccoes over the altar by Cosimo Fancelli, figures of L: *Faith* and R: *Religion* and the arms of Alexander VII[9]
2 to L: L. Gimignani, *Crucifixion with Sts Francis Xavier and Francis of Paola*[10]
1 to L: A. Camassei, *Calling of Sts Andrew and Peter*, 1634

In the niches are busts of benefactors of the college and congregation: R: Giovanni Savenier; Federico Cornelio and Cardinal Roberto Ubaldini and L: Juan Baptista Vives; Cardinal Antonio Barberini and Agostino Galamino[11].
Over door: C. Fancelli, allegorical figures of L: *Justice* and R: *Abundance* and the arms of Alexander VII[12]

Within the college the staircase and the corridor on the first floor contain fine stucco work certainly designed by Borromini. Off it opens the old oratory, now called the Cappella Newman (Cardinal Newman celebrated his first Mass there), the vault of which (partly frescoed by Giovanni Ventura Borghesi) is articulated into a remarkably formed series of panels to designs by Borromini.

S. Rita da Cascia *see* S. Maria delle Vergini
Via delle Vergini, 23

S. Rita da Cascia (S. Biagio in Campitelli)
Via Montanara

The church was originally built at the foot of the Aracoeli steps, but was pulled down in the clearance around the Piazza Aracoeli in 1928 and re-erected on its present site in 1940. In the process it lost most of its interior decoration. For its appearance before it was moved, see *Capitolium*, XL, 1965, p. 218.

The church was built by 1653. The architect is unknown (Hager has suggested that it may be Felice della Greca, but he was only born c. 1626). The most interesting feature of the church is the façade, added by Carlo Fontana, to whom the whole church is usually, but wrongly, ascribed (he was only born in 1638). The lower part of the façade has a door and niches with false perspective soffits (cf. the top loggia at Palazzo Barberini) and the upper storey breaks back in concave bays in a highly original manner (cf. Bernini's design for the Cornaro tomb[1]). The exact date at which the façade was built is uncertain, but it must be before 1667 since it has the *monti* of Alexander VII and it must have been at least designed before 1665 since it appears in Plate 11 of Falda's *Nuovo teatro*, published that year, though one must bear in mind the fact that engravers often showed incomplete buildings as if they were finished.

S. Rocco
Via Ripetta, 74

The church was built in 1500-02 for the Confraternita di S. Rocco, founded in 1499. It was dedicated to St Martin and had its entrances at the east end. To it was attached a hospital administered by the confraternity. The church was rebuilt between 1645 and 1680 for Cardinal Odoardo Vecchiarelli and then Francesco Barberini. During the first year, the work was conducted by Pietro Maraldi and another unidentified architect, possibly Girolamo Rainaldi (Mola), but they do not seem to have achieved very much and the church is really a creation of G. A. de'

Rossi, who took over in 1646. The alignment of the church was reversed so that the façade came above the Porto di Ripetta. The façade was added by Giuseppe Valadier in 1834.

INTERIOR
In the aisles De' Rossi has copied the depressed arches used by Maderno in the aisles of St Peter's, a detail typical of his non-Baroque tendencies. The interior was extensively restored in 1852-64 when the nave was frescoed and the fictive marbling added. The Stations of the Cross date from 1864.

Vault: Achille Scaccioni, *St Roch Pays Homage to the Supreme Authority of the Church*, 1864

Above entrance: organ originally by Giacomo and Giovanni Antonio Alari and organ case carved by Girolamo Carpi, 1721[1]

To right of R entrance door: monument to Giuseppe Vitelli (d. 1830) by Giuseppe de' Fabris, 1830-33[2]

1 to R: Cappella di S. Francesco di Paola/S. Maria Goretti: altarpiece: Antonio Mercurio Amorosi, *Ecstasy of St Francis of Paola before the Blessed Sacrament*, 1719[3]

2 to R: Cappella di S. Rocco: R wall: Antonio Gregolini, *St Vincent Ferrer Raises a Dead Woman*, 1720[4]. Lunettes: scenes from the *Life of St Roch*, Andrea Belloli, before 1864

3 to R: Cappella di S. Giuliano: R Lunette: *Crucifixion*; L lunette: *Expulsion from Eden*, F. Bigioli, 1864

End of R aisle: Cappella Paracciani/Madonna delle Grazie: built for Gaspare Morelli by De' Rossi, 1655-57. The rich marbling may be part of a later restoration carried out in 1722. The dome of the chapel has an unusual form, with flattened sides and ends, used by De' Rossi in S. Maria in Campo Marzio. Altar: *Glory of Cherubs* by N. Menghini; R wall: monument to Cardinal

Domenico Parracciani, who completed the decoration of the chapel in 1638. Dome: *Assumption* by G. A. Carosi, 1657
Presbytery: high altar designed by G. A. de' Rossi, executed by Giuseppe Giorgetti, 1673[5]; altarpiece: Brandi, *St Roch Received into Heaven*, c.1663-65[6]; side walls decorated by C. Mariani, R: *Charity of St Martin* and L: *St Roch Succours the Plague Victims*, 1888[7]
Sacristy: built in 1651 by De' Rossi; altarpiece: Baciccio, *Virgin and Child with Sts Roch and Anthony Abbot*, 1663-66[8]. Vault: F. Cozza, *The Virgin Appearing to St Roch*, c. 1650-51[9]
L of sacristy door: monument to Francesco Orioli (d. 1856) designed by A. Cipolla
R of sacristy door: *Sts Peter and Paul*, probably the painting by L. Stern left to the church by Cardinal Riminaldi in 1789[10]
L transept: Altare di S. Martino: altarpiece: Donato da Formello, *St Martin and the Beggar*[11]; L lunette: *St Aloysius Gonzaga Renounces his Inheritance*, F. Bigioli
3 to L: Cappella di S. Antonio: altarpiece: G. Preti, *St Anthony of Padua*[12]. Lunettes: F. Rosa, R: *Death of St Anthony of Padua* and L: *St Anthony Leaves the Canons Regular and is Invested as a Franciscan*; dome: *St Anthony Received into Heaven*, c.1660-63[13]
2 to L: Cappella del Presepe: altarpiece: B. Peruzzi, *Adoration of the Shepherds*, c.1514-15[14]. L wall: Francesco da Castello, *Virgin with St Roch*[15].

SS. Rufina e Seconda
Via della Lungaretta, 92

A church has stood on this site since very early times. It was restored in 1602 but was recently stripped back to its original state. It contains a monument to Bianca Maria Nerli (d. 1697).

S. Sabina
Piazza di S. Pietro d'Iliria

In 1219 Honorius III gave the church, which was built in the 5th century, to the Dominicans, who still serve it. The interior was decorated by Domenico Fontana in 1587, but these later additions were removed in the present century and the church was restored to what remained of its original form. It contains, however, some 17th and 18th century paintings and monuments. Within the portico of the church is a statue of *St Rose of Lima* by an unknown artist, set up shortly after her canonisation in 1668[1].

INTERIOR
L of entrance: monument to Cardinal Arcangelo Bianchi (d. 1580)
R aisle: monument to Cardinal Alessandro Bichi (d. 1657) and his brother Celio (d. 1657)[2]. Further: Cappella di S. Giacinto/Ascoli[3]: built for Cardinal Girolamo Bernerio in 1600; altarpiece: Lavinia Fontana, *The Virgin Appears to St Hyacinth*, 1599[4]; wall frescoes by Federico Zuccaro, L wall: *St Hyacinth of Cracow Receiving the Habit from St Dominic*; R wall: *Canonisation of St Hyacinth*; vault: *Assumption*, 1600[5]
Apse: Taddeo Zuccaro, *Christ in Glory*, 1559[6]
L aisle: monuments to Giuseppe (d. 1670) and Monsignor Ignazio Ciantes (d. 1667)[7]. Further: Cappella di S. Caterina/Elci: built by G. A. Contini, 1671[8]; altarpiece: Sassoferrato, *Madonna of the Rosary*, 1643[9]. Morandi's painting of the same subject, once on the altar, is now housed in the monastery buildings. Dome frescoes: G. Odazzi, *Christ Crowning St Catherine of Siena in the Presence of Saints and Angels*; pendentives: *St Catherine Receiving the Stigmata*; *St Catherine Receiving the Crown of Thorns*; *St Catherine Receiving the Host from Christ*; *Sacred Heart*, 1686[10]; L wall:

monument to Cardinal Scipione d'Elci (d. 1670) and R wall: monument to Cardinal Ranieri d'Elci (d. 1761). Further: monuments to Cardinal Pietro Bertano (1588), Filippo Spinola (d. 1593) and Pietro Maria Passerini (d. 1677)

Within the monastery are two chapels, one in the cell occupied by St Dominic, the other in that of Pius V when a monk in the monastery.

The chapel of St Dominic, decorated on the orders of Clement IX, was attributed to Borromini in the 1765 edition of Roisecco's guide[11] and Hempel[12] hesitantly accepts the attribution, though he points out that the marble wall decoration with Ionic pilasters is quite unlike Borromini's style. He also says that according to the inscription in the chapel the decoration was finished in 1669, that is to say, two years after Borromini's death. Actually it says it was 'executed' (*aptari et exornari fecit*) in that year and being a very small work, it is unlikely to have taken longer than one year. The chapel has recently been attributed to Bernini[13].

The chapel of Pius V was decorated in 1710 with very elaborate stucco work, including naturalistic garlands of flowers and fruit which recall those on the vault of S. Maria dell'Orto. The altarpiece of *St Pius V* is by D. Muratori.

In the museum of the convent: L Baldi, *St Rose of Lima and Christ*, c.1668[14]. In the monastery cloister are frescoes by G. B. Leonardi, removed from the church during the 1919 restoration[15].

Oratory of the SS. Sacramento
see **S. Maria in Via (Oratory of)**
Piazza Poli

S. Salvatore in Campo
Piazza di S. Salvatore in Campo

Rebuilt in 1639-40 by Francesco Peparelli for Cardinal Francesco Barberini.

The church, which is rarely open, does not apparently contain any works of art of interest.

S. Salvatore delle Coppelle
Via delle Coppelle, 72b

The rebuilding of the church, which took place in 1740-43, is attributed in the early guides to Carlo de' Dominicis. The façade is of unexpectedly classical simplicity for him.

Now the church of the Romanian Catholic community and usually open on Sunday morning for Mass.

INTERIOR
Completely altered in 1863.
L of entrance: monument to Filippo Boschetti, (d. 1740)
L aisle: monument to Cardinal Giorgio Spinola, Abbot of Subiaco (d. 1739), signed by Bernardino Ludovisi, 1744[1].

S. Salvatore in Lauro
Piazza di S. Salvatore in Lauro

The old church, which belongs to the Celestine Canons Regular of S. Giorgio in Alga, Venice, was burnt down in 1591. Rebuilding of the church began immediately and two 17th century writers, Totti (1638) and Baglione (1642), attribute the new church to Mascarino, though Totti in the 'Emendationi e aggiunte' writes 'il disegno è del Padre Massimano' and in the 1652 edition the name of Mascarino is discarded altogether. The attribution to Mascarino, in fact, seems very insecure. In the first place there are no drawings for the church among the vast number which he bequeathed to the Accademia di S. Luca and which cover almost every building with which he was connected. Secondly, the nave, with its bold coupled columns – single shafts of travertine – reminiscent of Palladio, is quite unlike his dry and timid style. Indeed, on entering the church one has the impression of being in Venice rather than Rome and it seems likely that a design for the church was sent from the parent house, presumably by a follower of Palladio.

In the first building campaign, only the nave appears to have been built. When the Celestines were suppressed in 1688 the church was handed over to the Marchigian community of Rome and rebuilding was resumed in 1699 under Francesco Fontana. Fontana erected the crossing to the level of the entablature but lack of funds stopped work in 1701. Work began again in 1727 under Ludovico Rusconi Sassi, who was responsible for the dome and the apse. The interior was completed in 1731. The façade was only begun in 1845 by Antonio Sarti, but was unfinished until Camillo Guglielmetti's design was built at the beginning of the 1860's[1]. In 1858 the two transept altars were redesigned by Pietro Lancioni (completed 1862), a new floor was laid and the four prophets on the pendentives (*Moses*, *David*, *Isaiah* and *Ezekiel*) were painted by Luigi Fontana. The bas-relief on the façade of the *Transport of the Santa Casa* is by Rinaldo Rinaldi, 1862.

INTERIOR

R of entrance wall: monument to Cardinal Gaspare Bernardo Pianetti (d.1862) designed by L. Poletti and executed by by I. Jacometti[2]
L of entrance: monument to Cardinal Antonio Matteucci (d. 1868) by L. Fontana
1 to R: Cappella della Pietà/Paroni: architecture by Carlo Bizzacheri, 1693-94[3]; vault: *Angels* by Camillo Rusconi[4]; paintings by Giuseppe Ghezzi, altarpiece: *Pietà*; L wall: *St James of the Marches*; R wall: *St Nicholas of Tolentino*; vault: *God the Father*, c. 1694[5]
2 to R: Cappella di S. Carlo: altarpiece: Alessandro Turchi, *Virgin and Child with Sts Francis and Charles Borromeo*. The monuments to R: the Marchese Girolamo Pallavicini Montoro (d. 1645) and L: Monsignor Giovanni Castellani (d. 1646) were set up many decades after their deaths and are ascribed in the *Guide rionali* to Mario Asprucci and in *Roma sacra* to G. D. Pioselli
3 to R: Cappella della Natività/Orsini: altarpiece: Pietro da Cortona, *Adoration of the Shepherds*, 1628[6]
R transept: altarpiece: P. Gagliardi, *Sts Nicholas of Tolentino, James of the Marches and Emidius*, 1862. L wall: monument to Cardinal Raniero Simonetti, Governor of Rome under Benedict XIV (d. 1749), designed by Gerolamo Theodoli with sculpture by Carlo Monaldi, 1756[7]. R wall: monument to Niccolò Grimaldi (d. 1845) by Luigi Ferucci
High altar: originally designed by L. R. Sassi with a painting by Giovanni Peruzzini, which was removed in 1792 (now in the sacristy). The present high altar, designed to house a venerated image of the Virgin of Loreto, is by Antonio Asprucci with a *Glory of Angels* by Vincenzo Pacetti, 1792. The putti over the pediment by Pietro Paolo Campi belong to the original altar[8]
L transept: Cappella del Crocifisso: R wall: monument to Cardinal Prospero Marefoschi, Cardinal Vicar in Rome under Benedict XIII (d. 1732), designed by G. Theodoli with sculpture by C. Monaldi, 1751[9]. L wall: monument to Giuseppe Camillo Valentini (d. 1757)
3 to L: Cappella di S. Lutgarda/Tiracoda: altarpiece: Angelo Massarotti, *St Lutgard with Christ*; L wall: *Vision of St Lutgard*; R wall: *St Lutgard Flees her Tormentors*, 1679[10];

marble decorations by P. A. Ripoli, 1680
2 to L: Cappella di S. Giuseppe: redecorated and marbled in 1773[11]. Altarpiece: P. L. Ghezzi, *Sts Joachim and Anne with Joseph*, 1731[12]
1 to L: Cappella di S. Pietro in Vincoli: altarpiece: I. Grammatica, *Liberation of St Peter*, 1624[13]; side walls by D. Corvi, R: *St Peter Freed from Prison* and L: *St Peter Baptises Processus and Martinian*[14]
Sacristy: Giovanni Peruzzini, *Holy House of Loreto*; 1673; P. L. Ghezzi, *Sts Emidius, James of the Marches, Philip Neri, Sylvester, Sophie, Margaret and Seraphinus*, 1731[15]; O. Borgianni, *Lamentation over the Dead Christ*[16]

To the left of the church is the late 15th century cloister, behind which is the *sala dei piceni*, the former refectory. Within the *sala dei piceni*: back wall fresco: F. Salviati, *Marriage at Cana*, 1552-53[17].

who had it restored and the façade rebuilt. The church retains much of its medieval character in spite of the restoration.

INTERIOR
The interior was restored under the direction of L. Carimini with decorations by C. Mariani and stucco by D. d' Amico, 1877-78.
R side: Cappella della Vergine/Cassetta: decorated by C. Mariani, R of altar: *Annunciation* and *Esther and Ahasuerus*; L of altar: *Immaculate Virgin with Sts Francis, Anthony of Padua and Judith and Holofernes*, 1875-76
End of R aisle: Altar by Gioacchino Morichini, 1856. Maximilian Seitz, *Sts Cosmas and Damian with St Joseph and the Christ Child*[1]
End of L aisle: over the altar is a relief of *The Virgin Appearing to St Alexius and Euphemianus* by an unknown artist, c.1846.

S. Salvatore ai Monti (S. Salvatore de' Suburra)
Via Madonna dei Monti, 37

A small church next to the conventual buildings of S. Maria ai Monti; the façade is dated 1762. Within the church on the right wall is a monument to Agostino Masucci (d. 1746). The church is rarely open.

S. Salvatore in Onda
Via dei Pettinari, 59

A small church recorded since the early 12th century. At some date before 1684 a project was put forward by G. Tommasini to rebuild the church nearer the Tiber and so make a worthy end to the via Giulia[1]. The scheme was not carried out. The church was restored for Benedict XIII in 1725. In 1844 it was given by Gregory XVI to Vincenzo Pallotti,

S. Salvatore de'Suburra *see* S. Salvatore ai Monti

S. Sebastiano fuori le Mura
Via Appia Antica, 135

Built by Constantine over the famous catacomb which was believed to have contained the bodies of Sts Peter and Paul. The church also covered the tomb of St Sebastian. From 1431 onwards it was served by the Cistercians. In 1608 Cardinal Scipione Borghese began a complete remodelling of the church and the crypt to the designs of Flaminio Ponzio and under the artistic direction of Reni. According to Martinelli, he built the church as far as the cornice and at his death in 1613 it was completed by G. Vasanzio. The façade, however, which is dated 1612, is by Ponzio.

INTERIOR
The vault dates from the restoration ordered by Cardinal Scipione Borghese, executed by Annibale Durante to a design traditionally ascribed to Giovanni Vasanzio, 1612[1].

1 to R: Cappella delle Reliquie: built at the expense of Maximilian I, duke of Bavaria, 1625. Further: monument to Cardinal Giambattista Maria Gabrielli (d. 1711)

R entrance to catacomb: (no longer in use) Antonio Carracci: *God the Father and Saints*

2 to R: Altare di S. Francesca Romana: Filippo Frigiotti, *The Virgin and Child Appear to St Frances of Rome*[2]

3 to R: Altare di S. Girolamo: Archita Ricci, *St Jerome*, c. 1613

4 to R: Cappella di S. Fabiano/Albani[3]: built by Clement XI between 1706 and 1712 to the designs of Carlo Fontana, assisted by Alessandro Specchi and Filippo Barigioni; over the altar: statue of *St Fabian* by Pietro Papaleo, 1710-12[4]; apse stuccoes by P. Porciani[5]; R wall: Giuseppe Passeri, *St Fabian Anointing the Emperor Philip*, 1712[6]; L wall: P. L. Ghezzi, *Election of St Fabian*, 1712[7]

High altar: designed by F. Ponzio; altarpiece: I. Tacconi, *Crucifixion*, 1614[8]

1st bay: monument to Altobello d'Ense (d. 1615)[9]

Choir: busts of Sts Peter and Paul by Nicholas Cordier, 1608[10]. Pietro Sigismondi, *St Sebastian Prepares for Martyrdom*, 1618[11]

3 to L: altarpiece: *St Francis in Prayer*, attributed to Girolamo Muziano, which conceals the original altarpiece of the *Virgin with St Bernard* by A. Ricci

2 to L: Altare di S. Carlo Borromeo: *St Charles Borromeo Intercedes for the Plague Victims* by Marcantonio Bassetti[12]

Sacristy: built by M. Fontana, 1727, and decorated by Marco Tullio Montagna, wall: *Virgin with Sts Sebastian and Lucina*, 1627-28; vault: *God the Father with Saints*, though Merz[13] gives this fresco to Cortona and dates it 1618

1 to L: Cappella di S. Sebastiano: commissioned in 1672 by Cardinal Francesco Barberini after the saint's relics were found beneath the floor; designed by Ciro Ferri[14]; statue of *St Sebastian* by Giuseppe Giorgetti to a design by Ferri, altar bronze work cast by Carlo Spagna[15].

S. Sebastiano al Palatino
Via di S. Bonaventura, 1

A church stood on this site from very early times and played an important part in the 10th-14th centuries owing to its dependence on the Frangipani family (frescoes of the late 10th century survive in the apse). It was restored by Luigi Arigucci in 1630 on the orders of Cardinal Francesco Barberini and the first Mass was said here in January 1631.

INTERIOR

Choir lunette: frescoes by B. Gagliardi, *St Sebastian Tended by St Irene*; vault: *God the Father*; pendentives: allegorical figures of *Faith* and *Charity*, 1633-36. High altar by L. Arigucci

L wall: A. Camassei, *Martyrdom of St Sebastian*, 1633[1].

SS. Sergio e Bacco (Madonna del Pascolo)
Piazza della Madonna dei Monti, 3

A church is recorded on this site from about 800. In 1641 it was given to a body of Basilian monks and rebuilt in 1741-45 to the designs of Francesco Ferrari. The façade was rebuilt in 1880.

INTERIOR
Decorated with painted marble.

Vault: Sebastiano Ceccarini, *Assumption*, 1741[1]
1 to R: I. Stern, *St Basil*, 1741[2]
1 to L: I. Stern, *Sts Sergius and Bacchus*, 1741.

S. Silvestro in Capite
Piazza di S. Silvestro

The church was founded by Paul I in 761 and till 1285 was served by Benedictine monks. In that year it was given to the Poor Clares who served it till it was suppressed in 1871. In 1885 it was handed over to the English Pallottini fathers.

Of the medieval building only the 12th-13th century campanile and parts of the outer walls survive, though the forecourt presumably replaced an earlier atrium of the same type. In 1518 Pietro Soderini offered a new altar, the design of which was submitted to Michelangelo, though the existing altar shows none of the characteristics of his style. In 1591 a design for a new church was commissioned by Cardinal Franz von Dietrichstein from Francesco da Volterra and building began in 1594. In the same year Volterra died and was succeeded by Maderno, who modified his predecessor's plans, adding a third chapel to each side of the nave and making the transepts narrower, so that Volterra's dome had to be elongated. The building was finished in 1596 and consecrated in 1601. The decoration continued till 1604.

In 1680, when Carlo Rainaldi was the architect of the church, the nuns decided on a new campaign of decoration. This was continued after Rainaldi's death in 1691 by Mattia de' Rossi. On De' Rossi's death the role of architect passed to Domenico de' Rossi with general artistic supervision of the chapels given to Ludovico Gimignani.

The new façade was built by Domenico de' Rossi, 1703. Of the statues on the façade, *St Sylvester* is by Lorenzo Ottoni, *Pope Stephen I* by M. Maglia, *St Francis* by V. Felici and *St Clare* by B. Mazzuoli, between 1702-08[1].

INTERIOR
The interior is interesting as a completed decorative scheme dating from the last two decades of the 17th century. The organ and choir loft were probably designed by C. Rainaldi, 1685-86. The organ was built by Girolamo Galli and Giacomo Alari. The crossing, tribune and transept stuccoes were executed under Mattia de' Rossi's supervision. The stucco figures of angels and putti around the transept window and those supporting the central *tondi* on the transept vault, as well as those on the arches of the nave and the tribune vault, are by C. Rusconi (to R) and M. Maglia (to L), 1689-90, and those over the altar by Lorenzo Ottoni[2]
Vault of nave: Giacinto Brandi, *Assumption with Sts John the Baptist, Sylvester and other Saints*, 1683-84[3], enclosed by a stucco frame with *Sibyls* at each corner by Girolamo Gramignoli, 1681-83[4]
Dome fresco: C. Roncalli, *God the Father*[5]; pendentives: *Evangelists* by Cristofano Casolani and Giuseppe Agellio[6]
1 to R: Cappella di S. Antonio da Padova/Tedallini: decorated by Giuseppe Chiari, altarpiece: *Virgin and Child with Sts Anthony of Padua and Stephen*; L wall: *St Stephen Destroys the Idols*; lunette: *Martyrdom of St Stephen*; R wall: *St Anthony Resurrects a Dead Man*; lunette: *St Anthony Prophesying*; vault: *Angels in Glory*, 1695. Putti above altar by Lorenzo Ottoni[7]
Between 1 and 2 to R: monument to Cardinal Luigi Bottiglia (d. 1838) by A. M. Laboureur, 1838[8]
2 to R: Cappella di S. Francesco/Savelli: altarpiece: O. Gentileschi, *St Francis Receiving the Stigmata, c.* 1615[9]; wall and vault frescoes by Luigi Garzi, L wall: *St Francis Preaching*;

R wall: *St Francis Renouncing his Worldly Goods*; vault: *Glory of St Francis*, c.1695[10]

3 to R: Cappella dello Spirito Santo/Laurelino: decorated by Giuseppe Ghezzi, altarpiece: *Pentecost*; R wall: *St John Baptising the People*; lunette: *Pope Paul I*; L wall: *Baptism of Christ*; lunette: *St Gregory*, c.1696-97[11]

R transept: Cappella Colonna: altarpiece: Baccio Ciarpi, *Virgin and Child with Sts Louis, John the Baptist, Philip Neri and Dionysius*, c.1622[12]. Vault frescoes: L. Gimignani, L: *Image of Edessa Brought to King Abgar*; C: *Glory of Angels*; R: *St Sylvester Called by Constantine*, 1688-90[13]

Confessio: built in 1906

Apse: paintings of L: *Calling of St Sylvester* and R: *Martyrdom of St Stephen* by a Neapolitan follower of Caravaggio[14]. Tabernacle by C. Rainaldi, 1660-67.

Semi-dome of apse: L. Gimignani, *St Sylvester Baptises Constantine*

High altar: designed by Michelangelo for Piero Soderini to house the relic of St John the Baptists's head, and executed by Piero Rosselli, 1518, but altered by C. Rainaldi, who added the tabernacle consisting of four columns and a pediment[15]

L transept: altarpiece: Terenzio Terenzi, *Virgin and Child with Sts Paul, Nicholas, Mary Magdalen and Catherine of Alexandria*[16]. Vault frescoes: L. Gimignani, L: *St Stephen Preaching against Idols*; C: *Glory of Angels*; R: *St John the Baptist Preaching*[17]

3 to L: Cappella dell' Immacolata: decorated by Ludovico Gimignani, altarpiece: *Immaculate Conception*; R lunette: *Nativity*; L lunette: *Annunciation*, 1697[18]; side walls by Pier Francesco Morazzone, R wall: *Adoration of the Magi* and L wall: *Visitation*[19]

2 to L: Cappella di SS. Giuseppe e Marcello/Odeschi: altarpiece: Luigi Garzi, *Vision of St Marcellus*; 1705; side walls by L. Gimignani, L wall: *Death of St Joseph* and R wall: *Virgin and Child with Sts Elizabeth, Joseph and Zachariah*; vault: *Angels in Glory*, c. 1695[20]; putti over altar by Lorenzo Ottoni

1 to L: Cappella del Crocifisso/Timotei-Salviati: decorated by Francesco Trevisani, altarpiece: *Crucifixion with Mary Magdalen, St John and the Virgin*; L wall: *Flagellation*; lunette: *Mocking of Christ*; R wall: *On the Road to Calvary*; lunette: *In the Garden of Gethsemane*; vault: *Triumph of the Cross and Instruments of the Passion*, 1695-96[21].

SS. Silvestro e Martino ai Monti
see S. Martino ai Monti

S. Silvestro al Quirinale
Via XXIV Maggio, 9

Founded in the 11th century, the church belonged to the Dominican nuns of S. Marco in Florence from 1507. Vittoria Colonna lived in the convent and it was there that she held her conversations with Michelangelo. In 1555 Paul IV gave the church to the Theatines who rebuilt it (consecrated in 1566). The two chapels nearest the façade were cut off in 1877 when the via 24 Maggio was cut through at the present low level; the existing façade dates from the same time. A drawing in the Ashmolean for a projected façade of the church, identified as being by G. A. Dosio after Guglielmo della Porta, probably made in the late 1550's, was published by Carolyn Valone[1].

INTERIOR

The nave arcade and piers are decorated with painted marble. The wooden ceiling dates from the time of Pius V.

End wall (originally the entrance): monuments to L: Cardinal Federico Cornaro (d. 1591) by Domenico Fontana, erected by

Gregory XIV in 1591[2], and R: Prospero Farinaci (d. 1618), made as an exact pair to the other[3]. Between them is a bas-relief of the *Baptism* by Luigi Fontana[4]

Oval paintings in nave: Stefano Pozzo, R wall: *Holy Family with St John the Baptist*; *Guardian Angel*; L wall: *Trinity*; *St Michael Archangel*; entrance wall: L: *St Peter*; R: *St Paul*[5]

1 to R: Cappella di S. Silvestro/Nelli: altarpiece: Avanzino Nucci, *St Sylvester Baptises Constantine*, 1608-10[6]; vault: Giacomo Beltrami, scenes from the *Life of St Sylvester*; R wall: *Constantine Meets Pope Sylvester*; L wall: *St Sylvester Hides on Mount Soreactum*, 1868

2 to R: Cappella della Madonna della Catena: altarpiece: Giacinto Gimignani: *Pius V and Cardinal Alfonso Carafa Adore the Picture of the Madonna della Catena*[7]; vault: C. Nebbia, R: *Annunciation*; C: *Pentecost*; L: *Visitation*; R wall: *Birth of the Virgin*; L wall: *Presentation of Jesus in the Temple*

R transept: Cappella di S. Gaetano da Thiene: altarpiece: Antonio Barbalonga, *Vision of Sts. Cajetan and Andrew Avellino*, 1630[8]; side walls by Pietro Angeletti, R: *The Blessed John Marinoni Refuses the Bishopric of Naples from Paul IV*: L: *The Blessed Paul Burali Comforts Pius V at his Death*, 1782[9]

Choir: the pilasters are of marble. The frescoes of the choir vault were begun by Giovanni Alberti in 1598 and continued after his death in 1601 by his brother Cherubino. The rest of the choir was frescoed by G. Agellio, who painted the vault: *God the Father with Angels*, lunette: *St Sylvester Discovered by Constantine's Soldiers in a Cave on Mount Soreactum* and figures of *Isaiah* and *Jeremiah* and *Evangelists* to designs by C. Roncalli, 1602. The fictive architecture is by Matteo Zaccolino, completed 1603[10]. R wall: B. Betti, *Christ among the Doctors*[11]; L wall: Lazzaro Baldi, *The Virgin Appears to St Cajetan Thiene*, 1695-c. 97[12]

L transept: Cappella dell'Assunta/Bandini: by Mascarino, 1579[13]; altarpiece: Scipione Pulzone, *Assumption*, 1585[14]; statues of *St John the Evangelist* and *Mary Magdalen* by Algardi[15]; *St Joseph* and *St Martha*, attributed to Mochi[16]. *Tondi* in pendentives by Domenichino, *King David before the Ark*; *Judith with the Head of Holofernes*; *Esther Swooning in front of Ahasuerus*; *Solomon and Bathsheba Enthroned*, 1628[17]. Monuments to L: Cardinal Ottavio Bandini (d. 1629) with bust by G. Finelli and R: Pietro Antonio and Cassandra Bandini, 1629-34/35 (d. 1588, 1582), the latter by Finelli and the former by his workshop[18]

2 to L: Cappella del Presepe/Orsini/Ghisleri: founded by Francesca Baglioni Orsini, who financed the decoration of the chapel[19]. Altarpiece: *Adoration of the Shepherds* by Marcello Venusti, 1573[20]. Vault frescoes by Raffaellino da Reggio, R: *Joseph's Dream* and *Flight into Egypt*; C: *Holy Ghost*; L: *Massacre of the Innocents*; side walls attributed to Jacopo Zucchi, L wall: *Adoration of the Magi* and R wall: *Circumcision*[21]

1 to L: Cappella di Fra Mariano[22]: decorated by Polidoro da Caravaggio, executed in an imitation of the ancient technique of encaustic paintings and the earliest pure landscapes in Roman art; on either side of altar: R: *St Mary Magdalen* and L: *St Catherine of Siena*, 1525-27. The *putti* below are by Polidoro and Maturino da Firenze[23]. The marbling, stucco and frescoes were added later for Cardinal Giacomo Sannesio, 1604-05. Vault: Giuseppe Cesari, L: *St Stephen Preaching*; C: *St Stephen in Glory*; R: *Martyrdom of St Stephen*, 1525-27[24]

There is door in the left transept, with steps leading to a terrace, originally the cemetery, with a small oratory dating from the 18th century.

S. Simeone Profeta (destroyed)

The church stood in the Piazza Lancellotti and was restored about 1610 by Orazio Lancellotti. In the 19th century it was secularized and was pulled down about 1940.

S. Sisto Vecchio

Piazza Numa Pompilio, Via di Porta S. Sebastiano

A church has stood on this site since the 4th century, but was several times restored or rebuilt. It was originally a basilica in plan but towards the end of the 16th century it was reduced to its present form with a single nave, and the apse and wooden roof were built. A further restoration, which gave the church its present appearance, was carried out by F. Raguzzini for Benedict XIII, 1725-27.

INTERIOR
1 to R: Emmanuele Alfani, *Virgin and Child with Sts Dominic, Thomas Aquinas, Hyacinth, Catherine of Siena, Rose of Lima and Pius V,* c. 1727[1]
2 to R: E. Alfani, *Madonna of the Rosary with Sts Dominic, Philip Neri, Thomas Aquinas and Agnes of Montepulciano*
Choir: frescoes attributed to Bartholomaeus Spranger of scenes from the *Lives of Sts Lawrence and Sixtus II,* R: *St Sixtus Baptises whilst in Prison;* L: *Charity of St Lawrence;* C: *Holy Trinity with Angels*[2]
2 to L: E. Alfani, *Virgin with an Image of St Dominic together with Mary Magdalen and St Catherine of Alexandria*
1 to R: E. Alfani (attributed), *St Vincent Ferrer*
   Within the cloister are a series of paintings by Andrea Casali depicting scenes from the *Life of St Dominic,* 1727[3].
Sala capitolare: scenes from the *Life of St Dominic* by Hyacinth Besson, 1852-59[4].

Spirito Santo dei Napoletani

Via Giulia, 34

An earlier church on this site was presented to the Neapolitan colony by Gregory XIII in 1572. Ottaviano Mascarino made a number of elaborate plans for the church, some based on an oval with an arcade of coupled columns, but it was ultimately built on a simple rectangular plan, possibly but not certainly by Mascarino. In about 1649 the façade was built by the Neapolitan architect Cosimo Fanzago[1] but it was replaced in 1853 by the existing façade by Antonio Cipolla, who also transformed the interior, completed in 1862[2].

INTERIOR
Remodelled by C. Fontana in 1666-68 and again in 1702-08[3]. The dome of the *Trinity in Glory with Saints and Angels* was frescoed by G. Passeri, 1707-08[4]. Pietro Gagliardi was responsible for the interior decorations during the 1853 renovations, when the walls were decorated with painted marble.
1 to R: Cappella di S. Francesco di Paola: altarpiece: Bonaventura Lamberti, *St Francis of Paola Restores the Facial Features to a Deformed Child*[5]. L wall: monument to Giuseppe Benedetto Dusmet by Pietro Canonica
Between 2 and 3 to R: monument to Cardinal Giambattista de' Luca, Governor of Rome under Innocent XI (d. 1683), probably designed by Fontana, 1690-93, with figures of *Justice* and *Prudence* and *The Cardinal in Prayer* by D. Guidi[6]
3 to R: Cappella del Crocifisso: altarpiece: P. Gagliardi, *Crucifixion*
High altar: by C. Fontana, 1709, but it has recently been attributed to F. Raguzzini[7]; apse: P. Gagliardi, *Annunciation;* triumphal arch: *Pentecost*
Over side doors: Vincenzo Felice and

Giuseppe Napolini, *Miracle of St Francis of Paola*
3 to L: Cappella di S. Gennaro: Luca Giordano, *Martyrdom of St Januarius*, c. 1702[8]
1 to L: Cappella di S. Tommaso d'Aquino: D. M. Muratori, *St Thomas Aquinas Healing a Child*, 1720-22[9]; L wall: monument to Pietro Corso, c.1680.

S. Spirito in Sassia
Largo Gregori, Borgo S. Spirito

The Confraternita di S. Spirito in Sassia was founded in France as a lay hospital Order in 1174 but later moved to Rome under Innocent III. The hospital was greatly enlarged by Sixtus IV, who built the nucleus of the existing structure, which was extended in the late 16th century by Ottaviano Mascarino. The church was built between 1538 and 1545 by Antonio da Sangallo the Younger and the façade was completed by Mascarino during the pontificate of Sixtus V to Sangallo's designs. The interior decoration was begun immediately after the rebuilding was completed. Restored in 1791, when the new pavement was laid[1], and again in 1856 for Pius IX by V. Vespignani[2].

INTERIOR
The carved wooden ceiling dates from the 16th century, but was restored for Pius IX. In 1582 Jacopo Zucchi was commissioned to fresco the whole church on a programme devised by P. Ignazio Danti, but only part of the scheme was carried out. It was completed c.1588[3].
Dome apse: *Risen Christ with the Holy Spirit in Glory and Saints*
Vault over high altar: *God the Father*; outer bands: *St Peter and Paul Converting the Infidels by Blessing them with the Holy Spirit*
Apse walls: *Pentecost*

Over front of tribune: *David and Isaiah*
Zucchi's frescoes in the apse constitute an unusually bold piece of illusionism, particularly in the use of architecture in the scenes of Pentecost and in the fact that the action spreads over two frescoes of the wall and the half dome, so that light emanating from the Holy Spirit in the upper zone flows into the lower.
Façade wall: *Pentecost* by A. Calcagnadoro; *Putti* and *Prophets* by Cesare Conti[4]
1 to R: Cappella dello Spirito Santo/Tolfa: built by Ottaviano Mascarino for the Marchesa Vittoria Tolfa and decorated by J. Zucchi; altarpiece: *Pentecost*, 1587-88; L wall: *St John the Baptist*; R wall: *Prophet Joel*; semi-dome oculus: *God the Father* and centre panel: *Risen Christ*; either side: *Angels*
2 to R: Cappella dell'Assunta/Glorieri: decorated for Cesare Glorieri. The altar has Salomonic columns, which were extremely rare in church architecture until they were used by Bernini in the *baldacchino* of St Peter's. Livio Agresti, who was active in the chapel till his death in 1579, was responsible for the stucco designs and the altarpiece: *Assumption*; apse: L: *Annunciation*; C: *Coronation of the Virgin*; R: *Visitation*; L wall: Giovanni Battista Montano, *Birth of Mary* and R wall: Simone de' Magistris, *Circumcision*[5]
Side entrance: side walls: putti and architectural paintings by C. Conti, 1590; scenes from the *Passion*, R: *Agony in the Garden*; below: *Washing of the Feet*, above door: *Last Supper*, all attributed to Litardo Piccioli, 1578-80; L: *Ecce Homo*[6] attributed to J. Stella
Between 3 and 4 to R: monument to Bernardino Cirillo (d. 1575)
4 to R: Cappella della Trinità: frescoes and stucco designs by Livio Agresti, L wall: *Healing of the Paralytic*; R wall: *Healing of the Blind*; semi-dome: C: *Abraham and Three Angels*; R: *Tobias Heals his Father*; L: *Elisha*

Cures Naaman of Leprosy, 1573-75. Stuccoes executed by Marcantonio Petta di Capranica, 1573-76
Between 4 and 5 to R: monument to Domenico Zoilo (d. 1576)
5 to R: Cappella dell'Ascensione/Neroni: frescoes and stuccoes by Giuseppe Valeriano; altarpiece: *Ascension*, 1570; L wall: *St Philip*; R wall: *St James the Lesser*; semi-dome: *Pentecost*, 1569-71
To L of 5 to R: monument to Antonio Vargas y Laguna (d. 1824) by Adam Tadolini, 1827[7]
To R of high altar: monument to Antonio Crisolino (d. 1669)
High altar: the steps to the high altar were laid in 1749[8]. Tabernacle by 'Monsu Lorenzo Tedesco'[9] but the design has recently been attributed to G. P. Schor and the carving to G. M. Giorgetti, *c*. 1680[10]
To L of high altar: monuments to Pietro Lavina Leponzio (d. 1779) by Raffaello Secini and Francesco Maria Ceccoli (d. 1677) by Pietro Antonio Ripoli, probably to the designs of his brother, Giovanni Tommaso, 1678[11]
5 to L: Cappella di S. Giovanni Evangelista/Landis: decorated for Francesco Landis, *c*.1545. Altarpiece: A. Giorgini, *St John the Baptist*, 1835[12]. Frescoes by Marcello Venusti of scenes from the *Life of St John the Evangelist*, R wall: *St John in the Cauldron of Boiling Oil*; L wall; *St John Raises a Dead Man*[13]
Between 4 and 5 to L: monument to Filippo Calligaria (d. 1581)
4 to L: Cappella della Pietà/Gonzaga: decorated for Giulio Cesare Gonzaga of Novellara, Patriarch of Alexandria. Oil paintings and stucco by Livio Agresti; altarpiece: *Pietà*; L wall: *Adoration of the Shepherds*; R wall: *Resurrection*; semi-dome: L: *Temptation of Adam*; R: *Expulsion from the Garden of Eden*, flanked by *Prophets*; L of altar: stucco figure of *Fortitude*; R of altar: stucco figure of *Mercy*, 1554-57[14]

3 to L: Cappella del Crocifisso/Guidiccioni: decorated for Alessandro Guidiccioni, 1546-49. Frescoes attributed to Pedro de Rubiales (Roviale Spagnolo), completed by 1551; L wall: *Crowning with Thorns*; C: *Christ before Pilate*; R wall: *Christ Carrying the Cross*; semi-dome: R: *Flagellation*; C: *Before the High Priests*; L: *Arrest of Christ*
2 to L: Cappella della Deposizione/Cirillo: decorated for Fra Nicola Cirillo. Stuccoes by Pompeo Cesura, who was also commissioned to paint the frescoes but died before he could begin. Altarpiece: Cesare Nebbia, *Coronation of the Virgin*; *tondi* L and R of altar: *Angel of the Annunciation* and *The Virgin*. Entrance pillar: *Evangelists*, Andrea Lilli. Nebbia also helped Lilli to paint the L wall: *St Augustine*; R wall: *St Monica*; semi-dome: L: *Dream of St Augustine*; C: *Baptism of St Augustine*; R: *St Augustine Contemplates the Trinity*. L wall: monument to Vincenzo Fontanello (d. 1610)
1 to L: Cappella della Vergine/Migliori: frescoes by Cesare Nebbia and stucco designed by Nebbia, executed by Giovanni Caselano and Michele Lucchesino, 1594. Altarpiece: *St Aloysius Gonzaga*, Ignazio Jacometti, 1880
L entrance wall: *Conversion of Paul* by Pedro de Rubiales, 1545
R entrance wall: *Visitation* by M. Pino[15]
Sacristy: built by Pietro Perini. Altarpiece: *Exaltation of the Cross*, J. Zucchi. Fine wooden cupboards by Pietro Perini; upper wall frescoes of scenes from the *History of the Hospital and Confraternity* and vault frescoed with scenes connected with the *Holy Spirit* by G. Abbatini[16]; vault stuccoes by Giovanni Maria Ferrera and Battista Besano, 1647

The buildings to the left of the church, stretching down to the Tiber, are part of the hospital begun by Sixtus IV, later enlarged and altered, but partially restored in the present century to what was believed to be their original condition.

The main entrance is in the Palazzo del Commendatore, immediately to the left of the church, which was built by Ottaviano Mascarino in the last years of the 16th century[17].

From a second cloister (to the left) a passage leads to the Quattrocento block containing two large wards, between which is an octagonal chapel (visible from the outside) containing a *baldacchino* persistently but wrongly ascribed to Palladio. It dates from the late 16th century, but was altered under Clement VIII.

Beyond this cloister is the museum which contains a pharmacy with 17th century blue and white maiolica drug jars and a wooden model for one of the wings of the Ospedale degli Incurabili.

Of the two doors built by Bernini[18], one was destroyed in the present century and the other, slightly altered, was built in the via dei Penitenzieri, which runs along the side of the church, leading to the Porta di S. Spirito.

Under Benedict XIII Fuga added a wing and a cemetery with a chapel dedicated to the Madonna del Rosario, but this was destroyed when the 20th century additions to the hospital were made[19].

Oratory of S. Spirito in Sassia *see* Oratory of the Annunziata
Lungotevere Vaticano, 1

S. Stanislao dei Polacchi
Via delle Botteghe Oscure, 15-16

A medieval church on this site was granted to the Polish community by Gregory XIII in 1578 and was rebuilt between 1580 and 1582. The present church dates from 1712-14 and is by Francesco Ferrari. It was restored by Ignazio Brocchi in 1777[1].

INTERIOR
Nave vault: fresco of *St Stanislaus in Glory* by Ermenegildo Costantini, 1774-77[2]
L of entrance: monument to Eustacy Adam Sluska (d. 1639)[3]
R of entrance: monument to Canon Marcin Katlewski (d. 1656)[4]
1 to R: Franciszek Smuglewicz, *St Casimir Stops a Battle*, 1765-77
2 to R: Thaddaus Kuntz, *Miracle of Bishop Stanislaus of Cracow*[5]
High altar: A. Grammatica, *Sts Stanislaus, Adalbert and Hyacinth with Christ in Glory*, before 1597[6]
Before 2 to L: monument to Giacomo Raffaelli (d. 1836) by Carlo Canigga[7]
2 to L: S. Czechowicz, *St Hedwig Adores the Cross*, 1742[8]
1 to R: S. Monosilio, *St John Kanty Distributes Alms*, 1767.

S. Stefano del Cacco
Via di S. Stefano del Cacco, 25

The medieval church was given by Pius IV in 1563 to the Silvestrine Benedictines, who still serve it. The church was restored in 1607-17, when the apse was rebuilt, and again in 1638-41 and in 1725. The façade dates from c.1640. The church is open for Sunday morning Mass.

INTERIOR
After 2 to R Pierino del Vaga, *Pietà*, c.1520[1]
Choir: high altar: C. Nebbia, *Martyrdom of St Stephen*[2]; apse frescoes by Cristofano Casolani, R: *St Frances of Rome*; L: *The Virgin and Child Appear to St Charles Borromeo*; above: *Trinity*; stuccoes by Rocco Solari, 1608-13
1 to L: side walls by Baglione, R: *Sts Paul the Hermit and Stephen*; L: *Sts Charles Borromeo and Philip Neri*, c.1639[3]

3 to L: Cappella di S. Matteo: altarpiece: C. Mariani, *St Matthew*. The altars have good *scagliola* frontals
Sacristy: G. Odazzi, *St Nicholas of Bari with the Virgin and Child* and *St Aurea Led to her Martyrdom* attributed to G. M. Morandi[4].

S. Stefano Rotondo
Via di S. Stefano Rotondo, 7

The church was founded during the reign of Pope Simplicius (468-483) and later restored by Nicholas V in 1453 under the direction of Bernardo Rossellino. After various religious occupants, the church and the convent were given by Gregory XIII to the German and Hungarian Jesuits in 1580.

INTERIOR
The arcades of the ambulatory walls are frescoed by Niccolò Circignani and Matteo da Siena and depict graphic scenes of the martyrdom of early saints, 1582. The frescoes, thirty in number, start on the south-east wall, on the first arcade to the right of the chapel of St Paul the Hermit and St Stephen and end on the north-east arcade immediately to the left of the vestibule entrance. Two 18th century frescoes by Marcello Leopardi, *Martyrdom of St Polycarp* and *Martyrdom of St Margaret*, were painted to replace damaged frescoes in 1794.
To L of entrance: over sacristy door: Antonio Tempesta, *Massacre of the Innocents* and opposite: *Madonna Addolorata*
Choir: Chapel of Sts Primus and Felician: altar by F. Barigioni[1]; scenes from the *Life of Sts Primus and Felician* by Antonio Tempesta
Cappella di SS. Stefano re d'Ungheria e Paolo primo eremita: built in 1777-78 to replace the demolished church of S. Stefano degli Ungari; frescoes by Giuseppe Midossi, 1794.

Stimmate di S. Francesco
Largo delle Stimmate

An earlier church on this site was given by Clement VIII in 1597 to the Congregazione della Stimmate di S. Francesco, founded in 1594. The church was rebuilt from 1714 onwards to the designs of G. B. Contini[1], though the vestibule and the façade were added later by A. Canevari (1719) when the church was consecrated. The statue of *St Francis* over the door is by B. Cametti, 1718-21.
In vestibule: L wall: monuments to Palmira Pulieri Petracchia (d. 1844) and Enrico Pulieri (d. 1830) by Adamo Tadolini[2].

INTERIOR
A single nave with side chapels. The corners of the nave are rounded as in Borromini's chapel of the Collegio di Propaganda Fide. Restored by Giuseppe Valadier, 1828-29.
Nave vault: fresco: L. Garzi, *St Francis in Glory Accompanied by Allegorical Figures of Charity, Humility, Faith and Poverty*, 1719[3]
1 to R: Cappella della Redenzione: built for Gianluigi di Torre Magno in 1725. Altarpiece: Francesco Mancini, *Madonna Addolorata*; vault: G. Odazzi, *Symbols of the Passion*, after 1726; R wall: M. Benefial, *Flagellation*, 1731[4]; L wall: D. Muratori, *Crowning with Thorns*, 1731[5]
2 to R: Cappella di S. Michele Arcangelo: copy of Reni's *St Michael*; above altar: P. Galli, relief of *The Virgin's Vision of God the Father, David and Isaiah*[6]
3 to R: Cappella S. Giuseppe Calesanzio: altarpiece: Marco Caprinozzi, *The Virgin and Child Appear to St Joseph Calasanctius*, c.1748[7]
Sacristy: vault: G. Pesci, *The Virgin with St John the Baptist and the Evangelists Appear to St Francis*, c.1730[8]; T. Salini, *Death of St Francis*[9]

High altar: Trevisani, *St Francis Receiving the Stigmata*, 1719[10]; stucco group of angels above by Pietro Bracci[11]
L transept: monument to Wladyslaw Constantino Waza, son of King Wladyslaw IV of Poland (d. 1698), commissioned by Cardinal Francesco Albani from B. Cametti, 1698-1700[12]
3 to L: Cappella di S. Antonio da Padova: altarpiece: F. Trevisani, *Vision of St Anthony of Padua*, c.1721-24[13]
1 to L: Cappella dei SS. Quaranta Martiri: altarpiece: G. Brandi, *The Forty Martyrs of Sebaste*, before 1663[14]; monument to Domenico and Michele Lavaggi, attributed to V. Luccardi, c.1837.

Within the church is a banner of the Confraternita delle Stimmate by I. Hugford showing *St Francis Receiving the Stigmata* and *The Virgin and Child Appearing to St Francis*, 1750.
Oratory: vault: Filippo Lauri, *Ecstasy of St Francis*; wall decorations by Paolo Gamba[15] (Giovanni V, p. 293).

SS. Sudario dei Piemontesi
Via del Sudario, 47b

The Arciconfraternita del SS. Sudario, named after the Holy Shroud preserved in Turin, was founded in 1597. The church was begun in 1604 to the designs of the Piedmontese architect Carlo di Castellamonte and was finished in the following year. In 1657 it was decided to enlarge the church and work was begun in 1660 under the direction of Carlo Rainaldi. It was, however, soon suspended and the main remodelling of the church took place between 1682 and 1692 under the direction of Pier Francesco Garola, during which time the façade and high altar were built. The church is usually open for Sunday morning Mass.

INTERIOR
The choir is decorated with Sicilian jasper, the nave with unusually fine *scagliola*. The vault was repainted at the restoration of 1874, but the church retains much of its Baroque character.
Vault: C. Maccari, *The Blessed Amedeus, Louise, Humbert, Bonifice and Margaret of Savoy in Glory*, 1870-71
R transept: Carlo Cesi, *St Francis of Sales*
High altar: A. Gherardi, *Sts Maximus of Turin, Maurice, the Blessed Amedeus, the Blessed Margaret and the Blessed Louise of Savoy in Adoration of the Dead Christ Lying on the Holy Shroud*, 1680-82[1], with a fine stucco group of *God the Father and Angels Holding the Holy Shroud* over it designed by Gherardi but executed by Pietro Mantinovese, 1688-89[2]. Side wall decorated by C. Maccari, R: *Urban II Presides over the Council of Bari*; R: *Meeting of St Francis of Sales and the Blessed John Ancina*
L Transept: altarpiece: G. D. Cerrini, *The Blessed Amedeus of Savoy Renounces his Throne before the Virgin and Child*, 1680
Sacristy: L. Baldi, *Nativity* and *Circumcision*, c.1690[3]
Corridor between sacristy and convent: monument to Principe Benedetto Maurizio di Savoia (d. 1808) by F. Festa, 1809[4].

S. Susanna
Via XX Settembre, 14

A church of basilical form stood from a very early date on this site, which incorporated the remains of a Roman house said to be that of Pope Caius (282/3-295/6), uncle of St Susanna, and the scene of her martyrdom. It underwent frequent restorations, including one under Sixtus IV in 1474-77, when three nave arches were removed.

Cardinal Girolamo Rusticucci, who became titular cardinal of the church in 1570, had certain alterations carried out by Domenico Fontana, notably in the chapel of St Lawrence, (after 1580), which was frescoed by G. B. Pozzo (d. 1589).

In 1586 Sixtus V gave the church to a newly reformed group of Cistercian nuns called the Foglianti, who rebuilt the convent to the designs of Francesco da Volterra. In 1589 the parish of S. Sebastianello was transferred to the church of S. Susanna, since the site was needed for the construction of S. Andrea della Valle. S. Susanna thus became the centre of a new parish in the recently built up area on top of the Quirinal. A nuns' choir was built behind the apse of the existing church.

In 1593 a complete remodelling of the church was carried out by Rusticucci under the direction of Maderno. In the first document Domenico Fontana is mentioned, but his name does not appear again and the existing church is the work of Maderno, though he used the outer shell of the old church.

The contract for the façade was signed in 1597 and the façade was completed in 1603. The statues of *Sts Susanna* and *Felicity* are attributed to Paracca and *Sts Caius* and his brother *Gabinus* to Stefano Maderno.

The façade makes an important step towards the Baroque type of façade. Though the walls are all in parallel planes, the architect has contrived a strong emphasis on the central bay by the movement forward of the wall, the increase in the plasticity of the order (pilaster to half column to full column) and the increasing richness of the sculpture.

The foundation stone of the conventual buildings was laid by Cardinal Francesco Barberini in 1638[1].

INTERIOR
The chancel was begun in 1593, the stuccoes being by Francesco de' Rossi and his sons, Bastiano and Battista. The nave was transformed by Maderno, who removed two transverse arches and roofed the new nave with a carved and gilded ceiling. On the truncated piers four prophets attributed to Paracca were added; R: *Jeremiah* and *Isaiah*; L: *Daniel* and *Ezekiel*.

Nave and entrance wall frescoes: Baldassare Croce, scenes from the *Life of the Old Testament Susanna* commissioned in 1598. R wall: 2nd bay: *Susanna is Spied on while Bathing*; 1st bay: *Susanna is Accused Unjustly by the Two Elders*; entrance wall to R: *Daniel Interrogates the Two Elders* and to L: *Daniel Defends Susanna*; L wall: 1st bay: *The Two Elders are Stoned to Death for their Lies*; 2nd bay: *Susanna Enters the Temple*. The illusionistic architecture is by Matteo Zaccolini

1st bay: monument to Filippo della Valle (d. 1768) and his daughter Camilla

R side chapel: Cappella della Madonna: vault fresco: Domenico Parodini, *Angels with the Instruments of the Passion*, c.1708

High altar: commissioned in 1596 from Matteo Castello and Francesco de' Rossi with a painting by Tommaso Laureto, *Martyrdom of St Susanna*

Choir: apse: frescoes by Cesare Nebbia, to L: *St Susanna Rebuffs Diocletian's Son*; to R: *St Susanna Refuses to Worship the Idols*; apse: *St Susanna in Glory*. L wall: B. Croce, *Martyrdom of St Gabinus*; R wall: P. Nogari, *Martyrdom of St Felicity*

Confessio: the *confessio* below the choir, which contains the relics of St Susanna, was remodelled in 1595 by Maderno to include Cardinal Rusticucci's tomb (d. 1603), an early example of the Counter Reformation cult of Early Christian martyrs. Altarpiece: *Sts Susanna, Felicity and Gabinus* by B. Croce

The triumphal arch over the choir is dated 1595.

L side chapel: Cappella di S. Lorenzo/ Peretti: built by D. Fontana for Camilla Peretti, sister

of Sixtus V, in 1590-92. Altarpiece: C. Nebbia, *Martyrdom of St Lawrence*; frescoes by G. B. Pozzo, L wall: *Baptism of St Genesius*; R wall: *Martyrdom of St Eleutherius*; vault: *Coronation of the Virgin*; intrados: scenes from the *Life of St Lawrence*[2]
Nuns' choir: frescoes of scenes from the *Old Testament* by Francesco Mezzetti.

S. Teodoro al Palatino
Via di S. Teodoro, 5-7

A circular church built on the site of a pagan temple dedicated to Romulus and Remus. It was extensively restored under Hadrian I, c.772 and Nicholas V, 1450, and again for Clement XI (1703-04) by C. Fontana. Fontana was also responsible for the small *piazza* in front of the church and the two-tiered staircase which descends from the road above. Restored again in the 1720's and 1780's when the altars were rebuilt. Fontana's work was further modified in 1825 and 1852.

INTERIOR
1 to R: P. L. Ghezzi, *St Crescentius of Urbino Slays the Dragon*, 1707[1]
1 to L: Francesco Manno, *Triumph of the Heart of Jesus with Sts Leonard of Port Maurice and Hyacinth of Mariscotti*, 1807[2].

S. Tommaso di Canterbury
Via Monserrato, 45

A hospital and hospice for English pilgrims are known on this site as early as the 12th century. A new church was built in 1496-97 and consecrated in 1501. Gregory XIII instituted the *Venerabile Collegio Inglese di Roma* in 1579 with a view to training English priests for the English mission. The church was decorated with a cycle showing the martyrdoms of English saints by Niccolò Circignani.

The church was desecrated during the French invasion and pulled down in 1834. The present church was erected by V. Vespignani in 1866-68[1].

INTERIOR
Entrance wall: L: monument to Martha Swinburne (d. 1778) by Christopher Hewetson, 1780[2]
High altar: Durante Alberti, *God the Father with the Dead Christ, St Thomas Becket and St Edmund*, c.1580[2]
L aisle: monument to Sir Thomas Dereham (d. 1739) with allegorical figures of L: *Religion* and R: *Fidelity* by Filippo della Valle, 1739-41[3]

The galleries contain 19th century copies by S. Capparoni of Circignani's lost frescoes.
Cappella del Sodalizio di Nostra Signora: ceiling fresco of the *Assumption* by Andrea Pozzo

Within the refectory: Pozzo, *Jesus Dining with Simon the Pharisee*, 1700. The ceiling fresco of *St George and the Dragon*, by an unknown pupil of Pozzo, is most probably based on Pozzo's design[4].

S. Tommaso de' Cenci
Via Monte de' Cenci, 14

In 1554 Rocco Cenci obtained from Julius III the jurispatronage of this early medieval church and this was confirmed again by Paul IV in 1559. Thereafter the church was radically restored, work being completed in 1562. The church is open in the morning of the second Sunday in the month.

INTERIOR
1 to L: Cappella della Madonna della Sbarra: decorated by Sicciolante, altarpiece: *Adoration of the Shepherds*; to L: *David*; to R: *Isaiah*; L wall: *Birth of the Virgin*; R wall:

Annunciation; vault: L: *Joachim and Anne Meet at the Golden Gate*; C: *Joachim and the Angel*; R: *Joachim Expelled from the Temple*, 1565[1]
2 to L: Cappella di S. Francesco: frescoes of scenes from the *Life of St Francis* by an unknown artist, *c.*1612
High altar: Giuseppe Vermiglio, *Incredulity of St Thomas*, 1612[2]
Above the entrance to the sacristy is an anonymous 16th century painting of the *Virgin with Sts Anthony Abbot, Lucy and Francis*[3].

S. Tommaso in Formis
Via di S. Paolo della Croce, 10

A small medieval church attached to a hospital, restored in 1633 on the orders of Alexander VII and again in 1787. The monastery buildings contain the room in which St John of Matha died (d. 1213). The church is open for Sunday morning Mass.

INTERIOR

1 to L: Sicciolante; *Virgin and Child with Sts Boniface of Tarsus and Francis and Pope Boniface VIII*, *c.*1574[1]
2 to L: Tommaso Luini, *Incredulity of St Thomas*[2].

S. Tommaso in Parione
Via Parione, 32-37

An earlier church, consecrated in 1139, stood on this site and was given to the Confraternity of Scribes and Copyists in 1561, who rebuilt it at the expense of Mario and Camillo Cerrini. De' Rossi ascribes the rebuilding to Francesco da Volterra and later writers repeat this attribution. It has a simple 17th century façade.

INTERIOR

L of entrance: monument to Giuseppe Ceccacci (d. 1831) by A. Francia, 1833
1 to L: the altarpiece by G. Passeri, *Immaculate Virgin*, before 1686, has been removed[1]
High altar: built in 1748.

SS. Trinità ai Monti
Piazza Trinità ai Monti

Founded by King Charles VIII of France for the Order of Minims created by St Francis of Paola. The church and convent were begun in 1502 in a French gothic style (still visible in the vault over the crossing), largely completed in *c.*1585 and consecrated ten years later. The façade was mainly built in 1570 (the date on the tower), but the door and the towers were not finished till 1587. The façade is, without documentary evidence, ascribed to Giacomo della Porta. The steps were added by D. Fontana for Sixtus V, 1586-87.

INTERIOR

1 to R: Cappella di S. Giovanni Battista/Altoviti: built by Giovanni Antonio Dosio, who also designed the stuccoes; frescoes of scenes from the *Life of St John the Baptist* by Giovanni Battista Naldini; altarpiece: *Baptism of Christ*; flanking the altar: *Isaiah* and *Zachariah*; L wall: *Dance of Salome*; lunette: *Beheading of the Baptist*; R lunette: *St John in Prison*; vault: *Nativity*; *Visitation*; *Childhood*; *Preaching*[1]
3 to R: Cappella dell'Assunzione/Rovere: altarpiece: *Assumption*, Daniele da Volterra, 1548-50; above: *Annunciation*, Giovanni Paolo Rossetti, 1548-50; R wall: *Presentation in the Temple*, Daniele da Volterra, paid 1553; lunette: *Birth of the Virgin*, Gasper Becerra; L wall: *Massacre of the Innocents* by Michele Alberti from Volterra's cartoon, 1548-53; lunette: *Presentation in the Temple*,

G. P. Rossetti, 1548-59; vault: M. Pino, *Coronation of the Virgin*; *Meeting of Anne and Joachim*; Tibaldi, *Rest on the Flight into Egypt*²
4 to R: Cappella Orsini/Massimo: altarpiece: L. Pallière, *Flagellation*, 1817. Frescoes by Paris Nogari, R lunette: *Christ Carrying the Cross*; L lunette: *Flagellation*, 1575³. Vault: *Last Supper*; *Washing of the Feet*; *Agony in the Garden*; *Jesus before Pilate*. Stuccoes by G. A. Paracca and Prospero Antichi⁴. L wall: monument to Cardinal Rodolfo Pio da Carpi (d. 1564) by Leonardo Sormani, 1568; R wall: monument to Cecilia Orsini di Carpi (d. 1575)
5 to R: Cappella Mariac: decorated by Michele Grechi; altarpiece: *Adoration of the Shepherds*; L of altar: *St Peter and a Donor*; R of altar: *St Paul*; L wall: *Circumcision*; lunette: *Baptism of Christ*; R wall: *Adoration of the Magi*; lunette: *Flight into Egypt*; vault: *David*; *Daniel*; *Isaiah* and *Jeremiah*⁵. The vault frescoes have also been attributed to Michiel Coxie⁶
7 to R: Cappella di S. Michele/Chateauvilliers: decorated for Cardinal Chateauvilliers, French ambassador to Leo X. Frescoes by an unknown Sicilian artist; vault: *Sibyls and Prophets*; R wall: *The Archangel Michael Appears to St Gregory to Indicate the End of the Plague in Rome*⁷
8 to R: Cappella di S. Francesco di Sales/Verospi: rebuilt in 1739-54; L wall: Domenico Corvi, *St Michael the Archangel*, c.1758⁸
High altar: designed by G. Rinaldi, 1676; stucco work by G. Ruggeri and two angels by G. Rinaldi, 1679, but the rest of his sculpture was removed in 1807⁹
Choir: Cesare Nebbia, *Crucifixion*¹⁰
Sacristy and Ante-Sacristy: built by B. Breccioli, 1617-22; in the latter, stucco decoration with the arms of France and Navarre, apparently late 17th century
8 to L: F. Zuccaro, *Coronation of the Virgin*

7 to L: Cappella della Coronazione/Pucci/Cauco: frescoes begun for Cardinal Lorenzo Pucci by Perino del Vaga; over entrance arch: *Isaiah and Daniel*; arch: *Adam and Eve*; *Creation of Adam*; *Fall of Man*; vault: *Nativity of the Virgin*; *Presentation in the Temple*; *Meeting of Anne and Joachim*; *Annunciation*; altar lunette: *Visitation*; L lunette: *Charity and Faith*, 1524-26. In 1563 Giacomo Caucho, Bishop of Corfu, commissioned Taddeo Zuccaro to complete the frescoes; L wall: *Death of the Virgin*, begun 1565-66 and completed by his death in 1566; altarpiece: *Assumption* begun by Taddeo Zuccaro and completed by Federico Zuccaro in 1589; upper wall: *Sibyl Showing a Vision of the Virgin and Child to Augustus*; lower wall: *God the Father Supporting the Dead Christ* and *Angels Holding Instruments of the Passion*, both by Federico¹¹
6 to L: Cappella del Sacro Cuore/Turchi: decorated by A. M. Seitz; altarpiece: *Virgin and Child*; R wall: *Return of the Prodigal Son*; L wall: *Wise and Foolish Virgins*, 1858¹²
4 to L: Cappella di S. Giuseppe/Cardelli: altarpiece: J. M. Langlois, *St Joseph with the Christ Child*, c.1825
3 to L: Cappella dell'Immacolata/Orsini: altarpiece: Philipp Veit, *Coronation of the Virgin*; side walls by Wilhelm Steinle, completed by Joseph Turner, L wall: *Annunciation*; R wall: *Visitation*, 1830¹³
2 to L: Cappella Aldobrandini: altarpiece: Daniele da Volterra, *Deposition*, after 1541¹⁴; R wall: Cesare Arbasia, *Adoration of the Shepherds*; L wall: Paolo Céspedes, *Expulsion of Adam and Eve*; vault: *Evangelists*; lunettes: *Story of the Virgin*, between 1571 and 1577¹⁵
1 to L: Cappella della Pietà/Borghese: ceded to Marcantonio Borghese in 1573. Frescoes by Cesare Nebbia, R wall: *Christ Carrying the Cross*; lunette: *Flagellation*; R of altar: *St Catherine*; L of altar: *St Francis*; vault: *Scenes from the Passion*, c.1590¹⁶. Plaster copy of the

Deposition by Wilhelm Achtermann, 1850[17]
Refectory: frescoed by A. Pozzo, 1694[18]
Cloister: astronomical table by E. Maignan, 1637
Corridor: anamorphic frescoes – i.e. designs in steep perspective – by J. F. Nicéron representing *St John on Patmos* and *St Francis of Paola as a Hermit*[19]

A room in the upper part of the convent was decorated by Charles-Louis Clérisseau for Thomas Lesueur, a scientifically minded father, with an illusionist effect of ruins and landscape.

SS. Trinità in Palazzo Monte di Pietà
Piazza di Monte di Pietà

The Roman Monte di Pietà, which lent money on security, was founded by Paul III in 1539. It was moved to its present site in 1605 and installed in the Palazzo Santacroce, built by Ottaviano Mascarino. The palace was enlarged by Maderno, who was responsible for the tabernacle and coat of arms on the façade. It was again enlarged about 1740 by Nicola Salvi to whom it owes its present appearance externally. Requests to visit the chapel should be made to the *portiere*.

INTERIOR
Hibbard has shown that Maderno's chapel was in a different part of the palace and the present chapel is by F. Peparelli, 1639-42, with interior decorations by G. A. de' Rossi, 1660-70. By 1686 the walls had been marbled with *giallo antico* and Sicilian jasper, but the decoration of the dome had still not been completed when C. F. Bizzacheri took over the project in 1696.

With its rich marbles on the walls, elaborate gilt and white stuccoes on the dome and white marble reliefs and lifesize statues, the chapel is one of the most splendid late Baroque ensembles. It is, however, surprising as a work designed by G. A. de' Rossi, whose style is generally simple and severe. It may well be that the chapel was originally planned to be simple and that the rich decoration was only imposed on the architect by the wealthy commissioning body.

Entrance vestibule: built by C. F. Bizzacheri, 1700-02. Stuccoes by A. Berrettoni, G. M. Galli and F. Ferrari; vault: M. Maglia, *God the Father*; L wall: Domenico Guidi, *St Charles Borromeo*, c.1660

Vault: stucco reliefs by L. Ottoni, *Sixtus V Points out the Palazzo del Monte to the Needy*; *Clement VII Consigns the Plans for the Monte di Pietà to Cardinal Pietro Aldobrandini*; M. Maglia, *Paul III Confirms the Privileges of the Monte di Pietà in the Presence of Cardinal Santacroce and Father Giovanni Calvi*; S. Giorgini, *Pius IV Confirms the Privileges of the Institution of the Monte di Pietà*; C: M. Maglia, *Dove of the Holy Spirit*. Other stuccoes by Andrea Bertoni and A. Berrettoni

1st niche to R: Francesco Moderati, *Faith*, 1724

To R: P. Legros, *Tobit Lending Money to Gabael*, 1702-05[1]

2nd niche to R: Bernardino Cametti, *Almsgiving*, 1721-25

High altar: Domenico Guidi, *Pietà*, designed in 1659 but its execution was – for unknown reasons – stopped and the relief was carried out on a new model in 1676

To L: J. B. Théodon, *Joseph Giving Grain to the Egyptians*, 1702-05

2nd niche to L: Giuseppe Mazzuoli, *Charity*, 1723

1st niche to L: Agostino Cornacchini, *Hope*, 1721-24.

SS. Trinità dei Pellegrini
Piazza Trinità dei Pellegrini

The medieval church of S. Benedetto in Aurenula was granted by Paul IV in 1558 to the Confraternita della SS. Trinità dei Pellegrini e dei Convalescenti, which had been founded in 1548 by Philip Neri and his confessor, Persiano Rosa, to provide lodgings for pilgrims and the sick, and which originally met in S. Girolamo della Carità. The church was rebuilt between 1587 and 1597 to the designs of Martino Longhi the Elder. The façade was not executed at this time, but the projected design is recorded in a drawing by G. P. Maggi, probably based on Longhi's ideas. The new church was consecrated in 1616 and rededicated to the Trinity and St Benedict. At this stage the interior was entirely articulated with pilasters under the direction of Giovanni Paolo Maggi, but in 1690 cracks appeared in the dome and Giovanni Battista Contini added eight travertine columns at the crossing which carried supporting arches. The existing façade, a skilful variant of Carlo Fontana's S. Marcello, was built by Giuseppe Sardi to a design by Francesco de' Sanctis in 1722-23[1]. The statues of the *Four Evangelists* are by Bernardino Ludovisi, 1723[2].

INTERIOR
The church was restored in 1849-53 by Antonio Sarti, when the columns and the vault were covered with yellow *scagliola* and the vault and much of the walls repainted[3].
Dome: lantern: *God the Father* by G. Reni, 1612-15[4]; pendentives: *Four Evangelists* by G. B. Ricci
1 to R: Cappella del Crocifisso/Lucatelli: decorated soon after 1630
2 to R: Cappella di S. Filippo Neri/Salomoni: restored by A. Sarti; decorated by Filippo Bigioli, altarpiece: *The Virgin and Child Appear to St Philip Neri*; altar lunette: *Death of St Philip Neri*; L: *St Philip Neri Healing the Sick*; R: *St Philip Neri Preaching*; vault: R: *Charity of St Philip*; L: *St Philip Washing the Feet of Pilgrims*; C: *Apotheosis of St Philip*, 1853
3 to R: Cappella di S. Giovanni Battista de' Rossi/Maffioli: altarpiece: Antonio Bianchini, *St John de' Rossi with Christ, the Virgin and Sts Philip Neri and John the Baptist*, 1882. Chapel decorations by G. B. Ricci: frescoes of scenes from the *Life of St Julius of Novara* to whom the chapel was once dedicated; L wall: *St Julius Heals a Carpenter whose Finger is Cut off*; R wall: *St Julius Exorcises a Demon*
R transept: Cappella di S. Matteo Apostolo: built by G. B. Mola. The altar has a fine marble sculpture of *St Matthew and the Angel*. The figure of St Matthew was commissioned from J. C. Cobaert in 1587 for the Contarelli chapel in S. Luigi dei Francesi, but was rejected when submitted in 1602. The angel was added by Pompeo Ferrucci when the group was set up in the Trinità c.1615[5]. The altar frontal was given in 1731
Sacristy: by G. B. Mola, 1644. Altarpiece: G. B. Ricci, *Annunciation*. To side of altar: L: *St Charles Borromeo* and R: *St Philip Neri* by F. Lanfranco, 1774; opposite wall: *Ecce Homo*; Jacopo Zucchi, *Last Mass of St Gregory*, 1572-c.75[6]; Angelo Papi, *St Philip Neri Caring for the Pilgrims* and *St Philip Preaching*, 1786. Over a door leading off the sacristy is a monument to Alessandro Raimondi (d. 1718) by Giuseppe Riccardi to a design by Francesco de' Sanctis, 1723-24[7]
Choir: high altar designed by Antonio de' Battisti and executed by Domenico Pozzi, 1616, but remodelled in the 1853 restoration; it contains Reni's painting of the *Holy Trinity*, 1625[8]. The tabernacle dates from 1853. On either side of the choir are magnif-

icent candlesticks by Orazio Censore, 1616[9]
L transept: built in 1613-16 by Tullio Solari and D. Pozzi to the designs of an unknown architect. Altarpiece: G. B. Ricci, *St Joseph and St Benedict*, incorporating an earlier miraculous image of the *Virgin and Child*, 1613

3 to L: Cappella di S. Gregorio Magno/Parisi: decorated by B. Croce, 1604-06; altarpiece: *St Gregory Freeing Souls from Purgatory*; altar lunette: *Mass of St Gregory*; R wall: *St Gregory Feeding the Poor*; L wall: *St Gregory and the Angel*; vault: R: *St Gregory with the Virgin and Child*; L: *St Gregory Inspired by the Dove of the Holy Spirit*

2 to L: Cappella di SS. Agostino e Francesco d'Assisi/Radice: altarpiece: Giuseppe Cesari, *Virgin and Child with Sts Augustine and Francis*, shortly before 1605[10]; chapel decoration by B. Croce, altar lunette: *Apostles around the Virgin's tomb*; vault: R: *St Clare Receives the Veil from St Francis*; C: *Assumption*; L: *Sts Clare and Francis*; side walls: *Ecstasy of St Francis* and *St Augustine*. R wall: monument to Augustus Maria Radice (d. 1869) by E. Granchelli

1 to L: Cappella di S. Carlo Borromeo/Altimani: altarpiece: Guglielmo Cortese, *Virgin and Child with Sts Charles Borromeo, Dominic Guzman, Philip Neri and Anthony of Padua*, c.1677[11]; Giovanni Battista Ferretti, R wall: *St Philip Neri in the Hospital*; L wall: *Charity of St Charles Borromeo*; vault: L: *St Dominic Resurrects Napoleone Orsini*; R: *St Felix Cantalice Receives the Virgin and Christ Child*; C: *Christ in Glory*, 1677[12]

To the left of the church (now a shop) is the old refectory of the hospital (of which the remainder was pulled down in 1940), with a series of memorials to popes, and a door above which is a bust of St Philip Neri in a setting by Cosimo Fanzago[13]. The sculptures in the memorials to the popes were lost during the French Occupation and replaced by plaster casts. That to Urban VIII was by Bernini and that to Innocent X by Algardi, who designed the surviving setting. These were in bronze but later busts were in marble[14].

SS. Trinità degli Spagnuoli
Via Condotti, 41

Founded in 1731 by the Spanish Trinitarians and built in 1741 to the designs of the Portuguese architect Emanuele Rodriguez. Giuseppe Sardi was in charge of the actual construction. The church was consecrated in 1750. The plan is oval with the long axis leading to the high altar and with six side chapels. The façade, completed in 1746, is on a slight concave curve, like that of S. Marcello, and culminates in a complicated and not altogether harmonious system of broken pediments, one curved, one rectilinear. The *Angels with Slaves* over the door are by P. Pacilli; in the niches: *St John of Matha* and *St Felix of Valois*, founders of the Trinitarian Order, by Pascal Latour, 1747[1].

INTERIOR
The effect of the interior is seriously damaged by the coarse painted marbling. The altars, including the high altar, and the interior stucco decorations were designed by José de Hermonsilla. Stucco executed by B. Mattei.
Vault fresco: Gregorio Guglielmi, *Mission of the Trinitarian Order*, 1748, enclosed by a stucco frame designed by P. Pacilli[2]
R side chapel: A. Velásquez, *The Good Shepherd*, c.1750[3]
Coretto ceiling: G. Guglielmi, *Virgin with Sts John of Matha and Felix of Valois*[4]
1 to R: Cappella di S. Caterina d' Alessandria: altarpiece: G. Paladino, *Martyrdom of St Catherine of Alexandria*, 1750; side walls: A. Casali, L: *St Catherine Survives her*

Torture and R: *Death of St Catherine*
2 to R: Cappella di S. Felice di Valois: decorated by Andrea Casali, altarpiece: *St Felix of Valois Liberates Slaves*, 1775. Side walls: L: *St John of Matha*, 1779 and R: *St Felix of Valois*, 1775
3 to R: decorated by A. Casali, altarpiece: *Pietà*, 1776; L wall: *Flagellation*; R wall: *Christ Falling under the Cross*[5]
High altar: C. Giaquinto, *Trinity with Liberated Slaves*, 1749[6]
Choir: decorated by A. Velásquez; L oval: *Innocent III Approves the Order of the Discalced Trinitarians of Castile;* R oval: *St John of Matha and Felix of Valois as Hermits*, 1750. Dome: Velásquez, *Story of Job, Abraham and Sarah*; pendentives: *Moses, St John* and *Two Prophets*, 1748-50
Sacristy: built on a design by Emanuele Rodriguez, who also designed the altar, 1749, and the *lavamani*, executed by Juan de Jouza, 1746. Over door: monument to Diego Morcillo (d. 1739) by G. Sibilla, 1760. Sacristy cupboards designed by Marco David and made by Giuseppe Alberici, 1750-60. Vault: fresco by G. Guglielmi, *St Ambrose with the Founding Saints of the Order*, 1746-47[7]
Corridor off church: F. Preciado de la Vega, *Vision of the Blessed Simon de Roxas*, 1757, formerly over the high altar[8]; Giuliano Presutti, *Ascension*, 1548[9]; A. Casali, *St Michael*
3 to L: altarpiece: F. Preciado de la Vega, *Immaculate Virgin*, 1750; side walls by Miguel Espinosa, R: *Annunciation* and L: *Assumption*
2 to L: Cappella di S. Giovanni di Matha: altarpiece: Gaetano Lapis, *St John of Matha Liberates Slaves*, 1750[10]; walls: A. Casali, R: *The Virgin Appears to St John of Matha* and L: *St John's Vision during Mass*[11]
1 to L: Cappella di S. Agnese: altarpiece: Marco Benefial, *Martyrdom of St Agnes*, 1750[12]; side wall by A. Casali, R: *St Agnes Taken to her Martyrdom* and L: *St Agnes Appears to her Parents*, 1773.

SS. Venanzio e Ansovino (destroyed)

The church, also called S. Giovanni in Mercatello, which stood below the steps leading up to the Capitol, was given in 1675 to the Comunità dei Camerinesi by Clement X, who had been Bishop of Camerino and who paid for its restoration to the designs of Antonio Liborio Raspantini. It was pulled down in 1928, but its façade is recorded in Vasi's engraving.

SS. Vincenzo e Anastasio
Piazza di Fontana di Trevi

The church was given by Paul V in 1612 to the Hieronomites, who began to build their monastery in 1614. In 1640 Urban VIII, who was planning a new Trevi Fountain, issued a brief allowing the monks to rebuild their church. According to Borromini, correcting Martinelli, the architect was Gaspare de' Vecchi (d. 1643). It is possible that Cardinal Mazarin financed this operation, but his certain contribution was the building of the façade begun by Martino Longhi the Younger in 1646 and probably finished by 1650. Mola says that he also built part of the church. According to Passeri, Longhi intended to have panels on either side of the door filled with bas-reliefs. Mazarin's coat of arms and the angels supporting it are by A. Raggi, 1647[1]. The choir and sacristy were built by Giuseppe Ferroni, 1760/62-67.

INTERIOR
Nave vault: Francesco Manno, *Sts Vincent and Anastasius with St Camillus de Lellis in Glory*, 1818[2]

Entrance wall: R: monuments to Flavia Foschi (d. 1826) by A. Tadolini, 1826[3], and Christian Schlosser (d. 1829) by Christina Lotsch[4]. Above: organ originally installed by J. C. Werle, 1772-76[5]

3 to R: Cappella di S. Camillo de Lellis: altarpiece: Gaspare Serenari, *Christ Appears to St Camillus*. Chapel decoration by Silverio Capparoni of scenes from the *Life of St Camillus*; L wall: *St Camillus Helps the Sick*; R wall: *St Camillus's Dream*; vault: C: *St Camillus in Glory*; R: *St Camillus Prays in the Woods*; L: *St Camillus Helps Orphans*, 1876[6]

4 to R: baptistery by G. Ferroni with vault stuccoes by G. Ferrari, reliefs of *St John the Baptist Baptising*, *St Peter Baptising* and *Baptism of St Paul*

High altar: designed by G. M. Ferroni, 1764; however, it is also given to Antonio Cioli, 1775[7]. Altarpiece: Francesco Pascucci, *Sts Vincent and Anastasius*, 1778[8]

3 to L: built by Giacomo Monaldi, 1846

2 to L: Cappella di S. Giuseppe: altarpiece: Giuseppe Tommasi, *Death of St Joseph*; R wall: monument to Alessandro Maria Tassoni (d. 1818) designed by L. Baldi with bust by Giuseppe Pacetti, 1819[9]

The monastic buildings (entrance in the via del Lavatore, 38), about which no documents have been published, appear to date from the early 18th century, and the door[10], vestibule and steps leading to the cloister show a rare understanding of Borromini's method of design. It is known that Bizzacheri worked on the building and the design of this part may be due to him[11].

S. Vitale
Via Nazionale, 192

A church has stood on this site since the early 5th century. It was rebuilt by Sixtus IV in 1475. In 1598 it was given by Clement VIII to the Jesuits and attached to their noviatiate of S. Andrea al Quirinale. The Jesuits restored the church in 1599-1603 and set up four altars supported on marble columns. They decorated the walls with a bold scheme of illusionistic frescoes, articulated with pairs of fictive giant Ionic columns flanking the altars. Between the pairs the wall is divided into two zones: above are fictive niches with figures of prophets and below are landscapes with scenes of martyrdoms of hermit saints devised by G. B. Fiammeri and executed by Tarquino Ligustri, final payment 1603[1]. All this work was made possible by the patronage of Isabella della Rovere, whose coat of arms is on the high altar. The carved wooden doors date from after 1611. The church was restored for Pius IV in 1858[2].

INTERIOR

Entrance wall: R: *Martyrdom of Sts Victor and Corona in Syria*; above: *Micah*; L: above: *Joel*

From R: *St Andrew and his Troops*; above: *Daniel*

1 to R: G. B. Fiammeri, *Sts Ursula, Agnes, Catherine, Agatha, Martha, Margaret, Thecla, Lucy, Barbara, Cecilia, Anastasia, Prisca, Bibiana and Emerentiana*[3]; *Martyrdom of St Paphnutius in Egypt*; above: *Jeremiah*; *Martyrdom of Sts Marcellinus and Peter*

2 to R: attributed to Fiammeri, *Immaculate Conception*; *Martyrdom of St Ignatius*

3 to R: A. Ciampelli, *St Vitalis Buried Alive*[4]

Presbytery: apse: Andrea Commodi, *Christ Carrying the Cross*; R wall: *Beheading of St Protasius*; L wall: *Flagellation of St Gervasius*, 1599-1600[5]. The four stucco statues of L: *St Jerome* and *St Gregory* and R: *St Augustine* and *St Ambrose* date from 1611; *Martyrdom of St Clement*

3 to L: A. Ciampelli, *Torture of St Vitalis*[6]; *Martyrdom of St Januarius*; *Martyrdom of the*

Forty Martyrs; above: *Isaiah*
1 to L: attributed to J. Heintz, *Sts Silvester, John Chrysostom, Basil, Gregory Nazianzen, Ambrose, Augustine, Jerome, Bernard*; *Martyrdom of St Saturninus and Martinian and their Brothers*; above: *Zacharias*.

SS. Vito e Modesto
Via di S. Vito

An early church stood on this site from the late 7th century next to the Arch of Gallienus. It was rebuilt by Sixtus IV in 1477. The Baroque façade is shown in Vasi's engraving, but it was removed in the 19th century. Restored by Pietro Camporese in 1830 for Gregory XVI. The interior was stripped of all decoration at some date after the Second World War.

INTERIOR
L wall: monument to Cardinal Carlo Visconti (d. 1565).

BIBLIOGRAPHIES AND REFERENCES

AA	Acta ad Archaeologiam et Artium Historiam Pertinenta	LU	L'Urbe
ARN	Acta Romani Norvegiae	MAH	Mélanges d'archéologie et d'histoire
AAM	Arte antica e moderna	MD	Master Drawings
AB	Art Bulletin	MEFRIM	Mélanges de l'École Française de Rome, Italie et Méditerranée
ABA	Antologia di Belle Arti	MJBK	Münchner Jahrbuch der bildenden Kunst
AC	Arte Cristiana	MKIF	Mitteilungen des Kunsthistorischen Institutes in Florenz
AD	Arte Documento		
AdI	Archivi d'Italia	MNIR	Mededelingen van het Nederlands Institut te Rome
AH	Art History		
AI	Arte Illustrata	MPARA	Memorie della Pontificia Accademia Romana di Archeologia
AJ	Art Journal		
AeH	Artibus et Historiae	NBAC	Nuovo Bollettino di Archeologia Cristiana
AK	Allgemeines Künstlerlexikon		
AQ	Art Quarterly	NPA	Notizie da Palazzo Albani
AR	Alma Roma	Pala.	Palatino
Arch.	Architettura	Pall.	Palladio
ASD	Architettura, storia e documenti	PA	Paragone Arte
ASRSP	Archivio della Societa Romana di Storia Patria	Panth.	Pantheon
		Pros.	Prospettiva
AV	Antichità Viva	QISA	Quaderni dell'Instituto di Storia dell'Architettura
b.	born		
BdA	Bollettino d'Arte	RA	Rassegna d'Arte
BCN	Bollettino del Centro Nazionale di Studi di Storia dell'Architettura	RAU	Rassegna di Architettura e Urbanistica
		RD	Regnum Dei
BM	Burlington Magazine	RdA	Revue de l'Arte
BUSA	Bollettino della Unione storia del Arte	RdL	Revue du Louvre
c.	circa	rec.	recorded
Cap.	Capitolium	RHM	Römische historische Mitteilungen
cat.	catalogue	RINASA	Rivista dell'Istituto Nazionale d'Archeologia e Storia dell'Arte
CdR	Chiese di Roma		
Comm.	Commentari		
d.	died	RJBH	Römisches Jahrbuch der Bibliotheca Hertziana
diss.	dissertation		
DKD	Deutsche Kunst und Denkmalplege	RJK	Römisches Jahrbuch für Kunstgeschichte
exhib. cat.	exhibition catalogue	RMC	Roma moderna e contemporanea
FA	Fede e Arte	RSA	Ricerche di Storia dell'Arte
GBA	Gazette des Beaux-Arts	S.	Santo/Santa/Sant'
GR	Guide Rionali di Roma	SdA	Storia dell'Arte
icon.	iconography	SdR	Strenna dei Romanisti
JSAH	Journal of the Society of Architectural Historians	SR	Studi Romani
		SS.	Sante, Santi, Santissima, Santissimo
JWCI	Journal of the Warburg and Courtauld Institutes	St/Sts	Saint/Saints
		WJK	Wiener Jahrbuch für Kunstgeschichte
KT	Konsthistorisk Tidskrift	ZfK	Zeitschrift für Kunstgeschichte
Loth.	Lotharinga		

S. Adriano
Bibliography: Nibby, p. 27; Angeli, p. 3; O. Ozzi, *Le veneranda chiesa di S. Andrea al Forno*, Rome, 1924; Pugliese and Rigano, p. 67; J. Varriano, *RJK*, 13, 1971, p. 287; Racheli, p. 356; Lombardi, p. 223

1 Boselli, p. 29, 59v; Bacchi, figs. 237, 238; Ferrari, p. 1

S. Agata dei Goti
Bibliography: Pollak, I, p. 19; Roisecco, 1750, II, p. 582; Titi, 1763, p. 272; S. Piale, *Della subura antica ... e della chiesa di S. Agata dei Goti*, Rome, 1833; Angeli, p. 5; C. Huelsen et al., *S. Agata dei Goti*, Rome, 1924; Ferrari, *Lo Stucco*, pl. CCIX; *Diario di Roma*, 1837, No. 14; L. Lotti, *AR*, 16 (1-2), 1975, p. 91; Buchowiecki, I, p. 279; Buchowiecki, I, p. 279; Pinelli, No. 12; Tesei, p. 18; Lombardi, p. 53; M. Bevilacqua, *Pall.*, 8, 1991, p. 19; Chracas, II, No. 7647; *GR*, I, III, p. 158; Pocino, p. 123; Racheli, p. 186; Wolfe, p. 62

1 *Organi*, p. 54
2 Mallory, *Rococo*, p. 131; M. G. Gargano, *SdA*, 17, 1973, p. 85

S. Agata in Trastevere
Bibliography: Venuti, p. 430; Nibby, p. 37; Angeli, p. 6; U. Vichi, *Sant'Agata in Trastevere*, Rome, 1961; Portoghesi, *Roma Barocca*, pls. 326-29; Elling, pl. 33; *GR*, XIII, II, 2°, p. 176; Dunn, p. 483; Kuhn-Forte, p. 243

1 W; Poensgen, p. 87, fig. 53
2 W; but rejected by V. Casale, *PA*, 341, 1978, p. 64
3 W; R
4 W

S. Agnese in Agone
Bibliography: Tessin, p. 162; De Brosses, II, p. 122; Magni, I, pls. 63-66; Hempel, p. 138; Angeli, p. 15; Lavagnino, *Altari*, p. 139; Fasolo, p. 119; G. Eimer, *S. Agnese*; Portoghesi, *Borromini*, pls. LXXIII-LXXIV, 123-31, 418-421; R. Preimesberger, *Colloqui del Sodalizio*, series 3, 1970-72, p. 44; F. Trevisani, *SdA*, 23, 1975, p. 61; R. Preimesberger, *RJK*, 17, 1978, p. 159; Blunt, *Borromini*, p. 156; *GR*, VI, I, p. 36; Montagu, *Algardi*, p. 433; *Chiese dal Rinascimento*, p. 239; *Piazza Navona*, p. 226; M. Raspe, 'Borromini und S. Agnese', *RJK*, 31, 1996, p. 313; *Organi*, p. 56; *Roma Sacra*, 7, 1996, p. 45; S. Bettini, *Arch.*, 45, 1999, p. 319; *Borromini e l'universo barocco*, p. 184

1 Eimer, I, p. 91
2 Hempel, pl. 90
3 Garms, p. 68, document 353
4 Davis, p. 20
5 Enggass, *Baciccio*, pp. 9, 140; *Pittura barocca romana*, p. 62
6 Ferrari, *La Tomba*, pl. CLVI; Montini, p. 364
7 Bacchi, fig. 732
8 Ferrari and Papaldo, p. 2
9 Bacchi, fig. 242; Ferrari and Papaldo, p. 8
10 Bacchi, fig. 374
11 Ferrari and Papaldo, p. 3
12 Bacchi, fig. 374
13 Ferrari and Papaldo, p. 4
14 *Pietro da Cortona*, p. 271
15 Ferrari and Papaldo, p. 8
16 A. Bacchi, *BM*, CXXXVII, 1995, p. 842
17 Enggass, *Sculpture*, p. 177; Ferrari and Papaldo, p. 5
18 Bacchi, fig. 699; Ferrari and Papaldo, p. 6
19 Enggass, *Sculpture*, p. 180
20 Sorgiovanni, p. 112
21 Bacchi, fig. 257; Ferrari and Papaldo, p. 6
22 Bissell, p. 121

S. Agostino
Bibliography: Titi, 1763, p. 400; A. Ronci, *S. Agostino in Campo Marzio*, Rome, n.d.; G. Urban, *RJK*, 9/10, 1964, p. 274; M. Breccia Fratedocchi, *S. Agostino in Roma, arte storia documenti*, Rome, 1980; R. U. Montini and D. G. Cavallero, *CdR*, Nuova Serie, 22; Nibby, p. 51; Pinelli, No. 13; Buchowiecki, I, p. 296; J. Connors, *RJK*, 25, 1989, p. 207; R. Samperi, *QISA*, 22, 1993, p. 37; Lombardi, p. 190; *Organi*, p. 58; *Roma Sacra*, 7, 1996, p. 8; R. Samperi, *L'Architettura di S. Agostino a Roma (1296-1483): Una chiesa mendicante tra Medioevo e Rinascimento*, Rome, 1999

1 *Giornale di Rome*, 1681, No. 241, Oct. 19; id., 1868, No. 90, 20 April; id., 1868, No. 91, 21 April
2 C. P. Ridolfini, *Bollettino dei Musei Comunali di Roma*, XIX, 1972, p. 27
3 M. Hirst, *BM*, 1972, CXIV, p. 162; Boucher, p. 320
4 Sorgiovanni, p. 114
5 Ferrari and Papaldo, p. 10
6 V. A. Bonito, *BM*, CXXII, 1980, p. 805; Pope-Hennessy, p. 455
7 A. Nava Cellini, *PA*, 105, 1958, p. 17; Ferrari and Papaldo, p. 10
8 Russo, p. 4; Kamp, p. 114
9 Ferrari and Papaldo, p. 12
10 *Roma di Sisto V*, p. 189
11 Del Bufalo, p. 86
12 W
13 Titi, p. 338
14 Ferrari and Papaldo, p. 19
15 Seta, p. 33
16 W
17 Titi, p. 392; Enggass, *Sculpture*, p. 116; Ferrari and Papaldo, p. 12
18 Dombrowski, p. 283
19 Ferrari and Papaldo, p. 11
20 Salerno, p. 257
21 Bernini, p. 112
22 De' Rossi, *Architettura Civile*, II, pl. 52; Magni, I, pl. 57; Chracas, II, No. 4383; Gradara, p. 103; Ferrari, *La Tomba*, pl. CLXVI; C. Kelly, 'Paolo Posi', in, *An Architectural Progress*, p. 817; González-Palacios, p. 101
23 *Roma di Sisto V*, p. 191; Zuccari, p. 91
24 M. Gregori, Paragone, 475, 1989, p. 52
25 Dombrowski, p. 283
26 Wittkower, *Bernini*, p. 191; Dombrowski, p. 314; Ferrari and Papaldo, p. 13
27 Gradara, p. 24
28 Titi, p. 390
29 Gere and Pouncey, p. 150
30 *Pittura in Italia: L'Ottocento*, p. 830
31 Bernini, p. 44; Schleier, p. 49
32 Titi, p. 390; Ferrari and Papaldo, p. 14
33 de' Rossi, *Architettura Civile*, II, pl. 15; Eimer, *S. Agnese*, II, fig. 277; Ferrari and Papaldo, p. 15
34 R. Preimesberger and M. Weil, *RJK*, 15, 1975, p. 183
35 Enggass, *Sculpture*, p. 98; Ferrari

and Papaldo, p. 17
36 Titi, p. 392
37 Titi, p. 392
38 Ferrari and Papaldo, p. 11
39 W
40 Di Giammaria, p. 155
41 F. Petrucci, *SdA*, 96, 1999, p. 176
42 R
43 *Fagiolo dell'Arco*, cat. no. 92; Lavin, *Bernini*, pp. 54, 193; Borsi, p. 310
44 W
45 *Roma di Sisto V*, p. 191; Andrea Lilli, p. 115
46 A. Nava Cellini, *PA*, 147, 1962, p. 24; Ferrari and Papaldo, p. 18
47 Marini, p. 222
48 Vasi, *Magnificenze*, pl. 123; Magni, II, pl. 101 and Pane, in, R. De Fusco et al., *Luigi Vanvitelli*, Naples, 1973, p. 62; A. S. Schiavo, *SR*, XXII, 1974, p. 316
49 Fleming and Honour, p. 255

SS. Alessio e Bonifazio all'Aventino

Bibliography: Venuti, p. 371; Titi, 1674, p. 65; Nibby, p. 59; Angeli, p. 23; Mallory, *Notizie*, No. 5505; *Le scienze e le arte*, vol. I, n.n. Letarouilly, pl. 150 (266); L. Zambarelli, *CdR*, 9; Buchowiecki, I, p. 475; *GR*, XII, II, p. 50; Lombardi, p. 250; S. Carbonara, 'L'architettura "temperata" di Tommaso de' Marchis' in, Roma borghese, p. 61; Bevilacqua, *Nolli*, p. 152; M. Bevilacqua, *Pall.*, 21, 1998, p. 103

1 Mallory, *Notizie*, III, p. 125
2 Ferrari and Papaldo, p. 62
3 Gunter, p. 327; Ferrari and Papaldo, p. 63
4 Marmorari e argentieri, p. 16
5 Weil, p. 148; Bacchi, fig. 446
6 R
7 Lavagnino, *Altari*, p. 209; Chracas, II, No. 5874

S. Ambrogio della Massima

Bibliography: Totti, p. 175; Mola, p. 89; Nibby, p. 72; Hibbard, *Maderno*, p. 138; Buchowiecki, I, p. 308; G. Gurisatti and D. Picchi, *QISA*, XXVII/ 169-174, 1982, p. 49; De Tomasso, p. 132; L. Lotti, *AR*, 11 (3), 1970, p. 26; Lombardi, p. 240; M. De Dreuille, *S. Ambrogio della Massima: Casa paterna di S. Ambrogio*, Parma, 1996; *Roma Sacra*, 15, 1999, p. 6

1 W; Trezzani, p. 28; Sorgiovanni, p. 66
2 Boselli, p. 40, 155v
3 R
4 G. Papi, *SdA*, 62, 1988, p. 7; M. Lafranconi, *Pros.*, 93-94, 1999, p. 123

S. Anastasia al Palatino

Bibliography: Totti, p. 154; Martinelli, p. 14; Mola, pp. 81, 113; Nibby, p. 73; Falda, *Nuovo teatro*, III, p. 128; G. M. Crescimbeni, *L'istoria della Basilica di S. Anastasia*, Rome, 1722; Titi, 1763, p. 78; Venuti, p. 398; Angeli, p. 29; F. Cappello, *Brevi Notizie di S. Anastasia di Roma*, Rome 1722; Pollak, I, p. 20; Ferrari, *Lo Stucco*, pl. CXLVI; Chracas, II, No. 743; W. J. Doheny, *St Anastasia: The Saint and Her Basilica in Rome*, Rome, 1956; Portoghesi, *Roma Barocca*, pl. 411; Buchowiecki, I, p. 322; *GR*, X, IV, p. 30; Lombardi, p. 220

1 Portoghesi p. 541
2 Titi, 1763; Mallory, I, p. 111; Chracas, II, No. 743, 819
3 R
4 *Giovanni V*, p. 335
5 *Pier Francesco Mola*, p. 169
6 W; Pampalone, p. 46
7 *Giornale di Roma*, 154, 1870
8 Di Federico, p. 62
9 Bacchi, fig. 774; Gunter, p. 324
10 Pampalone, p. 53
11 Titi, p. 110; Gunter, p. 348, n. 122

S. Andrea delle Fratte

Bibliography: Falda, *Nuovo teatro*, I, pl. 9; Titi, 1763, p. 342; Venuti, p. 121; Nibby, p. 77; Angeli, p. 23; Letarouilly, pl. 142 (265); Hempel, *Borromini*, pp. 167ff.; J. Zänker, *Arch.*, IV, 1974, p. 165; F. A. Salvagnini, *La basilica di S. Andrea delle Fratte*, Rome, 1967; Racheli, p. 196; Portoghesi, *Borromini*, pls. 178-89; id. *Roma Barocca*, pls. 161-68; M. D. Onofrio, *S. Andrea delle Fratte*, Rome, 1971; Blunt, *Borromini*, pl. 195; *GR*, III, III, p. 38; Buchowiecki, I, p. 332; Pinelli, No. 15; S. Bettini, *Arch.*, 45, 1999, p. 385; V. Zanchettin, *Annali di architettura*, 9, 1997, p. 112; *Roma Sacra*, 5, 1996, p. 18; *Borromini e l'universo barocco*, p. 284

1 Hibbard, *Licenze*, p. 100
2 Drawing in the Albertina, Hempel, p. 169, fig. 61
3 Reproduced Blunt, *Borromini*, p. 78, fig. 26
4 Blunt, op. cit., p. 46, fig. 37
5 *Diario di Roma*, 25, 1827
6 Titi, p. 326; Chracas, II, No. 4986
7 Gradara, p. 55; Chracas, II, No. 4947
8 W
9 *Roma la città*, p. 279
10 Titi, p. 323
11 Sorgiovanni, pp. 90, 91
12 Chracas, II, No. 6486
13 B. S. Groseclose, *American Art Journal*, 12, 1980, p. 78
14 Lilli, p. 51
15 Caracciolo, p. 336; Clark, p. 133; Chracas, III, No. 1856
16 Lilli, p. 53
17 Lilli, p. 88
18 Sorgiovanni, p. 94
19 Lilli, p. 156
20 A. M. Gunter, *SR*, XLV, 1997, p. 97
21 W
22 Titi, p. 326
23 Wittkower, *Bernini*, p. 248; Weil, p. 46
24 R
25 R
26 *Pietro da Cortona*, p. 216
27 Di Federico, p. 45
28 W; M. Casella, 'La decorazione di S. Andrea delle Fratte', in, *L'Arte per i giubilei*, p. 71
29 see also V. Casle, *Scritti di storia dell' arte in onore di Federico Zeri*, p. 736
30 De Fusco et al., *Luigi Vanvitelli*, 1973, figs. 195-99; J. Garms, *WJK*, XXVII, 1974, p. 140; de Seta, p. 298
31 R
32 J. Montagu, *MD*, 31, 1993, p. 454
33 Hubert, p. 428; Lilli, p. 80
34 Lilli, p. 76
35 W; Trezzani, p. 37; Sorgiovanni, p. 64
36 *Pittura in Italia: L'Ottocento*, p. 736
37 Lavagnino, p. 373
38 *Borromini nella cultura europea*,

figs. 284ff; Heimbürger Ravalli, *Archivio Spada*, p. 75, figs. 60ff; Ferrari and Papaldo, p. 28
39 Heimbürger Ravalli, pp. 48, 68, etc.
40 ibid., p. 82
41 M. Pupillo, *SdA*, 85, 1995, p. 395
42 R. Contini, *Panth.*, LVII, 1999, p. 104

S. Andrea al Quirinale

Bibliography: Falda, *Nuovo teatro*, III, pl. 13: Tessin, p. 161, pls. 83, 84; de' Rossi, *Architettura Civile*, I, pl. 107 and II, pl. 4; De Brosses, II, p. 310; Titi, 1763, p. 302; Franco Borsi, *La chiesa di S. Andrea al Quirinale*, 1967; Portoghesi, *Roma Barocca*, pls. 62-69; Eimer, *S. Agnese*, II, p. 271-73; J. Connors, *JSAH*, 41, 1982, p. 15; C. L. Frommel, 'S. Andrea al Quirinale: genesi e struttura', in, *Gian Lorenzo Bernini architetto e l'architettura europea del Sei-Settecento*, Florence, 1983, p. 211; J. E. Barclay Lloyd, *JSAH*, 45, 1986, p. 197; Scribner, pls. 30-31; *Chiese dal Rinascimento*, p. 206; J. M. Smyth-Pinney, *JSAH*, 48, 1989, p. 53; T. A. Marder, *Arch.*, 20 (21), 1990, p. 108; Careri, p. 87; L. Lanzetta, *CdR*, Nuova Serie, 30; P. M. Gijsbers, *MNIR*, LV, 1996, p. 293; Marder, p. 187; *Roma Sacra*, 16, 1999, p. 43

1 Eimer, *S. Agnese*, I, p. 328
2 Eimer, *S. Agnese*, pl. 271
3 *Diary of Alexander VII*, entries 226, 235, 238, 241, 331
4 *Diary of Alexander VII*, entry 235
5 Westin, p. 157
6 Ferrari and Papaldo, p. 30
7 Enggass, *Baciccio*, pp. 25, 141
8 Lavagnino, *Altari*, p. 89
9 Rodino, p. 60
10 Montagu, *Gold*, p. 47
11 Lilli, p. 79
12 J. K. and R. H. Westin, *Carlo Maratti and his Contemporaries. Figurative drawings of the Roman Baroque*, Pennsylvania State University, 1975, p. 67
13 W
14 R. Santucci, *AI*, 59, 1974, p. 352
15 Titi, p. 298
16 W
17 Gloton, pl. LII
18 M. B. Guerrieri Borsoi, *AV*, XXII/1, 1983,

p. 11; V. Casale, *PA*, 389, 1982, p. 33; Guerrieri Borsoi, loc. cit., p. 21
19 Bissell, p. 73; Ferrari and Papaldo, p. 31
20 *Disegni di Tommaso Minardi*, II, Galleria Nazionale d'Arte Moderna, Rome, 1982, p. 200

S. Andrea della Valle

Bibliography: Falda, *Nuovo teatro*, I, pl. 25; Titi, 1763, pp. 136, 467; Venuti, p. 261; Nibby, p. 86; Angeli, p. 39; de' Rossi, *Prospectus*, pls. 41-44; de' Rossi, *Architettura Civile*, III, p. 38; De Brosses, II, p. 115; F. Fassolo, *Pall.*, 1, 1951, p. 34; *Tesori d'arte cristiana*, vol. 5, p. 113; Hibbard, *Maderno*, p. 146; S. Ortolani, *CdR*, 4; K. Schwager, *RJK*, XV, 1975, p. 122; Buchowiecki, I, p. 349; *GR*, VIII, p. 72; Magnuson, I, p. 147; *Organi*, p. 60; *Roma Sacra*, 10, 1997, p. 19; Schlimme, p. 198; A. Costamagna, D. Ferrara and C. Grili, *La chiesa di S. Andrea della Valle. I Committenti, I documenti, le opera*, Milan, 2000

1 *Rainaldi*, p. 243
2 Noehles, *Fasolo*, p. 175
3 Montagu, *Roman*, p. 92; Ferrari and Papaldo, pp. 32-34
4 de' Rossi, *Altari*, pls. 38, 39; Magni, I, pl. 22; Donati, figs. 382-87, 392, 393; Ferrari, *La Tomba*, pl. CLXXVIII; P. Cavazzini, *BM*, CXLI, 1999, p. 401
5 de' Rossi, *Altari*, pls. 6, 7; Magni, I, pl. 25; M. Adrower, *RD*, 36, 1980, p. 81
6 Sisto V, p. 556
7 *Diario di Roma*, No. 16, 1819
8 *Diario di Roma*, No. 95, 1825; Stringa, p. 85
9 W
10 Cecchelli, p. 168
11 Mola, p. 91
12 Hibbard, pl. 37a
13 W; Preti, 22; J. Clifton and J. T. Spike, *SdA*, 1989, 65, p. 48
14 Ferrari and Papaldo, p. 38
15 Spear, p. 242; *Domenichino*, p. 284
16 B. Buscaroli Fabbri, *Carlo Cignani*, Padua, 1991, p. 113
17 Schleier, p. 117; Bernini, p. 70
18 N. Turner, *SdA*, 12, 1971, p. 297; A. Blunt, *AH*, I, 1978, p. 73
19 Venuti, p. 264

20 *Tesori d'arte*, p. 158; *Roma, la città degli anni santi*, p. 346
21 Tosini, p. 325
22 O. Michel, *RD*, 1972, p. 225; Chracas, II, No. 8208
23 Bacchi, fig. 469, p. 811; Ferrari and Papaldo, p. 39
24 *Giornale di Roma*, No. 285, 1869, Dec. 15
25 Tosini, p. 330
26 Lilli, p. 142
27 Martinelli, p. 19; *Marmorari*, p. 23
28 Abromson, p. 221; Chiappini di Sorio, p. 113
29 J. Varriano, *PA*, 465, 1988, p. 31; Kunze, p. 155
30 Baglione, p. 178
31 Martinelli, p. 19
32 I. Lavin, *AB*, LII, 1968, p. 223; Mochi, p. 67; Ferrari and Papaldo, pp. 40-43
33 Cantelli; Nissman, p. 304
34 *Pietro Bernini*, p. 48
35 *Marmorari*, p. 33
36 Montagu, *Giorgetti*, p. 290
37 Ferrari and Papaldo, p. 42
38 Nissman, p. 304
39 D. di Castro, *ABA*, 43-47, 1993, p. 150; Ferrari and Papaldo, p. 42
40 Connors, *Oratory*, p.108

S. Andrea in via Flaminia

Bibliography: Baglione, p. 7, n. 4; Falda, *Nuovo teatro*, III, p. 37; Portoghesi, *Renaissance*, pls. 241-42; W. Lotz, *RJK*, 7, 1955, p. 37; Ackerman-Lotz, p. 12; J. Coolidge, W. Lotz et al., *La vita e le opere di Jacopo Barozzi da Vignola*, Vignola, 1974, figs. 23-33; Tesei, p. 482; Lewine, p. 120; De Tomasso, p. 186; Lombardi, p. 404; J. Vicioso, 'Il tempietto del Vignola', *BdA*, 89-90, 1995, p. 59

1 *Descritione de le chiese di Roma*, Rome, 1554
2 Hunter, p. 146

S. Andrea in Vincis (destroyed)

Bibliography: Armellini, I, p. 683; M. J. Lewine, 'The Roman Church Interior 1527-1580' (diss., Columbia University, 1960), p. 124

SS. Andrea e Bartolomeo

Bibliography: *GR*, I, I, p. 96; G.

BIBLIOGRAPHIES AND REFERENCES

Curcio, *SdA*, 32, 1978, p. 23; Buchowiecki, I, p. 366; Tesei, p. 52; Lombardi, p. 55; Pocino, p. 234

SS. Angeli Custodi
(destroyed)
Bibliography: Armellini, II, p. 1246; G. Matthiae, 'Due chiesette romane del seicento', *Pall.*, V, 1941, p. 41

S. Angelo in Pescheria
Bibliography: Mola, p. 77; Titi, 1674, p. 96; Roisecco, 1745, I, p. 282; Venuti, p. 356; Nibby, p. 95; Buchowiecki, I, p. 384; Pinelli, No. 20; Tesei, p. 322; Lombardi, p. 241; I. Salvagni, *RSA*, 56, 1995, p. 73; I. Salvagni, *Rivista storica del Lazio*, 7, 1997, p. 91; R. Tancred, *Opus*, 1996, 5, 1996, p. 279; *Roma Sacra*, 14, 1998, p. 58; P. Pellegrineschi, 'Carlo Maratti e la direzione dei lavori nella chiesa di S. Angelo in Pescheria', in, *L'Arte per i giubilei*, p. 63

1 *Diario di Roma*, No. 78, 1808; F. Pansecchi, *Pros.*, 33-36, 1983-84, p. 327
2 Titi, p. 116
3 A. Brogi, *PA*, XLVI, 1995, p. 27; F. d'Amico, *RSA*, 13-14, 1981, p. 13
4 D. Scrase, *BM*, CXXVII, 1985, p. 89
5 *Quadri Romani*, p. 79
6 G. Falcidia, *PA*, 343, 1978, p. 24
7 Ferrari and Papaldo, p. 44

S. Anna dei Bresciani
See **SS. Faustino e Giovita**
(destroyed)

S. Anna dei Palafrenieri
Bibliography: Titi, 1763, p. 428; Baglione, p. 8, n. 16; M. Lewine, p. 141; Lotz, *Die ovalen Kirchenräume*, p. 7; A. Cecinelli, *Le chiese di Roma*, 110; J. Coolidge, W. Lotz et al., *La vita e le opere di Jacopo Barozzi da Vignola*, Vignola, 1974, figs. 86-91; De Tomasso, p. 160; *Guide del Vaticano: La città; Parte orientale*, ed. C. Pietrangeli, Rome, 1989

1 *Diario di Roma*, No. 96, 1842
2 Kowa, p. 172

SS. Annunziate
Bibliography: Baglione, *Le nove chiese*, p. 97; Lombardi, p. 422; D. Ambrosini et al., *La Chiese dell'Annunziatella in Roma e i suoi dintorni*, 1994, Rome

1 A. Negro, *BdA*, 83, 1994, p. 65
2 *Pietro da Cortona*, 237

Oratory of the SS. Annunziate (Oratory of S. Spirito in Sassia)
Bibliography: Titi, 1763, p. 29; Vasi, 1792, p. 597; Portoghesi, *Roma Barocca*, pls. 422, 433; Elling, pl. 57; Mallory, *Notizie*, Nos. 4248, 4404, 4422 and 4503; Tesei, p. 410; Lombardi, p. 305; Varagnoli, p. 81; G. Scarfone, *AR*, 25 (4-5), 1984, p. 51; *GR*, XIV, III, p. 10

SS. Annunziata a Tor de' Specchi
Bibliography: *GR*, X, I, p. 54; Buchowiecki, I, p. 706; n.a. *Ieri e oggi Francesca Romana segno dei tempi*, Rome, 1984; Lombardi, p. 226; *Roma Sacra*, 15, 1999, p. 29

1 R. Bösel, *Pros.*, 15, 1978, p. 29
2 F. Pansecchi, *BdA*, 37-38, 1986, p. 129; Cleri, p. 90
3 Titi, pp. 225, 228; Cleri, pp. 85-87
4 Cavallaro, p. 211

S. Antonio Abate
Bibliography: Angeli, p. 50; Baglione, p. 42, n. 8, p. 47, n. 24; A. C. Ward, *Rivista d'Archeologia*, 10, 1933, p. p. 71; Buchowiecki, I, p. 404; R. Enking, *CdR*, 83; Lombardi, p. 313; *Roma di Sisto V*, p. 194

1 Titi, p. 258

S. Antonio dei Portoghesi
Bibliography: Mola, p. 63; Titi, 1763, p. 398; Nibby, p. 101; Martinelli, p. 22; de' Rossi, p. 1697, p. 486; Nibby, p. 103; de' Rossi, *Architettura Civile*, III, pls. 35-37; anon., *S. Antonio dei Portoghesi*, Rome, 1931; G. R. Ansaldi, *Cap.*, IX, 1933, p. 616; Buchowiecki, I, p. 412; Longhi, p. 101; Varriano, p. 25; S. Vasco Rocca and G. Borghini eds., *S. Antonio dei Portoghesi*, Rome, 1992; Lombardi, p. 117; *Organi*, p. 62; A. Pinto Cardoso, *S. Antonio dei Portoghesi in Roma*, Rome, 1996; *Roma Sacra*, 6, 1996, p. 60

1 *Roma di Sisto V*, p. 420
2 Ferrari and Papaldo, p. 46
3 Lilli, p. 61
4 Titi, p. 385; Graf, p. 36
5 *Claude Lorrain e i pittori lorenesi*, p. 433; Titi, p. 385
6 V. Martinelli, *Comm.*, X, 1959, p. 149; Ferrari and Papaldo, p. 47
7 *Diario ordinario*, No. 262, 1803
8 W; Graf, p. 48
9 *Giovanni V*, pp. 299, 304
10 P. Ferris, 'La capella Sampajo', in, *Giovanni V*, p. 203
11 A. Schiavo, *ASRSP*, XCV, 1972, p. 143; J. Garms, *RHM*, 17, 1975, p. 187
12 Guerrieri Borsoi, p. 38
13 Chracas, II, Nos. 5505, 6153; Minor, p. 237
14 Chracas, III, No. 860; Sestieri, p. 60
15 Cavallaro p. 235
16 Russo, p. 6; Kamp, p. 115
17 Kamp, p. 115

S. Apollinare
Bibliography: Titi, 1763, p. 405; Nibby, p. 106; Vasi, *Magnificenze*, pl. 264; C. M. Mancini, *CdR*, 93; Bianchi, *Fuga*, p. 75; Pane, p. 79; Portoghesi, *Roma Barocca*, pls. 430-33; Elling, pls. 49, 52; L. Lotti, *AR*, 12 (5-6), 1971, p. 31; Buchowiecki, I, p. 417; Bösel, p. 228; Kieven, p. 64; R. Bösel and J. Garms, *RHM*, 23, 1981, p. 335; Chracas, II, Nos. 3915, 4353, 4542, 4800; Lombardi, p. 136; *Roma Sacra*, 7, 1996, p. 51

1 *Diario di Roma*, No. 20, 1827
2 Chracas, II, No. 4806
3 *Notizie del Giorno*, 25, 1828
4 Poensgen, p. 88, fig. 47
5 *Organi*, p. 23
6 Titi, p. 392
7 Titi, p. 392
8 *Tesori d'arte sacra*, No. 405
9 Bissell, p. 63
10 *Roma la città*, p. 331
11 *Giovanni V*, p. 389
12 Titi, p. 392
13 *Tesori d'arte sacra*, No. 334
14 Gaus, p. 138; Titi, p. 394
15 Clark, p. 64

S. Apollonia (destroyed)
Bibliography: Titi, 1686, p. 35; Roisecco, 1750, I, p. 181; Vasi, *Magnificenze*, pl. 154; Armellini, II, p. 852

SS. Apostoli
Bibliography: Titi, 1763, p. 318; de' Rossi, *Architettura Civile*, III, pls. 17-19; Venuti, p. 104; Chracas, I, No. 1115; Nibby, p. 108; Angeli, p. 55; Letarouilly, pl. 167, (271); Magni, I, pls. 71, 72; F. Santilli, *CdR*, 15; E. Zocca, *La basilica dei SS. Apostoli*, Rome, 1959; Buchowiecki, I, p. 638; Dunn, p. 507; L. Finocchi Ghersi, *SdA*, 73, 1991, p. 332; Racheli, p. 200; Lombardi, p. 76; *Il complesso dei SS. Apostoli*, ed. by C. Arcieri, Rome, 1992; *Roma Sacra*, 4, 1995, p. 14; *GR*, II, VII, p. 19

1. Noehles, *Fasolo*, p. 176
2. S. Rudolph, *Labyrinthos*, III/5-6, 1984, p. 54; Lilli, p. 59; *Diario ordinario*, 9, 1807; id., 77, 1807
3. Riccoboni, p. 396
4. Bacchi, p. 811
5. Enggass, *Baciccio*, pp. 100, 147
6. Enggass, *Sculpture*, pp. 85, 141; Bissell, p. 87
7. Minor, *Diario*, No. 8296; Sestieri, p. 101
8. Cavallaro, p. 184
9. Chracas, I, No. 58; V. H. Minor, *AB*, LXV, 1983, p. 485
10. Gabrielli, p. 50
11. Riccoboni, p. 395
12. Minor, p. 157
13. Donati, fig. 328
14. Kelly, p. 80; Bowron, p. 221; Sestieri, p. 135
15. Ceschi, p. 94; Priori and Tabarrini, p. 48
16. Titi, p. 307
17. Weil, p. 148
18. Boselli, p. 39, f. 140; Bacchi, fig. 681; Ferrari and Papaldo, p. 50
19. *Organi*, p. 70
20. Sciolla, p. 88
21. Cellini, p. 67
22. J. Daniels, *Sebastiano Ricci*, Hove, 1976, p. 104
23. W
24. V. Minor, *ABA*, 1978, p. 234
25. Mallory, *Notizie*, No. 5055
26. *Diario di Roma*, Nos. 75, 76, 1822; Lilli, p. 119
27. Caracciolo, p. 200; Minor, *Diario*, No. 452; Chracas, III, No. 452
28. Ceschi, p. 119
29. Riccoboni, p. 396

S. Atanasio dei Greci
Bibliography: Totti, p. 343; Baglione, p. 80; Martinelli, p. 23; Falda, *Nuovo teatro*, III, pl. 91; Titi, 1763, p. 381; de' Rossi, *Prospectus*, pl. 60; Roisecco, 1750, II, p. 148; Lewine, p. 166; *GR*, IV, III, p. 194; Longhi, p. 48; Tiberia, p. 36; D. A. Bedon, *AV*, XXII, 1983, p. 49; Tesei, p. 130; A. Di Giuseppe, *BdA*, 66, 1991, p. 82; Racheli, p. 202; Lombardi, p. 118; *Roma di Sisto V*, p. 199; *Roma Sacra*, 6, 1996, p. 28; R. Tancredi, 'La costruzione della chiesa di S. Atanasio dei Greci a Roma 1578-1583', *Pall.*, 21, 1998, p. 13

1. I. Faldi, *BdA*, XXXVIII, 1953, p. 45

S. Balbina
Bibliography: Titi, 1763, p. 73; Venuti, p. 389; Angeli, p. 60; *GR*, XXI, II, p. 110; Pinelli, No. 26; Tesei, p. 12; L. Lotti, *AR*, 13 (2-3), 1972, p. 1; C. Ferreri, *AR*, 37 (1), 1996, p. 27; Buchowiecki, I, p. 424; Macioce, p. 148; Lombardi, p. 368

1. Abromson, p. 199; A. Negro, *BdA*, 83, 1994, p. 65

Bambino Gesù
Bibliography: Titi, 1763, p. 269; Nibby, p. 119; Chracas, I, No. 2984; Matthiae, p. 19; Pane, p. 56; Bianchi, pp. 35, 77; Elling, pl. 50; Angeli, p. 60; J. Garms, *CdR*, 135; Pinelli, No. 5; Kieven, p. 47; Tesei, p. 466; P. Mancini, *AR*, 12 (4), 1971, p. 1; Buchowiecki, I, p. 431; A. L. Trabucchi, *BUSA*, 32, 1989, p. 77; De Tomasso, p. 12; Lombardi, p. 50; Spagnesi, p. 36; Racheli, p. 204; Pocino, p. 280; *GR*, I, III, p. 142

1. Titi, p. 270
2. A. Donò and A. Marino, in, *L'Architettura da Clemente XI*, p. 97
3. Titi, p. 270; M. B. Guerrieri Borsoi, *AV*, XXII, 1983, p. 11; id., *Zoboli*, p. 32

4. *Pittura in Italia: L'Ottocento*, p. 858
5. *Diario di Roma* No. 155, 1856 9 July; Cecchelli, p. 160

S. Barbara dei Librai
Bibliography: Titi, 1763, p. 101; Roisecco, 1745, I, p. 398; *Architettura minora*, II, pl. 17; Nibby, p. 120; Angeli, p. 61; G. Morelli, *La chiesa di S. Barbara de' Librai*, Rome, 1929; Buchowiecki, I, p. 433; *GR*, VI, II, p. 164; Tesei, p. 194; Racheli, p. 206; Lombardi, p. 153; *Roma Sacra*, 13, 1998, p. 44

1. Ferrari and Papaldo, p. 53
2. W
3. Titi, p. 124

S. Bartolomeo all' Isola
Bibliography: Mola, p. 81; Martinelli, p. 24; Titi, 1674, p. 61 and 1763, p. 58; Venuti, p. 363; Nibby, p. 123; Angeli, p. 63; *GR*, XII, I, p. 30; Letarouilly, pl. 163 (270); Pinelli, No. 28; Buchowiecki, I, p. 435; *Longhi*, p. 65; C. Gerlini, *AR*, 17 (5-6), 1976, p. 73; Tesei, p. 332; Lombardi, p. 251

1. F. Frisoni, *PA*, 367, 1980, p. 22; S. M. Bailey, *MD*, 37, 1999, p. 277
2. R
3. A. Giannotti, *Notizie da Palazzo Albani*, XX, 1991, p. 183; C. Witcombe, *BdA*, 76, 1992, p. 53
4. U. Hiesinger, *ABA*, 13-14, 1980, p. 78
5. F. Frisoni, *PA*, 367, 1980, p. 22

SS. Bartolomeo e Alessandro dei Bergamaschi (S. Maria della Pietà)
Bibliography: Titi, 1763, p. 355; Nibby, p. 122; Ferrari, *Lo Stucco*, pl. CXLII; U. Vichi, *SS. Bartolomeo e Alessandro*, Rome, 1965; Fasolo, *Palladio*, N.S., I, 1951, p. 186; *Via del Corso*, p. 199; Mallory, *Rococo*, pp. 144, 132; Angeli, p. 62; Buchowiecki, III, p. 97; Pinelli, No. 27; Lewine, p. 359; M. G. Gargano, *SdA*, 17, 1973, p. 85; *GR*, III, II, p. 28; Lombardi, p. 100; L. Marcucci and B. Torresi, *Pall.*, 12, 1993, p. 59; A. Capriotti, D. Frascarelli and L. Testa, *L'arciconfraternita dei Bergamaschi*, Rome, 1989; P.

Salera, 'Il complesso architettonico di S. Maria della Pietà', in, *Ospedale dei pazzi di Roma*, p. 207; L. Picchiotti, 'G. B. Contini nei disegni inediti dell' archivio di S. Maria della Pietà', in, ibid, p. 221; Racheli, p. 212; *Roma Sacra*, 2, 1995, p. 19; D. Fracarelli and L. Test, 'Alcuni documenti sulla chiesa', in, *Architettura città territorio*, p. 39.

1 *Diario di Roma*, No. 51, 1839
2 R; Titi, p. 337
3 Roli, p. 116

S. Basilio

Bibliography: Titi, 1686, p. 305; Roisecco, 1750, II, p. 300; *GR*, II, I, p. 62; L. Lotti, *AR*, 14 (5-6), p. 14; Buchowiecki, I, p. 445; Pinelli, No. 29; Lombardi, p. 81; *Roma Sacra*, 5, 1996, p. 38

S. Bernardino ai Monti

Bibliography: Titi, 1763, p. 271; Venuti, p. 86; Nibby, p. 129; Angeli, p. 68; O. Montenovesi, *AdI*, S.II. IX, 1942, p. 79; L. Salerno, *Pala.*, S.III, IX, 1965, p. 128; Buchowiecki, I, p. 448; Lombardi, p. 60; *GR*, I, III, p. 346; Pocino, p. 153

1 Gloton, pl. XXV
2 E. Riccomini, *Il Seicento Ferrarese*, p. 53; C. Guglielmi, *BdA*, XXXIX, 1953, p. 311
3 M. G. Aurigemma, *SdA*, 80, 1994, p. 23; Möller, p. 129

S. Bernardo alle Terme

Bibliography: Titi, 1763, p. 298; Venuti, p. 73; S. Ortolani, *CdR*, 8; Pinelli, No. 30; Buchowiecki, I, p. 450; De Tomasso, p. 168; *Le scienze e le arti*, vol. I, n. n.; A. M. Affanni, M. Cogotti and R. Vodret, *S. Susanna e S. Bernardo alle Terme*, Rome, 1993; Valone, p. 138; Lombardi, p. 342; *Roma Sacra*, 17, 2000, p. 16

1 Burns, pp. 84, 163
2 W
3 Sacchi, p. 110
4 Bacchi, fig. 359; Ferrari and Papaldo, p. 57
5 Ferrari and Papaldo, p. 56
6 Geller, p. 43
7 Cavina, p. 116
8 *Giornale di Roma*, No. 224, 1857 5th Oct

9 R
10 Ferrari and Papaldo, p. 56

S. Biagio in Campitelli See S. Rita da Cascia

S. Biagio della Pagnotta

Bibliography: Vasi, *Magnificenze*, pl. 71; Titi, 1763, p. 419; Chracas, I, No. 2074; Nibby, p. 132; Angeli, p. 70; *GR*, V, IV, p. 52; Tesei, p. 174; *Via Giulia*, p. 323; M. Escobar, *LU*, LII (3-4) 1989, p. 47; G. Grillo, *AR*, 28 (5-6), 1987, p. 144; Buchowiecki, p. 457; Lombardi, p. 139; *Roma Sacra*, 11, 1997, p. 48

1 *Diario di Roma*, No. 49, 1834

SS. Biagio e Carlo ai Catinari See S. Carlo ai Catinari

SS. Biagio e Cecilia dei Materassai See Madonna del Divino Amore

S. Bibiana

Bibliography: Pollak, I, p. 22; Martinelli, p. 29; Falda, Nuovo teatro, III, pl. 23; de' Rossi, Architettura Civile, III, pl. 40; De Brosses, II, p. 319; Fagiolo dell'Arco, Bernini, cat. nos. 34, 35; Wittkower, Bernini, pp. 189; G. C. Bauer, Gian Lorenzo Bernini: The Development of an Architectural Iconography, diss., Princeton, 1974, pp. 11ff.; Briganti, pp. 167ff.; S. Vasco Rocca, *CdR*, Nuova Serie, 14; P. Zampa, *ASD*, July-Dec., 1986, p. 55; Scribner, pl. 12; Merz, p. 113ff.; Lombardi, p. 316; Marder, p. 47

1 Dombrowski, p. 301
2 *Pietro da Cortona*, p. 316
3 *Pietro da Cortona*, p. 291
4 Titi, p. 251

SS. Bonaventura e dei Lucchesi See SS. Croce e Bonaventura dei Lucchesi

S. Bonaventura al Palatino

Bibliography: Titi, 1686, p. 183; Venuti, p. 394; Pinelli, No. 31; Tesei, p. 308; Buchowiecki, I, p. 473; Lombardi, p. 227; R. Sbardella, *S.* *Leonardo da Porto Maurizio*, Rome, 1976; M. Escobar, *SdR*, 39, 1978, p. 137; *Roma Sacra*, 3, 1995, p. 36

1 *Diario di Roma*, No. 56, 1839
2 W; M. A. Pavone, *Pros.*, 1986, 46, p. 31
3 W; G. Nicodemi, *AC*, 754, 1993, p. 35; Graf, p. 40
4 Titi, p. 230
5 W
6 G. Nicodemi, *AC*, 754, 1993, p. 35
7 Titi, p. 230

S. Brigida

Bibliography: Mola, p. 63; Titi, 1764, p. 122 and 1763, p. 116; Roisecco, 1750, I, p. 622; *GR*, VII, II, p. 86; Tesei, p. 218; Buchowiecki, I, p. 485; M. A. De Angelis, *CdR*, Nuova Serie, 25; *Roma Sacra*, 12, 1998, p. 24

1 *Urbe Architectus*, p. 418
2 Gunter, p. 328
3 V. Casale, *PA*, 341, 1978, p. 64
4 Chracas, II, No. 7950

S. Caio (destroyed)

Bibliography: Baglione, p. 129; Titi, 1686, p. 268 and 1763, p. 299; Armellini, II, p. 1015; *GR*, II, 1, p. 35

S. Callisto

Bibliography: Totti, p. 62; Venuti, p. 446; Nibby, p. 140; Angeli, p. 77; G. Mano, *Relazione sui lavori di restauro della Chiesa di S. Calisto in Roma*, Rome, 1938; *GR*, XIII, II, 2°, p. 130; Pinelli, No. 34; Tesei, p. 380; Lombardi, p. 275; Kuhn-Forte, p. 269

1 Bernini, No. 161; Ferrari and Papaldo, p. 64
2 Titi, p. 68; Lo Bianco, p. 120
3 M. Pupillo, *SdA*, 85, 1995, p. 395
4 *Seicento Fiorentino*, p. 219

Cappuccini See S. Maria della Concezione

Oratorio del Caravita (S. Francesco Saverio)

Bibliography: Nibby, p. 768; Angeli, p. 78; Pollak, I, p. 243; Buchowiecki, I, p. 722; Lombardi, p. 216; M. Escobar, *SdR*, 41, 1980, p. 188; G. Scarfone

AR, 21, 1981, p. 17; *Roma Sacra*, 2, 1995, p. 35

1 Pampalone, p. 41
2 Bösel, p. 244
3 A. Lo Bianco, in, *L'arte per i papi*, vol. II, p. 115
4 Jennifer Montagu

SS. Carlo e Ambrogio al Corso

Bibliography: Titi, 1763, p. 371; de' Rossi, *Prospectus*, pls. 50-52; de' Rossi, *Architettura Civile*, III, pl. 27; Vasi, *Magnificenze*, pl. 140; G. Tonga, *Sunto storia della chiesa archiconfraternita e spedale dei santi Ambrogio e Carlo*, 1884, Rome; Nibby, p. 67; Angeli, p. 79; Letarouilly, pl. 222 (286); G. Drago and L. Salerno, *CdR*, 96; *Via del Corso*, p. 146; J. L. Varriano, *The Roman Ecclesiastical Architecture of Martino Longhi the Elder*, Ph.D. diss., University of Michigan, 1970; Buchowiecki, I, p. 312; Dunn, p. 170; De Tomasso, p. 54; Lombardi, p. 112; A. Spiriti, 'Luigi Alessandro Omodei e la riqualificazione di S. Carlo al Corso', *SdA*, 84, 1995, p. 269; *Roma Sacra*, I, 1995, p. 49; Schlimme, p. 159

1 Longhi, p. 87
2 Mallory, *Rococo*, p. 44; id., Bizzacheri, pp. 38, 45
3 Claude du Molinet, *Historia summorum pontificum*, Paris, 1679, pl. 28, No. XIII
4 Claude du Molinet, p. 148
5 Ferrari, *Lo Stucco*, pls. CXXVff.
6 Poensgen, p. 89, fig. 30
7 A. Blunt, *Kunsthistorische Forschungen. Otto Pächt zu seinem 70 Geburtstag*, Salzburg, 1972, p. 258
8 Gunter, p. 316
9 F. Petrucci, *SdA*, 96, 1999, p. 176
10 Stringa, p. 149
11 *Notizie del Giorno*, No. 49, 1845; Lilli, p. 49
12 *Imago Mariae*, p. 143
13 R. R. Villani, *PA*, 359-361, 1980, p. 60
14 R. Carloni, *BdA*, 55, 1989, p. 57
15 *L'Idea del Bello*, p. 472
16 Montagu, *Algardi*, p. 332
17 *Notizie del Giorno*, No. 28, 1831; Lilli, p. 121; González-Palacios, p. 101
18 F. d'Amico, *ABA*, 25-28, 1985, p. 90
19 Chiappini di Sorio, p. 113
20 Lilli, p. 82
21 Titi, p. 356
22 Lilli, p. 109
23 F. Petrucci, *SdA*, 96, 1999, p. 176
24 *La Pittura in Italia: Il Settecento*, p. 568
25 Cocke, p. 60, No. 55; Pier Francesco Mola, p. 169
26 F. Petrucci, *SdA*, 96, 1999, p. 176
27 Enggass, *Sculpture*, p. 200
28 F. d'Amico, *BdA*, 3, 1979, p. 79
29 G. Panofsky, *JWCI*, 56, 1993, p. 119
30 *Diario di Roma*, No. 13, 1821
31 S. Ceccarelli, *RSA*, 68, 1999, p. 81
32 *Quadri dal Silenzio*, p. 12

S. Carlo ai Catinari (SS. Biagio e Carlo ai Catinari)

Bibliography: Mola, p. 102; Titi, 1763, p. 96; Falda, *Nuovo teatro*, I, pl. 24; Martinelli, p. 31; de' Rossi, *Prospectus*, pl. 48; de' Rossi, *Architettura Civile*, III, pls. 23, 24; Vasi, *Magnificenze*, pl. 136; Magni, I, pls. 25, 28; Venuti, p. 219; L. Cacciari, *Memorie intorno alla chiesa de' SS. Biagio e Carlo*, Rome, 1861; Buchowiecki, I, p. 460; G. Delfini, *CdR*, Nuova Serie, 16; *GR*, VIII, I, p. 11; J. Connors, *RJK*, 25, 1989, p. 204; Ringbeck, p. 98; Nibby, p. 141; *Roma Sacra*, 13, 1998, p. 50

1 Gigli, p. 23
2 *Giornale di Roma*, No. 42, 1860; ibid., Nos. 257, 269, 1861
3 Preti, p. 17
4 Spear, p. 274
5 Bernini, p. 49
6 W; A. Pampalone *BdA*, 1, 1973, p. 123
7 *La pittura in Italia: L'Ottocento*, p. 434
8 T. Pickrel, *SdA*, 61, 1987, p. 237; id., *ABA*, 23-24, 1984, p. 27; id., *Gherardi*, pp. 174, 232; P. Ferraris, *SdA*, 2, 1991, p. 213; Ferrari and Papaldo, p. 58
9 Titi, p. 121; *Notizie del Giorno*, No. 46, 1841
10 Schleier, p. 220
11 M. Fagiolo dell'Arco, 'L'altare Colonna in S. Carlo', in, *Studi in Onore di Giulio Carlo Argan*, Florence, 1994, p. 218; Alessandra Anselmi, 'The high altar of S. Carlo ai Catinari, Rome', *BM*, CXXXVIII, 1996, pp. 660-67
12 Longhi, p. 118; *La Roma dei Longhi*, p. 83; Boselli, p. 61, 61v
13 Stringa, p. 124
14 Briganti, p. 268
15 Jennifer Montagu
16 Eimer, *S. Agnese*, I, pp. 407, 409
17 Montagu, *Algardi*, p. 332
18 Röttgen, p. 101
19 Papi, *Commodi*, p. 97; *Pittura barocca romana*, p. 84
20 Hunter, p. 151
21 Pepper, p. 227
22 W; Fischer, p. 144
23 Lilli, p. 123
24 Harris, *Sacchi*, p. 97
25 Stringa, p. 66
26 *Diario ordinario*, No. 276, 1803
27 Titi, p. 122; Chracas, II, No. 6672
28 A. Avagnano, *SdA*, 89, 1997, p. 100
29 Fischer, p. 182

S. Carlo al Corso
See SS. Carlo e Ambrogio al Corso

S. Carlo alle Quattro Fontane

Bibliography: Falda, *Nuovo teatro*, III, pl. 2; de' Rossi, *Architettura Civile*, I, pl. 101 and II, pls. 18-26; De Bosses, II, p. 310; Magni, I, pls. 60-62; Pollak, I, p. 36; Hempel, pp. 32ff.; L. Steinberg, *Borromini's S. Carlo alle Quattro Fontane*, New York, 1977; Portoghesi, *Borromini*, pls. 14-33, 205-13; A. Blunt, review of Portoghesi, *BM*, 1971, CXIII, p. 670; C. P. Ridolfi, *S. Carlo alle Quattro Fontane*, Rome, n.d.; Blunt, *Borromini*, p. 52; *Tesori d'arte cristiana*, vol. 5, p. 169; J. Connors, in, *Macmillan Encyclopedia of Architects*, ed. A. L. Placzek, vol. I, New York, 1982; Pocino, p. 183; *Roma Sacra*, 16, 1999, p. 51; M. Kahn-Rossi and M. Franciolli, eds., *Il giovane Borromini: Dagli esordi a S. Carlo alle Quattro Fontane*, Milan, 1999; *Borromini e l'universo barocco*, p. 106

1 Albertina 171, 173, 175, 186; Portoghesi, figs VIII, IX, X, XII
2 Westin, p. 201
3 *Notizie del Giorno*, No. 41, 1867
4 W

5 L. Barroero, *Pros.*, 33-36, 1983-84, p. 334
6 E. Borea, *Pros.*, 12, 1978, p. 4
7 Nicolson, p. 25; Papi, *Borgianni*, p. 125

S. Caterina dei Funari
Bibliography: de' Rossi, *Prospectus*, pl. 67; Martinelli, p. 35; Nibby, p. 148; Angeli, p. 82; G. Giovannoni, *Saggi sulla architettura del Rinascimento*, 2nd ed. Milan, 1935, p. 179; Buchowiecki, I, p. 502; Kummer, p. 80; Pinelli, No. 36; Lewine, p. 178; B. Sabatine, *The Church of Santa Caterina dei Funari and the Vergini Miserabili of Rome*, diss., University of California, 1992; Lombardi, p. 242; Evers, p. 131; B. Fedeli, 'Madri "gravate di figli inhutili" poverissime di robbe et d'honore: I prima cento anni del Conservatorio delle vergini miserabili di S. Caterina dei Funari', in, *Ospedale dei pazzi di Roma*, p. 317; *Roma Sacra*, 14, 1998, p. 27; Luchinat, vol. II, p. 43; L. Lazar, 'E faucibus daemonis', in, *Confraternites and the Visual Arts*, p. 259; L. Smith Bross, 'She is among all virgins the queen', in, ibid., p. 280

1 Posner, pp. 46, 47; *The Age of Correggio and Carracci*, exhibition cat., Washington, 1986, p. 289; *L'Idea del Bello*, II, p. 206
2 *L'Immagine di San Francesco*, p. 52, fig. 18; M. J. Lewine, *AB*, XLVII, 1965, p. 199; Di Giammaria, p. 137; Luchinat gives all the arch paintings to Zuccaro
3 A. Melograni, *SdA*, 67, 1989, p. 219
4 Russo, p. 13; Kamp, p. 116; Evers, p. 157

S. Caterina della Rota
Bibliography: Titi, 1763, p. 118; Chracas, I, No. 2032; Vasi, *Magnificenze*, pl. 111; Venuti, p. 237; Tesei, p. 9; Angeli, p. 83; Buchowiecki, I, p. 508; Nibby, p. 150; *Via Giulia*, p. 444; Wasserman, p. 49; Elling, pl. 42; *GR*, VIII, II, p. 46; Pinelli, No. 38; Tesei, p. 216; G. Marincola-Mauro, *AR*, 15 (5-6), 1974, p. 53; Lombardi, p. 167; *Roma Sacra*, 12, 1998, p. 38

1 J. A. Gere, *BM*, CVIII, 1966, p. 417; di Giammaria, p. 130
2 B. F. Davidson, *AB*, XLVI, 1964, p. 550
3 Nicolson, p. 109

S. Caterina da Siena
Bibliography: Portoghesi, *Roma Barocca*, pl. 424; G. Zandri, *Comm.*, XXII, 1971, p. 241; Chracas, II, No. 7818; Minor, *Diario*, Nos. 8208, 96; Nibby, p. 153; Angeli, p. 84; *Via Giulia*, p. 415; *GR*, VII, III, p. 36; G. Borghini, *SdA*, 52, 1984, p. 205; *L'arte degli anni santi*, p. 459; Tesei, p. 212; Buchowiecki, I, p. 510; Lombardi, p. 168; *Roma Sacra*, 12, 1998, p. 8

1 R
2 R
3 R
4 R
5 Faldi, p. 363; *Domenico Corvi*, p. 128
6 S. P. Guicciardi, *ABA*, 35-38, 1990, p. 59
7 Bianchi and Giunta, p. 450 but see Riedel, p. 28, n. 83
8 A. Negro, *PA*, 477, 1989, p. 107
9 A. M. Petrioli, *PA*, 177, 1964, p. 48

S. Caterina da Siena a Magnanapoli
Bibliography: Totti, p. 498; Mola, p. 94; Falda, *Nuovo teatro*, I, pl. 12 and III, pl. 16; Titi, 1674, p. 313 and 1763, p. 275; Venuti, p. 58; Nibby, p. 152; de' Rossi, *Architectura Civile*, III, pls. 8-10; Magni, I, pls. 102, 103; Lavagnino, *Altari*, pp. 29, 135; Buchowiecki, I, p. 514; Pinelli, No. 37; Dunn, p. 149; Ringbeck, p. 78; M. Bevilacqua, *S. Caterina da Siena a Magnanapoli: arte e storia di una comunità religiosa romana nell' età della Controriforma*, Rome, 1993; Valone, p. 131; M. Ricci, *Annali di architettura*, 7, 1995, p. 39; Racheli, p. 238; *Roma Sacra*, 16, 1999, p. 8; Pocino, 116

1 Hibbard, *Licenze*, p. 101
2 Ferrari and Papaldo, p. 67
3 Titi, 1686, p. 250
4 W; Poensgen, p. 90, fig. 34
5 Bowron, pp. 124, 279
6 Bianchi and Giunta, p. 502; Graf, *Passeri*, p. 69

7 Titi, p. 275; Graf, *Passeri*, p. 73
8 Bacchi, fig. 258; Ferrari and Papaldo, p. 67
9 Gradara, p. 107
10 M. Bevilacqua, in, *Carlo Marchionni*, p. 145; Montagu, *Gold*, p. 52; Chracas, III, No. 1290
11 W
12 Graf, *Passeri*, p. 71
13 Dombrowski, p. 416
14 Ehrlich, p. 82
15 Graf, *Passeri*, p. 70
16 Clark, p. 45; Graf, *Passeri*, p. 69

S. Cecilia
Bibliography: Titi, 1763, p. 53; Venuti, p. 435; Angeli, p. 86; Nibby, p. 155; Chracas, I, No. 872; Vasi, *Magnificenze*, pl. 145; G. Matthiae, *CdR*, 113; Matthiae, p. 78; Pane, p. 98; Portoghesi, *Roma Barocca*, pl. 414; *Restauri a Roma Santa Cecilia, Villa Doria Pamphili, Sant' Eusebio*, ed. L. Tubell, Rome, 1988, p. 13; Macioce, p. 128; Lombardi, p. 266; P. Vitti, *Pall.*, 12, 1993, p. 115; Kuhn-Forte, p. 279; P. Marchetti, *S. Cecilia in Trastevere: storia e restauro*, 1999, Rome

1 E. Bentivoglio, *QISA*, XVII-XIX, 1975, p. 133
2 Ferrari, *La Tomba*, pl. CIV; Hibbard, *Maderno*, p. 237
3 Ferrari and Papaldo, p. 70
4 F. Würtenberger, *RJK*, 4, 1940, p. 59
5 Sciolla, p. 91
6 Conca, p.148
7 La Regola, p. 534
8 D. Radeglia, *BdA*, 46, 1987, p. 93
9 B. W. Meijer, *BdA*, 100 (supplement), 1997, p. 117
10 Faldi, p. 207
11 Titi, p. 88; Ghezzi, p. 22
12 R; Titi, p. 86; Seta, pp. 8, 297
13 Chracas, II, No. 7950
14 M. Ceccopieri, *SdR*, 1996, p. 137
15 Lavagnino, *Altari*, pp. 19, 49; A. Nava Cellini, *PA*, 227, 1969, p. 18; M. Smith O'Neil, *ABA*, 25-26, 1985, p. 9; Pope-Hennessy, p. 532; Ferrari and Papaldo, p. 71
16 Giovanni V, p. 485; Ferrari and Papaldo, p. 72
17 Möller, p. 98
18 L. Barroero, *BdA*, 19, 1983, p. 1
19 Möller, p. 99

20 Titi, p. 88; Ghezzi, p. 47
21 A. Czére, *MD*, 1998, p. 378

SS. Celso e Giuliano

Bibliography: Venuti, p. 175; Vasi, *Magnificenze*, pl. 109; Chracas, I, No. 2906; Nibby, p. 167; G. Segui, C. Thoenes, L. Mortari, *CdR*, 88; F. Fasolo, *QISA*, 4, 1953, p. 1; Portoghesi, *Roma Barocca*, pls. 383-85; Mallory, *Rococo*, p. 136; *GR*, V, III, p. 36; Tesei, p. 168; G. Cannizzaro, *AR*, 15 (1-2), 1974, p. 56; Buchowiecki, I, p. 519; De Tomasso, p. 80; Racheli, p. 240; Lombardi, p. 137; *Roma Sacra*, 11, 1997, p. 22

1 M. G. Gargano, *SdA*, 1973, 17, p. 85
2 S. Jacob, *Zeichnungen*, No. 798
3 *Giornale di Roma*, No. 285, 1868
4 R
5 Titi, p. 406
6 Clark, *Batoni*, p. 214
7 Sestieri, p. 38
8 R
9 R
10 Titi, p. 408
11 Ferrari and Papaldo, p. 73

S. Cesareo

Bibliography: Baglione, p. 60, n. 40; Nibby, p. 167; G. Matthiae, *S. Cesareo 'de Appia'*, Rome, 1955; P. Tomassi, *San Cesareo in Palatio*, Rome, 1965; Buchowiecki, I, p. 525; Pinelli, No. 39; Tesei, p. 472; *GR*, XXI, II, p. 76; Macioce, p. 139; Lombardi, p. 369

1 *La città degli anni santi*, p. 220
2 Cavallaro, p. 220

Chiesa Nuova
See **S. Maria in Vallicella**

S. Chiara

Bibliography: Baglione, pp. 48, 309; Vasi, *Magnificenze*, pl. 156; Titi, 1763, p. 153; A. Eschbach, *Le séminaire pontifical français de Rome*, Rome, 1903; J. B. Frey, *Le séminaire français à Rome*, Rome, 1919; Angeli, p. 93; *GR*, IX, II, p. 16; Pinelli, No. 340; Buchowiecki, I, p. 537; Marcucci, p. 136; Lombardi, p. 208; *Roma sacra*, 8, 1996, p. 15; Priori and Tabarrini, p. 94

SS. Claudio e Andrea de' Borgognoni

Bibliography: Roisecco, 1745, II, p. 21; Titi, 1763, p. 350; Chracas, I, II, Nos. 1696, 2122, 8258; Nibby, p. 170; Angeli, p. 95; Buchowiecki, I, p. 538; Elling, pl. 45; Valesio, p. 121; De Tomasso, p. 46; *GR*, II, VI, p. 20; Lombardi, p. 80; C. Cozzolino, *Pall.*, 4, 1989, p. 77; *Roma sacra*, 5, 1996, p. 6

1 H. Hager, 'Il Modelle di L. Rusconi Sassi del Concorso per la facciata di S. Giovanni in Laterano', *Comm.*, XXII, 1971, p. 50, and fig. 9
2 Clark, p. 66; R
3 Titi, p. 334; Negro, p. 206
4 Titi, p. 334
5 Sestieri, p. 20

S. Clemente

Bibliography: Titi, 1763, p. 231; Nibby, p. 170; L. Nolan, *The basilica of S. Clemente in Rome*, Rome, 1910; Letarouilly, pls. 247-49 (303-05); C. Cecchelli, *CdR*, 24/25; Buchowiecki, I, p. 541; U. Vichi, *AR*, 17, (1-2), 1976, p. 83; *GR*, I, II, p. 5; Johns, *Papal Art*, p. 94; Pocino, p. 213

1 Elling, pl. 31
2 J. Gilmartin, *BM*, CXVI, 1974, p. 305
3 R
4 Croke, p. 435
5 Conca, p. 106
6 R
7 F. Caglioti, *FKIF*, XLI, 1997, p. 213
8 R
9 M. Bradshaw-Nishi, *Masolino's Saint Catherine chapel in San Clemente, Rome: style, iconography, patron, and date*, diss., Indiana University, 1984
10 R; Conca, p. 102
11 A. Vannugli, *Pros.*, 75-76, 1994, p. 161

S. Cosimato (SS. Cosma e Damiano in Mica Aurea)

Bibliography: *GR*, XIII, IV, p. 64; p. 276; Kuhn Forte, p. 347; J. Barclay Lloyd and K. Bull Simonsen Einaudi, *Ss. Cosma e Damiano in Mica Aureas*, Rome, 1998

1 Pampalone, p. 76
2 Titi, p. 118; *GR*, XIII, V, p. 34; G. di Domenico Cortese, *Palatino*, XII (4), 1968, p. 394

SS. Cosma e Damiano

Bibliography: Pollak, I, p. 116; Totti, p. 427; Nibby, p. 182; Martinelli, p. 39; Mola, p. 103; Angeli, p. 103; Venuti, p. 354; G. Matthiae, *CdR*, 59; P. Chioccioni, *La basilica e il convento dei Santi Cosma e Damiano in Roma*, Rome, 1963; Pinelli, No. 45; Buchowiecki, I, p. 586; Lombardi, p. 221

1 Ferrari and Papaldo, p. 74
2 Verena Fischer Pace, p. 139
3 Verena Fischer Pace, p. 144
4 Möller, p. 147
5 Nicolson, p. 109
6 Gere and Pouncey, p. 26
7 Di Giammaria, p. 156
8 Gere and Pouncey, p. 26
9 Dombrowski, p. 417

SS. Cosma e Damiano de' Barbieri (Gesù Nazareno)

Bibliography: Roisecco, 1745, p. 189; Nibby, p. 181; Venuti, p. 266; G. Marincola Mauro, *AR*, 11 (4-5), 1970, p.1; G. Scarfone, *AR*, 24 (1-2), 1981, p. 45; *GR*, VIII, I, p. 32; Lewine, p. 207; Pinelli, No. 44; Buchowiecki, III, p. 503; Lombardi, p. 187; *Roma Sacra*, 13, 1998, p. 59

1 Negro, p. 206

S. Crisogono

Bibliography: Martinelli, p. 40; Nibby, p. 190; Mola, p. 58; Titi, 1763, p. 56; Angeli, p. 111; Falda, *Nuovo teatro*, III, pl. 32; de' Rossi, *Architettura Civile*, II, pl. 42; Letarouilly, pl. 343 (353); Magni, I, pls. 26, 27; M. Mesnard, *La basilique de S. Chrysogone à Rome*, 1935, Rome; J. Mandl, *Die Kirche des Hl. Chrysogonus in Rom*, Graz, n.d.; B. M. Apollonj Ghetti, *CdR*, 92; *GR*, XIII, II, p. 184; Tesei, p. 384; Ringbeck, p. 35; Lombardi, p. 270; R. Luciani and S. Settecasi, *S. Crisogono*, Rome, 1996; Kuhn-Forte, p. 365; Hill, pp. 108, 211

1 Salerno, p. 169
2 Cantelli
3 D. d'Amico, *RSA*, 22, 1984, p.

BIBLIOGRAPHIES AND REFERENCES

71
4 Titi, 1686, p. 461
5 de' Rossi, *Architettura Civile*, II, pls. 13, 14
6 Fagiolo dell'Arco, *Bernini*, cat. no. 243
7 Ferrari and Papaldo, p. 75
8 Fischer, p. 181
9 *Giornale di Roma*, No. 92, 1863, 24th April
10 Chracas, II, No. 6690; C. H. Minor, *Apollo*, CXIII/224, 1988, p. 44

S. Croce in Gerusalemme

Bibliography: Baglione, *Le nove chiese*, p. 141; Titi, 1763, p. 223; Venuti, p. 21; Chracas, II, Nos. 3783, 4017, 4092, 4146, 4236; Vasi, 1753, III, p. XIX and 1777, p. 207; Magni, I, pl. 101; Nibby, p. 194; S. Ortolani, *CdR*, 106; Portoghesi, *Roma Barocca*, pls. 409, 410, 415-20; Mallory, *Rococo*, p. 155; S. Negro, *Nuovo album romano*, Rome, 1964, pl. 160; Buchowiecki, I, p. 603; E. A. Plummer, *The Eighteenth-Century Rebuilding of S. Croce in Gerusalemme*, Rome, diss., University of Michigan, 1983; Lombardi, p. 314; C. Varagnoli, *S. Croce in Gerusalemme. La basilica restaurato e l'architttura del Settecento romano*, Rome, 1995; A. M. Affanni, *La basilica di S. Croce in Geru- salemme a Roma: quando l'antico è futuro*, Viterbo, 1997

1 E. Plummer, *JSAH*, XLIII, 1984, p. 356
2 Chracas, II, No. 4185; V. H. Minor, *Source*, 11/4, 1983, p. 21
3 Matthiesen, 1987, p. 150; S. Vasco, in, *Corrado Giaquinto (1703-1766)*, ed. P. Amato, Mezzana, 1985, p. 97; Gabrielli, p. 43
4 W
5 *Bernardino Mei*, p. 97
6 Cavallaro, p. 263; M. J. Gill, *SdA*, 83, 1995, p. 28
7 Chracas, II, No. 5433; S. Vasco, op. cit.
8 Boucher, p. 326
9 *Roma di Sisto V*, p. 201; Macioce, p. 140
10 L. dal Prà, *Iconografia di S. Bernardo di Clairvaux in Italia*, vol. II, 1991, Rome, p. 237
11 Bacchi, fig. 433; Ferrari and Papaldo, p. 77
12 W
13 W; Graf, *Passeri*, p. 43
14 Gaus, p. 140

SS. Croce e Bonaventura dei Lucchesi

Bibliography: Pollak, I, p. 124; Titi, 1763, p. 312; *Le scienze e le arti*, vol. II, n.n.; Nibby, p. 206; Venuti, p. 102; Angeli, p. 75; U. Vichi, *Santa Croce de' Lucchesi*, Rome, 1964; Elling, pl. 27; *GR*, II, II, 2°, p. 116; G. Marchesi, *Cenni sulla chiesa del SS. Crocefisso e di S. Bonaventura de' Lucchesi*, Rome, 1863; Menichella, p. 81; Buchowiecki, I, p. 625; Dunn, p. 236; Tesei, p. 78; Lombardi, p. 82; *Roma Sacra*, 4, 1995, p. 42

1 Barry, n. 203
2 *Giornale di Roma*, No. 100, 1863, 4th May
3 Ferrari and Papaldo, p. 76
4 W; Titi, p. 305; Ferrari and Papaldo, p. 76
5 R
6 R
7 Chracas, II, No. 4431
8 R. de Gennaro, *Pros.*, 43, 1985, p. 26
9 Lilli, p. 137
10 Lilli, pp. 122, 151

S. Croce alla Lungara (S. Croce delle Scalette)

Bibliography: Baglione, p. 181; Titi, 1686, p. 27; Nibby, p. 207; Angeli, p. 117; *GR*, XIII, I, p. 56; Pinelli, No. 46; Tesei, p. 360; Lombardi, p. 277

Oratorio del SS. Crocifisso

Bibliography: J. von Henneberg, *AB*, LII, 1970, p. 157; id., L'Oratorio dell' Arciconfraternita del Santissimo Crocifisso di San Marcello, Rome, 1974; Lewine, p. 210; Tesei, p. 82; Buchowiecki, I, p. 630; Robertson, p. 176; P. Mancini and G. Scarfone, *L'Oratorio del SS. Crocifisso*, Rome, 1983; *Roma Sacra*, 4, 1995, p. 32

1 Lewine, p. 212

S. Dionigi alle Quattro Fontane (destroyed)

Bibliography: G. Matthiae, 'Due chiesette romane del seicento', *Pall.*, V, 1941, p. 39

SS. Domenico e Sisto

Bibliography: Mola, p. 119; Venuti, p. 57; Angeli, p. 125; Falda, *Nuovo teatro*, I, pl. 12 and III, pl. 15; Tessin, p. 162; de' Rossi, *Architettura Civile*, III, pls. 5-7; Vasi, *Magnificenze*, pl. 149; Magni, I, pl. 40; Pollak, I, p. 125; Wittkower, *Art and Architecture*, Vol. II, p. 107, note 25; B. R. Ontini, *La chiesa di S. Domenico in Roma*, Rome, 1952; D'Onofrio, *Scalinate*, p. 259; V. Bernardini and G. Verdesi, *BdA*, 50-51, 1988, p. 123; Pinelli, No. 48; Buchowiecki, I, p. 668; Dunn, p. 119; V. Bernardini, A. Draghi and G. Verdesi, SS. Domenico e Sisto, *CdR*, Nuova Serie, 26; C. M. McOmber, 'Recovering Female Agency: Roman Patronage and the Dominican Convent of SS. Domenico e Sisto', diss., University of Iowa, 1997; Racheli, p. 258; Pocino, p. 21; *Roma Sacra*, 16, 1999, p. 15; Schlimme, p. 217

1 Ferrari and Papaldo, p. 78
2 Gloton, p. 92, pl. LII-LV; Stagni, pp. 81, 175ff.
3 Lavagnino, *Altari*, p. 99
4 de' Rossi, *Altari*, pl. 20; Wittkower, *Bernini*, p. 223; Borsi, p. 34; Ferrari and Papaldo, p. 79
5 Westin, p. 137
6 Cocke, p. 60, No. 56; *Pier Francesco Mola*, p. 154
7 *Bernini*, cat. no. 87
8 Stagni, loc. cit.
9 W; Fischer Pace, *Baldini*
10 Fischer Pace, *Baldini*
11 L. Motori, *AI*, 50, 1972, p. 305; *Bernini*, p. 126

Domine Quo Vadis (S. Maria in Palmis)

Bibliography: Venuti, p. 385; Nibby, p. 453; Pollak, p. 126; G. B. Lugari, *NBAC*, VII, 1901, p. 5; Angeli, p. 367; Orbaan, I, p. 126; Pinelli, No. 6; Tesei, p. 500; Lombardi, p. 420

S. Dorotea

Bibliography: Venuti, p. 426; Nibby, p. 210; Angeli, p. 126; Chracas, II, Nos. 5139, 6120; Portoghesi, *Roma Barocca*, p. 401; J. Zänker, *Arch.*, IV, 1974, p. 165; Elling, pl. 51; G. Marincola-Mauro, *AR*, 14 (1-4), 1973, p. 13; *GR*, XIII, I, p. 94; De Tomasso, p.

148; Lombardi, p. 279; Kuhn-Forte, p. 413

1 R
2 R
3 Chracas, II, No. 7206; R
4 Titi, p. 58
5 Titi, p. 58
6 Chracas, II, No. 6690
7 R; E. Borsellino, *BdA*, 10, 1981, p. 49

S. Egidio (S. Maria del Carmelo)

Bibliography: Venuti, p. 451; Nibby, p. 211; Angeli, p. 127; Totti, p. 70; de' Rossi, *Prospectus*, pl. 69; Titi, 1674, p. 47; Roisecco, 1750, I, p. 173; Vasi, *Magnificenze*, pl. 147; G. d' Arrigo, *SdR*, 30, 1969, p. 119; *GR*, XIII, II, p. 54; Tesei, p. 368; Lombardi, p. 278; Kuhn-Forte, p. 425

1 Braham and Hager, p. 97; Ferrari and Papaldo, p. 81
2 Harris, *Camassei*, p. 49
3 Chiappini di Sorio, p. 114

S. Eligio dei Ferrari

Bibliography: Titi, 1763, p. 82; Nibby, p. 212; Venuti, p. 402; Angeli, p. 128; E. Venier, G. Zandri and C. de Vita, *CdR*, 127; *GR*, XII, I, p. 86; Buchowiecki, I, p. 677; Tesei, p. 336; Lombardi, p. 256; Lewine, p. 219; *Roma di Sisto V*, p. 204; n.a., *L'Arciconfraternita di S. Eligio de' Ferrari e la sua chiesa di S. Eligio in Roma*, Rome, 1998

1 P. Anderson, *Panth.*, LVII, 1999, p. 90
2 Lewine, p. 219
3 Hunter, p. 149
4 Clark, *Batoni*, p. 244

S. Eligio degli Orefici

Bibliography: Titi, 1763, p. 464; Portoghesi, *Renaissance*, pls. 46-47; C. L. Frommel, *Stil und Überlieferung. Akten des 17ten Kongresses für Kunstgeschichte*, Bonn, 1967; *Via Giulia*, p. 431; D. De Simoni, *S. Eligio degli Orefici*, Rome, 1984; Buchowiecki, I, p. 680; Lewine, p. 219; *I luoghi di Raffaello a Roma*, ed. L. Cassanelli and S. Rossi, Rome, 1983, p. 157; G. Delfini and R. Pentrella, in, *Fabriche romane del primo '500 cinque secoli di restauri*, Rome, 1984, p. 357; S. Valtieri, 'L'originario impianto a croce non iscritta di S. Eligio degli Orefici', in, *Raffaello a Roma*, ed. C. L. Frommel and M. Winner, Rome, 1986, p. 323; Racheli, p. 260; Lombardi, p. 169; *Roma Sacra*, 11, 1978, p. 59; S. Valtieri, *ASD*, 2, 1985, p. 71

1 W
2 P. Leone de Castris, *BdA*, 84-85, 1994, p. 71
3 W
4 Tosini, p. 307

S. Eligio dei Sellari (destroyed)

Bibliography: Armellini, II, p. 838; *Architettura minora*, I, pl. 46

S. Eufemia (destroyed)

Bibliography: Vasi, *Magnificenze*, pl. 142; Titi, 1763, pp. 233, 476; Armellini, I, pp. 206, 211

S. Eusebio

Bibliography: Venuti, p. 26; Vasi, *Magnificenze*, pl. 142; Titi, 1763, p. 227; Angeli, p. 132; Armellini, I, pp. 206, 211; Chracas, II, No. 6771; Nibby, p. 214; E. Iezzi, *La chiesa di S. Eusebio all'Esquilino*, Rome, 1977; *GR*, XV, p. 106; Buchowiecki, I, p. 685; *Restauri a Roma: Santa Cecilia, Villa Doria Pamphili, Sant' Eusebio*, ed. L. Tubello, Rome, 1988, p. 133; Pinelli, No. 51; G. Fusciello, *Pall.*, 13, 1994, p. 57; Lombardi, p. 317

1 Voss, p. 651; Poensgen, p. 93, fig. 48
2 Gere and Pouncey, p. 160
3 Martinelli, p. 44
4 Titi, p. 251

S. Eustachio

Bibliography: Titi, 1763, p. 151; Venuti, p. 250; Angeli, p. 130; Chracas, I, II, Nos. 959, 989, 1990, 3492; Nibby, p. 25; Vasi, *Magnificenze*, pl. 113; C. Appetiti, *CdR*, 82; *GR*, VII, IV, p. 24; Buchowiecki, I, p. 692; Pinelli, No. 52; Lombardi, p. 188; C. Varagnoli, *Quaderni del Dipartimento Patrimonio Architettonico e Urbanistico Storia cultura progetto*, 3, 1992, p. 51; C. Ciafrone and S. Ventura, *RSA*, 52, 1994, p. 87; G. Sacchi, *RSA*, 52, 1994, p. 88; *Roma Sacra*, 8, 1996, p. 19

1 Del Bufalo, p. 96
2 del Bufalo, p. 96
3 Lilli, p. 47
4 *Organi*, p. 72
5 JM
6 *Pittura in Italia: L' Ottocento*, p. 837
7 Dombrowski, p. 423
8 *Notizie del Giorno*, 23, 1826
9 Guerrieri Borsoi, *Zoboli*, p. 23
10 R; *Roma città degli anni santi*, p. 331
11 M. B. Guerrieri Borsoi, *Zoboli*, p. 23
12 Minor, *Diario*, No. 8272
13 Natoli and Scarpati, p. 14
14 Titi, p. 170; E. Russo de Caro, *SdR*, 1999, 60, 497
15 W

SS. Faustino e Giovita (S. Anna dei Bresciani) (destroyed)

Bibliography: Coudenhove-Erthal, p. 21 and pl. 3; H. Hager, 'Le Facciate di SS. Faustino e Giovita e di S. Biagio in Campitelli a Roma', *Comm.*, XXIII, 1972, p. 261; Tafuri, *Via Giulia*, pp. 233, 530; M. Myers, *Architectural and Ornament Drawings* (Metropolitan Museum), New York, 1975, p. 24

S. Filippo Neri

Bibliography: Venuti, p. 233; Angeli, p. 135; *Architettura minora*, I, pl. 29; Rotili, p. 54; L. dell'Olio, *Della chiese di S. Filippo Neri nella via Giulia*, Rome, 1854; V. Fasole, *La chiesa di S. Filippino in via Giulia*, Rome, 1943; G. Lizzari, *LU*, XXVI, 1963, p. 1; G. Matteocci, *AR*, 31, p. 220; *GR*, VII, III, p. 16; *Giornale di Roma*, No. 146, 1854; Buchowiecki, I, p. 705; Elling, pl. 41; Lombardi, p. 170; *Roma Sacra*, 11, 1997, p. 54; *In Urbe*, p. 367; F. Ferri, 'La fabbrica all'Arco dei Banchi: un opera dellí architetti, Giovanni Francesco Fiori', in, *Roma borghese*, p. 77; E. Russo de Caro, *SdR*, 60, 1999, p. 497; I. Pagani, 'La chiesa di S. Filippo Neri' in, *L'Arte per i giubilei*, p. 257

S. Filippo Neri, Oratory of

See **S. Maria in Vallicella**

BIBLIOGRAPHIES AND REFERENCES

S. Francesca Romana (S. Maria Nova)
Bibliography: Mola, pp. 87, 110; Tesei, p. 204; Venuti, p. 2; Nibby, p. 763; Angeli, p. 136; Falda, *Nuovo teatro*, III, pl. 9; De Brosses, II, p. 232; Magni, I, pl. 12; P. Lugano, *CdR*, 1; Buchowiecki, III, p. 33; Pinelli, No. 53; Tesei, p. 300; Lombardi, p. 224; *Roma Sacra*, 3, 1995, p. 40

1 G. Tancioni, 'Intorno a quattro disegni di Francesco Ferrari', in, *L'Architettura da Clement XI*, p. 33
2 Sestieri, p. 161
3 Pepper, p. 224
4 de' Rossi, *Altari*, pl. 29
5 Gigli, p. 179
6 *Giornale di Roma*, No. 33, 1866, 10th Feb
7 *Giornale di Roma*, No. 127, 1869, 10th June
8 Bacchi, fig. 368; Ferrari and Papaldo, p. 84
9 Wittkower, *Bernini*, p. 213; Fagiolo dell'Arco, cat. no. 124; Lavin, *Bernini*, pp. 58, 185; Borsi, p. 312; Marder, p. 104
10 W
11 *Roma di Sisto V*, p. 413
12 Sestieri, p. 150
13 Subleyras, p. 287
14 W
15 W
16 *L'arte degli anni santi*, p. 383
17 Gloton, p. 160, note 1, plate LIX
18 R
19 Sestieri, p. 172
20 *L'arte degli anni santi*, p. 419
21 W's attribution, but rejected by Stagni, p. 227

S. Francesco d'Assisi a Monte Mario
Bibliography: L. Pallottino, *Pala.*, IV, 1960, p. 46; Elling, pl. 39b; Pinelli, No. 54; Tesei, p. 476; Lombardi, p. 452; Varagnoli, p. 80; G. Aldo Rossi, *Monte Mario*, Rome, 1996, p. 95

S. Francesco di Paola
Bibliography: Pollak, I, p. 126; Totti, p. 479; Baglione, p. 181; Titi, 1674, p. 266 and 1763, p. 476; Venuti, p. 39; Angeli, p. 138; Roisecco, 1750, II, p. 493; Nibby, p. 221; Magni, I, pl. 70 (wrongly labelled S. Vincenzo di Paola); D. Taccone Gallucci, *Monografia della chiese di S. Francesco di Paola dei Calabresi in Roma*, Rome, 1916; Ferrari, *Lo Stucco*, pl. CXXXIII; Eimer, *S. Agnese*, I, figs. 7-9; Buchowiecki, I, p. 718; Garms, No. 444; G. Cannizzaro, *AR*, 23 (1-2), 1982, p. 4; *GR*, I, II, p. 92; Tesei, p. 42; A. Valeriani, *BdA*, 82, 1993, p. 49; Racheli, p. 274; Pocino, p. 216

1 Minor, *Diario*, No. 7347
2 W
3 W; Gloton, pl. XLIV; Titi, p. 413
4 Titi, p. 414; C. Legrand, *PA*, 1992, XLIII, p. 36
5 Matthiae, p. 50; Pane, p. 115
6 Eimer, *S. Agnese*, I, p. 123 and II, fig. 261; Barry, n. 48
7 W
8 Clark, p. 100
9 Sorgiovanni, p. 86
10 Titi, p. 419
11 Titi, p. 414
12 Chracas, III, Nos. 1316, 1854; S. Papaldo, *SdA*, 30/31, 1977, p. 187

S. Francesco a Ripa
Bibliography: Venuti, p. 443; Nibby, p. 219; Angeli, p. 139; Martinelli, p. 49; B. Pesci, *CdR*, 49; A. Menichella, *San Francesco a Ripa*, Rome, 1981; *GR*, XIII, IV, p. 128; Pinelli, No. 56; Menichella, pp. 48, 79; Lombardi, p. 280; Kuhn-Forte, p. 441

1 Ferrari and Papaldo, p. 85
2 Ferrari and Papaldo, p. 85
3 Lilli, p. 167
4 Titi, p. 68
5 Ferrari and Papaldo, p. 85
6 Titi, p. 68
7 W; Graf, *Passeri*, p. 76
8 Lilli, p. 118
9 Lavagnino, *Altari*, pp. 43, 199; Portoghesi, *Roma Barocca*, pl. 366
10 J. Pinto, 'Il modello della cappella Pallavicini Rospigliosi', in, *In Urbe Architectus*, p. 50
11 R. and J. Westin, *BM*, CXVI, 1974, p. 36; A. Negro, *BdA*, 44-45, 1987, p. 157
12 R
13 Titi, p. 60
14 *In Urbe Architectus*, pp. 348, 366, 443

15 Chracas, II, No. 4551
16 Montagu, *Algardi*, p. 332
17 Lavagnino, *Altari*, pp. 27, 93; S. K. Perlove, *Bernini and the Idealization of Death: The Blessed Ludovica Albertoni and the Altieri Chapel*, 1990, University Park; Wittkower, *Bernini*, p. 257; A. Blunt, *AH*, I, 1978, p. 67; C. M. Johns, *SdA*, 50, 1984, p. 43; Careri, p. 51; Marder, p. 296; M. Beltramme, *SR*, XLVI (1-2), 1998, p. 29
18 Gloton, pl. XIII
19 *BM*, CXXIII, 1981, p. 63
20 Enggass, *Baciccio*, pp. 24, 142
21 Bacchi, fig. 372; Ferrari and Papaldo, p. 88
22 Mola, p. 87
23 Bacchi, p. 786, fig. 215; Mola, p. 87; Ferrari and Papaldo, p. 88
24 Enggass, *Ottoni*, p. 315; Bacchi, fig. 672; Ferrari and Papaldo, p. 88
25 Cheney, p. 337; Mortari, p. 107
26 Enggass, *Sculpture*, p. 97; Ferrari and Papaldo, p. 90
27 *Fiamminghi a Roma*, p. 250
28 *Imago Mariae*, pp. 130, 153; Vouet, p. 212
29 C. Klemm, *GBA*, XCIII, 1979, p. 159
30 Nicolson, p. 209; A. Lo Bianco, *RdA*, 114, 1996, p. 81

S. Francesco di Sales
See **S. Maria della Visitazione**

S. Francesco Saverio
See **Oratorio del Caravita**

S. Gallicano
Bibliography: Vasi, *Magnificenze*, pl. 174; P. de Angelis, *L'ospedale di Santa Maria e San Gallicano*, Rome, 1966; Rotili, p. 34; Portoghesi, *Roma Barocca*, p. 359; Chracas, I, No. 1433; *L'arte degli anni santi*, p. 451; G. Falcidia, *PA*, 343, 1978, p. 24; Lombardi, p. 282; A. Rocca de Amicis, *Pall.*, 10, 1992, p. 55; Kuhn-Forte, p. 491

Il Gesù (SS. Nome di Gesù)
Bibliography: Titi, 1763, p. 172; Baglione, p. 8, n. 8; id, p. 81, n. 19, 23; Venuti, p. 282; Nibby, p. 224; de'

Rossi, *Prospectus*, pls. 18-20; Tessin, p. 161; de' Rossi, *Architettura Civile*, II, pls. 2, 3; De Brosses, II, p. 108; Letarouilly, pl. 198 (282); Magni, I, pls. 73-78; P. Pecchiai, *Il Gesù di Roma*, 1952; J. Ackerman, in, Wittkower and Jaffe, *Baroque Art: The Jesuit Contribution*, p. 15; Hibbard, ibid, p. 29; C. P. Ridolfini, *Roma, Chiesa del Gesù*, Rome, 1975 (with useful plates); Buchowiecki, III, p. 416; *GR*, IX, I, p. 38; *Tesori d'arte cristiana*, vol. 5, p. 1; Bösel, p. 160; Kummer, pp. 185ff; A. Dionisi, *Il Gesù di Roma*, Rome, 1982; *Chiese dal Rinascimento*, p. 182; *Saint, Site and Sacred Strategy: Ignatius Rome and Jesuit Urbanism*, exhibition cat., ed. T. M. Lucas, Vatican City, 1990; Macioce, p. 118; Robertson, p. 181; Lombardi, p. 212; *Roma di Sisto V*, p. 168ff; *Mamorari*, p. 20; *Organi*, p. 80; A. Dionisi, *Il Gesù*, Rome, 1996; Schlimme, p. 181; G. A. Bailey, 'The Jesuits and Painting in Italy, 1550-1690', in, *Saints and Sinners*, p. 151; C. Robertson, 'Two Farnese Cardinals and the Question of Jesuit Taste', in, *The Jesuits: Cultures, Sciences, and the Arts 1540-1773*, ed. J. O'Malley et al, Toronto, 1999, p. 134

1   The plan reproduced as Michelangelo's by Pecchiai (pl. III) and others is by Nanni Lippi, and only a small scribbled variant is by Michelangelo, see Ackerman, *Michaelangelo*, II, Cat., p. 141; cf. S. Jacob, *Italienische Zeichnungen der Kunstbibliothek Berlin*, Berlin, 1972, no. 22
2   Harris, *Sacchi*, pl. 113
3   A. Blunt, *Neapolitan Baroque and Rococo Architecture*, London, 1975, p. 38
4   Haskell, in, *Baroque Art: The Jesuit Contribution*, p. 51
5   For an ingenious interpretation of the iconography of the early decoration see H. Hibbard, 'Ut picturæ sermones', in, Wittkower and Jaffe, *Baroque Art: The Jesuit Contribution*, p. 29
6   Enggass, *Baciccio*, pp. 31, 135
7   Donati, *Artisti ticinesi*, figs. 397-406
8   Weil, p. 142; Ferrari and Papaldo, pp. 93, 94
9   Dieter Graf, *Die Handzeichnungen von G. Cortese und G. B. Gaulli*, Düsseldorf, 1976, No. 241
10 La Regola, p. 506
11 Burns, p. 161
12 de' Rossi, *Altari*, pl. 47
13 W
14 Titi, p. 194; *La pittura a Genova*, p. 270, where the frescoes are dated 1673-78
15 Titi, 1686, p. 150
16 Clark, *Batoni*, p. 306; C. Johns, *GBA*, CXXXII, 1998, p. 19
17 Abromson, p. 232; Lewine, p. 260; *Fiamminghi a Roma*, p. 219; B. W. Meijer, *BdA*, 100 (supplement), 1997, p. 117
18 J. D. C. Masheck, *BM*, CXII, 1970, p. 110
19 Pozzo, *Perspectiva pictorum*, II, Rome, 1700, pl. 71
20 Jacob, *Zeichnungen*, Nos. 811ff.
21 Lilli, p. 133
22 Wittkower, *Bernini*, p. 182; *Gian Lorenzo Bernini*, p. 322; Ferrari and Papaldo, p. 94
23 Mola, p. 117
24 Lilli, p. 140
25 Titi, 1686, p. 152
26 Baglione, p. 83, n. 35; ibid, p. 40, n. 28; Lewine, p. 258
27 Montagu, *Algardi*, p. 387; *Algardi* cat., p. 104
28 Lavagnino, *Altari*, p. 169; Kerber, p. 140; M. Gargano, in, *Andrea Pozzo: Architettura e illusione*, V. De Feo, Rome, 1988, p. 77ff; *Andrea Pozzo*, p. 114ff.; E. A. Levy, 'A Canonical Work of an Uncanonical Era. Re-reading the Chapel of St Ignatius (1695-1699) in the Gesù of Rome', diss. Princeton University, 1993; Ferrari and Papaldo, p. 95
29 E. Neumann, *Panth.*, XXXV, 1977, p. 318; Montagu, *Algardi*, pp. 104, 387
30 Bissell, p. 40; *Diario ordinario*, No. 28, 1804
31 Bissell, p. 36
32 Enggass, *Sculpture*, pp. 67, 81, 107, 108, 120, 133, 153
33 Enggass, p. 153; Franz-Duhme, pp. 40, 192
34 Enggass, *Sculpture*, p. 97
35 Ferrari and Papaldo, p. 102
36 R. Enggass, *BM*, CXVI, 1974, p. 178
37 G. Pflug, *Zeitschrift für Schweizerische Archäologie und Kunstgeschichte*, XLIII/2, 1986, p. 203
38 A. Zuccari, *SdA*, 50, 1984, p. 27; B. W. Meijer, *BdA*, 100 (supplement), 1997, p. 117
39 Abromson, p. 226
40 Ferrari and Papaldo, p. 103
41 Montagu, *Algardi*, pp. 150, 424
42 Minor, p. 98
43 Ferrari and Papaldo, p. 104
44 Cocke, *Mola*, p. 59, no. 53; *Pier Francesco Mola*, p. 215
45 *Giornale di Roma*, No. 263, 1862, 18th Nov; W
46 Wittkower, *Bernini*, p. 271; *Effigies and Ecstasies*, p. 148
47 S. Pepper, *PA*, 211, 1967, p. 69; Möller, p. 107
48 E. Giffi Ponzi, *Pros.*, 50, 1987, p. 71
49 *Pietro da Cortona*, p. 447
50 P. Tacchi Venturi, *La prima casa di S. Ignazio di Loyola a Roma*, Rome, 1951; Kerber, p. 50; *Andrea Pozzo*, p. 42
51 Fasolo, p. 40
52 G. Papi, *SdA*, 62, 1988, p. 71; Papi, *Commodi*, p. 83

Gesù e Maria

Bibliography: Pollak, I, p. 130; Mola, p. 119; Titi, 1686, p. 349; Venuti, p. 155; Nibby, p. 230; de' Rossi, *Architettura Civile*, III, pls. 33, 34; de' Rossi, *Altari*, pl. 48; Magni, I, pls. 19, 35-37; Lavagnino, *Altari*, p. 149; *Via del Corso*, p. 141; Fasolo, p. 232; F. Trevisani, *SdA*, XI, 1971, p. 163; I. Barbagallo, *La chiese di Gesù e Maria in Roma. Cenni storico-artistici*, Rome, 1985; Buchowiecki, III, p. 476; Pinelli, No. 7; Tesei, p. 124; A. L. Palmer, *The Gesù e Maria on the Via del Corso: Building in Rome after the Counter-Reformation*, diss., State University of New Jersey-Brunswick, 1994; id, *Augustinian Studies*, XXVIII, 1997, p. 111; id., 'The first building campaign of the church Gesù e Maria', *Arch.*, 27, 1997, p. 1; Gunter, p. 318ff.; Angelini, p. 260; *Roma Sacra*, 1, 1995, p. 38; Schlimme, p. 146

1   Donati, figs. 427-32; Ferrari, *La Tomba*, pls. CXLIXff.
2   *Organi*, p. 82

3   Lilli, p. 129
4   de' Rossi, *Architettura Civile*, II, pl. 54
5   Chracas, III. No. 2150
6   Minor, *Diario*, No. 7500
7   Bacchi, figs. 563, 564
8   Pampalone, p. 93
9   Titi, p. 320
10 Mallory, *Bizzacheri*, pp. 35, 45; *Le statue*, p. 216; Chracas, III, Nos. 1954, 1962
11 Ceschi, I, p. 45; Valadier, p. 339
12 W
13 Titi, p. 362

S. Gesù Nazareno
See **SS. Cosma e Damiano de' Barbieri**

S. Giacomo Augusta
See **S. Giacomo degli Incurabili**

S. Giacomo degli Incurabili (S. Giacomo in Augusta)
Bibliography: Titi, 1763, p. 384; Venuti, p. 156; Falda, *Nuovo teatro*, III, pl. 26; de' Rossi, *Prospectus*, pls. 56-58; Magni, I, pl. 19; P. Pecchiai and R. U. Montini, *CdR*, 46; Salerno, *Via del Corso*, p. 128; Nibby, p. 232; M. Zocca, *La cupola di S. Giacomo in Augusta*, Rome, 1945; Lotz, p. 58; Wittkower, *Italian Baroque*, p. 24; Buchowiecki, II, p. 34; M. Heinz, 'Das Hospital S. Giacomo in Augusta', *SdA*, 41, 1981, p. 31; Benedetti and Zander, p. 531; Macioce, p. 151; De Tomasso, p. 58; Marcucci, p. 251; Lombardi, p. 120; L. Nasto, '"Qui è di Franza il dilettevol male e di S. Lazzaro la lebbra gioconda": l'arcispedale di S. Giacomo degli Incurabili', in, *Ospedale dei pazzi di Roma*, p. 365; A. Bona, Basilica parrocchiale S. Giacomo in Agusta, Rome, n.d.; *Roma Sacra*, 1, 1995, p. 44

1   Hibbard, *Licenze*, p. 106
2   Chiappini di Sorio, p. 114
3   Bissell, p. 108
4   Graf, *Passeri*, p. 109
5   Nissman, p. 322; Thomas, p. 113
6   *Marmorari*, p. 33
7   Abromson, p. 166; *Roma la città degli anni santi*, p. 220
8   *Organi*, p. 84
9   Papi, *Grammatica*, p. 121; Riedl, p. 168
10 Bacchi, fig. 244; Ferrari and Papaldo, p. 126

S. Giacomo alla Lungara (S. Giacomo in Settimiano)
Bibliography: Baglione, p. 181; Martinelli, p. 51; Titi, 1674, p. 38 and 1763, p. 33; Angeli, p. 154; Vasi, *Magnificenze*, pl. 72; Roisecco, 1750, I, p. 141; *GR*, XIII, II, p. 62; Lombardi, p. 281; Kuhn-Forte, p. 497

1   B. Kerber, *Giessener Beiträge zur Kunstgeschichte*, IV, 1979, p. 1
2   J. Montagu, 'Antonio and Gioseppe Georgetti ...', *AB*, LII, 1970, p. 282, note 29
3   Wittkower, *Bernini*, p. 210; Montagu, *Georgetti*, p. 282, n. 29; Ferrari and Papaldo, p. 127
4   A. Blunt, *AH*, I, 1978, p. 67

S. Giacomo in Settimiano
See **S. Giacomo alla Lungara**

S. Giacomo degli Spagnuoli (Nostra Signora del Sacro Cuore)
Bibliography: Venuti, p. 257; Güthlein, *Familienarchiv Spada*, p. 219; *GR*, VI, I, p. 22; F. Russo, *CdR*, 105; Buchowiecki, III, p. 485; Pinelli, No. 57; *Piazza Navona*, p. 287; Lombardi, p. 156; *Roma Sacra*, 7, 1996, p. 40

1   G. Spagnesi, *Bollettino del Centro di Studi per la Storia dell'Architettura*, 25, 1979, p. 51; Prior and Tabarrini, p. 62
2   B. F. Davidson, *BM*, CXII, 1970, p. 78; F. Sricchia Santoro, *Pros.*, 33-36, 1983-84, p. 166

SS. Gioacchino e Anna
Bibliography: Totti, p. 516; Titi, 1686, p. 269; Thieme-Becker, *s.v.*, *Maruscelli*; Tesei, p. 32; Buchowiecki, I, p. 398; Lombardi, p. 63; P. Mancini, *AR*, 23 (5-6), 1982, p. 46; *GR*, I, IV, p. 100; *Roma Sacra*, 16, 1999, p. 49

1   Titi, p. 294
2   *Giornale di Roma*, No. 232, 1862, 11th Oct

S. Gioacchino in Selci
Bibliography: Vasi, 1791, I, p. 211; Eimer, p. 115; *GR*, I, II, p. 78; Minor, *Diario*, No. 538; Buchowiecki, II, p. 48; P. Mancini, *La chiese di S. Gioacchino ai Monti*, Rome, 1979; Lombardi, p. 62

1   Chracas, III, No. 538

S. Giorgio in Velabro
Bibliography: Nibby, p. 234; A. Giannettini and C. Venanzi, *CdR*, 95; Angeli, p. 167; Buchowiecki, II, p. 49; Lombardi, p. 257

S. Giovanni Battista dei Genovesi
Bibliography: Titi, 1763, p. 53; *Architettura minore*, I, pl. 39; Angeli, p. 167; Nibby, p. 240; C. Kouma and D. Paganelli, *CdR*, Nuova Serie, 18; Tesei, p. 386; E. Carreras Amato, *AR*, 17 (5-6), 1976, p. 45; A. Manodori, *S. Giovanni Battista dei Genovesi*, Rome, 1983; Lombardi, p. 284; Kuhn-Forte, p. 509

1   Titi, p. 85
2   C. Strinati, *SdA*, 38-40, 1980, p. 319
3   Titi, p. 85
4   Chracas, II, No. 3175
5   R; Titi, p. 85; *Giovanni V*, p. 304

S. Giovanni Calabita
Bibliography: Titi, 1763, pp. 60, 457; Venuti, p. 365; Vasi, Magnificenze, pl. 173; Chracas, II, Nos. 3840, 3843; L. Huetter, R. U. Montini, CdR, 37; Angeli, p. 163; Buchowiecki, II, p. 68; *GR*, XII, I, p. 22; n. a., Vita ospedaliera, 37 (8), 1982; G. Andreotti, Il Tevere sotto il letto: quattro secoli di asssistenza a Roma nell' opera dei Fatebenefratelli, Rome, 1982; Lombardi, p. 258; G. Micheli, *L'Isola Tiberina e i Fatebenefratelli*, Milan, 1995

1   Albertina, 356, 358, 359
2   J. Varriano, *AB*, LII, 1970, p. 71
3   Gabrielli, p. 43
4   Poensgen, p. 95, fig. 45
5   Titi, p. 90; *Un'antologia*, p. 37; *Pittura barocca romana*, p. 101
6   R
7   *Pittura del Seicento: Ricerche in*

Umbria, ed. L. Borroero et al., c.1989, p. 302
8 Titi, p. 90; *Un'antologia*, p. 134
9 Titi, p. 92
10 Preti, p. 160
11 Pio, 1977, p. 153, and review by Waterhouse, *BM*, CXXII, 1980, p. 202
12 Ehrlich, p. 88

S. Giovanni Decollato

Bibliography: Venuti, p. 400; Nibby, p. 236; V. Moschini, *CdR*, 26; E. Lavagnino, *La chiese di Santo Spirito in Sassia*, Rome, 1962, p. 61; M. Hirst, *Studies in Renaissance and Baroque Art presented to Anthony Blunt on his 60th Birthday*, London, 1967, p. 34; Letarouilly, pl. 171 (273); Lewine, p. 266; Buchowiecki, II, p. 76; *GR*, XII, I, p. 96; J. S. Weisz, 'Caritas/Controriforma', in, *Crossing the Boundaries*, ed. K. Eisenbichler, Kalamazoo, 1991, p. 221; Lombardi, p. 259; *Roma di Sisto V*, p. 204ff.

1 I. Toesca, *BM*, CXVII, 1975, p. 668
2 Baglione, p. 46, n. 2
3 *Roma la città degli anni santi*, p. 346; L. Mocci, *BdA*, 96-97, 1996, p. 127
4 Corti, p. 80
5 S. M. Guida, *Pros.*, 31, 1982, p. 35
6 S. M. Guida, *Pros.*, 31, 1982, p. 35

Oratorio di S. Giovanni Decollato

Bibliography: Lewine, p. 279; M. Hirst, in, *Studies in Renaissance and Baroque Art presented to Anthony Blunt on his 60th Birthday*, London, 1967, p. 34; J. S. Weisz, *Oratory of S. Giovanni Decollato*, Michigan, 1984; J. S. Weisz, *Pittura e misericordia: The Oratory of S. Giovanni Decollato in Rome*, Ann Arbor, 1984; Cheney, p. 339; R. Keller, *Das Oratorium von San Giovanni Decollato in Rom. Ein Studie seiner Fresken*, Neuchatel, 1976, reviewed by L. W. Partridge, *AB*, 1978, LX, p. 171; *Francesco Salviati*, 23; Hall, pp. 141ff.

1 Mortari, pp. 107, 119; M. Clayton, *Apollo*, 457, 2000, p. 9
2 A. Nova, *MD*, 30, 1992, p. 83

3 *Roma di Sisto V*, p. 205

S. Giovanni dei Fiorentini

Bibliography: Titi, 1763, p. 422; Venuti, p. 178; de' Rossi, *Architettura Civile*, III, pls. 25, 26; Magni, I, pl. 100; Nibby, p. 238; A. Nava, *Archivio della Romana Deputazione di Storia Patria*, LIX, 1936, p. 337; H. Siebenhüner, *Kunstgeschichtliche Studien für Hans Kauffmann*, Berlin, 1956, p. 174; E. Rufini, *CdR*, 39; Hibbard, *Maderno*, p. 142; *Via del Corso*, p. 201; *GR*, V, IV, p. 16; Buchowiecki, II, p. 87; S. Benedetti, in, *Firenze e la Toscana dei Medici nell' Europa del' 500*, Florence, 1983, p. 959; *Chiese dal Rinascimento*, p. 150; J. Vicioso, *BdA*, 72, 1992, p. 73; M. Kersting, *S. Giovanni dei Fiorentini in Rom und die Zentralbauideen des Cinquecento*, Worms, 1994; H. Günther 'A History of the Construction of S. Giovanni dei Fiorentini', in, *The Renaissance from Brunelleschi to Michelangelo*, p. 550; S. M. Germond, *Florentine Patronage in Rome in the Church of S. Giovanni dei Fiorentini, 1593-1822*, diss., Stanford, 1995; *Roma Sacra*, 11, 1997, p. 27; D. Lorenzi, *Pall.*, 9, 1997, p. 27

1 For the interior of the dome see Gloton, pl. XXI.
2 *Le Statue*, p. 250
3 Chracas, II, No. 5280; Minor, pp. 146, 219
4 *Organi*, p. 86
5 S. Major Germond, *BM*, CXXXV, 1993, p. 754
6 Gian Lorenzo Bernini, pp. 318, 322
7 Minor, p. 181
8 Chracas, III, No. 2140
9 A. Negro, *PA*, 477, 1989, p.109
10 J. Spalding, *Santo di Tito*, New York, 1982, p. 445
11 Faranda, p. 143
12 Nissman, p. 279; Thomas, p. 45
13 Stringa, p. 57; *Notizie del Giorno*, No. 32, 1821
14 Enggass, *Sculpture*, p. 122; Ferrari and Papaldo, p. 131
15 Titi, 1763, p. 424
16 Montagu, *Algardi*, p. 425
17 Montagu, *Gold*, p. 9
18 A. Negro, *BdA*, 83, 1994, p. 65
19 Pollak, p. 131; Blunt, *Borromini*, p. 201
20 K. Noehles, *MJBK*, N.S.XX,

1969, p. 182, and *SS. Luca e Martina*, pp. 13, 29; *Effigies and Ecstasies*, p. 146; J. Connors, *Annali di architettura*, 9, 1998, p. 97; Ferrari and Papaldo, p. 132
21 Westin, p. 166; Bacchi, fig. 702
22 Titi, p. 395
23 de' Rossi, *Altari*, pls. 15, 16; de' Rossi, *Architettura civile*, II, pl. 52
24 Bacchi, fig. 456
25 Ferrari and Papaldo, p. 136
26 Bacchi, fig. 384
27 Portoghesi, *Borromini*, pls. 198-99, 200-204
28 Angelini, p. 463
29 Portoghesi, *Borromini*, pls. 200-03; for measured drawings of this chapel and the tombs see G. Perugini, *Modelli Borrominiani in S. Giovanni dei Fiorentini*, Rome, 1961-62.
30 *Fünf Architecta aus fünf Jahrhunderten*, Kunstbibliothek, Berlin, 1976, No. 22
31 S. Ostrow, *SdA*, 92, 1998, p. 27
32 Schleier, p. 140; Bernini, p. 61
33 Ferrari and Papaldo, p. 138
34 Dombrowski, p. 331; *Gian Lorenzo Bernini*, p. 331; Ferrari and Papaldo, p. 138
35 Minor, p. 143
36 Ferrari, *La Tomba*, pl. CLXXX; Chracas, II, No. 4554; Matthiae, p. 53
37 Baglione, p. 41, n. 42; *Roma di Sisto V*, p. 210
38 *Notizie del Giorno*, No. 39, 1827
39 S. P. Valenti, *PA*, 265, 1972, p. 80
40 Pio, p. 20; A. Vannugli, *SdA*, 48, 1983, p. 101
41 P. Barocchi, *AAM*, 1965, 31-32, p. 244
42 *Notizie del Giorno*, No. 3, 1828
43 S. M. Guida, *Pros.*, 31, 1982, p. 35
44 *Seicento Fiorentino*, p. 292

S. Giovanni in Laterano

Bibliography: Baglione, *Le nove chiese*, p. 113; Titi, 1763, p. 210; Martinelli, p. 60; Chracas, I, Nos. 166, 450, 2553; Venuti, p. 9; Nibby, p. 241; de' Rossi, *Architettura Civile*, I, pls. 64-70; Letarouilly, pls. 223-28 (254-58); Magni, I, pls. 92-95; S. Ortolani, *CdR*, 13; *GR*, I, I, p. 22 and XV, p. 151; Buchowiecki, I, p. 61; J. Freiberg,

BIBLIOGRAPHIES AND REFERENCES

The Lateran and Clement VIII, diss., New York University, 1988; id., *ZfK*, 54, 1991, 66; id., *The Lateran in 1600: Christian Concord in Counter-Reformation Rome*, Cambridge, 1995; Fruhan, p. 30; Magnuson, p. 35; *Chiese dal Rinascimento*, p. 232; C. Pietrangeli, *San Giovanni in Laterano*, Florence, 1990; *Marmorari*, p. 168; A. Roca de Amicis, *Pall.*, 18, 1996, p. 51. For the early history of the church: R. Krautheimer et al., *Corpus basilicarum christianarum Romæ*, Rome (Vatican), 1937-77, V, p. 1. For Borromini's restoration of the interior: Hempel, p. 91; Portoghesi, *Borromini*, pls. LVII-LXXII, 92-122; Heimbürger Ravalli, *Archivio Spada*, p. 217; Blunt, *Borromini*, p. 134; Güthlein, *Familienarchiv Spada*, pp. 206-19, 227-50; R. Echols, *JSAH*, LI, 1992, p. 146; A. Roca de Amicis, *L'opera di Borromini in S. Giovanni in Laterano; gli anni della fabbrica, 1646-1650*, Rome, 1995; A. Roca de Amicis, *Pall.*, 18, 1996, p. 51; id., *Pall.*, 20, 1997, p. 61; G. C. Argan, *Arch.*, 45, 1999, p. 251; *Borromini e l'universo barocco*, p. 208. For the designs submitted for the façade: A. Prandi, *Roma*, XXII, 1944, p. 23; A. Schiavo, *La fontana di Trevi e le altre opere di Nicola Salvi*, Rome, 1956, p. 27; E. Kieven, 'Il ruolo del disegno', in, *In Urbe Architectus*, p. 78; V. Golzio, *Miscellanea Bibliothecæ Hertzianæ*, Munich, 1961, p. 450; H. Hager, *BM*, CXVII, 1975, p. 105; id., *Comm.*, XXII, 1971, p. 36; S. Jacob, *ZfK*, XXXV, 1972, p. 100; Mallory, *Rococo*, p. 112, note 16; Volker Hoffmann, *RJK*, 17, 1978, p. 1

1 O. Brunetti, *Pall.*, 21, 1998, p. 71
2 *Le statue*, p. 251; A. Desmas, *MEFRIM*, 110, 1998, p. 755
3 A. Desmas, *MEFRIM*, 110, 1998, p. 755
4 Entries 32, 34, 37, 168; also Güthlein, *Familienarchiv Spada*, p. 216
5 Chracas, III, No. 1400
6 A. Roca de Amicis, *SR*, XLVI, (1-2), p. 91
7 Gigli, p. 278
8 Heimbürger Ravalli, *Archivio Spada*, p. 220
9 P. Anderson, *Panth.*, LVII, 1999, p. 9; see Barolsky, p. 111, for a ceiling design attributed to Daniele da Volterra
10 Chracas, III, No. 1400
11 Güthlein, pp. 238ff.
12 Güthlein, *Familienarchiv Spada*, I, p. 230
13 Entries 175, 314, 315, 345
14 Enggass, *Sculpture*, passim; Braham and Hager, p. 86; M. Conforti, *Studies in Italian Art and Architecture*, American Academy in Rome, 1980, p. 243; Johns, *Papal Art*, p. 75
15 Bissell, p. 83
16 Bissell, p. 85
17 Titi, pp. 234-36
18 Heimbürger Ravalli, *Archivio Spada*, p. 232; Westin, pp. 38, 133; Montagu, *Algardi*, p. 343; Ferrari and Papaldo, p. 141
19 A. Busiri Vici, *SdR*, 40, 1979, p. 118
20 de' Rossi, *Architettura Civile*, I, pl. 69
21 Chracas, II, No. 3888
22 B. Steindl, 'Una committenza Torlonia: la cappella Torlonia', in, *Thornvaldsen: L'Ambiente, l'influsso, il mito*, ed. P. Kragelund and M Nykjær, Rome, 1991, p. 77; id., *Mäzenatentum im Rom des 19 Jarhunderts*, Hildesheim, 1993, p. 130
23 *Notizie del Giorno*, No. 2, 1845
24 *Notizie del Giorno*, No. 37, 1845
25 K. Schwager, *RJK*, 15, 1975, p. 120
26 Hunter, p. 355
27 Diaries of Alexander VII, entries 105, 286, 309, 362; Ferrari and Papaldo, p. 146
28 Ferrari and Papaldo, p. 146
29 Visentini, *Osservazioni*, p. 6
30 W
31 Martinelli, p. 675
32 Baglione, p. 79, n. 26 and p. 8, n. 13
33 Fruhan, p. 267
34 Ferrari and Papaldo, p. 153
35 Enggass, *Sculpture*, p. 154; Ferrari and Papaldo, p. 147
36 Hempel, *Borromini*, pl. 67; de' Rossi, *Architettura Civile*, III, pls. 48, 49
37 No. 123 for 22.viii.1657
38 *Le scienze e le arti*, vol. I, n. n.
39 Martinelli, p. 64; Mola, p. 68; *Organi*, p. 44
40 *Diario ordinario*, No. 32, 1804
41 Montini, p. 210
42 J. Wilton-Ely, *Piranesi as Architect and Designer*, New York, 1993, p. 63ff.
43 F. Tamburini, *AHP*, 34, 1996, p. 245
44 Ferrari and Papaldo, p. 148
45 Montini, p. 414
46 P. Lotti, *SdR*, 1996, p. 391
47 M. C. Abromson, *AB*, LX, 1978, p. 531
48 A. Desmas, *GBA*, CXXXI, 1998, p. 235
49 Vaudo, p. 21
50 Kamp, p. 117
51 Röttgen, p. 97
52 *Roma di Sisto V*, p. 120
53 *Fiamminghi a Roma*, p. 273
54 A. Desmas, *MEFRIM*, 110, 1998, p. 755
55 Martinelli, p. 66
56 Pio, p. 108
57 Bacchi, fig. 486; Ferrari and Papaldo, p. 149
58 Titi, 1763, p. 213 lists all the artists involved in the scheme
59 Burns, p. 192
60 Benedetti, p. 77; D. Frascarelli and L. Testa, *BdA*, 70, 1992, p. 123
61 Martinelli, p. 67
62 L. Russo, 'Notizie su Guglielmo Cortese', in, *Innocenzo X*, p. 193
63 Bissell, p. 60
64 de' Rossi, *Altari*, pl. 45
65 Hibbard, *Maderno*, p. 124
66 G. A. Spagnesi, de' Rossi, p. 104; Titi, p. 244; Ferrari and Papaldo, p. 150
67 Titi, p. 244
68 Mola, p. 69; Martinelli, p. 66; *Longhi*, p. 85
69 Dombrowski, p. 335
70 F. Sricchia Santoro, *Pros.*, 1, 1975, p. 35
71 Chracas, III, No. 222
72 Ferrari, *La Tomba*, pls. CLVII-lff.; C. Filippo, *Carmelus*, XXI, 1974, p. 281; Enggass, *Sculpture*, pp. 16ff.; Titi, p. 238; Chracas, I, Nos. 2311, 2541, 2843, 2966; E. Kieven, 'Überlegungen zu Architektur und Ausstattung der Cappella Corsini', in, *L'Architettura da Clemente XI*, p. 69; Minor, p. 29
73 Pepper, p. 269
74 Minor, p. 130
75 Montagu, *Gold*, p. 143
76 R
77 *Giovanni V*, p. 459

78 JM
79 JM

The Baptistery (S. Giovanni in Fonte)
Bibliography: Baglione, *Le nove chiese*, p. 115; Nibby, pp. 262, 751; Marucci, p. 75; M. Romana, *BdA*, 70, 1992, p. 31; S. Previtero, *Opus*, 5, 1996, p. 7; Pocino, p. 219

1 Martinelli, p. 69; A. Blunt, *RJK*, 20, 1983, p. 17
2 Harris, *Sacchi*, pp. 87ff.
3 Harris, *Sacchi*, p. 84
4 Montagu, *Roman*, p. 86
5 Minor, *Diario*, No. 7326
6 Chracas, II, Nos. 6630, 6894; F. Zeri, *ABA*, 25-26, 1985, p. 56
7 Chracas, II, No. 7767; F. Zeri op. cit.
8 Bacchi, fig. 353; Ferrari and Papaldo, p. 154
9 Chracas, III, No. 536
10 Freiberg, p. 634

The Scala Santa
Bibliography: Letarouilly, pl. 57 (246); C. D'Onofrio, *Scalinate*, p. 99; M. Cempanari and T. Amodei, *CdR*, Nuova Serie, 23: G. Scavizzi, *BdA*, 45, 1960, p. 111; C. L. C. Ewart Witcombe, *JSAH*, XLIV, 1985, p. 368; id., *GBA*, CXXIX, 1987, p. 61; Zuccari, p. 103ff.; *Il Palazzo Apostolico Lateranese*, ed. Carlo Pietrangeli, Florence, 1991, p. 121ff.; *Roma di Sisto V*, p. 127; L. Donadono, *RMC*, 2, 1994, p. 249; Hall, p. 260; Pocino, p. 173; L. Donadono, *La Scala Santa a S. Giovanni in Laterano*, in press

The Triclinium of Leo III
Bibliography: Matthiae, p. 41; Pane, p. 100 and fig. 77; Chracas, II, No. 4164

S. Giovanni in Mercatello (destroyed) See SS. Venanzio e Ansovino

S. Giovanni in Oleo
Bibliography: Venuti, p. 386; Nibby, p. 270; Angeli, p. 188; Hempel, p. 182; G. Matthiae et al., *CdR*, 51; Portoghesi, *Borromini*, pls. CXXXIX, 195-96; M. L. Polidori, *Monumenti e mecenati francesi in Roma*, Viterbo, 1969, p. 59; Buchowiecki, II, p. 110; Blunt, *Borromini*, p. 198; Lombardi, p. 355

1 Hempel, op. cit., pl. 119
2 Pampalone, p. 16; *Pietro da Cortona*, p. 214

S. Giovanni della Pigna
Bibliography: Totti, p. 387; Titi, 1674, p. 165, 1686, p. 132 and 1763, p. 155; Nibby, p. 269; Angeli, p. 197; de' Rossi, 1697, p. 542; Venuti, p. 277; Buchowiecki, II, p. 113; *GR*, IX, II, p. 88; Tesei, p. 276; Lombardi, p. 214; *Roma Sacra*, 9, 1997, p. 40

1 M. B. Guerrieri Borsoi, *AV*, XXII/I, 1983, p. 11
2 M. B. Guerrieri Borsoi, 'Nicola La Piccola', in, *Alessandro Albani*, p. 141
3 W
4 Titi, p. 172

SS. Giovanni e Paolo
Bibliography: Titi, 1763, p. 76; Venuti, p. 393; Chracas, I, Nos. 1322, 1361; Nibby, p. 266; Angeli, p. 191; C. Ballerio, *Pall.*, VI, 1942, p. 81; S. dell' Addolorata, *La basilica celimontana dei SS. Giovanni e Paolo*, Rome, 1930; S. Ortolani, *CdR*, 29; A. Prandi, *CdR*, 38; C. Gerlini, *AR*, 10 (2), 1969, p. 7; B. M. Margarucci Italiani, *Il titolo di Pammachio, Santi Giovanni e Paolo*, Rome, 1967; Pinelli, No. 62; Buchowiecki, II, p. 125; Lombardi, p. 350; M. Bevilacqua, *Pall.*, 8, 1991, p. 19; *GR*, XIX, I, p. 84

1 R
2 Gradara, p. 17
3 Minor, *Diario*, No. 14
4 Titi, p. 103
5 Ricconi, p. 400
6 Voss, p. 161; Titi, p. 103
7 Lilli, p. 155
8 R
9 *Pittura in Italia: L'Ottocento*, p. 766; De Tomasso, p. 174
10 Lilli, p. 67
11 *Roma di Sisto V*, p. 212
12 *Roma, la città degli anni santi*, p. 311; Titi, p. 103
13 D. C. Miller, *BdA*, XLVIII, 1964, p. 54; Titi, p. 105
14 Conca, p. 44
15 Chracas, III, No. 1936
16 Titi, p. 105

17 R. Roli, *AAM*, 27, 1964, p. 341

SS. Giovanni e Petronio dei Bolognesi
Bibliography: Titi, 1763, p. 105; Nibby, p. 268; *Via Giulia*, p. 489; Wasserman, p. 51; *GR*, VII, III, p. 58; Pinelli, No. 63; Buchowiecki, II, p. 154; Tesei, p. 228; Lombardi, p. 170; *Roma Sacra*, 12, 1998, p. 19

1 *La Scuola di Guidi Reni*, ed. E. Negro and M. Pirondini, Modena, 1992, p. 368

S. Giovanni a Porta Latina
Bibliography: Titi, 1763, pp. 72, 460; Nibby, p. 269; Angeli, p. 199; n. a. *Il collegio missionario A. Rosmini a Roma ed il restauro dell basilica di S. Giovanni a Porta Latina*, Rome, 1951; Buchowiecki, II, p. 116; G. Matthiae et al., *CdR*, 51; *GR*, XIX, II, p. 58; Lombardi, p. 351

S. Girolamo della Carità
Bibliography: Titi, 1763, p. 116; Nibby, p. 271; Venuti, p. 237; S. Papaldo, *CdR*, 132; C. Baggio and P. Zampa, *QISA*, XXV, 1979, p. 21; Tesei, p. 214; Buchowiecki, II, p. 157; J. Variano, 'Domenico Castelli's Façade', in, *Hortus Imaginum: Essays in Western Art*, ed. R. Enggass, Lawrence, 1974, p. 139; Lombardi, p. 172; F. F. Ardizzon, *S. Girolamo della Carità. Storia, arte, spiritualità per una chiesa nel cuore di Roma*, Vatican City, 1987; *Roma Sacra*, 12, 1998, p. 33; S. Isgrò, in, *L'Arte per i giubilei*, p. 273

1 L. Ponnelle and L. Bordet, *Saint Philippe Neri*, Paris, 1928, p. 119
2 *Fasolo*, p. 175
3 Variano, p. 95; Longhi, p. 105
4 Hempel, p. 182; Lavagnino, *Altari*, p. 115; Portoghesi, *Borromini*, pls. 190-94; Montagu, *Giorgetti*, p. 279; M. Heimbürger Ravalli, *Archivio Spada*, pp. 82ff.; and *PA*, 329, 1977, p. 39; Blunt, *Borromini*, p. 207; R. Bösel, *Pros.*, 15, 1978, p. 29; Ferrari and Papaldo, p. 156
5 Titi, 1686, p. 95
6 Gere and Pouncey, p. 24

7 Titi, 1686, p. 95; Fasolo, p. 98
8 Spear, p. 175; *L'Idea del Bello*, II, p. 328
9 Ferrari and Papaldo, p. 162
10 Lavagnino, *Altari*, pl. 193; R. Preimesberger, *RHM*, X, 1966-67, p. 203; Portoghesi, *Roma Barocca*, pls. 394, 395; S. Boscarino, *Juvarra architetto*, Rome, 1973, p. 418; M. L. Myers, *Architectural and Ornamental Drawings*, exhibition cat., Metropolitan Museum, 1975, p. 33; G. Gritella, *Juvarra: L'Architettura*, vol. I, Modena, 1994, p. 104; Bissell, p. 96; G. Bissell, 'A "dialogue" between sculptor and architect', in, *The Sculpted Object 1400-1700*, ed. S. Currie and P. Motture, Aldershot, 1997, p. 12
11 *Roma di Sisto V*, p. 420
12 Titi, p. 144; Pio, p. 172
13 *Quadri Romani*, p. 43
14 R; Titi, p. 146
15 Pollak, I, p. 245; E. Longo, *Pall.*, 3 (5), 1990, p. 25
16 Gradara, p. 34
17 C. Strinati, 'Il cropo', in, *La Regola*, p. 28

S. Girolamo degli Schiavoni (S. Girolamo dei Croati)

Bibliography: Mola, p. 81; Titi, 1763, p. 396; Falda, *Nuovo teatro*, III, pl. 38; de' Rossi, *Prospectus*, p. 64; Magni, I, pl. 11; G. Koksa, *CdR*, 120/121; Longhi, p. 647; Angeli, p. 146; Pinelli, No. 64; Buchowiecki, II, p. 163; M. Caperna, 'Influssi lombardi a Roma', in, *L'Architettura a Roma*, p. 219; Lombardi, p. 122; *Chiesa Sistina, 1589-1989*, vol. I, 1989, vol. II, ed. R. Peric, Rome; *Roma di Sisto V*, p. 145; *Organi*, p. 90; *GR*, IV, VI, p. 61; M. Caperna, *Storia architettura*, 1, 1992, p. 255; *Roma Sacra*, 6, 1996, p. 43; *Giornale di Roma*, Nos. 20, 59, 60, 1853, 26th Jan., 14th and 15th March

1 *La pittura in Italia: L'Ottocento*, p. 340
2 *Andrea Lilli*, p. 43
3 Ferrari and Papaldo, p. 163
4 Titi, p. 384
5 H. Röttgen, *Panth.*, XLII, 1984, p. 320
6 Ricceboni, p. 391

7 *Roma, la città degli anni santi*, p. 322
8 Ferrari and Papaldo, p. 163
9 L. Rebecchini, *SdR*, 60, 1999, p. 453
10 Röttgen, op. cit.
11 *Andrea Lilli*, p. 43

S. Giuliano dei Fiamminghi

Bibliography: de' Rossi, 1697, p. 510; Nibby, p. 275; Angeli, p. 202; Magni, I, pl. 26; *GR*, VIII, I, p. 50; Pinelli, No. 65; Buchowiecki, II, p. 171; Tesei, p. 256; D. Bodart, 'Les fondations hospitalières', in, *Les fondations nationales*, p. 61; Lombardi, p. 191; *Roma Sacra*, 14, 1998, p. 5; J. De Brabandere, B. De Groof and J. Ickx, *1000 Jaar San Giuliano dei Fiamminghi*, Brugge, 1996. F. Barry, 'L'insediamento dei Fiamminghi a Romaí in, *Roma, le case, la città*, ed. E. Debendeti, Rome 1998

1 E. Croft-Murray, *The English Miscellany*, I, 1950, p. 221
2 Lilli, p. 154
3 Lilli, p. 91
4 R. Bösel, *Pros.*, 15, 1978, p. 29; Ferrari and Papaldo, p. 164

S. Giuseppe a Capo le Case

Bibliography: Pollak, I, p. 144; Totti, p. 304; Titi, 1674, p. 372 and 1721, pp. 341, 484; Nibby, p. 276; Venuti, p. 119; Angeli, p. 199; Racheli, p. 284; Vasi, *Magnificenze*, pl. 146; *GR*, III, III, p. 66; Buchowiecki, II, p. 177; Pinelli, No. 66; Lombardi, p. 101; C. Andretta, *AR*, 21 (5-6), p. 1; F. Trinchieri Camiz, 'Virgo non sterilis: nuns as artists in seventeenth century Rome', in, *Picturing Women in Renaissance and Baroque Italy*, ed. G. Johnson and S. F. Matthews Grieco, Cambridge, 1997, p. 139; *Roma Sacra*, 5, 1996, p. 60

1 Baglione, p. 347; Martinelli, p. 57
2 Harris, *Sacchi*, p. 100; *Pittura barocca romana*, p. 132
3 *Artisti ticinesi*, p. 326

S. Giuseppe dei Falegnami

Bibliography: Venuti, p. 350; Nibby, p. 277; Angeli, p. 200; T. Piatti, *Il carcere Mamertino. La chiesa di S. Giuseppe dei Falegnami*, Rome, 1925;

G. Zandri, *CdR*, 118; L. Lotti, *AR*, 11 (4-5), 1970, p. 32; D'Onofrio, *Scalinate*, p. 230; V. Tiberio, *Pall.*, XXI, 1971, p. 184; Buchowiecki, II, p. 179; *GR*, X, I, p. 92; Lombardi, p. 228; *Roma Sacra*, 3, 1995, p. 8

1 Ferrari and Papaldo, p. 166
2 *Organi*, p. 92
3 W
4 W; *Ghezzi*, p. 13
5 *Cesare Mariani*, p. 31
6 W
7 F. d'Amico, *Prosp.*, 15, 1978, p. 19
8 M. Pozzi, 'Riscoperta di un pittore Velletrano', in, *Lunario Romano, X, Seicento e Settecento nel Lazio*, ed. R. Lefevre, 1980, p. 111
9 Titi, p. 224; *Lo Bianco*, p. 111; *Ghezzi*, p. 125
10 Ferrari and Papaldo, p. 167
11 Normand, p. 283

S. Giuseppe alla Lungara

Bibliography: Venuti, p. 411; Chracas, I, No. 2011; D. Vizzari, *La chiesa di San Giuseppe alla Lungara*, Rome, 1966; Portoghesi, *Roma Barocca*, pls. 397, 400; *GR*, XIII, I, 32; Angeli, p. 201; E. Carreras, *AR*, 21, 1980, p. 11; Kelly, p. 152; n.a., *La chiesa di San Giuseppe alla Lungara*, Rome, 1976; Tesei, p. 356; S. Iacobini, 'Le vicende contruttive di S. Giuseppe alla Lungara', in, *L'Architettura da Clemente XI*, p. 49; Lombardi, p. 283; Kuhn-Forte, p. 535

1 C. Paul, *AB*, LXXIV, 1992, p. 297
2 M. B. Guerrieri Borsoi, *BdA*, 50-51, 1988, p. 161
3 Titi, p. 56

Oratorio del Gonfalone (See also S. Lucia del Gonfalone)

Bibliography: *Via Giulia*, p. 344; Baglione, p. 19, n. 18; *Oltre Raffaello*, p. 145; B. L. Wollesen-Wisch, *The Archiconfraternita del Gonfalone and its oratory in Rome: Art and Counter-Reformation Spirtual Values*, diss., University of California, 1985; B. Wisch, 'The Passion of Christ', in, *Crossing the Boundaries*, ed. K. Eisenbichler, Kalamazoo, 1991, p. 237;

Lombardi, p. 147; D. De Grazia, *Bertoia, Mirola and the Farnese Court*, Rome, 1991, p. 92; D. Estivell, *AC*, 758, 1993, p. 357; Hall, p. 208; *Roma Sacra*, 11, 1987, p. 42

1 Luchinat, vol. II, p. 50

S. Gregorio al Celio

Bibliography: Totti, p. 143; Titi, 1763, pp. 74, 459; Venuti, p. 391; Angeli, p. 203; Falda, *Nuovo teatro*, III, pl. 17; de' Rossi, *Prospectus*, pl. 71; Roisecco, 1750, I, p. 422; Nibby, p. 279; Letarouilly, pl. 163 (270); V. Moschini, *CdR*, 17; Magni, I, pl. 24; Tesei, p. 450; Ringbeck, p. 83; A. M. Pedrocchi, *S. Gregorio al Celio: Storia di una Abbazia*, Rome, 1993; Lombardi, p. 356; A. M. Pedrocchi, *S. Gregorio al Celio Roma*, Rome, 1995; *GR*, XIX, I, p. 108; G. Miarelli Mariani, 'Architettura fra Cinque e Seicento', in, *Dopo Sisto V*, p. 181

1 H. H. Brummer, *Konsthistorisk Tidskrift*, XLII, 1978, p. 101
2 Blunt, *The other side*, p. 65
3 Ferrari and Papaldo, p. 168
4 Dombrowski, Bolgi
5 R. Spinelli, *FM*, XXXVI, 1993, p. 329
6 *Longhi*, p. 95
7 Chracas, I, No. 1606; Poensgen, p. 98, fig. 42
8 Titi, p. 100
9 R; G. Sestieri, *SdA*, 29, 1977, p. 67
10 Clark, p. 85
11 A. Negro, *BdA*, 83, 1994, p. 65
12 A. Valeriani, *BdA*, 82, 1993, p. 49
13 Chracas, II, Nos. 2849, 3642
14 Stringa, p. 117
15 Marcucci, p. 187; M. Eichberg, *Pall.*, 13, 1994, p. 41
16 *Maderno*, p. 121
17 *Marmorari*, p. 33
18 Posner, p. 57
19 Abromson, p. 177; Macioce, p. 136
20 Titi, p. 103; G. Sestieri, *SdA*, 29, 1977, p. 67
21 Clark, *Batoni*, p. 209
22 Titi, p. 103
23 M. S. O'Neil, 'The Patronage of Baronio at San Gregorio Magno', in, *Baronio e l'arte, atti del convegno internazionale di studio*, ed. R. De Maio et al.,

Sora, 1985, p. 147; Hill, pp. 153, 203
24 Pressouyre, p. 368; Ferrari and Papaldo, p. 168
25 Spear, p. 155; *Domenichino*, p. 271
26 Pepper, p. 225
27 *Bernini*, p. 30
28 *Chiappini di Soria*, p. 115
29 Pepper, p. 224
30 Pepper, p. 223
31 Pressouyre, p. 372

S. Gregorio a Ponte Quattro Capi

Bibliography: Roisecco, 1750, I, p. 22; Chracas, I, Nos. 1660, 1897; Nibby, p. 283; Venuti, p. 366; Angeli, p. 206; Elling, pl. 43; Buchowiecki, II, p. 194; Tesei, p. 324; G. Scarfone, *AR*, 17 (1-2), 1976, p. 58; M. Carè, E. Comelli and M. Damiani, *Roma, Chiesa di S. Gregorio a Ponte quattro capi*, Rome, 1990; Lombardi, p. 243; *Roma Sacra*, 14, 1998, p. 55

1 R

S. Ignazio

Bibliography: Titi, p. 675; Venuti, p. 269; Pollak, I, p. 144; Falda, *Nuovo teatro*, III, pls. 21, 22; Tessin, p. 161; de' Rossi, *Prospectus*, pls. 24-26; de' Rossi, *Architettura Civile*, III, pl. 28; Nibby, p. 283; De Brosses, II, p. 110; Magni, I, pls. 29, 30; D. Frey, *WJK*, III, 1924-25, p. 11; Hibbard, *Maderno*, p. 232; G. Martinelli (*CdR*, 97; unreliable on the history of the building); Thelen, I, p. 39, II, pls. C.32; Letarouilly, 1857, pl. 273 (274); F. Calvo, *Chiesa di S. Ignazio di Roma*, Rome, 1968; *Saint, Site and Sacred Strategy: Ignatius Rome and Jesuit Urbanism*, exhibition cat., ed. T. M. Lucas, Vatican City, 1990; Buchowiecki, II, p. 199; *Tesori d'arte cristiana*, vol. 5, p. 225; *GR*, IX, III, p. 24; Lombardi, p. 210; Z. Carlucci, *La chiesa di S. Ignazio di Loyola*, Rome, 1995; *Roma Sacra*, 2, 1995, p. 22; Z. Carlucci, *LU*, LVII, 1997, p. 211

1 Rome, 1651, p. 177
2 C. Thelen, 32 and Hibbard, pl. 100b
3 Montagu, *Algardi*, p. 456
4 Kerber, p. 54
5 Chracas, II, No. 7236; Minor, p.

262
6 J. Pinto, *JSAH*, XXXVIII, 1979, p. 375
7 Di Federico, p. 54
8 Titi, p. 192
9 W
10 R. Hemphill, *MD*, XXXIII, 1995, p. 36
11 Andrea Pozzo, p. 114; B. Contardi, ' Il modello di S. Andrea Pozzo, in, *In Urbe Architectus*, p. 23; *The Triumph of the Baroque: Architecture in Europe 1600-1750*, exhib. cat. ed. H. Milon, Venice, 1999, p. 558
12 Bissell, p. 44
13 Bissell, p. 104; *Pittura barocca romana*, p. 128
14 Enggass, *Sculpture*, pp. 86, 95, 144; Ferrari and Papaldo, p. 173
15 *Quadri dal Silenzio*, pp. 35, 36
16 Enggass, *Sculpture*, p. 112; Ferrari and Papaldo, p. 174
17 Enggass, *Sculpture*, pp. 104, 208
18 A. Chiavo, *ASRSP*, XCV, 1972, p. 151
19 Minor, p. 122
20 Chracas, II, Nos. 5088, 5199; Gradara, p. 59
21 N. Spinosa, *Pittura napoletana del Settecento*, Naples, 1987, vol. 2, p. 145
22 F. A. Salvagnini, *I pittori Borogognone Cortese (Courtois)*, Rome, 1936, p. 123

SS. Ildefonso e Tommaso di Villanova

Bibliography: Titi, 1674, p. 371; de' Rossi, 1697, p. 395; Roisecco, 1750, p. 293; Angeli, p. 207; Buchowiecki, II, p. 220; *GR*, III, III, p. 74; Pinelli, No. 70; Tesei, p. 100; M. Escobar, *SdR*, 45, 1984, p. 157; Lombardi, p. 102; Bevilacqua, p. 19; *Roma Sacra*, 5, 1996, p. 58

1 Bacchi, fig. 440

S. Isidoro

Bibliography: Mola, p. 102; Martinelli, p. 73; Titi, 1763, p. 339; Nibby, p. 289; Venuti, p. 83; Angeli, p. 213; Magni, I, pl. 103; A. Daly, *CdR*, 119; H. Quinn, *S. Isidore's Church and College of the Irish Franciscans*, Vatican City, 1950; Buchowiecki, II, p. 224; Mallory, *Rococo*, p. 42; id., *Bizzacheri*, pp. 37, 46; Pinelli, No. 71;

De Tomasso, p. 178; G. Cannizzaro, *AR*, 17 (3-4), 1976, p. 24; Lombardi, p. 328; *Roma Sacra*, 5, 1996, p. 52; *GR*, XVI, IV, p. 104

1 Enggass, *Sculpture*, p. 112; Ferrari and Papaldo, 176
2 R
3 Riccoboni, p. 383
4 L. Borroero, *PA*, 347, 1979, p. 3; *Pietro da Cortona*, p. 195
5 A. Nava Cellini, *PA*, 131, 1960, p. 9; Ferrari and Papaldo, 177
6 Dombrowski, p. 438
7 W
8 Brauer and Wittkower, pp. 139-41, pls. 103, 174; Ferrari and Papaldo, 178
9 Wittkower, *Bernini*, p. 243
10 de' Rossi, *Architettura Civile*, II, pls. 16, 17
11 *Bernini*, cat. no. 190
12 Fischer, p. 168
13 Harris, *Sacchi*, p. 50
14 Ferrari and Papaldo, 180
15 Bacchi, p. 841, fig. 733
16 Mallory, *Bizzacheri*, pp. 31, 45, and *Rococo*, p. 37; R. Bösel, *Pros.*, 15, 1978, p. 29
17 W; E. Borea, *Pros.*, 12, 1978, p. 4
18 *Diario di Roma*, No. 39, 1830
19 Bodart, vol. 1, p. 177
20 Ferrari and Papaldo, 180
21 W; C. Legrand, *BM*, CXXXVI, 1994, p. 348
22 Montagu, *Algardi*, p. 332

S. Ivo della Sapienza

Bibliography: Pollak, I, p. 159; Falda, *Nuovo teatro*, I, pls. 19, 20; P. Ferrerio, *Palazzi di Roma*, I, pl. 30, n.d.; *Opera del Cavaliere Francesco Borromini*, Rome, 1720; de' Rossi, *Architettura Civile*, I, pls. 98-100; Visentini, pp. 22, 35; Magni, I, p. 67; Hempel, p. 114; Portoghesi, *Borromini nella cultura europea*, pls. 46-74 and *Borromini*, pls. L-LVI, 75-91; H. Thelen, *Miscellanea Bibliothecae Hertzianae*, Vienna, 1961, p. 285; *Ragguagli Borrominiani*, pp. 131, 225; L. Benevolo, *QISA*, 3, 1953; ibid., 13, 1956, p. 1; H. Ost, *Zeitschrift für Kunstgeschichte*, 1967, p. 101; P. de la Ruffinière du Prey, ibid., XXXI, 1968, p. 215; E. Battisti, *Studi sul Borromini*, I, p. 229; Portoghesi, *Roma Barocca*, pls. 125-41; W. Hauptman, *JSAH*, XXXIII, 1974, p. 73; L. Benevolo, 'Il problema dei pavimenti Borrominiani in bianco e nero', *QISA*, 13, 1956, p. 1; V. Poulson, *The Iconography of Francesco Borromini's Church of S. Ivo della Sapienza in Rome*, diss., Oslo, 1976; M. Malmanger, *ARN*, VIII, 1978, p. 237; Blunt, *Borromini*, p. 111; J. Bedlon Scott, *JSAH*, 41, 1982, p. 294; A. Herz, *JSAH*, XLVIII, 1989, p. 150; *Chiese dal Rinascimento*, p. 228; F. Rangoni, *CdR*, Nuova Serie, 24; J. Connors, *JSAH*, 55, 1996, p. 38; id., *BM*, CXXXVIII, 1996, p. 668; C. Brandi, *Arch.*, 45, 1999, p. 119; R. Stalla, 'L'Opera architettonica di Francesco Borromini', in, *Borromini e l'universo barocco*, ed. R. Bösel and C. L. Frommel, Milan, 2000, p. 23; *Borromini e l'universo barocco*, p. 250

1 Briganti, p. 265; *Effigies and Ecstasies*, p. 128; *Pittura barocca romana*, p. 86
2 see also S. Macioce, 'La chiocciola di S. Ivo', in *Innocenzo X*, p. 75
3 see *Borromini e l'universo barocco* for the most recent bibliography

S. Lorenzo in Damaso

Bibliography: Venuti, p. 201; Nibby, p. 291; Angeli, p. 216; G. Urban, *RJK*, 9/10, 1961-62, p. 219; A. Schiavo, *Il palazzo della Cancelleria e la chiesa di S. Lorenzo in Damaso*, Rome, n.d.; *GR*, VI, II, p. 108; Buchowiecki, II, p. 247; S. Valtieri, *La basilica di S. Lorenzo in Damaso*, Rome, 1984; Robertson, p. 162; J. Montagu, 'Antonio and Giuseppe Giorgetti ...', *AB*, LII, 1970; *Roma Sacra*, 10, 1997, p. 38

1 Pollak, I, p. 164; Fagiolo dell'Arco, *Bernini*, no. 89; Portoghesi, *Roma Barocca*, fig. 60
2 Titi, 1763, p. 122
3 *Diario di Roma*, No. 72, 1818
4 Wittkower, *Bernini*, p. 210; Montagu, *Giorgetti*, p. 282, note 29
5 R. Spinelli, *MKIF*, XXXVI, 1993, p. 329
6 Bacchi, fig. 517
7 A. Schiavo, p. 105, pl. XXXV; Mallory, *Notizie*, Nos. 4107, 4116, 4137
8 Titi, p. 416; Gabrielli, p. 47
9 Voss, p. 137
10 J. Montagu, *AB*, LII, 1970, p. 278
11 *Notizie del Giorno*, No. 46, 1839
12 Lilli, p. 84
13 Lilli, p. 147
14 *Giornale di Roma*, No. 199, 1851, 30th Aug
15 *Giornale di Roma*, No. 192, 1851, 22nd Aug
16 Mundy, cat. nos. 60-61; Luchinat, vol. 1, p. 272
17 Pollak, I, p. 163 and Del Piazzo, No. 154
18 C. Valone, *AB*, LVIII, 1976, p. 528; R. Spinelli, *MKIF*, XXXVI, 1993, p. 329
19 A. Schiavo, p. 104, pl. XXXIV; Kelly, p. 230
20 Titi, p. 149
21 Noehls, SS. *Luca e Martina*, p. 14 and pl. 22

S. Lorenzo in Fonte

Bibliography: Totti, p. 494; Titi, 1647, p. 308 and 1763, p. 269; Nibby, p. 295; Angeli, p. 218; Pinelli, No. 74; Buchowiecki, II, p. 263; Tesei, p. 26; G. Marincola Mauro, *AR*, 10 (3-4), 1969, p. 6; Lombardi, p. 67; *GR*, I, III, p. 39

1 Chracas, II, No. 8498
2 L. Barroero, *BdA*, LXIV, 1979, p. 65
3 *Gian Lorenzo Bernini*, p. 327; Ferrari and Papaldo, p. 183

S. Lorenzo in Lucina

Bibliography: Titi, 1763, pp. 367, 485; *Le scienze e le arti*, vol. I, n. n.; Venuti, p. 145; Nibby, p. 301; Angeli, p. 225; L. Huetter and E. Lavagnino, *CdR*, 27; *Via del Corso*, p. 157; Buchowiecki, II, p. 266; R. Bösel, *Pros.*, 15, 1978, p. 29; *GR*, III, I, p. 92; Pinelli, No. 75; M. E. Bertoldi, *CdR*, Nuova Serie, 28; Racheli, p. 292; *Roma Sacra*, 2, 1995, p. 6

1 *Giornale di Roma*, No. 150, 1858, 7th July
2 Kempfer, p. 139
3 Lilli, p. 144
4 *Diario di Roma*, No. 47, 1809; U. Hiesinger, *ABA*, 13-14, 1980, p. 78; F. Pansecchi, *Pros.*, 33-36, 1984, p. 327
5 Lilli, p. 171
6 Ferrari and Papaldo, p. 187
7 Chracas, III, Nos. 1422; 1526
8 R
9 Mola, p. 115; Eimer, I, fig. 85, p.

860
10 Bodart, I, p. 407
11 Lilli, p. 100
12 Chracas, III, No. 986
13 de' Rossi, *Altari*, pls. 44, 50; J. Dobias, *BM*, CXX, 1978, p. 65; A. Blunt, *AH*, I, 1978, Wittkower, *Bernini*, p. 256; Scribner, pl. 36, p. 80; Borsi, p. 335; Careri, p. 11; Marder, p. 292; *Gian Lorenzo Bernini*, p. 361
14 Fischer, p. 169
15 de' Rossi, *Altari*, pl. 49
16 Bacchi, p. 794, fig. 282
17 Chracas, II, No. 3870; Ricconboni, p. 310
18 *Diario di Roma*, No. 23, 1805
19 Pepper, p. 237
20 Ricconboni, p. 385
21 Clark, p. 85
22 Vouet, p. 212
23 F. Panescchi, *Pros.*, 33-36, 1984, p. 327
24 Ricconboni, p. 312
25 Nicolson, p. 171; Cavina, p. 117
26 Ferrari and Papaldo, p. 187
27 Portoghesi, *Roma Barocca*, pl. 332; Mallory, *Rococo*, p. 56
28 R; C. Legrand, *PA*, 1992, XLIII, p. 36
29 Sestieri, p. 17; Titi, p. 348
30 *Architettura minore*, I, pl. 41; Mallory, *Bizzacheri*, pp. 28, 45

S. Lorenzo in Miranda

Bibliography: Mola, p. 110; Titi, 1686, p. 179; Nibby, p. 303; Venuti, p. 353; Angeli, p. 228; Buchowiecki, II, p. 282; C. Strinati, *BUSA*, 26 (1-2), 1983, p. 13; R. M. Dal Mas, *S. Lorenzo de' Speziali in Miranda*, Rome, 1998; D'Onofrio, *Scalinate*, p. 272; Lombardi, p. 229; *Roma Sacra*, 3, 1995, p. 22

1 S. Jacob, *Italienische Zeichnungen der Kunst-bibliothek Berlin*, 1975, Nos. 280ff.
2 Ferrari and Papaldo, p. 188
3 Spear, p. 101; *Classicismo e natura*, p. 169
4 Tosini, p. 319
5 R. M. Dal Mas, 'Il Martirio di S. Lorenzo', in, *Pietro da Cortona: Atti del convegno*, p. 336
6 *Pietro da Cortona*, p. 364
7 Spear, p. 266
8 cf. a note by Caylus in the *Memoires inédits ... des membres de L'Académie Royale de peinture et de sculpture*, Paris, 1877, I, p. 117, note 1; Ferrari and Papaldo, p. 189
9 Spear, p. 266

S. Lorenzo fuori le Mura

Bibliography: Baglione, *Le nove chiese*, p. 219; Titi, 1763, pp. 225, 475; *Diario di Roma*, No. 52, 1819; *Giornale di Rome*, No. 178, 1862, 6th Aug.; ibid., No. 40, 1863, 19th Feb.; ibid, No, 28, 1864, 5th Feb., ibid., No. 229, 1869, 8th Oct.; ibid., No. 135, 1870, 15th July; Venuti, p. 23; Nibby, p. 296; Angeli, p. 219; *Le scienze e le arti*, vol. I, n. n.; Letarouilly, pls. 268-72 (320-24); G. Matthiae, *CdR*, 89; G. da Bra, *San Lorenzo fuori le Mura*, Rome, 1952; C. F. Guglielmi, *Basilica di S. Lorenzo al Verano*, Milan, 1966; Pinelli, No. 77; Tesei, p. 490; Lombardi, p. 398; J. Montagu, 'Antonio and Giuseppe Giorgetti ...', *AB*, LII, 1970; S. Mulder, 'Image Building by Means of Church Restoration', in, *The Power of Imagery*, p. 83

1 F. d'Amico, *BdA*, 3, 1979, p. 79
2 Serodine: la pittura oltre Caravaggio, ed. R. Chiappini, Milan, 1987, p. 106
3 Noehles, *SS. Luca e Martina*, pp. 83ff., with reproductions of Cortona's drawings for the monuments; Montagu, *Giorgetti*, p. 280; *Pietro da Cortona*, p. 454; Ferrari and Papaldo, p. 184
4 Ferrari and Papaldo, p. 184

S. Lorenzo in Panisperna

Bibliography: Totti, p. 494; Titi, 1674, p. 309 and 1763, p. 270; de' Rossi, 1697, p. 655; Nibby, p. 305; Angeli, p. 230; Vasi, *Magnificenze*, pl. 152; Hibbard, *Maderno*, p. 29; Levine, p. 286; Andrea da Rocca di Papa, *Memorie storiche della chiesa e monastero di S. Lorenzo in Panisperna*, Rome, 1893; P. Tomassi, *Chiesa di S. Lorenzo in Panisperna*, Rome, 1967; C. Lotti, *AR*, 1973, XIV, 5/6, p. 14; Buchowiecki, II, p. 286; Pinelli, No. 78; Tesei, p. 22; Marcucci, p. 91; Racheli, p. 294; *GR*, I, III, p. 148

1 Chracas, II, No. 6258
2 R; Negro, p. 206
3 R

4 *Roma di Sisto V*, p. 421
5 R; Titi, p. 737
6 R
7 M. Zerbi Fanna, *AR*, 28 (3-4), 1987, p. 59; *Roma di Sisto V*, p. 215
8 Mallory, op. cit.; Titi, p. 272
9 Natoli and Scarpati, p. 14
10 R
11 R

S. Lorenzo in Piscibus

Bibliography: Armellini, II, p. 964; Nibby, p. 306; Angeli, 232; R. Battaglia, *BdA*, XXXI, 1937-38, p. 370; *GR*, XIV, II, 124; G. Scarfone, *AR*, 37, 3/4, 1986, p. 122; Lombardi, p. 305.

SS. Luca e Martina

Bibliography: Pollak, I, p. 185; Nibby, p. 539; Falda, *Nuovo teatro*, pl. 5; de' Rossi, *Altari*, pls. 17, 18; de' Rossi, *Architettura Civile*, I, pls. 41, 42; Visentini, *Osservazioni*, p. 6; Magni, I, pls. 46-48; Vasi, *Magnificenze*, pl. 42; Lavagnino, *Altari*, pp. 31, 103; K. Noehles, *La chiesa dei SS. Luca e Martina*, Rome, 1969; Buchowiecki, III, p. 330; *Chiese dal Rinascimento*, p. 214; *Pietro da Cortona*, p. 133; M. Gallo, *SdA*, 93-94, 1998, p. 312; M. Villani, *Pall.*, 20, 1997, p. 43; J. M, 'SS. Luca e Martina reconsidered', in, *Pietro da Cortona: Atti del convegno*, p. 231

1 Noehles, pls. 37, 38, 43
2 ibid., pl. 61
3 ibid., pls. 48, 55
4 As yet unpublished
5 Noehles, pl. 91
6 Merz in *Atti del convegno internazionale Pietro da Cortona*, 1998. pp. 236-37
7 Noehles, pls. 84, 86
8 ibid., pls. 102,.103
9 Montagu, *Giorgetti*, p. 391
10 Noehles, p. 109
11 Minor, p. 111
12 Chracas, III, No. 238
13 W; Pampalone, p. 63
14 J. Connors, *An Architectural Progress*, p. 392
15 Riedel, p. 174
16 Ferrari and Papaldo, p. 190
17 Chracas, I, Nos. 2532, 3623
18 Montagu, *Algardi*, p. 364
19 Dombrowski, p. 424
20 Montagu, *Algardi*, p. 346

21 Ferrari and Papaldo, p. 194
22 D. Dombrowski, *BM*, CXL, 1998, p. 824
23 *Pietro da Cortona*, p. 441; Ferrari and Papaldo, p. 192
24 Montagu, *Algardi*, p. 354
25 Bacchi, fig. 417; Ferrari and Papaldo, p. 196

S. Lucia del Gonfalone (See also Oratorio del Gonfalone)

Bibliography: Titi, 1763, p. 486; Vasi, 1791, II, p. 584; Nibby, p. 309; Angeli, p. 237; Donati, fig. 332; *GR*, VII, II, p. 11; Chracas, II, Nos. 6831, 7224, 7554; *Via Giulia*, p. 353; Buchowiecki, II, p. 295; Lombardi, p. 171; Racheli, p. 298; G. Matteocci, *AR*, 32 3-4, 1991, p. 106; *Roma Sacra*, 12, 1998, p. 57

1 Stringa, p. 114
2 Riccoboni, p. 410
3 R
4 *Cesare Mariani*, p. 54
5 Mariani, p. 31
6 Minor, *Diario*, No. 7812

S. Lucia in Selci

Bibliography: Baglione, p. 339; Titi, 1763, p. 242; Nibby, p. 310; Venuti, p. 41; Angeli, p. 239; Hibbard, *Maderno*, p. 136; Portoghesi, *Borromini nella cultura europea*, p. 205; ibid., *Borromini*, pls. 34-36; *GR*, I, II, p. 72; Pinelli, No. 80; Buchowiecki, II, p. 299; Lombardi, p. 65; Pocino, p. 259

1 Schleier, p. 154
2 L. Barroero, *BdA*, 1, 1979, p. 65
3 L. Barroero, loc. cit.
4 F. Sricchia Santoro, *Pros.*, 1, 1975, p. 35; *Pietro da Cortona*, p. 285

S. Lucia della Tinta

Bibliography: Titi, 1763, p. 398; Venuti, p. 172; Nibby, p. 311; Angeli, p. 240; E. Schleier, *AC*, 727, 1988, p. 303; Buchowiecki, II, p. 306; G. Marincola Mauro, AR, 10 (1), 1969, p. 33; G. Scarfone, *AR*, 29 (5-6), 1988, p. 167; Pinelli, No. 81; *GR*, IV, V, p. 7; Lombardi, p. 119; *Roma Sacra*, 6, 1996, p. 51

S. Luigi dei Francesi

Bibliography: Totti, p. 360; Baglione, p. 81, n. 37; Mola, p. 88; Martinelli, p. 80; Venuti, p. 254; Nibby, p. 311;

Falda, *Nuovo teatro*, III, pl. 24; de' Rossi, *Prospectus*, pl. 37; De Brosses, II, p. 119; A. D'Armailhacq, *L'Eglise nationale de Saint Louis des Français à Rome*, Rome, 1894; Magni, I, pl. 15; A. Cametti, *BdA*, XXI, 1918, p. 170; M. L. Polidori, *Monumenti e Mecenati francesi a Roma, 1492-1527*, Viterbo, 1969, p. 21; G. Giovannoni, *Pall.*, III, 1939, p. 97; J. Lesellier, *MAH*, XLVIII, 1931, p. 223; Bousquet, p. 119; *Tesori d'arte cristiana*, vol. 5, p. 113; Buchowiecki, II, p. 308; C. L. Frommel, 'S. Luigi dei Francesi: das Meisterwerk des Jean de Chènevières', in, *'Il se rendit en Italie': Etudes offertes à André Chastel*, 1987, Paris, p. 169; A. Le Normand, 'Un siècle de monuments', in, *Les fondations nationales*, p. 225; Organi, p. 96; Lombardi, p. 194; *Roma Sacra*, 7, 1996, p. 24; J. Montagu, *Gold, Silver and Bronze*, New Haven/London, 1996, pp. 35-46

1 Fontana, *Della Traportatione dell'obelisco Vaticano*, Rome, 1590, p. 42
2 Schwager, 'Die Porta Pia in Rom', *MJBK*, XXIV, 1973, p. 59
3 Enggass, *Sculpture*, p. 218
4 D. Lavalle, 'Une décoration à Rome', in, *Les fondations nationales*, p. 249
5 Chracas, II, No. 6105; Sestieri, p. 29; Negro, p. 206
6 Wright, p. 221; Titi, p. 168
7 Spear, p. 178; *Domenichino*, p. 237
8 Pepper, p. 212
9 Lilli, p. 116
10 Lilli, p. 107
11 Lilli, p. 105; *Notizie del Giorno*, No. 6, 1841
12 Pugliatti, p. 86; Hunter, p. 153; B. F. Davidson, *AB*, XLVIII, 1966, p. 55
13 Lilli, p. 102
14 Lilli, p. 125
15 Lilli, p. 81
16 Enggass, *Sculpture*, p. 217
17 Clark, *Batoni*, p. 274
18 W
19 *La Pittura in Italia: Il Seicento*, p. 457
20 *Roma di Sisto V*, p. 216
21 Chracas, II, No. 5499
22 C. E. Gilbert, *Caravaggio and his Two Cardinals*, University

Park, 1995, p. 59ff.
23 M. Kitson, *Caravaggio*, London, 1969, p. 93; M. Marini, pp. 182, 184, 202; B. Treffers, *SdA*, 67, 1989, p. 241; F. T. Camiz, *AeH*, 22, 1990, p. 89
24 A. M. Wagner, *BM*, CXXI, 1979, p. 725
25 E. Schleier, *BM*, CXVIII, 1976, p. 837; J. Thuillier, 'Charles Mellin', in, *Les fondations nationales*, p. 583; O. Michel, 'Giuseppe Manno', in, *Les fondations nationales*, p. 173
26 Baglione, p. 404; Möller, p. 142
27 J. Varriano, in, *An Architectural Progress*, p. 267
28 Titi, p. 166
29 Montagu, *Gold*, p. 53
30 W
31 Wright, p. 241
32 La Regola, p. 517
33 Kummer, p. 273
34 *Notizie del Giorno*, No. 30, 1840
35 Lilli, p. 92
36 Lilli, p. 110
37 Natoli and Scarpati, p. 62; O. Michael, op. cit.
38 Ferrari, *Lo Stucco*, pl. CLXVII; Mallory, *Bizzacheri*, pp. 36, 46 and *Rococo*, p. 46

S. Macuto

Bibliography: Vasi, *Magnificenze*, pl. 165; Nibby, p. 316; Angeli, p. 244; B. Pocqet du Haut-Jassé, *MAH*, XXXVI, 1916-17, p. 85; *GR*, III, II, p. 22 and IX, II, p. 46; Lewine, p. 298; Bösel, p. 223; Pinelli, No. 82; G. Scarfone, AR, 29 (1-2), 1988, p. 69; Buchowiecki, II, p. 323; Tesei, p. 116; Marcucci, p. 80; Lombardi, p. 103; L. Marcucci and B. Toresi, *Pall.*, 12, 1993, p. 59; *Roma Sacra*, 2, 1995, p. 38

1 Titi, p. 217
2 Titi, p. 217
3 R

Madonna dell'Archetto
See S. Maria dell'Archetto

Madonella di S. Marco
See Madonna delle Grazie

Madonna del Divino Amore (SS. Biagio e Cecilia dei Materassai)

Bibliography: Nibby, p. 132; Angeli, p. 124; Chracas, I, No. 2107; P.

Mancini, *La Madonna del Divino Amore in Campo Marzio*, Rome, 1976; Rotili, p. 56; Tesei, p. 144; A. P. Mancini, AR, 14 (3-4), 1973, p.1; Buchowiecki, II, p. 325; Lombardi, p. 115; *Roma Sacra*, 9, 1997, p. 36

1 Clark, p. 66

Madonna delle Grazie (Madonella di S. Marco)
Bibliography: Nibby, p. 405; Angeli, p. 329; Coudenhove-Erthal, p. 58; *GR*, IX, III, p. 122; *Palazzo Venezia: Paolo II e le fabbriche di S. Marco*, Rome, 1980, p. 141; Buchowiecki, II, p. 329; *Roma Sacra*, 15, 1999, p. 63; Ferrari and Papaldo, p. 205

1 Bacchi, figs. 273, 274
2 Titi, p. 215; Sorgiovanni, p. 72

Madonna dei Monti
See **S. Maria dei Monti**

Madonna del Pascolo
See **SS. Sergio e Bacco**

SS. Marcellino e Pietro
Bibliography: Vasi, *Magnificenze*, pl. 50; Chracas, I, No. 5151; C. Cecchelli and E. Persico, *CdR*, 36; Braham and Hager, p. 88; *GR*, I, II, p. 34; Pinelli, No. 83; Tesei, p. 50; Buchowiecki, II, p. 331; Spesso, p. 123; De Tomasso, p. 16; Lombardi, p. 66; Pocino, p. 127

1 R
2 R
3 Pepper, p. 295

S. Marcello
Bibliography: Titi, 1763, pp. 321, 484; Nibby, p. 316; Venuti, p. 111; Angeli, p. 245; de' Rossi, *Prospectus*, pl. 36; Nibby, p. 316; Tessin, p. 164; Magni, I, pl. 58; Coudenhove-Erthal, p. 51; Portoghesi, *Renaissance*, pls. 115-16; *Via del Corso*, p. 22; J. Zänker, *Arch.*, IV, 1974, p. 177; B. Massi, *Le chiese dei Serviti*, Rome, 1941, p. 11; H. Hager, *Comm.*, XXIV, 1973, p. 58; Buchowiecki, II, p. 339; L. Gigli, *CdR*, Nuova Serie, 29; *Oltre Raffaello*, p. 93; Lombardi, p. 83; *Roma Sacra*, 2, 1995, p. 52; Schlimme, p. 209

1 For the preliminary designs, see Hagar
2 Portoghesi, *Borromini*, pl.

XXIX
3 J. Varriano 'Martino Longhi the Younger and the façade of S. Giovanni Calabita in Rome', *AB*, LII, 1970, p. 71
4 Westin, p. 202
5 Gunter, pp. 317, 327; Ferrari and Papaldo, p. 199
6 Riccoboni, p. 192; Ceschi, p. 77; Ferrari and Papaldo, p. 201
7 Boucher, p. 368
8 Lilli, p. 130
9 Pampalone, p. 65
10 Gloton, pl. XLIX
11 Chracas, I, No. 1591
12 Kowa, p. 174
13 Enggass, *Sculpture*, p. 156
14 *Roma la città*, p. 280; Weil, p. 146; Ferrari and Papaldo, p. 201
15 Mortari, p. 128; L. Mortari, *PA*, 401-3, 1983, p. 100; J. Moffitt, *AC*, 730, 1989, p. 57
16 Riccoboni, p. 486; Ceschi, p. 73
17 A. Vinnugli, *Ricerche per la storia religiosa di Roma*, 3, 1984, p. 42
18 Mallory, *Bizzacheri*, p. 26
19 Pugliatti, p. 30; Armani, p. 260
20 Barolsky, p. 53
21 *Diario di Roma*, No. 67, 1831
22 Lilli, p. 124
23 Chracas, I, No. 1825; Kelly, p. 103; Gradara, p. 23; H. Hager, *Comm.*, XXII, 1971, p. 62, n. 51
24 R. Roli, *AAM*, 1964, 27, p. 34; Roli, p. 115
25 Minor, *Diario*, No. 144
26 Lo Bianco, p. 116
27 Gere and Pouncey, p. 166
28 Luchinat, vol. I, p. 62; Hall, p. 184
29 Cavallero et al., p. 397, n. 1
30 Montagu, *Algardi*, p. 426; *Algardi* p. 132; Ferrari and Papaldo, p. 202
31 Negro. p. 206
32 Chracas, II, No. 7053; Matthiesen, 1987, p. 101; Titi, p. 312; *Domenico Corvi*, p. 108
33 Chracas, I, No. 1486; Clark, p. 100
34 Fischer Pace, *Baldini*
35 Lilli, p. 139
36 V. Casale, *ABA*, 9-12, 1979, p. 113

S. Marco
Bibliography: Venuti, p. 287; Mallory, *Notizie*, Nos. 2759, 4017; Nibby, p. 321; Angeli, p. 247; F. Hermanin,

CdR, 30; G. Urban, *RJK*, 9-10, 1961-62, p. 125; L. Lotti, AR, 17 (5-6), 1976, p. 95; *GR*, IX, III, p. 130; Buchowiecki, II, p. 359; C. L. Frommel, *RJK*, 21, 1984, p. 71; *Organi*, p. 98; Lombardi, p. 202; *Roma Sacra*, 15, 1999, p. 54

1 w
2 V. Tiberia, *AR*, XXIX, 1-2, 1988, p. 3
3 W
4 W
5 *Pier Francesco Mola*, p. 213
6 W
7 W
8 W
9 Enggass, *Sculpture*, p. 187
10 Lilli, pp. 135, 152
11 W
12 W; Pio, p. 641
13 Ferrari and Papaldo, p. 203
14 Titi, p. 212; Ferrari and Papaldo, p. 203
15 Lilli, p. 73
16 Stringa, p. 88
17 V. Casale, *Comm.*, XX, 1969, p. 93
18 del Piazzo, No. 85
19 Titi, 1763, p. 180
20 Venuti, 1767, p. 287
21 Rodino, p. 25; *Pietro da Cortona*, pp. 224, 230
22 Venuti, p. 686
23 *La Pittura in Italia: Il Quattrocento*, ed. F. Zeri, Milan, p. 709
24 Chracas, II, Nos. 3599, 3633
25 W
26 W
27 Sciolla, p. 92
28 L. Russo, 'Notizie su Guglielmo Cortese', in, *Innocenzo X*, p. 193
29 Faldi, p. 272; E. Schleier, *The Age of Caravaggio*, exhib. cat., New York, p. 26
30 *Pietro da Cortona*, p. 230
31 V. Tiberia, *BdA*, 64, 1990, p. 71
32 Chracas, III, No. 2404; Lilli, p. 77
33 Bacchi, fig. 272; Ferrari and Papaldo, p. 204
34 *Pier Francesco Mola*, p. 184
35 Ferrari, *La Tomba*, pl. CLVXXV
36 M. L. Chappell, *Southeastern College Art Conference Review*, IX/2, 1977, p. 62
37 Chracas, II, No. 7461
38 *Diario ordinario*, No. 49, 1801,

ibid. No. 154, 1802; G. Pavanello, *ABA*, 35-38, 1990, p. 13
39 D. L. Bershad, *BM*, CXIX, 1977, p. 114
40 Westin, p. 27
41 Titi, 1674, p. 201; Ferrari and Papaldo, p. 204

S. Margherita in Trastevere

Bibliography: Titi, 1763, p. 43; Chracas, I, No. 1756; Roisecco, 1750, I, p. 182; Nibby, p. 328; Venuti, p. 429; Angeli, p. 251; H. Hager, *Comm.*, XXV, 1974, p. 225; Tesei, p. 374; Lombardi, p. 285; Kuhn-Forte, p. 551

1 *Pittura del '600 e '700: ricerche in Umbria*, Treviso, 1976, vol. 2, p. 455
2 Titi, p. 64; F. Pansecchi, *Scritti di storia dell'arte in onore di Federico Zeri*, p. 725
3 Enggass, *Baciccio*, pp. 29, 143

S. Maria degli Angeli

Bibliography: Titi, 1763, pp. 285, 480; Venuti, p. 69; Nibby, p. 329; Letarouilly, pl. 316 (300); Magni, I, p. 13; G. Matthiae, *CdR*, Nuova Serie, 13; Ackerman, *Michelangelo*, p. 260; B. Salvetti, *S. Maria degli Angeli alle Terme e Antonio lo Duca*, 1965, Rome; Buchowiecki, II, p. 383; R. de Fusco et al., *Luigi Vanvitelli*, Naples, 1973, pls. 173-92; *S. Maria degli Angeli e dei Martiri: incontro di storie*, ed. C. Blasetti, Rome, 1991; Lombardi, p. 344

1 Enggass, *Sculpture*, p. 116; Ferrari and Papaldo, p. 206
2 Pugliatti, p. 172
3 Pio, p. 20
4 *Luigi Vanvitelli*, No. 20
5 Ferrari and Papaldo, p. 206
6 Chracas, II, No. 7997
7 Freedburg, p. 500; Di Giammaria, p. 61
8 Di Federico, p. 66
9 Chracas, III, No. 378
10 Titi, p. 280; M. G. Guerrieri Borsoi, *BdA*, 50-51, 1988, p. 161
11 Titi, p. 280; Guerrieri Borsoi, loc. cit.
12 Negro, p. 206
13 Titi, p. 281; Roli, p. 120
14 Geller, p. 35
15 Guerrieri Borsoi, loc. cit.

16 Möller, p. 124
17 Spear, p. 268
18 W
19 Chiappini di Sorio, p. 115
20 J. Varriano, *PA*, 465, 1988, p. 31; Kunze, p. 128
21 Montini, p. 330
22 Titi, p. 285
23 Pugliatti, p. 204; Sandro Benedetti, *Saggi in onore di Guilielmo de Angelis d'Ossat*, Rome, 1987, p. 245; Cavallero et al., p. 211
24 R
25 R
26 Titi, p. 288; Guerrieri Borsoi, loc. cit.
27 Titi, p. 286
28 W
29 Di Federico, p. 66
30 W
31 Negro, p. 206
32 *Subleyras*, p. 333
33 Clark, p. 261
34 Guerrieri Borsoi, loc. cit.
35 Roisecco, 1750, II, p. 606
36 Wasserman, *Mascarino*, p. 83
37 reproduced by Pane in De Fusco et al., *Luigi Vanvitelli*, Naples, 1973, fig. 176
38 Gradara, *Bracci*, p. 94, pl. XXXII)

S. Maria dell'Anima

Bibliography: Titi, 1763, p. 411; Martinelli, p. 84; Nibby, p. 362; Venuti, p. 192; Angeli, p. 257; Letarouilly, pls. 68, 69 (251, 252); J. Scmidlin, *Gesichte der deutschen Nationalkirche in Rom: S. Maria dell'Anima*, Freiburg, 1906; J. Lohninger, *S. Maria dell'Anima, die deutsche Nationalkirche in Rom*, Rome, 1909; R. Urban, *RJK*, 9-10, 1961-62, p. 73; *GR*, V, II, p. 62; G. Cannizzaro, *AR*, 17 (5-6), 1976, p. 79; K. Weil - Garris Posner, *SdA*, 6, 1970, p. 121; G. Knopp and W. Hansmann, *S. Maria dell'Anima*, Münchengladbach, 1979; Buchowiecki, II, p. 407; Tesei, p. 160; Lombardi, p. 140; *Roma Sacra*, 8, 1996, p. 5; B. Baumüller, *S. Maria dell' Anima in Rom. Ein Kirchenbau im politischen Spannung der Zeit um 1500: Aspekte einer historischen Architekturbefragung*, Berlin, 2000

1 Nicolson, p. 171
2 Fischer, p. 140

3 W
4 Montagu, *Algardi*, p. 444
5 D. Bershad, *ABA*, I, 1977, p. 18; Ferrari and Papaldo, p. 207
6 Hunter, p. 158
7 Bacchi, fig. 327; Ferrari and Papaldo, p. 201
8 Mallory, *Notizie*, No. 5196
9 Montini, p. 314; Frommel, p. 119; A. Angelini, *Pros.*, 91-92, 1998, p. 127
10 *Fiamminghi a Roma*, p. 47
11 C. L. Ewart Witcombe, *GBA*, CXXXI, 1989, p. 51
12 Martinelli, p. 87; Mola, p. 120; Connors, *Borromini and the Roman Oratory*, p. 108
13 W
14 Chracas, III, No. 760
15 Bodart, vol. 1, p. 59
16 Ferrari and Papaldo, p. 214
17 Montagu, *Giorgetti*, p. 281; Ferrari and Papaldo, p. 211
18 *Roma di Sisto V*, p. 421
19 Cheney, p. 386; Mortari, p. 118
20 J. Hunter, *SdA*, 59, 1987, p. 15
21 M. H. Stone, *Michael Coxie in Rome*, New York University, 1957, p. 98; A. Gnann and D. Laurenza, *MD*, XXXIV, 1996, p. 293
22 Bacchi, fig. 425; Ferrari and Papaldo, p. 210
23 Ferrari and Papaldo, p. 214
24 Ferrari and Papaldo, p. 213
25 Ferrari and Papaldo, p. 213
26 Lilli, p. 115
27 Nicolson, p. 171
28 Bodart, I, p. 405; U. V. Fischer Pace, in, *Poussin et Roma*, ed. O. Bonfait et al., Paris, 1996, p. 137
29 Dombrowski, p. 353
30 Ferrari and Papaldo, p. 212

S. Maria Annunziata delle Turchine (destroyed)

Bibliography: Vasi, *Magnificenze*, pl. 157; Armellini, p. 280

S. Maria Antiqua (S. Maria Liberatrice)

Bibliography: Falda, *Nuovo teatro*, III, pl. 27; Titi, 1686, p. 181; ibid., 1763, p. 205; Venuti, p. 397; Angeli, p. 260; Vasi, *Magnificenze*, pl. 54; W. de Grüneisen, *Sainte-Marie-antique*, Rome, 1911; P. Romanelli, *S. Maria Antiqua*, Rome, 1964; Buchowiecki, II, p. 433; Lombardi, p. 231; *Roma Sacra*, 9, 1997, p. 12

S. Maria in Aquiro

Bibliography: Titi, 1763, p. 359; Minor, *Diario*, Nos. 8480, 76; *Giornale di Roma*, No. 33, 1866, 10th Feb., ibid., 1866, No. 289, 19th Dec.; Nibby, p. 388; Venuti, p. 134; Angeli, p. 264; M. D'Onofrio and C. M. Strinati, *CdR*, 125; U. Vichi, *AR*, 16 (5- 6), 1975, p. 1; *GR*, III, II, p. 62; Buchowiecki, II, p. 469; De Tomasso, p. 48; Marcucci, p. 169; Lombardi, p. 104; Racheli, p. 304; *Roma Sacra*, 9, 1997, p. 12

1. Hibbard, *Maderno*, p. 121 and *Licenze*, p. 100
2. C. Pietrangeli, *SdR*, 1988, p. 381
3. *Cesare Mariani*, p. 39
4. Ferrari and Papaldo, p. 215
5. R. Contini, *PA*, 529-33, 1994, p. 191
6. *Roma Sacra*, 10, 1997, p. 5
7. Nicolson, p. 170
8. Cecchelli, p. 168
9. Menichella, p. 76
10. Ricconboni, p. 397
11. Cecchelli, p. 169
12. P. Cuzin, *BM*, CXXI, 1979, p. 301; Nicolson, p. 61; G. Papi, *PA*, 479-81, 1990, p. 47; G. Papi, *PA*, 22, 1998, p. 3
13. G. Papi, *PA*, 483, 1990, p. 94
14. Geller, p. 39
15. C. Strinati, 'Il cropo', in, *La Regola*, p. 30
16. Ferrari and Papaldo, p. 215
17. Priorri and Tabarrini, p. 46
18. *Quadri Romani*, pp. 74, 59
19. *Classicismo e natura*, p. 177

S. Maria in Aracoeli

Bibliography: Padre Casimiro da Roma, *Memorie istoriche della chiesa e convento di S. Maria in Araceli di Roma*, Rome, 1736; Titi, 1763, pp. 189, 472; Venuti, p. 341; Angeli, p. 260; M. Carta and L. Russo, *CdR*, Nuova Serie, 22; C. Pietrangeli and L. Salerno, *Cap.*, XI, 1965, p. 187; *GR*, X, II, p. 144; Buchowiecki, II, p. 478; J. E. L. Heideman, *The Cinquecento Chapel Decorations in S. Maria in Aracoeli in Rome*, Amsterdam, 1982

1. Hunter, p. 171
2. Pollak, I, p. 165; Wittkower, *Bernini*, p. 206
3. Ferrari and Papaldo, p. 216; Wittkower, ibid., p. 195
4. F. Caglioti, *FKIF*, XLI, 1997, p. 213
5. *Roma di Sisto V*, p. 422
6. Graf, *Passeri*, p. 44
7. P. Seabury Albright, *Pinturicchio's frescoes in the San Bernardino chapel in S. Maria in Aracoeli, Rome*, diss., University of California, 1980
8. *Un'antologia*, p. 42
9. J. E. Heideman, *PA*, 369, 1980, p. 28; *Chiappini di Sorio*, p. 115; *Roma di Sisto V*, p. 218
10. *Roma di Sisto V*, p. 423
11. *RSA*, 6, 1977, p. 51
12. Heideman, p. 125
13. Harwood, p. 519
14. Hunter, p. 168
15. *Classicismo e natura*, p. 171
16. J. E. Heideman, *BM*, CXIX, 1977, p. 686; *Roma di Sisto V*, p. 222
17. Lilli, p. 98
18. del Bufalo, p. 86
19. Bacchi, fig. 531
20. Titi, pp. 218, 221
21. Tosini, p. 325
22. Heideman, p. 130
23. R. Spinelli, *MKIF*, XXXVI, 1993, p. 329
24. Harwood, p. 518
25. W; J. Varriano, *PA*, 465, 1988, p. 31; Kunze, p. 99
26. Titi, pp. 219, 220; Gunter, p. 332
27. Ferrari and Papaldo, p. 217
28. Rotili, p. 56
29. Di Federico, p. 64; R
30. Giovanni V, p. 367
31. Titi, 1686, p. 206
32. Titi, p. 220; R
33. Titi, 1686, p. 169
34. Pickrel, pp. 155, 210
35. W; Ghezzi, p. 108
36. Ferrari and Papaldo, p. 219
37. J. E. L. Heideman, *PA*, 455, 1988, p. 51
38. *Diario ordinario*, No. 78, 1801
39. Chracas, II, No. 8228
40. Cavallero et al., p. 430
41. P. Rotondi, *Cap.*, X, 1934, p. 267
42. Russo, p. 10
43. Cavallero et al., p. 355
44. Baglione, p. 156; *Longhi*, p. 95
45. Heideman, p. 142
46. G. Falcidia, *PA*, 343, 1978, p. 24
47. J. Heideman, *AV*, XXVI (1), 1987, p. 24
48. J. Heideman, *RHM*, 36, 1994, p. 207
49. R. Carloni, *BdA*, 55, 1989, p. 57
50. Heideman, p. 111
51. J. Heideman, *ABA*, 19-20, 1981, p. 143; *Chiappini di Sorio*, p. 116; *Roma di Sisto V*, p. 224
52. Mallory, *Rococo*, p. 165
53. Di Federico, p. 69
54. Heideman, p. 127; G. Falcidia, *Scritti di Storia dell' Arte in onore di Federico Zeri*, ed. M. Natale, Milan, 1984, p. 640
55. J. E. L. Heideman, *BM*, CXXV, 1983, p. 4

S. Maria in Aventino
See **S. Maria del Priorato**

S. Maria in Campitelli

Bibliography: Falda, *Nuovo teatro*, I, pl. 32; Titi, 1763, p. 83; Nibby, p. 357; Venuti, p. 345; Angeli, p. 283; Magni, I, pls. 31-33; Ferrari, *Lo Stucco*, pls. CXVIIff.; Wittkower, *Italian Baroque*, p. 279; Fasolo, p. 147; Spagnesi, p. 115; Portoghesi, *Roma Barocca*, pls. 221-30; Eimer, II, figs. 304-14; H. Hager, *RJK*, 11, 1967-68, p. 297; Buchowiecki, II, p. 527; M. Pedroli Bertoni, *CdR*, Nuova Serie, 21; J. Connors, *RJK*, 25, 1989, p. 207; K. Güthlein, *RJK*, 26, 1990, p. 187; *Chiese dal Rinascimento*, p. 244

1. *Diario di Roma*, No. 59, 1824
2. Ricconboni, p. 364
3. Voss, p. 137
4. N. Spinosa, *Pittura napoletana del Settecento*, Naples, 1988, vol. 1, p. 101
5. Ferrari and Papaldo, p. 220
6. *Giornale di Roma*, No. 212, 1862, 19th Sep.
7. Lavagnino, *Altari*, pp. 39, 145; Ferrari and Papaldo, p. 222
8. Spagnesi, p. 119
9. see also Montagu, *Roman*, p. 94
10. Enggass, *Baciccio*, p. 143
11. de' Rossi, *Altari*, pl. 10; Portoghesi, *Roma Barocca*, pl. 398
12. W
13. Titi, p. 112; Ferrari and Papaldo, p. 223
14. de Bufalo, p. 87
15. Portoghesi, *Roma Barocca*, pl. 399; A. Anselmi, 'Sebastiano Cipriani, la cappella Altieri', in,

Alessandro Albani, p. 203; Ferrari and Papaldo, p. 224
16 Graf, *Passeri*, p. 74
17 W; Graf, 64
18 A. Negro, *PA*, 477, 1989, p. 109

S. Maria in Campo Carleo (destroyed)
Bibliography: Vasi, *Magnificenze*, pl. 102; Armellini, I, p. 215

S. Maria in Campo Marzio
Bibliography: Titi, 1763, p. 364; Vasi, *Magnificenze*, pl. 141; Nibby, p. 361; Angeli, p. 285; M. Bosi, *CdR*, 61; Buchowiecki, II, p. 550; Spagnesi, pp. 167ff.; F. Borsi, *L'insula millenaria. Il monastero di Santa Maria in Campo Marzio e la camera dei deputati*, Rome, 1984; F. Borsi and P. Boccardi Storoni, *Santa Maria in Campo Marzio*, Rome, 1987; Lombardi, p. 125; *Roma Sacra*, 9, 1997, p. 22

1 Portoghesi, p. 544
2 W
3 G. Sestieri, *Comm.*, XXIII, 1972, p. 89
4 Clark, p. 58
5 Montagu, *Algardi*, p. 332
6 Titi, p. 344
7 F. Sricchia Santoro, *Pros.*, 2, 1975, p. 18

S. Maria in Camposanto
Bibliography: Titi, 1763, p. 24; A. Tönnesmann and U. V. Fischer, *Santa Maria della Pietà: die Kirche des Campo Santo Tutonico in Rom*, vol. II, Freiburg, 1988; Lombardi, p. 388

1 Ferrari and Papaldo, p. 584
2 Ferrari and Papaldo, p. 584

S. Maria dei Cappuccini
See S. Maria della Concezione

S. Maria del Carmelo
See S. Egidio

S. Maria del Carmine
Bibliography: *GR*, XI, p. 50; Angeli, p. 289; Pinelli, p. 44; Buchowiecki, II, p. 559; Lombardi, p. 239; *Roma Sacra*, 14, 1998, p. 31

S. Maria del Carmine alle Tre Cannelle
Bibliography: Roisecco, 1745, II, p.

558; Chracas, II, Nos. 5133, 8396; Nibby, p. 365; P. Mancini, *AR*, XV, 15 (1-2), 1974, p. 31; *GR*, II, II, 2°, p. 80; Pinelli, No. 89; Tesei, p. 85; Buchowiecki, II, p. 557; Lombardi, p. 85; *Roma Sacra*, 16, 1999, p. 2

1 *Roma la città degli anni santi*, p. 349
2 A. Negro, *PA*, 36, 1992, p. 50
3 *Quadrini dal Silenzio*, p. 15

S. Maria della Concezione (Cappuccini)
Bibliography: Pollak, I, p. 165; Mola, p. 101; Martinelli, p. 93; Venuti, p. 84; Angeli, p. 291; Vasi, *Magnificenze*, pl. 132; Nibby. p. 177; Domenico da Isnello, *Il convento della Santissima Concezione de' padri Cappuccini in Piazza Barberini di Roma*, Viterbo, 1923; Buchowiecki, II, p. 559; Braham and Hager, p. 179; B. Brizzi, *Album di Roma*, 1980, Rome, pp. 62ff., 71, 80ff.; Pinelli, No. 91; M. D'Alatri and L. Cattaneo di Ciccia, *La chiese e il cimitero della SS. Concezione*, Rome, 1988; *Roma Sacra*, 5, 1996, p. 46; *GR*, XVI, IV, p. 78; Wolfe, p. 50

1 Poensgen, p. 97
2 Pepper, p. 272; *L'Idea del Bello*, II, p. 353
3 Nicolson, p. 123; G. Papi, *PA*, 479-81, 1990, p. 47; Judson and Ekkart, p. 87
4 W; *Bernini*, p. 80
5 Spear, p. 28
6 *Diario ordinario*, No. 66, 1806
7 W
8 Harris, *Sacchi*, p. 70
9 *Diario di Roma*, No. 41, 1824; Lilli. p. 95
10 Enggass, *Sculpture*, p. 103
11 Harris, *Sacchi*, p. 78
12 Harris, *Camassei*, p. 49
13 Di Giammaria, p. 143
14 L. Manzatto, *Fra Semplice da Verona pittore del Seicento*, Verona, 1973, cat. no. 16
15 Merz, p. 200
16 *Pietro da Cortona*, p. 338
17 M. Marini, *SdR*, 49, 1988, p. 463
18 *Quadri dal Silenzio*, p. 18
19 Hunter, p. 156
20 A. Cera, *La pittura emiliana del' 600*, Milan, 1982
21 A. Sutherland Harris, *MD*, 37, 1999, p. 3
22 Hunter, p. 252

23 *The Age of Caravaggio*, New York, 1985, p. 294
24 JM
25 *Diario ordinario*, No. 31, 1807

S. Maria della Consolazione
Bibliography: Titi, 1763, p. 185; Martinelli, p. 94; Nibby, p. 366; Venuti, p. 349; F. Riese, *CdR*, 98; Buchowiecki, II, p. 569; Nibby, p. 366; G. B. Proja, *AR*, 20 (5-6), 1979, p. 40; C. W. Brentano, *The Church of S. Maria della Consolazione in Rome*, diss., University of California, 1967; Longhi, p. 59; Tesei, p. 294; Marcucci, p. 292; Buchowiecki, II, p. 232

1 *Diario di Roma*, No. 87, 1828
2 Luchinat, p. 44
3 Kummer, p. 270; C. Strinati, *Pros.*, 9, 1977, p. 69; *L'Immagine di S. Francesco*, p. 44
4 Baglione, p. 404; Möller, p. 143
5 Cavallaro, p. 181
6 Chiappini di Sorio, p. 118
7 E. Giffi, *BdA*, 19, 1983, p. 17
8 P. Fehl, *AB*, LIII, 1971, p. 326
9 *Quadri Romani*, p. 74
10 F. Todini, *ABA*, 6, 1978, p. 121
11 Riccoboni, p. 77

S. Maria in Cosmedin
Bibliography: Venuti, p. 367; Angeli, p. 295; Vasi, *Magnificenze*, p. 56; Nibby, p. 367; Buchowiecki, II, p. 582; Letarouilly, pl. 68 (251); G. Massimi, *La chiesa S. Maria in Cosmedin*, Rome, 1989; Johns, *Papal Art*, p. 117; Lombardi, p. 252; Racheli, p. 308

1 Mallory, *Rococo*, p. 54
2 Elling, p. 32

S. Maria di Costantinopli
See S. Maria d'Itria

S. Maria in Domnica
Bibliography: Titi, 1763, p. 207; Venuti, p. 3; Angeli, p. 302; Letarouilly, pl. 5 (237); *GR*, XIX, II, p. 19; G. Matthiae, *CdR*, 56; Pinelli, No. 93; Tesei, p. 456; Buchowiecki, II, p. 620; Lombardi, p. 354; Pocino, p. 137; S. Magister, 'I restauri del Raguzzini nelle chiese romane', in, *L'Arte per i giubilei*, p. 227

BIBLIOGRAPHIES AND REFERENCES

S. Maria delle Grazie alle Fornaci
Bibliography: de' Rossi, 1727, p. 85; Roisecco, 1750, I, p. 115; Nibby, p. 371; A. F. Caiola, *CdR*, 109; Elling, pl. 44; Lombardi, p. 444; *In Urbe Architectus*, p. 407

1 Valesio, p. 120
2 Roisecco
3 J. Montagu, *MD*, 31, 1993, p. 454; JM
4 Fleming and Honour, p. 255
5 W
6 Mallory, *Notizie*, No. 1442
7 Pascoli, p. 214
8 W
9 G. Falcidia, *PA*, 343, 1978, p. 24
10 M. B. Guerrieri Borsoi, *BdA*, 50-51, 1988, p. 161
11 A. Pampalone, *SdA*, 84, 1995, p. 244

S. Maria delle Grazie a Porta Angelica (destroyed)
Bibliography: Titi, 1763, p. 428; Vasi, *Magnificenze*, VI, p. XIII; Armellini, II, pp. 975, 1354

S. Maria di Grottapinta
Bibliography: Nibby, p. 376; Angeli, p. 308; *Architettura minora*, pl. 46; *GR*, VI, II, p. 170; Buchowiecki, II, p. 631; Lombardi, p. 155; *Roma Sacra*, 13, 1998, p. 48

S. Maria d'Itria
Bibliography: Nibby, p. 369; Angeli, p. 309; *Diario di Roma*, No. 87, 1840; Lewine, p. 524; Buchowiecki, II, p. 633; *GR*, III, III, p. 86; G. Marincola Mauro, *AR*, 16 (1-2), 1975, p. 39; R. Carloni, ibid., 30 (3-4), 1989, p. 55; Lombardi, p. 102; *Roma Sacra*, 5, 1996, p. 26

1 *Diario di Roma*, No. 74, 1841

S. Maria delle Lauretane
See **S. Maria di Loreto**

S. Maria Liberatrice
See **S. Maria Antiqua**

S. Maria di Loreto
Via di S. Giovanni in Laterano, 33
Bibliography: *Architettura minora*, I, pl. 32; Buchowiecki, II, p. 638; Lombardi, p. 68.

S. Maria di Loreto
Piazza Madonna di Loreto, 26
Bibliography: Titi, 1763, p. 277; Nibby, p. 378; Venuti, p. 60; De' Rossi, *Prospectus*; Magni, I, pl. 9; S. Benedetti, pp. 115, 460; ibid., *CdR*, 100; R. Bertucci, in, *Antonio da Sangallo*, p. 265; C. Jobst, loc. cit., p. 277; Buchowiecki, II, p. 638; Portoghesi, *Renaissance*, pls. 145-48; Tesei, p. 90; *Chiese dal Rinascimento*, p. 144; C. Jobst, *Die Planungen Antonios da Sangallo des Jüngeren für die Kirche S. Maria di Loreto in Rom*, Worms, 1991; *Roma Sacra*, 3, 1995, p. 58; Racheli, p. 310; *GR*, II, VIII, p. 106

1 H. Hager, *RJK*, 11, 1967-68, p. 234, note 107; S. Benedetti, *Letture di architettura. Saggi sul Cinquecento romano*, Rome, 1987, p. 65
2 Blunt, *Borromini*, pp. 15, 34
3 *Cesare Mariani*, p. 46
4 *Roma la città degli anni santi*, p. 222
5 *Roma di Sisto V*, p. 227
6 Baglione, p. 41, n. 40; Röttgen, p. 139
7 Ferrari and Papaldo, p. 226
8 Dombrowski, p. 322
9 Ferrari and Papaldo, p. 229
10 Ferrari and Papaldo, p. 229
11 Priori and Tabarrini, p. 53
12 *Diario ordinario*, No. 4, 1807

S. Maria Liberatrice
See **S. Maria Antiqua**

S. Maria della Luce
Bibliography: Roisecco, 1750, I, p. 184; Vasi, 1777, p. 354; Melchiorri, p. 545; Fasolo, *Trastevere*, pp. 70ff.; Nibby, p. 694; Angeli, p. 311; Portoghesi, *Roma Barocca*, p. 367; D. Gallavotti and G. Testa, *CdR*, 129; E. Carreras, *AR*, 18 (3-4), 1977, p. 57; ibid., *Breve storia della Chiesa di Santa Maria della Luce*, Rome, 1980; Mallory, *Rococo*, p. 105; Lombardi, p. 297; Kuhn-Forte, p. 603

1 Conca, p. 43
2 Minor, *Diario*, No. 8005
3 Voss, p. 137
4 W
5 Chracas, II, No. 5568; R

S. Maria Maddalena
Bibliography: Titi, 1763, p. 363; Nibby, p. 533; Venuti, p. 139; Angeli, p. 313; Vasi, *Magnificenze*, pl. 138; Magni, I, pls. 140-47; Spagnesi, pp. 204ff.; Portoghesi, *Roma Barocca*, pls 258-61, 333-36, 352; Buchowiecki, III, p. 307; Mallory, *Rococo*, p. 67; *GR*, III, II, p. 36; Valesio, p. 123; L. Mortari, *CdR*, 104; Lombardi, p. 105: A. Marino, *QISA*, 15-20, 1990-92, p. 789; ibid., *ASD*, 3, 1987, p. 69; ibid., *La Chiesa e il Convento della Maddalena*, Pescara, 1995; *Roma Sacra*, 8, 1996, p. 48

1 Ferrari, *Lo Stucco*, pls. CXXVI-Iff.
2 A. Donó and A. Marino, in, *L'Architettura da Clement XI*, p. 106
3 *Organi*, p. 23
4 Chracas, I, No. 2332; Poensgen, p. 100
5 Enggass, *Sculpture*, p. 185; *Le statue*, p. 221; Titi, p. 341; Ferrari and Papaldo, p. 230
6 W
7 W; *Ghezzi*, p. 17
8 Chracas, II, No. 8124; *L'Oro di Valadier*, ed. A. Gonzàlez-Palacios, Rome, 1997, p. 199
9 R
10 *Conca*, p. 228
11 Chracas, II, Nos. 5145, 6240
12 R; R. Enggass, *BM*, CXVIII, 1976, p. 491; A. Russo, *AR*, XXXVI (3), 1995, p. 161
13 Mallory, *Bizzacheri*, pp. 32, 45; ibid., *Rococo*, p. 38; Menichella, p. 81
14 R; P. Petraroia, *RINASA*, III/IV, 1981, p. 279
15 R
16 Pio, p. 140
17 R
18 Mallory, *Bizzacheri*, pp. 29, 45

S. Maria Maggiore
Bibliography: Baglione, *Le nuove chiese*, p. 163; Titi, 1763, pp. 249, 479; De Brosses, II, p. 319; Martinelli, p. 99; Venuti, p. 47; Nibby, p. 380; Vasi, *Magnificenze*, pl. 48; Letarouilly, pls. 308-11 (329-37); Magni, I, pls. 86-91; E. Lavagnino and V. Moschini, *CdR*, 7; Buchowiecki, I, p. 237; K. Schwager, *Miscellanea Bibliothecæ Hertzianæ*, Munich, 1961, p. 324; G. Urban, *RJK*, 9-10, 1961-62, p. 96; Kieven, p. 61; K. Schwager, *RJK*, 21, 1983, p. 241; *Santa Maria Maggiore a*

287

Roma, ed. C. Pietrangeli, Florence, 1988; S. F. Ostrow, *Art and Spirituality in Counter-Reformation Rome: The Sistine and Pauline Chapels in S. Maria Maggiore*, Cambridge, 1996; *S. Maria Maggiore e Roma*, ed. R. Luciani, Rome, 1996; Bellini, *Pall.*, 15, 1995, p. 49; *GR*, I, III, p. 74; Pocino, p. 239

1. Martinelli, p. 99; Mola, p. 75
2. Braham and Hager, fig. 475
3. Matthiae, p. 75; Pane, p. 84 and figs. 61-71; for drawings see Bianchi, *Fuga*, p. 65
4. Enggass, *Sculpture*, p. 173; D. S. M. Jones, *The eighteenth-century sculptural program for the façade of S. Maria Maggiore, Rome*, diss., University of Southern California, 1984; A. Anselmi, *RSA*, 40, 1990, p. 61
5. H. Hibbard, *The Architect of the Palazzo Borghese*, Rome, 1962, p. 46
6. M. C. Dorati, *Comm.*, XVIII, 1967, p. 231
7. S. F. Ostrow, *AB*, LXXIII, 1991, p. 89
8. Enggass, *Sculpture*, p. 174; Gradara, p. 53; A. Anselmi, op cit.
9. O. Ostrow, *SdA*, 92, 1998, p. 27
10. Montagu, *Gold*, p. 136
11. P. J. Jacks, *RJK*, 22, 1985, p. 62; P. Anderson, *Panth.*, LVII, 1999, p. 9
12. Macioce, p. 114
13. Montini, p. 370; Olivier Michel, *SdR*, LIX, 1998, p. 265; Ferrari and Papaldo, p. 235
14. *Roma di Sisto V*, p. 403
15. *Roma di Sisto V*, p. 426
16. Montagu, *Algardi*, p. 440
17. H. Röttgen, *Panth.*, XLII, 1984, p. 320
18. Ferrari and Papaldo, p. 237
19. Titi, 1686, p. 226
20. *Diario di Roma*, No. 1, 1827; Valadier, p. 337
21. *Pietro Bernini*, p. 45
22. Montagu, *Algardi*, p. 442
23. Ferrari and Papaldo, p. 239
24. Pollak, I, p. 174; Bacchi, fig. 271; Ferrari and Papaldo, p. 240
25. Nissman, p. 319; Thomas, p. 208
26. Clark, p. 233
27. Titi, p. 258
28. Titi, 1763, p. 252
29. Clark, *Batoni*, p. 233
30. K. Schwager, *Miscellanea Bibliothecæ Hertz-ianæ*, Munich, 1961, p. 324; A. Herz, *SdA*, 43, 1981, p. 241; S. F. Ostrow, *The Sistine chapel at S. Maria Maggiore, Sixtus V and the Art of the Counter Reformation*, diss., Princeton, 1987; Zuccarri, p. 9ff.; *Roma di Sisto V*, pp. 137, 383; Marmorari, p. 19; R. Eitel-Porter, *BM*, CXXXIX, 1997, p. 452
31. Montagu, *Gold*, p. 19
32. Bissell, p. 42
33. Ferrari and Papaldo, p. 242
34. *Roma di Sisto V*, p. 425
35. Minor, p. 228
36. *Giornale di Roma*, No. 249, 1862, 31st Oct, id., No. 238, 1863, 21st Oct; *Le scienze e le arti*, vol. II, n. n.
37. *Diario ordinario*, Nos, 207, 208, 1802
38. *Roma la città degli anni santi*, p. 370
39. *Roma di Sisto V*, p. 424
40. Martinelli, p. 107
41. M. Heimbürger, *PA*, 237, 1967, p. 59
42. A. Nava Cellini, *PA*, 147, 1962, p. 24
43. Dombrowski, p. 338
44. Harwood, p. 398; Fruhan, p. 82; A. Herz, op. cit.; G. P. Wolf, *RJK*, 27-28, 1991-92, p. 283; Evers, p. 238; Ferrari and Papaldo, p. 243
45. Bacchi, p. 833
46. *Pietro Bernini*, p. 46
47. Bacchi, p. 833
48. Burns, p. 184
49. Röttgen, p. 42
50. Cigoli, p. 169; Faranda, pp. 93, 169
51. B. W. Meijer, *MD*, 1993, 31, p. 414
52. Nissman, p. 324; Thomas, p. 208
53. Ackerman, *Michelangelo*, pp. 234, 328; Tiberia, p. 27
54. Baglione, p. 80, n. 4
55. Hunter, p. 178
56. ibid., p. 178
57. Blunt, *Borromini*, p. 29
58. Ackerman, I, pl. 73b
59. G. Sestieri, *PA*, 491, 1991, p. 67
60. Titi, p. 266; Cleri, p. 96
61. Longhi, p. 29
62. Hunter, p. 310
63. W
64. *Pietro da Cortona*, p. 259

65. Pope-Hennessy, p. 500
66. Ferrari and Papaldo, p. 258
67. Stringa, p. 135
68. de' Rossi, *Architettura Civile*, II, pl. 48; Ferrari and Papaldo, p. 258
69. S. F. Ostrow, *RSA*, 21, 1983, p. 87

S. Maria ad Martyres (The Pantheon)

Bibliography: Titi, 1763, p. 360; Nibby, p. 406; Venuti, p. 136; Angeli, p. 330; V. Bartoccetti, *CdR*, 47; Buchowiecki, II, p. 654; A. Lo Biancio, *BdA*, 42, 1987, p. 91; Lombardi, p. 204; S. Pasquali, *Il Pantheon, Architettura e Antiquaria nel Settecento a Roma*, Modena, 1996; Marder, p. 225

1. Pollak, I, p. 178; Thelen, p. 36; S. Bardini, *QISA*, 79-84, 1963, p. 53; Hibbard, *Maderno*, p. 230; T. Thieme, *Pall.*, N.S.XX, 1970, p. 73
2. Bacchi, fig. 617; Ferrari and Papaldo, p. 261
3. Bacchi, fig. 652; Ferrari and Papaldo, p. 260
4. I. Lavin, *AB*, LII, 1970, p. 132
5. Enggass, *Ottoni*, p. 322
6. Chracas, I, Nos. 1000, 1131; T. A. Marder, *BM*, CXXII, 1980, p. 30; Spagnesi, p. 35
7. *Diario di Roma*, No. 79, 1824; *Bertel Thorvaldsen*, p. 187; Lilli, p. 149
8. *Le statue*, p. 210
9. Sorgiovanni, p. 116
10. *La pittura a Genova e in Liguria*, p. 270
11. F. Petrucci, *SdA*, 96, 1999, p. 176
12. Titi, p. 338
13. Enggass *Sculpture*, p. 186
14. Titi, p. 338
15. Harris, *Camassei*, p. 49

S. Maria sopra Minerva

Bibliography: Titi, 1763, p. 155; Venuti, p. 273; Nibby, p. 414; Angeli, p. 335; J. J. Berthier, *L'Eglise de la Minerve à Rome*, 1910; *Giornale di Roma*, No. 238, 1854, 19th Oct.; S. Spinelli, *CdR*, 19; I. P. Grassi, *Basilica di S. Maria sopra Minerva*, Rome, n.d.; *GR*, IX, II, p. 52; Buchowiecki, II, p. 691; L. Lotti, *AR*, 13 (1), 1972, p. 1; G. Palmerio and G. Villetti, *Storia edilizia di S. Maria sopra Minerva in Roma, 1275-1870*, Rome, 1989; G.

Villetti and G. Palmerio, *S. Maria sopra Minerva in Roma: Notizie dal Cantiere*, Rome, 1994; S. Mulder, *RAU*, 69-70, 1989-90, p. 96; U. Kleefisch-Jobst, *Die römische Dominikanerkirche S. Maria sopra Minerva*, Münster, 1991; Lombardi, p. 206; *Roma Sacra*, 8, 1996, p. 24

1 Harwood, p. 499
2 Ferrari and Papaldo, p. 262
3 Rotili, *Raguzzini*, p. 31
4 I. Lavin, *AB*, LII, 1970, p. 132; J. Hess, *BdA*, XXIX, 1936, p. 309; Ferrari and Papaldo, p. 262
5 Ferrari and Papaldo, p. 262
6 Lilli, p. 146
7 Hill, pp. 105, 220
8 Enggass, *Baciccio*, p. 144
9 Gere and Pouncey, p. 48
10 Pampalone, p. 28; *Pietro da Cortona*, p. 216
11 Vicario, p. 628
12 Bacchi, fig. 453
13 Titi, p. 175; P. Petraroia, *RINASA*, III/IV, 1981, p. 279
14 A. Coliva, *AD*, 6, 1992, p. 197; *Roma la città degli anni santi*, p. 171; M. Carta, *AD*, 6, 1992, p. 207; Di Giammaria, p. 125
15 C. Davis, *BM*, CXVIII, 1976, p. 472
16 Dombrowski, *Bolgi*
17 Pio, p. 30
18 Cavallaro, p. 203
19 Ferrari and Papaldo, p. 265
20 Montini, p. 344; Fruhan, p. 141
21 Lavagnino, *Altari*, pp. 15, 17; Hibbard, *Maderno*, p. 133; Fruhan, p. 55; Pressouyre, pp. 375ff.; Harwood, p. 251; *Marmorari*, p. 25; Ferrari and Papaldo, p. 266
22 Emiliani, p. 377
23 Burns, p. 107
24 Fruhan, p. 164
25 Bacchi, p. 833
26 M. C. Abromson, *AB*, LX, 1978, p. 531
27 Lilli, p. 126
28 G. Wiedmann, *SR*, XLIV, 1996, p. 321
29 F. Caglioti, *FKIF*, XLI, 1997, p. 213
30 Ceschi, p. 102
31 J. Hunter, *SdA*, 59, 1987, p. 15; Hunter, p. 182
32 G. L. Geiger, 'Filippino Lippi's Carafa Chapel', diss., Michigan, 1986; E. Parlato, 'La decorazione della cappella Carafa', in, *Roma, centro ideale della cultura dell'antico nei secoli XV e XVI*, ed. S. Danesi Squarzina, Milan, 1989, p. 169
33 Ferrari, *La Tomba*, pl. CVI; Cavallero et al., p. 395; *Marmorari*, p. 18
34 T. Magnuson, vol. II, p. 301
35 Enggass, *Baciccio*, p. 145
36 Buchowiecki, II, p. 720; Ferrari and Papaldo, p. 272
37 *Organi*, p. 106
38 Tosini, p. 313; S. E. Wegner, 'Painted Records of Two Companies of St Catherine', in, *Confraternite*, p. 755; J. Heideman, 'Giovanni de' Vecchi's Fresco Cycle', in, *The Power of Imagery*, p. 149; *Roma di Sisto V*, p. 230; Hall, p. 211
39 Russo, p. 12; Kamp, p. 119; Evers, p. 152; *Roma di Sisto V*, p. 230
40 Bianchi and Giunta, p. 37
41 Riccoboni, p. 393
42 Montini, p. 316
43 Montini, p. 310; U. Kleefisch-Jobst, *ZfK*, 4, 1988, p. 524
44 Cavallero et al., p. 341
45 Bacchi, fig. 387; Ferrari and Papaldo, p. 275
46 Baglione, p. 81, n. 32; Fruhan, p. 92; Ferrari and Papaldo, p. 273
47 Wittkower, *Bernini*, p. 227; Borsi, p. 319
48 Kamp, p. 118
49 D. Bodart, *SdA*, 12, 1971, p. 327; S.R.
50 Harris, *Sacchi*, p. 79
51 Martinelli, p. 110
52 *Pietro da Cortona*, p. 192
53 B. de Lavergnée, 'Simon Vouet à Rome', in, *Scritti di archeologia e storia dell'arte in onore di Carlo Pietrangeli*, 1996, p. 29
54 Harris, loc. cit.; Blunt, *The Other Side*, Wolfe, p. 93
55 Cavallaro, p. 227
56 J. A. Pinto, *The Trevi Fountain*, New Haven and London, 1986, p. 96
57 Varriano, p. 74
58 Rotili, p. 30
59 Chracas, II, No. 3365; Gradara, p. 35
60 Titi, p. 175
61 Bacchi, fig. 439; Ferrari and Papaldo, p. 276
62 Croke, p. 435
63 W
64 Pampalone, p. 40
65 Titi, p. 175
66 Wittkower, *Bernini*, p. 212; Lavin, *Bernini*, p. 67; J. Bernstock, *AB*, LXII, 1980, p. 243; *Bernini in Vaticano*, p. 115; *Gian Lorenzo Bernini*, p. 349
67 A. Blunt, *AH*, I, 1978, p. 72
68 *Roma di Sisto V*, p. 427
69 A. Gonzáles-Palacios, *RSA*, 1-2, 1976, p. 216; Dombrowski, p. 288; Ferrari and Papaldo, p. 276
70 Russo, p. 6; Kamp, p. 121
71 Riccoboni, p. 365; Ceschi, p. 101
72 M. Gallo, *SR*, XLV, 1997, p. 88
73 R. Erbentraut, *Der genueser Maler Bernardo Castello 1557?-1629. Leben und Gemälde*, Freren, 1989, p. 69
74 Wittkower, *Bernini*, p. 175; Ferrari and Papaldo, p. 278
75 Titi, 1763, p. 161
76 H. Hibbard, *Bernini*, London, 1965, p. 66; Burns, p. 175
77 Fruhan, p. 38
78 Lavin, *Bernini*, pp. 66, 182; Ferrari and Papaldo, p. 280
79 A. Nava Cellini, *PA*, 65, 1955, p. 23; ibid., 147, 1962, p. 24; Dombrowksi, p. 444
80 S. Amadio, *SR*, XLV (3-4), 1997, p. 314
81 *Roma di Sisto V*, p. 428
82 Ferrari and Papaldo, p. 282
83 Enggass, *Sculpture*, p. 98; Ferrari and Papaldo, p. 282
84 F. Zeri, 'Gli affreschi dell Sant'Uffizio', *ABA*, 3, 1979, p. 266
85 Connors, p. 109

S. Maria dei Miracoli
See **S. Maria di Montesanto and S. Maria dei Miracoli**

S. Maria di Monserrato
Bibliography: Martinelli, p. 111; Nibby, p. 434; Venuti, p. 235; Angeli, p. 349; de' Rossi, *Prospectus*, p. 66; J. Fernàndez Alonso, *CdR*, 103; *Via Giulia*, p. 445; *GR*, VII, II, p. 32; *Notizie del Giorno*, No. 31, 1822; Pinelli, No. 100; Buchowiecki, II, p. 752; G. Lerza, 'Un contributo a Francesco da Volterra', in, *L'Architettura a Roma*, p. 253; U. Vichi, *AR*, 13 (1), 1972, p. 53; G. Cannizzaro, *AR*, 22 (1-2), 1981, p. 9; G. Lerza,

QISA, 11, 1988, p. 77; Marcucci, p. 142; Lombardi, p. 173; G. Lerza, 'I progetti di Antonio da Sangallo', in, *Antonio da Sangallo*, p. 119; G. Lerza, *S. Maria di Monserrato a Roma dal Cinquecento sintetista al purismo dell' Ottocento*, Rome, 1996; Racheli, p. 318; *Roma Sacra*, 12, 1998, p. 48

1. del Bufalo, p. 87
2. JM
3. Posner, p. 74; *Dominichino*, p. 545
4. *Roma la città*, p. 243
5. Chracas, I, No. 7980
6. Bodart, vol. 1, p. 161
7. Hunter, p. 166
8. Wittkower, *Bernini*, p. 181; Ferrari and Papaldo, p. 283
9. M. Cali, *Pros.*, 57-60, 1989-90, p. 399
10. Boucher, p. 321
11. Lilli, pp. 43, 134
12. Riccoboni, p. 53
13. Dombrowski, p. 419

S. Maria di Monterone

Bibliography: Roisecco, 1750, I, p. 546; Chracas, I, No. 1698; Nibby, p. 438; Venuti, p. 265; *Architettura minora*, I, p. 99; Buchowiecki, II, p. 773; Elling, pl. 22; Lombardi, p. 193; *Roma Sacra*, 10, 1997, p. 15

1. Ferrari and Papaldo, p. 285, though it has also been given by *Roma Sacra* to Francesco Bianchi, 1735
2. Ferrari and Papaldo, p. 285
3. *Giornale di Roma*, No. 275, 1859, 3rd Dec

S. Maria di Montesanto and S. Maria dei Miracoli

Bibliography: Letarouilly, pl. 233 (287); Titi, 1763, p. 385; Golzio, *AdI*, VIII, 1941, p. 122; Magni, I, p. 34; M. L. Casanova, *CdR*, 58; G. Matthiae, *Piazza del Popolo*, Rome, 1946; *Via del Corso*, p. 117; H. Hager, *RJK*, XI, 1967-68, p. 189; Wittkower, *Italian Baroque*, pp. 94ff.; Braham and Hager, p. 64; Eimer, *S. Agnese*, I, figs. 42-44; G. Ciucci, *La piazza del Popolo*, Rome, 1974; Buchowiecki, pp. 744, 776; R. Luciani, *S. Maria dei Miracoli e S. Maria di Montesanto*, Rome, 1990; Hager, p. 128; Kempfer, p. 86

1. Spesso, p. 174

S. Maria dei Miracoli

Bibliography: de' Rossi, *Architettura Civile*, III, pls. 31, 32; Nibby, p. 433; Angeli, p. 348; *GR*, IV, I, p. 152; *Roma Sacra*, 1, 1995, p. 35

1. Ceschi, p. 122
2. Westin, p. 186
3. de' Rossi, *Architettura Civile*, II, pl. 53; Bacchi, p. 816; Ferrari and Papaldo, p. 294
4. Titi, p. 378
5. Ceschi, p. 77

S. Maria di Montesanto

Bibliography: Venuti, p. 159; de' Rossi, *Architettura Civile*, III, pls. 29, 30; Nibby, p. 441; Portoghesi, *Roma Barocca*, pl. 99; *GR*, IV, I, p. 142; *Roma Sacra*, 1, 1995, p. 29

1. Titi, p. 376; Ferrari and Papaldo, p. 288
2. Titi, p. 370; Ferrari and Papaldo, p. 289
3. M. G. Sassoli, *BdA*, 55, 1989, p. 75; *Diario di Roma*, No. 61, 1825
4. *Roma la città degli anni santi*, p. 358
5. Mallory, *Bizzacheri*, pp. 31, 45; ibid., *Rococo*, p. 36
6. Titi, p. 370; W
7. Bacchi, p. 816
8. Wittkower, *Bernini*, p. 186
9. W; Titi, p. 376
10. *Imago Mariae*, p. 163
11. J. Varriano, *PA*, 465, 1988, p. 31; Kunze, p. 89
12. A. Czére, *SdA*, 86, 1996, p. 94
13. Enggass, *Baciccio*, pp. 95, 145
14. W
15. W; Titi, p. 374
16. *Le statue*, p. 206; Ferrari and Papaldo, p. 296
17. *Diario di Roma*, No. 83, 1832; Lilli, p. 96

S. Maria dei Monti (Madonna dei Monti)

Bibliography: Totti, p. 475; Baglione, p. 80, n. 30; Titi, 1674, p. 261; Martinelli, p. 111; Nibby, p. 443; Venuti, p. 36; Angeli, p. 355; Falda, *Nuovo teatro*, III, pl. 30; de' Rossi, *Prospectus*, pl. 72; Letarouilly, pl. 27 (241); Magni, I, pl. 6; Kummer, p. 227; Pinelli, No. 101; Tiberia, p. 35; Tesei, p. 36; De Tomasso, p. 14; Buchowiecki, II, p. 793; G. Alterio and F. Rocchi, *La chiesa Madonna dei Monti a Roma*, Rome, 1979; Lombardi, p. 52; *Roma di Sisto V*, p. 231ff.; Evers, p. 187; *GR*, I, III, p. 38; Pocino, p. 111

1. Poensgen, p. 37, fig. 23
2. Gloton, pl. VIII
3. L. Barroero, *ABA*, 19-20, 1981, p. 169
4. Fischer, p. 176
5. M. B. Guerrieri Borsoi, *PA*, 1-2, 1995, p. 115
6. Riccoboni, p. 387
7. F. d'Amico, op. cit.
8. Pollak, I, p. 207

S. Maria in Monticelli

Bibliography: Titi, 1763, p. 99; Chracas, I, Nos. 1744, 1735, 1750, 1756; Nibby, p. 439; Venuti, p. 223; Angeli, p. 356; Vasi, *Magnificenze*, pl. 112; n.a. *La chiese e parrocchiale di S. Maria in Monticelli*, Rome, 1860; *Le scienze e le arti*, vol. I, n.s.; Giornale di Roma, Nos. 30, 42, 1860, 7th, 21st Feb.; Braham and Hager, p. 180; Donati, fig. 327; *GR*, VII, I, 2°, p. 42; Pinelli, No. 102; Buchowiecki, II, p. 801; Tesei, p. 232; Johns, p. 217; Johns, *Papal Art*, p. 124; Lombardi, p. 174; *Roma Sacra*, 13, 1998, p. 28

1. An alternative project by Domenico Antonio de' Sanctis is at Windsor, cf. Braham and Hagar.
2. *Cesare Mariani*, p. 28
3. Titi, p. 129
4. Sestieri, p 154
5. Titi, p. 129; F. Sricchia Santoro, *Pros.*, 1, 1975, p. 35; W
6. Titi, p. 129
7. G. Falcidia, *BdA*, 65, 1991, p. 133

S. Maria Nova
See **S. Francesca Romana**

S. Maria della Neve

Bibliography: Roisecco, 1750, p. 490; Nibby, p. 84; Angeli, p. 359; Donati, fig. 258, *Architettura minora*, II, p. 15; Portoghesi, *Roma Barocca*, p. 344; H. Hager, *Comm.*, XXII, 1971, p. 36; Buchowiecki, III,

p. 31; Mallory, *Rococo*, p. 63; *GR*, I, II, p. 104; Lombardi, p. 67; Pocino, p. 58

S. Maria dell'Orazione e della Morte

Bibliography: Titi, 1763, p. 462; Chracas, I, II, Nos. 2473, 3157; Nibby, p. 445; Matthiae, p. 13; Pane, p. 42; Lewine, p. 353; *Via Giulia*, p. 460; H. Hager, *CdR*, 79; Lavagnino, *Altari*, p. 197; Buchowiecki, III, p. 58; De Tomasso, p. 98; Lombardi, p. 175; Racheli, p. 320; *Roma Sacra*, 12, 1998, p. 13

1   A. Witte, BM, CXLII, 2000, p.423
2   Chracas, II, No. 3768
3   Lo Bianco, p. 132
4   *Imago Mariae*, p. 40
5   E. Schleier, *PA*, 177, 1964, p. 10

S. Maria dell'Orto

Bibliography: Falda, *Nuovo teatro*, III, pl. 36; de' Rossi, *Prospectus*, pl. 65; Titi, 1763, p. 51; Venuti, p. 439; Nibby, p. 446; G. Giovannoni, *Saggi sull' architettura del Rinascimento*, Milan, 1935; F. Fasolo, *La fabbrica cinquecentesca di S. Maria dell'Orto*, Rome, 1944; Ferrari, *Lo Stucco*, pls. CXLff.; L. Barroero, *CdR*, 130; Portoghesi, *Roma Barocca*, pls. 317-21; F. R. Milone, *QISA*, XXII, 1976, p. 127; *GR*, XIII, IV, p. 74; Tesei, p. 396; Marcucci, p. 77; Lombardi, p. 287; Kuhn-Forte, p. 621; Ferrari and Papaldo, p. 295; S. de Cavi, 'S. Maria dell'Orto in Trastevere (1699-1727)', in, *L'Arte per i giubilei*, p. 97

1   *Descritione de la chiese di Roma*
2   C. Berna, *AC*, 782, 1997, p. 357
3   Graf, *Calandrucci*, p. 73
4   Poensgen, p. 98, fig. 36; Gloton, pl. XXXII
5   Titi, p. 82
6   A. Ciccarese, *SdA*, 58, 1986, p. 205; Luchinat, vol. I, p. 131
7   R
8   R; Titi, p. 76; G. Scarfone, *SdR*, 44, 1983, p. 459
9   Baglione, p. 404; M. G. Aurigemma, *SdA*, 1994, 80, p. 23; Möller, p. 143
10 Titi, p. 81
11 Pio, p. 87; Graf, *Calandrucci*, p. 71
12 Gere and Pouncey, p. 174

13 W
14 Bissell, p. 67
15 P. Becchetti, *SdR*, 42, 1981, p. 27
16 *Da Sodoma a Marco Pino: Pittori a Siena nella prima metà del Cinquecento*, ed. F. Sricchia Santoro, Siena, 1988, p. 16
17 Luchinat, vol. I, p. 103
18 Baglione, p. 401; Möller, p. 95; M. Smith O'Neil, MD, XXXVI, 1998, p. 355
19 L. Turcic, *BM*, CXXVII, 1985, p. 795; W
20 Enggass, *Sculpture*, p. 136
21 Baglione, p. 405; A. Forastieri, *AR*, 1989, 30, (3-4), p. 71; Möller, p. 149
22 Mallory, *Rococo*, p. 125
23 Gabrielli, p. 50
24 Nicolson, p. 59; Möller, p. 137

S. Maria della Pace

Bibliography: Falda, *Nuovo teatro*, I, pls. 26-28; Titi, 1686, p. 384, 1763, p. 414; Nibby, p. 448; Venuti, p. 189; Angeli, p. 362; de' Rossi, *Architettura Civile*, III, pls. 2-4; C. Fea, *Pro-memoria per la venerabile chiesa di S. Maria della Pace*, Rome, 1809; Letarouilly, pls. 63-66 (247-50); Magni, I, pl. 42; G. Urban, *RJK*, 9/10, 1961-62, p. 176; H. Ost, ibid., 13, 1971, p. 231; Portoghesi, *Roma Barocca*, pls. 190-99; Güthlein, *Familienarchiv Spada*, pp. 190, 201; P. Basso and E. Cappella, *Il chiostro di S. Maria della Pace*, Rome, 1987; Buchowiecki, III, p. 67; L. Kugler, *Studien zur Malerei*, p. 519; *Chiese dal Rinascimento*, p. 218; M. L. Riccardi, *Quaderni*, 163-168 (XXVI), 1981, p. 5; Lombardi, p. 142; *Pietro da Cortona*, p. 466ff.; M. Dal Mas, 'Artifizi per una nuova spazialità', in, *Pietro da Cortona: Atti del convegno*, p. 324; *Roma Sacra*, 11, 1997, p. 2

1   Ost, p. 268, fig. 45
2   Ferrari and Papaldo, p. 296
3   Blunt and Cooke, *Roman Drawings at Windsor Castle*, London, 1960, No. 593
4   Ferrari and Papaldo, p. 297
5   Urban, fig. 181
6   M. Hirst, *JWCI*, XXIV, 1961, p. 161; C. Gould, *GBA* CXX, 1992, p. 78
7   J. Montagu, *BM*, CXXXVI, 1994, p. 836; Ferrari and Papaldo, p. 298

8   E. A. Carroll, *Rosso Fiorentino: Drawings, prints and decorative arts*, Washington, 1987, p. 66
9   *Pietro da Cortona*, p. 432
10 *I luoghi di Raffaello a Roma*, p. 123; J. Hunter, *SdA*, 59, 1987, p. 15; J. Hunter, p. 161
11 W
12 Frommel, p. 125; Stollhans, p. 97
13 *Roma di Sisto V*, p. 429
14 Bissell, p. 139; *Gentileschi*, p. 139
15 *Bernardino Mei*, p. 171
16 Hibbard, *Maderno*, p. 189
17 Bacchi, fig. 518; Ferrari and Papaldo, p. 296
18 Cantaro, p. 216
19 Nissman, p. 327
20 C. Pugliese, *Francesco Albani*, New Haven and London, 1999, p. 128
21 Cantaro, p. 220
22 J. Hunter loc. cit.; J. Hunter, p. 164
23 Ferrari and Papaldo, p. 300
24 Russo, p. 9; Kamp, p. 121
25 Sestieri, p. 104
26 C. Frommel, *Il Vasari*, XXI, 1963, p. 144
27 M. V. Brugnoli, *BdA*, LVIII, 1973, p. 113
28 N. Dacos, *Scritti di storia dell'arte in onore di Federico Zeri*, Milan, 1984, p. 332; Stollhans, p. 57, ascribes these frescoes to Peruzzi

S. Maria in Palmis
See **Domine Quo Vadis**

S. Maria del Pianto

Bibliography: Baglione, p. 365; Totti, p. 182; Martinelli, p. 121; Mola, p. 105; Titi, 1686, p. 83; 1763, p. 94; Nibby, p. 454; Venuti, p. 222; Buchowiecki, III, p. 93; *GR*, VII, I, 2°, p. 54; P. Ferraris, *SdA*, 58, 1986, p. 247; De Tomasso, p. 100; C. Gröbner and P. L. Tucci, *CdR*, Nuova Serie, 27; Lombardi, p. 176; *Roma Sacra*, 14, 1998, p. 37

1   Pampalone, p. 95
2   Chracas, III, No. 105; Montagu, *Roman*, p. 212, note 33
3   *Il Seicento Fiorentino*, p. 149

BIBLIOGRAPHIES AND REFERENCES

S. Maria della Pietà
See SS. Bartolomeo e Alessandro dei Bergamaschi

S. Maria del Popolo
Bibliography: Titi, 1763, p. 368; Nibby, p. 456; Venuti, p. 161; Angeli, p. 371; Falda, *Nuovo teatro*, I, pl. 8; Letarouilly, pls. 97, 98 (287-98); R. Colantuoni, *La chiese di S. Maria del Popolo negli otto secoli dalla sua prima fondazione*, Rome, 1899; Magni, I, pls. 55, 56; E. Lavagnino, *CdR*, 20; G. Urban, *RJK*, 9-10, 1961-62, p. 154; Wittkower, *Bernini*, p. 232; Fagiolo dell'Arco, *Bernini*, p. 160; E. Bentivoglio and S. Valtieri, *Santa Maria del Popolo*, Rome, 1976; Buchowiecki, III, p. 102; *GR*, IV, I, p. 70; *Umanesimo e primo Rinascimento in Maria del Popolo*, ed. R. Cannatà, A. Cavallaro and C. Strinati, Rome, 1981; *Chiese dal Rinascimento*, p. 131; F. Ackermann, 'Berninis Umgestaltung des Innenraumes von S. Maria del Popolo', *RJK*, 31, 1996, 369; Angelini, p. 133; *Roma Sacra*, 1, 1995, p. 12

1 cf. Ferrari, *Lo Stucco*, pls. XCVII ff.
2 For a view of the church before the façade was altered see J. Shearman, 'The Chigi chapel in S. Maria del Popolo', *JWCI*, XXIV, 1961, pl. 21a. For a more complete transformation of the façade see S. Jacob, 'Zu Zwei römischen Architekturzeichnungen der Berliner Kunstbibliothek', Römisches Jahrbuch, XIII, 1976, p. 291.
3 Westin, p. 72; Montagu, *Roman*, p. 134; Ferrari and Papaldo, p. 302
4 Sciolla, p. 93
5 Ceschi, p. 121
6 Lavagnino, *Altari*, p. 157; H. Hager, *Comm.*, XXV, 1974, p. 47; Hager, p. 132; F. Ceccopieri Maruffi, *SdR*, LV, 1994, p. 93; Ferrari and Papaldo, p. 306
7 W
8 Gunter, p. 320
9 J. Variano, *PA*, 465, 1988, p. 31; Kunze, pp. 94, 98
10 W
11 Bacchi, figs. 74, 286
12 *Pittura del Seicento e del Settecento: Ricerche in Umbria*, Vol. 1, ed. V. Casale et al., Spoleto, 1976, p. 59
13 Cavallero et al., p. 314
14 Lilli, p. 90
15 Lilli, p. 131
16 Pressouyre, p. 450
17 G. and L. Bauer, *AB*, LXII, 1980, p. 115; *Organi*, p. 29
18 Westin, p. 146
19 W
20 Ferrari and Papaldo, p. 308
21 Pope-Hennessy, p. 500
22 Lilli, p. 132
23 *Pittura in Italia. L' Ottocento*, p. 718
24 Ferrari and Papaldo, p. 303
25 W; *Bernardino Mei*, p. 94
26 Ferrari and Papaldo, p. 311
27 Boucher, p. 314
28 Pope-Hennessy, p. 452; Cavallero et al., p. 320
29 A. Brogi, *PA*, XLVI, 1995, p. 27
30 Ferrari and Papaldo, p. 313
31 Posner, p. 55
32 Marini, pp. 192, 194; L. Steinberg, *AB*, XLI, 1959, p. 183
33 Ferrari and Papaldo, p. 313
34 Vicario, p. 1027
35 Titi, p. 332; C. Strinati, *BdA*, 1, 1979, p. 27; Pugliatti, p. 200; Evers, p. 140
36 Ferrari and Papaldo, p. 308
37 *Bernardino Mei*, p. 168
38 *Roma di Sisto V*, p. 430
39 Busiri Vici, p. 6
40 W
41 Enggass, *Sculpture*, p. 84
42 Walker, p. 99
43 Montagu, pp. 437, 439
44 Ferrari and Papaldo, p. 315
45 Bacchi, fig. 448; Ferrari and Papaldo, p. 315
46 J. Shearman, *JWCI*, XXIV, 1961, p. 129; Angelini, p. 140
47 Hirst, p. 139; Mortari, p. 123
48 C. Magnusson, *Konsthistorisk Tidskrift*, LVI, 1987, p. 19; Pope-Hennessy, p. 449
49 Wittkower, *Bernini*, p. 232; Scribner, pl. 27; Marder, p. 283; *Gian Lorenzo Bernini*, p. 235ff.
50 Chracas, II, No. 8404; L. Paardekooper, *Laby-rinthos*, 29-30, 1996-97, p. 261; A. González Palacios, *ABA*, 55-58, 1998, p. 155
51 Ferrari and Papaldo, p. 322
52 Sestieri, p. 164
53 Harwood, p. 510
54 F. Pesenti, *SdR*, 44, 1983, p. 385; J. Connors, in, *An Architectural Progress*, p. 391
55 Chracas, II, No. 5034

S. Maria Porta Paradisi
Bibliography: Titi, 1763, p. 393; Nibby, p. 472; Angeli, p. 381; Spagnesi, pp. 32ff.; Buchowiecki, III, p. 151; M. Heinz, *SdA*, 41, 1981, p. 31; Portoghesi, *Renaissance*, pls. 70-72; G. Marincola Mauro, *AR*, 20 (3-4), 1979, p. 20; P. Pecchiai and R. U. Montini, *CdR*, 46; Pinelli, No. 105; S. Placidi, in, *Antonio da Sangallo il Giovane*, p. 131; Benedetti and Zander, p. 530; *Roma Sacra*, 6, 1996, p. 35

1 Spagnesi, pp. 32ff.
2 Frommel, p. 124
3 W
4 Bacchi, p. 840, fig. 729; Ferrari and Papaldo, p. 324
5 Bacchi, fig. 241; Ferrari and Papaldo, p. 324
6 Bacchi, fig. 339; Ferrari and Papaldo, p. 325
7 Bacchi, fig. 340; Ferrari and Papaldo, p. 325
8 *La Regola*, p. 32

S. Maria in Portico (S. Galla) (destroyed)
Bibliography: Vasi, *Magnificenze*, pl. 177; Titi, 1763, p. 61; Armellini, II, p. 773; L. Pasquali, *S. Maria in Portico*, Rome, 1904

S. Maria del Priorato (S. Maria in Aventino)
Bibliography: Chracas, II, Nos. 7404, 7695; Nibby, p. 473; Magni I, pls. 136, 137; K. Körte, *ZfK*, II, 1933, p. 16; Wittkower, *Italian Baroque*, p. 27; M. Salmi, *Pall.*, XX, 1970, p. 157; Lavagnino, *Altari*, p. 213; Portoghesi, *Roma Barocca*, pls. 469-75; J. Wilton-Ely, *Piranesi as Architect and Designer*, New York, 1993, p. 87ff.; Tesei, p. 348; Bucho-wiecki, III, p. 187; Minor, *Diario*, p. 230; D. Gallavotti Cavallero and R. U. Montini, *CdR*, Nuova Serie, 15; *Piranesi e l'Aventino*, ed. B. Jatta, Milan, 1998

1 Chracas, III, No. 596; Lilli, p. 45
2 Harris, *Sacchi*, p. 82

S. Maria in Publicolis
Bibliography: Titi, 1763, p. 95; Venuti, p. 361; Nibby, p. 474; Angeli, p. 384; Spagnesi, p. 27; *GR*, VIII, I, p. 24; Tesei, p. 262; Buchowiecki, III, p. 167; Lombardi, p. 196; *Roma Sacra*, 14, 1998, p. 32

1. J. Montagu, *BM*, CXXXIX, 1997, p. 849
2. *Pietro da Cortona*, p. 424
3. W; A. Negro, *PA*, 477, 1989, p. 109
4. W

S. Maria della Purificazione (destroyed)
Bibliography: Vasi, *Magnificenze*, pl. 155; Armellini, I, p. 267

S. Maria della Quercia
Bibliography: Titi, 1763, p. 108; Chracas, I, II, Nos. 1582, 2131, 3250; Nibby, p. 475; Venuti, p. 244; *Architettura minore*, I, pl. 31; A. Martini, *CdR*, 67; Rotili, p. 44; Lewine, p. 370; Buchowiecki, III, p. 173; G. Cannizzaro, *AR*, 14 (5-6), 1973, p. 28; Portoghesi, *Roma Barocca*, pl. 358; Elling, pl. 40; Tesei, p. 222; De Tomasso, p. 102; *Roma Sacra*, 13, 1998, p. 2

1. D. M. Habel, *PA*, 455, 1988, p. 62
2. Titi, p. 138

S. Maria del Rosario sul Monte Mario
Bibliography: Chracas, I, Nos. 1367, 1382; Angeli, p. 387; Vasi, *Magnificenze*, VII, p. XXXIX; *Architettura minore*, p. 76; Nibby, p. 477; A. Zucchi, *Roma domenica*, Florence, 1940, II, p. 40; L. Lotti, *AR*, 16 (5-6), 1975, p. 18; C. Faccioli, *SdR*, 29, 1968, p. 151; Tesei, p. 364; De Tomasso, p. 180; Lombardi, p. 456; 'La chiese del SS. Rosario', in, *Cronache e fioretti del monastero di S. Sisto all' Appina*, ed. R. Spiazzi, Bolonga, 1993, p. 743; L. Frapiselli, *Monte Mario: Finestra su Roma*, Rome, 1998, p. 295

1. Sestieri, p. 50

S. Maria della Scala
Bibliography: Martinelli, p. 134; Mola, p. 61; Venuti, p. 452; Nibby, p. 479; Angeli, p. 389; Falda, *Nuovo teatro*, III, pl. 35; Titi, 1763, p. 41; E. Carreras, *AR*, 19 (3-4), p. 5; de' Rossi, *Prospectus*, pl. 68; M. Escobar, *SdR*, 42, 1981, p. 173; Wasserman, p. 56; Tesei, p. 364; Lombardi, p. 288; Kuhn-Forte, p. 653

1. Ferrari and Papaldo, p. 327
2. Nicolson, p. 123; G. Papi, *PA*, 479-81, 1990, p. 47; L. Lorizzo, *Fiamenghi che vanno e vengono*, p. 159; Judson and Ekkart, p. 70
3. W
4. JM
5. Titi, p. 60; Minor, p. 160; Chracas, II, No. 4407
6. Enggass, *Sculpture*, p. 173; Westin, p. 143
7. Fleming and Honour, p. 255
8. F. Fasolo, *FA*, VII, 1960, p. 302; Eimer, *S. Agnese*, I, fig. 26 and p. 147
9. *Le statue*, p. 212
10. Titi, p. 60; D. Germano, *BdA*, 65, 1991, p. 127
11. E. Borsook, *BM*, XCVI, 1954, p. 270
12. Titi, p. 62; D. Germano, loc. cit.
13. Montagu, *Algardi*, p. 442; Ferrari and Papaldo, p. 329
14. Weil, p. 148; Ferrari and Papaldo, p. 328
15. Titi, p. 62
16. Sestieri, p. 187
17. Titi, p. 64
18. Fasolo, p. 48
19. Cavina, p. 118; P. Askew, *Caravaggio's Death of the Virgin*, Princeton, 1990
20. Abromson, p. 209; Chiappini di Sorio, p. 118

S. Maria Scala Coeli
(See also **S. Paolo alle Tre Fontane**)
Bibliography: K. Schwager, 'Santa Maria Scala Coeli in Tre Fontane bei Rom', in, *Praestant Interna Festschrift für Ulrich Hausmann*, Tübingen, 1982, p. 394; Tiberia, p. 37; F. Bellini, *QISA*, 14, 1989, p. 31; G. Mulazzani, *L'abbazia delle Tre Fontane*, Milan, 1988; De Tomasso, p. 182; Robertson, p. 197; *Roma di Sisto V*, p. 238; *Abbazia delle Tre Fontane*, G. Belardi et al., Rome, 1995

1. *Pittura del Seicento: Ricerche in Umbria*, ed. L. Barroero et al., 1989, p. 114
2. Tosini, p. 332

S. Maria dei Sette Dolori
Bibliography: Venuti, p. 415; Nibby, p. 482; M. Bosi, *CdR*, 117; Perugini, *Architettura Borromini sulla S. Maria dei Sette Dolori*, Rome, 1959-60; E. Carreras, *AR*, 20 (5-6), 1979, p. 25; Portoghesi, *Borromini*, pls. 70-74; Blunt, *Borromini*, p. 129; *GR*, XIII, p. 10; A. Gunnarsjaa, *AA*, III, 1983, p. 231; Lombardi, p. 289; Kuhn-Forte, p. 683; M. Dunn, 'Spiritual Philanthropists', in, *Women and Art*, p. 164

1. C. Furlan, *Il Pordenone*, Milan, 1988, p. 182
2. W

S. Maria del Suffragio
Bibliography: Titi, 1686, p. 391; 1763, p. 419; Nibby, p. 483; Venuti, p. 181; Angeli, p. 392; *Via Giulia*, p. 332; Fasolo, p. 230; *GR*, V, IV, p. 56; P. Mancini, *AR*, 19 (5-6), 1978, p. 14; Buchowiecki, III, p. 182; Tesei, p. 172; Lombardi, p. 141; *Roma Sacra*, 11, 1997, p. 50

1. Titi, 1686, p. 391
2. Bacchi, p. 804, fig. 390; Ferrari and Papaldo, p. 329
3. W
4. Del Bufalo, p. 86
5. Bacchi, figs. 657, 658; Ferrari and Papaldo, p. 330
6. W
7. F. Pansecchi, *Scritti di storia dell'arte in onore di Federico Zeri*, p. 724
8. M. A. Pavone, *Pros.*, 46, 1986, p. 31
9. W
10. W; Pavone, loc. cit.
11. Chracas, II, No. 5640; F. Pansecchi, *BdA*, 28, 1984, p. 61
12. Minor, *Diario*, No. 906
13. W; J. Varriano, *PA*, 465, 1988, p. 31; Kunze, p. 73
14. Titi, p. 404

S. Maria in Traspontina
Bibliography: Baglione, p. 99; Martinelli, p. 135; Falda, *Nuovo teatro*, III, pl. 34; Titi, 1686, p. 401; Nibby, p. 485; Venuti, p. 457; Angeli, p. 393; de' Rossi, *Prospectus*, pl. 63; Magni, I, pls. 7, 8; Pollak, I, p. 184; C. Catena, *Traspontina. Guida storica e artistica*,

Rome, 1956; Wasserman, p. 59; Lewine, p. 382; Tesei, p. 408; *Organi*, p. 114; *GR*, XIV, I, p. 90; Lombardi, p. 308

1. E. Kieven, 'Eine Vignola Zeichnung fur S. Maria in Traspontina', *RJK*, XIX, 1981, p. 245
2. Pollak, I, p. 184
3. *Roma la città degli anni santi*, p. 224
4. J. Varriano, *PA*, 465, 1988, p. 31; Kunze, p. 95
5. Titi, p. 408
6. R. Bösel, *Pros.*, 15, 1978, p. 29
7. *Roma di Sisto V*, p. 241
8. *La Regola*, p. 32
9. E. Giffi, *BdA*, 19, 1983, p. 17; G. Papi, *PA*, 483, 1990, p. 95
10. Titi, p. 410; Ferrari and Papaldo, p. 332
11. W; E. Borea, *Pros.*, 12, 1978, p. 4
12. de' Rossi, *Altari*, p. 27; Coudenhove-Erthal, p. 42
13. M. B. Guerrieri Borsoi, *BdA*, 61, 1990, p. 99
14. *Le Statue*, p. 210; Ferrari and Papaldo, p. 331
15. L. Barroero, *PA*, 347, 1979, p. 3
16. E. Longo, *Pall.*, 3 (5), 1990, p. 25
17. L. Barroero, loc. cit.; *Pietro da Cortona*, p. 192
18. Titi, p. 410; S. Radino, *MD*, XVIII/4, 1980, p. 351
19. Gere and Pouncey, p. 150
20. Pickrel, pp. 188, 240
21. Graf, *Calandrucci*, p67
22. W
23. *I premiati dell'Accademia, 1682-1754*, ed. Angela Cipriani, Rome, 1989, p. 60
24. G. Tancioni, in, *Carlo Marchionni*, p. 153
25. W

S. Maria in Trastevere

Bibliography: Martinelli, p. 136; Titi, 1763, p. 43; Nibby, p. 488; Venuti, p. 448; Angeli, p. 394; Letarouilly, pl. 327 (302); C. Cecchelli, *CdR*, 31, 32; Pinelli, No. 111; Johns, p. 251; *Organi*, p. 116; Lombardi, p. 268; Kuhn-Forte, p. 699

1. Braham and Hager, p. 77
2. Enggass, *Sculpture*, p. 69
3. Mola, p. 58; Bellori, p. 350
4. Spear, p. 189; *Domenichino*, p. 253
5. Bevilacqua, p. 19; M. Villani, *SR*, XLIV, 1996, p. 321
6. M. B. Guerrieri Borsoi, *AV*, XXII, 1983, p. 11; ibid., *Zoboli*, p. 20; G. Falcidia, *Pros.*, 1983-84, 33-36, p. 287
7. Titi, p. 66
8. Titi, p. 66
9. *Pittura in Italia. Il Settecento*, p. 808
10. Minor, p. 197; Titi, p. 236
11. Frommel, p. 121; A. Angelini, *Pros.*, 91-92, 1998, p. 127
12. Pollak, I, p. 184
13. Spear, p. 278; *Domenichino*, p. 278
14. Montagu, *Algardi*, p. 453; Ferrari and Papaldo, p. 334
15. *Roma di Sisto V*, p. 430
16. B. Torresi, *QISA*, XXII, 1976, p. 95; Longhi, p. 61; H. Friedel, *RJK*, 1978, p. 89; Evers, p. 173; *Roma di Sisto V*, p. 242
17. González-Palacios, p. 371
18. Pickrel, pp. 170, 217
19. *L'Immagine di S. Francesco*, p. 55, fig, 22; G. Scavizzili, *BdA*, XLV, 1960, p. 111
20. W
21. Rotili, p. 39
22. G. Borghini, *Comm.*, XXIII, 1972, p. 385
23. Elling, pl. 36; *Architettura minora*, p. 67

S. Maria in Trivio

Bibliography: Magni, I, p. 24; Benedetti, p. 155, pls. 123-47; Titi, 1763, p. 354; Nibby, p. 505; Lewine, p. 398; Buchowiecki, III, p. 188; Letarouilly, pl. 97 (293); G. Scarfone, *S. Maria in Trivio*, Rome, 1976; M. Lange, *AA*, I, 1981, p. 275; T. Pickrel, *ABA*, 7-8, 1978, p. 216; ibid., *SdA*, 47, 1983, p. 57; M. Escobar, *SdR*, 52, 1991, p. 167; Pinelli, No. 112; Dunn, p. 17; *GR*, II, V, p. 98; Lombardi, p. 86; Racheli, p. 326; *Roma Sacra*, 4, 1995, p. 53

1. cf. Blunt, *Borromini*, p. 39
2. T. Frangenberg, *SdA*, 96, 1999, p. 165
3. W
4. Lewine, p. 404
5. *Architettura minore*, II, p. 103

S. Maria dell'Umiltà

Bibliography: Baglione, p. 310; Titi, 1763, p. 327; Nibby, p. 524; Venuti, p. 114; A. Cicinelli, *CdR*, 111; Portoghesi, *Roma Barocca*, pl. 353; Pugliese and Rigano, p. 36; Braham and Hager, 86; Buchowiecki, III, p. 195; Pinelli, No. 113; Valone, p. 140; Lombardi, p. 84; *GR*, II, VII, p. 27; M. Dunn, 'Spiritual Philanthropists', in, *Women and Art*, p. 158

1. Ferrari and Papaldo, p. 338
2. Poensgen, fig. 41, p. 98
3. Westin, p. 130; Ferrari and Papaldo, p. 338
4. M. di Macco, 'Note su Antonio Mariani', in, *Studi in onore di Giulio Carlo Argan*, Florence, 1994, p. 192
5. Bacchi, fig. 235; Ferrari and Papaldo, p. 339
6. Gunter, p. 320; Ferrari and Papaldo, p. 339
7. Titi, p. 316
8. Titi, 1686, p. 297; Dunn, p. 119
9. Gunter, p. 320; Ferrari and Papaldo, p. 340

S. Maria in Vallicella (Chiesa Nuova)

Bibliography: Pollak, I, p. 423; Titi, 1763, p. 124; Venuti, p. 204; de' Rossi, *Prospectus*; *Architettura Civile*, II, pls. 5, 6; ibid., III, pls. 20-22; Magni, I, pl. 41; M. Guidi, *RA*, XXI, 1921, p. 158; E. Strong, *La Chiesa Nuova*, Rome, 1923; Letarouilly, pl. 109 (243); M. T. Russo, *SR*, XIII, 1965, p. 21; J. Hess, *Kunstgeschichte Studien*, Rome-Vienna, 1967, I, p. 353; H. Hager, *Comm.*, XXIV, 1973, p. 300; Buchowiecki, III, p. 205; *Tesori d'arte cristiana*, p. 337; R. Lefevère, *Oratorium*, IV, 1973, p. 42; Connors, *Borromini and the Roman Oratory*; *GR*, VI, II, p. 10; Longhi, p. 45; Kummer, p. 113; Lombardi, p. 158; C. Barber, S. Barchiesi and D. Ferrara, *S. Maria in Vallicella*, Rome, 1995; D. Ferrara, 'Artisti e committenza alla Chiese Nuova', in, *La Regola*, p. 108; S. Barchiesi, 'S. Filippi Neri e l'iconografia mariana', in, *La Regola*, p. 130; *La Chiesa Nuova la facciata, il restauro*, ed. C. Molteni, 1994, Rome; *Algardi: L'altra faccia del barocco*, exhibition cat., ed. Jennifer Montagu, Rome, 1999; M. Tafuri, *Arch.*, 45, 1999, p. 471, *Roma Sacra*, 10, 1997, p. 44

1. L. Ponnelle and L. Bordet, *Saint*

Philippe Neri, Paris, 1928, pp. 118ff.
2 cf. Ponnelle and Bordet, p. 363
3 M. Dunn, *AB*, LXIV, 1982, p. 601
4 M. A. Lavin, *The Place of Narrative: Mural Decoration in Italian Churches, 1431-1600*, Chicago, 1990, p. 225
5 Briganti, pp. 248, 261, 267; Kugler, p. 65; A. Ronen, *RJK*, 25, 1989, p. 179; P. Montorsi, *BdA*, 64, 1990, p. 93
6 Ferrari and Papaldo, p. 341
7 W; Kunze, p. 91
8 M. Chiarini, *MD*, XIV, 1976, 4, p. 303
9 Bernini, p. 58
10 T. Troy, *Studies in Iconography*, 12, 1988, p. 61
11 C. S. Salerno, *SdA*, 76, 1992, p. 346
12 B. W. Meijer, *BdA*, 100 (supplement), 1997, p. 117
13 *Roma di Sisto V*, p. 246
14 Röttgen, p.125
15 D. L. Butler, *The Spada Chapel in Santa Maria in Vallicella, Rome: A Study of Late Baroque Patronage, Taste, and Style*, diss., Washington, 1991; D. Butler, *JSAH*, 1994, 53, p. 61; A. Pampalone, in, *An Architectural Progress*, p. 353; A. Pampalone, *La cappella della famiglia Spada nella Chiesa Nuova. Testimonianze documentarie*, Rome, 1993
16 B. La Greca, in, *Studi in onore di Giulio Argan*, Rome, 1984, p. 355
17 Titi, p. 152
18 *Organi*, p. 120
19 I. von zur Mühlen, 'S. Maria in Vallicella. Zur Geschichte des Hauptaltars', *RJK*, 31, 1996, p. 245
20 Strong, pl. XXIV
21 Montagu, *Roman*, p. 89; Gold, p. 56
22 A. Costamagna, 'La più bella et superba', in, *La Regola*, p. 150
23 Lavagnino, *Altari*, p. 57
24 Longhi, p. 49
25 G. Incisa della Rocchetta, *Oratorium*, III, 1972, p. 49
26 Chiappini di Sorio, p. 119; ibid., 'Cristoforo Roncalli alla Chiese Nuova', in, *Baronio e l'arte*, Sora, 1985, p. 137; F. Papi, *Roma moderna e contemporanea*, 4 (3), 1996, p. 725
27 *Marmorari*, p. 21
28 Olsen, p. 148; Emiliani, p. 347
29 Baglione, p. 595, n. 29; Fruhan, p. 261
30 Montagu, *Algardi*, p. 380; *Algardi* cat., p. 144
31 Montagu, *Algardi*, p. 427
32 Briganti, p. 205; Merz, p. 233
33 *In corso d'opera situazioni e progetti*, ed. R. B. Amidei et al., Rome, 1988
34 Salerno, p. 289
35 Pepper, p. 229
36 Pampalone, p. 53
37 *Bernardino Mei*, p. 117
38 A. Broschi, *Pala.*, S. IV, XII, 1968, p. 13
39 Nissman, p. 238; Thomas, p. 16
40 Strong, pp. 84ff.; Lilli, p. 44; *Roma di Sisto V*, p. 250
41 Olsen, p. 140; Emiliani, p. 217
42 Cavina, p. 121
43 *Roma di Sisto V*, p. 249
44 Chiappini di Sorio, p. 121
45 F. Sricchia Santoro, *Pros.*, 2, 1975, p. 18

The Oratory

Bibliography: Borromini's own ideas – partly seen through the eyes of his friend, Virgilio Spada, the prior of the Oratorians – are to be found in the *Opus architectonicum*, published in Rome in 1725 with magnificent engravings of the whole building (facsimile edition, London, n.d.); on the text see Giovanni Incisa dell Rocchetta, 'Un dialogo del P. Virgilio Spada sulla Fabbrica dei Filippini', *ASRSP*, XC, 1968, pp. 165ff.; Pollak, I, p. 437; Falda, *Nuovo teatro*, I, pls. 21-3; De' Rossi, *Architettura Civile*, I, pls. 85-97 and II, pl. 7; Magni, I, pl. 41, Hempel, pp. 61ff.; Portoghesi, *Borromini*, pls. XXX-XLIX, 37-65; Blunt, *Borromini*, p. 85; Connors, *Oratory*; J. Connors, 'Virgilio Spada's defence of Borromini', *BM*, CXXXI, 1989, p. 76; *Algardi: L'altra faccia del barocco*, exhibition cat., ed. Jennifer Montagu, Rome, 1999; M. Tafuri, *Arch.*, 45, 1999, p. 471; *Borromini e l'universo barocco*, p. 296

1 Windsor Castle, Royal Library
2 Blunt, *Borromini*, p. 34
3 A. Pandolfi, *BdA*, 84-85, 1994, p. 105; C. Cancellieri, *BdA*, 84-85, 1994, p. 121
4 J. Connors, *BM*, 1989, p. 131
5 Montagu, *Algardi*, p. 361
6 J. B. Scott, *SdA*, 55, 1985, p. 295
7 Montagu, *Algardi*, p. 353; *Algardi* cat., p. 186

S. Maria delle Vergini (S. Rita da Cascia)

Bibliography: Totti, p. 292; Martinelli, p. 127; Titi, 1674, p. 358; ibid., 1763, p. 326; de' Rossi, 1697, p. 377; Nibby, p. 515; Venuti, p. 113; Vasi, *Magnificenze*, pl. 144; Portoghesi, *Roma Barocca*, pl. 396; G. Marincola Mauro, *AR*, 16 (5-6), 1975, p. 33; Buchowiecki, III, p. 241; Dunn, p. 346; Tesei, p. 74; Lombardi, p. 91; *GR*, II, VII, p. 18; *Roma Sacra*, 4, 1995, p. 35; Barry, n. 252

1 E. Longo, *Pall.*, 3 (5), 1990, p. 25
2 Titi, p. 314
3 *Pietro da Cortona*, p. 266
4 Menichella, p. 75
5 Titi, p. 316; *Le statue*, p. 207; Ferrari and Papaldo, p. 348

S. Maria in Via

Bibliography: Baglione, p. 81, n. 35; Mola, p. 95; Titi, 1763, p. 350; Buchowiecki, III, p. 243; Venuti, p. 125; Angeli, p. 407; B. Massi, *Le chiese dei Serviti*, Rome, 1942, p. 9; Magni, I, p. 11; Longhi, p. 44; C. Cecchelli, *CdR*, 14; Marcucci, p. 279; *GR*, II, VI, p. 30; Lombardi, p. 87; *Roma Sacra*, 4, 1995, p. 57

1 Fasolo, p. 429
2 Esaperanzi, p. 65
3 G. Papi, *PA*, 15-16, 1997, p. 64
4 Röttgen, p. 64
5 Abromson, p. 44
6 Witcombe, p. 175
7 Titi, p. 334
8 Zuccari, p. 95

S. Maria in Via (Oratorio del SS. Sacramento)

Bibliography: Magni, I, pl. 107; Portoghesi, *Roma Barocca*, pl. 421; Nibby, p. 516; Mallory, *Rococo*, p. 146; P. Mancini and G. Scarfone, *L'Oratorio del SS. Sacramento di S. Maria in Via*, Rome, 1973; Chracas, I, II, Nos. 1501, 1975, 2203; Lewine, p. 448; L. Lotti, *AR*, 13 (1), 1972, p. 72; C. Varagnoli, 'Ricerche sull' opera architettonica di Gregorini e Passalacqua', *ASD*, 1-2, 1988, p. 21; *GR*, II, VI, p. 5; Lombardi, p. 94; Kuhn-Forte, p. 173; Varagnoli, p. 74; Racheli, p. 330; *Roma Sacra*, 4, 1995, p. 62

1 W: Di Federico, p. 65

S. Maria in Via Lata
Bibliography: Falda, *Nuovo teatro*, I, pl. 17; Titi, 1763, p. 318; Venuti, p. 110; Nibby, p. 519; Angeli, p. 409; Vasi, *Magnificenze*, pl. 44; *Le scienze e le arti*, vol. 1, n. n.; L. Cavazzi, *La diaconia di S. Maria in Via e il monastero di S. Ciriaco*, Rome, 1908; Magni, I, pls. 43, 44; Pollak, I, p. 184; *Via del Corso*, p. 246; Wittkower, *Art and Architecture*, p. 224; Buchowiecki, III, p. 255; C. Bertelli and C. Galassi Paluzzi, *CdR*, 114; R. Bösel, *Pros.*, 15, 1978, p. 29; *GR*, IX, III, p. 48; D. Metzger Habel, *Arch.*, 21, 1991, p. 121; Lombardi, p. 205; *Roma Sacra*, 2, 1995, p. 43; L. Lozza, *Chiese di S. Maria in Via*, Rome, 1998; Wittkower, *Art and Architecture*, vol. II, p. 71; Wittkower, Rudolf, *Art and Architecture in Italy 1600-1750*, three volumes, 6th ed revised by Joseph Connors and Jennifer Montagu, New Haven and London, 1999

1 Lavin, *Bernini*, pp. 50, 169
2 *Diary of Alexander VII*, 564, 755, June-July 1661
3 ibid., 693, 13 June 1663
4 ibid., 808
5 D. R. Marshall, *SdA*, 56, 1986, p. 49
6 W
7 W; Titi, p. 308
8 W
9 Esaperanzi, p. 65
10 R
11 S. Rudolph, *Labyrinthos*, III/5-6, 1984, p. 54
12 Lilli, p. 54
13 Lavin, *Bernini*, p. 169; D. Metzger Habel, *AB*, LXXIX, 1997, p. 291
14 A. Nava Cellini, *PA*, 147, 1962, p. 24; Dom-browski, *Finelli*, p. 420; Dombrowski, *Bolgi*, p. 299
15 Bacchi, p. 801, fig. 362
16 W
17 Riccoboni, p. 364; Ceschi, p. 102
18 R
19 V. Casale, *Scritti di storia dell'arte in onore di Federico Zeri*, p. 736; V. Casale, *Pros.*, 57-60, 1989-90, p. 327
20 R; D. Graf, *MD*, 1993, 31, p. 441
21 Esaperanzi, p. 65
22 Ferrari and Papaldo, p. 351
23 Bachi, fig. 345; Ferrari and Papaldo, p. 351

S. Maria della Visitazione (S. Francesco di Sales)
Bibliography: Venuti, p. 412; Nibby, p. 525; Angeli, p. 412; *Diario ordinario*, No. 248, 1803; *GR*, XIII, I, p. 34; Lombardi, p. 291

1 del Bufalo, p. 88

S. Maria della Vittoria
Bibliography: Baglione, p. 308; Titi, 1763, pp. 294, 481; Venuti, p. 88; Nibby, p. 526; Angeli, p. 413; Falda, *Nuovo teatro*, III, pl. 10; Tessin, p. 162; de' Rossi, *Prospectus*, pl. 70; Vasi, *Magnificenze*, pl. 148; Marcellino di S. Teresa, *Guida di S. Maria della Vittoria alle Terme*, Rome, 1915; Magni, I, pls. 49-52; G. Matthiae, *CdR*, 84; Buchowiecki, III, p. 280; Hibbard, *Maderno*, pp. 140ff.; Organi, p. 122; *GR*, XVII, p. 11; Dunn, p. 466; Ringbeck, p. 68; Lombardi, p. 357; *Roma Sacra*, 17, 2000, p. 34

1 Baglione, p. 308
2 W
3 Spear, p. 282; *Domenichino*, p. 330
4 Bacchi, p. 805, fig. 401; Ferrari and Papaldo, p. 352
5 del Bufalo, p. 87; R. Canuti, 'La Cappella di S. Giuseppe in S. Maria della Vittoria', in, *L'Arte per i giubilei*, p. 41
6 Bacchi, fig. 483; Ferrari and Papaldo, p. 353
7 Enggass, *Sculpture*, p. 82
8 R; P. Petraroia, *RINASA*, III/IV, 1981, p. 279
9 Matthiae, p. 80; Pane, p. 115
10 Ferrari and Papaldo, p. 354
11 E. Giffi Ponzi, *Pros.*, 50, 1987, p. 71; G. Papi, *PA*, 479-81, 1990, p. 47; L. Lorizzo, *Fiamenghi che vanno e vengono*, p. 159; Judson and Ekkart, p. 92
12 *Notizie del Giorno*, No. 11, 1834
13 Wittkower, *Bernini*, p. 216; Lavagnino, *Altari*, pp. 25, 83; A. Blunt, *AH*, I, 1978, p. 73; R. Preimesberger, *ZfK*, 49, 1986, p. 190; C. Napoleone, *FMR*, 83, 1996, p. 20; Marder, p. 110; C. Napoleone, *ABA*, 55-58, 1998, p. 172
14 Montagu, *Algardi*, p. 201, n. 22; p. 453
15 W
16 Salerno, p. 261
17 Pepper, p. 303
18 *Imago Mariae*, p. 162
19 Pepper, p. 249

S. Marta
Bibliography: Falda, *Nuovo teatro*, I, pl. 18; Titi, 1763, p. 23; de' Rossi, *Architettura Civile*, III, pl. 41; Nibby, p. 536; H. Hager, *Comm.*, XXV, 1974, p. 225; Buchowiecki, III, p. 325; *GR*, IX, I, p. 76; M. R. Dunn, *AB*, LXX, 1988, p. 451; Pinelli, No. 114; Lombardi, p. 209; *Roma Sacra*, 2, 1995, p. 40

1 M. B. Guerrieri Borsoi, *BdA*, 61, 1990, p. 99; Ferrari and Papaldo, p. 358

S. Marta in Vaticano (destroyed)
Bibliography: Vasi, *Magnificenze*, pl. 166; Titi, 1721, p. 29; Armellini, *Chiese*, II, p. 939; G. Bossi, *La Chiesa di S. Marta al Vaticano*, Rome, 1883; Wasserman, 'Santa Marta al Vaticano', *Cap.*, XXXVI, 9. 1961, p. 23; Wasserman, *Mascarino*, p. 64

S. Martino ai Monti (SS. Silvestro e Martino ai Monti)
Bibliography: Titi, 1686, p. 218; Venuti, p. 42; Nibby, p. 543; Angeli, p. 417; Chracas, III, Nos. 1906, 2282; Letarouilly, pls. 252, 253 (308, 309); Magni, I, p. 45; E. Bogga, *Cap.*, XXXI, 1956, p. 280; M. Metraux, *The Iconography of S. Martino ai Monti in Rome*, diss., Boston University, 1979; E. Boaga, *Il titolo di equizio e la basilica di S. Martino ai Monti*, Rome, 1988; G. C. Miletti and S. Ray, *Pala.*, XI, 1967, p. 3; *Organi*, p. 124; *GR*, I, II, p. 42; Pinelli, No. 115; Tesei, p. 28; Lombardi, p. 46; Pocino, p. 134

1 Ferrari and Papaldo, p. 359
2 S. J. Bandes, *SdA*, 26, 1976, p. 45; A. B. Sutherland, *BM*, CVI, 1964, p. 58; J. Heideman, ibid.,

CXXII, 1980, p. 540; M. Boisclair, *SdA*, 53, 1985, p. 87
3   Natoli and Scarpati, p. 64
4   Chracas, III, No. 2388
5   W
6   W
7   Ferrari and Papaldo, p. 361
8   *La Regola*, p. 86
9   Di Giammaria, p. 156
10 *Pietro Testa, 1612-1650. Prints and Drawings*, ed. E. Copper, Philadelphia, 1988, p. 193
11 Bodart, I, p. 404

SS. Michele e Magno
Bibliography: Venuti, p. 511; M. Bosi and P. Becchetti, *CdR*, 126; Nibby, p. 553; Pinelli, No. 116; M. Bosi, *AR*, 17 (1-2), 1976, p. 66; Tesei, p. 414; M. Muskens, *SS. Michele e Magno dei Frisoni*, Rome, 1993; Lombardi, p. 307; *GR*, VXIV, IV, p. 24

1   Titi, p. 48
2   Titi, p. 49
3   Geller, p. 92

SS. Michele e Magno
Bibliography: Venuti, p. 511; M. Bosi and P. Becchetti, *CdR*, 126; Nibby, p. 553; Pinelli, No. 116; Tesei, p. 414; M. Muskens, *SS. Michele e Magno dei Frisoni*, Rome, 1993; Lombardi, p. 307; *GR*, VXIV, IV, p. 24

1   Titi, p. 48
2   Titi, p. 49
3   Geller, p. 92

SS. Nereo e Achilleo
Bibliography: Venuti, p. 388; J. Urban, *RJK*, 9-10, 1961-62, p. 91; Nibby, p. 555; G. Matthiae, *Cap.*, XLIV, 1969, p. 154; Letarouilly, pl. 266 (319); A. Zuccari, *SdA*, 42, 1981, p. 171; A. Guerriri, *La chiese dei SS. Nereo e ed Achilleo*, Rome, 1951; Buchwiecki, III, p. 350; A. Herz, *AB*, LXX, 1988, p. 590; Macioce, p. 126; Abromson, p. 124; Pinelli, No. 117; *GR*, XXI, II, p. 88; Lombardi, p. 371; A. Zuccari, 'Cesare Baronio, Le immagini', *La Regola*, p. 80; M. Grazia Turco, *Pall.*, 14, 1994, p. 215; ibid, *Il Titulus dei SS. Nero e Achilleo emblema della reforma cattolica*, Rome, 1997; ibid, *BdA*, 88, 1994, p. 93

1   Gere and Pouncey, p. 24; *La Regola*, p. 502

2   *Chiappini di Sorio*, p. 122

S. Nicola in Arcione (destroyed)
Bibliography: *GR*, II, 1, p. 112

S. Nicola in Carcere
Bibliography: Baglione, p. 81, n. 25; Vasi, *Magnificenze*, pl. 118; Buchwiecki, III, p. 373; G. Fiocco, *Pall.*, 4, 1945, p. 131; G. B. Proja, *CdR*, Nuova Serie, 112; Macioce, p. 153; Pinelli, No. 119; Tesei, p. 326; Lombardi, p. 238; *Roma Sacra*, 15, 1999, p. 23; Racheli, p. 344

1   *La pittura in Italia: L'Ottocento*, p. 441
2   Salerno, p. 261
3   Cavallaro, p. 232
4   Chracas, III, No. 1272; Stella Rudolph, *Labyrinthos*, III/5-6, 1984, p. 54; Lilli, p. 87
5   *Roma la città degli anni*, p. 226; Möller, p. 96
6   Posner, p. 55

S. Nicola degli Incoronati (destroyed)
Bibliography: C. P. Planca Incoronati, 'La Chiesa di S. Nicola degli Incoronati in Roma', *Archivio della R. Deputazione romana di storia patria*, LXI, 1938, p. 193

S. Nicola dei Lorenesi
Bibliography: Titi, 1763, p. 410; Nibby, p. 561; F. Bonnard, *Histoire de l'église de Saint-Nicolas de la Confraternité des Lorrains à Rome*, 1932; Ferarri, *Lo Stucco*, pls. CXXIff.; M. de Dumast, *L'église Saint Nicolas des Lorrains à Rome*, Rome, n.d.; Venuti, p. 193; Chracas, II, No. 5052; Buchwiecki, III, p. 368; *GR*, VI, I, p. 76; Bousquet, *Recherches*, p. 125; P. Violette, 'La décoration de l'église', in, *Les fondations nationales*, p. 487; Tesei, p. 180; Lombardi, p. 157; H. Collin, 'L'église S. Nicola-des-Lorrains', *Loth.*, 5, 1993, p. 301; *Roma Sacra*, 8, 1996, p. 2

1   Poensgen, p. 100; P. Violette, in, *Corrado Giaquinto (1703-1766)*, ed. P. Amato, Messina, 1985, p. 113; Gabrielli; p. 36
2   Titi, p. 398

S. Nicola dei Prefetti
Bibliography: Titi, 1763, p. 366; Nibby, p. 562; Venuti, p. 144; Angeli, p. 429; Vasi, *Magnificenze*, pl. 106; G. Drago, *CdR*, 55; Buchwiecki, III, p. 401; Pinelli, No. 122; *GR*, IV, V, p. 78; Lombardi, p. 127; *Roma Sacra*, 9, 1997, p. 30

1   Priori and Tabarrini, p. 31

S. Nicola da Tolentino
Bibliography: Totti, p. 297; Falda, *Nuovo teatro*, III, pl. 14; Titi, p. 1686, p. 302 and 1763, p. 334; Nibby, p. 562; Venuti, p. 88; de' Rossi, *Architettura Civile*, III, pls. 11-13; F. Fasolo, *FA*, XI, 1963, p. 66; H. Hager, *Comm.*, XXII, 1971, p. 36; Buchwiecki, III, p. 407; *GR*, II, I, p. 44; G. Zandri, *CdR*, Nuova Serie, 19; Pinelli, No. 123; Tesei, p. 58; De Tomasso, p. 34; Lombardi, p. 88; *Algardi: L'altra faccia del barocco*, exhibition cat., ed. Jennifer Montagu, Rome, 1999; Racheli, p. 346; *Roma Sacra*, 5, 1996, p. 39

1   *Agnese*, II, p. 522
2   C. C. Kelly, *JSAH*, L, 1991, p. 57
3   Ferrari and Papaldo, p. 368
4   *Le statue*, p. 204; Ferrari and Papaldo, p. 362
5   *Le statue*, p. 222; Weil, p. 142
6   Titi, p. 320; *Pietro da Cortona*, p. 251
7   W; Fischer Pace, *Baldini*
8   Salerno, p. 298
9   Chracas, II, No. 96
10 Enggass, *Baciccio*, p. 147
11 Ferrari and Papaldo, p. 363
12 W; N. Dunn-Czak, *Apollo*, CII/1972, 1975, p. 110
13 Fischer Pace, *Baldini*, p. 3
14 Montagu, *Algardi*, p. 367; *Algardi* cat., p. 180; Ferrari and Papaldo, p. 364; *L'Idea del Bello*, p. 393
15 Fischer Pace, *Baldini*; *Pietro da Cortona*, pp. 192, 398
16 Caracciolo, p. 334
17 Chracas, III, No. 1586
18 Lavagnino, *Altari*, p. 107; Briganti, p. 70; Davis, p. 29ff.; *Von Bernini bis Piranesi: Römische Architekturzeichnungen des Barock*, ed. E. Kieven, Stuttgart, 1993, cat. no. 49; *Pietro da Cortona*, p. 442; A. Rocca de

Amicis and C. Varagnoli, 'La cappella dei Gavotti', in, *Pietro Cortona: Atti del convegno*, p. 353
19 Westin, p. 175

SS. Nome di Gesù
See Il Gesù

SS. Nome di Maria
Bibliography: Titi, 1763, p. 278; Nibby, p. 564; Venuti, p. 59; A. Martini and M. C. Casanova, *CdR*, 70; Buchowiecki, III, p. 465; W. Oeshsli, *QISA*, 16, 1969, p. 47; De Tomasso, p. 36; M. di Tanna, *AR*, 38 (1), 1997, p. 11; C. Cozzolino, *Pall.*, 2, 1989, p. 77; Lombardi, p. 89; *GR*, II, VIII, p. 113; *Roma Sacra*, 3, 1995, p. 53

1 Minor, p. 177
2 Titi, p. 277; Chracas, II, No. 6222
3 Chracas, II, No. 6270; Titi, p. 277
4 Chracas, II, No. 5880
5 Chracas, II, No. 5139
6 R

Nostra Signora del Sacro Cuore See S. Giacomo degli Spagnuoli

S. Omobono
Bibliography: Nibby, p. 565; Venuti, p. 402; Angeli, p. 433; A. M. Colini, M. Bosi and L. Huetter, *CdR*, 57; *GR*, XII, I, p. 53; Buchowiecki, III, p. 506; Lewine, p. 528; Tesei, p. 334; De Tomasso, p. 142; Lombardi, p. 261

1 Nicolson, p. 110

S. Onofrio
Bibliography: Titi, 1763, p. 29; Nibby, p. 566; Venuti, p. 407; G. Caterbi, *La chiese di S. Onofrio*, Rome, 1858; Letarouilly, pl. 275 (326); L. Huetter, E. Lavagnino et al., *CdR*, 40; G. Urban, *RJK*, 9-10, 1961-62, p. 79; *GR*, XIII, p. 156; Pinelli, No. 125; Lombardi, p. 292; Macioce, p. 141; O. Mandolesi, 'S. Onofrio al Gianicolo', in, *L'Arte per i giubilei*, p. 203

1 Spear, p. 137; *Domenichino*, p. 178
2 Santiago Godos, 'La fachada de la Capilla del Rosario', in, *Homenaje al profesor Martin Gonzàlez*, Valladolid, 1995, p. 683
3 T. Pugliatti, *Agostino Tassi tra conformismo e libertà*, Rome, 1977, p. 56
4 Titi, p. 56
5 A. Caliva, in, *L'arte per i papi*, vol. 2, p. 31
6 J. Montagu, 'Claudio Ridolfi in the cloister of S. Onofrio' in *Claudio Ridolfi. Un pittore vento nelle Marche del Seicento*, ed. C. Costanzi, Corinaldo, 1997, p. 185
7 Bacchi, fig. 318
8 Cavallaro, p. 228
9 Posner, p. 68; *Angels from the Vatican: Invisible Made Visible*, exhibition cat. ed A. Duston and A. Nesselrath, Arnold, 1998, p. 250
10 L. Spezzaferro, 'I Madruzzi a Roma', 'La cappella Madruzzo in S. Onofrio', and in, *I Madruzzo e l'Europa*, exhibition cat. ed L. Dal Prà, Florence, 1993, pp. 683, 695
11 Di Federico, p. 63
12 R
13 Stollhans, p. 12; L. Testa, *SdA*, 66, 1989, p. 171
14 M. Faietti and K. Oberhuber, *RSA*, 34, 1988, p. 55; M. Faietti 'Jacopo Ripanda, il suo collaboratore', in, *Dal disegno all' opera compiuta: Atti del convegno internazionale Torgiano*, Torgiano, 1987, p. 19; H. Wohl, *The Aesthetics of Italian Renaissance Art: A Reconsideration of Style*, Cambridge, 1999, p. 5
15 Stringa, p. 95; *Giornale di Roma*, No. 95, 1858, 21st April; id., No. 162, 1856, 17th July; *Le scienze e le arti*, vol. I, n.n.

S. Pancrazio
Bibliography: Nibby, p. 569; Venuti, p. 425; Angeli, p. 438; n. a. *Della basilica di S. Pancrazio martire*, Rome, 1838; M. Cecchelli, *CdR*, 124; O. Pietro-bono, *S. Pancrazio a Via Aurelia Antica*, Rome, n. d.; L. Lotti, *AR*, 12 (5- 6), 1971, p. 24; Tesei, p. 494; Lombardi, p. 434

1 Ferrari and Papaldo, p. 369
2 S. M. Rainaldi, *Palma il Giovane*, Milan, 1984, p. 106

S. Pantaleo
Bibliography: Titi, 1763, p. 233; Nibby, p. 572; Venuti, p. 215; Spagnesi, *de Rossi*, pp. 193ff.; id., *CdR*, 94; Buchowiecki, III, p. 519; G. Scarfone, *AR*, 24 (3-6), 1983, p.40; *GR*, VI, I, p. 112; M. Dunn, *RJK*, 29, 1994, p. 187; Lombardi, p. 160; *Roma Sacra*, 10, 1997, p. 33

1 Ferrari and Papaldo, p. 369
2 *Diario ordinario*, No. 105, 1806; Valadier, p. 47
3 Poensgen, p. 101, fig. 33
4 Enggass, *Sculpture*, p. 122
5 J. Daniels, *Sebastiano Ricci*, Wayland, 1976, p. 105
6 R. De Fusco et al., *Luigi Vanvitelli*, Naples, 1973, p. 76; *Architettura del Settecento*, p. 79; Seta, p. 301
7 *Diario ordinario*, No. 138, 1802; Hubert, p. 170; M. Ingendaay Rodio, *AC*, 74, 1986, p. 393
8 *Diario ordinario*, No. 70, 1807
9 Titi, p. 160
10 Dunn, p. 203, n. 121
11 Chracas, II, No. 6678

Pantheon See S. Maria ad Martyres

S. Paolo fuori le Mura
Bibliography: There are a great number of journal entries relating to the rebuilding of S. Paolo; these are some of the more important entries. *Diario di Roma*, No. 56, 1823; No, 1, 102, 1826; No. 50, 1827; No. 56, 1823; No. 85, 1835; No. 87, 1836; No. 84, 1839; No. 83, 1840, Nos. 53, 86, 1845; Nos. 54, 85, 1847; *Giornale di Roma*, No. 149, 1851; No. 150, 1852,; Nos. 147, 148, 1853; Nos. 148, 283, 1854; No. 149, 1856; No. 146, 1858; No. 147, 1859; No. 166, 1861; No. 170, 1862; No. 140, 1863; No. 150, 1864; No. 153, 1866; No. 153, 1868; No. 153, 1869; *Notizie di Roma*, No. 32, 1834; *Le scienze e le arti*, vol. I, n. n.; Nibby, p. 577; Angeli, p. 442; *S. Paolo fuori le Mura*, ed. C. Pietrangeli, Florence, 1988; Buchowiecki, I, p. 214; E. Lavagnino, *CdR*, No. 12; M. F. Fischer, *DKD*, 38, 1980, p. 6; Lombardi, p. 432; E. Pallottino, 'La nuova architttura paleocristiana', *RSA*, 56, 1995, p. 30

1 J. Huber, *SdA*, 36-37, 1979, p.

2 M. H. Ravalli, *PA*, 383-85, 1982, p. 15; F. Barocelli, ibid., p. 43
3 Faranda, p. 176

S. Paolo Primo Eremita

Bibliography: de' Rossi, 1727, p. 694; Titi, 1763, pp. 65, 70; Vasi, *Magnificenze*, pl. 122; Vasi, 1777, p. 138; M. Vasi, 1814, p. 183; Nibby, p. 575; Ladislao Toth, *Atti del II° Congresso Nazionale di Studi Romani*, 1931, II, p. 371; P. Mancini, *AR*, 24 (3-6), 1983, p. 22; F. A. Salvagnini, *I pittori Borgognoni*, Rome, 1936, p. 159; A. Schiavo, *Cap.*, XXXVI, 1961, p. 8; Buchowiecki, III, p. 531; Pinelli, No. 127; Lombardi, p. 69; P. Guerrini, 'Clemente Orlandi architetto', in, *Architettura città territorio*, p. 93

S. Paolo alla Regola

Bibliography: Titi, 1686, p. 435 and 1763, p. 100; Chracas, I, No. 1741; Vasi, *Magnificenze*, p. 131; Roisecco, 1750, I, p. 592; Venuti, p. 224; Nibby, p. 576; P. G. Parisi, *S. Paolo alla Regola*, Rome, 1931; G. Cannizzaro, *AR*, 26, 1985, p. 130; Buchowiecki, III, p. 534; Elling, pl. 34; *GR*, VII, I, p. 32; Tesei, p. 230; De Tomasso, p. 104; Lombardi, p. 178; *Roma Sacra*, 13, 1998, p. 21

1 Titi, p. 129
2 W; Titi, p. 130
3 Titi, p. 129; Voss, p. 624; D. N. Roio, *AV*, XXXII (6), 1993, p. 42
4 W
5 Ferrari and Papaldo, p. 372
6 Kowa, p. 175; Sestieri, p. 167
7 W; Titi, p. 129
8 Sestieri, p. 155
9 Graf, *Calandrucci*, p. 69; Sestieri, p. 155
10 Chracas, II, No. 4680; Titi, p. 130
11 Graf, *Calandrucci*, p. 68
12 Titi, p. 130

S. Paolo alle Tre Fontane (See also S. Maria Scala Coeli)

Bibliography: Baglione, p. 81; Totti, p. 118; Titi, 1686, p. 56; Nibby, pp. 585, 755; Venuti, p. 380; Letarouilly, pl. 339 (352); Tesei, p. 496; Benedetti and Zander, p. 546; Macioce, p. 134; L. Maggi, *Pall.*, 13, 1994, 25; ibid, *Giacomo della Porta: il S. Paolo alle Tre Fontane*, Rome, 1996

1 Harwood, p. 535: Ferrari and Papaldo, p. 373
2 Ferrari and Papaldo, p. 373
3 C. Höper, *Bartolomeo Passarotti (1529-1592)*, Worms, 1987, Part II, p. 221

S. Pasquale Baylon (SS. Quaranta Martiri)

Bibliography: Titi, 1763, p. 50; Chracas, II, Nos. 4191, 4653; Venuti, p. 445; Vasi, *Magnificenze*, p. 169; Nibby, p. 681; Portoghesi, *Roma Barocca*, pls. 343, 345; Mallory, *Rococo*, p. 61; G. Cannizzaro, *La chiesa dei SS. Quaranta Martiri e S. Pasquale Baylon*, Rome, 1977; Elling, pl. 58; *GR*, XIII, V, p. 6; Pinelli, No. 128; Kuhn-Forte, p. 1091

1 Titi, p. 74
2 R
3 R
4 R
5 R
6 Chracas, II, No. 4596
7 Chracas, II, No. 7350
8 Titi, p. 76
9 R

S. Pietro in Montorio

Bibliography: Titi, 1763, p. 239; Nibby, p. 587; Venuti, p. 416; Falda, *Nuovo teatro*, III, pl. 31; Magni, I, pl. 96; Letarouilly, pls. 44, 103-5, 322, 323 (338-43); Portoghesi, *Renaissance*, pls. 17-20; B. Pesci and E. Lavagnino, *CdR*, 42; *GR*, XIII, I, p. 124; A. M. Compagna, in, *Fabbriche romane del primo '500 cinque secoli di restauri*, Rome, 1984, p. 17; *Oltre Raffaello*, p. 67; Pinelli, No. 130; P. L. Vannicelli, *S. Pietro in Montorio*, Rome, 1971; *Chiese dal Rinascimento*, p. 139; L. Gigli, *Il complesso Gianicolense di S. Pietro in Montorio*, Rome, 1987; Lombardi, p. 294; Kuhn-Forte, p. 935; F. Cantatore, *QISA*, 24, 1994, p. 3

1 S. Spinelli, *MKIF*, XXXVI, 1992, p. 333
2 Hirst, p. 49
3 Pio, p. 76
4 Corti, p. 82
5 Baglione, p. 12; A. Nova, *AB*, LXVI, 1984, p. 150; Pope-Hennessy, p. 483
6 Barolsky, p. 103
7 Pugliatti, fig. 356
8 Hall, p. 188
9 Pugliatti, p. 167
10 Nicolson, pp. 54, 119; C. Grilli, *BdA*, 84-85, 1994, p. 157; id, *PA*, 11, 1997, p. 32; V. White, *Fiamenghi che vanno e vengono*, p. 168
11 Cavallaro, p. 247
12 Lavagnino, *Altari*, p. 77; Lavin, *Bernini*, pp. 22, 188; Borsi, p. 307; Marder, p. 106; Ferrari and Papaldo, p. 374
13 Wittkower, *Bernini*, p. 213
14 Bacchi, p. 780
15 W
16 Tosini, p. 325; Macioce, p. 152
17 G. Belardinelli, *BdA*, 68-69, 1991, p. 13; *Roma di Sisto V*, p. 253

S. Pietro in Vaticano

Bibliography: Titi, 1763, pp. 1, 449; Venuti, p. 462; Nibby, p. 593; W. Lotz, *Architecture in Italy, 1400-1600*, rev. D. Howard, New Haven/London, 1994, pp. 17, 23, 31, 54, 98; F. Wolff-Metternich, *Die Entstehung der Peterskirche zu Rom im 16. Jahrhundert*, Vienna-Munich, 1972; A. Bruschi, C. L. Frommel, F. G. Wolf Metternich and C. Thoenes, *San Pietro che non'É da Bramante a Sangallo il Giovane*, Milan, 1996; C. B. McClendon, 'The History of the Site of St Peter's', *Perspecta*, 25, 1989, p. 32; C. L. Frommel, 'St Peter's: The Early History', in, *The Renaissance from Brunel-leschi to Michelangelo*, p. 399; Buchowiecki, I, p. 103; C. Galassi-Paluzzi, *CdR*, 74, 75, 76, 77; Ackerman, *Michelangelo*, pp. 193, 317; A. C. Carpiceci, *BdA*, 68-69, 1991, p. 23; Pollak, II; *Chiese dal Rinascimento*, p. 192; E. Francia, *Storia della costruzione del nuovo San Pietro da Michelangelo a Bernini*, Rome, 1989; *La basilica di San Pietro*, ed. C. Pietrangeli, Florence, 1989; G. Delfini Filippi, *Guide de Vaticano: San Pietro, La Basilica*, Rome, 1989; H. Tratz, *RJK*, 27-28, 1991-92, p. 337; L. Rice, *The Altars and Altarpieces of New St Peter's: Outfitting the Basilica, 1621-1660*, New York, 1998; F. R. Di Federico, *The Mosaics of Saint Peter*, Pennsylvania, 1983; G. L. Hersey, *High Renaissance Art in St Peter's and the Vatican. An Interpretative Guide*, Chicago, 1993; S. Schütze, *RJK*, 29, 1994, p. 213; *L'Architettura della Basilica di S. Pietro: Storia e Costruzione*, ed. G. Spagnesi, Rome, 1997; V. Noè, *I santi fondatori nella basilica Vaticano*, Modena, 1996; *S. Pietro: Arte e storia nella Basilica Vaticano*, ed. G. Rocchi Coopmans De Yoldi, Bergamo, 1996; Bacchi, Andrea and Stefano Tumidei, *Bernini. La Scultura in S. Pietro*, Milan, 1998; *Algardi: L'altra faccia del barocco*, exhibition cat., ed. Jennifer Montagu, Rome, 1999

1. Hibbard, *Maderno*, pp. 65, 155
2. Chracas, III, No. 1566; Collins, p. 236
3. Hibbard, *Maderno*, pp. 160ff.
4. Bacchi, *Bernini*, p. 112; G. C. Bauer, *ZfK*, 1, 2000, p. 15
5. Wittkower, *Bernini*, p. 251; Scribner, pl. 32; T. Marder, *Bernini's Scala Regia at the Vatican Palace. Architecture, Sculpture, and Ritual*, Cambridge, 1997
6. Enggass, *Sculpture*, p. 200
7. R. Enggass, *AB*, LX, 1978, p. 96; R. Enggass, *Apollo*, 113, 1981, p. 74
8. Wittkower, *Bernini*, p. 216
9. Braham and Hager, p. 61; Johns, *Papal Art*, p. 55
10. Enggass, *Sculpture*, pp. 139, 181, 182, 184, 186, 191, 203
11. Chracas, II, No. 5790; Minor, p. 233
12. Chracas, II, No. 6216
13. Chracas, II, No. 5964
14. Bissell, p. 79
15. *Diario di Roma*, No. 20, 1834
16. D. L. Bershad, *ABA*, 23-24, 1984, p. 76
17. Chracas, II, No. 4374; Minor, p. 203
18. Chracas, II, No. 5661
19. Chracas, II, No. 5607
20. Enggass, *Sculpture*, p. 202
21. *La Confessione nella basilica di San Pietro in Vaticano*, ed. A. M. Pergolizzi, Milan, 1999
22. Lavin, *Bernini*, p. 19
23. Wittkower, *Bernini*, p. 189; Montagu, *Roman*, p. 70; W. C. Kirwin, in, *Gian Lorenzo Bernini Architetto*, p. 53; W. C. Kirwin, *Powers Matchless: The Pontificate of Urban VIII, the Baldachin, and Gian Lorenzo Bernini*, New York, 1996; G. Bauer, 'Bernini and the Baldacchino', *Arch.*, 26, 1996, p. 144; Dom-browski, p. 301; Bacchi, p. 72; for iconography see H. Kauffmann, *MJBK*, VI, 1955, p. 222; W. C. Kirwin, *RJK*, 19, 1981, p. 141; W. C. Kirwin and P. Fehl, *Icon.*, VII/VIII, 1981-82, p. 323. For the complicated question of the origin of the design and the share of Borromini in it, see I. Lavin, *Bernini and the Crossing of St Peter's*, New York, 1968; H. Thelen, *Die Entstehungsgeschichte der Hochaltararchitektur von St Peter in Rom*, Berlin, 1967
24. *Diario di Roma*, No. 10, 1819
25. Ferrari and Papaldo, p. 554
26. Ferrari and Papaldo, p. 552
27. Ferrari and Papaldo, p. 553
28. Bacchi, *Bernini*, p. 84
29. Bacchi, *Bernini*, p. 92
30. Sutherland and Harris, pp. 71ff
31. Schleier, p. 141
32. Braham and Hager, p. 56
33. Enggass, *Sculpture*, p. 68; Montagu, *Gold*, p. 125
34. *Diario di Roma*, No. 86, 1835, No. 103, 1836, No. 14, 1837; Stringa, p. 121
35. Briganti, p. 252
36. Spear, p. 268
37. Braham and Hager, p. 51
38. Matthiae, p. 53
39. Minor, p. 205
40. Wittkower, *Bernini*, p. 201; *Bernini in Vaticano*, p. 110; Bacchi, *Bernini*, p. 104; C. Schmid, *Incontri*, 13, 1998 (1998), p. 41
41. M. Visona, *PA*, 1-2, 1995, p. 81
42. M. Carta, 'L'Architettura del Ciborio berniniano', in, *L'Ultimo Bernini*, p. 37; L. Falaschi, 'Il Ciborio del Santissimo Sacramento in S. Pietro', ibid., p. 29; Marder, p. 299; Bacchi, *Bernini* p. 168; M. Beck, *Apollo*, 449, 1999, p. 35
43. Hempel, p. 11; M. Fagiolo, *Studio sul Borromini*, II, pl. 8; G. Scarfone, *SdR*, XXXVIII, 1977, p. 372
44. Briganti, p. 187; Merz, p. 204
45. Wittkower, *Bernini*, p. 260; K. Noehles, *RJK*, 15, 1975, p. 169; Borsi, p. 238; Scribner, pl. 40; Montagu, *Gold*, p. 62
46. Spear, p. 281
47. Enggass, *Sculpture*, p. 102; F. den Broeder, *BM*, CXX, 1978, p. 542; F. Martin, *ZfK*, 1, 1998, p. 77; S. Androssov, *SdA*, 96, 1999, p. 238
48. Spear, p. 175
49. Baglione, p. 80, n. 26
50. *Notizie del Giorno*, No. 17, 29th April, No. 38, 23rd Sept, No. 78, 28th Sept., 1847
51. Gradara, p. 72
52. Chracas, II, No. 8057; Montini, p. 393
53. Montini, p. 393
54. L. Rice, *BM*, CXXXIV, 1992, p. 428
55. Montini, p. 372; Ferrari and Papaldo, p. 565
56. Wittkower, *Bernini*, p. 198; Fagiolo dell'Arco, *Bernini*, cat. no. 63; Bacchi, *Bernini*, p. 118; *Bernini in Vaticano*, p. 108; Pope-Hennessy, p. 523
57. W. Gramberg, *RJK*, 21, 1984, p. 253
58. H. Tratz, *RJK*, 23-24, 1988, p. 395; Bacchi, *Bernini*, p. 142; Pope-Hennessy, p. 529; Angelini, p. 23; Ferrari and Papaldo, p. 555
59. F. den Broeder, *BM*, CXX, 1978, p. 542; E. J. Olszeski, *SdA*, 91, 1997, p. 367
60. Montagu, *Algardi*, p. 358
61. Wittkower, *Bernini*, p. 254; Borsi, p. 348; Bacchi, *Bernini*, p. 178; *Bernini in Vaticano*, p. 148; Pope-Hennessy, p. 524; K. Zollikofer, *Berninis Grabmal für Alexander VII. Fiktion und Repräsentation*, Worms, 1994; Marder, p. 314; Angelini, p. 185
62. A. Blunt, in, *Essays in the History of Art Presented to Rudolf Wittkower*, London, 1967, p. 230
63. J. Montagu, *MD*, 31, 1993, p. 454
64. Collins, p. 196; Gaus, p. 67; S. Ceccarelli, in, *Carlo Marchionni*, p. 57
65. *Gian Lorenzo Bernini*, p. 332; Ferrari and Papaldo, p. 574
66. Chracas, III, No. 932
67. A. Vannugli, *Pros.*, 75-76, 1994, p. 161
68. F. Caglioti, *Pros.*, 86, 1997, p. 37
69. *Giornale di Roma*, No. 44, 1857,

24th Feb; ibid., No. 15, 1866, 19th Jan.; *Montini*, p. 410
70 *Marmorari*, p. 23
71 Baglione, p. 81, n. 22
72 *Notizie del Giorno*, No. 45, 1829; *Bertel Thorvaldsen*, p. 105
73 Montagu, *Algardi*, p. 434; *Algardi* cat., p. 112
74 Enggass, *Sculpture*, p. 83; Walker, p. 117; Ferrari and Papaldo, p. 573
75 Hempel, p. 11
76 *Montini*, p. 416
77 *Canonica scultore e musicista*, ed. N. Cardano, Rome, 1985, p. 219
78 Chracas, II, No. 3960; Gradara, p. 45; Gonzàlez-Palacios, p. 101
79 *Diario di Roma*, Nos. 42, 46, 49, 1819
80 F. di Federico, *SdA*, 6, 1970, p. 153
81 Braham and Hager, p. 39; Hager, p. 133; Montagu, *Gold*, p. 121

The Piazza

Bibliography: C. Thoenes, 'Studien zur Geschichte des Peterplatzes', *ZfK*, XXVI, 1963, p. 97; D'Onofrio, *Acque e Fontane*, p. 316. For Bernini's schemes, see Brauer and Wittkower, p. 64; Witt-kower, *Italian Baroque*, pp. 53, 61; T. Kitao, *Circle and Oval in the Square of St Peter's*, New York, 1973; A. G. Marino, 'Il Colonnato di San Pietro', *Pall.*, XXIII, 1973, p. 81; T. Thieme, 'La Geometria di Piazza San Pietro', ibid., p. 129; H. W. Kruft, ' The Origin of the Oval in Bernini's Piazza S. Pietro', *BM*, CXXI. 1979, p. 796; P. Rietbergen, 'A Vision Come True', *MNIR*, XLIV-XLV, p. 111; R. Carloni, in, *An Architectural Progress*, p. 655; H. Hagar, 'Bernini, Carlo Fontana e la fortuna del "terzo braccio" del colonnato di piazza San Pietro in Vaticano', *QISA*, 25-30, 1995-97 (1997), p. 337. T. Marder, *Bernini's Scala Regia at the Vatican Palace: Architecture, Sculpture and Ritual*, Cambridge, 1997, p. 82; Marder, p. 126. For the statues on colonnade, see *Le statue berniniane del Colonnato di San Pietro*, ed. Valentino Martinelli, Rome, 1987; Marder, p. 126

1 G. Pomodoro, *Geometria Prattica*, Rome, 1599, pl. XXVIII
2 Ferrari and Papaldo, p. 587

Cappella Sistina

Bibliography: L. D. Ettlinger, *The Sistine Chapel before Michelangelo*, Oxford, 1965; *The Sistine Chapel: The Art, the History, and the Restoration*, C. Pietrangeli et al., New York, 1986; *Michelangelo: Selected Scholarship in English*, vols 2, 'The Sistine Chapel' and 4, 'Tomb of Julius II and Works in Rome' ed. W. E. Wallace, New York, 1995; C. F. Lewine, *The Sistine Chapel Walls and the Roman Liturgy*, University Park, 1993; L. Partridge, *Michelangelo: The Sistine Chapel Ceiling*, Rome and New York, 1996; B. Barnes, *Michelangelo's Last Judgment: The Renaissance Response*, Berkeley, 1998

S. Pietro in Vincoli

Bibliography: Titi, 1763, pp. 239, 478; Venuti, p. 37; Nibby, p. 663; Letarouilly, pl. 140 (263); L. Lotti, *AR*, 13 (1) 1972, p.25; Buchowiecki, III, p. 548; G. Matthiae, *CdR*, 54; *GR*, I, II, p. 80; Racheli, p. 260; Lombardi, p. 43; Pocino, p. 251

1 P. Bagni, *Benedetto Gennari e la bottega del Guercino*, Padova, 1986, p. 241
2 Ferrari and Papaldo, p. 376
3 Spear, p. 133
4 Spear, p. 143; Ferrari and Papaldo, p. 376
5 Pope-Hennessy, p. 425
6 Salerno, p. 291
7 *Roma la città degli anni santi*, p. 193
8 Titi, 1686, p. 216; Barry, n. 106
9 Mallory, *Bizzacheri*, pp. 35, 45; id., *Rococo*, p. 41; D. L. Bershad, *ABA*, 7-8, 1978, p. 323

S. Prassede

Bibliography: Titi, 1763, p. 245; Nibby, p. 670; Venuti, p. 43; Angeli, p. 510; Letarouilly, pl. 329 (344); B. M. Apollonj Ghetti, *CdR*, 66; Buchowiecki, III, p. 591; *GR*, I, II, p. 66; Tesei, p. 24; Lombardi, p. 44; M. Caperna, *Pall.*, 12, 1993, p. 43; Pocino, p. 247, Racheli, p. 368; P. Gallo, *La Basilica di S. Prassede*, Genoa, 1998; M. Caperna, *La Basilica di S. Prassede: Il significato della vicenda architettonica*, Rome, 1999

1 Abromson, p. 115
2 R; Titi, p. 255

3 R; Esaperanzi, p. 65
4 Rodino, p. 36
5 W; Davis, p. 13; *Pietro da Cortona*, p. 225
6 Montagu, *Algardi*, pp. 379, 383
7 Wittkower, *Bernini*, p. 173; D'Onofrio, *Roma vista*, p. 114; Scribner, pl. 1; Ferrari and Papaldo, p. 379
8 Chracas, I,No. 2813; Bevilacqua, p. 19
9 Enggass, *Sculpture*, p. 208
10 C. Spetia, *Notizie da Palazzo Albani*, XVI (2), 1987, p. 121
11 W
12 Titi, p. 256
13 Rodino, p. 41
14 Tosini, p. 323
15 Cavallero et al., p. 286; *Fiamminghi a Roma*, p. 23
16 *Roma di Sisto V*, p. 257; Röttgen, p. 29; *Longhi*, p. 72
17 Luchinat, vol. II, p. 180
18 Ferrari and Papaldo, p. 380
19 Sestieri, p. 143
20 R
21 Titi, p. 258

S. Prisca

Bibliography: Titi, 1686, p. 60, 1763, p. 73; Venuti, p. 390; Nibby, p. 675; Angeli, p. 516; Buchowiecki, III, p. 629; G. Sangiorgi, *CdR*, 101; *GR*, XII, II, 2°, p. 16; Macioce, p. 132; Tesei, p. 350; Lombardi, p. 262

1 Nissman, p. 284
2 Abromson, p. 159; Cantelli

S. Pudenziana

Bibliography: Titi, 1763, p. 267; Venuti, p. 53; Nibby, p. 677; Angeli, p. 518; R. U. Montini, *CdR*, 50; Buchowiecki, III, p. 650; Pinelli, No. 132; De Tomasso, p. 22. Marcucci, p. 160; Lombardi, p. 45; L. Marcucci, *Pall.*, 14, 1994, p. 181; Racheli, p. 372; *GR*, I, III, p. 122

1 Ceschi, p. 125
2 Titi, p. 314
3 Pampalone, p. 89
4 Titi, p. 270
5 *Roma di Sisto V*, p. 264
6 *Diario ordinario*, No. 28, 1806
7 *Roma la città*, p. 227; Möller, p. 94
8 A. C. Beccarini, *QISA*, 127-132, 1975, p. 143; Marcucci, p. 180;

301

R. Senecal, *Apollo*, 401, 1995, p. 37; Bacchi, p. 833; O. Ferrari, *ABA*, 52-55, 1996, p. 73; Ferrari and Papaldo, p. 382
9   Hibbard, *Maderno*, p. 127
10 Luchinat, vol. II, pp. 191, 234
11 Burns, p. 157
12 Burns, p. 159
13 Bacchi, figs. 239, 538, 540
14 *La Regola*, p. 515

SS. Quaranta Martiri
See S. Pasquale Baylon

SS. Quattro Coronati
Bibliography: Titi, 1763, p. 230; Nibby, p. 682; Venuti, p. 49; Angeli, p. 524; Buchowiecki, III, p. 677; G. Cannizzaro, R. M. Apollonj Ghetti, *CdR*, 81; Pinelli, No. 133; M. G. Barberini, *I Santi Quattro Coronati a Roma*, Rome, 1989; Lombardi, p. 352; F. Caraffa, *AR*, 20 (5-6), 1979, p. 40; *GR*, XIX, I, p. 42; *Roma Sacra*, 3, 1995, p. 48

1   Ferrari and Papaldo, p. 387
2   S. Neuburger, *SdA*, 58, 1986, p. 207
3   Möller, p. 145

Oratorio di S. Silvestro

1   Gere and Pouncey, p. 145; Neuburger, op. cit.

SS. Quirico e Giulitta
Bibliography: Titi, 1763, p. 235; Chracas, II, No. 2026; Nibby, p. 684; Angeli, p. 526; Venuti, p. 35; *Architettura minora in Italia*, II, p. 89; A. Rava, *SS. Quirico e Giulitta*, Rome, 1934; M. Bosi, *CdR*, 60; Rotili, p. 10; Mallory, *Rococo*, p. 126; Pinelli, No. 134; Tesei, p. 40; Lombardi, p. 70; C. Harada, *Pall.*, 7, 1991, p. 107; Pocino, p. 272; Racheli, p. 374; F. Guglielmi, *LU*, LVII, 1997, p. 293

1   Poensgen, p. 102
2   *Mattia Preti*, p. 161

SS. Re Magi
Bibliography: Pollak, I, p. 211; Mola, pp. 120, 132; de' Rossie, *Architettura Civile*, I, pls. 72-84; Falda, *Nuovo teatro*, I, pl. 9 and IV, pls. 51, 52; Hempel, p. 157; Güthlein, p. 217; G. Antonazzi, 'La Sede della Sacra Congregazione e del Collegio Urbano', in, *Sacra Congregationis de Propaganda Fide memoria rerum*, ed. J. Meller, Rome, 1971, p. 306; Buchowiecki, III, p. 718; Portoghesi, *Borromini*, pl. 166-69; Blunt, *Borromini*, p. 183; *GR*, III, Il, p. 60; R. Stalla, *RJK*, 29, 1994, p. 289; Lombardi, p. 107; Marder, p. 63; *Roma Sacra* 6, 1996, p. 2; *Borromini e l'universo barocco*, p. 296

1   Hempel, figs. 55-59
2   Hempel, fig. 56
3   Hempel, pls. 5104, 105
4   Martinelli, p. 201
5   W; *Bernini in Vaticano*, Rome, 1981, p. 64
6   W
7   Fischer, p. 136
8   W
9   Lavagnino, *Altari*, p. 127
10 W
11 Ferrari and Papaldo, p. 388
12 Ferrari and Papaldo, p. 288

S. Rita da Cascia See S. Maria delle Vergini

S. Rita da Cascia (S. Biagio in Campitelli)
Bibliography: Falda, *Nuovo teatro*, I, pl. 11; de' Rossi, *Architettura Civile*, III, pl. 44; Nibby, p. 685; Coudenhove-Erthal, p. 21; Buchowiecki, III, p. 729; H. Hager, *Comm.*, XXIII, 1972, p. 261; Elling, pl. 24; *GR*, XI, I, p. 66; Lombardi, p. 245; *Roma Sacra*, 15, 1999, p. 21

1   Wittkower, *Bernini*, p. 216

S. Rocco
Bibliography: Mola, p. 113; Titi, 1763, p. 394; Venuti, p. 267; Nibby, p. 685; Angeli, p. 529; *Giornale di Roma*, No. 240, 1864, 21st Oct.; L. Salerno and G. Spagnesi, *La chiesa di San Rocco all'Augusteo*, Rome, 1962; Buchowiecki, III, p. 732; Spagnesi, p. 36; Pinelli, No. 136; Tesei, p. 140; De Tomasso, p. 72; *Organi*, p. 128; Lombardi, p. 129; *GR*, IV, VI, p. 68; *Roma Sacra*, 6, 1996, p. 37

1   *Organi*, p. 128
2   Lilli, p. 70
3   Chracas, I, No. 288; Titi, p. 384
4   V. Casale, *Scritti di storia dell'arte in onore di Federico Zeri*, p. 736
5   Montagu, *Giorgetti*, p. 292
6   A. Pampalone, *BdA*, 58, 1973, p. 123
7   *Mariani*, p. 43
8   Enggass, *Baciccio*, pp. 15, 47
9   W; Trezzani, p. 43
10 Chracas, III, No. 1548
11 *Quadri Romani*, p. 33; Gere and Pouncey, p. 69
12 F. Petrucci, *SdA*, 96, 1999, p. 176
13 W
14 Frommel, p. 78
15 C. Strinati, *Pros.*, 15, 1978, p. 61

SS. Rufina e Seconda
Bibliography: Nibby, p. 687; Venuti, p. 8; Angeli, p. 531; Armellini, pp. 850, 1426; Tesei, p. 376; E. Iezzi, *Studio storico della Chiesa e del Monastero delle SS. Rufina e Seconda*, Rome, 1980; Lombardi, p. 296

S. Sabina
Bibliography: Titi, 1763, p. 64; Angeli, p. 533; Buchowiecki, III, p. 767; Venuti, p. 369; Nibby, p. 688; F. M. Darsy, *CdR*, 63-64; *La chiese dal Paleocristiano al Gotico*, ed. A. Piva, Novara, 1987, p. 60; Lombardi, p. 254; Racheli, p. 384

1   Ferrari and Papaldo, p. 390
2   Ferrari and Papaldo, p. 391
3   S. Schütze, *RJBH*, 32, 1997-98, p. 231
4   Cantaro, p. 194
5   Abromson, p. 188; Mundy, cat. nos. 99, 100
6   Luchinat, vol. I, p. 115
7   Ferrari and Papaldo, p. 391
8   del Bufalo, p. 84
9   *Giovan Battista Salvi 'Il Sassoferrato'*, ed. F. M. de Lepinay, Milan, 1990, p. 116
10 W
11 Roisecco, p. 256
12 Hempel, p. 185
13 M. Fagiolo and S. Roberto, *Pall.*, 3 (5), 1990, p. 63
14 *Pietro da Cortona*, p. 215
15 P. Ferraris, *BdA*, 66, 1991, p. 53

Oratory of the SS. Sacramento See S. Maria in Via (Oratory of)

BIBLIOGRAPHIES AND REFERENCES

S. Salvatore in Campo
Bibliography: Totti, p. 211; Martinelli. p. 170; Titi, 1721, p. 116; Roisecco, 1745, p. 344; Nibby, p. 693; Pollak, I, p. 193; Buchowiecki, III, p. 806; P. Macini, *AR*, 11 (2), 1979, p. 40; Elling, pl. 77; F. Pariset, *SdR*, 40, 1979, p. 451; E. Longo, 'Francesco Peparelli', *Pall.*, 3 (5), 1990, p. 25; Lombardi, p. 176; *Roma Sacra*, 13, 1998, p. 32

S. Salvatore delle Coppelle
Bibliography: Venuti, p. 142; Nibby, p. 693; Mallory, *Rococo*, p. 140; *Giornale di Roma*, No. 141, 1863, 25th June; L. Lotti, *San Salvatore alle Coppelle*, Rome, 1976; *GR*, VIII, IV, p. 102; L. Lotti, *AR*, 17 (1-2), 1976, p. 1; Buchowiecki, III, p. 810; Tesei, p. 242; Lombardi, p. 196; *Roma Sacra*, 8, 1996, p. 56

1 Chracas, II, No. 4167; *Giovanni V*, p. 433

S. Salvatore in Lauro
Bibliography: Totti, p. 251; Chracas, II, No. 2131; Baglione, p. 99; Titi, 1763, p. 407; Nibby, p. 695; Venuti, p. 184; *Architettura minora*, I, pl. 86; Wasserman, p. 191; C. Astolfi, *Storia del convento e chiesa di S. Salvatore in Lauro*, Pesaro, 1933; L. Lotti, AR, 14 (1-2), 1976, p. 31; E. Fanano, *CdR*, 52; *GR*, V, I, p. 62; Pinelli, No. 137; Buchowiecki, III, p. 813; Tesei, p. 166; De Tomasso, p. 86; E. Fanano, *S. Salvatore in Lauro*, Rome n.d.; G. Gandolfi, *RAU*, 69-70, 1989-90, p. 66; Lombardi, p. 144; Kelly, p. 129; *Roma Sacra*, 11, 1997, p. 14

1 *Giornale di Roma*, No. 282, 1862, 11th Dec.; G. Petrucci, *AV*, XVI/3 1977, p. 27
2 Vicario, p. 579
3 Mallory, *Bizzacheri*, pp. 31, 45; id., *Rococo*, p. 38
4 Enggass, *Sculpture*, p. 38
5 W; Titi, p. 394; Ghezzi, pp. 20, 50, 47, 49
6 *Pietro da Cortona*, p. 314
7 R. Pantanella, *SdA*, 90, 1997, p. 306; Spesso, p. 171
8 Enggass, *Sculpture*, p. 181
9 R. Pantanella, *SdA*, 90, 1997, p. 306
10 Titi, p. 396
11 Chracas, II, No. 8502
12 Titi, p. 396; Lo Bianco, p. 128;
Ghezzi, p. 28
13 *L'Arte per i papi*, vol. I, p. 50
14 *Domenico Corvi*, p. 126
15 M. V. Brugnoli, *BdA*, LII, 1967, p. 249; Lo Bianco, p. 128; *Ghezzi*, p. 55
16 Papi, *Borgianni*, p. 131
17 Mortari, p. 120; *Francesco Salviati*, p. 65

S. Salvatore ai Monti (S. Salvatore de'Suburra)
Bibliography: Totti, p. 476; *Giornale di Roma*, No. 141, 1864, 21st Jun.; Vasi, *Magnificenze*, pl. 169; Angeli, p. 543; Vasi, 1791, p. 344; L. Cavazzi, *S. Salvatore ai Monti*, Rome, 1941; Buchowiecki, III, p. 830; Pinelli, No. 139; Lombardi, p. 69; Pocino, p. 113; *Roma Sacra*, 13, 1998, p. 14

S. Salvatore in Onda
Bibliography: Salerno, *Via Giulia*, p. 505; *Notizie del Giorno*, No. 50, 1819; Nibby, p. 698; Buchowiecki, III, p. 831; L. Huetter, *CdR*, 41; *GR*, VII, III, p. 64; Lombardi, p. 179; Priori and Tabarrini, p. 57; *Roma Sacra*, 13, 1998, p. 14; V. Valerio, 'Commodità e maggior splendore', in, *L'Arte per i giubilei*, p. 161

1 The plan and elevation are reproduced in Salerno
2 Geller, p. 42

S. Salvatore de'Suburra
See **S. Salvatore ai Monti**

S. Sebastiano fuori le Mura
Bibliography: Mola, p. 76; Titi, 1763, p. 70; Baglione, *Le nove chiese*, p. 103; Martinelli, p. 26; Venuti, p. 382; Angeli, p. 550; Nibby, p. 704; A. Ferrua, *CdR*, 99; Tesei, p. 506; E. Fumagalli, *PA*, 483, 1990, p. 67; A. Zekagh, 'La chiese di S. Sebastiano fuori le Mura in Roma', *Pall.*, 3 (6), 1990, p. 77; Lombardi, p. 415; A. Antinori, *Scipione Borghese e l'Architettura. Programmi progetti cantieri alle soglie dell'età barocca*, Rome, 1995, p. 31; Michael Hill, 'Cardinal Scipione Borghesi's Patronage of Ecclesiastical Architecture, 1605-1633', diss., University of Sydney, 1998, pp. 70, 206

1 Ferrari and Papaldo, p. 393
2 Titi, p. 98; R
3 Johns, *Papal Art*, p. 159
4 Enggass, *Sculpture*, p. 76
5 A. Valeriani, *BdA*, 82, 1993, p. 49
6 W; G. Sestieri, *Comm.*, XXVIII, 1977, p. 114; Graf, *Passeri*, p. 102
7 Lo Bianco, p. 106; Titi, p. 97
8 F. d'Amico, *RSA*, 13-14, 1981, p. 139
9 Ferrari and Papaldo, p. 393
10 Pressouyre, p. 338; Harwood, p. 376; Ferrari and Papaldo, p. 394
11 *Pittura in Italia. Il Seicento*, p. 883
12 R. Contini, *PA*, 529-533, 1994, p. 191
13 Merz, p. 22
14 Davis, p. 35
15 Montagu, *Giorgetti*, p. 287; id., *Roman*, p. 84

S. Sebastiano al Palatino
Bibliography: Venuti, p. 395; Pollak, I, p. 193; Buchowiecki, III, p. 837; L. Gigli, *CdR*, 128; Gigli, p. 119; Lombardi, p. 234; *Roma Sacra*, 3, 1995, p. 32

1 W

SS. Sergio e Bacco (Madonna del Pascolo)
Bibliography: Titi, 1763, p. 213; Venuti, p. 37; Nibby, p. 712; Angeli, p. 556; Buchowiecki, II, p. 327; Pinelli, No. 141; Tesei, p. 34; Lombardi, p. 71; M. Escobar, 'La chiesa dei SS. Sergio e Bacco', *LU*, XLVIII, 1985, p. 81; Racheli, p. 396; *GR*, I, III, p. 52; Pocino, p. 109

1 F. Pansecchi, *BdA*, 28, 1984, p. 61; Cleri, p. 80
2 Kowa, p. 175

S. Silvestro in Capite
Bibliography: Titi, 1763, p. 346; Nibby, p. 713; Venuti, p. 122; Vasi, *Magnificenze*, pl. 153; J. S. Gaynor and I. Toesca, *CdR*, 73; Hibbard, *Maderno*, p. 125; I. Lavin, *BdA*, XLII, 1957, p. 44; Buchowiecki, III, p. 842; *GR*, III, III, p. 13; Pinelli, No. 142; Dunn, p. 366; Marcucci, p. 272; Lombardi, p. 106; *Roma Sacra*, 5, 1996, p. 10

1 Enggass, *Sculpture*, p. 320; *Le statue*, pp. 210, 216
2 Enggass, *Ottoni*, p. 320;

3 M. Dunn, *ABA*, 39-42, 1991-92, p. 120
4 *Le statue*, p. 212; Ferrari and Papaldo, p. 397
5 Chiappini di Sorio, p. 123
6 Abromson, p. 196
7 Titi, pp. 326, 328
8 Lilli, p. 97
9 Bissell, *Gentileschi*, p. 163
10 Titi, p. 326; W
11 W; *Ghezzi*, pp. 97-100
12 W; *La Regola*, p. 463
13 Titi, p. 332
14 Papi, *Borgianni*, p. 142
15 W. Wallace, *SCJ*, 30, 1999, p. 419
16 Abromson, p. 197
17 Titi, p. 332
18 W; Titi, p. 328
19 *Il Seicento Lombardo. Catalogo dei dipinte e della sculture*, Milan, 1973, p. 45; F. Bologna, *Pros.*, 93-94, 1999, p. 95
20 W
21 Di Federico, p. 42

SS. Silvestro e Martino ai Monti See S. Martino ai Monti

S. Silvestro al Quirinale

Bibliography: Titi, 1674, p. 317; Martinelli, p. 172; Nibby, p. 716; Venuti, p. 61; Angeli, p. 560; Vasi, *Magnificenze*, VII, p. lv; Buchowiecki, III, p. 866; E. Iezzi, *S. Silvestro al Quirinale*, Rome, 1975; *GR*, II, II, 2°, p. 14; Pinelli, No. 143; Tesei, p. 86; B. Torres, *Pall.*, 14, 1994, p. 167; Racheli, p. 402; Pocino, p. 285; *Roma Sacra*, 16, 1999, p. 25

1 'Paul IV, Guglielmo della Porta and the rebuilding of S. Silvestro al Quirinale', *MD*, XV, 1977, p. 243
2 Donati, fig. 51
3 Dombrowski, p. 288; Ferrari, p. 399
4 Donati, p. 644
5 Titi, p. 278
6 M. Pupillo, *SdA*, 85, 1995, p. 395; *Roma di Sisto V*, p. 267
7 Fischer, p. 153; W
8 J. C. Bell, *Source*, VII, 1988, p. 17
9 Minor, *Diario*, No. 778; S. P. Guicciardi, *ABA*, 35-38, 1990, p. 59

10 Witcombe, p. 138; M. C. Abromson, *AB*, LX, 1978, p. 531
11 *Quadri Romani*, p. 66
12 Titi, p. 278; Pampalone, p. 97
13 Wasserman, p. 45
14 Vaudo, p. 29; *Roma di Sisto V*, p. 266
15 Montagu, *Algardi*, p. 358
16 V. Martinelli, *Comm.*, II, 1951, p. 224; Ferrari and Papaldo, p. 400
17 Spear, p. 271; *Domenichino*, p. 318
18 Dombrowski, p. 323; Ferrari and Papaldo, p. 401
19 M. Dunn, 'Spiritual Philanthropists', in, *Women and Art*, p. 161
20 Kamp, p. 122
21 Gere and Pouncey, p. 145; E. Giffi Ponzi, *Pros.*, 57-60, 1989-90, p. 99
22 L. Ravelli, *Polidoro a San Silvestro al Quirinale*, Bergamo, 1987
23 L. Ravelli, *Polidoro a San Silvestro al Quirinale*, Bergamo, 1987; id., 'Polidoro in Silvestro al Quirinale', in, *Raffaello e l'Europa*, ed. M. Fagiolo and M. L. Madonna, Rome, 1990, p. 299
24 Abromson, p. 211

S. Simeone Profeta (destroyed)

Bibliography: C. Cecchelli, 'Necrologia di S. Simeone profeta', *Urbe*, V, 1940, no. 9, p. 5

S. Sisto Vecchio

Bibliography: Venuti, p. 387; Angeli, p. 562; G. Matthiae, *Cap.*, XLIV, 1969, p. 154; Rotili, p. 40; C. Strepi et al., *San Sisto Vecchio a Porta Capena*, Rome, 1975; M. Escobar, *SdR*, 48, 1987, p. 187; G. Cannizzaro, *AR*, 18 (3-4), 1977, p. 34; Elling, pls. 38, 39a; Pinelli, No. 145; Buchowiecki, III, p. 908; Tesei, p. 458; Titi, p. 98; Chracas, I, Nos. 1260, 1579; Lombardi, p. 353; *La chiesa e il monastero di S. Sisto all' Appia*, ed. R. Spiazzi, Bologna, 1992

1 *La Regola*, p. 280
2 *Roma la città degli anni santi*, p. 194
3 A. Lo Bianco, *Pros.*, 57-60, 1989-90, p. 316
4 *Pittura in Italia: L' Ottocento*, p. 431

Spirito Santo dei Napoletani

Bibliography: Mola, p. 120; Titi, 1763, p. 464; Nibby, p. 723; Angeli, p. 565; L. Lancellotti, *La regina chiesa dello SS. dei Napoletani in Roma*, Naples, 1868; *Via Giulia*, p. 392; Wasserman, p. 71; P. Pecchiai, *La chiesa dello Spirito Santo dei Napoletani*, Rome, 1953; G. Sacchi, *SdR*, 47, 1986, p. 495; Buchowiecki, III, p. 920; *GR*, VII, p. 24; L. Lotti, *AR*, 12 (5-6), 1971, p. 80; Pinelli, No. 159; Lombardi, p. 181; *Roma Sacra*, 11, 1997, p. 55

1 R. Bösel, *Pros.*, 15, 1978, p. 29
2 *Giornale di Roma*, Nos, 225, 230, 1862, 3rd and 9th Oct.
3 Braham and Hager, p. 71
4 W; G. Sestieri, *Comm.*, XXVIII, 1977, p. 114; Graf, *Passeri*, p. 67
5 Titi, p. 42; P. Petraroia, *RINASA*, III-IV, 1981, p. 279
6 Braham and Hager, p. 73; *Le statue*, p. 210; Ferrari and Papaldo, p. 402
7 P. Di Giammaria, 'Un problema di attribuzione l'altare maggiore della chiese dell Spirito Santo', in, *L'Arte per i giubilei*, p. 237
8 Titi, p. 143
9 Sestieri, p. 134

S. Spirito in Sassia

Bibliography: Mola, p. 155; Martinelli, p. 175; Titi, 1763, p. 26; Nibby, p. 721; Venuti, p. 512; Leta-rouilly, p. 236 (312); P. de Angelis, *L' Architetto e gli affreschi di Santo Spirito in Saxia*, Rome, 1961; E. Lavagnino, *La chiesa di Santo Spirito in Sassia*, Rome, 1962; Kummer, p. 23; Lewine, p. 451; Tesei, p. 416; L. S. Bross, *The Church of Santo Spirito in Sassia: A Study in the Development of Art, Architecture and Patronage in Counter Reformation Rome*, diss., University of Chicago, 1994; ibid., 'Patronage and Propaganda at S. Spirito in Sassia', in, *Confraternite*, p. 87; *Organi*, p. 130; Lombardi, p. 306; *Roma di Sisto V*, p. 268ff.; *GR*, XIV, III, p. 72

1 Chracas, III, p. 1718
2 *Giornale di Roma*, No. 244, 1856, 24th Oct.
3 E. Pillsbury, *BM*, CXVI, 1974, p. 404
4 Zuccari, p. 79
5 E. Giffi Ponzi, *Pros.*, 57-60,

1989, p. 99
6   D. Matteucci, *SdA*, 88, 1996, p. 301
7   Lilli, p. 138
8   Mallory, *Notizie*, II, No. 5037
9   Titi, 1763, p. 27; Lavagnino, *Altari*, pp. 41, 163
10 G. Casale, 'Variazioni manieristiche e barocche del ciborio', in, *L'Ultimo Bernini*, p. 21; Ferrari and Papaldo, p. 403
11 Barry, n. 107
12 Natoli and Scarpati, p. 42
13 Russo, p. 1
14 Baglione, p. 19, n. 40; L. Bross, *BM*, CXXXV, 1993, p. 338; Evers, p. 106
15 A. Zezza, *Pros.*, 73-74, 1994, p. 144
16 B. Toscano, *PA*, 177, 1964, p. 36
17 Baglione, p. 99; Martinelli, p. 253
18 cf. Fagiolo dell'Arco, *Bernini*, No. 193
19 Armellini, II, p. 807; Pane, p. 100; Matthiae, p. 43

Oratory of S. Spirito in Sassia See Oratory of the Annunziata

S. Stanislao dei Polacchi
Bibliography: Totti, p. 389; Titi, 1686, p. 159 and 1763, p. 183; Venuti, p. 281; Nibby, p. 724; G. Marincola-Mauro, *AR*, XV, 1974, p. 62; Lewine, p. 484; Buchowiecki, III, p. 927; Pinelli, No. 146; Lombardi, p. 245; Bevilacqua, *Pall.*, 8, 1991, p. 19; *Roma Sacra*, 14, 1998, p. 22

1   Chracas, III, Nos. 244, 246
2   Poensgen, p. 103, fig. 50; Minor, *Diario*, No. 246
3   Ferrari and Papaldo, p. 404
4   Ferrari and Papaldo, p. 404
5   Titi, p. 217
6   A. Marino, *L'Arte*, 3-4, 1968, p. 47; Papi, *Grammatica*, p. 85
7   Vicario, p. 240
8   Titi, p. 217

S. Stefano del Cacco
Bibliography: Totti, p. 395; Martinelli, p. 177; Titi, 1674, p. 186; Venuti, p. 285; Nibby, p. 725; Buchowiecki, III, p. 931; *GR*, IX, I, p. 82; E. Iezzi and L. Roncaioli, *BUSA*, 33, 1990, p. p. 51; ibid., 34, 1991, p. 57; Lombardi, p. 214; C. Tudert, *Inter fratres*, 1991, p.

55; ibid., *Inter fratres*, 42, 1992, p. 107; *Roma Sacra*, 9, 1997, p. 44

1   Armani, p. 25
2   *Roma di Sisto V*, p. 278
3   Möller, p. 128
4   W

S. Stefano Rotondo
Bibliography: Baglione, p. 41, n. 15; Nibby, p. 727; L. H. Monssen, *AA*, 1982, II, p. 175; id., 1983, III, p. 11; *MPARA*, XV, 1982, p. 107; F. Banfi, *La chiese di S. Stefano sul Monte Celio a Roma*, Florence, 1947; L. Benedetti, *S. Stefano Rotando*, Rome, 1962; Buchowiecki, III, p. 943; C. Ceschi, *Stefano Rotondo*, Rome, 1982; *GR*, I, I, p. 110; A. Vannugli, *SdA*, 48, 1983, p. 101; M. Nimmo, *RSA*, 25, 1985, p. 91; Lombardi, p. 47; Pocino, p. 256

1   *In Urbe Architectus*, p. 320

Stimmate di S. Francesco
Bibliography: Mola, p. 122; Titi, 1721, p. 165, 1763, p. 165; Chracas, I, No. 343; Nibby, p. 730; Pascoli, III, p. 534; Venuti, p. 278; Vasi, *Magnificenze*, pl. 179; F. Fasolo, *BCN*, IV, 1945, p. 13; Buchowiecki, III, p. 982; *GR*, IX, II, p. 98; Tesei, p. 280; D. Baldini, et al., *Chiesa delle SS. Stimmate di Francesco d'Assisi in Roma: guida storico-artistica*, Rome, 1982; F. Ferraris, *SdA*, 65, 1989, p. 69; del Bufalo, p. 96; Lombardi, p. 215; *Roma Sacra*, 10, 1997, p. 6

1   del Bufalo, p. 96
2   Lilli, p. 141
3   W; Poensgen, p. 103
4   R
5   W; Titi, p. 180
6   G. Scarfone, *SdR*, 40, 1979, p. 544
7   R; L. Barroero, *BdA*, I, 1979, p. 65
8   R. Enggass, *BM*, CXVIII, 1976, p. 491
9   G. Papi, *PA*, 485, 1990, p. 73
10 Di Federico, p. 61
11 Gradara, p. 82
12 *Le statue*, p. 205; Ferrari and Papaldo, p. 408
13 Di Federico, p. 61
14 W; A. Pampalone, *BdA*, 1, 1973, 123
15 *Giovanni V*, p. 293

SS. Sudario dei Piemontesi
Bibliography: Titi, 1686, p. 112; Venuti, p. 265; Nibby, p. 732; Angeli, p. 576;G. Croset Mouchet, *La chiesa ed arciconfraternita del SS. Sudario*, Pinerlo, 1870; U. Vichi, *La chiesa del SS. Sudario dei Piemontesi in Roma*, Rome, n.d.; Fasolo: p. 193; Buchowiecki, III, p. 989; *GR*, VIII, I, p. 58; Tesei, p. 254; Lombardi, p. 196; *Roma Sacra*, 14, 1998, p. 2

1   A. Mezzetti, *PA*, 401-403, 1983, p. 127
2   T. C. Pickrel, *ABA*, 7-8, 1979, p. 216; M. Lange, *AA*, 1, 1981, p. 275
3   Pampalone, p. 89
4   Natoli and Scarpati, p. 35; Lilli, p. 78

S. Susanna
Bibliography: Falda, *Nuovo teatro*, III, pl. 11; Titi, 1763, p. 297; Nibby, p. 732; Venuti, p. 91; de' Rossi, *Prospectus*, pl. 62; Vasi, *Magnificenze*, pl. 148; Magni, I, pls. 17, 18; Pollak, I, p. 265; Hibbard, *Maderno*, pp. 38-43, 110-14; Buchowiecki, III, p. 994; B. M. Apollonj Ghetti, *CdR*, 85; Macioce, p. 144; Marcucci, p. 241; A. M. Affanni, M. Cogotti and R. Vodret, *S. Susanna e S. Bernardo alle Terme*, Rome, 1993; Valone, p. 134

1   Pollak, I, p. 206
2   *Roma di Sisto V*, p. 279; Baglione, p. 40, n. 22

S. Teodoro al Palatino
Bibliography: Titi, 1763, p. 206; Venuti, p. 397; Nibby, p. 736; F. and O. Fasolo, *Pall.*, 5, 1941, p. 112; Braham and Hager, p. 79; Tesei, p. 304; Johns, *Papal Art*, p. 225; Lombardi, p. 233; Kuhn-Forte, p. 3

1   R; *Ghezzi*, p. 125
2   U. Hiesinger, *ABA*, 13-14, 1980, p. 78

S. Tommaso di Canterbury
Bibliography: Baglione, p. 14, n. 18; Nibby, p. 738; Anon., *The Venerable English College*, Rome, 1967; Lewine, p. 489; M. E. Williams, *The Venerable English College Rome. A History 1579-1979*, Dublin, 1979; Bösel, p. 251; C. Cristallini and M. Noccioli, *I*

'Libra delle case' di Roma: il catasto del Collegio Inglese (1630), Rome, 1987; L. Lotti, AR, 17 (1-2), 1976, p. 138; L. Lotti and P. L. Lotti, La comunità cattolica inglese di Roma. La sua chiesa e il suo collegio, Rome, 1978; Kuhn-Forte, p. 21; Racheli, p. 413

1 Giornale di Roma, No. 30, 1866, 7th Feb
2 Chracas, III, No. 462
2 Gere and Pouncey, p. 24
3 Minor, p. 171
4 B. Kuhn, RHM, 26, 1984, p. 417

S. Tommaso dei Cenci

Bibliography: Titi, 1763, p. 95; Venuti, p. 223; Lewine, p. 495; E. Lotti, 15 (5-6), 1974, p. 44; E. Iezzi, San Tommaso ai Cenci, Rome, 1975; Restauro della Cappella Cenci eseguita da Hugette Girauds, Rome, n.d.; GR, VIII, I, p. 60; Tesei, p. 326; Lombardi, p. 181; Kuhn-Forte, p. 33; Roma Sacra, 14, 1998, p. 43; S. Sbardella, '"Riattamenti", lavori di manutenzione, paramenti e suppellettili sacra tra I giubilei del 1770 e 1725 nella chiesa di S. Tommaso ai Cenci', in, L'Arte per i giubilei, p. 195

1 Hunter, p. 184
2 Nicolson, p. 206
3 Quadri Romani, p. 68

S. Tommaso in Formis

Bibliography: Nibby, p. 738; Angeli, p. 582; F. Caraffa, AR, 19 (3-4), p. 20; Antonio dell'Assunta and R. di S. Teresa, S. Tommaso in Formis, Isola dei Liri, 1927; Lombardi, p. 355; GR, XIX, I, p. 78; Kuhn-Forte, p. 43

1 Hunter, p. 188
2 F. d'Amico, ABA, 25-26, 1985, p. 90

S. Tommaso in Parione

Bibliography: Totti, p. 229; Titi, 1674, p. 137 and 1763, p. 129; de' Rossi, 1697, p. 240; Nibby, p. 739; Venuti, p. 208; Angeli, p. 584; Diario di Roma, No. 41, 1830; Vasi, Magnificenze, pl. 110; Roisecco, 1750, II, p. 9; M. Lumbroso and A. Martini, FA, IX, 1961, p. 424; Elling, pl. 19; GR, VI, 1, 2°, p. 21; Pinelli, No. 150; Lombardi, p. 161; Kuhn-Forte, p. 55; Roma Sacra, 11, 1997, p. 9

1 W; G. Sestieri, Comm., XXVIII, 1977, p. 114; Graf, Passeri, p. 43

SS. Trinità dei Monti

Bibliography: Titi, 1763, p. 375; Martinelli, p. 180; Venuti, p. 151; Falda, Nuovo teatro, III, pl. 18; Nibby, p. 742; P. Pecchiai, La Scalinata di Piazza di Spagna, Rome, 1941; C. Salerno, Piazza di Spagna, Rome, 1967; Letarouilly, pl. 9 (239); Diario di Roma, No. 72, 1816; G. Cannizzaro, AR, 17 (1-2), 1976, p. 79; R. Luciani and A. Casula, SdR, 53, 1992, p. 375; L. Salerno, Chiesa e convento della Santissima Trinità dei Monti in Roma, Bologna, 1968; GR, IV, II, p. 74; Bousquet, Recherches sur le sojour des peintres français à Rome au XVIIe siècle, Monpellier, 1980, p. 127; Pinelli, No. 151; Lombardi, p. 130; Kuhn-Forte, p. 79; Roma Sacra, 6, 1996, p. 5

1 P. Barocchi, AAM, 31-31, 1965, p. 244
2 Barolsky, p. 83; Pugliatti, p. 65; G. Albers and P. Morel, BdA, 48, 1988, p. 69
3 Baglione, p. 89, n. 2; Gere and Pouncey, p. 136
4 Roma la città degli anni santi, p. 194
5 B. F. Davidson, AB, XLVI, 1964, p. 550
6 D. Laurenza, RdL, 31, 1994, p. 30
7 A. Chastel, 'La chapelle de Saint Michel', in, Les fondations nationales, p. 479
8 Domenico Corvi, p. 100
9 de' Rossi, Architettura Civile, III, pl. 52; L. Falaschi, 'Il ciborio del Santissimo', in, L'Ultimo Bernini, p. 69; Montagu, Gold, p. 227, n. 116
10 Gere and Pouncey, p. 133
11 Gere, p. 123; Armani, p. 258; Mundy, cat. no. 44-46; Roma di Sisto V, p. 283; Luchinat, vol. I, p. 265
12 Ceschi, p. 53
13 Geller, pp. 33, 41
14 Barolsky, p. 55; C. Valone, AeH, 22, 1990, p. 79
15 Roma la città degli anni santi, p. 194; Evers, p. 30
16 V. Moccagatta, AAM, 27, 1964, p. 320
17 Thorvaldsen, p. 264
18 Kerber, p. 75

19 L. Cassanelli, in, Studi in onore di Giulio Carlo Argan, Rome, 1984, p. 293

SS Trinità in Palazzo Monte di Pietà

Bibliography: Baglione, p. 99; De' Rossi, Altari, pl. 46; Titi, 1763, p. 100; D. Tamilio, Il Sacro Monte di Pietà, Rome, 1900; Magni, I, pls. 97-99 and II, pl. 59; Hibbard, Maderno, p. 218; Spagnesi, p. 165; M. Tosi, Il Sacro Monte di Pietà, Rome, 1937; A. Schiavo, La Fontana di Trevi e le altre opere di Nicola Salvi, Rome, 1956; Wasserman, p. 116; Portoghesi, Roma Barocca, pls. 251, 252; L. Salerno, La Cappella del Monte di Pietà, Rome, n.d.; Mallory, Bizzacheri, pp. 34, 45; id., Rococo, p. 39; M. Costa, 'C. F. Bizzacheri e la cappella del Monte di Pietà', BdA, S.VI, No. 6, 1979, p. 49; Enggass, Sculpture, pp. 71, 139, 156, 177, 202; Kuhn-Forte, p. 167; M. Carta, La cappella del Monte di Pietà di Roma, 1996, Rome; Roma Sacra, 13, 1998, p. 37

1 Bissell, p. 67

SS. Trinità dei Pellegrini

Bibliography: Titi, 1674, pp. 121, 414 and 1763, p. 103; Roisecco, 1745, I, p. 305; Nibby, p. 748; Venuti, p. 225; Vasi, Magnificenze, pl. 126; Magni, I, pl. 9; S. Vasco Rocca, CdR, 133; GR, VII, I, p. 26; S. Vasco Rocca, SdA, 38-40, 1980, p. 285; Roma Sancta, ed. M. Fagiolo and M. L. Madonna, Rome, 1985, p. 101; C. Benocci, RSA, 26, 1985, p. 106; C. Benocci, RSA, 1986, p. 104; Tesei, p. 224; Lombardi, p. 182; A. Lemoine, SdA, 85, 1995, p. 416; ibid., BdA, 86-87, 1994, p. 111; Kuhn-Forte, p. 123; Roma Sacra, 13, 1998, p. 6; F. Salamone, 'Preparativi per il giubilei del 1725', in, L'Arte per i giubilei, p. 215

1 Mallory, Rococo, p. 78
2 Titi, p. 134
3 Giornale di Roma, Nos. 154, 155, 1853, 11th, 12th July
4 Pepper, p. 227
5 Bacchi, p. 795, fig. 298
6 L'arte degli anni santi, p. 390
7 F. Salamone, 'Il monumento funebre ad Alessandro Raimondi', in, L'Arte per i giubilei, p. 223

8 Pepper, p. 250
9 Ferrari and Papaldo, p. 407
10 Gere and Pouncey, p. 29
11 Rodino, p. 68; Titi, p. 136; *La Regola*, p. 559
12 Titi, p. 134; *La Regola*, p. 568
13 R. Bösel, *Pros.*, 15, 1978, p. 29
14 Montagu, *Algardi*, p. 430; *Effigies and Ecstasies*, p. 150; JM

SS. Trinità degli Spagnuoli

Bibliography: Vasi, *Magnificenze*, pl. 129; Chracas, II, Nos. 4584, 4684, 5181; Nibby, p. 740; P. C. Blanco, *CdR*, 28; Pinelli, No. 152; De Tomaso, p. 74; Lombardi, p. 131; Kuhn-Forte, p. 149; *GR*, IV, VII, p. 81; *Roma Sacra*, 1, 1995, p. 58

1 *Roma la città degli anni santi*, p. 335
2 R
3 R
4 E. Borsellino, *BdA*, 10, 1981, p. 49
5 Chracas, III, No. 236; E. Schleier, *AI*, 27-29, 1970, p. 92
6 R; Gabrielli, p. 50
7 V. Palma, 'La Sacrestia della SS. Trinità degli Spagnuoli', in *L'Arte per i giubilei*, p. 289
8 Chracas, II, No. 7797; R
9 B. Montevecchi, *Notizie da Palazzo Albani*, XIII/I, 1984, p. 180
10 R
11 Chracas, III, No. 466
12 R; Voss, p. 161

SS. Vincenzo e Anastasio

Bibliography: Martinelli, p. 185; Mola, p. 104; Titi, 1763, p. 328; Nibby, p. 757; Venuti, p. 77; Falda, *Nuovo teatro*, III, pl. 25; de' Rossi, *Architettura Civile*, III, pl. 39; Passeri, p. 230; Magni, I, pl. 16; Pugliese and Rigano, p. 45; Longhi, p. 113; Varriano, p. 377; Lombardi, p. 93; *GR*, p. II, V, p. 86; Kuhn-Forte, p. 183; *Roma Sacra*, 4, 1995, p. 49; G. Bonaccorso, 'L' opera architettonica di Giuseppe Ferroni', in, *Architettura città territorio*, p. 149

1 Ferrari and Papaldo, p. 409
2 U. Hiesinger, *ABA*, 13-14, 1980, p. 78
3 Lilli, p. 136
4 Geller, p. 32
5 *Organi*, p. 136
6 *Pittura in Italia. L'Ottocento*, p. 736
7 Chracas, II, No. 8; *Roma la città degli anni santi*, p. 344
8 Chracas, III, No. 414; B. Kuhn, *RHM*, 28, 1986, p. 387
9 *Diario di Roma*, No. 18, 1819; Lilli, p. 198
10 *Architettura minora*, II, pl. 80; Elling, pl. 66
11 Varriano, in, Mallory, *Bizzacheri*, p. 45

SS. Venanzio e Ansovino (destroyed)

Bibliography: Titi, 1721, p. 97; Roisecco, 1750, I, p. 318; Vasi, *Magnificenze*, pl. 116

S. Vitale

Bibliography: L. Huetter and V. Golzio, *CdR*, 35; Nibby, p. 758; *Le scienze e le arti*, vol. I, n. n.; Macioce, p. 122; Pinelli, No. 156; Tesei, p. 6; Valone, p. 137; C. Valone, *Piety and Patronage in Creative Women in Medieval and Early Modern Italy*, ed. A. Matter and J. Coakley, Philadelphia, 1994, p. 157; Lombardi, p. 48; Kuhn-Forte, p. 201; Racheli, p. 422; Pocino, p. 144; Pocino, p. 144; G. A. Bailey, 'The Jesuits and Painting in Italy, 1550-1690', in, *Saints and Sinners*, p. 151; *Saints and Sinners: Caravaggio and the Baroque Image* exhibition cat. ed. Franco Mormando, Boston College, 1999

1 Abromson, p. 240; Faldi, p. 269; L. Monssen, *AA*, III, 1983, p. 204
2 *Giornale di Roma*, No. 93, 1858, 26th April
3 Bianchi, p. 387
4 Cantelli, p. 44
5 Papi, *Commodi*, p. 76
6 Cantelli, p. 44

SS. Vito e Modesto

Bibliography: Vasi, *Magnificenze*, pl. 126; *Diario di Roma*, No. 54, 1837; Nibby, p. 760; Angeli, p. 602; P. Odescalchi, *De' nuovi lavori esguiti nella diaconia de' SS. Vito e Modesto* Rome, 1837; Armellini, pp. 1002, 1473; Pinelli, No. 157; Tesei, p. 436; Lombardi, p. 320; Kuhn-Forte, p. 227

BIBLIOGRAPHY

Amato, Pietro, 'Disegni inediti di C. Giaquinto in casa Spadavecchia', in, *Atti Convegno di Studi su C. Giaquinto*, Molfetta 3-5 Gennaio 1969, Molfetta 1971, pp. 29-42

Arisi, Ferdinando, *Gian Paolo Pannini e i fasti della Roma del '700*, Roma, Bozzi (1986)

L'Arte per i giubilei e tra giubilei del Settecento. Arciconfraternità, chiese, artisti, I, ed Elisa Debenedetti, Rome, 1999

Barbera, Gioacchino, 'Ricci, Trevisani, De Matteis e Batoni per la chiesa delle Anime del Purgatorio di Messina', *Quaderni dell'Istituto di Storia dell'arte Medievale e Moderna*, 4. 1980, pp. 41-45

Barry, Fabio, '"Building History": the Baroque remodellings of S. Anastasio al Palatino', *Storia dell' Arte*, 95, 1999, p. 45

Bellini, Paolo, 'Pietro De Pietri (con un elenco dei disegni)', *Arte cristiana*, N.S. 74 (1986), pp. 315-332

Bernardino Mei e la pittura barocca a Siena [Mostra, 1987], Firenze, S.P.E.S. 1987

Bershad, D, 'Pierre-Etienne Monnot newly discovered sculpture and document', *Antologia di belle arti*, N.S., 23/24 (1984), pp. 72-75

Bevilacqua, Nerina, 'Documenti su A. Raffaello Mengs. S. Conca, L. Vanvitelli, G.B. Piranesi', in, *Le arti figurative a Napoli nel Settecento*, 1979, pp. 13-28

Bevilacqua, Nerina, 'Documenti su R. Mengs, S. Conca, L. Vanvitelli, in, *Le arti figurative a Napoli nel Settecento*, 1979, pp. 13-28

Bon, Caterina, 'Una proposta per la cronologia delle opere giovanili di Giovanni Baglione', *Paragone. Arte*. 32. 1981, 373, pp. 17-48

Borghini G, *Un'antologia di restauri* ... [Cat. Mostra], Roma, 1982, p. 134

Borghini, Gabriele, 'Giacinto Brandi: un documento ed alcuni dipinti inediti', *Commentari*, N.S. 23.1972,4, pp. 385-393

Borromini e l'universo barocco. Catalogo ed. R. Bösel and C. L. Frommel, Milan, 2000

Bowron, Edgar P., *The painting of B. Luti 1666-1724*, New York/N.Y. University, diss., 1979

Bowron, Edgar Peters, *The painting of Benedetto Luti (1666-1724)*, New York/N.Y., New York University, diss., 1979

Brejon DeLavergnee, Arnauld, 'Plaidoyer pour un peintre "de pratique": le séjour de Paolo de Matteis en France (1702-1705)', in, *Revue de l'art*, 1990, H.88, pp. 70-7

Briganti, Giuliano. *Pietro da Cortona o della Pittura Barocca*, Firenze: Sansoni (1982) 438 S.

Brigstocke, Hugh, 'A Pietro da Cortona landscape for Edinburgh', *The Burlington Magazine*, 122, 1980, 926, pp. 342-344

Busiri Vici, A., 'Due dipinti di Placido Costanzi', *Antichita' viva*, 22. 1983, 3 ('84), pp. 5-8

Busiri Vici, A., "Opere romane di Jean de Troy" in *Antichita' viva*, IX, 2, 1970, pp. 2-20

Cappelletti, Francesca-Testa, Laura, E per me pagate a Michelangelo a Caravaggio. Nuove date per i dipinti Mattei, *Art e dossier*, 5 (1990) H. 42, pp. 4-7

Casale, Gerardo, 'Giuseppe Nicola Nasini pittore senese: opere conservate a Roma', *Annuario dell'Istituto di Storia dell'Arte*, Univ. della Sapienza, Roma 1981/82, pp. 43-52

Casale, Gerardo, 'Le fonti, gli studi moderni sui Ghezzi', in, *Giuseppe e Pier Leone Ghezzi*, Roma 1990, pp. 21-43

Cassanelli, L. and Rossi S., *I luoghi di Raffaello Sanzio a Roma. Mostra. La Farnesina, S. Eligio degli Orefici, S. Maria del Popolo, S. Maria della Pace, S. Agostino*, Roma, 1983

Cellini, Marina, 'Un nuovo Cantarini', *Paragone Arte*, N.S. 38 (1987) H. 2, pp. 40-44

Chappell, Miles, 'On the identification of "Crocino pittore di grand'aspettazione and the early career of Ludovico Cigoli', *Mitteilungen des Kunsthistorischen Institutes in Florenz*, 26, 1982, 3, pp. 325-338

Chiarini, Marco, Postilla al Cerrini (Giovanni Domenico), *Antologia di belle arti*, 4. 1980, 15-16, pp. 253

Chiarini, Marco, 'Tableaux inconnus ou peu connus de L. Giordano et de Sebastiano Ricci dans les musees francais', in, *Le revue du Louvre et des Musées de France*, 33 (1983), pp. 1-4

Chirico, Mariateresa, 'Pietro De Pietri', *Rassegna di studi e di notizie*, 10 (1982), pp. 243-262

Clark, A., 'Painting in Italy in the 18th c. Rococo to Romanticism. Rome and the Papal States', *Catalogo della Mostra*, Chicago, 1970

Clark, Anthony Morris. 'S. Conca and the Roman Rococo', in, *Studies in Roman 18th c. painting*, 1981, pp. 1/10

Clark, Anthony Morris, 'Agostino Masucci: a conclusion and a reformation of the Roman baroque', *Studies in 18th c. painting*, 1981, pp. 90-102

Clark, Anthony Morris, 'Batoni's professional carrer and style', *Studies in Roman eighteenth-century painting*, 1981, pp. 103-118

Conforti M., 'Pierre Legros and the vote of sculptors as designers in late Baroque Rome', *The Burlington Magazine*, 119 (1977), pp. 557-560

Confraternities and the Visual Arts in Renaissance

Italy: Ritual, Spectacle, Image ed. Barbara Wisch and Diane Cole Ahl, Cambridge, 2000

Cropper, Elizabeth, 'New documents concerning Domenichino's "Last Communion of St. Jerome"', *The Burlington Magazine*, 126, 1984, 972, pp.149-151

Curcio, Giovanna, 'Giacomo e Giovanni Battista Mola: due diversi modi di essere architetti a Roma nella prima meta' del XVII secolo', in, *P. F. Mola, 1612-1666* [Mostra], Milano (1989), pp. 28-39

D'Orsi, M., *Corrado Giaquinto*, Roma, 1958

Dania, Luigi, 'Alcuni dipinti inediti di C. Giaquinto', *Antichita' Viva*, 14, 1975, 5, pp. 13-17

Dania, Luigi, 'Nuove aggiunte a C. Giaquinto', *Scritti in onore di F. Zeri*, 2, 1984., pp. 820-823

Dania, Luigi, 'Alcuni inediti di Corrado Giaquinto', *Romagna arte e storia*, 9 (1989) H. 26, pp. 17-32

Dania, Luigi, 'Inediti di C.Giaquinto', *Paragone*, 20. 1969, 225, pp. 63-68

Davis, Bruce William, *The drawings of Ciro Ferri*, o.O.u.J. XIX, 322, S. Barbara (California), University of Calif., diss., 1982

De Angelis d'Ossat, G., 'Tre progetti del Peruzzi per chiese romane', in, *B. Peruzzi. Pittura, scena, architettura nel Cinquecento*, Roma, (1987), pp. 263-307

Del Bufalo, Alessandro, *G.B. Contini e la tradizione del tardomanierismo nell'architettura tra 600' e 700'*, Roma, 1982

Delfino, Antonio, 'Documenti inerenti a L. Giordano tratti dall'Archivio di Stato di Napoli', *Ricerche sul '600 napoletano*, Milano 1991, pp. 19-32

Di Domenico Cortese,Gemma, 'Due Maddalene inedite del Trevisani', *Bollettino dei Musei Comunali di Roma*, 24, 1977, pp. 73-78

Di Gioia, Elena Bianca, 'Un bozzetto del "San Longino" di G.L. Bernini ritrovato nella bottega di Francesco Antonio Fontana', *Antologia di belle arti*, N.S. 1984, 21-22, pp. 65-69

Dirani, Maria Teresa, 'Mecenati, pittori e mercato dell'arte nel Seicento. Il "Ratto di Elena" di Guido Reni e la "Morte di Didone" del Guercino nella corrispondenza del cardinale Bernardino Spada', *Ricerche di storia dell'arte*, 1982, 16, pp. 83-94

Disegni di Guglielmo Cortese detto il Borgognone nelle collezioni del Gabinetto Nazionale delle Stampe{Mostra], Roma: De Luca (1979)

Disegni di Lazzaro Baldi nelle collezioni del Gabinetto Nazionale delle Stampe.[Mostra]. Istituto Nazionale per la Grafica, Roma, De Luca (1979)

Dreyer, Peter, 'Notizen zum malerischen und reichnerischen Oeuvre der Maratta-Schule, Giuseppe Chiari, Pietro de Pietri, Agostino Masucci', *Zeitschrift fur Kunstgeschichte*, 34. 1971, 3, pp. 184-207

Edwards, Nancy E, 'The Renaissance 'stufetta' in Rome: the circle of Raphael and the recreation of the antique', Minneapolis/Minn., University of Minnesota, Phil. diss., 1982

Enggass, Robert, 'Settecento Sculpture in St. Peter: An Encyclopedia of Styles', *Apollo* (1981), 112, pp. 748

Enggass, Robert, 'Bernardino Ludovisi : a new attribution', *The Burlington Magazine*, 120, 1978, 901., pp. 229-230

Faldi, I., 'Gli inizi del Neoclassicismo in Pittura nella Prima meta del Settecento', in, *Atti del Convegno Internazionale dell'Accademia Nazionale dei Lincei*, Roma, 1977, pp. 495-523

Ferrari, Oreste and Serenita Papaldo, *Le sculture del Seicento a Roma*, Rome, 1999

'Fiamenghi che vanno e vengono non li si puol dar regola' Paesi Bassi e Italia fra Cinquecento e Seicento; pittura, stora (sic or storia?) e cultura degli emblemi, ed. Irene Baldriga, Rome, 1995

Finocchi Ghersi, Lorenzo, [Rezension] Mark Wilson Jones, 'The tempietto and the roots of coincidence', in, *Architectural history. Journal of the Society of Architectural Historians of Great Britain*, 33 (1990), pp. 1-28; in, *Roma nel Rinascimento*, 7 (1991), pp. 246-247

Fiorani, Luigi, 'Monache e monasteri romani nell'eta' del quietismo', in, *Ricerche per la Storia religiosa di Roma*, 1, 1977, 63-111, especially 107

Fisher Pace, Ursula V., Disegni di Giacinto e Ludovico Gimignani nelle collezioni del Gabinetto Nazionale delle Stampe [Mostra], Roma, De Luca (1979). 460 S

Franz-Duhme, Helga Nora, *Angelo De Rossi ein bildhauer um 1700 in Rom*, Berlin 1986, diss., Berlin

Freeman, Linda B., 'L'inventario dei beni di A. Pomarancio e alcune note sulla vita e l'opera del pittore', *Bollettino d'arte*, Ser.6. , 68. 1983, 19, pp. 31-34

Friedman, Terry, 'Lord Harrold in Italy 1715-16: four frustrated commissions to Leoni, Juvarra, Chiari and Soldani', *The Burlington Magazine*, 130 (1988), pp. 836-845

Frommel C., 'Raffaels architektonische Laufbahn', in, *Raffael. Das architektonische Werk*, Stuttgart (1987), pp. 13-46

BIBLIOGRAPHY

Frommel, C., 'S.Andrea al Quirinale: Genesi e struttura', *Atti del Convegno.... Gian Lorenzo Bernini*, Rome

Frommel, Christoph, 'Raffaels architektonische Arbeiten in Vatikan', in, *Raffael. Das architektonische Werk*, Stuttgart (1987), pp. 357-358

Golzio V, 'La facciata di S.Giovanni in Laterano e l'architettura del settecento', in *Miscellanea Bibliotheca Hertzianae*, ed. L. Bruns, F. G. W. Metternich and L. Schuat, Munich 1961, pp. 450-463

González-Palacios, Alvar, *Il Gusto dei Principe. Atre di corte del XVII e del XVIII secolo*, Milan, 1993

Graf, Dieter, Giuseppe Passeris Zeichnungen und Olskizzen. Zu fresken in romischen Kirchen. *Munchen Jahrbuch der bildenden Kunst*, F.3 41 (1990), pp. 61-122

Guercino Drawings. From the collections of Denis Mahon and the Ashmolean Museum, Catalogue, compiled by D. Mahon and D. Ekserdjian, Oxford 1986

Guerrieri Borsoi,Maria Barbara, *Per la conoscenza di Domenico Maria Muratori*, Annuario dell'Istituto di Storia dell'Arte-Univ. La Sapienza, Roma, 1982/83, pp. 32-45

Die Handzeichnungen von Giacinto Calandrucci (Catalogue), Dusseldorf 1986, Kunstmuseum Dusseldorf

Harris, Ann Sutherland, Andrea Sacchi's 'Portrait of a Cardinal', *Bulletin, The National Gallery of Canada*, 14, 1969 (1971), pp. 9-15

Harris, A. S., *Academy drawing by A.Sacchi*: addenda *Master Drawings*, 11.1973, 2, pp. 160-161

Harris, A. S., "New drawings by A. Sacchi": addenda. *The Burlington Magazine*. 120. 1978, 906, pp. 600-602

Harris, Ann S., *Drawings by Andrea Sacchi*: additions and problems, Master Drawings. 9.1971, 4, pp. 384-391

Heinzl Brigitte, The Luti collection – Towards the Reconstruction of a 17th Century Roman Collection of Master Drawings, *Connoisseur*, 1966, (161), pp. 17-22

Judson, Richard and R. E. O. Ekkart, *Gerrit von Honthorst, 1592-1656*, Doornspijk, 1999

Jurcic, Lawrence, Niccolo' Circignani, called il Pomarancio: drawings for some Roman projects. *Master drawings*. 21.1983,3, pp. 271-274.

Kitao, T., " Bernini's Church Facades : Method of Design and the Contrapposti", in *Journal of the Society of Architectural Historians*, 24 (1965), pp. 263-284.

Kugler, L. *Vier Hauptwerke Pietro da Cortona nach 1630 in Rom. Eine gattungsubergreifende Analyse zum Illusionismus im Barock*. o.O.u.J, Bochum,Ruhr Universitat, Diss. 1983.

Kunza, Matthias, *Daniel Seiter 1647-1705*, Munich, 2000

La Cappella Sistina. La volta restaurata: il trionfo del colore. Ed. Istit. Geografico De Agostini (1992).

Laskin M., " Corrado Giaquinto's St Helena and the Emperor Constantine presented by the Virgin to the Trinity ". *Museum Monographs: City Art Museum of St. Louis*, 1, 1968, pp. 29-42

Lazzareschi, Luigi, Delle rappresentazioni di Francesco Bufalini e Carlo Fontana. In: *G. L. Bernini architetto e l'architettura europea del Sei-Settecento.*, 2.1984, pp. 413-416

Liversidge, Michael, A drawing by Cortona for the Chiesa Nuova, *The Burlington Magazine*, 122. 1980, 926, pp. 341-342

Luchinat, Cristina Acidini, *Taddeo e Federico Zuccari fratell pittori del Cinquecento*, two volumes, Rome, 1998, 1999

Magnanimi Giuseppina, Inventari della Collezione Romana dei Principi Corsini, in *Bollettino d'Arte*, 7, 1980, pp. 91-126; 8, 1980, pp.73-114.

Mahon D. and Turner N.,.*The Drawings of Guercino in the colection of Her Majesty the Queen at Windsor Castle*, 1989

Mancigotti,Mario. *Simone Cantarini il Pesarese*. Pesaro; Cinisello Balsamo: Pizzi 1975., 296 .

Mancinelli,Fabrizio, Colalucci G.L., Gabrielli N. Rapporto sul "Giudizio" (Stato delle conoscenze e delle indagini in data 31-3-91). *Bollettino. Monumenti, Musei e Gallerie Pontificie*, 11 (1991), pp. 219-249

Martellacci, Rosamaria, Ciro Ferri per la Cappella dei Principi in San Lorenzo. In: *Qua*. s.a.r., 1, 1989, pp. 64-66

Martinelli, Valentino. Il busto originale di Maria Barberi nipote di Urbano VIII, di G.L. Bernini e Giuliano Finelli. *Antichità viva*, 26 (1987) H.3,pp. 27-36

Martinelli, Valentino. Il busto originale di Maria Barberini,nipote di Urbano VIII, di G.L. Bernini e Giuliano Finelli. *Antichità viva*, 26 (1987), H.3, pp. 27-36

Martinelli, Valentino. Un altro dipinto di G.L.

BIBLIOGRAPHY

Bernini: un ritratto giovanile del cardinale Antonio Barberini junior. *Studi in onore di Giulio Carlo Argan*. 1. 1984, pp, 259-268

Meroni, Ubaldo. *Lettere ed altri documenti intorno alla storia della pittura. Giovanni Benedetto Castiglione detto il Grechetto, Salvatore Rosa, Gian Lorenzo Bernini.* Monzambano: Ed. per le Fonti di Storia della Pittura, 1978

Micheli, Maria Elisa, 'Le raccolte di antichita' di A. Canova', *Rivista dell'Istituto Nazionale d'Archeologia e Storia dell'Arte*, Ser. 3, 8/9 (1985-86), pp. 205-322

Mochi Onori, Lorenzo. Una versione inedita dell' Erminia tra i pastori di Giovanni Lanfranco proveniente dalla collezione Barberini. *Bollettino d'arte*, Ser. 6, 77 (1991) H.65, pp. 121-126.

Montagu, Jennifer. Mattia Preti in S.Andrea della Valle: an unfulfilled contract, *The Burlington Magazine*, 133 (1991), pp. 708-710

Mueler, Barbara. Die Casa Zuccari in Florenz und der Palazzo Zuccari in Rom. Kunstlerhauser und Haus der Kunst. In: *Kunstlerhaus von der Renaissance bis zur Gegenwart*, Zurich, 1985, pp. 101-120

Nava Cellini, Antonio. Nota per alcune sculture romane di Lorenzo Merlini. *Imagination und Imago.* 1983. pp. 229-234

Nava Cellini, Antonia. Ritratti di Andrea Bolgi. *Paragone.Arte*. 13. 1962,147,pp. 24-40

A. Nava Cellini, *La Scultura del 700'*, Torino 1982, pp. 47-49

Nissman, Joan Lee, *'Domenico Cresti, Il Passignano, 1559-1638: a Tuscan painter in Florence and Rome'*, New York, N.Y., Columbia University, Phil. diss., 1979

Noack, F. Die Kunstlerfamilie Stern in Rom, in *Monatshefte fur Kunstwissenschaft* XIII, 1920, fasc. 2, pp. 166-173

Pacelli,Vincenzo. Inediti del Solimena e del Giordano al Monte dei Poveri. *Scritti di storia dell'arte*, Napoli (1988), pp. 273-280.

Pansecchi,Fiorella. Giuseppe Ghezzi: tre quadri fuori sede. *Scritti di storia dell'arte in onore di F. Zeri*, 2.1984., pp. 724-729.

Petraroia, Pietro. Ventura Lamberti. *Rivista dell'Istituto Nazionale d'Archeologia e Storia dell'Arte*, Ser.3. 4. 1981-82,pp. 279-318.

Pickrel, Thomas Carl. *Antonio Gherardi, painter and architect of the late baroque in Rome*. Lawrence/Kan., University of Kansas, Phil. diss., February 1981

Pier Francesco Mola (1612-1666) [exhibition catalogu], Milano, Electa (1989)

Pinto, John Abel. *Nicola Michetti circa 1675-1758 and 18th century architecture in Rome and St. Petersburg.* Cambridge, Mass. Harvard Univ., diss., 1976.

Pittura barocca romana. Dal Cavalier d'Arpino a Fratel Pozzo. La collezione Fagrolo, [exhibition catalogue] Milan, 1999

Princeton Raphael Symposium. Science in the service of art history. Edited by J. Sherman and Marcia Brown Hall, Princeton University Press (1990)

Raffaelo Sanzio e l'Europa. A cura di Marcello Fagiolo e Maria Luisa Madonna. Roma: Istituto Poligrafico e Zecca dello Stato 1990

Roettgen, Steffi, Guido Reni e la pittura romana nel Seicento e nel Settecento. in: *G. Reni e l'Europa. Fama e fortuna.* [exhibition catalogue] Frankfurt 1988, pp. 548-573.

Roli, Renato, Due inediti di S. Conca. *Studi di storia dell'arte in memoria di M. Rotili.* 2, Napoli 1984, p. 481-483

Roma Sacra. Guida alle Chiese della Città Eterna, Naples, 1995

Rosenberg, Pierre. Un carton de Baroche et un dessin d'Annibale Carrache inedits. *Per A. E. Popham*, 1981, pp. 131-135

Schleier, Erich, *Disegni di Giovanni Lanfranco (1582-1647)*, [exhibition catalogue], 1983

Schleier, Erich, Un affresco poco noto e due modelli inediti di G. Odazzi. *Paragone. Arte*. 29.1978, 339, pp. 63-67.

Schlimme, Hermann, *Die Kirchenfassade in Rom: 'Reliefierte Kirchenfronten' 1475-1765*, Petersberg, 1999

Sebastiano Conca. 1680-1764. (exhibition catalogue) Palazzo De Vio, Gaeta: luglio-ottobre 1981.Centro storico culturale "Gaeta", Gaeta 1981, 426 S. (Reviewed *The Burlington Magazine*, 125, 1983, 961, pp. 231-232

Shearman, J. Gli arazzi di Raffaello per la Cappella Sistina. In: *La Cappella Sistina. I primi restauri: la scoperta del colore.* Novara (1986), pp. 88-91

Shearman, J. Raphael's clouds and Correggio's. In: *Studi su R. Atti del Congresso Intern. di Studi.* Urbino (1987), pp. 657-688

Simone Cantarini. Disegni, incisioni e opere di riproduzione.. *Cataloghi del Centro Studi Salimbeni.* 2., San Severino Marche (1987).

Siracusano, C. Disegni inediti di C.Giaquinto in una raccolta siciliana. *Atti della Accademia Peloritana dei Pericolanti. Lettere, Filosofia e Belle Arti*, Messina. 50. 1972.

Spagnesi, Gianfranco. L'immagine di Roma Barocca

da Sisto V a Clemente XII: la pianta di G.B. Nolli del 1748. *Immagini del barocco. Bernini e la cultura del Seicento*. 1982, pp. 156

Spear, Richard E., *Domenichino*, 2 Volumes. New Haven: Yale University Press 1982

Spinosa, Nicola, *Paolo De Matteis a Guardia Sanframondi* (exhibition catalogue) 1989, pp. 19-33

Spinosa, Nicola, 'Notizie su C. Giaquinto, sui lavori per la Reggia di Caserta', *Le arti figurative a Napoli nel Settecento*, 1979., pp. 385-391

Stagni, Simonetta, Disegni del Canuti, *Paragone. Arte*, 32.1981 ,377, pp. 37-44

Stone, David Marshall. *Guercino. Catalogo completo dei dipinti.* Firenze, Centini (1991).

Studi su Raffaello. Atti del Congresso Intern. di studi. A cura di M. Sambucco Hamoud e M.L. Strocchi. Urbino: Quattroventi (1987).

Tancioni, G., *Luigi Garzi*, tesi di laurea, Universita' agli Studi di Roma, La Sapienza, aa 1989-1990.

Tancioni, Gianluca. Oratorio di Traspontina: la commissione del cardinale Sacripante e l'attivita' di Michetti, Garzi e Giovanni Conca. In: *Carlo Marchionni: architettura, decorazione e scenografia contemporanea*, Roma 1988, pp. 153-171.

Thoenes, Christof, La lettera a Leone X. In: *Raffaello Sanzio a Roma. Il convegno del 1983.* (Roma 1986), pp. 373-381

Trezzani,Ludovica. *Francesco Cozza (1605-1682)*. Roma: Multigrafica Ed. 1981

Trimarchi,Michele. *Giovanni Odazzi pittore romano 1663-1731*. Roma 1979

Trinchieri Camiz,Franca, 'Music and painting in Cardinal del Monte's household', *Metropolitan Museum Journal*, 26 (1991), pp. 213-226

Turcic, Lawrence, 'Drawings for A.Masucci's "Education of the Virgin", *Master Drawings*, 20, 1982, 3, pp. 275-278

Turner, Nicholas, 'Drawings by Giovanni Angelo Canini', *Master Drawings*, 16.1978, 4, pp. 387-397

Turner, Nicholas, Rome, Lanfranco at the Farnesina. *The Burlington Magazine*, 126.1984,972. pp. 177-181

Turner, Nicholas, Rome[Exibition]: Disegni del seicento romano di Lazzaro Baldi, Guglielmo Cortese, Giacinto e Ludovico Gimignani, *The Burlington Magazine*, 122. 1980,923, pp. 150-153

Ventura, Aleandro, Un bozzetto barocco riscoperto: una nuova attribuzione per Melchiorre Caffa'. *Ricerche di storia dell'arte*, 45 (1991),pp. 77-84.

Villani, Elena, A proposito di una mostra su Simone Cantarini, in, *Arte cristiana*, N.S. 76 (1988), pp. 315-321

Vitzhum, Walter, *Il Barocco a Roma*, (1978)

Wallace,William, 'An unpublished Michelangelo document', *The Burlington Magazine*, 129 (1987), pp. 181-184

Waterhouse, E.K., *Introduction to Painting in Italy in the 18th Century: Rococo to Romanticism*, Chicago, 1970

Westin, Robert H., 'Antonio Raggi: a documentary and stylistic investigation of his life, work, and significance in 17th century Roman baroque sculpture', University Park/Pa, Pennsylvania State Univ., Phil. diss., 1978.

Winner, Matthias, ' ... una certa idea", Maratta zitiert einen Brief Raffaels in einer Zeichnung. In: *Der Kunstler uber sich in seinen work'*, International Symposium der B. Hertziana Roma 1989. (Weinheim) 1992, pp. 511-570

Wittkower, Rudolph, *G.L. Bernini. The sculpture of the roman baroque*, 3 edition, revised by Howard Hibbard, Thomas Martin, Margot Wittkower, Oxford: Phaidon (1981)

Wittkower, Rudolf. *Bernini. Lo scultore del Barocco Romano*, Milano (Electa 1990)

Wolk Simon, Linda, 'Fame, paragone and the cartoon : the case of Perino del Vaga', *Master drawings*, 30 (1992) H 1, pp. 61-82

Wolk Simon, Linda, 'La "deposizione" perduta di Perino del Vaga per S.Maria sopra Minerva', in, *Raffaello e l'Europa*, Roma 1990, pp. 229-242

Zanella, Andrea, *Canova a Roma*, Roma, Palombi (1991)

Zuccari, Alessandro e Morace, Stefania, *Innocenzo X Pamphilj, Arte e Potere a Roma nell'Eta' Barocca*, Roma, 1990

INDEXES

INDEX OF ARTISTS

Abbatini, Guido Ubaldo (c. 1600–56)
   S. Agostino
   S. Maria della Vittoria
   S. Pietro in Montorio
   S. Spirito in Sassia
Accardi, Michelangelo (rec. 1750)
   S. Maria in Aracoeli
Achtermann, Theodor Wilhelm (1799–1884)
   S. Maria in Camposanto
   SS. Trinità dei Monti
Acquisti, Luigi Antonio (1745–1823)
   Il Gesú
   S. Pantaleo
Adam, Lambert Sigisbert (1700–59)
   S. Giovanni in Laterano
Agellio, Giuseppe (c. 1570–c. 1650)
   S. Silvestro in Capite
   S. Sivestro in Quirinale
Agnolo di Donnino called il Maziere (1466–1513)
   S. Pietro in Vaticano, Cappella Sistina
Agresti, Livio (c. 1508–79)
   Oratorio del Gonfalone
   S. Maria della Consolazione
   S. Spirito in Sassia
Agricola, Filippo (1795–1857)
   S. Giovanni in Laterano
Agricola, Luigi Antonio (1759–1821)
   S. Antonio dei Portoghesi
Aimo, Domenico (1460/70–1539)
   S. Maria in Aracoeli
Alari, Giacomo (c. 1645–1727)
   S. Maria in Vallicella
   S. Rocco
   S. Silvestro in Capite
Alari, Giovanni Antonio (1685–72)
   S. Rocco
Albacini, Achille (1841–1914)
   S. Maria dei Monti
Albani, Francesco (1578–1660)
   S. Maria della Pace
Alberici, Giuseppe (rec. 1750–60)
   SS. Trinità degli Spagnuoli
Alberizi, Oratio (rec. 1612–51)
   S. Pietro in Vaticano
Alberti, Antonio (1603–49)
   S. Maria della Concezione
Alberti, Cherubino (1553–1615)
   S. Giovanni in Laterano and Scala Santa
   S. Maria sopra Minerva
   S. Maria in Via in Largo Chigi
   S. Silvestro al Quirinale
Alberti, Durante (1538–1616)
   SS. Bartolomeo e Alessandro dei Bergamaschi
   Il Gesù
   S. Girolamo della Carità
   S. Maria della Consolazione
   S. Maria dei Monti
   S. Maria in Vallicella
   SS. Nero e Achilleo
   S. Tommaso di Canterbury
Alberti, Giovanni (1558–1601)
   S. Giovanni in Laterano and Scala Santa
   S. Silvestro al Quirinale
Alberti, Michele (rec. 1535–82)
   S. Maria degli Angeli
   S. Pietro in Montorio
   SS. Trinità dei MontiAlbertino, Innocenzo
   S. Pietro in Vaticano
Albertini, Innocenzo (17th century)
   S. Pietro in Vaticano
Albertini, Matteo (rec. 1638–40)
   S. Maria sopra Minerva
Albertoni, Paolo (active c. 1670–95)
   SS. Carlo e Ambrogio al Corso
   S. Marta
Aldini, Nicolangelo (rec. 1702–50)
   S. Maria dell'Orto
Aleggiani, Giuseppe (19th century)
   S. Maria in Via, Largo Chigi
Alessi, Galeazzo (1512–72)
   Il Gesù
Alfani, Emanuele (active 1730–1774)
   SS. Celso e Giuliano
   S. Sisto Vecchio
Algardi, Alessandro (1598–1654)
   S. Agnese in Agone
   SS. Carlo e Ambrogio al Corso
   S. Carlo ai Catinari
   S. Francesco a Ripa
   Il Gesù
   S. Giovanni dei Fiorentini
   S. Giovanni in Laterano
   S. Ignazio
   S. Isidoro
   SS. Luca e Martina
   S. Marcello
   S. Maria dell' Anima
   S. Maria in Campo Marzio
   S. Maria Maggiore
   S. Maria del Popolo
   S. Maria della Scala
   S. Maria in Trastevere
   S. Maria in Vallicella and Oratory
   S. Maria della Vittoria
   S. Nicola da Tolentino
   S. Pietro in Vaticano
   S. Prassede
   S. Silvestro al Quirinale
   SS. Trinità dei Pellegrini
Alignini, Antonio (rec. 1702–06)
   S. Pietro in Vaticano, Piazza
Allegrini, Flaminio (1587 ?–1663)
   SS. Cosma e Damiano
Allegrini, Francesco (1614?–after 1679)
   S. Agnese in Agone
   SS. Cosma e Damiano
   SS. Domenico e Sisto
   S. Marco
   S. Maria sopra Minerva
   S. Maria dell'Umiltà
Allori, Alessandro (1535–1607)
   SS. Annunziata a Tor de' Specchi
Allori, Cristofano (1577–1621)
   S. Marco
Altobelli, Gaetano (rec. 1734–37)
   S. Giovanni dei Fiorentini
   S. Lorenzo in Lucina
Alvarez Bouquel, José Antonio (1805–30)
   S. Maria di Monserrato
Alvarez Cubero, José (1768–1827)
   S. Maria di Monserrato
Amati, Giacomo (1643–1732)
   S. Maria in Trivio
Amato, Paolo (1634–1714)
   S. Maria Maddalena
Armellini, Francesco (18th century)

INDEX OF ARTISTS

    S. Prassede
Amici, Luigi (1817– 97)
    S. Pietro in Vaticano
Amico, Domenico d' (19th century)
    S. Maria in Aquiro
    S. Maria di Loreto
    S. Salvatore in Onda
Ammanati, Bartolomeo (1511–92)
    Il Gesù
    S. Maria sopra Minerva
    S. Pietro in Montorio
Amorosi, Antonio Mercurio
    (1660–1738)
    S. Bernardino ai Monti
    S. Rocco
Andreozzi, Antonio Francesco
    (1663–1730)
    S. Maria del Popolo
Angeletti, Pietro (c. 1737–98)
    S. Caterina da Siena
    S. Maria in Vallicella, Oratory
    S. Silvestro al Quirinale
    S. Pietro in Vaticano
Angelini, Giuseppe (1738–1811)
    S. Maria del Priorato
    S. Pietro in Vaticano and Piazza
Angelis, Amalia de (rec. 1847)
    S. Carlo allle Quattro Fontane
Angelis, Desiderio de (rec. 1787–1808)
    S. Maria Scala Coeli
Angelo da Pietrafitta, Fra'
    (d. before 1699)
    S. Francesco a Ripa
Angelo di Mariano (b. 1491)
    S. Maria dell' Anima
    S. Maria Porta Paradisi
Angelo di Pellegrino (rec. 1623)
    S. Cecilia
Angelo di Siena (rec. 1524)
    S. Maria in Trastevere
Angelo d'Orvieto (rec. 1585–c. 90)
    S. Giovanni in Laterano,
      Scala Santa
    S. Maria Maggiore
Angiolini, Benigno (mid 17th century)
    S. Maria del Pianto
Angiolo d'Orvieto see Angelo
    d'Orvieto
Anguier, Michel (1612– 86)
    S. Giovanni dei Fiorentini
    S. Giovanni in Laterano
Anguilla, Giovanni (rec. 1599–1600)
    S. Maria dei Monti
Antichi, Prospero (Prospero
    Bresciano) (?–1591)
    S. Giovanni dei Fiorentini
    S. Maria Maggiore
    S. Pietro in Vaticano
    SS. Trinità dei Monti
Antoniazzo Romano, (Antonio

    Aquili) (1452–1508/12)
    S. Annunziata a Tor de' Specchi
    S. Antonio dei Portoghesi
    SS. Apostoli
    S. Cesareo
    S. Croce in Gerusalemme
    S. Maria della Consolazione
    S. Maria sopra Minerva
    S. Nicola in Carcere
    S. Onofrio
    S. Pietro in Montorio
Antonio della Cornia (late 15th
    century)
    S. Francesco a Ripa
Antonio del Massaro, il Pastura
    (c. 1450– before 1516)
    S. Cecilia
    S. Cosimato
Antonini, Giovanni Battista
    (rec. 1697–1703)
    Il Gesù
    S. Pietro in Vaticano
Antoniozzi, Francesco (rec. 1730)
    S. Nicola dei Lorenesi
Aprile, Francesco (c. 1654–84)
    S. Anastasia
    Gesù e Maria
    S. Giovanni dei Fioretini
    S. Maria sopra Minerva
Aquili, Antonio see Antoniazzo
    Romano
Arconio, Mario (1575–1623)
    S. Eufemia
    S. Isidoro
    S. Maria in Vallicella, Oratory
    S. Maria della Vittoria
Arbasia, Cesare (1547–1607)
    SS. Trinità dei Monti
Arcucci, Camillo (c. 1617–67)
    S. Giuliano dei Fiamminghi
    S. Maria del Rosario sul Monte
      Mario
    S. Maria in Vallicella and Oratory
Aretino, Andrea (rec. 1584–89)
    Il Gesù
Ari, Girolamo (rec. 1665–66)
    S. Maria in Traspontina
Arigucci, Luigi (1575– c. 1654)
    S. Anastasia
    SS. Cosma e Damiano
    S. Giacomo alla Lungara
    S. Sebastiano al Palatino
Armellini, Francesco (18th century)
    S. Prassede
Armellini, Tito (rec. 1869–78)
    S. Maria del Suffragio
Arnolfo di Cambio (c. 1245–1302)
    S. Cecilia
    S. Maria Maggiore
Arrigo Fiammingo see Hendrik Van

    den Broecke
Artusi, Giovanni (d. 1676)
    S. Pietro in Vaticano
Artusi, Nicola (1646–1712)
    S. Pietro in Vaticano, Piazza
Ascenzi, Carlo (second half of 17th
    century)
    SS. Carlo e Ambrogio al Corso
Asprucci, Antonio (1732–1808)
    S. Maria Maggiore
Asprucci, Mario (rec. 1727– d. 1750)
    S. Giuliano dei Fiamminghi
    S. Salvatore in Lauro
Astorri, Pier Enrico (1882–1926)
    S. Pietro in Vaticano
Atanasio da Coriano (d. 1843)
    S. Maria in Aracoeli
Augero, Angelo (19th century)
    S. Angelo in Pescheria
Avellino, Onofrio (c. 1674–1741)
    S. Francesco di Paola
    S. Lorenzo in Lucina
    S. Maria delle Grazie alle Fornaci
    S. Maria della Luce
Azzurri, Francesco (1827–1901)
    S. Lucia del Gonfalone
    S. Maria in Monticelli
Azzurri, Giovanni (1792–1858)
    S. Giovanni in Laterano, Scala Santa
Baburen, Dirck van (c. 1595–1624)
    S. Pietro in Montorio
Baciccio, Giovanni Battista Gaulli
    called (1639–1709)
    S. Agnese in Agone
    S. Andrea al Quirinale
    SS. Apostoli
    S. Francesco a Ripa
    Il Gesù
    S. Margherita in Trastevere
    S. Maria in Campitelli
    S. Maria Maddalena
    S. Maria sopra Minerva
    S. Maria di Montesanto
    S. Marta
    S. Nicola da Tolentino
    S. Rocco
Badalocchio, Sisto (1585–after 1620)
    S. Gregorio al Celio, Oratorio di
      S. Sylvia
Baglione, Giovanni (c. 1566–1643)
    S. Bernardino ai Monti
    S. Cecilia
    SS. Cosma e Damiano
    Il Gesù
    S. Giovanni in Laterano and
      Sancta Scala
    S. Luigi dei Francesi
    S. Maria degli Angeli
    S. Maria della Consolazione
    S. Maria Maggiore

S. Maria dell'Orto
S. Nicola in Carcere
S. Pudenziana
SS. Quattro Coronati
S. Stefano del Cacco
Baini, Felice (active 1816–36)
S. Paolo fuori le Mura
Balassi, Mario (1604–67)
S. Maria della Concezione
Balbi, Filippo (1806–90)
S. Onofrio
Baldi, Antonio (rec. 1791)
S. Maria dell' Anima
Baldi, Bernardino (1557–1612)
Il Gesù
Baldi, Filippo (rec. 1781)
S. Maria dell' Anima
Baldi, Filippo (19th century)
S. Paolo fuori le Mura
Baldi, Lazzaro (1622–1703)
S. Anastasia
S. Andrea delle Fratte
Oratorio del Caravita
S. Cosimato
SS. Croce e Bonaventura dei Lucchesi
Gesù e Maria
S. Giovanni Calabita
S. Giovanni in Laterano
S. Giovanni in Oleo
SS. Luca e Martina
S. Marcello
S. Maria in Campo Marzio
S. Maria sopra Minerva
S. Maria del Pianto
S. Maria in Vallicella
S. Pudenziana
SS. Re Magi
S. Sabina
S. Silvestro al Quirinale
SS. Sudario dei Piemontesi
Baldi, Luigi (rec. 1818)
SS. Vincenzo e Anastasio
Baldini, Pietro Paolo (Ubaldini or Naldini) (1611–50)
SS. Domenico e Sisto
S. Isidoro
S. Marcello
S. Maria sopra Minerva
S. Maria Porta Paradisi
S. Maria in Traspontina
S. Nicola da Tolentino
Balducci, Giovanni (c. 1560–after 1631)
S. Giovanni Decollato
S. Giovanni dei Fiorentini
S. Prassede
Balestra, Antonio (1666–1740)
S. Gregorio al Celio
Balestra, Pietro Maria (1645–1729)
S. Maria in Vallicella

Baltard, Victor (1805–74)
S. Luigi dei Francesi
Balzico, Alfonso (1825–1901)
S. Maria in Vittoria
Bandinelli, Baccio (1493–c. 1560)
S. Maria sopra Minerva
Baragiolio, Marcantonio (mid 17th century)
S. Francesco d'Assisi a Monte Mario
Baratta, Andrea (b. 1639–rec. 1657–1700)
S. Agnese in Agone
S. Nicola da Tolentino
S. Pietro in Vaticano, Piazza
Baratta, Francesco (c. 1590/1600–66)
S. Girolamo della Carità
S. Nicola da Tolentino
S. Pietro in Montorio
Baratta, Francesco (d. c. 1728/30)
SS. Croce e Bonaventura dei Lucchesi
Baratta, Giovanni Maria (c. 1620–79/80)
S. Agnese in Agone
S. Agostino
S. Andrea al Quirinale
S. Nicola da Tolentino
S. Pietro in Vaticano, Piazza
Barattone, Luigi (c. 1670-1731)
S. Cecilia
S. Francesco di Paola
S. Eligio dei Ferrari
S. Maria dell'Orto
Barba, Giuseppe (active 1830–50)
S. Eustachio
S. Giovanni in Laterano
Barbalonga, Antonio (1603–49)
SS. Croce e Bonaventura dei Lucchesi
S. Maria della Vittoria
S. Silvestro al Quirinale
Barbault, Jean (1718–62)
SS. Giovanni e Paolo
Barberi, Giuseppe (1746–1809)
S. Maria degli Angeli
Barberi, Michelangelo (1787–1867)
S. Lorenzo in Damaso
Barbiani, Domenico (rec. 1729–36)
S. Maria Maddalena
Barbieri, Giovanni Francesco see Guercino
Barbieri, Pietro Andrea (1684–1730)
SS. Claudio e Andrea de' Borgognoni
S. Giovanni e Paolo
S. Girolamo della Carità
S. Marcello
S. Maria della Quercia
Bardi, Bartolomeo de' (d. before 1607)

S. Maria in Vallicella
Barigioni, Filippo (1672–1753)
S. Andrea delle Fratte
S. Gregorio a Ponte Quattro Capi
S. Marco
S. Pietro in Vaticano
S. Sebastiano fuori le Mura
S. Stefano Rotondo
Barlocci, T. (rec. 1857)
S. Maria sopra Minerva
Barocci, Federico (1535–1612)
S. Maria sopra Minerva
S. Maria in Vallicella
Bartoli, Papirio (16th/17th century)
S. Pietro in Vaticano, Piazza
Bartolini, Domenico (1827–84)
S. Isidoro
S. Paolo fuori le Mura
Bartolini, Matteo (Matteo da Castello) (c. 1530–89)
S. Maria della Scala
S. Maria in Vallicella
Bascapé, Ruggero (d. 1600)
S. Maria in Aracoeli
Bassani, Lorenzo (rec. 1585–98)
S. Maria Maggiore
Bassano, Francesco (Francesco dal Ponte) (1549–92)
Il Gesù
S. Luigi dei Francesi
Bassetti, Marcantonio (1586–1630)
S. Maria in Aquiro
S. Sebastiano fuori le Mura
Basso, Bartolomeo (rec. 1575–1619)
S. Andrea della Valle
Il Gesù
S. Giacomo degli Incurabili
S. Gregorio al Celio
S. Lucia in Selci
S. Maria Maggiore
S. Maria in Vallicella
Basso, Piero (1441–1525)
S. Pietro in Vaticano, Cappella Sistina
Bassano, Francesco (Francesco dal Ponte) (1549–92)
Il Gesù
S. Luigi dei Francesi
Bastiani, Giuseppe (c. 1560–c. 1630)
S. Maria sopra Minerva
Batisti, Antonio de (active c.1600–22/24)
S. Trinità dei Pellegrini
Batoni, Pompeo Girolamo (1708–87)
SS. Celso e Giuliano
S. Eligio dei Ferrari
Il Gesù
S. Gregorio al Celio
S. Luigi dei Francesi
S. Maria degli Angeli

317

INDEX OF ARTISTS

S. Maria Maggiore
Bazzani, Cesare (1873–1939)
  S. Andrea della Valle
Bazzi, Giovanni Antonio see Sodoma
Bea, Alfredo (19th century)
  S. Maria in Monticelli
Becerra, Gaspar (Becerra Spagnuolo) (c. 1520–68)
  SS. Trinità dei Monti
Beinaschi, Giovanni Battista (1636–88)
  S. Bonaventura al Palatino
  SS. Carlo e Ambrogio al Corso
  S. Maria del Suffragio
Belcari, Salvatore see Salvatore Bercari
Belletti, Domenico (d. 1715)
  S. Maria degli Angeli
Bellevia, Marcantonio (17th century)
  S. Andrea delle Fratte
Belli, Francesco (rec. 1796)
  S. Martino ai Monti
Belli, Gioacchino (rec. 1796)
  S. Martino ai Monti
Belli, Michele (rec. 1796)
  S. Martino ai Monti
Belli, Pasquale (1752–1833)
  S. Andrea delle Fratte
  S. Maria della Consolazione
  S. Paolo fuori le Mura
Belloli, Andrea (1822–81)
  R. Rocco
Belloni, Paolo (1815–89)
  S. Francesco a Ripa
  S. Nicola dei Prefetti
Beltramelli, Francesco (17th century)
  S. Pietro in Vaticano
Beltrami, Giacomo (rec. 1868)
  S. Silvestro al Quirinale
Benaglia, Francesco (1809–68)
  SS. Carlo e Ambrogio al Corso
  S. Maria dei Miracoli
Benaglia, Paolo (c. 1694–1739)
  S. Giovanni dei Fioretini
  S. Giovanni in Laterano
  S. Maria ad Martyres
  S. Maria sopra Minerva
  S. Maria in Via, Piazza Poli
Benaglia, Pietro (rec. 1845)
  S. Giovanni dei Fiorentini
Benamati, Stefano (17th century)
  S. Maria in Vallicella
Bencari, Salvatore
  SS. Nome di Maria
Bencivenga, P. (19th century)
  S. Maria in Aquiro
Benedetti, Flavia see Maria Eufrasia della Croce
Benefial, Marco (1684–1764)
  S. Angelo in Pescheria *
  S. Gallicano
  S. Giovanni dei Fiorentini

S. Giovanni in Laterano
SS. Giovanni e Paolo
S. Lorenzo in Lucina
S. Maria in Aracoeli
S. Maria delle Grazie alle Fornaci
S. Maria della Quercia
S. Pietro in Vaticano
Stimmate di S. Francesco
SS. Trinità degli Spagnuoli
Benincampi, Teresa (1778–1830)
  S. Andrea delle Fratte
Bentinelli, Francesco (17th century)
  S. Maria in Traspontina
Benzoni, Giovanni Maria (1809–73)
  S. Anastasia
  S. Andrea delle Fratte
  S. Isidoro
Bercari, Salvatore (rec. 1743–71)
  S. Marco
Berettoni, Luigi see Luigi Barattone
Bergondi, Andrea (d. 1789)
  S. Agostino
  SS. Alessio e Bonifazio all'Aventino
  SS. Annunziata a Tor de' Specchi
  S. Marco
  SS. Nome di Maria
  S. Paolo Primo Eremita
  S. Pietro in Vaticano
Bergonzoni, Giovanni Battista (c. 1628–92)
  S. Paolo alla Regola
Bernardi, Mario (rec. 1704–75)
  S. Maria del Pianto
Bernini, Gian Lorenzo (1598–1680)
  S. Agnese in Agone
  S. Agostino
  S. Andrea delle Fratte
  S. Andrea al Quirinale
  S. Andrea della Valle
  S. Bernardino ai Monti
  S. Bibiana
  S. Calisto
  S. Crisogono
  SS. Domenico e Sisto
  S. Francesca Romana
  S. Francesco a Ripa
  Il Gesù
  S. Giacomo alla Lungara
  S. Giovanni dei Fiorentini
  S. Isidoro
  S. Lorenzo in Damaso
  S. Lorenzo in Fonte
  S. Lorenzo in Lucina
  S. Maria in Aracoeli
  S. Maria Maggiore
  S. Maria ad Martyres
  S. Maria sopra Minerva
  S. Maria di Monserrato
  S. Maria dei Miracoli and

S. Maria di Montesanto
S. Maria del Popolo
S. Maria in Via Lata
S. Maria in Vittoria
S. Pietro in Montorio
S. Pietro in Vaticano and Piazza
S. Prassede
SS. Re Magi
S. Sabina
S. Spirito in Sassia
Bernini, Luigi (1612–81)
  S. Pietro in Vaticano
Bernini, Pietro (1562–1629)
  S. Andrea della Valle
  Il Gesù
  S. Giovanni dei Fiorentini
  S. Maria Maggiore
Berrettini, Luca (1609–80)
  Il Gesù
  SS. Luca e Martina
  S. Marco
Berrettini, Pietro see Pietro da Cortona
Berrettini, Vincenzo (rec. 1774–1818)
  S. Lorenzo in Damaso
Berrettoni, Andrea (18th century)
  SS. Trinità in Palazzo Monte di Pietà
Berrettoni, Niccolò (1637–82)
  S. Marcello
  S. Maria di Montesanto
Berthelot, Guillaume (c. 1580–1648)
  S. Maria Maggiore
  S. Maria in Vallicella
Bertoia, Jacopo, il Zanguidi (1544–74)
  Oratorio del Gonfalone
Bertoni, Andrea (early 18th century)
  SS. Croce e Bonaventura dei Lucchesi
  S. Isidoro
  SS. Trinità in Palazzo Monte di Pietà
Bertosi, Francesco (rec. 1691–1760)
  S. Maria in Aracoeli
Bertosi, Giuseppe, (rec. 1724 -25)
  S. Pietro in Vaticano
Besano, Battista (rec. 1647)
  S. Spirito in Sassia
Besson, Hyacinthe (1816–61)
  S. Sisto Vecchio
Betocchi, Alessandro (1823–1909)
  S. Andrea in Pescheria
Betti, Biagio (1545–1615)
  S. Silvestro al Quirinale
Bettini, Angelo (rec. 1863)
  S. Stefano del Cacco
Bevilacqua, Andrea (19th century)
  S. Antonio dei Portoghesi
Bezzi, Angelo (rec. 1830–55)
  S. Giovanni in Laterano

Bianchedi, Girolamo (1802–49)
   S. Maria sopra Minerva
Bianchi, Francesco (rec. 1703–48)
   S. Maria in Monterone
Bianchi, Giuseppe (rec. 1589–1604)
   S. Eligio dei Ferrari
Bianchi, Orazio (17th century)
   S. Giuseppe dei Falegnami
Bianchi, Pietro (1694–1740)
   SS. Bartolomeo e Alessandro
     dei Bergamaschi
   S. Maria degli Angeli
   S. Maria delle Grazie alle Fornaci
   S. Pietro in Vaticano
Bianchi, Salvatore (1821–84)
   S. Maria in Via Lata
Bianchini, Antonio (1803–84)
   SS. Trinità dei Pellegrini
Bianchini, Francesco (rec. 1702)
   S. Maria degli Angeli
Bicchierai, Antonio (1688–1766)
   SS. Claudio e Andrea
     de' Borgognoni
   SS. Cosmos e Damiano
     de' Barbieri
   S. Lorenzo in Panisperna
   S. Luigi dei Francesi
   S. Marcello
   S. Maria degli Angeli
Bido, Francesco (rec. 1650–66)
   S. Maria in Traspontina
Bigatti, Giovanni (1784–c. 1817)
   S. Eustachio
   S. Lorenzo in Panisperna
   S. Maria in Via, Largo Chigi
Bigeri, Marcello (rec. 1715)
   S. Maria in Via Lata
Bigioli, Filippo (1798–1878)
   S. Rocco
   SS. Trinità dei Pellegrini
Biglioschi, Leandro (rec. 1813–23)
   S. Maria in Via Lata
Bigot, Trophime (1579–1650)
   S. Marco
   S. Maria in Aquiro
Bilancioni, Giuseppe (rec. 1691–1703)
   S. Carlo ai Catinari
   S. Maria dell'Orto
   S. Maria in Traspontina
Biliverti, Giovanni (1576/85–1644)
   S. Calisto
Bisetti, Antonio (rec. 1840–55)
   S. Maria della Concezione
Bizzacheri, Carlo Francesco
   (1655–1721)
   SS. Carlo e Ambrogio al Corso
   Gesù e Maria
   S. Isidoro
   S. Lorenzo in Lucina
   S. Luigi dei Francesi

S. Marcello
S. Maria Maddalena
S. Maria sopra Minerva
S. Maria di Montesanto
S. Pietro in Vincoli
S. Salvatore in Lauro
SS. Trinità in Palazzo
   Monte di Pietà
SS. Vincenzo e Anastasio
Bizzacheri, Francesco (rec. 1625–26)
   S. Maria di Monserrato
Blasi, Luca (c. 1545–1609)
   S. Giovanni in Laterano
   S. Maria di Loreto
Blasi, Pietro (rec. 1749)
   S. Apollinare
   S. Girolamo degli Schiavoni
   S. Lucia in Selci
Blasij, Antonio (rec. 1725)
   S. Eligio dei Ferrari
Bolangier, Flaminio see Flamen
   Boulanger
Boldrini, Luigi (1795–1868)
   S. Carlo ai Catinari
Bolgi, Andrea (1606–56)
   S. Agostino
   S. Antonio dei Portoghesi
   S. Francesco a Ripa
   S. Gregorio al Celio
   S. Maria in Aracoeli
   S. Maria Maggiore
   S. Maria sopra Minerva
   S. Maria in Via Lata
   S. Pietro in Montorio
   S. Pietro in Vaticano
Boli, Rocco (rec. 1559–62)
   S. Agnese in Agone
Bolognese, Ercolino (rec. 1585–1590)
   S. Maria Maggiore
Bombelli, Gioacchino (19th century)
   Madonna del Divino Amore
Bompiani, Roberto (1821–1908)
   S. Lorenzo in Lucina
   S. Paolo fuori le Mura
Bon, Melchiorre von (rec. 1613)
   S. Giuseppe dei Falegnami
Bonacina, Carlo Mauro
   S. Ignazio
Bonarelli, Matteo (d. 1654)
   S. Maria dell' Anima
   S. Pietro in Vaticano
Bonatti, Giovanni (c. 1635–81)
   S. Croce in Gerusalemme
   S. Maria dell' Anima
   S. Maria in Vallicella
Bonazzino, Ambrogio (?–1602)
   S. Giovanni in Laterano
   Oratorio del Gonfalone
Bonazzini, Giovanni Maria
   (rec. 1606–16)

S. Anastasia
S. Eligio degli Orefici
Bonfreni, Giovanni Battista
   (rec. 1717–95)
   S. Gregorio al Celio
   S. Pietro in Vaticano
Bonifazi, Ennio (c. 1592–1654)
   S. Maria sopra Minerva
   S. Stefano del Cacco
Bonnassieux, Jean Marie Bienaimé
   (1810–92)
   S. Giuseppe dei Falegnami
Boncori see
   Giovan Battista Buoncuore
Bonocoro, Giovan Battista see
   Giovan Battista Buoncuore
Bonola, Francesco (rec. 1885)
   S. Onofrio
Bonvicino, Ambrogio see
   Buonvicino
Bonzi, Paolo (1573–1636)
   S. Maria ad Martyres
Borghese, Girolamo (rec. 1633–61)
   S. Giacomo degli Incurabili
Borghesi, Giovanni Ventura
   (1640–1708)
   S. Ivo della Sapienza
   S. Nicola da Tolentino
   SS. Re Magi
Borghini, Gabriele (18th century)
   S. Giovanni Calabita
Borgianni, Orazio (c. 1578–1616)
   S. Carlo alle Quattro Fontane
   S. Salvatore in Lauro
Borgo, Filippo dal (rec. 1569)
   SS. Bartolmeo e Alessandro
     dei Bergamaschi
Borgognone see Guglielmo Cortese
Borgognoni, Salvatore (1768–1830)
   S. Apollinare
Boroni, Bartolomeo (1703–87)
   S. Maria del Popolo
Boroni, Giuseppe (1741–1820)
   S. Martino ai Monti
Borromini, Francesco (1599–1667)
   S. Agnese in Agone
   S. Anastasia
   S. Andrea delle Fratte
   SS. Carlo e Ambrogio al Corso
   S. Carlo alle Quattro Fontane
   S. Eustachio
   S. Giovanni Calabita
   S. Giovanni dei Fiorentini
   S. Giovanni in Laterano and
     Baptistery
   S. Giovanni in Oleo
   S. Girolamo della Carità
   S. Ignazio
   S. Ivo della Sapienza
   S. Lucia in Selci

INDEX OF ARTISTS

S. Maria Maggiore
S. Maria ad Martyres
S. Maria dei Sette Dolori
S. Maria in Vallicella
S. Pietro in Vaticano
SS. Re Magi
S. Sabina
Boscoli, Tommaso (1503–74)
S. Maria di Monserrato
S. Pietro in Vincoli
Boselli, Orfeo (1597–1667)
S. Adriano
S. Ambrogio della Massima
S. Carlo ai Catinari
S. Maria dell'Umiltà
Bosi, Bartolomeo (18th century)
S. Pantaleo
Botta, Ida (18th century)
S. Lorenzo in Miranda
Bottani, Giuseppe (1717–84)
S. Andrea delle Fratte
Botticelli, Sandro (1445–1510)
S. Pietro in Vaticano,
Cappella Sistina
Boucoiran, Numa (1805–69)
S. Luigi de' Francesi
Boudard, Jean Batista (rec. 1739–41)
SS. Nome di Maria
Boulangier, Flamen (Boulangier,
Flaminio) (rec. 1552–90)
SS. Crocifisso, Oratorio del
S. Giovanni in Laterano
S. Maria in Aracoeli
Bracci, Alessandro (1730–d. before 94)
S. Nicola da Tolentino
Bracci, Antonio (rec. 1764–67)
S. Pantaleo
Bracci, Filippo (1727–?)
S. Andrea al Quirinale
S. Girolamo degli Schiavoni
S. Nicola da Tolentino
Bracci, Pietro (1700–73)
S. Agostino
S. Andrea delle Fratte
S. Caterina da Siena a
Magnanapoli
S. Giovanni dei Fiorentini
S. Giovanni in Laterano
SS. Giovanni e Paolo
S. Girolamo della Carità
S. Gregorio a Ponte Quattro Capi
S. Ignazio
S. Marcello
S. Maria Maggiore
S. Maria sopra Minerva
S. Pietro in Vaticano
Stimmate di S. Francesco
Bracci, Virgino (1737–1815)
S. Nicola da Tolentino
Braccioli, Filippo (17th century)

S. Francesco di Paola
Bramante, Donato (1444–1514)
S. Biagio della Pagnotta
SS. Celso e Giuliano
SS. Faustino e Giovita
S. Maria della Pace
S. Maria del Popolo
S. Pietro in Montorio
S. Pietro in Vaticano
Brandi, Giacinto (1621–91)
S. Agostino
S. Andrea del Quirinale
S. Carlo al Quirinale
SS. Carlo e Ambrogio al Corso
S. Carlo ai Catinari
S. Francesca Romana
Gesù e Maria
S. Margherita in Trastevere
S. Maria del Suffragio
S. Maria in Trastevere
S. Maria in Via Lata
S. Rocco
S. Silvestro in Capite
Stimmate di S. Francesco
Brandini, Tommaso (active 1716–50)
S. Croce in Gerusalemme
S. Giovanni in Laterano
Brasca, Andrea (rec. 1589)
S. Maria Maggiore
Breccioli, Bartolomeo (d. after 1637)
S. Giuseppe a Capo le Case
S. Maria della Scala
SS. Trinità dei Monti
Breccioli, Filippo (1574–d. after 1627)
S. Maria in Aquiro
Brefort, Adam Claude (d. 1673)
S. Pudenziana
Bregno, Andrea (1418–1503)
SS. Apostoli
S. Clemente
S. Maria in Aracoeli
S. Maria sopra Minerva
S. Maria del Popolo
Bresciano, Prospero see
Prospero Antichi
Breton, Luc-François (1731–1800)
SS. Claudio e Andrea de'
Borgognoni
Bricci, Plautilla (1616–after 1700)
S. Luigi dei Francesi
Bril, Paul (1554–1626)
S. Cecilia
Il Gesù
S. Giovanni in Laterano and
Scala Santa
Brocchi, Ignazio (rec. 1738–1802)
S. Giovanni Decollato
S. Stanislao dei Polacchi
Broecke, Hendrik van den (Arrigo
Fiammingo) (c. 1519–97)

S. Maria degli Angeli
S. Maria Maggiore
S. Pietro in Vaticano,
Cappella Sistina
Brughi, Giovan Battista (c.
1660–1730)
S. Angelo in Pescheria
S. Barbara dei Librai
S. Francesco di Paola
Brumidi, Costantino (1805–80)
S. Maria dell'Archetto
S. Nicola in Carcere
Brunetti, Francesco Maria
(d. after 1721)
S. Maria in Aracoeli
S. Maria Porta Paradisi
S. Maria in Via Lata
S. Pietro in Vaticano
Bruschi, Domenico (1840–1910)
SS. Apostoli
Bruschini, Bastiono (16th century)
S. Maria sopra Minerva
Bucci, Michele (late 17th century)
S. Dorotea
Bufalini, Francesco Antonio
(rec. 1688–1716)
S. Maria delle Grazie alle
Fornaci
Bugiardini, Giuliano (1475–1554)
S. Pietro in Vaticano,
Cappella Sistina
Buoncuore, Giovan Battista (1643–99)
SS. Carlo e Ambrogio al Corso
S. Maria in Aracoeli
Buonvicino, Ambrogio (1552–1622)
S. Andrea della Valle
S. Giovanni in Laterano and
Baptistery
S. Maria Maggiore
S. Maria sopra Minerva
S. Maria dei Monti
S. Maria del Popolo
S. Pietro in Vaticano and Piazza
S. Pudenziana
Buonvisi, Francesco (1625–1700)
SS. Croce e Bonaventura del
Lucchesi
Buratti, Carlo (c. 1651–1734)
Bambino Gesù
SS. Luca e Martina
Buratti, Giovanni (rec. 1662–63)
S. Agnese in Agone
Busiri Vici, Andrea (1818–1911)
S. Francesca Romana
S. Giovanni in Laterano
S. Lorenzo in Lucina
S. Maria della Quercia
S. Maria dell'Umiltà
Busini Vici, Carlo (1856–1925)
S. Eligio dei Ferrari

Butio, Carlo see Carlo Buzzi
Buzio (Buzzi), Ippolito (1562–1634)
  S. Giacomo degli Incurabili
  S. Giovanni in Laterano
  S. Maria in Aracoeli
  S. Maria Maggiore
  S. Maria sopra Minerva
  S. Paolo alle Tre Fontane
Buziot, Stefano (rec. 1600)
  S. Paolo alle Tre Fontane
Buzzi, Carlo (Carlo Butio)
  (17th century)
  Gesù e Maria
Cacci, Giuseppe (mid 17th century)
  S. Francesco d'Assisi
    a Monte Mario
Caccia, Girolamo (1650–1728/29)
  S. Francesco a Ripa
Caccianiga, Francesco (1700–81)
  SS. Celso e Giuliano
Cades, Giuseppe (1750–99)
  S. Andrea delle Fratte
  S. Antonio dei Portoghesi
  SS. Apostoli
  S. Nicola da Tolentino
Cafà, Melchiorre (1638–67)
  S. Agnese in Agone
  S. Agostino
  S. Caterina da Siena
    a Magnanapoli
  S. Maria in Campitelli
Caffieri, Gian Giacomo (1725–92)
  S. Luigi dei Francesi
Caisotti, Tommaso Amadeo
  (17th century)
  S. Pantaleo
Calandra, Giovanni Battista
  (1586–1644)
  S. Lorenzo fuori le Mura
  S. Maria sopra Minerva
Calandrucci, Giacinto (1646–1707)
  S. Antonio dei Portoghesi
  S. Bonaventura al Palatino
  S. Carlo ai Catinari
  S. Maria dell'Orto
  S. Maria del Suffragio
  S. Maria in Traspontina
  S. Paola alla Regola
Calandrucci, Giovanni Battista
  (?–1749)
  S. Maria in Traspontina
Calcagnadoro, Antonino (1874–1934)
  S. Spirito in Sassia
Calcagni, Domenico
  S. Agnese in Agone
Calcagni, Tiberio (1532–65)
  S. Caterina dei Funari
  S. Giuseppe dei Falegnami
  S. Maria Maggiore
Caldarani, Mariano (rec. 1775)
  S. Maria in Aracoeli
Calderari, Carlo (rec. 1762–64)
  S. Maria Maddalena
Calliano, Antonio Raffaele
  (1785–1824)
  S. Prassede
Camassei, Andrea (1602–49)
  S. Egidio
  S. Giovanni in Laterano,
    Baptistery
  S. Lorenzo in Fonte
  S. Lucia in Selci
  S. Maria della Concezione
  S. Maria ad Martyres
  S. Maria in Via Lata
  SS. Re Magi
  S. Sebastiano al Palatino
Cametti, Bernardino Agostino
  (1669–1736)
  SS. Apostoli
  Il Gesù
  S. Giovanni Calabita
  S. Giovanni in Laterano
  S. Marcello
  S. Maria ad Martyres
  S. Maria in Vallicella
  S. Pietro in Vaticano and Piazza
  Stimmate di S. Francesco
  SS. Trinità in Palazzo
    Monte di Pietà
Campana, Paolo (18th century)
  S. Giovanni in Laterano
  S. Maria Maddalena
Campanelli, Angelo (1748–1811)
  Gesù e Maria
Campi, Pietro Paolo (1688–1764)
  S. Agnese in Agone
  SS. Nome di Maria
  S. Pietro in Vaticano and Piazza
  S. Salvatore in Lauro
Camporese, Giuseppe (d. 1822)
  S. Maria di Monserrato
Camporese, Pietro the Elder
  (1726–81)
  S. Brigida
  S. Maria in Aquiro
  S. Nicola da Tolentino
Camporese, Pietro the Younger
  (1792–1873)
  S. Apollinare
  S. Maria di Monserrato
  S. Maria di Monterone
  S. Maria Porta Paradisi
  S. Maria in Trastevere
  SS. Vito e Modesto
Camuccini, Pietro (1761–1833)
  S. Maria della Vittoria
Camuccini, Vincenzo (1771–1844)
  S. Paolo fuori le Mura
  S. Pietro in Vaticano
Canarte, Filippo (18th century)
  S. Maria Maddalena
Canevari, Antonio Giacomo
  (1681–1764)
  S. Eustachio
  SS. Giovanni e Paolo
  Stimmate di S. Francesco
Caniggia, Carlo (1802–52)
  S. Stanislao dei Polacchi
Canini, Giovanni Angelo
  (c. 1609/17–66)
  S. Francesca Romana
  S. Giovanni dei Fiorentini
  S. Marco
  S. Maria in Aracoeli
  S. Maria Maggiore
  S. Martino ai Monti
Canini, Marc Antonio (1622–?)
  SS. Domenico e Sisto
Canonica, Pietro (1869–1959)
  S. Pietro in Vaticano
  Spirito Santo dei Napoletani
Canova, Antonio (1757–1822)
  S. Antonio dei Portoghesi
  SS. Apostoli
  Il Gesù
  S. Pietro in Vaticano
Canusi, Fabio (rec. 1703)
  S. Pietro in Vaticano, Piazza
Canuti, Domenico Maria
  (1626–84)
  SS. Domenico e Sisto
  S. Francesca Romana
Capalti, Alessandro (1807–68)
  Il Gesù
Caporale, Francesco (rec. 1606–20)
  S. Maria Maggiore
Capparoni, Giuseppe (c. 1800–79)
  S. Andrea delle Fratte
Capparoni, Silverio (1831–1907)
  S. Andrea della Valle
  S. Giacomo degli Incurabili
  S. Marcello
  S. Tommaso di Canterbury
  SS. Vincenzo e Anastasio
Cappelletti, Antonio (1772–1838)
  S. Apollinare
Capponi, Luigi (late 15th century)
  S. Clemente
  S. Gregorio al Celio
Capriano da Volterra, Francesco see
  Francesco da Volterra
Caprinozzi, Marco (1711–78)
  S. Lorenzo in Fonte
  Stimmate di S. Francesco
Capronnier, Jean-Baptste
  (1814–1891)
  S. Giuliano dei Fiamminghi
Carapecchia, Romano Fortunato
  (c. 1661–1738 [41])

INDEX OF ARTISTS

S. Giovanni Calabita
Caravaggio, Michelangelo Merisi,
   called (1571–1610)
  S. Agostino
  S. Anna dei Palafrenieri
  S. Luigi dei Francesi
  S. Maria della Concezione
  S. Maria del Popolo
  S. Maria della Scala
  S. Maria in Vallicella *
  S. Pietro in Vaticano *
Carcani, Filippo (1644–88)
  S. Giovanni dei Fiorentini
  S. Giovanni in Laterano
  Madonna delle Grazie
  S. Marco
  S. Maria in Campitelli
  S. Maria Maggiore
  S. Maria sopra Minerva
  S. Maria di Montesanto
  S. Maria delle Vergini
  S. Pietro in Vaticano and Piazza
Cardani, Tommaso (rec. 1684–1711)
  S. Maria dell'Orto
Cardelli, Giuseppe (1769–1822)
  S. Marco
Cardi, Ludovico see Cigoli
Carimini, Luca (1830–90)
  SS. Apostoli
  S. Chiara
  S. Giacomo degli Spagnuoli
  S. Giovanni Battista dei
    Genovesi
  S. Maria in Aquiro
  S. Maria di Loreto
  S. Nicola dei Prefetti
  S. Salvatore in Onda
Carlione, Giovanni Antonio
   (1639–97)
  Il Gesù
  S. Maria ad Martyres
Carlini, Alberigo Clemente (1703–75)
  S. Bartolomeo all'Isola
Carloni, Marco (1742–96)
  S. Maria degli Angeli
Carmini, Luca (1830–90)
  SS. Apostoli
  S. Giovanni Battista dei Genovesi
Carnevale (rec. 1722)
  SS. Cosma e Damiano de' Barbieri
Carnevale, Giuseppe (rec. 1869)
  S. Girolamo degli Schiavoni
Carnevali, Augusto (second half of
   the 19th century)
  S. Maria della Consolazione
  S. Maria della Vittoria
Caroselli, Angelo (1585–1652)
  S. Francesca Romana
  S. Maria in Vallicella
  S. Pietro in Vaticano *

Caroselli, Cesare (1847–1927)
  S. Maria in Traspontina
Carosi, Giovanni Antonio
   (c. 1600–d. after 67)
  S. Rocco
Carpeaux, Jean-Baptiste (1827–75)
  S. Luigi dei Francesi
Carpi, M. (19th century)
  S. Maria in Aquiro
Carracci, Annibale (1560–1609)
  S. Caterina dei Funari
  S. Gregorio al Celio
  S. Maria di Monserrato
  S. Maria del Popolo
  S. Nicola in Carcere *
  S. Onofrio
Carracci, Antonio (1589–1618)
  S. Bartolomeo all'Isola
  S. Maria in Monticelli
  S. Sebastiano fuori le Mura
Carta, Natale (1800–88)
  S. Andrea delle Fratte
  S. Maria d'Itria
  S. Paolo fuori le Mura
Cartari, Giulio (rec. 1655–91)
  Gesù e Maria
  S. Giuliano dei Fiamminghi
  S. Isidoro
  S. Lorenzo in Lucina
  S. Pietro in Vaticano
Casa, A. (19th century)
  S. Agostino
Casali, Andrea (1705–84)
  S. Gregorio a Ponte Quattro Capi
  S. Lorenzo in Damaso
  S. Sisto Vecchio
  SS. Trinità degli Spagnuoli
Casali, Salvatore (c. 1715–95)
  S. Agata dei Goti
Casella, Annibale (rec. 1702–03)
  S. Pietro in Vaticano, Piazza
Casella, Giovanni Battista (d. 1695)
  S. Anastasia
  S. Maria dei Miracoli
  S. Maria di Montesanto
Casolani, Cristofano (1582–1629)
  S. Agostino
  S. Maria dei Monti
  S. Maria in Via, Largo Chigi
  S. Silvestro in Capite
  S. Stefano del Cacco
Casolano, Giovanni (rec. 1588–98)
  S. Maria dei Monti
  S. Spirito in Sassia
Casone, Antonio Felice (1559–1634)
  S. Isidoro
  S. Lucia in Selci
  S. Marcello
  S. Maria della Concezione
Casoni, Baldassare (rec. 1734–35)

S. Giovanni in Laterano
Caslano, Giovanni (rec. 1607–18)
  S. Pietro in Vaticano
Cassani, Alessandro (rec. 1677–79)
  S. Maria di Montesanto
Cassignola, Giovanni Battista
   (second half of the
   16th century)
  S. Agostino
  S. Maria sopra Minerva
Castellacci, Luigi (19th century)
  S. Maria della Vittoria
Castellamonte, Carlo di (1560–1641)
  SS. Sudario dei Piemontesi
Castelli, Pietro (rec. 1611)
  S. Maria in Vallicella
Castelli, Stefano (rec. 1631–76)
  S. Martino ai Monti
Castello, Bernardo (1557?–1629)
  S. Maria sopra Minerva
Castello, Bernardo (1643–1709)
  S. Carlo alle Quattro Fontane
Castello, Domenico (c. 1582–1657)
  S. Agata dei Goti
  S. Anastasia
  SS. Cosma e Damiano
  S. Francesco di Paola
  S. Giacomo alla Lungara
  S. Girolamo della Carità
  Oratorio del Gonfalone
  S. Isidoro
  S. Lorenzo in Fonte
Castello, Matteo (c. 1560–1632)
  S. Andrea della Valle
  S. Giovanni dei Fiorentini
  S. Susanna
Castello, Simone (rec. 1613–14)
  S. Giovanni dei Fiorentini
Castro, Filippo de (1711–75)
  S. Apollinare
Caterinazzo da Subiaco (rec. 1652)
  S. Maria in Via Lata
Cati, Pasquale (1537–1612)
  S. Lorenzo in Panisperna
  S. Maria in Trastevere
Cavaceppi, Bartolomeo (1716–99)
  S. Pietro in Vaticano
Cavaceppi, Paolo (1723–after 1804)
  SS. Apostoli
Cavagna, Giovanni (c. 1548–1613)
  S. Agostino
Cavalier d'Arpino see
   Giuseppe Cesari
Cavalleri, Fernando (1794–1865)
  S. Maria di Montesanto
Cavallini, Francesco (1645–90)
  SS. Carlo e Ambrogio al Corso
  Gesù e Maria
  S. Marcello
  S. Maria in Aracoeli

S. Maria del Popolo
S. Maria dell'Umiltà
Cavallini, Pietro
    (c. 1240/50–1330/40)
  S. Cecilia
  S. Maria in Trastevere
Cavallucci, Antonio (1752–95)
  S. Martino ai Monti
Cavarozzi, Bartolomeo (1588 ?–1625)
  S. Marco
Ceccarelli, Giovanni Battista
    (rec. 1768–88)
  S. Cecilia
  S. Giovanni in Laterano and
    Baptistery
Caccarini, Camillo (rec. 1856)
  S. Andrea della Valle
Ceccarini, Giovanni (c. 1790–1861)
  S. Giovanni dei Fiorentini
Ceccarini, Sebastiano (1703–83)
  SS. Annunziata a Tor de' Specchi
  S. Maria Maggiore
  S. Maria del Suffragio
  SS. Sergio e Bacco
Cecchino di Pietrasanta see
    Francesco di Pietrasanta
Cecco del Caravaggio
    (active in Rome 1610–c. 20)
  S. Maria in Vallicella
Cecconali bothers (rec. 1668)
  S. Stefano del Cacco
Ceci, Giacomo and Pietro
    (rec. 1733–34)
  S. Giovanni in Laterano
Celio, Gaspare (1571–1640)
  S. Carlo ai Catinari
  S. Francesco a Ripa
  Il Gesù
  S. Maria del Carmine alle
    Tre Cannelle
  S. Maria sopra Minerva
Cellini, Francesco (19th century)
  S. Giovanni Battista
    dei Genovesi
Cennini, Bartolomeo (d. 1674)
  S. Pietro in Vaticano and Piazza
Censore, Orazio (d. 1622)
  S. Maria Maggiore
  S. Pietro in Vaticano and Piazza
  SS. Trinità dei Pellegrini
Ceribelli, Francesco (18th century)
  SS. Bartolomeo e Alessandro
    dei Bergamaschi
Ceroti, Francesco (18th century)
  S. Maria in Trastevere
Cerrini, Gian Domenico called il
    Cavalier Perugino (1609–81)
  S. Carlo ai Catinari
  S. Carlo alle Quattro Fontane
  S. Francesca Romana

S. Isidoro
S. Maria in Traspontina
S. Maria in Vallicella
S. Maria della Vittoria
SS. Sudario dei Piemontesi
Cerruti, Francesco (rec. 1747)
  S. Ignazio
Cerruti, Michelangelo (1663–1748)
  S. Anastasia
  S. Antonio dei Portoghesi
  S. Girolamo degli Schiavoni
  S. Macuto
  S. Maria Maddalena
  S. Maria sopra Minerva
  S. Maria del Rosario sul
    Monte Mario
  S. Maria dell'Umiltà
  S. Maria in Via Lata
  Natività di Gesù
  S. Pietro in Montorio
  SS. Trinità dei Pellegrini
Cerulli, Giovanni (19th century)
  S. Maria del Popolo
Cesari, Bernadino (1571–1622)
  S. Angelo in Pescheria
  S. Giovanni in Laterano
Cesari, Giuseppe (Cavalier d'Arpino)
    (1568–1640)
  S. Atanasio dei Greci
  S. Carlo ai Catinari
  S. Cesareo
  SS. Cosma e Damiano *
  S. Crisogono
  S. Giovanni in Laterano
  S. Lorenzo in Damaso
  S. Lucia in Selci
  S. Luigi dei Francesi
  S. Maria di Loreto
  S. Maria Maggiore
  S. Maria sopra Minerva
  S. Maria della Scala
  S. Maria in Traspontina
  S. Maria in Vallicella
  S. Maria in Via, Largo Chigi
  S. Onofrio
  S. Pietro in Vaticano and Piazza
  S. Prassede
  S. Silvestro al Quirinale
  SS. Trinità dei Pellegrini
Cesi, Carlo (1626–86)
  S. Maria Maggiore
  S. Maria della Pace
  SS. Re Magi
  SS. Sudario dei Piemontesi
Céspedes, Paolo (1538–1608)
  SS. Trinità dei Monti
Cesura, Pompeo (d. 1571)
  S. Spirito in Sassia
Challe, Simon (1719–65)
  S. Luigi dei Francesi

Chelli, Carlo (1807–77)
  S. Maria in Aquiro
Chènevière, Jean de (1490–1527)
  S. Luigi dei Francesi
Chialli, Giuseppe (1800–39)
  S. Giovanni in Laterano
Chiari, Fabrizio (c. 1615–95)
  S. Anastasia al Palatino
  SS. Carlo e Ambrogio al Corso
  S. Marco
  S. Martino ai Monti
Chiari, Giuseppe Bartolomeo
    (1654–1727)
  S. Andrea al Quirinale
  SS. Apostoli
  S. Clemente
  S. Francesco di Paola
  S. Francesco a Ripa
  S. Giovanni in Laterano
  S. Ignazio
  S. Maria in Cosmedin
  S. Maria delle Grazie alle Fornaci
  S. Maria di Montesanto
  S. Maria del Suffragio
  S. Pietro in Vaticano
  S. Silvestro in Capite
Chiari, Tommaso (1668–1733)
  S. Clemente
  S. Francesco a Ripa
Ciampelli, Agostino (1565–1630)
  S. Bibiana
  Il Gesù
  S. Giovanni dei Fiorentini
  S. Giovanni in Laterano and
    Baptistery
  S. Maria del Pianto
  S. Maria in Trastevere
  S. Pietro in Vaticano
  S. Prassede
  S. Vitale
Cianchi, Giulio
  S. Lucia in Selci
Ciarpi, Baccio (1574–1654)
  S. Ambrogio della Massima
  Il Gesù
  S. Giovanni in Laterano
  S. Lucia in Selci
  S. Maria in Campo Marzio
  S. Maria della Concezione
  S. Maria in Monticelli
  S. Maria in Vallicella
  S. Silvestro in Capite
Cibocchi, Biagio (rec. 1688–1712)
  S. Maria del Pianto
Cienfuegos, Cardinal Alvaro de
  S. Bartolomro all' Isola
Cignani, Carlo (1628–1719)
  S. Andrea della Valle
Cigoli, Ludovico Cardi, called Il
    (1559–1613)

INDEX OF ARTISTS

S. Giovanni dei Fiorentini
S. Maria Maggiore
S. Paolo fuori le Mura
Cimini, Giovanni Battista (d. c. 1690)
S. Maria del Suffragio
Ciocchi, Giovan Battista (1658–1725)
S. Marcello
Cioli, Antonio (rec. 1775)
SS. Vincenzo e Anastasio
Cioli, Alessandro (active 1576–82)
S. Maria degli Angeli
S. Maria Maggiore
Ciolo, Giovambattista (rec.1697–1703)
S. Pietro in Vaticano, Piazza
Ciolli, Giacomo (d.1734)
S. Maria del Carmine alle
 Tre Cannele
S. Paola alla Regola
Cipolla, Antonio (1820–74)
S. Giuseppe alla Lungara
S. Maria Maddalena
S. Rocco
Spirito Santo dei Napoletani
S. Tommaso in Parione
Cippitelli, Michele (active c. 1700)
S. Pudenziana
Cipriani, Sebastiano (c. 1662–1738)
SS. Apostoli
S. Croce in Gerusalemme
S. Maria in Campitelli
Circignani, Antonio, called il
 Pomarancio (c. 1571–1629)
S. Cecilia
S. Maria in Aquiro
S. Maria della Consolazione
S. Maria in Traspontina
S. Maria in Via, Largo Chigi
Circignani, Nicolò
 (1530/35–96 [after 97])
S. Antonio Abate
S. Croce in Gerusalemme
SS. Crocifisso, Oratorio del
 Il Gesù
S. Giovanni dei Fiorentini
SS. Giovanni e Paolo
S. Maria di Loreto
S. Pudenziana
S. Pietro in Montorio
S. Stefano Rotondo
S. Tommaso di Canterbury
Ceribelli, Franesco (19th century)
SS. Bartolomeo e Alessandro
 dei Bergamaschi
Clérisseau, Charles-Louis (1721–1820)
SS. Trinità dei Monti
Cobaert, Jacob Cornelisz
 (1530/35–1615)
S. Luigi dei Francesi
SS. Trinità dei Pellegrini
Coccetti, Liborio (1739–1816)

S. Maria della Concezione
Cochetti, Luigi (1802–84)
S. Paolo fuori le Mura
Codazzi, Viviano (1603/04–70)
S. Maria in Via Lata
Coghetti, Francesco (1801–75)
S. Carlo ai Catinari
SS. Giovanni e Paolo
S. Paolo fuori le Mura
Coli, Giovanni (1636–81)
SS. Croce e Bonaventura
 dei Lucchesi
S. Nicola da Tolentino
Colombo, Bartolomeo
 (active 1648–72)
S. Giuseppe dei Falegnami
Cometti, Antonio (17th century)
SS. Ildefonso e Tommaso
 di Villanova
Commodi, Andrea (1560–1638)
S. Carlo ai Catinari
Il Gesù
S. Vitale
Conca, Giovanni (c. 1690–1771)
S. Maria della Luce
S. Maria della Scala
S. Maria in Traspontina
Conca, Sebastiano (1680–1764)
S. Agostino
S. Bonaventura al Palatino *
S. Cecilia
S. Clemente
S. Giovanni in Laterano
S. Lorenzo in Damaso
SS. Luca e Martina
S. Maria in Aracoeli *
S. Maria in Campitelli
S. Maria della Luce
S. Maria Maddalena
S. Pantaleo
Conca, Tommaso Maria (1734–1822)
S. Caterina da Siena
S. Eustachio
S. Giovanni in Laterano,
 Scala Santa
SS. Giovanni e Paolo
Concioli, Antonio (c. 1736–1820)
S. Antonio dei Portoghesi
S. Paolo Primo Eremita
Concioli, Faustina (rec. 1806–07)
S. Maria di Loreto
Consalvi, Valentino (rec. 1724–30)
S. Maria in Via, Largo Chigi
SS. Trinità dei Pellegrini
Consoni, Nicola (1814–84)
S. Paolo fuori le Mura
Conti, Cesare (c. 1550–1622)
S. Maria in Traspontina
S. Spirito in Sassia
Conti, Francesco (19th century)

S. Maria della Vittoria
Conti, Vincenzo (d. 1626)
S. Agostino
S. Giovanni in Laterano,
 Scala Santa
S. Maria dei Monti
Contini, Francesco Gaetano
 (1599–1669)
SS. Carlo e Ambrogio al Corso
Contini, Giovanni Battista
 (1642–1723)
S. Agostino
SS. Alessio e Bonifazio
 all'Aventino
SS. Bartolomeo e Alessandro
 dei Bergamaschi
S. Eustachio
S. Ivo della Sapienza
Madonna delle Grazie
S. Maria in Aracoeli
S. Maria in Campitelli
S. Maria di Monserrato
S. Maria dei Sette Dolori
S. Maria del Suffragio
S. Maria della Visitazione
S. Maria della Vittoria
S. Sabina
Stimmate di S. Francesco
SS. Trinità dei Pellegrini
Coppi, Jacopo (Giacomo del Meglio)
 (1523–91)
S. Pietro in Vincoli
Coraducci, Domenico (18th century)
S. Gioacchino in Selci
Corbelli, Giovanni (c. 1656–1700)
S. Francesco a Ripa
Corbellini, Sebastiano
 (late 17th century)
S. Agnese in Agone
Cordier, Nicolas (1567–1612)
S. Andrea della Valle
S. Giovanni in Laterano
S. Gregorio al Celio, Oratorio
 di S. Sylvia and S. Barbara
S. Maria Maggiore
S. Maria sopra Minerva
S. Pietro in Vaticano and Piazza
S. Sebastiano fuori le Mura
Cornacchini, Agostino (1686–c.1754)
SS. Carlo e Ambrogio al Corso
S. Giovanni in Laterano
S. Pietro in Vaticano
SS. Trinità in Palazzo
 Monte di Pietà
Cornaro, G. (rec. 1734–35)
S. Giovanni dei Fiorentini
Corpi, Girolamo (rec. 1721–49)
S. Apollinare
S. Girolamo degli Schiavoni
S. Rocco

Correa, Juan
    SS. Ildefonso e Tommaso
        di Villanova
Corsi, Antonio (rec. 1790–1809)
    S. Girolamo della Carità
Corsini, Agostino (1688–1772)
    S. Carlo ai Catinari
    S. Cecilia
    S. Croce in Gerusalemme
    S. Francesco di Paola
    S. Giovanni in Laterano
    S. Lorenzo in Lucina
    S. Maria Maggiore
    S. Maria della Vittoria
Corsini, Giuliano (19th century)
    S. Antonio dei Portoghesi
Cortese (Courtois), Francesco (second
    half of the 17th century)
    S. Andrea delle Fratte
Cortese, Giacomo called Il
    Borgognone (1621–75)
    Il Gesù, Casa Professa
    S. Ignazio
Cortese, Guglielmo (Guillaume
    Courtois) (1628–79)
    S. Andrea delle Fratte
    S. Andrea al Quirinale
    S. Cosimato
    Il Gesù
    S. Giovanni in Laterano
    S. Ignazio
    S. Marco
    S. Paolo Primo Eremita
    S. Prassede
    SS. Trinità dei Pellegrini
Cortona, Pietro see Pietro da Cortona
Corvara, Cesare (d. 1703)
    S. Antonio dei Portoghesi
    S. Eustachio
Corvi, Domenico (1721–1803)
    S. Caterina da Siena
    S. Marcello
    S. Marco
    S. Salvatore in Lauro
    SS. Trinità dei Monti
Coscia, Giulio (rec. 1702–05)
    S. Pietro in Vaticano, Piazza
Cosimo Piazza da Castelfranco
    S. Maria in Aquiro
Costa, Domenico (rec. 1743–87)
    SS. Domenico e Sisto
Costa, Lorenzo (c. 1537–83)
    S. Nicola in Carcere
Costantini, Ermenegildo (1731–91)
    S. Caterina da Siena
    Gesù e Maria
    S. Luca del Gonfalone
    S. Nicola da Tolentino
    S. Stanislao dei Polacchi
Costantini, Francesco (rec. 1766)

S. Luca del Gonfalone
Costanzi, Placido (1702–59)
    S. Apollinare
    SS. Claudio e Andrea
        de' Borgognoni
    S. Giovanni in Laterano
    S. Gregorio al Celio
    Madonna del Divino Amore
    S. Maria degli Angeli
    S. Maria in Aquiro
    S. Maria in Campo Marzio
    S. Maria Maddalena
    S. Maria Maggiore
    S. Pietro in Vaticano *
    SS. Trinità dei Pellegrini
Costanzi, Simone (d. 1709)
    S. Carlo ai Catinari
    SS. Croce e Bonaventura
        dei Lucchesi
Courtois see Cortese
Cousin, Louis see Luigi Gentile
Coxie, Michiel (1499–1592)
    S. Maria dell' Anima
    SS. Trinità dei Monti
Cozza, Francesco (1605–82)
    S. Agnese in Agone
    S. Agostino
    S. Ambrogio della Massima
    S. Andrea delle Fratte
    S. Carlo ai Catinari
    S. Francesco di Paola
    Madonna delle Grazie
    S. Maria in Aquiro
    S. Maria ad Martyres
    S. Maria della Pace
    S. Rocco
Crecolini, Giovanni Antonio
    (1675–1725)
    S. Andrea delle Fratte
    S. Clemente
    SS. Cosma e Damiano de' Barbieri
    S. Francesco di Paola
    S. Lorenzo in Lucina
Cremoni, Melchiorre
    (rec. 1567–1601)
    S. Maria in Vallicella
Creo, Cristoforo (rec. 1710–28)
    S. Paolo alla Regola
Crescenzi, Giovan Battista
    (1577–1635)
    S. Andrea della Valle
Cresti, Domenico (Il Passignano)
    (1599–1638)
    S. Andrea della Valle
    S. Giacomo degli Incurabili
    S. Giovanni dei Fiorentini
    S. Maria Maggiore
    S. Maria della Pace
    S. Maria in Vallicella
    S. Pietro in Vaticano

S. Prisca
Cristelli, Pietro (doc. 1694–1703)
    S. Pietro in Vaticano, Piazza
Cristofari, Fabio (d. 1689)
    S. Pietro in Vaticano
Cristofari, Pietro Paolo (1685–1743)
    S. Agostino
    S. Giovanni in Laterano
    S. Pierto in Vaticano
Croce, Baldassare (1558–1628)
    S. Eusebio
    Il Gesù
    S. Giovanni in Laterano and
        Scala Santa
    S. Luigi dei Francesi
    S. Maria Maggiore
    S. Maria dei Monti
    S. Prassede
    S. Susanna
    SS. Trinità dei Pellegrini
Cronè, Carlo Nicolò (rec. 1739–41)
    SS. Nome di Maria
Crovara, Cesare see Cesare Corvara
Curradi, Francesco (1570–1661)
    S. Giovanni dei Fiorentini
Cusart, Francesco di (rec. 1633)
    S. Maria della Scala
Czechowich, Szyman (1689–1775)
    S. Stanislao dei Polacchi
Dalmata, Giovanni
    (c. 1440–d. after 1509)
    S. Clemente
Dalmazzoni, Francesco (rec. 1725–38)
    S. Gregorio al Celio
Dal Ponte, Francesco see
    Francesco Bassano
Daniele (Ricciarelli) da Volterra
    (1509–66)
    S. Giovanni in Laterano
    S. Marcello
    S. Pietro in Montorio
    SS. Trinità dei Monti
Dantan, Antoine-Laurent (1798–1878)
    S. Luigi dei Francesi
Daria, Simone (rec. 1600–20)
    S. Pietro in Vaticano
Dario de Mezzana, Domenico
    (rec. 1574–78)
    SS. Domenico e Sisto
d'Arras, Nicolò see Nicolas Pippe
David, Ludovico Antonio
    (1648–1709)
    S. Andrea al Quirinale
David, Luigi Antonio
    (c. 1680–c. 1738)
    S. Maria della Scala
David, Marco (rec. 1739–65)
    S. Lucia del Gonfalone
    SS. Trinità degli Spagnuoli
Delaborde, Jean (rec. 1669–83)

INDEX OF ARTISTS

S. Andrea al Quirinale
Delaplache, Eugène (1836–91)
S. Luigi dei Francesi
Del Colle, Giovanni Paolo (rec. 1551)
S. Marcello
Del Conte, Jacopino (1510–98)
S. Francesca Romana
S. Giovanni Decollato, Oratory
S. Luigi dei Francesi
S. Maria sopra Minerva
Del Duca, Giacomo (c. 1520–1604)
S. Giovanni in Laterano
S. Maria degli Angeli
S. Maria in Aracoeli
S. Maria di Loreto
S. Maria in Trivio
Del Duca, Ludovico (?–after 1601)
S. Giovanni in Laterano
S. Maria Maggiore
Del Grande, Antonio (1625–71)
S. Giuseppe dei Falegnami
S. Maria dei Sette Dolori
del Grandis, Alessandro
  (rec. 1697–d. c. 1724)
S. Paolo alla Regola
del Rosso, Zenobio (1724–98)
S. Marcello
Dell' Abate, Pompeo (rec. 1589)
S. Maria in Trastevere
Della Cornia, Antonio (rec. 1634)
S. Maria dell'Umiltà
Della Greca, Felice (c. 1626–77)
S. Angelo in Custode
SS. Domenico e Sisto
S. Giovonni dei Fiorentini
S. Rita da Cascia
Della Greca, Vincenzo (rec. 1615–d.
  after 1650, before 1663)
S. Agostino
S. Caio
SS. Domenico e Sisto
Della Porta, Giacomo (1532–1602)
S. Agostino
S. Andrea della Valle
S. Atanasio dei Greci
S. Caterina dei Funari
S. Cesareo
Oratorio del SS. Crocifisso
SS. Domenico e Sisto
Il Gesù
S. Giovanni dei Fiorentini
S. Giovanni in Laterano
S. Ivo della Sapienza
S. Luigi dei Francesi
S. Maria in Aracoeli
S. Maria della Consolazione
S. Maria Maggiore
S. Maria sopra Minerva and
S. Maria dei Miracoli and
  S. Maria di Montesanto

S. Maria dei Monti
S. Maria dell'Orto
S. Maria Scala Coeli
S. Maria in Vallicella
S. Maria in Via, Largo Chigi
S. Nicola in Carcere
S. Nicola dei Lorenesi
S. Paolo alle Tre Fontane
S. Pietro in Vaticano
SS. Trinità dei Monti
Della Porta, Giovanni Battista
  (c. 1542–97)
S. Maria degli Angeli
S. Maria Maggiore
S. Maria dei Monti
S. Onofrio
S. Pudenziana
Della Porta, Giovanni Paolo
  (c. 1542–97)
S. Onofrio
Della Porta, Guglielmo (c. 1515–1577)
S. Caterina della Rota
S. Maria in Aracoeli
S. Pietro in Vaticano
Della Porta, Tommaso (c. 1545–1606)
SS. Carlo e Ambrogio al Corso
S. Giovanni in Laterano
S. Maria in Aracoeli
S. Maria sopra Minerva
S. Onofrio
Della Porta, Teodoro (1567–1638)
S. Giovanni in Laterano
Della Valle, Filippo (ottonare)
  (rec. 1746)
S. Apollinare
Della Valle, Filippo (1698–1768)
S. Antonio dei Portoghesi
SS. Apostoli
Il Gesù
S. Giovanni dei Fiorentini
S. Giovanni in Laterano
S. Ignazio
SS. Luca e Martina
S. Luigi dei Francesi
S. Maria Maggiore
S. Maria della Scala
S. Maria in Trastevere
SS. Nome di Maria
S. Pietro in Vaticano
S. Tommaso di Canterbury
Della Valle, Pietro (rec. 1775)
S. Giovanni Decollato
Dérizet, Antoine (1686–1768)
SS. Claudio e Andrea
  de' Borgognoni
S. Luigi dei Francesi
SS. Nome di Maria
de' Rossi see Rossi
Desprez, Luigi (1799–1870)
S. Lorenzo in Lucina

d'Este, Antonio (1754–1837)
S. Apollinare
S. Giovanni in Laterano
S. Marco
Diego da Careri, Fra' (rec. 1578–88)
S. Francsco a Ripa
Dies, Cesare (1830–after 1907)
S. Paolo fuori le Mura
Dieussart, Francois (d.1661)
S. Giovanni dei Fiorentini
S. Giuliano dei Fiamminghi
Dini, Lorenzo (rec. 1666)
S. Carlo alle Quattro Fontane
Diol, Giacomo (c. 1690–1759)
S. Paola alla Regola
Dobbelaer, Enrico (rec. 1853)
SS. Gioacchino e Anna
Dolci, Giovannino de' (d. before 1486)
S. Pietro in Vaticano,
  Cappella Sistina
Domenichino (Domenico Zampieri)
  (1581–1641)
S. Andrea della Valle
S. Carlo ai Catinari
S. Francesca Romana *
Il Gesù *
SS. Giovanni e Petronio dei
  Bolognesi *
S. Girolamo della Carità
S. Gregorio al Celio,
  Oratorio di S. Andrea
S. Ignazio
S. Lorenzo in Miranda
S. Luigi dei Francesi
S. Maria degli Angeli
S. Maria della Concezione
S. Maria in Trastevere
S. Maria in Vallicella
S. Onofrio
S. Pietro in Vaticano
S. Pietro in Vincoli
S. Silvestro al Quirinale
Domenico de Ario (rec. 1543)
S. Lorenzo in Fonte
Domenico da Modena (16th century)
Oratorio del Gonfalone
S. Maria degli Angeli
Dominicis, Andrea, de' (rec. 1790–93)
S. Martino ai Monti
Dominicis, Carlo de' (1696–1758)
S. Agatha dei Goti
S. Bartolomeo e Alessandro
  dei Bergamaschi
SS. Celso e Giuliano
S. Francesco a Ripa
S. Salvatore delle Coppelle
Dona, Giovanni Cesare (rec. 1662–76)
S. Carlo alle Quattro Fontane
Donato da Formello (c. 1530–d. not
  earlier than 1574)

S. Rocco
Donini, Tommaso see
   Tommaso Luini
Dori, Alessandro (1702–72)
   S. Maria dell'Umiltà
Dosio, Giovanni Antonio
   (1533–after 1609)
   S. Gregorio al Celio
   S. Lorenzo in Damaso
   S. Maria in Aracoeli
   S. Maria di Monserrato
   S. Maria in Vallicella
   S. Pietro in Montorio
   SS. Trinità dei Monti
Drouin, Siméon (b. 1659)
   S. Pietro in Vaticano
Duca, Giovanni Pietro del
   (17th century)
   Il Gesù
Dughet, Gaspard (1615–75)
   S. Martino ai Monti
du Jardin, François (active 1625–61)
   S. Nicola dei Lorenesi
Duquesnoy, François (1597–1643)
   S. Ambrogio della Massima
   S. Giovanni Decollato
   S. Girolamo della Carità
   S. Lorenzo fuori le Mura
   S. Maria dell' Anima
   S. Maria in Camposanto
   S. Maria di Loreto
   S. Onofrio
   S. Pietro in Vaticano
Dumont, Augustin Alexandre
   (1801–84)
   S. Luigi dei Francesi
Duran, Gioacchino (c. 1709–c. 75)
   S. Pasquale Baylon
Durante, Annibale (rec. 1601–21)
   S. Sebastiano fuori le Mura
Dussart, François see
   François Dieussart
Egidio della Riviera see
   Gillis van den Vliete
Elia, Alessio d' (rec. 1754–71)
   S. Andrea della Valle
   S. Caterina dei Funari
Elsken, Giuseppe Wander
   (mid 18th century)
   S. Caterina da Siena
Emanuele da Como Fra' (1625–1701)
   S. Francesco a Ripa
Enrico di San Martino, Carlo
   (rec. 1704)
   S. Pietro in Vaticano
Espinosa, Miguel (18th century)
   SS. Trinità degli Spagnuoli
Etex, Antoine (1808–88)
   S. Andrea delle Fratte
Evangelisti, Filippo Antonio

(1684–1761)
   Bambino Gesù
   SS. Marcello e Pietro
Fabi Atini, Francesco (1830–1906)
   S. Gregorio al Celio
   S. Maria in Campitelli
Fabris, Giuseppe de' (1790–1860)
   S. Andrea della Valle
   SS. Carlo e Ambrogio al Corso
   S. Carlo ai Catinari
   S. Giovanni dei Fiorentini
   SS. Giovanni e Paolo
   S. Gregorio al Celio
   S. Lucia del Gonfalone
   S. Marco
   S. Maria Maggiore
   S. Onofrio
   S. Pietro in Vaticano
   S. Rocco
Fabrizi, Gaetano (rec. 1716–49)
   S. Eligio dei Ferrari
Falconi, Andrea (rec. 1659)
   S. Agnese in Agone
Fancelli, Chiarissimo (d. 1632)
   S. Pietro in Vaticano
Fancelli, Cosimo (1618–88)
   SS. Carlo e Ambrogio al Corso
   Il Gesù
   S. Giovanni in Laterano,
      Baptistery
   S. Girolamo della Carità
   SS. Luca e Martina
   S. Marco
   S. Maria Maggiore
   S. Maria sopra Minerva
   S. Maria dei Miracoli
   S. Maria della Pace
   S. Maria Porta Paradisi
   S. Maria in Vallicella
   S. Maria in Via Lata
   S. Nicola da Tolentino
   S. Pietro in Vaticano
   SS. Re Magi
Fancelli, Francesco (1624–81)
   S. Maria Maggiore
Fancelli, Giacomo Antonio
   (1606–74)
   S. Andrea della Valle
   S. Bernardo alle Terme
   SS. Carlo e Ambrogio al Corso
   Il Gesù
   S. Maria dell' Anima
   S. Maria sopra Minerva
   S. Pietro in Vaticano, Piazza
Fangerilli, Francesco (rec. 1611–13)
   S. Giuseppe dei Falegnami
Fantasia, Antonio (rec. 1701–02)
   S. Pietro in Vaticano, Piazza
Fanzago, Cosimo (1591–1678)
   S. Agostino

SS. Annunziata a Tor de' Specchi
S. Girolamo della Carità
S. Giuseppe dei Falegnami
S. Isidoro
S. Lorenzo in Lucina
S. Maria in Traspontina
S. Maria in Via Lata
Spirito Santo dei Napoletani
SS. Trinità dei Pellegrini
Farrera, Giovanni Maria (rec. 1647)
S. Spirito in Sassia
Fedele di San Biagio (1717–1801)
   S. Ambrogio della Massima
Fedeli, Tommaso (rec. 1619–31)
   S. Andrea della Valle
Felici, Vincenzo (c. 1657–after 1715)
   S. Maria ad Martyres
   S. Maria in Traspontina
   S. Maria in Trastevere
   S. Maria dell'Umiltà
   S. Pietro in Vaticano, Piazza
   S. Silvestro in Capite
   Spirito Santo dei Napoletani
Feliciano (rec. 1585–86)
   Il Gesú
Fenzone, Ferraù (1562–1645)
   Il Gesù
   S. Giovanni in Laterano and
      Scala Santa
   S. Maria Maggiore
   S. Maria in Trastevere
Fernandi, Francesco, called
   Imperiali (1679–1740)
   S. Eustachio
   S. Gregorio al Celio
Ferrabosco, Giovanni Battista
   (rec. 1645–56)
   S. Nicola da Tolentino
   S. Stefano del Cacco
Ferrabosco, Martino (d. 1623)
   S. Pietro in Vaticano, Piazza
Ferrari, Cintio (rec. 1762)
   S. Antonio dei Portoghesi
   S. Marcello
Ferrari, Filippo (rec. 1725)
   S. Gregorio al Celio
   SS. Trinità in Palazzo
      Monte di Pietà
Ferrari, Francesco Martino
   (active 1703–50)
   S. Agata dei Goti
   S. Antonio dei Portoghesi
   SS. Apostoli
   S. Eligio dei Ferrari
   S. Francesca Romana
   SS. Giovanni e Paolo
   S. Gregorio al Celio
   SS. Ildefonso e Tommaso
      di Villanova
   S. Marcello

INDEX OF ARTISTS

S. Maria in Trastevere
S. Nicola dei Prefetti
S. Prassede
S. Sergio e Bacco
S. Stanislao dei Polacchi
Ferrari, Giacinto (18th century)
SS. Vincenzo e Anastasio
Ferraris, Francesco (rec. 1795)
Gesú e Maria
Ferrata, Ercole (1610–86)
S. Agnese in Agone
S. Agostino
S. Anastasia
S. Andrea della Valle
S. Francesca Romana
S. Francesco a Ripa
Gesù e Maria
S. Giovanni dei Fiorentini
S. Girolamo della Carità
S. Maria dell' Anima
S. Maria in Campitelli
S. Maria Maggiore
S. Maria sopra Minerva
S. Maria dei Miracoli
S. Maria della Pace
S. Maria del Popolo
S. Maria del Suffragio
S. Maria in Vallicella and Oratory
S. Nicola da Tolentino
S. Pietro in Vaticano
Ferrer, Giovanni Antonio (rec. 1625–26)
S. Maria di Monserrato
Ferreri, Antonio (rec. c. 1632)
S. Maria della Consolazione
Ferreri, Girolamo (rec. 1657–61)
S. Giovanni in Laterano
Ferrerio, Domenico (c. 1585/90–1630)
SS. Alessio e Bonifazio all'Aventino
S. Maria Maggiore.
Ferretti, Giovanni Battista (d. 1713)
SS. Trinità dei Pellegrini
Ferretti, Giuseppe (re. 1702–20)
S. Pietro in Vaticano, Piazza
Ferretti, Sigismund (rec. 1842)
S. Anna dei Palafrenieri
Ferri, Ciro (1633–89)
S. Agnese in Agone
SS. Carlo e Ambrogio al Corso
S. Giovanni dei Fiorentini
S. Giovanni in Laterano, Baptistery
SS. Luca e Martina
S. Marco
S. Maria dell'Orazione e della Morte
S. Maria in Vallicella
S. Nicola da Tolentino

S. Pietro in Vaticano
S. Prassede
S. Sebastiano fuori le Mura
Ferroni, Giuseppe Maria (1714–71)
SS. Vincenzo e Anastasio
Ferrucci, Pompeo (1565–1637)
SS. Luca e Martina
S. Maria di Loreto
S. Maria sopra Minerva
S. Maria della Vittoria
SS. Trinità dei Pellegrini
Ferruzzi, Francesco Claudio (1680–1745)
S. Andrea delle Fratte
S. Francesco a Ripa
S. Maria Maddalena
S. Maria in Trastevere
Ferucci, Luigi (19th century)
S. Salvatore in Lauro
Festa, Felice (1763/64–1825)
S. Andrea al Quirinale
S. Marco
SS. Sudario dei Piemontesi
Fiammeri, Giovanni Battista (1534/50–1617)
Il Gesù
S. Maria in Aquiro
S. Vitale
Fiammingo, Pietro (rec. 1588–89)
Il Gesù
Filarete, Antonio di Pietro Averlino (c. 1400–c. 69)
S. Pietro in Vaticano
Filippo dal Borgo (rec. 1569)
SS. Bartolomeo e Alessandro dei Bergamaschi
Finazzi, Giacomo (rec. 1651)
S. Maria in Traspontina
Finelli, Giuliano (1601–53)
S. Agostino
S. Bibiana
S. Caterina da Siena a Magnanapoli
SS. Cosma e Damiano
S. Eustachio
S. Giovanni in Laterano
S. Isidoro
SS. Luca e Martina
S. Maria dell' Anima
S. Maria di Loreto
S. Maria Maggiore
S. Maria sopra Minerva
S. Maria di Monserrato
S. Maria in Via Lata
S. Silvestro al Quirinale
Fiorani, Andrea (19th century)
S. Cosimato
Fiorentini, Domenico Antonio (1747–1820)
S. Bartolomeo all'Isola

Fiori, Giovanni Francesco (1709–84)
S. Gioacchino in Selci
S. Giuseppe alla Lungara
Fioriti, Bernardo (c. 1623–78)
S. Agostino
S. Filippo Neri
SS. Luca e Martina
S. Maria degli Angeli
Florestano di Fausto
S. Pietro in Vaticano
Florij, Lorenzo (rec. 1640–41)
S. S. Giacomo alla Lungara
S. Lorenzo in Damaso
Fontana, Antonio (second half of the 17th century)
S. Maria in Vallicella
Fontana, Carlo (1638–1714)
S. Andrea della Valle
SS. Apostoli
S. Carlo ai Catinari
S. Clemente
S. Egidio
SS. Faustino e Giovita
S. Francesco a Ripa
Il Gesù
S. Giovanni in Laterano
SS. Luca e Martina
SS. Marcellino e Pietro
S. Marcello
S. Margherita in Trastevere
S. Maria Maddalena
S. Maria dei Miracoli and S. Maria di Montesanto
S. Maria del Popolo
S. Maria in Traspontina
S. Maria in Trastevere
S. Maria dell'Umiltà
S. Marta
S. Pietro in Vaticano and Piazza
S. Rita da Cascia
S. Sebastiano fuori le Mura
Spirito Santo dei Napoletani
S. Teodoro al Palatino
Fontana, Carlo Stefano (c. 1675–1740)
S. Clemente
S. Eusebio
S. Giuseppe a Capo le Case
Fontana, Domenico (1543–1607)
S. Antonio Abate
S. Giovanni in Laterano and Scala Santa
S. Luigi dei Francesi
S. Maria Maggiore
S. Maria dei Miracoli and S. Maria Montesanto
S. Maria in Vallicella
S. Pietro in Vaticano, Piazza
S. Sabina
S. Silvestro al Quirinale
S. Susanna

SS. Trinità dei Monti
Fontana, Francesco (1668–1708)
  S. Andrea della Valle
  SS. Apostoli
  S. Maria della Neve
  S. Pietro in Vincoli
  S. Salvatore in Lauro
Fontana, Francesco (1819–83)
  S. Crisogono
Fontana, Francesco Antonio
  (1641–1700)
  S. Carlo alle Quattro Fontane
  S. Maria di Montesanto
  S. Pietro in Vaticano, Piazza
Fontana, Giovanni (1540–1614)
  S. Angelo in Pescheria
  S. Girolamo degli Schiavoni
Fontana, Giuseppe (rec. 1614)
  S. Pietro in Vaticano
Fontana, Lavinia (1552–1614)
  S. Maria della Pace
  S. Sabina
Fontana, Luigi (1827–1908)
  S. Andrea delle Fratte
  S. Andrea in Pescheria
  SS. Apostoli
  S. Lorenzo in Damaso
  S. Maria in Aquiro
  S. Salvatore in Lauro
  S. Silvestro al Quirinale
Fontana, Mauro (1701–67)
  S. Carlo ai Catinari
  S. Lorenzo in Panisperna
  SS. Nome di Maria
Fontana, Marcantonio
  (early 17th century)
  S. Crisogono
  S. Maria in Via, Largo Chigi
Fontana, Salvatore (d. 1590)
  S. Maria Maggiore
Fontebuoni, Anastasio (1571–1626)
  S. Balbina
  S. Giovanni dei Fiorentini
  S. Gregorio al Celio
  S. Lucia in Selci
  S. Prisca
Forlivesi, Teodoro (19th century)
  S. Clemente
Forno, Marcantonio del (rec. 1573–95)
  Oratorio del Gonfalone
Forti, Nicola (1714–1802)
  S. Ivo della Sapienza
Fortini, Alberto (rec. 1762)
  S. Marcello
Fortuna, Alessandro (c. 1596–1623)
  S. Lorenzo in Miranda
Franceschini, Marc' Antonio
  (1648–1729)
  S. Pietro in Vaticano
Francesco da Castello (1540/41–1621)

S. Maria di Monserrato
S. Rocco
Francesco da Volterra (c. 1535–94)
  S. Andrea della Valle
  S. Chiara
  S. Giacomo degli Incurabili
  S. Giovanni in Laterano,
    Baptistery
  S. Gregorio al Celio
  S. Lorenzo in Panisperna
  S. Macuto
  S. Maria in Aquiro
  S. Maria della Consolazione
  S. Maria di Monserrato
  S. Maria dell'Orto
  S. Maria della Scala
  S. Pudenziana
  S. Silvestro in Capite
  S. Susanna
  S. Tommaso in Parione
Francesco da Pietrasanta
  (rec. 1577–1611)
  S. Maria Maggiore
Francesco di Città di Castello see
  Francesco da Castello
Francesi, Alessandra (rec. 1710)
  S. Andrea della Valle
Francia, Alessandro (rec. 1833)
  S. Tommaso in Parione
François de Bar, Nicolas see
  Nicolas Lorrain
Francisi, Raffaele (1821–1901)
  S. Agostino
  S. Maria in Aquiro
Franco, Giovanni Battista (1565–1628)
  S. Giovanni Decollato, Oratory
  S. Maria sopra Minerva
Franco, Giuseppe (c. 1550–1627/28)
  S. Maria in Via, Largo Chigi
François, Stefano (recorded 1716)
  S. Andrea al Quirinale
Franucci, Francuccio (active 1602–56)
  Il Gesù
Franzoni, Francesco Antonio
  (1734–1818)
  S. Caterina da Siena
  S. Maria del Popolo
Frascari, Giuseppe Maria
  (rec. 1716–46)
  S. Francesco a Ripa
  S. Giovanni in Laterano
  S. Pietro in Vaticano, Piazza
Frémin, René (1672–1744)
  Il Gesù
Frigiotti, Filippo (rec. 1715–32)
  S. Sebastiano fuori le Mura
Frugoni, Valerio (rec. 1702–03)
  S. Pietro in Vaticano, Piazza
Fuccari, Stefano (17th century)

S. Maria in Trastevere
S. Pietro in Vaticano
S. Pudenziana
Fucigna, Andrea (c. 1661–1711)
  SS. Alessio e Bonifacio
    all'Aventino
  S. Antonio dei Portoghesi
  S. Brigida
  S. Marcello
  S. Maria in Campitelli
  S. Maria in Publicolis
  S. Pietro in Vaticano, Piazza
Fuga, Ferdinando (1699–1782)
  SS. Alessio e Bonifacio
    all'Aventino
  S. Apollinare
  Bambino Gesù
  S. Cecilia
  S. Francesco di Paola
  S. Giovanni dei Fiorentini
  S. Giovanni in Laterano and
    Triclinium
  S. Lorenzo in Lucina
  S. Maria Maggiore
  S. Maria dell'Orazione
    e della Morte
  S. Maria della Vittoria
  S. Pietro in Vaticano
  S. Spiritio in Sassia
Fuga, Giacomo (18th century)
  S. Andrea delle Fratte
Fusio, Francesco (rec. 1726)
  S. Maria delle Grazie alle Fornaci
Gabano, Antonio (rec. 1702–03)
  S. Pietro in Vaticano, Piazza
Gabet, Luigi (1823–79)
  SS. Apostoli
  SS. Nome di Maria
Gabrini, Cesare (19th century)
  S. Maria in Traspontina
Gabrini, Pietro (rec. 1856)
  S. Cesareo
Gagliardi, Agostino (rec. 1868)
  S. Maria Maddalena
Gagliardi, Bernardino (1609–60)
  S. Bernardino ai Monti
  Madonna delle Grazie
  S. Marcello
  S. Marco
  S. Maria Porta Paradisi
  S. Maria in Traspontina
  S. Sebastiano al Palatino
Gagliardi, Filippo (1606/08–59)
  S. Maria della Concezione
  S. Maria in Traspontina
  S. Martino ai Monti
Gagliardi, Giovanni (1838–1924)
  S. Agostino
  Il Gesù
  S. Maria di Monterone

INDEX OF ARTISTS

S. Nicola da Tolentino
Gagliardi, Leonardo (1729–98)
  SS. Carlo e Ambrogio al Corso
Gagliardi, Pietro (1809–90)
  S. Agostino
  S. Eustachio
  Il Gesù
  S. Girolamo degli Schiavoni
  S. Ignazio
  S. Lorenzo in Damaso
  S. Maria in Aquiro
  S. Paolo fuori le Mura
  S. Pudenziana
  SS. Quirico e Giulitta
  S. Salvatore in Lauro
  Spirito Santo dei Napoletani
Gai, Francesco (1835–1917)
  S. Prassede
Gaiassi, Vincenzo (1801–61)
  S. Giovanni in Laterano
  S. Isidoro
Galilei, Alessandro (1691–1737)
  SS. Celso e Giuliano
  S. Giovanni dei Fiorentini
  S. Giovanni in Laterano
Gallesini, Francesco (rec. 1702–03)
  S. Pietro in Vaticano, Piazza
Galletti, Stefano (1833–1905)
  S. Andrea della Valle
  Bambino Gesù
  S. Maria in Aquiro
Galli, Alberto (b. 1843)
  S. Maria Maggiore
Galli, Giacomo (recorded 1747–50)
  S. Apollinare
  S. Pietro in Vaticano
Galli, Giovanni Antonio called
    Lo Spadarino (1585 -1652)
  S. Caterina della Rota
  SS. Cosma e Damiano
  Il Gesù
  S. Omobono
  S. Pietro in Vaticano
Galli, Giovanni Maria (rec. 1700)
  SS. Trinità in Palazzo
    Monte di Pietà
Galli, Girolamo (17th century)
  S. Silvestro in Capite
Galli, Pietro (1804–77)
  S. Agostino
  S. Crisogono
  SS. Gioacchino e Anna
  S. Giovanni in Laterano
  S. Pietro in Vaticano
  Stimmate di S. Francesco
Galli, Pietro (rec. 1753)
  S. Giuseppe alla Lungara
Galvani, Alberto (rec. 1560–63)
  S. Macuto
Gamba, Paolo (1712–82)

Stimmate di S. Francesco
Gamberucci, Marco
  S. Giovanni dei Fiorentini
Ganassini, Marzio (1560–after 1621)
  S. Cecilia
  S. Maria in Aracoeli
  S. Maria della Consolazione
  S. Maria dei Monti
Garola, Pier Francesco (17th century)
  SS. Sudario dei Piemontesi
Garzi, Luigi (1638–1721)
  S. Barbara dei Librai
  S. Bonaventura al Palatino
  SS. Carlo e Ambrogio al Corso
  S. Caterina da Siena
    a Magnanapoli
  S. Croce in Gerusalemme
  S. Giovanni in Laterano
  S. Giovanni della Pigna
  S. Ignazio
  S. Marcello
  S. Maria degli Angeli
  S. Maria in Campo Marzio
  S. Maria di Montesanto
  S. Mara dell'Orto
  S. Maria del Popolo
  S. Maria in Traspontina
  S. Paolo alla Regola
  S. Silvestro in Capite
  Stimmate di S. Francesco
Garzi, Mario (d. before 1721)
  S. Maria dell'Orto
  Natività di Gesù
Gascard, Henry (1634/35–1701)
  S. Maria dei Miracoli
Gaulli, Giovanni Battista see
    Baciccio
Gauthier, Giovenale (rec. 1708)
  S. Maria in Publicolis
Gavardini, Carlo (1811–69)
  SS. Alessio e Bonifazio
    all'Aventino
  S. Maria in Aquiro
  S. Paolo fuori le Mura
Genga, Gerolamo (1476–1551)
  S. Caterina da Siena
Genaroli, Andrea (d. 1650)
  S. Giovanni Calabita
Gentile, Luigi (Louis Cousin)
    (1606–68)
  SS. Domenico e Sisto
  S. Marco
  S. Maria Maggiore
  S. Maria di Monserrato
Gentileschi, Orazio (1563–1639)
  S. Giovanni dei Fiorentini
  S. Giovanni in Laterano
  S. Maria Maggiore
  S. Maria dei Monti
  S. Maria della Pace

S. Silvestro in Capite
Gessi, Francesco (1588–1649)
  SS. Giovanni e Petronio
    dei Bolognesi
Gesuelli, Francesco (rec. 1756)
  S. Maria Maddalena
Gherardi, Antonio (1638–1702)
  S. Carlo ai Catinari
  S. Giovanni della Pigna
  S. Maria in Aracoeli
  S. Maria in Traspontina
  S. Maria in Trastevere
  S. Maria in Trivio
  S. Sudario dei Piemontesi
Gherardi, Filippo (1643–1704)
  S. Croce e Bonaventura
    dei Lucchesi
  S. Martino ai Monti
  S. Nicola da Tolentino
  S. Pantaleo
Gherardini, Giovanfrancesco
    (17th century)
  S. Giovanni dei Fiorentini
Ghetti, Santi (1589–1656)
  S. Agostino
  Il Gesù
Ghezzi, Giuseppe (1634–1721)
  S. Cecilia
  S. Cosimato
  S. Giuseppe dei Falegnami
  S. Margherita in Trastevere
  S. Maria in Aracoeli
  S. Maria Maddalena
  S. Maria del Suffragio
  S. Maria in Vallicella
  S. Maria in Via Lata
  S. Salvatore in Lauro
  S. Silvestro in Capite
Ghezzi, Pier Leone (1674–1755)
  S. Calisto
  S. Clemente
  S. Giovanni in Laterano
  S. Giuseppe dei Falegnami
  S. Marcello
  S. Maria dell'Orazione
    e della Morte
  S. Maria in Vallicella
  S. Maria in Via Lata
  S. Salvatore in Lauro
  S. Sebastiano fuori le Mura
  S. Teodoro al Palatino
Ghioldo, Battista (rec. 1567)
  S. Maria in Traspontina
Ghirlandaio, Domenico (1449–94)
  S. Pietro in Vaticano,
    Cappella Sistina
Ghisleni, Giovanni Battista
    (d. 1672)
  S. Maria del Popolo
Giacomo, Giovanni (rec. 1588)

S. Agostino
Giacomo del Meglio see
　　Jacopo Coppi
Giabazzi, Goivanni (rec. 1842)
　S. Giuliano dei Fiamminghi
Giani, Giovan Pietro (rec. 1628–29)
　S. Giuseppe dei Falegnami
Giansimoni, Nicola (c. 1725–1800)
　S. Maria dell'Orto
Giaquinto, Corrado (1703–66)
　SS. Apostoli
　S. Croce in Gerusalemme
　S. Giovanni Calabita
　S. Girolamo degli Schiavoni
　S. Lorenzo in Damaso
　S. Maria del Carmine
　　alle Tre Cannelle
　S. Maria dell'Orto
　S. Nicola dei Lorenesi
　SS. Trinità degli Spagnuoli
Giardé, Arrigo (rec. 1659)
　S. Maria del Popolo
Giardini, Francesco see
　　François du Jardin
Giardini, Giovanni (1646–1721)
　S. Pietro in Vaticano
Giardoni, Francesco (1692–1757)
　S. Giovanni in Laterano
　S. Maria Maggiore
　S. Pietro in Vaticano
Giardoni, Giuseppe (d. 1781)
　S. Caterina da Siena
　　a Magnanapoli
Giardoni, Niccola (18th century)
　S. Caterina da Siena
　　a Magnanapoli
Giarguzzi, P. (late 17th century)
　S. Carlo alle Quattro Fontane
Gillet, Nicolas (1709–22)
　S. Luigi dei Francesi
Gimac, Carlo (c. 1655–1703)
　S. Anastasia
Gimachi, Carlo see Carlo Gimac
Gimignani, Giacinto (1606–81)
　S. Agostino
　S. Carlo ai Catinari
　S. Crisogono
　S. Giovanni in Laterano,
　　Baptistery
　S. Isidoro
　S. Lorenzo in Lucina
　S. Maria dell' Anima
　S. Maria dei Monti
　SS. Re Magi
　S. Silvestro al Quirinale
Gimignani, Ludovico (1643–97)
　S. Andrea delle Fratte
　SS. Carlo e Ambrogio al Corso
　S. Lorenzo in Lucina
　S. Luigi dei Francesi

S. Maria in Campitelli
S. Maria Maggiore
S. Maria ad Martyres
S. Maria di Montesanto
S. Maria delle Vergini
S. Pudenziana
SS. Re Magi
S. Silvestro in Capite
Giordano, Luca (1634–1705)
　S. Maria in Campitelli
　S. Maria Maddalena
　Spirito Santo dei Napoletani
Giorgetti, Antonio (rec. 1657–69)
　S. Girolamo delle Carità
　S. Lorenzo fuori le Mura
　S. Maria dell' Anima
Giorgetti, Gioseppe (rec. 1658–79)
　S. Andrea della Valle
　S. Lorenzo in Damaso
　SS. Luca e Martina
　S. Rocco
　S. Sebastiano fuori le Mura
Giorgetti, Giovanni Maria
　　(mid 17th century)
　S. Spirito in Sassia
Giorgetti, Pietro Paolo
　　(17th century)
　S. Maria della Concezione
Giorgieri, Gaetano (rec. 1808–19)
　S. Andrea delle Fratte
Giorgini, Andrea (1768–1844)
　S. Spirito in Sassia
Giorgini, Giovanni Battista
　　(rec. 1700)
　S. Maria dell'Orto
Giorgini (Giorgi), Simone,
　　(rec. 1677–1706)
　S. Carlo ai Catinari
　S. Carlo alle Quattro Fontane
　S. Ignazio
　S. Isidoro
　S. Maria dell'Orto
　S. Maria della Scala
　SS. Trinità in Palazzo
　　Monte di Pietà
　S. Pietro in Vaticano, Piazza
Giorgio da Coldrerio (first half of
　　the 16th century)
　S. Maria Porta Paradisi
Giovanni da San Giovanni
　　(Mannozzi) (1592–1636)
　S. Andrea delle Fratte
　S. Crisogono
　S. Maria dei Monti
　S. Maria del Popolo
　SS. Quattro Coronati
Giovannini, Domenico (18th century)
　S. Agostino
Girolamo da Santacroce (1503–66)
　S. Maria in Vallicella

Gismondi, Paolo (1612–85)
　S. Agata dei Goti
　S. Agnese in Agone
Giulio (Pippi) Romano
　　(1492/99–1546)
　S. Maria dell' Anima
　S. Prassede
Giusani, Antonio
　　(early 17th century)
　S. Maria in Via, Largo Chigi
Giusti, Alessandro (rec. 1746)
　S. Apollinare
Gnaccarini, Filippo (1804–75)
　SS. Carlo e Ambrogio al Corso
　S. Giovanni in Laterano
　S. Lorenzo in Damaso
　S. Luigi dei Francesi
　S. Paolo fuori le Mura
Gnocchis, Carlo de
　SS. Bartolomeo e Alessandro
　　dei Bergamaschi
Godioli, Filippo (18th century)
　S. Martino ai Monti
Gonelli, Arcangelo (rec. 1628–44)
　S. Croce in Gerusalemme
　S. Maria sopra Minerva
　S. Mari a dell'Umiltà
Gonelli, Filippo (rec. 1638)
　S. Maria sopra Minerva
Gorgi, Giovanni Battista (rec. 1689)
　S. Maria in Camposanto
Gottardi, Giovanni (1733–1812)
　S. Agostino
Gozzoli, Benozzo (1420/22–97)
　S. Maria in Aracoeli
Gramiccia, Lorenzo (1702–95)
　SS. Annunziata a Tor de' Specchi
　S. Dorotea
　S. Pietro in Vaticano
Gramignoli, Girolamo
　　(1653/56–1736)
　SS. Carlo e Ambrogio al Corso
　Gesù e Maria
　S. Pietro in Vaticano, Piazza
　S. Silvestro in Capite
Grammatica, Antiveduto
　　(c. 1570–1626)
　S. Caterina da Siena
　S. Giacomo degli Incurabili
　SS. Luca e Martina
　S. Stanislao dei Polacchi
Grammatica, Imperiale (1599–1634)
　S. Salvatore in Lauro
Granacci, Francesco (1460–c. 1543)
　S. Pietro in Vaticano,
　　Cappella Sistina
Granchelli, E. (rec. 1869)
　SS. Trinità dei Pellegrini
Grandi, Francesco (1831–91)
　S. Antonio dei Portoghesi

INDEX OF ARTISTS

Bambino Gesù
SS. Croce e Bonaventura
    dei Lucchesi
S. Giacomo degli Incurabili
SS. Giovanni e Paolo
S. Paolo fuori le Mura
Grandjacquet, Guillaume Antoine
    (1731–1801)
SS. Claudio e Andrea
    de' Borgognoni
Grassi, Orazio (1583–1654)
    Il Gesù
    S. Ignazio
Grassia, Francesco
    (rec. 1661–d. after 1683)
    S. Girolamo degli Schiavoni
    SS. Ildefonso e Tommaso
        di Villanova
    S. Maria sopra Minerva
Graziani, Ciccio (17th century)
    S. Antonio dei Portoghesi
Graziani, Ercole, the Younger
    (1688–1765)
    S. Apollinare
    S. Maria degli Angeli
Grechi, Michele (rec. 1541–53)
    SS. Trinità dei Monti
Grecolini, Giovanni Antonio see
    Giovanni Antonio Crecolini
Gregolini, Antonio (rec. 1721)
    S. Rocco
Gregorini, Domenico (1692–1777)
    S. Croce in Gerusalemme
    S. Lorenzo in Damaso
    S. Maria in Aracoeli
    S. Maria in Monterone
    S. Maria del Popolo
    S. Maria della Quercia
    S. Maria in Via, Piazza Poli
Greppi, Giovanni Battista
    S. Martino ai Monti
Greppi de Casolano, Giovanni see
    Giovanni Casolano
Greuter, Lorenzo (1620–68)
    S. Maria Porta Paradisi
Grimaldi, Alessandro (c. 1630–c. 63)
    S. Madonna delle Grazie
    S. Maria in Publicolis
Grimaldi, Fabrizio (1543–1613)
    S. Andrea della Valle
Grimaldi, Giovanni Francesco
    (1606–80)
    S. Maria dell' Anima
    S. Maria in Publicolis
    S. Maria in Trivio
    S. Maria della Vittoria
    S. Martino ai Monti
Grossi, Giovanni Battista
    (mid 18th century)

SS. Apostoli
S. Croce in Gerusalemme
S. Nicola dei Lorenesi
Guercino (Barbieri, Giovanni
    Francesco) (1591–1666)
    S. Agostino
    S. Crisogono *
    S. Maria in Vallicella
    S. Maria della Vittoria
    S. Nicola in Carcere *
    S. Nicola da Tolentino *
    S. Pietro in Vaticano *
    S. Pietro in Vincoli
Guerra, Gaspare (c. 1560–1622)
    S. Andrea delle Fratte
    S. Antonio dei Portoghesi
Guerra, Giovanni (1544–1618)
    S. Maria Maggiore
    S. Maria in Vallicella
Guerra, Giovanni Battista
    (16th century)
    S. Maria in Vallicella
Guglielmetti, Camillo (19th century)
    S. Salvatore in Lauro
Guglielmi, Gregorio (1714–73)
    S. Agostino
    SS. Trinità degli Spagnuoli
Guidetti, Guidetto (active 1556–1628)
    S. Caterina dei Funari
    S. Maria dell'Orto
Guidi, Domenico (1625–1701)
    S. Agnese in Agone
    S. Agostino
    SS. Alessio e Bonifazio
        all'Aventino
    S. Andrea della Valle
    SS. Apostoli
    SS. Croce e Bonaventura
        dei Lucchesi
    S. Francesco a Ripa
    Il Gesù
    Gesù e Maria
    S. Giovanni dei Fiorentini
    S. Giovanni in Laterano
    S. Giuliano dei Fiamminghi
    S. Ivo della Sapienza
    S. Maria dell' Anima
    S. Maria Maggiore
    S. Maria sopra Minerva
    S. Maria del Popolo
    S. Maria della Scala
    S. Maria in Traspontina
    S. Maria in Vallicella, Oratory
    S. Maria della Vittoria
    S. Nicola da Tolentino
    Spirito Santo dei Napoletani
    SS. Trinità in Palazzo
        Monte di Pietà
Guidi, Guido (1835–1918)
    S. Andrea della Valle

S. Nicola in Carcere
Guidotti, Francesco (rec. 1682–1708)
    S. Apollinare
    S. Maria in Aracoeli
Guidotti, Paolo (c. 1560–1629)
    S. Crisogono
    S. Giovanni in Laterano,
        Scala Santa
    S. Girolamo degli Schiavoni
    S. Maria dei Monti
Haan, David de (c. 1585–1622)
    S. Pietro in Montorio
Haese, Maximilien de (d. 1760)
    S. Giuliano dei Fiamminghi
Haffner, Enrico (1640–1702)
    SS. Domenico e Sisto
Hallet, Gilles (1620–94)
    S. Gregorio a Ponte Quattro Capi
    S. Isidoro
    S. Maria dell' Anima
    S. Maria delle Grazie alle Fornaci
Haye, Luca de la (1625–82)
    S. Egidio
    S. Maria della Scala
Heintz, Joseph the Elder (1564–1609)
    Il Gesù
    S. Vitale
Helmbreker, Dirk (1633–96)
    S. Giuliano dei Fiamminghi
Hermosilla y Sandoval,
    Josè de (d. 1776)
    SS. Trinità degli Spagnuoli
Hernot, Giovanni (rec. 1739–41)
    SS. Nome di Maria
Herzog, Peter (1794–1864)
    S. Maria della Concezione
Hewetson, Christopher (c. 1736–98)
    S. Nicola in Carcere
    S. Tommaso da Canterbury
Hill, Thomas (19th century)
    S. Marcello
Hoffman, Karl (1816–72)
    S. Bernardo alle Terme
Holl, Pietro (1780–1856)
    S. Maria in Aracoeli
    S. Maria del Pianto
Honthorst, Gerrit van (1592–1656)
    S. Maria in Concezione
    S. Maria della Scala
    S. Maria della Vittoria
Hosmer, Harriet (1830–1908)
    S. Andrea delle Fratte
Houdon, Jean Antoine (1741–1828)
    S. Maria degli Angeli
Hugford, Ignazio (1703–78)
    Stimmate di S. Francesco
Iefimoff, Nicolai (rec. 1836)
    S. Andrea delle Fratte
Imperiali see Francesco Fernandi
Intralegni, Pietro (rec. 1611)

S. Maria in Vallicella
Ippolito di Poggio Bustone,
    Fra' (rec. 1861)
    S. Isidoro
Isaia da Pisa (active 1447–64)
    S. Giovanni in Laterano
Jacometti, Ignazio (1819–83)
    S. Giovanni in Laterano,
        Scala Santa
    S. Girolamo degli Schiavoni
    S. Maria Maggiore
    S. Maria in Via Lata
    S. Salvatore in Lauro
    S. Spirito in Sassia
Jacopo da Pietrasanta
    (active 1452–c. 1495)
    S. Agostino
Jacovacci, Domenico (1624–1701)
    S. Andrea delle Fratte
Jacopo, maestro (early 17th century)
    S. Maria in Aquiro
Jacquet, Alexander called Grenoble
    (1614–86)
    S. Giovanni in Laterano
Jouza, Giovanni de (rec. 1746)
    SS. Trinità degli Spagnuoli
Juvarra, Filippo (1678–1736)
    S. Girolamo della Carità
Kempeneer, Peter de (1503–80)
    S. Prassede
Kent, William (1685–1748)
    S. Giuliano dei Fiamminghi
Kessels, Mathieu (1784–1836)
    S. Giuliano dei Fiamminghi
Krahe, Lambert (1712–90)
    S. Pasquale Baylon
Kuchler, Alberto (1803–87)
    S. Bonaventura al Palatino
Kuntz, Thaddeus (1732–93)
    S. Caterina da Siena
    S. Lucia della Tinta
    S. Stanislao dei Polacchi
Laboureur, Alessandro Massimiliano
    (1800–61)
    S. Eustachio
    S. Maria in Aracoeli
    S. Maria di Montesanto
    S. Paolo fuori le Mura
    S. Silvestro in Capite
Laboureur, Francesco Massimiliano
    (1767–1831)
    S. Luigi dei Francesi
    S. Maria in Aracoeli
    S. Maria della Concezione
    S. Pietro in Vaticano
Labruzzi, Pietro (1738–1805)
    Gesù e Maria
    S. Maria della Luca
    S. Maria ad Martyres
Lambardi, Carlo (1544–1620)

    S. Francesca Romana
    S. Marcello
    S. Maria in Via, Largo Chigi
    S. Prisca
Lamberti, Bonaventura (1652–1721)
    S. Luigi dei Francesi
    S. Maria Maddalena
    S. Maria sopra Minerva
    S. Maria della Vittoria
    S. Pietro in Vaticano
    Spirito Santo dei Napoletani
Lambardo, Francesco
    (late 16th century)
    S. Maria in Via, Largo Chigi
Lancioni, Pietro (rec. 1858)
    S. Salvatore in Lauro
Landini, Francesco (rec. 1594–1659)
    S. Agnese in Agone
    S. Giovanni in Laterano
Landini, Taddeo (1557/58–96)
    S. Giovanni in Laterano and
        Baptistery
    SS. Trinità dei Pellegrini
Lanfranco, F. V. R. (rec. 1774)
    S. Agostino
Lanfranco, Giovanni (1582–1647)
    S. Agostino
    S. Andrea della Valle
    S. Carlo ai Catinari
    SS. Domenico e Sisto
    S. Giovanni dei Fiorentini
    S. Gregorio al Celio,
        Oratorio di S. Andrea
    S. Lucia in Selci
    S. Maria della Concezione
    S. Maria dell'Orazione
        e della Morte
    S. Maria in Vallicella
    S. Paola fuori le Mura
    S. Pietro in Vaticano
Langlois, Jérôme Martin (1799–1838)
    SS. Trinità dei Monti
Lapiccola, Nicola (1727–90)
    SS. Apostoli
    S. Caterina da Siena
    S. Giovanni della Pigna
    S. Lorenzo in Panisperna
    S. Pietro in Vaticano
Lapis, Gaetano (1706–76)
    S. Caterina da Siena
    SS. Celso e Giuliano
    S. Lucia in Selci
    SS. Marcellino e Pietro
    SS. Trinità degli Spagnuoli
Larcan, Philadelphus (rec. 1766)
    S. Bernardo alle Terme
Latour, Pascasio (Pascal) (1702–56)
    S. Giovanni in Laterano
    SS. Nome di Maria
    SS. Trinità degli Spagnuoli
Latre, Daniele (rec. 1649)

    S. Martino ai Monti
Lattre, Pierre de (1606–83)
    S. Ignazio
Laureto, Tommaso (c. 1530–1602)
    S. Susanna
Laurenzi, Bartolomeo de'
    S. Maria in Vallicella
Laurenzi, Filippo (early 18th century)
    S. Nicola da Tolentino
Laurenziano (Laurentiani),
    Giacomo (d. 1650)
    S. Giovanni in Laterano
    S. Maria Maggiore
    S. Pietro in Vaticano
Lauri, Filippo (1623–94)
    S. Francesca Romana
    S. Maria della Pace
    Stimmate di S. Francesco
Lavaggi, Giacomo Antonio
    (rec. 1683–c. 1705)
    Il Gesù
    S. Ignazio
    S. Maria in Campitelli
    S. Maria in Traspontina
    S. Maria in Vallicella
Lazzari, Ottaviano (17th century)
    S. Maria sopra Minerva
Lazzari, Paolo (rec. 1628)
    S. Maria di Loreto
Lazzoni, Giovanni (1618–after 1680)
    Il Gesù
    S. Giovanni in Laterano
Lazzoni, Giovanni Francesco
    (rec. 1734–35)
    S. Giovanni in Laterano
Lebrun, Andrè-Jean (1736–1811)
    SS. Carlo e Ambrogio al Corso
    C. Cecilia
Le Doux, Jean (active c. 1760–78)
    S. Marco
Legnani, Stefano Maria (il Legnannino)
    (1660–1713/15)
    S. Francesco a Ripa
Legnannino see Stefano Legnani
Legros, Pierre the Younger
    (1666–1719)
    S. Agnese in Agone
    S. Andrea al Quirinale
    S. Apollinare
    SS. Apostoli
    Il Gesù
    S. Giacomo degli Incurabili
    S. Giovanni in Laterano
    S. Girolamo della Carità
    S. Ignazio
    S. Maria Maggiore
    S. Maria dell'Orto
    S. Pietro in Vaticano
    SS. Trinità in Palazzo
        Monte di Pietà

INDEX OF ARTISTS

Lemoyne, Paul (1784–1873)
  SS. Carlo e Ambrogio al Corso
  S. Lorenzo in Lucina
  S. Luigi dei Francesi
Lenardi, Giovanni Battista
  (1656–1704)
  S. Andrea delle Fratte
  S. Giovanni Calabita
  S. Sabina
Leonardi, F. (19th century)
  S. Maria in Aquiro
Leoncino, Galeazzo (rec. 1640)
  S. Martino ai Monti
Leoni, Ottavio (1578–1630)
  S. Eustachio
  S. Maria sopra Minerva
Leonori, Aristide (1856–1928)
  S. Andrea della Valle
Leopardi, Marcello (c. 1750–95)
  S. Stefano Rotondo
Lestache, Pierre (c. 1688/9–1774)
  S. Croce in Gerusalemme
  S. Giovanni in Laterano
  S. Luigi dei Francesi
Leti, Filippo (active 1677–d. 1711)
  S. Francesca a Ripa
Levieux, Reynaud (c. 1620–90)
  S. Luigi dei Francesi
Ligorio, Pirro (c. 1513–83)
  S. Giovanni Decollato, Oratory
  S. Ivo della Sapienza
  S. Maria sopra Minerva
Ligozzi, Jacopo (1547–1627)
  S. Giovanni dei Fiorentini
Ligustri da Viterbo, Tarquino
  (early 17th century)
  S. Marcello
  S. Vitale
Lilio, Andrea see Andrea Lilli
Lilli, Andrea (c. 1570–1635)
  S. Agostino
  S. Giovanni in Laterano and
    Scala Santa
  S. Girolamo degli Schiavoni
  S. Maria Maggiore
  S. Maria in Vallicella
  S. Spirito in Sassia
Lint, Pieter van (1609–90)
  S. Maria del Popolo
Lipari, Biagio (rec. 1840)
  S. Maria d'Itria
Lippi, Annibale (active 1563–81)
  S. Marcello
Lippi, Filippino (1457 ?–1504)
  S. Maria sopra Minerva
Lironi, Giuseppe (1699–1749)
  S. Carlo ai Catinari
  S. Giovanni in Laterano
  S. Maria Maggiore
  S. Maria della Scala

  S. Pietro in Vaticano
Lironi, Lorenzo (rec. 1702–33)
  S. Pietro in Vaticano, Piazza
Lisandroni, Ferdinando (18th century)
  Oratorio del Gonfalone
  S. Maria in Aquiro
Lodovico di Mariano (b. 1486)
  S. Maria in Trastevere
Lobelli, Claude (rec. c. 1696)
  Il Gesù
Loffredo, Bonaventura (1830–1913)
  S. Bartolomeo all'Isola
  S. Cosimato
Lombardelli, Giovanni Battista
  (c. 1537–92)
  S. Antonio Abate
  S. Maria dei Monti
  S. Pietro in Montorio
Lambardo, Carlo see Carlo Lambardi
Lomi, Aurelio (1556–1622)
  S. Maria in Vallicella
Lomi, Orazio see Orazio Gentileschi
Longhi, Martino the Elder (1534–91)
  S. Angelo in Pescheria
  S. Atanasio dei Greci
  S. Bartolomeo all'Isola
  S. Girolamo degli Schiavoni
  S. Macuto
  S. Maria degli Angeli
  S. Maria in Aracoeli
  S. Maria della Consolazione
  S. Maria Maggiore
  S. Maria dell'Orto
  S. Maria in Trastevere
  S. Maria in Vallicella
  S. Maria in Via, Largo Chigi
  S. Prassede
  SS. Trinità dei Pellegrini
Longhi, Martino the Younger
  (1602–60)
  S. Adriano
  S. Antonio dei Portoghesi
  SS. Carlo e Ambrogio al Corso
  S. Carlo ai Catinari
  S. Giovanni Calabita
  S. Girolamo della Carità
  S. Maria sopra Minerva
  S. Maria dell'Umiltà
  SS. Vincenzo e Anastasio
Longhi, Niccolò (d. 1581)
  S. Pietro in Vaticano
Longhi, Onorio (1568–1619)
  S. Anastasia
  SS. Carlo e Ambrogio al Corso
  S. Eusebio
  S Francesca a Ripa
  S. Giovanni in Laterano
  S. Gregorio al Celio
  S. Maria in Antiqua
  S. Maria in Aracoeli

  S. Maria in Trastevere
  S. Maria in Vallicella
  S. Maria in Via, Largo Chigi
Longhi, Silla Giacomo
  (1560–1619 [17])
  Il Gesù
  S. Giovanni in Laterano
  S. Maria Maggiore
  S. Maria sopra Minerva
Longhi, Stefano (d. 1635)
  S. Cesareo
  S. Gregorio al Celio,
    Oratorio di S. Andrea
  S. Maria di Loreto
Longo, Stefano (rec. 1600–21)
  S. Maria in Vallicella
  S. Paolo alle Tre Fontane
Loo, Jean Baptiste van (1684–1745)
  S. Maria in Monticelli
Loon, Theodor van
  (1585–before 1660)
  S. Maria dell' Anima
Lorenzi, Stoldo (1534–83)
  S. Marcello
Lorenzetto, Lorenzo di Ludovico di
  Guglielmo called (1490–1541)
  S. Maria dell' Anima
  S. Maria ad Martyres
  S. Maria del Popolo
Lorrain, Nicolas (Nicolas François
  de Bar) (active 1627 onwards)
  S. Antonio dei Portoghesi
  S. Maria della Vittoria
  S. Nicola dei Lorenesi
Lotsch, Christina (1790–1873)
  SS. Vincenzo e Anastasio
Lucatelli, Pietro (c. 1637–1710)
  S. Agostino
  S. Maria delle Vergini
Luccardi, Vincenzo (1811–76)
  SS. Apostoli
  Stimmate di S. Francesco
Lucchesino, Michele (rec. 1594)
  S. Spirito in Sassia
Lucenti, Ambrogio (d. 1656)
  S. Maria in Vallicella
  S. Pietro in Vaticano
Lucenti, Girolamo (1627–98)
  S. Anastasia
  S. Maria Maggiore
  S. Maria dei Miracoli
  S. Maria di Montesanto
  S. Pietro in Vaticano
Luchetti, Giuseppe (1823–92)
  S. Giovanni in Laterano
  SS. Giovanni e Paolo
Ludovico di Siena (early 16th
  century)
  S. Maria in Trastevere
Ludovisi, Bernardino (1713–49)

S. Apollinare
SS. Apostoli
S. Croce in Gerusalemme
Il Gesù
S. Giovanni in Laterano
S. Ignazio
S. Maria degli Angeli
S. Maria Maggiore
SS. Nome di Maria
S. Salvatore delle Coppelle
SS. Trinità dei Pellegrini
Luigi da Crema, Fra (1763–18/1618)
S. Maria della Concezione
Luini, Tommaso (1601–1637)
SS. Carlo e Ambrogio al Corso
S. Maria in Via, Largo Chigi
S. Tommaso in Formis
Luraghi, Giuseppe and Giovan Battista (rec. 1718)
S. Maria Maddalena
Luti, Benedetto (1666–1724)
SS. Apostoli
S. Caterina da Siena a Magnanapoli
S. Giovanni in Laterano
Luzi, Filippo (1665–1720)
S. Francesco di Paola
S. Prassede
Maccarano, Paola (rec. 1643–46)
S. Maria dell'Umiltà
Maccari, Cesare (1840–1919)
SS. Sudario de Piemontesi
Machuca, Pietro (?–1550)
S. Maria della Pace
Maderno, Carlo (1556–1629)
S. Ambrogio della Massima
S. Andrea della Vale
S. Chiara
S. Giacomo degli Incurabili
S. Giovanni dei Fiorentini
S. Giovanni in Laterano
S. Gregorio al Celio
S. Ignazio
S. Lucia in Selci
S. Luigi dei Francesi
S. Maria in Aquiro
S. Maria ad Martyres
S. Maria sopra Minerva
S. Maria della Pace
S. Maria della Vittoria
S. Pietro in Montorio
S. Pietro in Vaticano, Piazza
S. Pudenziana
S. Silvestro in Capite
S. Susanna
SS. Trinità in Palazzo Monte di Pietà
Maderno, Stefano (c. 1576–1636)
S. Cecilia
SS. Domenico e Sisto

S. Lorenzo in Damaso
S. Maria di Loreto
S. Maria Maggiore
S. Maria sopra Minerva
S. Maria della Pace
S. Paolo fuori le Mura
S. Pietro in Vaticano
S. Susanna
Maella, Mariano (1739–1819)
S. Pasquale Baylon
Maffei, Tomaso see Tommaso Mattei
Maggi, Girolamo (17th century)
S. Maria in Vallicella, Oratory
Maggi, Giovan Paolo (d. 1613)
SS. Trinità dei Pellegrini
Magistris, Simone de (1538–c. 1611)
S. Spirito in Sassia
Maglia, Francesco (late 17th century)
Il Gesù
S. Maria in Vallicella
Maglia, François, (François Maille) (rec. 1716)
S. Francesco a Ripa
Maglia, Michele (Michel Maille) (c. 1643–after 1703)
S. Angelo in Pescheria
S. Anna dei Palafrenieri
S. Carlo ai Catinari
Il Gesù
Gesù e Maria
S. Giovanni dei Fiorentini
S. Maria in Aracoeli
S. Maria in Campitelli
S. Maria sopra Minerva
S. Maria dei Miracoli
S. Maria dell'Orto
S. Maria in Traspontina
S. Maria in Trastevere
S. Maria in Vallicella
S. Pietro in Vaticano and Piazza
S. Silvestro in Capite
SS. Trinità in Palazzo Monte di Pietà
Magnani, Domenico (18th century)
S. Antonio de Portoghesi
Magnoni, Carlo (d. 1653)
S. Giovanni in Laterano, Baptistery
Magny, Nicolas (late 17th century)
S. Maria sopra Minerva
Maignan, Emmanuel (rec. 1637)
SS. Trinità dei Monti
Mainardi, Lattanzio (c. 1564–c. 90)
S. Maria Maggiore
S. Maria dei Monti
Maini, Giovanni Battista (1690–1752)
S. Agnese in Agone

S. Agostino
S. Andrea delle Fratte
Oratorio del Caravita
S. Giovanni in Laterano
SS. Luca e Martina
S. Luigi dei Francesi
S. Maria della Concezione
S. Maria delle Grazie alle Fornaci
S. Maria Maggiore
S. Maria in Publicolis
S. Maria della Scala
SS. Nome di Maria
S. Pietro in Vaticano
Mainoni, Luigi (1804–53)
S. Giovanni in Laterano
Maioli, Clemente (rec. 1634–73)
S. Bernardino ai Monti
S. Ivo della Sapienza
S. Maria ad Martyres
Malavista, Carlo (rec. 1647–76)
S. Pudenziana
Mallerini, Prospero (rec. 1829)
S. Carlo alle Quattro Fontane
Malmeluzzi, Lucca (rec. 1659)
S. Maria in Traspontina
Mancini, Francesco (1679–1758)
S. Gregorio al Celio
S. Maria degli Angeli
S. Maria Maggiore
S. Maria della Scala
S. Pietro in Vaticano *
Stimmate di S. Francesco
Manetti, Orazio (17th century)
S. Pietro in Vaticano
Manfredi, Madredo (1859–1927)
S. Maria ad Martyres
Mangone, Giovanni (d. 1543)
S. Luigi dei Francesi
S. Maria dell' Anima
Maniscalchi, Giovanni (rec. 1647)
S. Maria della Scala
Manno, Antonio (1739–1810)
S. Pudenziana
Manno, Francesco (1752–1831)
S. Angelo in Pescheria
SS. Apostoli
S. Bartolomeo all'Isola
S. Francesco di Paola
S. Ignazio
S. Lorenzo in Lucina
S. Maria d'Itria
S. Teodoro al Palatino
SS. Vincenzo e Anastasio
Manno, Giuseppe (c. 1784–1865)
S. Luigi dei Francesi
Mannozzi, Giovanni see Giovanni da San Giovanni
Mantinovese, Pietro (recorded 1664–1703)

335

INDEX OF ARTISTS

S. Pietrio in Vaticano, Piazza
SS. Sudario dei Piemontesi
Manzolini, Domenico (rec. 1796)
S. Martino ai Monti
Maraldi, Pietro (rec. 1645)
S. Rocco
Maratta, Carlo (1625–1713)
S. Andrea al Quirinale
S. Angelo in Pescheria
SS. Annunziate *
SS. Carlo e Ambrogio al Corso
S. Croce in Gerusalemme
S. Francesca Romana *
Il Gesù
S. Giovanni dei Fiorentini *
S. Giovanni in Laterano and Baptistery
S. Giuseppe a Capo le Case
S. Giuseppe dei Falegnami
S. Isidoro
S. Luigi dei Francesi
S. Marcello
S. Marco
S. Maria degli Angeli
S. Maria in Cosmedin
S. Maria sopra Minerva
S. Maria di Montesanto
S. Maria della Pace
S. Maria del Popolo
S. Maria del Rosario
   sul Monte Mario
S. Maria dei Sette Dolori
S. Maria in Vallicella
S. Pietro in Vaticano
Maratta, Francesco
   (active 1697–1719)
S. Agostino
S. Giovanni in Laterano
S. Marco
S. Maria degli Angeli
S. Maria in Vallicella
Marcellini, Carlo (1646–1713)
S. Maria in Vallicella
Marchant, Julian (rec. 1739–41)
Marchetti, Giovanni Battista
   (1730–1800)
S. Caterina da Siena
Marchetti, Giuseppe
   (rec. 1716–d. 1778)
S. Maria di Monserrato
Marchionni, Carlo (1702–86)
S. Apollinare
S. Caterina da Siena
   a Magnanapoli
S. Crisogono
S. Croce in Gerusalemme
S. Maria Maddalena
S. Maria Maggiore
S. Maria sopra Minerva
S. Pietro in Vaticano

Marchionni, Francesco (18th century)
S. Pietro in Vaticano, Piazza
Marchis, Tommaso de' (1693–1759)
SS. Alessio e Bonifazio
   all'Aventino
Marcillat, Guillaume de
   (1468/70–1529)
S. Maria del Popolo
Mare, Mattia de (rec. 1764–70)
S. Andrea della Valle
Mari, Francesco (1641–after 1676)
S. Pietro in Vaticano, Piazza
S. Pudenziana
Mari, Giovanni Antonio (c. 1631–61)
S. Maria sopra Minerva
S. Maria del Popolo
Maria Eufrasia della Croce (Flavia
   Benedetti) (1597–1676)
S. Giuseppe a Capo le Case
Mariani, Antonio
S. Maria dell'Umiltà
Mariani, Camillo (1567–1611)
S. Bernardo alle Terme
Il Gesù
S. Giovanni in Laterano
S. Maria Maggiore
S. Maria sopra Minerva
S. Pietro in Vaticano
S. Pudenziana
Mariani, Cesare (1826–1901)
S. Giuseppe dei Falegnami
S. Lucia del Gonfalone
S. Maria in Aquiro
S. Maria di Loreto
S. Maria in Monticelli
S. Maria del Suffragio
S. Omobono
S. Paolo fuori le Mura
S. Rocco
S. Salvatore in Onda
S. Stefano del Cacco
Marin, Joseph Charles (1759–1834)
S. Luigi dei Francesi
Marini, Camillo (rec. 1817)
S. Maria del Pianto
Marini, Giuseppe (rec. 1673)
S. Maria in Traspontina
S. Pietro in Vincoli
Marini, Pasquale (rec. 1858)
S. Gregorio a Ponte Quattro Capi
Marini, Pasquale Andrea (1650–1712)
S. Andrea delle Fratte
S. Maria in Campo Marzio
Mariotti, Pietro (rec. 1746–49)
S. Nicola dei Lorenesi
Mariotti, Vincenzo (rec. 1668–1703)
S. Pietro in Vaticano, Piazza
Marmorelli, Liborio (1724/25–1794)
S. Dorotea
S. Maria in Camposanto

Maron, Anton von (1731–1808)
S. Eusebio
S. Maria dell' Anima
Marta, Ignazio (mid 18th century)
S. Caterina da Siena
Martinelli, Niccolò (il Trometta)
   (c. 1540–1611)
S. Maria in Aracoeli
S. Maria dell'Orto
Martini, Alberto (rec. 1601)
S. Onofrio
Martini, Simone (c. 1690–1763)
S. Giovanni dei Fiorentini
S. Giovanni in Laterano
Martinis, Simone see Simone Martini
Martinori, Luigi (rec. 1862–65)
S. Maria in Via, Piazza Poli
S. Nicola in Carcere
Martorana, Gioacchino (1735–79)
S. Dorotea
Martinucci, Filippo (rec. 1857–80)
S. Andrea della Valle
SS. Giovanni e Paolo
Martinucci, Vincenzo (rec. 1862)
S. Maria del Carmine
   alle Tre Cannele
Maruscelli, Paolo (1596–1649)
S. Andrea della Valle
S. Carlo ai Catinari
SS. Gioacchino e Anna
S. Maria dell' Anima
S. Maria dell'Umiltà
**S. Maria in Vallicella and
   Oratory**
S. Stefano del Cacco
Maruscelli, Pietro (1594–1649)
S. Maria sopra Minerva
Marziani, Giovanni Domenico
   (17th century)
S. Bibiana
Marzio di Colantonio see
   Marzio Ganassini
Mascarino, Ottaviano (1536–1606)
S. Caterina della Rota
SS. Giovanni e Petronio
   dei Bolognesi
S. Maria della Scala
S. Maria in Traspontina
S. Marta in Vaticano
S. Salvatore in Lauro
S. Silvestro al Quirinale
Spirito Santo dei Napoletani
S. Spirito in Sassia
SS. Trinità in Palazzo
   Monte di Pietà
Mascarotti see Angelo Massarotti
Masolino (Tommaso di Cristofano
   Fini) (1383–1440)
S. Clemente
Massari, Francesco (rec. 1665–1705)

S. Lorenzo in Piscibus
S. Maria dell'Orto
Massarotti, Angelo (c. 1645–1732)
SS. Annunziata, Oratory of the
S. Salvatore in Lauro
Masseri, Francesco see
    Francesco Massari
Massei, Girolamo (c. 1540–c. 1614)
    S. Luigi dei Francesi
    S. Martino ai Monti
    SS. Nero e Achilleo
    S. Prassede
Massi, Giovanni Antonio
    (rec. shortly before 1686)
    S. Dionigi alle Quattro Fontane
Massimano, Padre (rec. c. 1591)
    S. Salvatore in Lauro
Massimi, Camillo de' (17 century)
    S. Maria sopra Minerva
Masucci, Agostino (d. 1746)
    S. Francesco a Ripa
Masucci, Agostino (1691–1768)
    S. Francesco di Paola
    S. Marcello
    S. Maria Maggiore
    S. Maria del Popolo
    S. Maria in Via, Largo Chigi *
    S. Maria in Via Lata
    SS. Nome di Maria
Masucci, Lorenzo (d. 1785)
    S. Maria dell'Orazione
        e della Morte
    SS. Nome di Maria
    S. Pantaleo
Mattei, Ambrogio (rec. 1764)
    S. Eligio dei Ferrari
Mattei, Baldassare
    (mid 18th century)
    S. Croce in Gerusalemme
    SS. Trinità degli Spagnuoli
Mattei, Paolo (18th century)
    S. Maria in Aracoeli
Mattei, Tommaso (c. 1648–1726)
    S. Maria in Aracoeli
    S. Maria in Campo Marzio
    S. Maria in Cosmedin
    S. Maria in Domnica
    S. Maria di Montesanto
Matteini, Teodoro (1754–1831)
    S. Lorenzo in Lucina
Matteis, Paolo De (1662–1728)
    S. Maria sopra Minerva
Matteo da Castello see
    Matteo Bartolini
Matteo da Lecce (Matteo Pérez de
    Alesio) (1545/50–c. 1616)
    S. Eligio degli Orefici
    Oratorio del Gonfalone
    S. Pietro in Vaticano,
        Cappella Sistina

Matteo da Siena (1533–88)
    S. Stefano Rotondo
Maturino da Firenze
    (early 16th century)
    S. Silvestro al Quirinale
Mauri, Giovanni Pietro
    (rec. 1686–1703)
    Gesù e Maria
    S. Pietro in Vaticano, Piazza
Mauri, Michele (rec. 1702–03)
    S. Pietro in Vaticano, Piazza
Mazzanti, Lodovico (1686–1775)
    S. Andrea al Quirinale
    S. Apollinare
    S. Ignazio
Mazzoni, Giulio (1525–c. 1618)
    S. Maria degli Angeli
    S. Maria sopra Minerva
    S. Maria del Popolo
Mazzuchelli, Pier Francesco see
    Morazzone
Mazzuoli, Giuseppe (1644–1725)
    S. Cecilia
    S. Francesco a Ripa
    Gesù e Maria
    S. Giovanni in Laterano
    S. Maria in Campitelli
    S. Maria Maddalena
    S. Pietro in Vaticano
    S. Silvestro in Capite
    SS. Trinità in Palazzo
        Monte di Pietà
    S. Pietro in Vaticano
Meder, Christian (late 17th and
    early 18th century)
    S. Andrea delle Fratte
Mei, Bernardino Paolo (1612–76)
    S. Maria della Pace
    S. Maria del Popolo
Melchiorri, Giovanni Paolo
    (1664–1745)
    S. Giovanni in Laterano
    S. Maria in Traspontina
Meli, Giosuè (1807–93)
    S. Francesca Romana
    S. Giovanni in Laterano and
        Scala Santa
Mellan, Claude (1598–1688)
    S. Barbara dei Librai
Mellin, Charles (c. 1600–49)
    S. Luigi dei Francesi
    S. Maria in Aracoeli
Mellone, Carlo Francesco
    (active 1695–1726)
    S. Pietro in Vaticano
Melozzo da Forlì (1438–1494)
    S. Marco
Melussi, Domenico (c. 1653–1710)
    Il Gesù
Menghini, Niccolò (1610–65)

S. Giovanni in Laterano
SS. Luca e Martina
S. Pietro in Vaticano
S. Rocco
Mengozzi, Girolamo (c. 1688–c. 1766)
    S. Girolamo della Carità
Mengs, Anton Raphael (1728–79)
    S. Eusebio
Mercandetti, F. (rec. 1861)
    S. Bernardo alle Terme
Mercati, Giovanbattista (1591–1645)
    S. Bartolomeo all'Isola
    S. Crisogono
    S. Maria delle Vergini
Merelli, Bartolomeo (1644–1726)
    S. Maria in Trivio
Merlini, Lorenzo (1666–after 1740)
    Il Gesù
    S. Giovanni dei Fiorentini
    S. Pantaleo
Meucci, Vincenzo (1694/99- 1766)
    S. Dorote
Mezzetti, Francesco
    (active 1676–1706)
    S. Susanna
Michallon, Claude (1751–99)
    S. Maria in Via Lata
Michelangelo, Buonarroti (1475–1564)
    S. Andrea della Valle
    Il Gesù
    S. Giovanni dei Fiorentini
    S. Maria degli Angeli
    S. Maria in Aracoeli
    S. Maria Maggiore
    S. Maria sopra Minerva
    S. Pietro in Montorio
    S. Pietro in Vaticano and
        Cappella Sistina
    S. Pietro in Vincoli
    S. Silvestro in Capite
Michele da Bergamo (d. 1641)
    S. Maria della Concezione
Michele, Monsù see Michele Maglia
Micheli, Filippo (17th century)
    S. Bonaventura al Palatino
Michetti, Francesco (rec. 1747)
    S. Eustachio
Michetti, Nicola (c. 1675–1758)
    SS. Apostoli
    S. Francesco a Ripa
    S. Girolamo degli Schiavoni
    S. Ignazio
    S. Maria in Traspontina
Michi, Giovanni (rec. 1508–16)
    S. Pietro in Vaticano,
        Cappella Sistina
Micocca, Giovanni (1763–1825)
    S. Maria Maggiore
    S. Martino ai Monti
Micocchi, Giovanni see

INDEX OF ARTISTS

Giovanni Micocca
Midossi, Giuseppe (rec. 1794)
  S. Stefano Rotondo
Miel, Jan (1599–1663)
  S. Lorenzo in Lucina
  S. Maria dell' Anima
  S. Martino ai Monti
Mignard, Pierre (1612–95)
  S. Carlo alle Quattro Fontane
Milani, Aureliano (1675–1749)
  SS. Bartolomeo e Alessandro dei Bergamaschi
  SS. Giovanni e Paolo
  S. Marcello
  S. Maria Maddalena
  S. Maria Maggiore
Milone, Vincenzo (c. 1735–1805)
  S. Maria in Aracoeli
  S. Omobono
Minardi, Tommaso (1787–1871)
  S. Andrea al Quirinale
  S. Maria in Monticelli
Mino da Fiesole (1429–84)
  SS. Apostoli
  S. Cecilia
  S. Marco
  S. Maria del Popolo
  S. Pietro in Vaticano
Minossi, Raffael (1732–1805)
  Gesù e Maria
  S. Nicola da Tolentino
Mochi, Francesco (1580–1654)
  S. Andrea della Valle
  S. Bernardo alle Terme
  S. Giovanni dei Fiorentini
  S. Maria Maggiore
  S. Maria ad Martyres
  S. Maria sopra Minerva
  S. Paola alla Regola
  S. Pietro in Vaticano
  S. Silvestro in Capite
Moderati, Francesco (c. 1680–c. 1728)
  S. Agnese in Agone
  S. Anna dei Palafrenieri
  S. Francesco a Ripa
  S. Maria ad Martyres
  S. Pietro in Vaticano, Piazza
  SS. Trinità in Palazzo Monte di Pietà
Mola, Giacomo (1583–1650)
  S. Francesco a Ripa
  S. Maria del Pianto
Mola, Giovanni Battista (c. 1585–1665)
  S. Ambrogio della Massima
  S. Eligio dei Ferrari
  S. Maria del Pianto
  S. Nicola da Tolentino
  SS. Trinità dei Pellegrini
Mola, Pier Francesco (1612–66)

S. Anastasia
SS. Carlo e Ambrogio al Corso
SS. Domenico e Sisto
Il Gesù
S. Marco
Molinari, Guido (19th century)
  S. Maria della Quercia
Molto, Andrea (early 18th century)
  S. Maria delle Grazie alle Fornaci
Monacelli, Domenico (19th century)
  S. Barbara dei Librai
Monaldi, Carlo (c. 1683–1760)
  S. Giovanni in Laterano
  S. Marco
  S. Maria Maddalena
  S. Maria Maggiore
  S. Maria ad Martyres
  S. Maria di Monserrato
  S. Pietro in Vaticano
  S. Salvatore in Lauro
Monaldi, G. P. (rec. 1645–50)
  S. Francesco di Paola
Monaldi, Giacomo (1819–1905)
  SS. Vincenzo e Anastasio
Mondelli, Filippo (mid 18th century)
  S. Carlo ai Catinari
Monnot, Pierre Etienne (1657–1733)
  SS. Apostoli
  Il Gesù
  S. Giovanni in Laterano
  S. Ignazio
  S. Maria del Popolo
  S. Maria della Vittoria
  S. Pietro in Vaticano and Piazza
Monosilio, Salvatore (d. 1776)
  S. Caterina da Siena
  S. Lucia del Gonfalone
  S. Paola alla Regola
  S. Pasquale Baylon
  S. Pietro in Vaticano
  S. Stanislao dei Polacchi
Montagna, Giovanni Battista
  S. Agostino
Montagna, Marco Tullio (active 1618–d. before 42)
  S. Angelo in Pescheria
  SS. Cosmo e Damiano
  S. Giuseppe dei Falegnami
  S. Sebastiano fuori le Mura
Montano, Giovanni Battista (1534–1621)
  S. Giovanni in Laterano
  S. Giuseppe dei Falegnami
  SS. Luca e Martina
  S. Maria dell' Anima
  S. Maria della Consolazione
  S. Maria di Loreto
  S. Spirito in Sassia
Montauti, Antonio (c. 1685–rec. 1746)

S. Giovanni in Laterano
S. Pietro in Vaticano
Montenois, Pierre (rec. 1671)
  S. Maria Maggiore
Montesanti, Giuseppe (d. 1779)
  S. Lorenzo in Panisperna
  S. Maria in Via, Largo Chigi
Morandi, Giovanni Maria (1622–1717)
  S. Maria dell' Anima
  S. Maria della Pace
  S. Maria del Popolo
  S. Maria in Vallicella
  S. Sabina
  S. Stefano del Cacco
Morandi, G. (early 17th century)
  S. Ambrogio della Massima
Morani, Domenico (d. 1870)
  SS. Apostoli
  S. Francesco a Ripa
Morani, Vincenzo (1809–70)
  S. Paolo fuori le Mura
Moratilla, Filippo (1827-?)
  S. Maria di Monserrato
Morazzone, il (1573–1626)
  SS. Carlo e Ambrogio al Corso
  S. Silvestro in Capite
Morelli, Giovanni Battista (d. 1669)
  S. Giovanni in Laterano
  S. Pietro in Vaticano
Morelli, Larazzo (1619–90)
  S. Marco
  S. Maria dei Miracoli
  S. Maria di Montesanto
  S. Maria del Popolo
  S. Pietro in Vaticano and Piazza
Morelli, Lorenzo (1702–84)
  S. Pietro in Vaticano
Morelli, Paolo (d. 1719)
  S. Maria Maddalena
  S. Pietro in Vaticano, Piazza
Moretti, Antonio (rec. 1851)
  S. Lorenzo in Damaso
Moretti, Egido (rec. 1614)
  S. Pietro in Vaticano
Moretti, Scipione (rec. 1851)
  S. Lorenzo in Damaso
Mori, M. (rec. 1828)
  S. Giovanni dei Fiorentini
Morichini, Gaetano (d. 1895)
  S. Maria in Aquiro
  S. Salvatore in Onda
Mormorelli, Liborio see Liborio Marmorelli
Mosca, Simone (1492–1553)
  S. Maria della Pace
Moscatelli, Eraldo (1900–88)
  SS. Carlo e Ambrogio al Corso
Motta, Pietro della (d. 1603)
  S. Maria dell' Anima

Motte, Pierre, de la see
    Pietro della Motta
Multò, Francesco (rec. 1720–27)
    S. Maria della Grazie alle Fornaci
Muratori, Domenico Maria
    (1661–1742 [1744])
    SS. Apostoli
    Bambino Gesù
    SS. Croce e Bonaventura
        dei Lucchesi
    S. Francesco a Ripa
    S. Giovanni in Laterano
    S. Maria dell'Archetto
    S. Prassede
    S. Sabina
    Spirito Santo dei Napoletani
    Stimmate di S. Francesco
Murena, Carlo (1713/14–64)
    S. Agostino
    SS. Alessio e Bonifazio
        all'Aventino
    S. Antonio dei Portoghesi
    SS. Michele e Magno
    S. Pantaleo
Muti, Cristoforo (rec. 1692)
    S. Antonio dei Portoghesi
Muziano, Girolamo (1532–92)
    S. Agostino
    SS. Bartolomeo e Alessandro
        dei Bergamaschi
    S. Caterina dei Funari
    S. Caterina della Rota
    SS. Cosma e Damiano
    Il Gesù
    S. Giovanni Decollato *
    S. Luigi dei Francesi
    S. Maria degli Angeli
    S. Maria in Aracoeli
    S. Maria della Concezione
    S. Maria sopra Minerva
    S. Maria dei Monti
    S. Maria in Vallicella
    S. Martino ai Monti
    S. Pietro in Vaticano
    S. Sebastiano fuori le Mura
Naldini, Francesco (rec. 1610–28)
    S. Maria di Loreto
Naldini, Giovanni Battista
    (1537–91)
    S. Giovanni Decollato
    S. Giovanni dei Fiorentini
    SS. Trinità dei Monti
Naldini, Pietro Paolo (1614–91)
    Il Gesù
    Gesù e Maria
    S. Giovanni in Laterano and
        Baptistery
    S. Girolamo della Carità
    S. Marcello
    S. Maria ad Martyres

S. Maria di Montesanto
S. Maria del Popolo
S. Maria del Suffragio
S. Martino ai Monti
S. Nicola da Tolentino
S. Pietro in Vaticano
S. Pudenziana
Nanni di Baccio Bigio di
    Bartolomeo (d. 1568)
    Il Gesù
    S. Maria sopra Minerva
Nanni, Girolamo (?–after 1642)
    S. Caterina dei Funari
    S. Croce in Gerusalemme
Napoletano, Marcantonio
    (active mid 17th century)
    S. Maria in Aracoeli
Napolino, Giuseppe (d. 1720)
    SS. Apostoli
    S. Maria in Campitelli
    S. Pietro in Vaticano, Piazza
    Spirito Santo dei Napoletani
Nappi, Francesco (c. 1565–1630)
    S. Caterina nella Rota
    S. Croce in Gerusalemme
    S. Giacomo degli Incurabili
    S. Maria della Consolazione
    S. Maria sopra Minerva
    S. Maria di Monserrato
Nasini, Apollonio (1692–1786)
    S. Andrea delle Fratte
Nasini, Giuseppe Nicola
    (1657–1736)
    SS. Apostoli
    S. Giovanni in Laterano
    S. Lorenzo in Lucina
Natali, Giovanni Battista (1630–96)
    S. Maria del Suffragio
Natoire, Charles-Joseph (1700–77)
    S. Luigi dei Francesi
Nave, Alessandro (rec. 1623–40)
    S. Maria della Concezione
Navone, Filippo (rec. 1833–34)
    S. Biagio della Pagnotta
Navone, Francesco (1731–1804)
    S. Anna dei Palafrenieri
    S. Antonio dei Portoghesi
    S. Giuseppe alla Lungara
    S. Lorenzo in Piscibus
Navone, Domenico Giovanni
    (rec. 1706–70)
    S. Eustachio
    S. Lorenzo in Damaso
Nebbia, Cesare (c. 1536–c. 1614)
    SS. Crocifisso, Oratorio del
    S. Giovanni Decollato, Oratory
    S. Giovanni in Laterano
    Oratorio del Gonfalone
    S. Maria degli Angeli
    S. Maria della Consolazione

S. Maria Maggiore
S. Maria sopra Minerva
S. Maria dei Monti
S. Maria in Vallicella
S. Pietro in Vaticano
S. Silvestro al Quirinale
S. Spirito in Sassia
S. Stefano del Cacco
S. Susanna
SS. Trinità dei Monti
Nelli, Pietro (1672–1740)
    S. Caterina da Siena
        a Magnanapoli
    SS. Gioacchino e Anna
    S. Maria in Trastevere
Nessi, Antonio (active 1739–73)
    S. Lorenzo in Panisperna
    SS. Nome di Maria
Nicéron, Jean-François (1613–46)
    SS. Trinità dei Monti
Nicoletti, Filippo (
    S. Maria in Aracoeli
    (rec. 1728–1815)
Nicoletti, Francesco (1703/09–76)
    S. Maria Maddalena
Nicolini, Francesco (rec. 1573–1626)
    S. Eligio dei Ferrari
Nobili, Salvatore (19th century)
    S. Antonio dei Portoghesi
Nocchi, Bernardino (1741–1812)
    S. Pudenziana
Nogari, Paris (c. 1536–1601)
    S. Andrea delle Fratte
    SS. Crocifisso, Oratorio del
    S. Giovanni in Laterano and
        Scala Santa
    S. Maria Maggiore
    S. Maria dei Monti
    SS. Nereo e Achilleo
    S. Prassede
    S. Susanna
    SS. Trinità dei Monti
Noleti, Orsola
    S. Andrea delle Fratte
Nolli, Giovanni Battista (1701–56)
    SS. Alessio e Bonifazio
        all'Aventino
    S. Dorotea
Nucci, Avanzino (c. 1552–1629)
    S. Agostino
    S. Andrea delle Fratte
    S. Calisto
    S. Giovanni in Laterano,
        Scala Santa
    S. Maria in Aracoeli
    S. Silvestro al Quirinale
Nussbaumer, Michael (1785–1861)
    S. Maria dell' Anima
Nuvolone, Francesco (rec. 1686–96)
    Il Gesù

INDEX OF ARTISTS

S. Ignazio
S. Maria in Vallicella
Obici, Giuseppe (1807–78)
  S. Maria sopra Minerva
Odam, Girolamo (b. 1681)
  S. Onofrio
Odazzi, Giovanni (1663–1731)
  S. Andrea delle Fratte
  S. Andrea al Quirinale
  S. Antonio Abate
  S. Antonio dei Portoghesi
  SS. Apostoli
  S. Bernardo alle Terme
  S. Clemente
  S. Giovanni Battista
    dei Genovesi
  S. Giovanni in Laterano
  S. Maria degli Angeli
  S. Maria in Aracoeli
  S. Maria della Scala
  S. Maria in Via Lata
  S. Prisca
  S. Sabina
  S. Stefano del Cacco
  Stimmate di S. Francesco
Olivieri, Pietro Paolo (1551–99)
  S. Francesca Romana
  S. Giovanni in Laterano
  S. Maria in Aracoeli
  S. Maria Maggiore
  S. Pudenziana
Omodei, Luigi Alessandro
  (1608–85)
  SS. Carlo e Ambrogio al Corso
Orazi, Andrea Antonio
  (1670–after 1724)
  S. Maria Maddalena
  S. Maria dell'Orto
  S. Maria della Vittoria
Orazi, Giuseppe (early 18th century)
  S. Maria dell'Orto
  S. Maria della Vittoria
Orlandi, Clemente (1704–1775)
  Oratorio del Caravita
  S. Mara in Campo Marzo
  S. Nicola dei Lorenesi
  S. Paolo Primo Eremita
Orsi, Prospero (c. 1558–c. 1633)
  S. Giovanni in Laterano and
    Scala Santa
Ossani, Andrea (rec. 1783)
  S. Maria del Suffragio
Ottaviani, Michele (19th century)
  SS. Alessio e Bonifazio
    all'Aventino
Ottin, Auguste Louis Marie (1811–90)
  S. Luigi dei Francesi
Ottini, Felice (d. 1695)
  Gesù e Maria
Ottoni, Lorenzo (1648–1726)

S. Angelo in Pescheria
S. Carlo ai Catinari
SS. Croce e Bonaventura
  dei Lucchesi
S. Eustachio
S. Francesco a Ripa
Il Gesù
Gesù e Maria
S. Giovanni in Laterano
S. Lorenzo in Damaso
S. Maria in Aquiro
S. Maria in Camposanto
S. Maria in Campitelli
S. Maria ad Martyres
S. Maria in Publicolis
S. Maria in Trastevere
S. Pietro in Vaticano
S. Silvestro in Capite
SS. Trinità in Palazzo
  Monte di Pietà
Pace, Luigi (rec. 1516)
  S. Maria del Popolo
Pacetti, Camillo (1758–1826)
  S. Andrea delle Fratte
  S. Nicola da Tolentino
Pacetti, Giuseppe (1782–1839)
  SS. Vincenzo e Anastasio
Pacetti, Vincenzo (c. 1746–1820)
  S. Lorenzo in Lucina
  SS. Michele e Magno
  S. Maria del Pianto
  S. Salvatore in Lauro
Pacilli, Carlo (rec. 1734–35)
  S. Giovanni dei Fiorentini
Pacilli, Pietro (1716–72)
  SS. Carlo e Ambrogio al Corso
  S. Crisogono
  S. Marco
  S. Maria Maddalena
  S. Pietro in Vaticano
  SS. Trinità dei Spagnuoli
Paglia, Giuseppe (c. 1616–83)
  SS. Ildefonso e Tommaso
    di Villanova
  S. Maria sopra Minerva
Pagliari, Pompeo (early 17th century)
  S. Giovanni dei Fiorentini
Pagni, Giovanni (mid 17th century)
  S. Maria del Pianto
Paladino, Giuseppe (1721–94)
  SS. Trinità degli Spagnuoli
Palombini, Giuseppe (19th century)
  S. Maria Maddalena
Palazzi, Giuseppe (c. 1740–1810)
  S. Caterina da Siena
  S. Giovanni dei Fiorentini
Pallière, Luigi (early 19th century)
  SS. Trinità dei Monti
Palliotti, Vincenzo (d. 1894)
  S. Giuseppe alla Lungara

Palma il Giovane (c. 1548–1628)
  S. Pancrazio
Palma, Alessandro (rec. 1702–03)
  S. Pietero in Vaticano, Piazza
Palma, Joseph (rec. 1762)
  S. Maria Maddalena
Palombi (18th century)
  S. Bernardino ai Monti
Palombo, Bartolomeo see
  Bartolomeo Colombo
Panaria, Matteo
  (active 1747–d. after 1768)
  S. Pasquale Baylon
Panci, Pietropalo (rec. 1758–62)
  S. Maria in Aracoeli
Pannerio, Matteo see Matteo Panaria
Pannini, Giovanni Paolo
  (1691/92–1765)
  S. Croce in Gerusalemme
  S. Maria della Scala
Pannini, Giuseppe (1718–c. 1810)
  S. Maria della Scala
Pannozza, Giovanni
  (mid 18 century)
  S. Maria Maddalena
Paoletti, Pietro (1801–47)
  S. Isidoro
Paolini, Pio (1620–92)
  SS. Carlo e Ambrogio al Corso
Papaleo, Pietro (c. 1642–1718)
  SS. Apostoli
  S. Maria di Montesanto
  S. Maria della Scala
  S. Sebastiano fuori le Mura
Papi, Angelo (rec. 1760–86)
  S. Maria inTraspontina
  SS. Trinità dei Pellegrini
Paracca, Giovanni Antonio the
  Elder called Il Valsoldo
  (?–1597)
  S. Giovanni in Laterano
  S. Lorenzo in Panisperna
  S. Maria Maggiore
  S. Maria del Popolo
  S. Maria in Trastevere
  S. Maria in Vallicella
  S. Susanna
  SS. Trinità dei Monti
Paracca, Giovanni Antonio the
  Younger (rec. 1598–d. 1646)
  S. Maria Maggiore
  S. Maria sopra Minerva
  S. Pietro in Vaticano
  S. Pudenziana
Paradisi, Domenico (c. 1660–1727)
  S. Cecilia
  S. Maria in Via Lata
Parisi, Ambrogio (c. 1644–1719)
  S. Barbara dei Librai
  S. Pudenziana

Parker, John (1710–60)
    S. Gregorio al Celio
Parmigiano, Fabrizio
    (1555/60–1600/07)
    S. Cecilia in Trastevere
Parodi, Domenico (1672–1742)
    S. Maria dell'Orto
    S. Maria in Vallicella
    S. Susanna
Parodi, Filippo (17th century)
    S. Maria di Monterone
Parodi, Giovanni Battista
    (1674–1730)
    S. Maria dell'Orto
    S. Pietro in Vincoli
Parodini, Domenico (rec. c.1708)
    S. Susanna
Parrocel, Etienne (1696–1774)
    S. Anastasia
    SS. Annunziata a Tor de' Specchi
    S. Caterina da Siena
    S. Gregorio a Ponte Quattro Capi
    S. Luigi dei Francesi
    S. Maria Maddalena
    S. Maria in Monticelli
    S. Maria in Trastevere
    S. Prassede
Pascucci, Francesco (1748–after 1803)
    SS. Vincenzo e Anastasio
Pasqualini, Pasquale (d. c. 1649)
    S. Carlo ai Catinari
    S. Maria dell'Umiltà
Pasqualoni, Vincenzo (1820–1880)
    S. Chiara
    S. Maria in Aquiro
    S. Nicola in Carcere
    S. Nicola dei Prefetti
Passalacqua, Melchiorre
    (mid 18th century)
    S. Eustachio
Passalacqua, Pietro (1690–1748)
    SS. Annunziata, Oratory of the
    S. Croce in Gerusalemme
    S. Francesco d'Assisi a Monte Mario
Passarotti Passarotto
    (1562–after 1615)
    S. Paolo dell Tre Fontane
Passeri, Giuseppe (1654–1714)
    S. Barbara dei Librai
    S. Caterina da Siena a Magnanapoli
    S. Croce in Gerusalemme
    S. Francesco a Ripa
    S. Giacomo degli Incurabili
    S. Maria in Aracoeli
    S. Maria in Campitelli
    S. Maria in Vallicella
    S. Pietro in Vaticano *

S. Sebastiano fuori le Mura
Spirito Santo dei Napoletani
S. Tommaso in Parione
Passignano see Domenico Cresti
Pastura il, see Antonio Massaro
Patichio, Giacomo (rec. 1791)
    Gesù e Maria
Patriarca, Pietro Giacomo
    (rec. 1680–d. 1715)
    S. Brigida
Pavoni, Stefano (rec. 1499–1500)
    S. Maria del Popolo
Pécheux, Laurent (1729–1821)
    S. Caterina da Siena
Pedero de Rubiales (Pietro Roviale Spagnuolo) (1511?–c. 60)
    Oratorio del Gonfalone
    S. Maria di Monserrato
    S. Spirito in Sassia
Pellegrini, Carlo (1605–49)
    S. Pietro in Vaticano
    SS. Re Magi
Pellegrino da Modena
    (before 1465–c. 1523/24)
    S. Giacomo degli Spagnuoli
Penna, Agostino (rec. c. 1730–1800)
    SS. Carlo e Ambrogio al Corso
    S. Eustachio
    S. Maria del Popolo
    S. Martino ai Monti
    S. Paolo Primo Eremita
    S. Pietro in Vaticano
Penitz, Giuseppe see
    Joseph Heintz the Elder
Peparelli, Francesco (c. 1585–1641)
    SS. Annunziate
    S. Brigida
    S. Caio
    S. Francesco a Ripa
    Il Gesù
    S. Girolamo della Carità
    S. Maria in Traspontina
    S. Maria delle Vergini
    S. Salvatore in Campo
Peracca, Giovanni Antonio see
    Giovanni Antonio Paracca
Perfetti, Giovanni Antonio (d. 1754)
    S. Biagio della Pagnotta
    SS. Croce e Bonaventura dei Lucchesi
Perini, Francesco (rec. 1681–83)
    Gesù e Maria
Perini, Ottavio (rec. 1791)
    S. Maria dell'Anima
Perini, Francesco (17th century)
    S. Spirito in Sassia
Perino del Vaga (1501–47)
    S. Giovanni Decollato, Oratory
    S. Luigi dei Francesi
    S. Marcello

S. Stefano del Cacco
SS. Trinità dei Monti
Peroni, Giuseppe (1626–62)
    S. Agnese in Agone
    SS. Apostoli
    S. Maria del Popolo
Perrugini, Stefano (rec. 1645)
    S. Francesco di Paola
Perugino, Pietro Vannuci
    (c. 1450–1524)
    S. Pietro in Vaticano, Cappella Sistina
Peruzzi, Augusto (b. 1838)
    S. Lorenzo in Lucina
Peruzzi, Baldassare (1481–1536)
    S. Giacomo degli Incurabili
    S. Maria dell'Anima
    S. Maria della Pace
    S. Maria Porta Paradisi
    S. Maria in Trastevere
    S. Onofrio
    S. Rocco
Peruzzi, Salustio (d. 1573)
    S. Maria in Traspontina
Peruzzini, Giovanni (c. 1629–94)
    S. Salvatore in Lauro
Pesci, Girolamo (1679–1759)
    S. Giuseppe alla Lungara
    S. Maria Maddalena
    S. Onofrio
    Stimmate di S. Francesco
Petraglia, Battista (d. 1637)
    SS. Domenico e Sisto
Petraglia, Francesco (rec. 1639)
    SS. Domenico e Sisto
Petrarca, Antonio
    (late 16th century)
    S. Giovanni in Laterano
Petrazzi, Astolfo (1579–1665)
    S. Giovanni dei Fiorentini
Petta di Caprancia, Marcantonio
    (rec. 1573–76)
    S. Spirito in Sassia
Pettrich, Ferdinand (1789–1872)
    S. Maria degli Angeli
    S. Maria in Campitelli
Piancastelli, Giovanni
    (19th century)
    S. Giovanni in Laterano
Pianello, Giovan Battista
    (1812–after 66)
    S. Paolo fuori le Mura
Piastrini, Giovanni Domenico
    (1678–1740)
    S. Clemente
    SS. Giovanni e Paolo
    S. Maria in Via, Largo Chigi
    S. Maria in Via Lata
    S. Prassede
Piazza, Paolo (Padre Cosimoda

INDEX OF ARTISTS

    Bassano) (1560–1620)
  S. Maria in Trivio
Piccardi, Angelo (19th century)
  S. Prassede
Piccioli, Litardo (16th century)
  S. Spirito in Sassia
Piccioni, Niccola Lorenzo
  (rec. 1747–64)
  S. Eusebio
  S. Francesco di Paola
  S. Giovanni in Laterano,
    Baptistery
  S. Maria della Luce
Piccioni, Matteo (1615–1671)
  S. Maria in Vallicella
  S. Martino ai Monti
Piccoli, Carlo (19th century)
  S. Onofrio
Pichi, Francesco (rec. 1552)
  S. Maria in Aracoeli
Pieri, Stefano (1542–1629)
  S. Prassede
Piernicoli, Benedetto (rec. 1818)
  S. Macuto
Pieroni, Domenico (rec. 1869)
  S. Maria in Monterone
Pietri, Pietro de' (1663–1716)
  S. Clemente
  S. Maria delle Grazie
    alle Fornaci
  S. Maria in Via Lata
Pietro (Berrettini) da Cortona
  (1597–1669)
  S. Bibiana
  SS. Carlo e Ambrogio al Corso
  S. Carlo ai Catinari
  Il Gesù
  S. Giovanni dei Fiorentini
  S. Giovanni in Laterano
  S. Girolamo della Carità
  S. Ivo della Sapienza
  S. Lorenzo in Damaso
  S. Lorenzo in Miranda
  S. Lorenzo fuori le Mura
  SS. Luca e Martina
  S. Marco
  S. Maria della Concezione
  S. Maria sopra Minerva
  S. Maria della Pace
  S. Maria in Vallicella
  S. Maria in Via Lata
  S. Nicola da Tolentino
  S. Pietro in Vaticano
  S. Salvatore in Lauro
  S. Sebastiano fuori le Mura
  S. Stefano del Cacco *
Pilotti, Giovanni (rec. 1637)
  Il Gesù
Pincellotti, Bartolomeo (c. 1708–40)
  S. Agostino

  S. Giovanni in Laterano
  S. Lorenzo in Damaso
  S. Maria sopra Minerva
Pincellotti, Francesco (. 1672–1749)
  S. Francesco a Ripa
  S. Pietro in Vaticano, Piazza
Pino, Marco (1521–87/88)
  S. Eligio degli Orefici
  Oratorio del Gonfalone
  S. Maria in Aracoeli
  S. Maria della Concezione
  S. Spirito Sassia
  SS. Trinità dei Monti
Pinson, Nicolas (1640–after 1672)
  S. Luigi dei Francesi
Pinturicchio (c. 1454–1513)
  S. Maria in Aracoeli
  S. Maria del Popolo
  S. Pietro in Montorio
Pioselli, Giovanni Domenico
  (rec. 1696)
  S. Salvatore in Lauro
Pippi, Nicolas (Nicolò d'Arras)
  (?–1599)
  S. Alessio e Bonifazio
    all'Aventino
  S. Giovanni in Laterano
  S. Luigi dei Francesi
  S. Maria dell' Anima
  S. Maria Maggiore
  S. Maria del Popolo
  S. Maria in Trastevere
Piranesi, Giovanni Battista (1720–78)
  S. Giovanni in Laterano
  S. Maria del Priorato
Pirovani, Giuseppe (c. 1755–c. 1835)
  S. Francesca Romana
Pirri, Giovanni (rec. 1776)
  S. Maria del Carmine
    alle Tre Cannelle
Pistrucci, Camillo (1811–54)
  S. Francesco a Ripa
Plancic, Giuseppe
  S. Girolamo degli Schiavoni
Podesti, Francesco (1800–95)
  S. Paolo fuori le Mura
Poggi, Valerio (17th century)
  SS. Re Magi
Polenzani, Giovan Battista
  (19th century)
  S. Marcello
Poletti, Luigi (1792–1869)
  S. Maria del Popolo
  S. Paolo fuori le Mura
  S. Salvatore in Lauro
Poli, Francesco (rec. 1671)
  SS. Carlo e Ambrogio al Corso
Polidoro (Caldara) da Caravaggio
  (1499/1500–43)
  S. Maria in Camposanto

  S. Silvestro al Quirinale
Pollaiuolo, Antonio (1431/32–98)
  S. Pietro in Vaticano
Pomis, Giacomo (16th century)
  S. Maria dei Monti
Ponfreni, see Giovanni Battista
  Bonfreni
Pontelli, Baccio (c. 1450–1492)
  S. Agostino
  SS. Apostoli
  S. Maria della Pace
  S. Pietro in Montorio
  S. Pietro in Vaticano,
    Cappella Sistina
Ponti, Domenico (rec. 1677)
  S. Anastasia al Palatino
Ponzio, Flaminio (1560–1613)
  S. Anastasia
  S. Andrea della Valle
  S. Eligio degli Orefici
  S. Gregorio al Celio,
    Oratorio di S. Andrea
  S. Maria Maggiore
  S. Maria sopra Minerva
  S. Sebastiano fuori le Mura
Porciani, Carlo (early 18th century)
  S. Francesco di Paola
  S. Gregorio al Celio
  S. Maria dell'Orto
Porciani, Pietro (early 18th century)
  S. Francesco di Paola
  S. Prassede
  S. Sebastiano fuori le Mura
Porciani, Sebatiano (18th century)
  S. Giuliano dei Fiamminghi
Pordenone, Giovanni Antonio de
  Lodesan (c. 1484–1539)
  S. Maria dei Sette Dolori *
Porretti, Eugenio
  S. Lucia del Gonfalone
Posi, Paolo (1708–76)
  S. Agostino
  SS. Alessio e Bonifazio
    all'Aventino
  S. Andrea delle Fratte
  S. Andrea della Valle
  SS. Carlo e Ambrogio al Corso
  S. Caterina da Siena
  S. Maria dell' Anima
  S. Maria ad Martyres
  S. Maria dell'Orazione e della
    Morte
  S. Maria del Popolo
Possenet, Michele Paolini del
  (mid 18th century)
  S. Eustachio
Pourbus, Francesco (1569–1622)
  SS. Carlo e Ambrogio al Corso
Poussin, Claude (rec. 1644–61)
  Il Gesù

342

Poussin, Nicolas (1594–1665)
  S. Luigi dei Francesi
  S. Pietro in Vaticano *
Pozzi, Andrea (1777–1837)
  S. Egidio
Pozzi, Domenico (d. 1638)
  SS. Trinità dei Pellegrini
Pozzi, Francesco (1790–1844)
  SS. Apostoli
Pozzi, Jacomo (rec. 1680–82)
  S. Anastasia
Pozzo, Andrea (1642–1709)
  S. Apollinare
  S. Francesca Romana
  Il Gesù
  S. Ignazio
  S. Tommaso di Canterbury
  SS. Trinità dei Monti
Pozzo, Andrea (1777–1837)
  S. Maria in Campitelli
Pozzo, Giovan Battista (c. 1563–91)
  Il Gesù
  S. Giovanni in Laterano
  S. Maria Maggiore
  S. Susanna
Pozzo, Filippo (rec. 1600)
  S. Paolo alle Tre Fontane
Pozzo, Stefano (1699–1768)
  S. Apollinare
  S. Francesca Romana
  S. Francesco di Paola
  S. Ignazio
  S. Maria Maggiore
  SS. Nome di Maria
  S. Silvestro al Quirinale
Prata, Battista (rec. 1600–03)
  S. Cesareo
Preciado de la Vega, Francisco (1713–89)
  S. Maria Monserrato
  S. Pasquale Baylon
  SS. Trinità degli Spagnuoli
Prenner, Georg Kasper von (1720–66)
  S. Dorotea
Prestinaro, Domenico (rec. 1611–48)
  S. Crisogono
  S. Pietro in Vaticano
Presutti, Giuliano (rec. 1499–1554)
  SS. Trinità degli Spagnuoli
Preti, Gregorio (d. 1672)
  S. Carlo ai Catinari
  S. Giovanni Calabita
  SS. Quirico e Giulitta
  S. Rocco
Preti, Mattia (1613–99)
  S. Andrea della Valle
  S. Carlo ai Catinari
Prinoti, G. (17th century)
  S. Maria in Monticelli

Prinizi, Giuseppe (1833–93)
  S. Andrea della Valle
  S. Lorenzo in Damaso
Procaccini, Andrea (1671–1734)
  S. Giovanni in Laterano
  S. Maria degli Angeli
  S. Maria sopra Minerva
  S. Maria dell'Orto
  S. Pietro in Vaticano
Prosperi, Cristoforo (rec. 1793–1868)
  S. Carlo ai Catinari
  SS. Giovanni e Paolo
Prosperi, Filippo (1831–1913)
  Madonna del Divino Amore
Protopapa, Girolamo (rec. 1702–03)
  S. Pietro in Vaticano, Piazza
Provenzale, Ippolito (rec. 1624)
  S. Crisogono
Puccetti, Giovanni Battista (1693–1743)
  S. Giovanni in Laterano
  S. Maria in Monticelli
Puccini, Blasinus (rec. 1717)
  S. Bernardino ai Monti
Puccini, Biagio (1673–1721)
  S. Agata in Trastevere
  S. Brigida
  S. Caterina da Siena a Magnanapoli
  SS. Croce e Bonaventura dei Lucchesi
  S. Eustachio
  S. Maria Maddalena
  S. Maria di Montesanto
  S. Maria in Traspontina
  S. Paolo alla Regola
Puglia, Giuseppe, il Bastaro (c. 1600–36)
  S. Girolamo degli Schiavoni
  S. Giuseppe dei Falegnami
  S. Maria Maggiore
Pulzone, Scipione (c. 1550–98)
  S. Caterina dei Funari
  S. Eligio dei Ferrari
  Il Gesù
  S. Giovanni in Laterano
  S. Maria in Vallicella
  S. Silvestro al Quirinale
Quadri, Carlo (rec. 1696–99)
  S. Maria Maddalena
Quadroli, Pietro (19th century)
  S. Maria della Vittoria
Quagliata, Giovanni Battista (1603–c. 73)
  SS. Croce e Bonaventura dei Lucchesi
Quattrini, Enrico (1863–1950)
  S. Cecilia
Queirolo, Francesco (1704–62)
  S. Andrea delle Fratte

S. Giovanni dei Fiorentini
S. Maria Maggiore
SS. Nome di Maria
Rabacchi, T. (19th century)
  S. Agostino
Radi, Agostino (d. 1655)
  S. Bibiana
Raffaele da Roma (1805)
  S. Maria Concezione
Raffaelli, Giuseppe (rec. 1696–1731)
  S. Maria in Campitelli
  S. Maria Maddalena
  S. Maria in Vallicella
  S. Pietro in Vaticano
Raffaellino (Motta) da Reggio (1550–78)
  S. Caterina dei Funari
  Oratorio del Gonfalone
  SS. Quattro Coronati, Oratory
  S. Silvestro al Quirinale
Raffaello (Sinibaldi) da Montelupo (c. 1505–c. 66)
  S. Maria della Consolazione
  S. Maria sopra Minerva
  S. Maria della Pace
  S. Pietro in Vincoli
Raggi, Antonio (1624–86)
  S. Agnese in Agone
  S. Andrea al Quirinale
  S. Andrea della Valle
  S. Carlo ai Quattro Fontane
  SS. Domenico e Sisto
  Il Gesù
  S. Giovanni dei Fiorentini
  S. Giovanni in Laterano
  S. Girolamo della Carità
  S. Marcello
  S. Marco
  S. Maria sopra Minerva
  S. Maria dei Miracoli
  S. Maria della Pace
  S. Maria del Popolo
  S. Maria dell'Umiltà
  S. Nicola da Tolentino
  S. Pietro in Vaticano
  SS. Vincenzo e Anastasio
Ragusa, Francesco (rec. 1591–1665)
  S. Barbara dei Librai
  S. Maria del Popolo
  S. Maria Scala Coeli
Raguzzini, Filippo (rec. 1680–1771)
  SS. Bartolomeo e Alessandro dei Bergamaschi
  S. Filippo Neri
  S. Gallicano
  Madonna del Divino Amore
  S. Maria in Aracoeli
  S. Maria in Domnica
  S. Maria sopra Minerva
  S. Maria della Quercia

INDEX OF ARTISTS

S. Maria in Trastevere
SS. Quirico e Giulitta
S. Sisto Vecchio
Spirito Santo dei Napoletani
Raimond, Quintilliano
   (rec. 1838–50)
S. Giovanni in Laterano
Rainaldi, Carlo (1611–91)
  S. Agnese in Agone
  S. Andrea della Valle
  S. Angelo Custode
  S. Antonio dei Portoghesi
  SS. Apostoli
  S. Carlo ai Catinari
  Gesù e Maria
  S. Giovanni in Laterano,
    Baptistery
  S. Girolamo della Carità
  S. Ignazio
  S. Lorenzo in Lucina
  S. Maria in Aracoeli
  S. Maria in Campitelli
  S. Maria Maggiore
  S. Maria sopra Minerva
  S. Maria dei Miracoli and
  S. Maria di Montesanto
  S. Maria della Scala
  S. Maria del Suffragio
  S. Maria in Vallicella
  S. Maria in Via, Largo Chigi
  S. Nicola da Tolentino
  S. Silvestro in Capite
  SS. Sudario dei Piemontesi
Rainaldi, Domenico (1619–98)
  S. Lorenzo in Lucina
Rainaldi, Francesco
  (second half of the
  17th century)
  S. Ignazio
Rainaldi, Girolamo (1570–1655)
  S. Agnese in Agone
  S. Carlo ai Catinari
  S. Cecilia
  Il Gesù
  S. Giovanni in Laterano
  S. Maria in Aracoeli
  SS. Luca e Martina
  S. Maria Maggiore
  S. Maria sopra Minerva
  S. Maria della Scala
  S. Rocco
Rambotti, Sebastiano (rec. 1718- 49)
  SS. Apostoli
Ranucci, Giuseppe
  (c. 1690–d. after 1757)
  SS. Celso e Giuliano
  S. Lorenzo in Panisperna
  S. Maria dell'Orto
Raphael (Raffaello Santi)
  (1483–1520)

S. Agostino
S. Eligio degli Orefici
SS. Luca e Martina *
S. Luigi dei Francesi *
S. Maria dei Miracoli and
S. Maria di Montesanto
S. Maria della Pace
S. Maria del Popolo
S. Pietro in Montorio *
S. Pietro in Vaticano
Raspantini, Antonio Liborio
  SS. Venanzio e Ansovino
Rasina, Pietro (d. after 1716)
  S. Clemente
Ravaglini, Giuseppe (rec. 1793)
  SS. Giovanni e Paolo
Razzinello, Jacomo (17th century)
  S. Lorenzo in Damaso
Recalcati, Giacomo Onorato
  (1684–1723)
  S. Agata in Trastevere
  S. Maria in Trastevere
Regiani, Paolo (rec. 1693–1706)
  S. Pietro in Vaticano
Régnier, Nicolas (1591–1667)
  S. Giovanni Battista
    dei Genovesi
Reiffi, Pietro see Pietro Reyff
Reni, Guido (1575–1642)
  S. Angelo in Pescheria*
  S. Carlo ai Catinari
  S. Cecilia
  S. Francesca Romana*
  S. Francesco a Ripa*
  S. Giovanni in Laterano and
    Baptistery
  S. Gregorio al Celio,
    Oratorio di S. Andrea and
    S. Sylvia
  S. Lorenzo in Lucina
  S. Luigi dei Francesi
  SS. Marcellino e Pietro *
  S. Maria della Concezione
  S. Maria Maggiore
  S. Maria sopra Minerva
  S. Maria dell'Orazione
    e della Morte *
  S. Maria in Vallicella
  S. Maria della Vittoria *
  S. Paolo alle Tre Fontane *
  S. Pietro in Montorio
  S. Pietro in Vaticano *
  S. Sebastian fuori le Mura
  Stimmate di S. Francesco *
  SS. Trinità dei Pellegrini
Renzi, Cesare (rec. 1581)
  Oratorio del Gonfalone
Renzi, Filippo (17th century)
  Il Gesù
Reth, Gian Giacomo (rec. 1660)

S. Giacomo degli Incurabili
Retrosi, Emilio (1858–1911)
  SS. Bartolomeo e Alessandro
    dei Bergamaschi
Retti, Leonardo (rec. 1666–1714)
  S. Agnese in Agone
  Il Gesù
  S. Giovanni dei Fiorentini
  S. Maria dell'Orto
  S. Maria in Traspontina
  S. Marta
  S. Pietro in Vaticano
  S. Pudenziana
Revelli, Savatore (1816–59)
  S. Cecilia
Reyff, Pietro (1661–1711)
  Il Gesù
Riccardi, Giuseppe (rec. 1702–36)
  S. Giovanni in Laterano
  S. Pietro in Vaticano, Piazza
  SS. Trinità dei Pellegrini
Ricci, Archita (rec. 1599–1619)
  S. Sebastiano fuori le Mura
Ricci, Sebastiano (1659–1734)
  SS. Apostoli
  S. Pantaleo
Ricci da Novara, Giovanni Battista
  (1537/45 [c. 1550]–1627)
  S. Agostino
  S. Francesco a Ripa
  S. Giovanni in Laterano and
    Scala Santa
  S. Girolamo della Carità
  S. Gregorio al Celio
  S. Marcello
  S. Maria Maggiore
  S. Maria del Popolo
  S. Maria in Traspontina
  S. Onofrio
  S. Pietro in Vaticano
  SS. Trinità dei Pellegrini
Ricciolini, Michelangelo (1654–1715)
  S. Maria in Campitelli
Ricciolini, Nicolò (1687–1772)
  S. Giuseppe alla Lungara
  S. Maria degli Angeli
  S. Maria della Grazie
    alle Fornaci
  SS. Michele e Magno
  Natività di Gesù
  SS. Nome di Maria
  S. Pietro in Vaticano
Ridolfi, Claudio (1560–1644)
  S. Onofrio
Righetti, Francesco (1805–?)
  SS. Carlo e Ambrogio al Corso
Righetti, Luigi (1780–1852)
  SS. Carlo e Ambrogio al Corso
Righi, Angelo (rec. 1588–89)
  S. Giovanni in Laterano,

Scala Santa
Righi, Tommaso (1727–1802)
  S. Brigida
  SS. Carlo e Ambrogio al Corso
  S. Eusebio
  S. Filippo Neri
  S. Giovanni in Laterano,
    Baptistery
  SS. Luca e Martina
  S. Marcello
  S. Maria del Priorato
  S. Maria in Publicolis
  S. Paolo Prima Eremite
Rinaldi, Costantino (19th century)
  S. Maria in Aquiro
Rinaldi, Giovanni (rec. 1661–79)
  S. Andrea al Quirinale
  S. Pietro in Vaticano
  SS. Trinità dei Monti
Rinaldi, Giuseppe (19th century)
  S. Lucia de Gonfalone
Rinaldi, Rinaldo (1793–1873)
  S. Bernardo alle Terme
  S. Carlo ai Catinari
  SS. Croce e Bonaventura
    dei Lucchesi
  Gesù e Maria
  S. Luigi dei Francesi
  S. Marcello
  S. Maria sopra Minerva
  S. Maria in Trastevere
  S. Paolo fuori le Mura
  S. Salvatore in Lauro
Ripanda, Jacopo (c. 1490–1530)
Rioli, Francesco (rec. 1671)
  S. Marcello
  S. Onofrio
Ripoli, Giovanni Tommaso
    (rec. 1666–82)
  S. Anastasia
  S. Spirito in Sassia
Ripoli, Pietro Antonio
    (rec. 1673–82)
  S. Maria in Traspontina
  S. Pietro in Vincoli
  S. Salvatore in Lauro
  S. Spirito in Sassia
Rivi, I. (19th century)
  S. Lorenzo in Lucina
Rocca, Giacomo
    (active 1560–after 1596)
  Oratorio del Gonfalone
  S. Maria degli Angeli
  S. Pietro in Montorio
Rocca, Michele (1675–c. 1751)
  S. Francesca Romana
  S. Maria Maddalena
  S. Paolo alla Regola
Rodriguez, Emanuele
    (Manuel Rodriguez dos
Santos) (c. 1702–64)
  Bambino Gesù
  S. Maria Maddalena
  SS. Trinità degli Spagnuoli
Romagnoli, Domenico (rec. 1779)
  S. Antonio dei Portoghesi
  S. Maria dell' Anima
Romanelli, Giovanni Francesco
    (1610/11–62)
  S. Agostin
  S. Carlo ai Catinari
  S. Carlo alle Quattro Fontane
  SS. Domenico e Sisto
  S. Eligio degli Orefici
  S. Giacomo all Lungara
  S. Marco
  S. Maria degli Angeli
  S. Maria dell' Anima
  S. Maria in Vallicella, Oratory
  S. Pietro in Montorio
  Pietro in Vaticano
Romano, Gian Cristoforo
    (1470–1512)
  S. Maria del Popolo
Romano, Giovanni Francesco
    (rec. 1757)
  S. Lorenzo in Panisperna
Romano, Giulio see
    Giulio Romano
Romoli, Marcantonio
    (mid 18th century)
  S. Andrea delle Fratte
Ronca, Antonio
    (c. 1641–after 1686/87)
  S. Francesco di Paola
Roncalli, Carlo (rec. 1700–28)
  S. Clemente
  S. Maria sopra Minerva
Roncalli, Cristoforo (il Pomarancio)
    (1552–1626)
  S. Andrea della Valle
  SS. Carlo e Ambrogio al Corso
  SS. Crocifisso, Oratorio del
  S. Egidio
  S. Giacomo degli Incurabili
  S. Giovanni Decollato
  S. Giovanni in Laterano
  S. Gregorio al Celio
    Oratorio di S. Andrea
  S. Maria degli Angeli
  S. Maria in Aracoeli
  S. Maria della Consolazione
  S. Maria della Scala
  S. Maria in Vallicella
  SS. Nero e Achilleo
  S. Pietro in Vaticano
  S. Silvestro in Capite
  S. Silvestro in Quirinale
Roncati, Antonio (rec. 1674)
  S. Marta
Ronconi, Vittorio (d.1614)
  S. Gregorio al Celio
Rondone, Alessandro
    (rec. 1674–1710)
  S. Andrea della Valle
  S. Maria di Montesanto
  S. Maria in Traspontina
  S. Pietro in Vaticano, Piazza
Sordo d'Urbino see Antonio Viviani
Rosa, Francesco (1638–87)
  S. Agostino
  SS. Carlo e Ambrogio al Corso
  S. Caterina da Siena
    a Magnanapoli
  S. Maria ad Martyres
  S. Rocco
Rosa, Francesco Giuseppe
    (rec. 1715–50)
  S. Maria Maddalena
Rosa, Salvator (1615–73)
  S. Giovanni dei Fiorentini
Rosa, Sigismondo (rec. 1716)
  S. Lorenzo in Lucina
  Madonna del Divino Amore
Rosati, Rosato (c. 1560–1622)
  S. Carlo ai Catinari
Roselli, Piero (1473?–1531)
  S. Pietro in Vaticano,
    Cappella Sistina
  S. Silvesto in Capite
Rosis, Giovanni Battista de
    (1538–1610)
  Il Gesù
Rosselli, Cosimo (1439–1507)
  S. Pierto in Vaticano,
    Cappella Sistina
Rosselli, Piero di Jacopo
  S. Silvestro in Capite
Rossellino, Bernardo (1409–64)
  S. Stefano Rotondo
Rossetti, Cesare (c. 1565–1644)
  S. Cesareo
  S. Eusebio
  S. Maria in Traspontina
  S. Prassede
Rossetti, Giovan Paolo (d. 1586)
  SS. Trinità dei Monti
Rossetti, Paolo (active 1579–1621)
  S. Pudenziana
  S. Maria di Loreto
Rossi, Angelo de' (1671–1715)
  Il Gesù
  S. Giovanni in Laterano
  S. Pietro in Vaticano
Rossi, Bartolomeo de' (rec. 1625–34)
  S. Agata dei Goti
  S. Giuseppe dei Falegnami
  S. Pietro in Vaticano
Rossi, Bastiano and Battista de'
    (early 17th century)

INDEX OF ARTISTS

S. Susanna
Rossi, Casimiro de (1818–76)
  S. Maria del Popolo
  S. Paolo fuori le Mura
Rossi, Domenico (scalpellino)
  (rec. 1640)
  S. Carlo alle Quattro Fontane
Rossi, Domenico de' (sculptor)
  (rec. 1627–51)
  S. Giovanni in Laterano
  S. Maria di Loreto
  S. Maria Porta Paradisi
  S. Maria della Vittoria
  S. Pietro in Vaticano
Rossi, Domenico de' (architect)
  (1659–1703)
  S. Silvestro in Capite
Rossi, Francesco de' see
  Francesco Salviati
Rossi, Francesco de' (rec. 1640–77)
  S. Maria del Popolo
  S. Susanna
Rossi, Giovanni de' (1538–1610)
  Il Gesù
Rossi, Giovanni Antonio de'
  (1616–95)
  S. Francesco di Paola
  S. Giovanni in Laterano
  S. Giuseppe a Capo le Case
  S. Maria in Campitelli
  S. Maria in Campo Marzio
  S. Maria Maddalena
  S. Maria Porta Paradisi
  S. Maria in Publicolis
  S. Pantaleo
  S. Rocco
  SS. Trinità in Palazzo
    Monte di Pietà
Rossi, Giovanni Battista de'
  (first half of the
  18th century)
  S. Anna dei Palafrenieri
  S. Giovanni in Laterano
  S. Gregorio al Celio
  S. Maria degli Angeli
  S. Maria in Trastevere
Rossi, Giovanni Francesco de'
  (rec. 1640–77)
  S. Agnese in Agone
  S. Caterina da Siena
    a Magnanapoli
  S. Giovanni in Laterano
  S. Isidoro
  S. Marcello
  S. Maria sopra Minerva
  S. Maria in Vallicella
  S. Nicola da Tolentino
  S. Pietro in Vaticano
Rossi, Giovanni Maria de'
  (c. 1636–1704)

S. Marcello
S. Maria in Montesanto
S. Pietro in Vaticano, Piazza
Rossi, Girolamo (rec. 1748–50)
  S. Maria in Aracoeli
Rossi, Gregorio de'
  (c. 1570–1637/43)
  S. Andrea della Valle
  S. Maria Maggiore
  S. Pietro in Vaticano
Rossi, Mariano (1731–1807)
  S. Giuseppe alla Lungara
  S. Lucia del Gonfalone
  S. Maria in Aracoeli
  S. Maria dei Monti
Rossi, Mattia de' (1637–95)
  S. Anastasia
  S. Andrea al Quirinale
  S. Angelo in Custode
  S. Francesco di Paola
  S. Francesco a Ripa
  S. Maria in Aquiro
  S. Maria in Campitelli
  S. Maria Maddalena
  S. Maria di Montesanto
  S. Maria in Portico
  S. Maria delle Vergini
  S. Maria della Vittoria
  S. Pietro in Vaticano
  S. Silvestro in Capite
Rossi, Nardo de' (16th century)
  S. Salvatore in Lauro
Rossi, Pasqualino de' (1639–1722)
  SS. Carlo e Ambrogio al Corso
  S. Maria in Aracoeli
  S. Maria del Popolo
Rossi, Sebastiano de' (17th century)
  S. Maria in Aracoeli
Rossi, Vincenzo de' (1525–87)
  S. Maria ad Martyres
  S. Maria sopra Minerva
  S. Maria della Pace
  S. Salvatore in Lauro
Rossi, Zenobi (rec. 1762)
  S. Maria in Trastevere
Rosso Fiorentino (1495 -1540)
  S. Maria della Pace
Roversi, Luigi (rec. 1858–60)
  SS. Apostoli
  S. Lorenzo in Lucina
Roviale Spagnolo Pietro see
  Pedro de Rubiales
Sozzi, Marcello (19th century)
  S. Giovanni Calabita
  S. Paolo fuori le Mura
Rubens, Peter Paul (1577–1640)
  S. Croce in Gerusalemme
  S. Maria in Vallicella
Rubiales, Pedro de IPietro Roviale
  Spagnuolo) (1511?–c. 60)

Rubini, Giacomo
  S. Maria in Aracoeli
Rudiez, Pietro (rec. 1768)
  SS. Carlo e Ambrogio al Corso
  S. Maria Monserrato
Rues, Laurentius (d. 1690)
  S. Maria in Camposanto
Ruggeri, Giuseppe (second half
  of 17th century)
  SS. Trinità dei Monti
Ruggieri, Giovanni Battista
  (1606–1640?)
  S. Caterina da Siena
    a Magnanapoli
Rughesi, Fausto (rec. 1593–1606)
  S. Maria in Vallicella
Rugusa, Francesco (c. 1591–1665)
  S. Maria Scale Coeli
Rusconi, Camillo (1658–1728)
  S. Agostino
  S. Francesco a Ripa
  Il Gesù
  S. Giovanni in Laterano
  S. Ignazio
  S. Maria della Concezione
  S. Maria sopra Minerva
  S. Maria dell'Orto
  S. Maria in Vallicella
  S. Pietro in Vaticano
  S. Salvatore in Lauro
  S. Silvestro in Capite
Rusconi, Giuseppe (1687–c. 1738)
  S. Giovanni in Laterano
  S. Ignazio
  SS. Luca e Martina
  S. Pietro in Vaticano
  S. Prassede
Rusconi, Ludovico see
  Ludovico Rusconi Sassi
Ruspi, Erocole (rec. 1843–61)
  S. Carlo ai Catinari
  SS. Croce e Bonaventura
    dei Lucchesi
  SS. Quirico e Giulitta
Ruthart, Karl Andreas (1630 ?–after
  1703)
  S. Eusebio
Sacchi, Andrea (1599–1661)
  S. Agata dei Goti
  S. Bernardo alle Terme
  S. Carlo ai Catinari
  Il Gesù
  S. Giovanni in Laterano,
    Baptistery *
  S. Giuseppe a Capo le Case
  S. Isidoro
  S. Luigi dei Francesi
  S. Maria della Concezione
  S. Maria sopra Minerva
  S. Maria in Monticelli

S. Maria del Priorato
S. Pietro in Vaticano
Sacconi, Giuseppe (19th century)
SS. Bartolomeo e Alessandro
   dei Bergamaschi
Sala, Carlo Innocenzo (d. 1787)
SS. Bartolomeo e Alessandro
   dei Bergamaschi
Salpini, D. (19th century)
S. Maria in Via Lata
Sale, Nicolò (rec. 1630–50)
S. Lorenzo in Damaso
S. Pietro in Montorio
Sales, Giuseppe (rec. 1827)
S. Maria in Aracoeli
Salimbeni, Ventura (1568–1613)
S. Agostino
Il Gesù
S. Giovanni in Laterano
S. Maria Maggiore
Salimei, Luigi (rec. 1760)
S. Maria del Priorato
Salini, Alessandro (rec. 1763)
S. Ignazio
Salini, Tommaso (c. 1575–1625)
S. Agostino
Stimmate di S. Francesco
Sallaert, Antoon (c. 1580/85–1658)
S. Francesco a Ripa
Salvatori, Giovanni (rec. 1628–29)
S. Giuseppe dei Falegnami
Salvi, F. (early 19th century)
S. Cecilia
Salvi, Giovanni Battista see
   Sassoferrato
Salvi, Nicola (1697–1751)
S. Eustachio
S. Lorenzo in Damaso
S. Pantaleo
SS. Trinità in Palazzo
   Monte di Pietà
Salviati, Francesco (de' Rossi)
   (1510–63)
S. Francesco a Ripa
S. Giovanni Decollato and
   Oratory
S. Marcello
S. Maria dell' Anima
S. Maria del Popolo
S. Salvatore in Lauro
Sanctis, Domenico Antonio de
   (c. 1660–1740)
S. Maria in Monticelli
Sanctis, Francesco de (1679–1731)
SS. Trinità dei Pellegrini
Sanctis, Guglielmo de (1829–1911)
S. Paolo fuori le Mura
Sandart, Joachim von (1606–88)
S. Francesco a Ripa
Sandro, Jacopo di (rec. 1500–d. 54)

S. Pietro in Vaticano,
   Cappella Sistina
Sangallo, Antonio da, the Younger
   (1484–1546)
S. Giacomo degli Incurabili
S. Giacomo degli Spagnuoli
S. Giovanni dei Fiorentini
S. Giovanni in Oleo
S. Marcello
S. Maria di Loreto
S. Maria Maggiore
S. Maria sopra Minerva
S. Maria di Monserrato
S. Maria dei Miracoli and
S. Maria di Montesanto
S. Maria della Pace
S. Maria Porta Paradisi
S. Pietro in Vaticano
S. Spirito in Sassia
Sangallo, Aristotile da (1481–1551)
S. Pietro in Vaticano,
   Cappella Sistina
Sangallo, Battista da (d. 1552)
S. Giovanni Decollato
Sangallo, Francesco da (1494–1576)
S. Maria del Popolo
Sangallo, Giuliano da (c. 1445–1516)
S. Maria Maggiore
S. Pietro in Vaticano,
   Cappella Sistina
Sanni, S. (rec. 1734–35)
S. Giovanni dei Fiorentini
Sanquirico, Paolo (1565–1630)
S. Giovanni dei Fiorentini
S. Maria Maggiore
Sansovino, Andrea Contucci
   (1467–1529)
S. Agostino
S. Maria in Domnica
S. Maria del Popolo
Sansovino, Jacopo Tatti (1486–1570)
S. Agostino
S. Croce in Gerusalemme
S. Giacomo degli Spagnuoli
S. Marcello
S. Maria di Monserrato
S. Maria del Popolo
Santen, Jan van see
   Vasanzio Giovanni
Santi di Tito (1536–1603)
S. Giovanni dei Fiorentini
Santos, Manuel Rodriguez dos see
   Emanuele Rodriguez
Saraceni, Carlo (c. 1580–1620)
S. Bernardo alle Terme
S. Lorenzo in Lucina
S. Maria dell' Anima
S. Maria in Aquiro
S. Maria sopra Minerva
S. Maria della Scala

S. Maria in Vallicella
Sardi, Gaetano (1680–1753)
S. Maria degli Angeli
S. Maria delle Grazie
   alle Fornaci
Sardi, Giuseppe (1680–rec. 1768)
S. Lorenzo in Lucina
S. Maria in Cosmedin
S. Maria di Loreto,
   via di S. Giovanni Laterano
S. Maria Maddalena
S. Maria in Monticelli
S. Paolo alla Regola
S. Pasquale Baylon
SS. Trinità dei Pellegrini
SS. Trinità dei Spagnuoli
Sarrazin, Jaques (1592–1660)
S. Andrea della Valle
S. Lorenzo in Miranda
Sarrocchi, Gaetano (rec. 1836)
S. Marcello
Sarti, Antonio (1797–1880 [81])
S. Andrea delle Fratte
Il Gesù
S. Salvatore in Lauro
SS. Trinità dei Pellegrini
Sassi, Antonio (rec. 1633)
S. Ignazio
Sassi, Ludovico Rusconi
   (1678–1736)
SS. Apostoli
S. Francesco a Ripa
S. Giuseppe alla Lungara
S. Lorenzo in Damaso
S. Marcello
S. Salvatore in Lauro
Sassi, Matteo (1656–1723)
S. Girolamo della Carità
S. Lorenzo in Miranda
S. Maria in Monticelli
Sassi, Pietro (d. 1686)
S. Andrea al Quirinale
S. Nicola da Tolentino
S. Pietro in Vaticano
Sassoferrato, Giovanni Battista Salvi
   called (1609–85)
S. Clemente
S. Francesco di Paola
S. Giovanni in Laterano,
   Baptistery
S. Giuliano dei Fiamminghi *
S. Maria in Miracoli *
S. Sabina
Savini, Salvio (16th century?)
S. Giovanni dei Fiorentini
Savonanzi, Emilio (1580–1660)
S. Lorenzo fuori le Mura
Sbrenchio, Alesandro (rec. 1638)
SS. Gioacchino e Anna
Scaccioni, Achille (rec. 1858–65)

INDEX OF ARTISTS

S. Paolo fuori le Mura
S. Rocco
Scala, Giovanni Battista
   (rec. 1654–57)
  S. Girolamo della Carità
Scaramella, Modesta and Lazzaro
   (17th century)
  SS. Apostoli
Scaramuccia, Luigi (1616–80)
  S. Maria in Trivio
  S. Maria in Vallicella
Scaramucci, Domenico (d. 1758)
  S. Giovanni dei Fiorentini
  S. Giovanni in Laterano
  S. Maria delle Grazie
   alle Fornaci
  SS. Nome di Maria
Schor, Cristoforo (1655–1701)
  S. Antonio dei Portoghesi
Schor, Egid (1627–1701)
  S. Caterina da Siena a
  Magnanapoli
Schor, Johann Paul called Giovanni
   Paolo Tedesco (1615–74)
  S. Caterina da Siena a
  Magnanapoli
  S. Giovanni Calabita
  S. Maria in Campitelli
  S. Spirito in Sassia
Sebastiano Fiorentini (rec. 1483)
  S. Agostino
Sebastiano del Piombo (1485–1547)
  S. Maria della Pace
  S. Maria del Popolo
  S. Pietro in Montorio
Sebregondi, Niccolò (active 1612–51)
  S. Maria del Pianto
Secini, Raffaello (17th century)
  S. Spirito in Sassia
Secondo da Roma, Fra (rec. 1744–47)
  S. Francesco a Ripa
Seiter, Daniel (1649–1705)
  S. Andrea della Valle
  S. Maria degli Angeli
  S. Maria in Aracoeli
  S. Maria di Montesanto
  S. Maria del Popolo
  S. Maria del Suffragio
  S. Maria in Traspontina
  S. Maria in Vallicella
Seitz, Alexander Maximilian
   (1811–88)
  S. Salvatore in Onda
  SS. Trinità dei Monti
Seitz, Ludwig (1844–1908)
  S. Maria dell' Anima
  S. Maria in Aracoeli
Semenza, Giovanni Giacomo
   (1580–1636)
  S. Carlo ai Catinari

Semplice da Verona, Fra
   (c. 1589–c. 1654)
  S. Maria della Concezione
Serenari, Gaspare (1694–1759)
  S. Maria Maddalena
  SS. Vincenzo e Anastasio
Serene, Giuseppe (rec. 1858)
  S. Gregorio a Ponte Quattro Capi
  S. Paolo fuori le Mura
Sermei, Ferdinando (rec. 1586–99)
  S. Maria Maggiore
Serodine, Giovanni (1600 ?–30)
  S. Lorenzo fuori le Mura
Serra, Luigi (1846–88)
  S. Maria della Vittoria
Servi, Gaspare (rec. 1865)
  S. Nicola in Carcere
Severoni, A. (rec. 1717)
  S. Prassede
Sibilla, Gasparo (d. 1782)
  S. Agostino
  S. Antonio dei Portoghesi
  S. Giovanni in Laterano
  S. Maria in Trastevere
  S. Pietro in Vaticano
  SS. Trinità degli Spagnuoli
Sicciolante da Sermoneta,
   Girolamo (1521–75)
  S. Andrea in via Flaminia
  S. Carlo ai Catinari
  S. Eligio dei Ferrari
  S. Giovanni in Laterano
  S. Luigi dei Francesi
  S. Maria dell' Anima
  S. Maria in Aracoeli
  S. Maria Concezione
  S. Maria di Monserrato
  S. Maria Maggiore
  S. Maria sopra Minerva
  S. Maria della Pace
  S. Tommaso dei Cenci
  S. Tommaso in Formis
Signorelli, Luca (c. 1441–1523)
  S. Pietro in Vaticano,
   Cappella Sistina
Sigismondi, Pietro (?–1623)
  S. Sebastiano fuori le Mura
Sillani, Sillano (rec. 1662–1703)
  S. Carlo alle Quatrro Fontane
  S. Maria di Montesanto
  S. Pietro in Vaticano
Silvagni, Giovanni (1790–1853)
  S. Maria in Aracoeli
Silvestro, Giuseppe (rec. 1754–55)
  Il Gesù
  Gesù e Maria
Simoncelli, Francesco (rec. 1700)
  S. Maria del Pianto
Simonetti, Luigi (active 1830–60)
  Il Gesù

S. Maria dell'Archetto
S. Maria del Popolo
Simonetti, Michelangelo (1724–81)
  SS. Apostoli
Sintes, Francesco (rec. 1765)
  S. Marco
Slodtz, Michelangelo (1705–64)
  S. Giovanni dei Fiorentini
  S. Luigi dei Francesi
  S. Marco
  S. Maria della Scala
  SS. Nome di Maria
  S. Pietro in Vaticano
Smigliewicz, Franz (1745–1807)
  S. Stanislao dei Polacchi
Soccorsi, Angelo (early 18th century)
  S. Maria in Campo Marzio
  S. Prassede
Sodoma (Giovanni Antonio Bazzi)
   (1477–1549)
  S. Maria dell'Orto
Soens, Jan (1546–1611)
  S. Maria in Vallicella
Somazzi, Giovanni (Il Moretto)
   (mid 17th century)
  S. Andrea delle Fratte
Sola, Antonio (1787–1861)
  S. Maria di Monserrato
Solari, Giovanni Battista
   (c. 1581–1666)
  S. Maria di Loreto
  S. Maria dei Monti
  S. Pietro in Vaticano
Solari, Rocco (rec. 1608–18)
  S. Stefano del Cacco
  S. Pietro in Vaticano
Solari, Tullio (rec. 1613–22)
  SS. Trinità dei Pellegrini
Sorbi, Giovanni (1695–after 1764)
  S. Caterina dei Funari
  S. Caterina da Siena
  S. Maria della Scala
  S. Pasquale Baylon
Soria, Giovanni Battista
   (1581–1651)
  S. Carlo ai Catinari
  S. Caterina da Siena
   a Magnanapoli
  S. Crisogono
  SS. Domenico e Sisto
  S. Giuseppe dei Falegnami
  S. Gregorio al Celio
  S. Maria della Vittoria
  S. Onofrio
  S. Pietro in Vaticano
Sormani, Leonardo Milanese
   (before 1530–d. after 1589)
  S Girolamo della Carità
  S. Maria Maggiore
  S. Pietro in Montorio

SS. Trinità dei Monti
Sortini, Gaetano (rec. 1745–89)
   Oratorio del Caravita
   S. Carlo ai Catinari
   S. Maria del Suffragio
Soratini, Giuseppe Antonio
   (rec. 1725)
   S. Gregorio al Celio
Sosnowski, Oscar (1811–86)
   S. Giovanni in Laterano,
     Scala Santa
Soulacroix, Charles (1825 -?)
   S. Luigi dei Francesi
Sozzi, Marcello (active 1850–60)
   S. Francesco a Ripa
   S. Giovanni Calabita
   S. Maria in Campitelli
   S. Paolo fuori le Mura
Spada, Gregorio (mid 17th century)
   S. Maria Maggiore
Spada, Lionello (1576–1622)
   S. Maria della Concezione
Spada, Orazio (1613–87)
   S. Andrea delle Fratte
   S. Maria in Vallicella
Spada, Virgilio (1596–1662)
   S. Andrea delle Fratte
   S. Girolamo della Carità
Spadarino see Giacomo Galli
Spagna, Carlo (rec. 1672–78)
   S. Agostino
   S. Giovanni in Laterano,
     Baptistery
   S. Sebastiano fuori le Mura
Spagna, Giuseppe (1765–1839)
   S. Maria Maggiore
Spagnolo, Domenico
   (early 17th century)
   S. Agostino
Specchi, Alessandro (1666–1729)
   S. Anna dei Palafrenieri
     Bambino Gesù
   S. Maria ad Martyres
   S. Sebastiano fuori le Mura
Specchi, Michelangelo
   (c. 1684–after 1750)
   S. Maria del Carmine alle Tre
     Cannelle
Speranza, Giovanni Battista
   (c. 1600–40)
   S. Caterina da Siena
     a Magnanapoli
   SS. Cosma e Damiano
   S. Giuseppe dei Falegnami
   S. Girolamo della Carità
   S. Maria in Aquiro
   S. Maria sopra Minerva
Speranza, Stefano (rec. 1629–36)
   S. Maria in Aracoeli
   S. Pietro in Vaticano

Sperone, Alessandro (1694–1783)
   S. Eustachio
Spinazzi, Angelo (1700–67)
   S. Giovanni in Laterano
Spinazzi, Innocenzo (d. 1798)
   SS. Carlo e Ambrogio al Corso
   S. Croce in Gerusalemme
   Oratorio del Gonfalone
   S. Pietro in Vaticano
Spranger, Bartolomeo (1546–1611)
   S. Giovanni in Laterano
   S. Giovanni a Porta Latina
   S. Sisto Vecchio
Stanghellini, Antonio
   (rec. 1650–d. before 1686)
   S. Maria in Aracoeli
Stati, Cristoforo (1556–1619)
   S. Andrea del Valle
   S. Maria Maggiore
   S. Pietro in Vaticano
Steinle, Wilhelm (c. 1818–81)
   SS. Trinità dei Monti
Stella, Jacques (1545–c. 1630)
   S. Giovanni in Laterano and
     Scala Santa
   S. Maria Maggiore
   S. Maria sopra Minerva
   S. Spirito in Sassia
Stern, Ignazio (1679–1748)
   S. Anna dei Palafrenieri
   S. Giovanni in Laterano
   S. Marcello
   S. Paola alla Regola
   SS. Sergio e Bacco
Stern, Ludwig (1709–77)
   S. Agostino
   S. Lorenzo in Lucina
   S. Maria dell' Anima
   SS. Michele e Magno
   S. Prassede
   S. Rocco
Stocchi, Achille (1789–?)
   S. Giovanni in Laterano
   S. Marco
   S. Paolo fuori le Mura
Strada, Vespasiano (c. 1582–1622)
   S. Giacomo degli Incurabili
   S. Maria in Aracoeli
   S. Onofrio
Straet, van den (1532–1605)
   S. Giovanni Decollato, Oratory
Subleyras, Pierre (1699–1749)
   S. Ambrogio della Massima
   S. Francesca Romana
   S. Maria degli Angeli
   S. Pietro in Vaticano
Swanvelt, Herman van (c. 1600–1655)
   S. Maria sopra Minerva
Tacconi, Innocenzo (c. 1575–1624/25)
   S. Angelo in Pescheria

S. Caterina dei Funari
S. Maria dei Monti
S. Maria del Popolo
S. Sebastiano fuori le Mura
Tadolini, Adam (1788–1868)
   S. Carlo ai Catinari
   SS. Croce e Bonaventura
     dei Lucchesi
   Il Gesù
   S. Marcello
   S. Pietro in Vaticano
   S. Spirito in Sassia
   Stimmate di S. Francesco
   SS. Vincenzo e Anastasio
Tadolini, Giulio (1849–1919)
   S. Andrea della Valle
   S. Giovanni in Laterano
Tadolini, Scipione (1822–92)
   S. Andrea della Valle
   Il Gesù
   S. Lucia del Gonfalone
Tanari, Antonio (rec. 1635)
   S. Pudenziana
Tantardini, Carlo (1677–1748)
   S. Giovanni in Laterano
   SS. Nome di Maria
Targone, Pompeo (1575–1630)
   S. Giovanni in Laterano
   S. Maria Maggiore
Tarquini, Giuseppe (rec. 1784)
   S. Lorenzo in Lucina
Taruffi, Emilio (1633–96)
   S. Andrea della Valle
Tassi, Agostino (c. 1580–1644)
   S. Onofrio
Tavolaccio, Domenico
   (mid 17th century)
   SS. Luca e Martina
Tedesco, Lorenzo (late 16th century)
   S. Maria dei Miracoli
   S. Spirito in Sassia
Tedeschi, Filippo (rec. 1798)
   S. Maria di Loreto
Tedeschi, Pietro (c. 1750–after 1808)
   S. Francesca Romana
   S. Maria di Loreto
Tempesta, Antonio (1555–1630)
   S. Giovanni dei Fiorentini
   S. Giovanni in Laterano,
     Baptistery
   S. Prisca
   S. Stefano Rotondo
Teneranti, Giuseppe (1793–1866)
   S. Maria del Popolo
Teneranti, Pietro (1789–1869)
   S. Giovanni in Laterano
   S. Lorenzo in Damaso
   S. Lorenzo in Lucina
   S. Maria in Campitelli
   S. Maria sopra Minerva

INDEX OF ARTISTS

S. Maria in Via Lata
S. Paolo fuori le Mura
S. Pietro in Vaticano
Terenzi, Terenzio (Trentio da Urbino)
  (active 1578–1619/21)
S. Eligio dei Ferrari
S. Maria della Concezione
S. Silvestro in Capite
Testa, Filippo (1665–1726)
  S. Giuseppe dei Falegnami
Testa, Giovan Battista (1675–1753)
  Gesù e Maria
Testa, Giuseppe (1629–77)
  S. Maria del Popolo
Testa, Pietro (1612–50)
  S. Maria dell' Anima
  S. Martino ai Monti
Theodoli, Gerolamo (1677–1766)
  SS. Marcello e Pietro
  S Maria di Montesanto
  S. Nicola in Arcione
  S. Salvatore in Lauro
Théodon, Jean-Baptiste (1646–1713)
  S. Carlo ai Catinari
  Il Gesù
  S. Maria in Trastevere
  S. Pietro in Vaticano and Piazza
  SS. Trinità in Palazzo
    Monte di Pietà
Thorvaldsen, Bertel (1770–1844)
  S. Maria ad Martyres
  S. Pietro in Vaticano
Tibaldi, Pellegrino (1527–96)
  S. Giacomo degli Spagnuoli
  S. Luigi dei Francesi
  S. Marcello
  SS. Trinità dei Monti
Tiberio d'Assisi (1460/70–1524)
  S. Maria del Popolo
Tintore, Francesco del (1645–1718)
  SS. Croce e Bonaventura
    dei Lucchesi
Tittone, Filippo (c. 1645–1713)
  S. Angelo in Pescheria
  S. Maria del Pianto
Tofanelli, Agostino (1770–1834)
  SS. Carlo e Ambrogio al Corso
  SS. Croce e Bonaventura
    dei Lucchesi
Tojetti, Domenico (1831–c. 1901)
  S. Paolo fuori le Mura
Tombini, A. (19th century)
  S. Maria in Via Lata
Tomassini, Matteo (rec. 1702)
  S. Pietro in Vaticano, Piazza
Tommasi da Pesaro, Giuseppe
  (18th century)
  S. Marcello
Tommasi di Pietro Boscoli (1503–74)
  S. Pietro in Vincoli

Tommasi, Giuseppe
  (18th/19th century)
  SS. Vincenzo e Anastasio
Tommasini, Gregorio (d. 1698)
  S. Salvatore in Onda
Torelli, Cesare (d. 1615)
  S. Maria di Monti
  S. Maria in Vallicella
Torelli, Felice (1667–1748)
  SS. Giovanni e Paolo
Torni, Jacopo called l'Indaco
  Vecchio (1476–1526)
  S. Pietro in Vaticano,
    Cappella Sistina
Tornioli, Niccolò (1598–1651)
  S. Maria in Vallicella
Torriani, Carlo (rec. 1673)
  S. Marcello
Torriani, Niccolò (rec. 1609–36)
  SS. Domenico e Sisto
  S. Maria di Monserrato
Torriani, Orazio (active 1601–60)
  S. Agostino
  S. Ambrogio della Massima
  S. Andrea della Valle
  S. Bartolomeo all'Isola
  S. Calisto
  SS. Cosma e Damiano
  S. Lorenzo in Miranda
  S. Marco
Torrigiano, Bastiano (d. 1596)
  S. Maria Maggiore
Torrigiani, Pietro (early 16th century)
  S. Giacomo degli Spagnuoli
Torriti, Jacomo (13th century)
  S. Maria Maggiore
Torrone, Angelo (rec. 1663–90)
  S. Giovanni della Pigna
Tosi, Luigi (rec. 1747)
  S. Pasquale Baylon
Tozzi, Andrea (rec. 1587)
  S. Girolamo della Carità
Tittoni, Filippo (c. 1645–1713)
  S. Angelo in Percheria
  S. Maria del Pianto
Trabacchi, Giuseppe (1839–1909)
  S. Agostino
Traballesi, Francesco (1544–88)
  S. Atanasio dei Greci
Travani, F. (17th century)
  S Girolamo della Carità
Traversari (19th century)
  S. Maria in Via Lata
Traversi, Gaspare Giovanni
  (c. 1722–70)
  S. Paolo fuori le Mura
Trémolières, Pierre-Charles (1730–39)
  S. Maria degli Angeli
Trentio da Urbino see
  Terenzio Terenzi

Trevisani, Francesco (1656–1746)
  S. Ambrogio della Massima *
  S. Anastasia
  S. Andrea delle Fratte
  S. Giovanni in Laterano
  S. Ignazio
  S. Maria degli Angeli
  S. Maria in Aracoeli
  S. Maria in Via, Oratory
  S. Onofrio
  S. Pietro in Vaticano
  S. Silvestro in Capite
  Stimmate di S. Francesco
Tribolo, Niccolò (16th century)
  S. Maria del' Anima
Triga, Giacomo (1674–1746)
  SS. Celso e Giuliano
  S. Clemente
  SS. Giovanni e Paolo
  S. Lucia della Tinta
  S. Marcello
  S. Maria del Popolo
  S. Nicola dei Prefetti
Trignoli, Giovanni (d. 1522)
  S. Pietro in Vaticano,
    Cappella Sistina
Tristano, Giovanni (active 1558–75)
  Il Gesù
Trometta see Niccolò Martinelli
Troppa, Girolamo (1630–c. 1711)
  S. Agata in Trastevere
  SS. Carlo e Ambrogio al Corso
  S. Croce all Lungara
  S. Maria del Suffragio
  S. Marta
Troschel, Julius (1806–63)
  S. Maria del Popolo
Troy, Jean François de (1679–1752)
  SS. Alessio e Bonifazio
    all'Aventino
  SS. Claudio e Andrea
    de' Borgognoni
Trufamond, Teofilio see
  Trophine Bigot (1579–?)
Tuccimei, Raffaele (active 1815–44)
  S. Marco
Tuerlinck, Joseph Jean (1809–73)
  S. Giuliano dei Fiamminghi
Turchi, Alessandro (1578–1649)
  S. Lorenzo in Lucina
  S. Maria della Concezione
  S. Salvatore in Lauro
Turini, Pietro (rec. 1510)
  S. Omobono
Turner, Joseph (1792–1877)
  SS. Trinità dei Monti
Ubaldini see Pietro Paolo Baldini
Ubeleski, Alessandro (d. 1718)
  S. Maria in Traspontina
Umile da Foligno, Fra (d. 1709)

URIBESALGO—VESPIGNANI

S. Margherita in Trastevere
S. Maria in Aracoeli
Unterberger, Cristoforo (1732–98)
S. Nicola da Tolentino
Urbano, Pietro (rec. 1506–20)
S. Pietro in Vaticano,
Cappella Sistina
Uribesalgo, Isidoro (17th century)
S. Carlo alle Quattro Fontane
Vacca, Flaminio (1538–1605)
Il Gesù
S. Maria Maggiore
S. Maria in Vallicella
Vaccari, Pietro (1741–70)
S. Agostino
Vaiani, Alessandro (c. 1570–?)
S. Maria in Via, Largo Chigi
Valadier, Giuseppe (1762–1839)
S. Andrea delle Fratte
SS. Apostoli
SS. Bartolomeo e Alessandro
dei Bergamaschi
S. Eligio dei Ferrari
Gesù e Maria
S. Lorenzo in Damaso
S. Maria della Consolazione
S. Maria Maggiore
S. Maria dei Miracoli and
S. Maria di Montesanto
S. Pantaleo
S. Pietro in Vaticano
S. Rocco
Stimmate di S. Francesco
Valadier, Luigi (1726–85)
S. Maria Maddalena
Valadier, Luigi Maria (b. 1791)
S. Andrea delle Fratte
S. Apollinare
S. Maria in Via, Piazza Poli
S. Pietro in Vaticano
Valentin de Boulogne (1591–1632)
S. Pietro in Vaticano *
Valentini, Pietro (active 1591)
S. Carlo ai Catinari
Valeriani, Domenico (rec. 1624)
S. Crisogono
Valeriani, Giuseppe (c. 1708–62)
SS. Celso e Giuliano
Valeriano, Giuseppe (1542–96)
Il Gesù
S. Spirito in Sassia
Valesio, Giovanni
S. Maria d'Itria
Valperga, Bernardino (rec. 1601–03)
S. Maria di Monserrato
Valsoldo see
Giovanni Antonio Paracca
Valtellina, Giovanni Antonio
(rec. 1732)
SS. Bartolomeo e Alessandro
dei Bergamaschi
Valvassori, Gabriele (1683–1761)
S. Agnese in Agone
SS. Bartolomeo e Alessandro
dei Bergamaschi
S. Maria della Luce
S. Maria dell'Orto
SS. Quirico e Giulitta
Van den Broecke, Hendrik
see Broecke
Van Loo, Carl (1705–65)
S. Isidoro
Vannelli, G. B. (rec. 1714)
S. Giuseppe dei Falegnami
Vanni, Curzio (active c. 1585–1613)
S. Giovanni in Laterano
Vanni, Francesco (c. 1563–1610)
S. Maria degli Angeli
Vanni, Giovanni Battista (1600–60)
S. Giovanni dei Fiorentini
Vanni, Michelangelo (rec. 1662–63)
S. Giovanni in Laterano
Vanni, Raffaelle (1595–1673)
S. Andrea delle Fratte
SS. Annunziate
S. Caterina da Siena
S. Croce in Gerusalemme
S. Giovanni dei Fiorentini
S. Lorenzo in Miranda
S. Maria in Campitelli
S. Maria della Pace
S. Maria del Popolo
S. Maria in Publicolis
S. Maria in Vallicella, Oratory
S. Pietro in Vaticano
Vannini, Ottavio (1585–1644)
SS. Annunziate
Vanvitelli, Luigi (1700–73)
S. Agostino
S. Andrea delle Fratte
S. Antonio dei Portoghesi
S. Cecilia
S. Maria degli Angeli
S. Pantaleo
S. Pietro in Vaticano
Vasanzio, Giovanni (Jan van Santen)
(c. 1550–1621)
S. Crisogono
S. Sebastiano fuori le Mura
Vasari, Giorgio (1511–74)
S. Giovanni Decollato
S. Pietro in Montorio
Vasconi, Filippo (c. 1687–1730)
S. Caterina da Siena
a Magnanapoli
Vasconio, Giuseppe (rec. 1657)
S. Agostino
S. Maria in Trastevere
Vaudoyer, Louis (1803–72)
S. Lorenzo in Lucina
Vecchi, Francesco de (17th century)
Il Gesù
Vecchi, Gaspare de' (d. 1643)
S. Maria id Loreto
S. Maria dei Monti
SS. Re Magi
SS. Vincenzo e Anastasio
Vecchi, Giovanni de' (c. 1543–1615)
S. Andrea della Valle
S. Bernardino ai Monti
SS. Crocifisso, Oratorio del
S. Eligio degli Orefici
Il Gesù
S. Lorenzo in Miranda
S. Maria in Aracoeli
S. Maria sopra Minerva
S. Maria Scala Coeli
S. Pietro in Montorio
S. Pietro in Vaticano
S. Prassede
Vecchiarelli, Pietro (rec. c. 1639)
S. Maria dell'Umiltà
S. Pietro in Vincoli
Veit, Philipp (1793–1877)
SS. Trinità dei Monti
Velásquez, Antonio (1723–94)
SS. Trinità degli Spagnuoli
Venturi, Sergio (c. 1584–1646)
S. Crisogono
Venusti, Marcello (c. 1512–79)
S. Agostino
S. Antonio dei Portoghesi
S. Caterina dei Funari
S. Eligio dei Ferrari
S. Giovanni in Laterano
S. Maria in Aracoeli
S. Maria sopra Minerva
S. Maria della Pace
S. Silvestro al Quirinale
S. Spirito in Sassia
Venuti, Ludovico (1785–after 1824)
S. Maria di Montesanto
Vergara, Francesco (1713–61)
S. Pietro in Vaticano
Vermiglio, Giuseppe
(1587–after 1635)
S. Tommaso dei Cenci
Verona, Jacopo (17the century)
S. Bibiana
Verpoorten, Peter (d. 1659)
S. Pietro in Vatican
Verschaffelt, Peter Anton (1710–93)
S. Apollinare
S. Croce in Gerusalemme
Vespignani, Francesco (1842–99)
S. Antonio dei Portoghesi
Vespignani, Virginio (1808–82)
Bambino Gesù
S. Carlo ai Catinari
SS. Croce e Bonaventura

351

INDEX OF ARTISTS

dei Lucchesi
S. Croce alla Lungara
S. Giovanni in Laterano
S. Giovanni della Pigna
S. Lorenzo in Damaso
S. Lorenzo fuori le Mura
S. Marcello
S. Maria dell'Archetto
S. Maria Maggiore
S. Spirito in Sassia
Veyrassat, Antoine (1804–52)
SS. Giovanni e Paolo
Vicinelli, Odoardo (1681–1755)
S. Giovanni Battista
dei Genovesi
S. Maria delle Grazie alle Fornaci
S. Maria in Monticelli
Vico di Raffaelle (rec. 1564–66)
S. Giovanni in Laterano
Vignola, Giacinto Barozzi da
(c. 1540–after 1584)
S. Anna dei Palafrenieri
S. Caterina dei Funari
Il Gesù
S. Maria dell'Orto
Vignola, Jacopo Barozzi da (1507–73)
S. Andrea in via Flaminia
S. Anna dei Palafrenieri
Il Gesù
S. Giovanni in Laterano
S. Lorenzo in Damaso
S. Maria dell'Orto
S. Maria in Traspontina
Vincenzo da Bassiano (d. 1694)
S. Maria in Aracoeli
Vincenzo da Montepulciano
(late 16th century)
S. Maria in Aracoeli
Vinelli, Giovanni (18th century)
S. Gioacchino in Selci
Vitale, Alessandro (rec. 1662)
S. Marco
Vitale, Pietro (rec. 1655–56)
S. maria sopra Minerva
Vittoria, Vincenzo (1650–1712)
S. Maria in Aracoeli
Viviani, Antonio (1560–1620)

S. Girolamo degli Schiavoni
S. Gregorio al Celio,
Oratorio di S. Barbara
S. Maria dei Monti
Viti, Timoteo (1469–1523)
S. Maria della Pace
Vivo, Donato De (rec. 1848)
S. Maria di Monterone
Vliete, Gillis van den (Egidio della
Riviera) (d. 1602)
S. Giovanni in Laterano
S. Maria dell' Anima
S. Maria Maggiore
S. Maria in Vallicella
Vouet, Simon (1590–1649)
S. Francesco a Ripa
S. Lorenzo in Lucina
S. Maria sopra Minerva
Werle, Johann Conrad (1701–77)
S. Maria Maddalena
SS. Vincenzo e Anastasio
Wolff, Emil (1802–79)
S. Andrea delle Fratte
S. Maria in Aquiro
Zacchetti, Bernardino (rec. 1510–23)
S. Pietro in Vaticano,
Cappella Sistina
Zaccolini, Matteo (1574–1630)
S. Silvestro al Quirinale
S. Susanna
Zallone, Benedetto (1595–1644)
S. Pietro in Vincoli
Zampieri, Domenico see
Domenichino
Zanna, Giovanni, il Pizzica
(active c. 1600)
S. Caterina dei Funari
Zannoli, Giovanni Francesco
(c. 1666–1717)
S. Maria in Publicolis
Zapponi, Ippolito (d. 1894)
S. Maria in Aquiro
Zena, Agostino (rec. 1703–04)
S. Pietro in Vaticano, Piazza
Zoboli, Giacomo (1681–1767)
S. Andrea al Quirinale
S. Antonio dei Portoghesi

S. Apollinare
Bambino Gesù
SS. Carlo e Ambrogio al Corso
S. Eustachio
S. Giovanni della Pigna
S. Maria in Trastevere
S. Pietro in Vaticano
Zoppo, Stefano dello (rec. 1589)
S. Maria in Trastevere
Zuccaro, Federico (1540–1609)
S. Caterina dei Funari
S. Croce in Gerusalemme
Il Gesù
Oratorio del Gonfalone
S. Lorenzo in Damaso
S. Maria dell'Orto
S. Prassede
S. Pudenziana
S. Sabina
SS. Trinità dei Monti
Zuccaro, Taddeo (1529–66)
S. Marcello
S. Maria della Consolazione
S. Maria dell'Orto
S. Sabina
SS. Trinità dei Monti
Zucchetti, Filippo (d. 1712)
S. Eligio degli Orefici
S. Giovanni Battista
dei Genovesi
S. Maria dell'Orto
S. Maria della Scala
Zucchi, Francesco (c. 1562–1622)
S. Cesareo
S. Croce in Gerusalemme
S. Giacomo degli Incurabili
S. Giovanni in Laterano
S. Maria Scala Coeli
Zucchi, Jacopo (1540/42–1595/96)
S. Clemente
S. Giovanni Decollato
S. Maria in Via, Largo Chigi
S. Pietro in Vaticano
S. Silvestro al Quirinale
S. Spirito in Sassia
SS. Trinità dei Pellegrini

INDEX OF PATRONS AND BENEFACTORS

Acquaviva, Cardinal Francesco
   S. Cecilia
Agucchi, Cardinal
   S. Onofrio
Alaleoni, Sister Maria
   SS. Domenico e Sisto
Albani, Cardinal Annibale
   S. Maria in Cosmedin
Albani, Cardinal Francesco
   S. Brigida
   Stimmate di S. Francesco
Albertoni, Cardinal Angelo Paluzzi
   S. Francesco a Ripa
Albertoni, Marchese
      Baldassare Paluzzi
   S. Croce alla Lungara
Albertoni, Marchese
      Baldassare Paluzzi
   S. Francesco a Ripa
Albrecht, Archduke
   S. Croce in Gerusalemme
Aldobrandini –Pamphili,
      Donna Olimpia
   S. Francesco di Paola
Aldobrandini, Cardinal Ippolito
   S. Maria sopra Minerva
Aldobrandini, Cardinal Pietro
   S. Maria Scala Coeli
   S. Maria in Traspontina
   S. Maria in Trastevere
   S. Maria in Via, Largo Chigi
   S. Nicola in Carcere
   S. Paolo alle Tre Fontane
Alexander VI
   S. Maria Maggiore
Alexander VII
   S. Andrea al Quirinale
   S. Giovanni in Laterano
   S. Giovanni in Laterano,
      Baptistry
   S. Maria in Campitelli
   S. Maria dei Miracoli
   S. Maria Montesanto
   S. Maria della Pace
   S. Maria in Via Lata
   S. Pietro in Vaticano
   S. Rita da Cascia
   S. Tommaso in Formis

S. Paolo Primo Eremita
   S. Pancrazio
Altemps, Cardinal Marco Sittico
   S. Maria in Trastevere
Alvarez, Cardinal Juan
   S. Lorenzo in Fonte
Alvaro de Cienfuegos, Cardinal
   S. Bartolomeo all'Isola
Androsilla, Sister Costanza
   S. Cosimato
Antoniano, Cardinal Silvio
   S. Maria in Vallicella
Arrigoni, Cardinal Pompeo
   S. Balbina
Avila, Pietro Paolo
   S. Maria in Trastevere
Azzolini, Cardinal Decio
   S. Agnese in Agone
Baglioni Orsini, Francesca
   S. Silvestro al Quirinale
Baldi, Cesare
   S. Maria della Scala
Barberini, Cardinal Antonio
   S. Luigi dei Francesi
   S. Maria dei Monti
   S. Maria della Concezione
   S. Maria sopra Minerva
   SS. Re Magi
Barberini, Cardinal Francesco
   S. Bonaventura al Palatino
   S. Carlo alle Quattro Fontane
   SS. Cosma e Damiano
   Domine Quo Vadis
   S. Giacomo alla Lungara
   S. Lorenzo fuori le Mura
   S. Lorenzo in Damaso
   SS. Luca e Martina
   S. Maria della Purificazione
   S. Salvatore in Campo
   S. Sebastiano al Palatino
   S. Sebastiano fuori le Mura
Barberini, Cardinal Maffeo
   S. Andrea della Valle
   S. Onofrio
Barberini, Francesco
   S. Andrea della Valle
Barberini, Francesco
   S. Rocco

Barbo, Cardinal Pietro
   S. Marco
Baronio, Cardinal Cesare
   S. Cesareo
   S. Eufemia
   S. Gregorio al Celio
   SS. Nereo e Achilleo
Bellarmino, Cardinal
   S. Maria in Via, Largo Chigi
Benedict XIII
   S. Dorotea
   S. Gallicano
   S. Gregorio a Ponte Quattro Capi
   S. Maria in Aracoeli
   S. Maria in Domnica
   S. Pietro in Vaticano
   S. Salvatore in Onda
   S. Sisto Vecchio
   S. Spirito in Sassia
Benedict XIII
   SS. Quirico e Giulitta
Benedict XIV
   S. Croce in Gerusalemme
   S. Francesco di Paola
   S. Giovanni in Laterano,
      Triclinium
   S. Lorenzo in Lucia
   SS. Marcellino e Pietro
   S. Maria degli Angeli
   S. Maria Maggiore
   SS. Michele e Magno
Bernerio, Cardinal Girolamo
   S. Sabina
Bianchetti, Cardinal Ludovico
   S. Maria dei Monti
Bolognetti, Bishop Giorgio
   Gesù e Maria
Bombasi, Gabrielle
   S. Caterina dei Funari
Bonaparte, Cardinal Luciano
   S. Pudenziana
Boncompagni, Cardinal Giacomo
   S. Pietro in Vaticano
Borghese, Cardinal Scipione
   S. Carlo ai Catinari
   S. Caterina da Siena
      a Magnanapoli
   S. Crisogono

353

INDEX OF PATRONS AND BENEFACTORS

S. Gregorio al Celio
S. Maria della Vittoria
S. Maria delle Vergini
S. Maria sopra Minerva
S. Sebastiano fuori le Mura
Borghese, Prince Camillo
  S. Maria Maggiore
Borghese, Prince Marcantonio
  S. Lucia della Tinta
Borgia, Cardinal Rodrigo
  S. Maria del Popolo
Borromeo, Cardinal Carlo
  S. Martino ai Monti
  S. Prassede
Borromeo, Cardinal Federico
  S. Nicola in Carcere
Boschi, Cardinal
  S. Lorenzo in Lucia
Buccini, Andrea
  S. Maria dei Monti
Bufalo, Marchese Ottavio del
  S. Andrea delle Fratte
Bufalo, Marchese Paolo del
  S. Andrea delle Fratte
Buonvisi, Cardinal Francesco
  SS. Croce e Bonaventura
    dei Lucchesi
Buratti, Matteo
  S. Nicola da Tolentino
Caetini, Cardinal Enrico
  S. Pudenziana
Caffarelli, Prospero
  S. Maria sopra Minerva
Canuto, Bishop Andrea
  S. Caterina dei Funaris
Caroli, Domenico
  S. Bernardino ai Monti
Carpegna, Cardinal Gaspare
  S. Pantaleo
Carpegna, Cardinal Ulderigo
  S. Anastasia al Palatino
Carvajal, Cardinal Bernardino
  Lopez de
  S. Croce in Gerusalemme
Castelrodrigo, Marquis of
  S. Carlo alle Quattro Fontane
Caucho, Bishop Giacomo
  SS. Trinità dei Monti
Cecchini, Benedetto
  S. Maria in Trastevere
Cenci, Rocco
  S. Tommaso dei Cenci
Cerrini, Mario and Camillo
  S. Tommaso in Parione
Cerrini, Salustia
  Il Gesù
Cesi, Baron Federico
  S. Prassede
Cesi, Cardinal Federico
  S. Caterina dei Funaris

Cesi, Cardinal Pierdonato
  S. Maria in Vallicella
Cesi, Monsignor Angelo
  S. Maria in Vallicella
Ceuli, Tiberio
  S. Maria in Vallicella
Ceva, Ponzio
  S. Maria in Vallicella
Charlels VIII of France
  SS. Trinità dei Monti
Chateaubriand
  S. Lorenzo in Lucia
Chateauvilliers, Cardinal
  SS. Trinità dei Monti
Chiara, Maria
  S. Bernardino ai Monti
Chigi, Agostino
  S. Maria della Pace
  S. Maria del Popolo
Chigi, Cardinal Flavio
  S. Lucia del Gonfalone
Chores, Prior Jean von
  S. Antonio Abate
Cirillo, Nicolo
  S. Spirito in Sassia
Clemenet XI
  SS. Marcellino e Pietro
Clemenet XIII
  S. Maria in Via Lata
Clement IX
  Il Gesù
  S. Sabina
Clement VIII
  S. Cesareo
  S. Spirito in Sassia
  Stimmate di S. Francesco
  S. Vitale
Clement X
  S. Maria Maggiore
  S. Pietro in Vaticano
  SS. Venanzio e Ansovino
Clement XI
  S. Clemente
  S. Giovanni in Laterano
  S. Maria delle Grazie
    alle Fornaci
  S. Maria in Cosmedin
  S. Maria in Monticelli
  S. Maria in Trastevere
  S. Marta in Vaticano
  S. Sebastiano fuori le Mura
  S. Teodoro al Palatino
Clement XII
  Bambino Gesù
  SS. Celso e Giuliano
  S. Giovanni dei Fiorentini
  S. Giovanni in Laterano
  S. Giovanni in Laterano,
    Triclinium
  S. Maria Maggiore

Clement XIII
  S. Maria Maggiore
  SS. Michele e Magno
Colonna, Cardinal Pietro
  S. Giacomo degli Incurabili
Colonna, Contestabile Filippo
  S. Carlo ai Catinari
Colonna, Filippo
  S. Egidio
Consalvi, Cardinal Ercole
  S. Andrea delle Fratte
Contarelli, Cardinal Matteo
  S. Luigi dei Francesi
Cornaro, Cardinal Federico
  S. Maria della Vittoria
Cornelio, Federico
  SS. Re Magi
Corradini, Cardinal Piermarcellino
  S. Gallicano
Crema, Cardinal Giovanni de
  S. Crisogono
Cusano, Cardinal Agostino
  S. Maria in Vallicella
Cuside, Perod de
  S. Pietro in Montorio
d'Aste, Francesco
  S. Maria in Via Lata
d'Estouteville, Cardinal
  S. Agostino
Dietrichstein, Cardinal Franz von
  S. Silvestro in Capite
Doria, Cardinal Giorgio
  S. Cecilia
Durazzo, Cardinal Marcelo
  S. Pietro in Vincoli
Emilio Sfondrati, Cardinal Paolo
  SS. Carlo e Ambrogio al Corso
  S. Cecilia
Enckenvoort, Cardinal Willem van
  S. Maria dell' Anima
Eugenius III
  S. Maria Maggiore
Eugenius IV
  S. Pietro in Vaticano
Fabri, Domenico
  S. Nicola dei Lorenesi
Falconieri, Cardinal Alessandro
  S. Marcello
Falconieri, Orazio
  S. Giovanni dei Fiorentini
Farnese, Cardinal Alessandro
  SS. Crocifisso, Oratorio del
  Il Gesù
  Gonfalone, Oratorio del
  S. Maria Scala Coeli
Farnese, Cardinal Odoardo
  S. Maria del Carmine
    alle Tre Cannelle
Febei, Monsignor Francesco Maria
  S. Anastasia al Palatino

INDEX OF PATRONS AND BENEFACTORS

Felix IV
  SS. Cosma e Damiano
Ferdinand and Isabella of Spain
  S. Pietro in Montorio
Ferrari, Cardinal Tommaso
  S. Clemente
Filippini, Prior Giovanni Antonio
  S. Martino ai Monti
Fini, Cardinal Antonio
  S. Maria in Trastevere
Fonesca, Gabriele
  S. Lorenzo in Lucia
Galamino, Agostino
  SS. Re Magi
Gasparini, Prioress Maria
  S. Maria delle Vergini
Gastaldi, Cardinal Girolamo
  S. Margherita in Trastevere
  S. Maria di Monterone
  S. Maria Montesanto
Gavotti, Giovanni Battista
  S. Nicola da Tolentino
Gessi, Cardinal Berlingero
  S. Maria della Vittoria
Gesualdo, Cardinal Alfonso
  S. Andrea della Valle
Ginetti, Cardinal Marizio
  S. Maria delle Vergini
  S. Andrea della Valle
Giustiniani, Cardinal Benedetto
  S. Prisca
Giustiniani, Marchese Vincenzo
  S. Luigi dei Francesi
Glorieri, Cesare
  S. Spirito in Sassia
Gonzaga, Giulio Cesare
  S. Spirito in Sassia
Gravita, Father Pierto
  Caravita, Oratorio del
Gregory II
  S. Agata in Trastevere
Gregory VIII
  S. Agata in Trastevere
Gregory IX
  S. Francesco a Ripa
Gregory XI
  S. Giovanni in Laterano
Gregory XI
  S. Maria sopra Minerva
Gregory XIII
  S. Apollinare
  S. Atanasio dei Greci
  S. Carlo ai Catinari
  S. Giovanni Calabita
  S. Giovanni in Laterano, Baptistry
  S. Giovanni in Pigna
  SS. Giovanni e Petronio dei Bolognesi
  S. Maria in Vallicella

Spirito Santo dei Napoletani
S. Stanislao dei Polacchi
S. Stefano Rotondo
S. Tommaso di Canterbury
S. Pietro in Vaticano
Gregory XV
  S. Francesco di Paola
  S. Nicola dei Lorenesi
Gregory XVI
  S. Bonaventura al Palatino
  S. Salvatore in Onda
  SS. Vito e Modesto
Guidiccioni, Alessandro
  S. Spirito in Sassia
Hadrian I
  S. Teodoro al Palatino
Henriquez, Cardinal Enrico
  S. Eusebio
Honorius I
  S. Adriano
Honorius III
  SS. Alessio e Bonifazio
  S. Sabina
Howard, Cardinal Philip
  S. Giovanni e Paolo
Innocent II
  S. Maria in Trastevere
Innocent IV
  S. Maria in Aracoeli
Innocent VIII
  S. Maria della Pace
Innocent X
  S. Agnese in Agone
  S. Giovanni in Laterano
  S. Ivo
Innocent XI
  Il Gesù
  S. Basilio
  S. Maria di Monterone
Innocent XII
  S. Eustachio
Julius II
  S. Maria del Popolo
  S. Pietro in Vaticano
Julius III
  S. Andrea in via Flaminia
  S. Biagio della Pagnotta
  S. Pietro in Montorio
Lambertini, Cardinal Prospero
  S. Carlo ai Catinari
  S. Maria della Scala
Lancellotti, Orazio
  S. Simeone Profeta
Lancellotti, Prince Scipione
  S. Ignazio
Landini, Bishop Nicola Angelo Maria
  S. Agostino
Landis, Francesco
  S. Spirito in Sassia
Lante, Cardinal

S. Martia delle Grazie a Porta Angelica
Lante, Cardinal Marcello
  S. Giuseppe a Capo le Case
  S. Maria Antiqua
Leni, Antonia and Lucrectia
  SS. Domenico e Sisto
Leni, Cardinal Giovanni Battista
  S. Carlo ai Catinari
Leo III
  S. Giovanni in Laterano, Triclinium
Leo X
  S. Caterina da Siena
  S. Maria in Via, Largo Chigi
Leo XII
  S. Maria Maggiore
Lesueur, Père Thomas
  SS. Trinità dei Monti
Lucius II
  S. Croce in Gerusalemme
Ludovisi, Cardinal Ludovico
  S. Ignazio
Ludovisi, Principe Nicolò
  S. Ignazio
Mancini, Cardinal Francesco Maria
  S. Maria in Aracoeli
Marini, Luigi
  S. Maria in Aracoeli
Martin V
  SS. Alessio e Bonifazio
  S. Giovanni in Laterano
Masotti, Zenobio
  S. Barbara dei Librai
Massimo, Porzia (nèe Colonna)
  S. Caterina da Siena a Magnanapoli
Mazarin, Cardinal
  SS. Vincenzo e Anastasio
Medici, Cardinal Alessandro de'
  S. Prassede
Medici, Cardinal Giovanni de'
  S. Maria in Domnica
Medici, Cardinal Giulio de'
  S. Giovanni dei Fiorentini
Morelli, Gaspare
  S. Rocco
Muti Papazurri, Marchese Alessandro
  S. Maria dell'Archeto
Neri, Bartolomeo
  S. Francesco d'Assisi a Monte Mario
Nicholas III
  S. Giovanni in Laterano, Scala Santa
Nicholas IV
  S. Maria Maggiore
Nicholas V
  S. Girolamo degli Schiavoni
  S. Stefano Rotondo

INDEX OF PATRONS AND BENEFACTORS

S. Teodoro al Palatino
Nobili, Vincenzo
  S. Bernardo alle Terme
Nobili Sforza, Caterina de'
  S. Bernardo alle Terme
Nuñez da Cuña de Attayde, Cardinal
  S. Anastasia al Palatino
Odescalchi, Livo
  S. Pietro in Vaticano
Olgiati, Bernardo
  S. Prassede
Omodei, Cardinal Luigi
  SS. Carlo e Ambrogio al Corsos
Orsini
  S. Maria di Grottapinta
Ottoboni, Cardinal Pietro
  S. Lorenzo in Damaso
  S. Maria in Via, Piazza Poli
  S. Pietro in Vaticano
Pammphili, Prince Giovanni Battista
  S. Pietro in Vincoli
Pamphili Olimpia, Donna
  S. Agnese in Agone
Pamphili, Camillo
  S. Agnese in Agone
Pamphili, Cardinal Benedetto
  S. Giovanni in Laterano
Pamphili, Don Camillo
  S. Nicola da Tolentino
Pamphili, Giambattista
  S. Agnese in Agone
Pamphili, Prince Camillo
  S. Andrea al Quirinale
  S. Maria di Monterone
  S. Maria Montesanto
Paolucci, Cardinal Fabrizio
  SS. Giovanni e Paolo
  S. Marcello
Paolucci, Cardinal Francesco
  S. Giovanni in Oleo
Paolucci, Cardinal Renato
  S. Giorgio in Velabro
Paschal II
  S. Lorenzo in Lucia
  SS. Quattro Coronati
Paul I
  S. Silvestro in Capite
Paul II
  S. Marco
Paul III
  SS. Trinità in Palazzo
    Monte di Pietà
Paul IV
  SS. Trinità dei Pellegrini
Paul V
  S. Calisto
  S. Lorenzo in Lucia
  S. Lucia della Tinta
  S. Maria in Campitelli
  S. Maria Maggiore

S. Pietro in Vaticano
  SS. Vincenzo e Anastasio
Peretti, Camilla
  S. Susanna
Peretti, Cardinal Felice
  S. Maria Maggiore
Peretti-Montalto,
  Cardinal Alessandro
  S. Andrea della Valle
Petra, Cardinal
  S. Pietro in Vaticano
Piccolomini, Donna Constanza
  S. Andrea della Valle
Pico della Mirandola,
  Cardinal Lodovico
  SS. Nome di Maria
  S. Prassede
Pinelli, Cardinal Domenico
  S. Maria Maggiore
Pius IV
  S. Croce in Gerusalemme
  S. Ivo
  S. Maria degli Angeli
  S. Maria in Traspontina
  SS. Quattro Coronati
  S. Silvestro al Quirinale
  S. Stefano del Cacco
Pius IX
  S. Bernardo alle Terme
  S. Carlo ai Catinari
  SS. Croce e Bonaventura
    dei Lucchesi
  S. Giovanni in Laterano,
    Scala Santa
  S. Giacomo degli Incurabili
  S. Lorenzo fuori le Mura
  S. Maria dell'Umiltà
  S. Maria in Aquiro
  S. Maria Maggiore
  SS. Nome di Maria
  S. Nicola in Carcere
  S. Onofrio
  S. Spirito in Sassia
  S. Vitale
Pius V
  SS. Domenico e Sisto
  S. Giovanni in Laterano
  S. Nicola dei Prefetti
  S. Silvestro al Quirinale
Pius VI
  S. Giovanni in Laterano
  S. Pietro in Vaticano
  S. Paolo Primo Eremita
Pucci, Cardinal Lorenzo
  SS. Trinità dei Monti
Querini, Cardinal Angelo Maria
  S. Marco
Quiñones, Cardinal Francesco
  S. Croce in Gerusalemme
Quirini , Cardinal Angelo Maria

SS. Alessio e Bonifazio
Raimondi, Francesco
  S. Pietro in Montorio
Rezzonico, Abbondio
  S. Pietro in Vaticano
Rezzonico, Cardinal
  Giovambattista
  S. Maria del Priorato
Riario, Cardinal Raffaele
  S. Lorenzo in Damaso
Ricci, Cardinal Giovanni Battista
  S. Pietro in Montorio
Ridolfi, Canon Atanasio
  S. Maria in Via Lata
Riminaldi, Cardinal
  S. Rocco
Rovere, Cardinal Giuliano della
  S. Pietro in Vincoli
Rovere, Isabella della
  S. Vitale
Royas, Cardinal Sandoval y
  S. Anastasia al Palatino
Rues, Laurentius
  S. Maria in Campostanto
Ruffo, Cardinal Tommaso
  S. Lorenzo in Damaso
Ruiz, Abbot Filippo
  S. Caterina dei Funari
Ruspoli, Alessandro and Orazio
  S. Maria in Vallicella
Rusticucci, Cardinal Girolamo
  S. Susanna
Sacripanto, Cardinal Giuseppe
  S. Ignazio
Sacchi, Cardinal Antonio
  S. Maria del Popolo
Sagredo, Niccolò
  S. Marco
Salviati, Cardinal Antonio Maria
  S. Giacomo degli Incurabili
  S. Gregorio al Celio
  S. Gregorio al Celio
  S. Maria in Aquiro
Sannesio, Cardinal Giacomo
  S. Silvestro al Quirinale
Santacroce, Cardinal Marcello
  S. Maria in Publicolis
Santorio, Cardinal Giulio Antonio
  S. Bartolomeo all'Isola
Savelli, Camilla Virginia
  S. Maria dei Sette Dolori
Savelli, Cardinal Giacomo
  Il Gesù
Savenier, Giovanni
  SS. Re Magi
Severina, Cardinal Giulio Antonio
  S. Girolamo della Carità
Sfondrato, Cardinal
  S. Francesca Romana
Sforza, Cardinal Guido Ascanio

INDEX OF PATRONS AND BENEFACTORS

S. Maria Maggiore
Sforza, Fulvio
  S. Eufemia
Silvester I
  S. Lorenzo in Panisperna
Sirleto, Cardinal
  S. Lorenzo in Panisperna
  S. Maria dei Monti
Sistus IV
  S. Eusebio
  S. Maria del Popolo
  S. Pietro in Montorio
  S. Pietro in Vaticano,
    Cappella Sistina
  S. Spirito in Sassia
  S. Susanna
  S. Vitale
  SS. Apostoli
  SS. Carlo e Ambrogio al Corso
  SS. Vito e Modesto
Sixtus V
  S. Giovanni in Laterano
  S. Giovanni in Laterano,
    Scala Santa
  S. Girolamo degli Schiavoni
  S. Maria Maggiore
  S. Spirito in Sassia
  S. Susanna
  SS. Trinità dei Monti
Soderini, Piero
  S. Silvestro in Capite
Soderini, Pietro
  S. Carlo alle Quattro Fontane
Solano, Giovanni
  S. Caterina dei Funari

Soto, Francesco de
  S. Giuseppe a Capo le Case
Spada, Orazio
  S. Maria in Vallicella
Stoppani, Cardinal Giovan
  Francesco
  S. Andrea della Valle
Strozz, Ferdinando
  S. Andrea della Valle
Stuart, Cardinal Henry
  S. Maria in Trastevere
Terzi, Sister Diodora
  S. Cosimato
Theodoli, Bishop Girolamo
  S. Maria del Popolo
Tolfa, Marchesa Vittoria
  S. Spirito in Sassia
Torlonia, Duca Alessaandro
  S. Maria della Vittoria
Torlonia, Prince Giovanni
  Il Gesù
  S. Pantaleo
Torre Magno, Macerateso
  Gian Luigi di
  Stimmate di S. Francesco
Torres, Archbishop Ludovico de
  S. Caterina dei Funari
Torres, Cardinal Ludovicus de
  S. Pancrazio
Troiano, Cardinal
  S. Cecilia
Ubaldini, Cardinal Roberto
  S. Pietro in Vaticano
  SS. Re Magi
Urban III

  S. Giovanni in Laterano,
    Baptistry
Urban V
  S. Giovanni in Laterano
Urban VIII
  S. Anastasia al Palatino
  S. Bibiana
  S. Caio
  S. Caterina da Siena a
    Magnanapoli
  SS. Cosma e Damiano
  SS. Croce e Bonaventura
    dei Lucchesi
  S. Giacomo alla Lungara
  S. Giovanni in Laterano,
    Baptistry
  S. Lorenzo in Fonte
  SS. Re Magi
  SS. Vincenzo e Anastasio
  S. Pietro in Vaticano
Vecchiarelli, Cardinal Odoarda
  S. Rocco
Velli, Muzio
  S. Maria in Trastevere
Vico, Cardinal Raimondo de
  SS. Crocifisso, Oratorio del
Vitelli, Monsignor Giulio
  S. Marcello
Vives, Juan Bautista
  SS. Re Magi
Zacharias
  S. Maria sopra Minerva
Zavarroni, Francesco
  S. Francesco di Paola

POPES 1527-1870

1523 - 1534   Clement VII
Giulio de' Medici (S. Maria sopra Minerva)
1534 - 1549   Paul III
Alessandro Farnese (S. Pietro in Vaticano)
1550 - 1555   Julius III
Giovanni Maria Ciocchi del Monte (S. Pietro in Vaticano, crypt)
1555 -1555   Marcellus II
Marcello Cervini (S. Pietro in Vaticano, crypt)
1555 - 1559   Paul IV
Gian Pietro Carafa (S. Maria sopra Minerva)
1559 - 1565   Pius IV
Giovan Angelo de'Medici (S. Maria degli Angeli)
1566 - 1572   Pius V
Antonio Ghislieri (S. Maria Maggiore)
1572 - 1585   Gregory XIII
Ugo Boncompagni (S. Pietro in Vaticano)
1585 - 1590   Sixtus V
Felicia Perth (S. Maria Maggiore)
1590 - 1590   Urban VII
Giovanni Battista Casting (S. Maria sopra Minerva)
1590 - 1591   Gregory XIV
Nicole Sfondrati (S. Pietro in Vaticano)
1591 - 1591   Innocent IX
Giovanni Antonio Facchinetti (S. Pietro in Vaticano, crypt)

1592 - 1605   Clement VIII
Ippolito Aldobrandini (S. Maria Maggiore)
1605 - 1605   Leo XI
Alessandro de'Medici (S. Pietro in Vaticano)
1605 - 1621   Paul V
Camillo Borghese (S. Maria Maggiore)
1621 - 1623   Gregory XV
Alessandro Ludovisi (S. Ignazio)
1623 - 1644   Urban VIII
Maffeo Barberini (S. Pietro in Vaticano)
1644 - 1655   Innocent X
Giovanni Battista Pamphilj (S. Agnese in Agone)
1655 - 1667   Alexander VII
Fabio Chigi (S. Pietro in Vaticano)
1667 - 1669   Clement IX
Giulio Rospigliosi (S. Maria Maggiore)
1670 - 1676   Clement X
Emilio Altieri (S. Pietro in Vaticano)
1676 - 1689   Innocent XI
Benedetto Odescalchi (S. Pietro in Vaticano)
1689 - 1691   Alexander VIII
Pietro Ottoboni (S. Pietro in Vaticano)
1691 - 1700   Innocent XII
Antonio Pignatelli (S. Pietro in Vaticano)
1700 - 1721   Clement XI
Gian Francesco Albani (S. Pietro in Vaticano)

1721 - 1724   Innocent XIII
Michelangelo Dei Conti (S. Pietro in Vaticano)
1724 - 1730   Benedict XII
Pietro Francesco Orsini (S. Maria sopra Minerva)
1730 - 1740   Clement XII
Lorenzo Corsini (S. Giovanni in Laterano)
1740 - 1758   Benedict XIV
Prospero Lambertini (S. Pietro in Vaticano)
1758 - 1769   Clement XIII
Carlo Rezzonico (S. Pietro in Vaticano)
1769 - 1774   Clement XIV
Gian Vincenzo Ganganelli (SS. Apostoli)
1775 - 1799   Pius VI
Giovanni Angelo Braschi (S. Pietro in Vaticano, crypt)
1880 - 1823   Pius VII
Barnaba Gregorio Chiaramonti (S. Pietro in Vaticano)
1823 - 1829   Leo XII
Annibale Della Genga (S. Pietro in Vaticano)
1829 - 1830   Pius VIII
Francesco Saverio Castiglioni (S. Pietro in Vaticano)
1831 - 1846   Gregory XVI
Bartolomeo Alberto Cappellari (S. Pietro in Vaticano)
1846 - 1878   Pius IX
Giovanni Mastai Ferretti (S. Lorenzo fuori le Mura)

TOPOGRAPHICAL INDEX BY STREET

Acque Salvie, Via
  S. Maria Scala Coeli
Acque Salvie, Via
  S. Paolo alle Tre Fontane
Agostino, Piazza di S.
  S. Agostino
Agostino Depretis, 95, Via
  S. Paolo Primo Eremita
Alessio, Piazza di
  SS. Alessio e Bonifazio
    all'Aventino
Ambrogio, 3, Via S
  S. Ambrogio della Massima
Andrea delle Fratte, Piazza di S.
  S. Andrea delle Fratte
Andrea della Valle, Piazza di S.
  S. Andrea della Valle
Angelicum, Largo
  SS. Domenico e Sisto
Anicia, 3, Via
  S. Giovanni Battista dei Genovesi
Anicia, 9 - 10, Via
  S. Maria dell'Orto
Anima, 66, Via dell'
  S. Maria dell' Anima
Anna, Via di S.
  S. Anna dei Palafrenieri
Annunziatella, 99 Vicolo dell'
  SS. Annunziate
Apollonia, Piazza di
  S. Margherita in Trastevere
Apollinare, Piazza di S.
  S. Apollinare
Apostoli, Piazza dei
  SS. Apostoli
Appia Antica, 51, Via
  Domine Quo Vadis
Appia Antica, 135, Via
  S. Sebastiano fuori le Mura
Aracoeli, Piazza d'
  S. Maria in Aracoeli
Argentario, 1, Clivo
  S. Giuseppe dei Falegnami
Argentario, 3, Clivo
  SS. Luca e Martina
Artisti, 41, Via degli
  S. Isidoro
Babuino, 150b–c, Via del

S. Atanasio dei Greci
Balbina, 8, Piazza di
  S. Balbina
Banchi Vecchi, 12, Via dei
  S. Lucia del Gonfalone
Banco S. Spirito, 6, Via del
  SS. Celso e Giuliano
Barbieri, 22, Via dei
  SS. Cosma e Damiano de' Barbieri
Bartolomeo all'Isola, Piazza S. di
  S. Bartolomeo all' Isola
Basilio, 51, Via di
  S. Basilio
Benedetto Cairoli, Piazza
  S. Carlo ai Catinari
Bernardo, Piazza di S.
  S. Bernardo alle Terme
Bocca della Verità, Piazza della
  S. Maria in Cosmedin
Bonaventura, 1, Via di
  S. Sebastiano al Palatino
Bonaventura, 7, Via di
  S. Bonaventura al Palatino
Botteghe Oscure, 15 - 16, Via delle
  S. Stanislao dei Polacchi
Calisto, 16, Piazza di S.
  S. Calisto
Campitelli, 8 - 10, Piazza di
  S. Maria in Campitelli
Campo Marzio, 45, Piazza di
  S. Maria in Campo Marzio
Cancelleria, 1, Piazza della
  S Lorenzo in Damaso
Capranica, Piazza
  S. Maria in Aquiro
Caravita, 7, Via del
  Oratorio del Caravita
Carlo Alberto, 2, Via
  S. Antonio Abate
Carmine, Via del
  S. Maria del Carmine
    alle Tre Cannelle
Caterina della Rota, Piazza di. S.
  S. Caterina dell Rota
Cavalieri di Malta, 4, Piazza dei
  S. Maria del Priorato
Cecilia, Piazza di S.
  S. Cecilia

Chiara, Piazza di S.
  S. Chiara
Chiese Nuova, Piazza della,
  S. Maria in Vallicella
Chigi, Largo
  S. Maria in Via
Claudio, Piazza di S.
  SS. Claudio e Andrea
    de' Borgognoni
Clemente, Piazza di S.
  S. Clemente
Collegio Romano, 5, Piazza del
  S. Marta
Colonna, 361, Piazza
  SS. Bartolomeo e Alessandro
Colosseo, 19, Via del
  S. Maria della Neve
Conciliazione, 14, Via della
  S. Maria in Traspontina
Condotti, 41, Via
  SS. Trinità degli Spagnuoli
Consolazione, 84, Piazza della
  S. Maria della Consolazione
Coppelle, 72b, Via delle
  S. Salvatore delle Coppelle
Corso, 45, Via del
  Gesù e Maria
Corso, 128, Via del
  SS. Carlo e Ambrogio al Corso
Corso, 306, Via del
  S. Maria in Via Lata
Corso, 499, Via del
  S. Giacomo degli Incurabili
Costaguti, Piazza
  S. Maria del Carmine
Croce in Gerusalemme, Piazza di S.
  S. Croce in Gerusalemme
Crociferi, Piazza dei
  S. Maria in Trivio
Divino Amore, 12, Vicolo del
  Madonna del Divino Amore
Dorotea, 22, Via di S.
  S. Dorotea
Egidio, Piazza di S.
  S. Egidio
Eligio, 9, Via di
  S. Eligio degli Orefici
Eustachio, Piazza di S.

TOPOGRAPHICAL INDEX BY STREET

S. Eustachio
Farnese, Piazza
S. Brigida
Febo, 20, Largo
S. Nicola dei Lorenesi
Flaminia, 208, Via
S. Andrea in via Flaminia
Fontana di Trevi, Piazza di
SS. Vincenzo e Anastasio
Fori Imperiali, 1, Via dei
SS. Cosma a Damiano
Foro Traiano, 89, Piazza del
SS. Nome di Maria
Foro Romana
S. Adriano
Foro Romana
S. Maria Antiqua
Francesca Romana, 4, Piazza di S.
S. Francesca Romana
Francesco a Ripa, 20, Via di
S. Pasquale Baylon
Francesco Crispi, 22 - 24, Via
S. Giuseppe a Capo le Case
Francesco d' Assisi, Piazza di S.
S. Francesco a Ripa
Francesco di Sales, Via
S. Maria della Visitazione
Francesco di Paola, 10, Piazza di S.
S. Francesco di Paola
Funari, Via dei
S. Caterina dei Funari
Gallicano, 26, Via S.
S. Gallicano
Garibaldi, 27, Via
S. Maria dei Sette Dolori
Gesù, Piazza del
Il Gesù
Giolitti, 154, Via
S. Bibiana
Giovanni a Porta Latina, Via di
S. Giovanni a Porta Latina
Giovanni Decollato, 9, Via S.
S. Eligio dei Ferrari
Giovanni Decollato, 22, Via S.
S. Giovanni Decollato and Oratory
Giovanni e Paolo, Via dei SS.
S. Gregorio al Celio
Giovanni e Paolo, Via dei SS.
SS. Giovanni e Paolo
Giovanni in Laterano, 280a, Via S
SS. Andrea e Bartolomeo
Giovanni in Laterano, Via di S.
S. Clemente
Giovanni in Laterano, 33, Via di S.
S. Maria di Loreto
Giovanni in Laterano, Piazza di S.
S. Giovanni in Laterano
Giovanni de'Matha, Piazza
S. Agata in Trastevere
Giulia, 34, Via

Spirito Santo dei Napoletani
Giulia, 59 - 59a, Via
S. Maria del Suffragio
Giulia, 64, Via
S. Biagio della Pagnotta
Giulia, 134, Via
S. Filippo Neri
Giulia, 161, Via
S. Caterina da Siena
Giulia, 262, Via
S. Maria dell'Orazione
e della Morte
Gonfalone, 32, Via del
Oratorio del Gonfalone
Gregorio, Piazza di
S. Gregorio al Celio
Grotta Pinta, Via di
S. Maria di Grottapinta
Ignazio, Piazza di S.
S. Ignazio
Ildebrando Gregori, Largo
S. Spirito in Sassia
Jugario, Vicolo
S. Omobono
Librai, Largo dei
S. Barbara dei Librai
Lorenzo, Piazzale di S.
S. Lorenzo fuori le Mura
Lorenzo in Lucina, 6, Piazza di S.
S. Lorenzo in Lucina
Lucchesi, 1, Via dei
SS. Croce e Bonaventur
a dei Lucchesi
Luce, 68, Via della
S. Maria della Luce
Luigi dei Francesi, Piazza di S.
S. Luigi dei Francesi
Lungara, 19, Via della
S. Croce alla Lungara
Lungara, 43–46, Via della
S. Giacomo alla Lungara
Lungara, 140, Via della
S. Giuseppe alla Lungara
Lungaretta, 92, Via della
SS. Rufina e Seconda
Maddalena, Via della
S. Maria Maddalena
Madonna di Loreto, 26, Piazza
S. Maria di Loreto
Madonna dei Monti, 3, Piazza della
SS. Sergio e Bacco
Madonna dei Monti, 37, Via della
S. Salvatore ai Monti
Madonna dei Monti, 39–41, Via della
S. Maria dei Monti
Maggio, 9, Via XXIV
S. Silvestro al Quirinale
Magnanapoli, Piazza
S. Caterina da Siena
a Magnanapoli

Marcello, 41b, Via di S.
S. Maria dell'Archetto
Marcello, Piazza di S.
S. Marcello
Marco, Piazza di S.
S. Marco
Macuto, Piazza di
S. Macuto
Maria dell' Anima, 66, Via,
S. Maria dell' Anima
Maria de Calderari, 1b, Via di
S. Maria del Pianto
Maria alle Fornaci, Piazza di S.
S. Maria delle Grazie alle Fornaci
Maria in Monticelli, Via S. di
S. Maria in Monticelli
Maria in Trastevere, Piazza di S.
S. Maria in Trastevere
Maria Maggiore, Piazza di S.
S. Maria Maggiore
Martino ai Monti, 28, Via di S.
S. Prassede
Mascherone, 61a, Via del
SS. Giovanni e Petronio
Mazzarino, 16, Via
S. Agata dei Goti
Merulana, 161, Via
SS. Marcellino e Pietro
Minerva, Piazza della
S. Maria sopra Minerva
Monserrato, 45, Via
S. Tommaso di Canterbury
Monserrato, 62, Via
S. Girolamo della Carità
Monserrato, 115, Via
S. Maria di Monserrato
Montanara ,Via S. Rita da Cascia
Monte Brianzo, 62, Via di
S. Lucia della Tinta
Monte de' Cenci, 14, Via
S. Tommaso dei Cenci
Monte Gaudo, 8, Piazza
S. Francesco d'Assisi
a Monte Mario
Monte Oppio, 26 ,Viale
S. Martino ai Monti
Monte di Pietà, Piazza del
SS. Trinità in Palazzo
Monte di Pietà
Monte Savello, Via di
S. Gregorio a Ponte Quattro Capi
Monterone, 75, Via
S. Maria di Monterone
Navicella, Via della
S. Maria in Domnica
Navona, Piazza
S. Agnese in Agone
Navona, 105, Piazza
S. Giacomo degli Spagnuoli
Nazionale, 192, Via

TOPOGRAPHICAL INDEX BY STREET

S. Vitale
Nicola da Tolentino, Salita di S.
   S. Nicola da Tolentino
Numa Pompilio, 7, Piazza
   S. Sisto Vecchio
Onofrio, Piazzale di S.
   S. Onofrio
Ora, Piazza dell'
   S. Giovanni dei Fiorentini
Oratorio, Piazza dell'
   Oratorio del SS. Crocifisso
Ostiense, Via
   S. Paolo fuori le Mura
Pace, Piazza della
   S. Maria della Pace
Padre Pancrazio Pfeiffer, 24
   S. Lorenzo in Piscibus
Pancrazio, Piazza di S.
   S. Pancrazio
Panisperna, 90, Via
   S. Lorenzo in Panisperna
Panisperna, 257, Via
   S. Bernardino ai Monte
Pantaleo, Piazza di S.
   S. Pantaleo
Paolo della Croce, 10, Via di
   S. Tommaso in Formis
Paolo alla Regola, Piazza di S.
   S. Paolo alla Regola
Parione, 32 - 37, Via di
   S. Tommaso in Parione
Pasquino, Piazza di
   Natività di Gesù
Pettinari, 59, Via dei
   S. Salvatore in Onda
Pietro, Piazza di S.
   S. Pietro in Vaticano
Pietro d'Iliria, Piazza
   S. Sabina
Pietro in Montorio, Piazza di S.
   S. Pietro in Montorio
Pietro in Vincoli, Piazza di S.
   S. Pietro in Vincoli
Pigna, Piazza della
   S. Giovanni della Pigna
Poli, Piazza
   S. Maria in Via
Ponte Quattro Capi, 39, Via
   S. Giovanni Calabita
Popolo, Piazza del
   S. Maria del Popolo
Popolo, Piazza del
   S. Maria dei Miracoli
Popolo, Piazza del
   S. Maria di Montesanto
Porta Latina, Via di
   S. Giovanni in Oleo
Porta S. Sebastiano, 6, Via di S.
   S. Cesareo
Portoghesi, 2, Via del

S. Andrea dei Portoghesi
Prefetti, 35 - 36, Via dei
   S. Nicola dei Prefetti
Prisca, 11 - 13, Piazza di S.
   S. Prisca
Propaganda Fide, 1c, Via di
   SS. Re Magi
Protomartiri Cristiani, Piazza dei
   S. Maria in Camposanto
Publicolis, 23, Via in
   S. Maria in Publicolis
Quattro Coronati, 20, Via dei SS.
   SS. Quattro Coronati
Quercia, Piazza della
   S. Maria della Quercia
Quirinale, 23 - 25, Via del
   S. Carlo alle Quattro Fontane
Quirinale, 24 - 26, Via del
   SS. Gioacchino e Anna
Quirinale, 28 - 30, Via del
   S. Andrea al Quirinale
Repubblica, Piazza delle
   S. Maria degli Angeli
Rinascimento, Corso del
   S. Giacomo degli Spagnuoli
Rinascimento,40, Corso del
   S. Ivo della Sapienza
Ripetta, 63, Via di
   S. Maria Porta Paradisi
Ripetta, 74, Via di
   S. Rocco
Ripetta, 75, Via di
   S. Girolamo degli Schiavoni
Roma Libera, 76, Via
   S. Cosimato
Rotunda, Piazza dell
   S. Maria ad Martyres
Sacro al Forno Romano, Via
   S. Lorenzo in Miranda
Salvatore in Campo, Piazza di S.
   S. Salvatore in Campo
Salvatore in Lauro, Piazza di S.
   S. Salvatore in Lauro
Santo Uffizio, 21, Via del
   SS. Michele e Magno
Scala, Piazza della
   S. Maria della Scala
Selci, 82, Via in
   S. Lucia in Selci
Settembre, 14, Via XX
   S. Susanna
Settembre, 15, Via XX
   S. Maria della Vittoria
Silvestro, Piazza di S.
   S. Silvestro in Capite
Sistina, 11, Via
   SS. Ildefonso e Tommaso
     di Villanova
Stefano del Cacco, 25, Via di S.
   S. Stefano del Cacco

Stefano Rotondo, 7, Via S.
   S. Stefano Rotondo
Stimmate, Largo delle
   Stimmate di S. Francesco
Sudario, 40 - 42, Via del
   S. Giuliano dei Fiamminghi
Sudario, 47b, Via del
   SS. Sudario dei Piemontesi
Teatro di Marcello, 32, Via del
   SS. Annunziata a Tor de' Specchi
Teatro di Marcello, 46, Via del
   S. Nicola in Carcere
Teodoro, Piazza di S.
   S. Anastasia
Teodoro, 5 - 7, Via di S.
   S. Teodoro al Palatino
Terme di Caracalla, 28, Via delle
   SS. Nero e Achilleo
Tor de' Conti, 31a, Via
   SS. Quirico e Giulitta
Trastevere, 47, Viale
   S. Crisogono
Trevi, Piazza Fontana di Trevi
   SS. Vincenzo e Anastasio
Tribuna di Campitelli, 6, Via
   S. Angelo in Pescheria
Trinità dei Monti, Piazza della
   SS. Trinità dei Monti
Trinità dei Pellegrini, Piazza della
   SS. Trinità dei Pellegrini
Trionfale, 177, Via
   S. Maria del Rosario
Tritone, 80, Via del
   S. Maria d'Itria
Umiltà, 29, Via dell'
   S. Maria dell' Umiltà
Urbana, Via
   Bambino Gesù
Urbana, 50, Via
   S. Lorenzo in Fonte
Urbana, 158, Via
   S. Pudenziana
Vascellari, Via dei
   S. Cecilia
Vaticano, Lungotevere
   Oratory of the SS. Annunziata
Velabro, 3, Via del
   S. Giorgio al Velabro
Venezia, Piazza
   Madonna delle Grazie
Vergini, 23, Via delle
   S. Maria delle Vergini
Visconti di Venosta, Piazza
   SS. Gioacchino e Anna
Vito, Via di S.
   SS. Vito e Modesto
Vittorio Emanuele II, 12b, Piazza di
   S. Eusebio
Vittorio Veneto, 25, Via
   S. Maria della Concezione

TOPOGRAPHICAL INDEX BY RIONE

S. ANGELO XI
S. Ambrogio alla Massima
S. Angelo in Pescheria
S. Caterina dei Funari
S. Gregorio a Ponte Quattro Capi
S. Maria in Campitelli
S. Nicola in Carcere
S. Rita dei Casciani
S. Stanislao dei Polacchi

BORGO XIV
SS. Annunziata, Oratory of the
S. Lorenzo in Piscibus
S. Maria in Traspontina
SS. Michele e Magno
S. Spirito in Sassia

COLONNA III
S. Andrea delle Fratte
SS. Bartolomeo e Alessandro dei Bergamaschi
S. Giuseppe a Capo le Case
SS. Ildefonso e Tommaso di Villanova
S. Lorenzo in Lucina
S. Macuto
S. Maria in Aquiro
S. Maria d'Itria
S. Maria Maddalena
SS. Re Magi
S. Silvestro in Capite

CAMPITELLI X
S. Adriano
S. Anastasia
SS. Annunziata a Tor de' Specchi
S. Bonaventura al Palatino
SS. Cosma e Damiano
S. Francesca Romana
S. Giuseppe dei Falegnami
S. Lorenzo in Miranda
SS. Luca e Martina
S. Maria Antiqua
S. Maria in Aracoeli
S. Maria della Consolazione
S. Sebastiano al Palatino
S. Teodoro al Palatino

CAMPO MARZIO IV
S. Antonio dei Portoghesi
S. Atanasio
SS. Carlo e Ambrogio al Corso
SS. Gesù e Maria
S. Giacomo in Augusta
S. Girolamo degli Schiavoni
S. Lucia della Tinta
Madonna del Divino Amore
S. Maria in Campo Marzio
S. Maria dei Miracoli
S. Maria in Montesanto
S. Maria del Popolo
S. Maria in Porta Paradisi
S. Nicola dei Prefetti
S. Rocco
SS. Trinità dei Monti
SS. Trinità degli Spagnuoli

CASTRO PRETORIO XVIII
S. Bernardo alle Terme
S. Maria degli Angeli

CELIO XIX
S. Giovanni in Oleo
SS. Giovanni e Paolo
S. Giovanni a Porta Latina
S. Gregorio al Celio
S. Maria in Domnica
SS. Quattro Coronati
S. Sisto Vecchio
S. Tommaso in Formis

S. EUSTACHIO VIII
S. Agostino
S. Andrea della Valle
S. Carlo ai Catinari
SS. Cosma e Damiano de' Barbieri
S. Eustachio
S. Giuliano dei Fiamminghi
S. Ivo alla Sapienza
S. Luigi dei Francesi
S. Maria in Monterone
S. Maria in Publicolis
S. Salvatore delle Coppelle
SS. Sudario dei Piemontesi

ESQUILINO XV
S. Antonio Abate
S. Croce in Gerusalemme
S. Bibiana
S. Eusebio
SS. Vito e Modesto

FUORI LE MURA
S. Andrea in via Flaminia
SS. Annunziate
Domine Quo Vadis
S. Lorenzo fuori le Mura
S. Maria delle Grazie alle Fornaci
S. Maria del Rosario sul Monte Mario
S. Maria Scala Coeli
S. Pancrazio
S. Paolo fuori le Mura
S. Sebastiano

LUDOVISI XVI
S. Isidoro
S. Maria della Concezione

MONTI I
S. Agata dei Goti
SS. Andrea e Bartolomeo
S. Andrea al Quirinale
Bambino Gesù
S. Bernardino ai Monte
S. Carlo alle Quattro Fontane
S. Caterina da Siena a Magnanapoli
S. Clemente
SS. Domenico e Sisto
S. Francesco di Paola
S. Gioacchino e Anna in Selci
S. Giovanni in Laterano
S. Lorenzo in Fonte
S. Lorenzo in Panisperna
S. Lucia in Selci
SS. Marcellino e Pietro
S. Maria di Loreto
S. Maria dei Monti
S. Maria della Neve
S. Maria Maggiore
S. Martino ai Monti
S. Paolo Primo Eremita
S. Pietro in Vincoli

TOPOGRAPHICAL INDEX BY RIONE

S. Prassede
S. Pudenziana
SS. Quirico e Giulitta
S. Salvatore ai Monti
SS. Sergio e Bacco
S. Stefano Rotondo
S. Vitale

PARIONE VI
S. Agnese in Agone
S. Barbara dei Librai
S. Giacomo degli Spagnuoli
S. Lorenzo in Damaso
S. Maria di Grottapinta
S. Maria in Vallicella
Natività di Gesù
S. Nicola dei Lorenesi
S. Pantaleo
S. Tommaso in Parione

PIGNA IX
S. Chiara
S. Francesco Saverio
Il Gesù
S. Giovanni della Pigna
S. Ignazio
S. Marco
S. Maria ad Martyres
S. Maria sopra Minerva
S. Maria in Via Lata
S. Marta
S. Stefano del Cacco
SS. Stimmate di S. Francesco

PONTE V
Oratorio del Gonfalone
S. Apollinare
S. Biagio della Pagnotta
SS. Celso e Giuliano
S. Giovanni dei Fiorentini
S. Maria dell' Anima
S. Maria della Pace
S. Maria del Suffragio
S. Salvatore in Lauro

REGOLA VII
S. Brigida
S. Caterina della Rota
S. Caterina da Siena

S. Eligio degli Orefici
S. Filippo Neri
SS. Giovanni e Petronio dei Bolognesi
S. Girolamo della Carità
S. Lucia del Gonfalone
S. Maria in Monserrato
S. Maria in Monticelli
S. Maria dell' Orazione e Morte
S. Maria del Pianto
S. Maria della Quercia
S. Paolo alla Regola
S. Salvatore in Campo
S. Salvatore in Onda
Spirito Santo dei Napoletani
S. Tommaso di Canterbury
S. Tommaso dei Cenci
SS. Trinità in Palazzo Monte di Pietà
SS. Trinità dei Pellegrini

RIPA XII
SS. Alessio e Bonifazio all'Aventino
S. Bartolomeo all'Isola
S. Eligio dei Ferrari
S. Giorgio al Velabro
S. Giovanni Calabita
S. Giovanni Decollato
S. Maria in Cosmedin
S. Maria del Priorato
S. Omobono
S. Prisca
S. Sabina

S. SABA XXI
S. Balbina
S. Cesareo
SS. Nero e Achilleo
S. Saba

SALLUSTIANO XVII
S. Maria della Vittoria

TRASTEVERE XIII
S. Agata in Trastevere
S. Calisto
S. Cecilia
S. Cosimato
S. Crisogono

S. Dorotea
S. Egidio
S. Francesco a Ripa
S. Gallicano
S. Giacomo alla Lungara
S. Giovanni Battista dei Genovesi
S. Giuseppe alla Lungara
S. Margherita
S. Maria della Luce
S. Maria dell'Orto
S. Maria della Scala
S. Maria dei Sette Dolori
S. Maria in Trastevere
S. Maria della Visitazione
S. Onofrio
S. Pasquale Baylon
S. Pietro in Montorio
SS. Rufina e Seconda

TREVI II
SS. Apostoli
S. Basilio
SS. Claudio e Andrea de' Borgognoni
SS. Croce e Bonaventura dei Lucchesi
SS. Crocifisso, Oratorio del
S. Marcello
S. Maria del Carmine alle Tre Cannelle
S. Maria dell'Archetto
S. Maria di Loreto
S. Maria in Trivio
S. Maria dell'Umiltà
S. Maria delle Vergini
S. Maria in Via
S. Maria in Via (Oratory of the SS. Sacramento)
S. Nicola da Tolentino
SS. Nome di Maria
S. Silvestro al Quirinale
S. Susanna
SS. Vincenzo e Anastasio

VATICANO
S. Anna dei Palafrenieri
S. Maria in Camposanto
S. Pietro in Vaticano